THIRD EDITION

The Old Testament
Made Easier

PART ONE
GENESIS THROUGH EXODUS 19

THIRD EDITION

— THE OLD —
TESTAMENT
MADE EASIER

PART ONE
GENESIS THROUGH EXODUS 19

DAVID J. RIDGES

CFI, AN IMPRINT OF

SPRINGVILLE, UTAH

Dedication

To my wife, my eternal companion, Janette, who has supported and helped me every step of the way. We are just getting started on our eternal journey together.

© 2021 by David J. Ridges
All rights reserved.

No part of this book may be reproduced in any form whatsoever, whether by graphic, visual, electronic, film, microfilm, audio recording, or any other means, without prior written permission of the publisher, except in the case of brief passages embodied in critical reviews and articles.

This book is not an official publication of The Church of Jesus Christ of Latter-day Saints. The opinions and views expressed herein belong solely to the author and do not necessarily represent the opinions or views of Cedar Fort, Inc. Permission for the use of sources, graphics, and photos is also solely the responsibility of the author.

ISBN: 978-1-4621-4164-7

Published by CFI, an imprint of Cedar Fort, Inc.
2373 W. 700 S., Springville, UT 84663
Distributed by Cedar Fort, Inc., www.cedarfort.com

Library of Congress Control Number: 2021939516

Cover design by Shawnda T. Craig
Cover design © 2021 Cedar Fort, Inc.

Printed in the United States of America

10 9 8 7 6 5 4 3 2 1

Printed on acid-free paper

Contents

Foreword 1
The Use of the JST (Joseph Smith Translation
    of the Bible). 2
Genesis 3
Exodus 349
Sources 431
About the Author 433

Books by David J. Ridges

The Gospel Study Series

- *Your Study of The Book of Isaiah Made Easier, Second Edition*
- *The New Testament Made Easier, Second Edition, Part 1*
- *The New Testament Made Easier, Second Edition, Part 2*
- *Your Study of The Book of Mormon Made Easier, Part 1*
- *Your Study of The Book of Mormon Made Easier, Part 2*
- *Your Study of The Book of Mormon Made Easier, Part 3*
- *Book of Mormon Made Easier, Family Deluxe Edition, Volumes 1 and 2*
- *Your Study of The Doctrine and Covenants Made Easier, Second Edition, Part 1*
- *Your Study of The Doctrine and Covenants Made Easier, Second Edition, Part 2*
- *Your Study of The Doctrine and Covenants Made Easier, Second Edition, Part 3*
- *The Old Testament Made Easier, Third Edition, Part 1*
- *The Old Testament Made Easier—Selections from the Old Testament, Third Edition, Part 2*
- *The Old Testament Made Easier—Selections from the Old Testament, Third Edition, Part 3*
- *The Old Testament Made Easier—Selections from the Old Testament, Third Edition, Part 4*
- *Your Study of the Pearl of Great Price Made Easier*
- *Your Study of Jeremiah Made Easier*
- *Your Study of The Book of Revelation Made Easier, Second Edition*

Our Savior, Jesus Christ: His Life and Mission to Cleanse and Heal

Mormon Beliefs and Doctrines Made Easier

The Proclamation on the Family: The Word of the Lord on More than 30 Current Issues

Using the Signs of the Times to Strengthen Your Testimony

Doctrinal Details of the Plan of Salvation: From Premortality to Exaltation

FOREWORD

The Old Testament is a most valuable book of scripture. It is the source of many favorite Bible stories many of us heard when we were growing up, such as Adam and Eve in the Garden of Eden, Noah and the Flood, David and Goliath, Ruth, Daniel in the lions' den, and many more. However, far beyond these precious stories that remain in our hearts, the Old Testament is a rich source of gospel doctrines and teachings of the plan of salvation. It teaches the Creation, the Fall, and the Atonement of Christ in many ways and with rich illustrations, including in the law of Moses and daily worship and ritual. It teaches the mercy and willingness to forgive over and over, of Jehovah, the premortal Jesus Christ. It teaches and illustrates time and again what kinds of thinking and actions we need to avoid if we desire to remain firmly on the covenant path. And it teaches how to repent and return to Christ, whose arms of mercy are extended all the day long (Isaiah 65:2), inviting us to repent.

This study guide is designed to help you enjoy learning from the Old Testament. It is designed to help beginners as well as seasoned experts in scripture study. The format is simple. I provide brief commentary within the verses, in brackets with italics, as well as between the verses in a different font. I define many, many scriptural words and phrases right within the verses so that you naturally learn the vocabulary of the scriptures as you go along. In effect, you learn a new language—the language of the scriptures. This will help as you read and study the other "standard works" (the other scriptures) used by the Church. I also use the books of Moses and Abraham and the JST (the Joseph Smith Translation of the Bible), inserting them where they belong.

THIRD EDITION

This third edition has been expanded to four volumes in order to include verse-by-verse study of many more Old Testament books than previous editions. It includes most of the scripture reading blocks referenced in "Come, Follow Me" for Old Testament.

By the way, I almost always use "we" rather than "I," even though I am the one commenting. The reason is simple. My parents taught me from a young age to avoid "I" trouble (talking about myself too much).

—David J. Ridges

THE USE OF THE JST
(JOSEPH SMITH TRANSLATION OF THE BIBLE)
IN STUDY GUIDES BY DAVID J. RIDGES

Be aware that some of the JST references I use in my study guides are not found in the footnotes or in the JST section at the back of our Latter-day Saint version of the King James Bible (the one we use in the English-speaking part of the Church). The reason for this, as explained to me some years ago while writing curriculum materials for the Church, is simply that there is not enough room, for practical purposes, to include all of the JST additions and changes. As you can imagine, as was likewise explained to me, there were difficult decisions that had to be made by the Scriptures Committee and Church leaders as to which JST contributions were included and which were not.

The Joseph Smith Translation of the Bible in its entirety can generally be found in Latter-day Saint bookstores or ordered through them. It was originally published under the auspices of the Reorganized Church of Jesus Christ of Latter Day Saints in Independence, Missouri. The version of the JST that I prefer to use is a parallel column version entitled Joseph Smith's "New Translation" of the Bible, published by Herald Publishing House, Independence, Missouri, in 1970. This parallel column version compares the King James Bible with the JST side by side and includes only the verses that have changes, additions, or deletions made by the Prophet Joseph Smith.

By the way, some members of the Church have wondered whether we can trust the JST since it was published by a breakaway faction from our Church who retained the original manuscripts after the martyrdom of the Prophet Joseph Smith. They worry that some changes to the Prophet's original manuscript might have been made to support doctrinal differences between the RLDS Church (the Reorganized Church of Jesus Christ of Latter Day Saints) and us. This is not the case. Many years ago, Robert J. Matthews of the Brigham Young University Religion Department was teaching a summer school class I attended. He told us that he was given permission by leaders of the RLDS Church to come to their Independence, Missouri, headquarters to see their publication of the JST. Brother Matthews was thus, through his own laborious and exacting study, able to verify that they had been meticulously true to the Prophet's original work.

Genesis

The books of Moses and Abraham, in the Pearl of Great Price, are from the same Old Testament time period as Genesis. They contribute much to our understanding of this vital, foundational book of scripture. Consequently, we will quote much from them as we pursue our verse-by-verse study of Genesis.

First though, by way of background, if you look in your Bible at the headings for Genesis, Exodus, Leviticus, Numbers, and Deuteronomy, you will see that they are called the first, second, third, fourth, and fifth books of Moses respectively. In other words, Moses wrote all of these books, which cover from the creation of the earth until the time when the children of Israel were about to cross the Jordan River and enter into the promised land (basically, the area that we call "Israel" today).

One of our objectives in this study guide will be to point out the gospel of Jesus Christ in the Old Testament. Many Christian religions teach that Jesus Christ did not come on the scene until His birth in Bethlehem. They do not understand that He is Jehovah in the Old Testament as well as the mortal Jesus Christ in the New Testament. In other words, He is the God of the Old Testament, under the Father's direction (see 3 Nephi 15:5). They do not realize that Adam and Eve were taught the gospel of Jesus Christ and had the ordinances of exaltation.

The gospel and Atonement of Christ are symbolized in much of Old Testament law and ritual. An excellent example of this is found in Leviticus 14:1–9. We will pause a moment and study these nine verses now by way of preparation for recognizing Atonement symbolism elsewhere in the Old Testament.

Leviticus 14:1–9

In this example, the ritual cleansing, under the law of Moses, of a person once afflicted with leprosy who is now well and can be pronounced "clean" is used to symbolically represent each of us in terms of our need to be cleansed and healed from sin. Under the law of Moses, lepers were prohibited from direct physical contact with others (for fear of spreading the disease) and were required to live outside the camp of the children of Israel during their years in the wilderness. Later, after Israel had entered the promised land, lepers were forbidden to enter walled cities.

Leprosy itself was a much-dreaded and feared disease of the skin, considered to be a "living death" (see Bible Dictionary, under "Leper"). It led to nerve paralysis and deformation of the extremities of the body. The cleansing of the ten lepers in Luke 17:12–19 who were standing "afar off" from Christ is not only an example of the Savior's power over physical disease but also can symbolize His miraculous power to heal us spiritually, through our faith in Him (Luke 17:19), even when we are spiritually "afar off" from Him.

Here in these nine verses of Leviticus, we see His power to cleanse and heal us symbolized. Again, this is a powerful example of Old Testament Atonement symbolism, which teaches the power of the Atonement to cleanse and heal:

1 And the Lord spake unto Moses, saying,

2 This shall be **the law of the leper** [*the rules for being made clean; symbolic of serious sin and great need for help and cleansing*] **in the day of his cleansing** [*symbolic of the desire to be made spiritually clean and pure*]: **He shall be brought unto the priest** [*authorized servant of God; can be symbolic of our bishop, stake president, etc.*]:

3 And **the priest shall go forth out of the camp** [*the person with leprosy did not have fellowship with the Lord's people and was required to live outside the main camp of the children of Israel; the bishop, symbolically, goes out of the way to help sinners who want to repent*]; and **the priest shall look, and, behold,** *if* **the plague of leprosy be healed in the leper** [*the bishop serves as a judge to see if the repentant sinner is ready to return to full membership privileges*];

4 **Then shall the priest command to take for him that is to be cleansed** [*the person who has repented*] **two birds** [*one represents the Savior, the other represents the person who has repented*] alive and clean, and cedar wood [*symbolic of the cross*], and **scarlet** [*associated with mocking Christ before his crucifixion—Mark 15:17*], and **hyssop** [*associated with Christ on the cross—John 19:29*]:

5 And the priest shall command that **one of the birds** [*symbolic of the Savior*] be **killed in an earthen vessel** [*Christ was sent to earth to die for us*] **over running water** [*Christ offers "living water," the gospel of Jesus Christ—John 7:37–38—which cleanses us when we come unto Him*]:

6 **As for the living bird** [*representing the person who has repented*], **he** [*the priest—symbolic of the bishop, stake president, etc.*] **shall take it** [*the living bird*], **and the cedar wood**, and the **scarlet**, and the **hyssop** [*all associated with the Atonement*], **and shall dip them and the living bird in the blood of the bird** *that was* **killed over the running water** [*representing the Savior's blood, which was shed for us*]:

7 And he shall **sprinkle upon him that is to be cleansed from the leprosy** [*cleansed from sin, symbolically*] **seven times** [*seven is the number that, in biblical numeric symbolism, represents perfection*], **and shall pronounce him clean** [*he has been forgiven*], **and shall let the living bird** [*the person who has repented*] **loose into the open field** [*representing the wide-open opportunities again available in the kingdom of God for the person who truly repents*].

8 And **he that is to be cleansed shall wash his clothes** [*symbolic of*

cleaning up your life from sinful ways and pursuits—compare with Isaiah 1:16], and **shave off all his hair** [*symbolic of becoming like a newborn baby; a fresh start*], and **wash himself in water** [*symbolic of baptism*], **that he may be clean: and after that he shall come into the camp** [*rejoin the Lord's people in full fellowship*], and shall tarry abroad out of his tent seven days.

9 But it shall be on the seventh day, that **he shall shave all his hair off his head and his beard and his eyebrows, even all his hair he shall shave off** [*symbolic of being "born again"*]: and he shall wash his clothes, also he shall **wash his flesh in water** [*symbolic of baptism*], and **he shall be clean** [*a simple fact, namely, that we can truly be cleansed and healed by the Savior's Atonement*].

If you keep the above Atonement symbolism in mind as you study the Old Testament, you will see much of the gospel of Jesus Christ in this marvelous book of scripture.

As members of the Church, we have a tremendous advantage over others in understanding the Old Testament because we study its pages through eyes and hearts that understand the Father's plan of salvation and the central role of the Atonement of Jesus Christ. As stated above, we know Jesus Christ is the God of the Old Testament. He is Jehovah. We understand that prior to the Fall of Adam and Eve, the Father was much involved, but that after the Fall, it is almost always Jehovah who is referred to as "God," the "Lord," etc.

We have the additional advantage of having the light and knowledge shed on Genesis by the books of Moses and Abraham in the Pearl of Great Price. And we are blessed by clarifications and additions from the Joseph Smith Translation of the Bible (the "JST"). In addition, we have the inspired writings and teachings of modern prophets, as well as contributions to our understanding made by the Book of Mormon (which is an Old Testament time period record, up until the Savior's appearance to the Nephites in Third Nephi) and the Doctrine and Covenants.

One example of such contributions is 2 Nephi 3, which gives us much additional detail about Joseph who was sold into Egypt (Genesis 37), especially some prophecies he made about Joseph Smith and the Restoration of the gospel in the last days.

Thus, we are in a good position to study and appreciate the Old Testament. Since Moses wrote the first five books of the Old Testament, we will begin by getting better acquainted with him by studying Moses, chapter one, in the Pearl of Great Price. There is no equivalent for this in Genesis or Exodus.

MOSES 1

(Revealed to Joseph Smith in June 1830)

The Book of Moses was given to the Prophet Joseph Smith by direct revelation between June 1830 and February 1831. You may wish to underline or highlight this fact in your own scriptures in the heading to the Book of Moses.

Moses, which consists of eight chapters in the Pearl of Great Price, was given to the Prophet during the time he was working on Genesis in his inspired translation of the King James Bible, which is now referred to as the Joseph Smith Translation of the Bible, or the JST. During these months, the Prophet completed his translation of Genesis 1:1 through 6:13, which now appears in the Pearl of Great Price as Moses, chapters 1–8.

As you will see as we proceed with our study, a great deal has been left out of this part of the Bible. The information found in Moses 1 is not found in Genesis at all. Moses 2–8 add much to the account found in Genesis, up to the Flood.

The events spoken of in Moses, chapter 1, take place after the "burning bush" and before Moses returns to Egypt to lead the children of Israel out of Egyptian bondage. See Moses 1:17, 25–26. Thus, we are given to understand that the Lord gave Moses tremendous strength and perspective, not recorded in the Bible, before sending him to accomplish the extremely difficult task of leading the Israelites into the wilderness and toward the promised land. We will proceed now with our verse-by-verse study of Moses, chapter 1, using bold for teaching emphasis.

As we do so, we will be introduced to many gospel concepts and doctrines. Indeed, the Book of Moses is filled with understanding and facts, in concentrated form, that can greatly enhance our understanding of the plan of salvation, other scriptures and how God operates.

Beginning with verse 1, we see God, who, in this case is Jehovah, the premortal Jesus Christ, taking Moses to a "high mountain," which, among other things, is symbolic of a place where one can be privileged to see as God sees. Thus, Moses is given perspective and enabled to lead his people, many of whom are rebellious and crude, with the patience of God, who sees all things from a "high mountain" perspective and knows our potential to become like Him. We will say more about this as we continue. Now, Moses, chapter one.

1 **The words of God** [*Jehovah, the premortal Jesus Christ*], **which he spake unto Moses** at a time when Moses was **caught up into an exceedingly high mountain** [*symbolic, among other things, of being given the perspectives that God has*],

We do not know whether the "high mountain" in verse 1, above, is literal or symbolic. Suffice it to say that it represents a place of instruction, strengthening, and being given the perspectives of God, in order to see as He sees and do His work as He would do it in leading people toward exaltation.

Next, we are told that Moses saw the premortal Christ face to face. We understand that Jesus Christ is the God of the Old Testament, working under the direction of His Father. Joseph Fielding Smith explained this. He said:

"All revelation since the fall has come through Jesus Christ, who is the Jehovah of the Old Testament. . . . He is the God of Israel, the Holy One of Israel; the one who led that nation out of Egyptian bondage, and who gave and fulfilled the law of Moses. The Father has never dealt with man directly and personally since the Fall, and he has never appeared except to introduce and bear record of the Son" (*Doctrines of Salvation,* Vol. 1, page 27).

2 And **he saw God face to face**, and **he talked with him**, and the glory of God was upon Moses; therefore Moses could endure his presence.

> Did you notice the brief explanation, in verse 2, above, as to why Moses could survive being in the direct presence of God, even though he was only a mortal? It said that Moses had the glory of God upon him. Verses 11 and 14 give us a gospel vocabulary word for this. The word is "transfigured." A mortal can be transfigured by the power of the Holy Ghost in order to survive the direct glory and presence of God. Elder Bruce R. McConkie explained this. He said:
>
> "Transfiguration is a special change in appearance and nature which is wrought upon a person or thing by the power of God. This divine transformation is from a lower to a higher state; it results in a more exalted, impressive, and glorious condition. . . .
>
> "By the power of the Holy Ghost many prophets have been transfigured so as to stand in the presence of God and view the visions of eternity" (Mormon Doctrine, page 803).
>
> In fact, the righteous Saints who are living upon the earth at the time of the Savior's Second Coming will be transfigured and caught up to meet Him (see Doctrine and Covenants 88:96). If they were not transfigured, their mortal bodies would be burned by the glory that will accompany Him as He comes to cleanse the world of wickedness and to rule and reign on earth for a thousand years.
>
> In verse 3, next, the Savior formally introduces Himself to Moses.

3 And **God spake unto Moses, saying:** Behold, **I am the Lord God Almighty**, and **Endless is my name**; for **I am without beginning of days or end of years**; and is not this endless?

> Perhaps you have noticed that often in the scriptures, the Savior speaks directly for the Father, without formally notifying us that He is going to do so. This is called "divine investiture." We see an example of this next, in verses 4–7 (especially verse 6), where Jesus Christ speaks directly for the Father.

4 And, behold, **thou art my son**; wherefore look, and **I will show thee the workmanship of mine hands; but not all,** for my works are without end [*including worlds without number*], **and also my words, for they never cease** [*the doctrine of continuous revelation*].

5 Wherefore, **no man** [*no mortal*] **can behold** [*see*] **all my works**, except he behold all my glory; and **no man can behold all my glory, and afterwards remain in the flesh on the earth.**

In verse 6, next, the Savior, speaking for the Father, informs Moses that he has a role that is symbolic of the Savior's role. Moses is to be a savior to his people, just as Jesus Christ is the Savior of all. Moses is to free his people, the children of Israel, from the spiritual darkness and wickedness that has overcome them during many generations in the bondage of Egyptian slavery. He will lead them through the waters of the Red Sea (symbolic of baptism) and into the promised land (symbolic of heaven). This is similar to the Savior's role of leading us from a world of sin to the cleansing waters of baptism and, through our obedience to His commandments and leadership thereafter, on to the promised land (celestial exaltation).

Watch, now, as Moses is tenderly told that his role is symbolic of the Savior's.

6 And **I have a work for thee, Moses, my son**; and **thou art in the similitude of mine Only Begotten** [*Moses's role is symbolic of the Savior's role*]; **and mine Only Begotten is and shall be the Savior,** for he is full of grace [*He is filled with the ability to help us*] and truth; but **there is no God beside me** [*remember, the Savior is speaking for the Father; Heavenly Father is the Supreme God—see Ephesians 4:6*], and all things are present with me, for I know them all.

You can see another example of such divine investiture, in which Jesus speaks for the Father, in Doctrine and Covenants 29:1, 42, and 46. In Moses 5:9, there is even an example of divine investiture in which the Holy Ghost speaks directly for the Savior.

Just a quick additional comment about the phrase "there is no God beside me" in verse 6, above. Remember that Moses was raised in Egypt, a culture where the people considered their many idols to be gods. In fact, the Pharaoh was considered by his people to be a god. Thus, the statement "there is no God beside me" could be a simple reminder to Moses that idols are not gods, that Pharaoh is not a god, and that there is one true God, Heavenly Father, who rules and reigns supreme.

Next, Moses is told that he will be shown details about this earth upon which we live.

7 And now, behold, **this one thing** [*our earth*] **I show unto thee, Moses, my son**, for thou art in the world, and now I show it unto thee.

In verse 8, next, by the power of the Holy Ghost, Moses is enabled to comprehend and understand far more than a mortal would otherwise be capable of. One of the lessons we can learn from this verse is that through the power of the Holy Ghost, we can be enabled to know and understand far beyond our mortal capabilities and limitations. We will continue to use **bold** for teaching emphasis.

8 And it came to pass that Moses looked, and beheld the world upon which he was created; and **Moses beheld the world and the ends thereof, and all the children of**

men [*all the people*] **which are, and which were created**; of the same he greatly marveled and wondered [*he was astonished*].

> Beginning with verse 9, next, the stage is set for Satan's coming onto the scene and attempting to persuade Moses to worship him, taking advantage of the fact that Moses is no longer in the direct presence of God. Certainly, there is symbolism in this. Having come to earth, we are no longer in the direct presence of God, and Lucifer does everything he can to take advantage of that fact.
>
> Before Satan enters the scene in verse 12, we are given additional perspective and doctrine in verses 9–11. For instance, a lesson for us in verse 9 might be that when left to ourselves, without the power of God in our lives, we are basically helpless.

9 And **the presence of God withdrew from Moses,** that **his glory was not upon Moses;** and **Moses was left unto himself**. And as he was left unto himself, he **fell unto the earth**.

> In verse 10, next, one lesson or perspective for us is the power of God compared to that of man. For Moses, this apparently came as a surprise. He had been reared for forty years as an Egyptian prince and was a mighty man in that culture (see Acts 7:22). Among other things, according to the Jewish historian Flavius Josephus, he had gained great fame as a successful military leader (see *Antiquities of the Jews,* book 2, chapters 9 and 10). In light of this background of being a "mighty" man associated with great and powerful leaders and being accustomed to commanding and being obeyed for the first forty years of his life, no wonder Moses was startled, as expressed at the end of verse 10 and the beginning of verse 11.

10 And it came to pass that it was for the space of many hours before Moses did again receive his natural strength like unto man; and **he said unto himself**: Now, for this cause **I know that man is nothing, which thing I never had supposed**.

> Over my years of teaching, students have often asked how the observation that "man is nothing" can be reconciled with the great "worth of souls" taught in Doctrine and Covenants 18:10. The answer is simple. It deals with context. Moses had discovered that "man is nothing" when compared to God, not that man has no worth. In fact, he will express his faith in the value and worth of souls shortly, in verse 13, as he bears witness of his great worth as a "son of God."
>
> Continuing, verse 11 explains how Moses could survive in the direct presence of God. As quoted previously, he was transfigured by the Holy Ghost, which enabled him to be in the direct presence of God without withering and dying.

11 **But now mine own eyes have beheld God**; but not my natural, but my spiritual eyes, for my natural eyes could not have beheld; for **I should have** [*would have*] **withered**

and died in his presence; but his glory was upon me; and I beheld his face, for **I was transfigured** before him.

Once in a while, students get a bit confused between the words "transfigured" and "translated" in reference to people. We will briefly define each of these gospel vocabulary words:

Transfigured

To be temporarily changed and enabled by the power of the Holy Ghost to be in the direct presence of God while still in a mortal body. This is what happened to Moses.

Translated

To be changed for a longer period of time in order to remain on earth and fulfill a special mission, such as is the case with John the Apostle and the Three Nephites. In Third Nephi, chapter 28, we read that the mortal bodies of the Three Nephites were changed such that they could remain on earth, were no longer subject to physical pain, and were no longer subject to the power of Satan. These four translated beings (John and the Three Nephites) will continue ministering on earth until the Second Coming of the Savior, at which time they will "be changed in the twinkling of an eye from mortality to immortality" (3 Nephi 28:8).

Shifting our attention now to verse 12, next, we see Satan approaching Moses to tempt him. Remember, in verse 6, that Moses was told that God had a "work" for him to do and that his mission was symbolic of the mission of Jesus Christ. In conjunction with this, it is interesting to note that as the Savior embarked on His mission to save His people, Satan approached Him and attempted to detour Him by tempting Him, among other things, to "fall down and worship me" (Matthew 4:3–10).

So, likewise, as Moses was about to return to Egypt to save his people, Lucifer approached him in an attempt to stop him from fulfilling his mission. As seems to be quite typical of Satan, he starts out somewhat suave and mild in verse 12, inviting Moses to worship him, but as things move along, he will show his true nature as he yells and rants in verse 19.

12 And it came to pass that when Moses had said these words, behold, **Satan came tempting him, saying: Moses, son of man, worship me**.

By the way, did you notice the put-down used by the devil in verse 12? Satan addresses Moses as "son of man" rather than as a "son of God," implying that Moses does not have a divine nature or eternal worth. Moses will set the record straight in verses 13–15, next.

13 And it came to pass that **Moses looked upon Satan and said: Who art thou?** [*perhaps meaning "Who do you think you are?"*] For behold, **I am a son of God**, in the similitude of his Only Begotten; and **where is thy glory, that I should worship thee?**

14 For behold, **I could not look upon God, except his glory should come upon me, and I were transfigured**

before him. But I can look upon thee in the natural man [*in other words, Moses could look upon Satan without needing to be transfigured*]. Is it not so, surely?

15 Blessed be the name of my God, for his Spirit hath not altogether withdrawn from me, or else **where is thy glory, for it is darkness unto me?** And I can judge [*discern*] between thee and God; for God said unto me: Worship God, for him only shalt thou serve.

> Among the vital lessons we can learn from verses 16–22, next, is the fact that we cannot overcome the devil by ourselves. We must have the help of the Savior. As you will see, it is not until his fourth attempt to have Lucifer depart that Moses commands in the name of Jesus Christ (verse 21). Then Satan departs.
>
> It appears that perhaps at first, Moses felt that he could handle the situation by himself, so he commanded Lucifer to leave, much the same perhaps as he had done as a crown prince and military leader in Egypt in commanding his subordinates. It didn't work. The attempts in verses 16, 18, and 20 were unsuccessful. We will number these attempts as we proceed. We will also deal with other subjects and add notes about them as we go along.
>
> As stated above, Moses makes his first attempt to command the devil to depart in verse 16.

16 **Get thee hence, Satan [1]**; deceive me not; for God said unto me: Thou art after the similitude of mine Only Begotten [*the fact that Moses knows that he is a child of God and has eternal worth is a great source of strength to him in his quest to overcome the devil*].

> Verse 17, next, provides the timing of this event in the life of Moses. As you can see, the interview with Jehovah (JST Exodus 3:2) at the "burning bush" had already taken place (Exodus 3:1–10). Moses uses this as part of his defense against the devil here.

17 And he [*the Lord, Jehovah, Jesus Christ, speaking for the Father through divine investiture*] also gave me commandments **when he called unto me out of the burning bush**, saying: Call upon God in the name of mine Only Begotten, and worship me.

> Another great lesson for us here is that Moses emphasizes his determination to keep the commandments of God, including calling "upon God in the name of mine Only Begotten" and worshipping the Father. You can feel the determination of Moses to do so in verse 18, next.
>
> Yet another lesson for us is that keeping the commandments opens up additional opportunities for us to inquire of Him and thus continue our celestial education.

18 And again Moses said: **I will not cease to call upon God, I have other things to inquire of him**: for his glory has been upon me, wherefore I can judge between him and thee. **Depart hence, Satan [2]**.

Satan will still not depart from Moses. As mentioned earlier, Lucifer started out somewhat calm and sophisticated as he began his initial temptation of Moses (verse 12). Now, however, as he sees that he is failing, his true vicious nature comes out, and he desperately yells and rants against him, even commanding him—an attempt to counterfeit God!

19 And now, **when Moses had said these words, Satan cried with a loud voice, and ranted** upon the earth, **and commanded**, saying: I am the Only Begotten, worship me [*this, of course, is an outright lie; one of Satan's titles might well be "the Great Counterfeiter"*].

It appears that at this point, Moses begins to realize that it is not so easy to get rid of Satan, and fear enters his heart as he sees the devil and his evil kingdom in their awful reality. Moses will attempt yet a third time to make Lucifer depart. He will still not succeed.

20 And it came to pass that **Moses began to fear exceedingly; and as he began to fear, he saw the bitterness of hell**. Nevertheless, calling upon God, he received strength, and he commanded, saying: **Depart from me, Satan [3]**, for this one God only will I worship, which is the God of glory [*Satan has no glory at all*].

Next, we are clearly taught that "there is none other name given under heaven save it be this Jesus Christ, of which I have spoken, whereby man can be saved" (2 Nephi 25:20). It is a simple fact that it is only through the Savior that we can overcome the devil.

21 And now Satan began to tremble, and the earth shook; and Moses received strength, and called upon God, saying: **In the name of the Only Begotten** [*in other words, in the name of Jesus Christ*]**, depart hence, Satan [4]**.

This time, because of the power of Christ, Satan departs (verse 22, next). In so doing, he displays great frustration and anger at being obligated by God's power to obey such a command. One of the important and comforting lessons we learn from this scene is that God does have power over Lucifer.

22 And it came to pass that **Satan** cried with a loud voice, with weeping, and wailing, and gnashing of teeth [*this sounds very much like a tantrum*]; and he **departed** hence, even from the presence of Moses, that he beheld him not.

As mentioned in the introduction to this chapter, many things were left out of Genesis over the centuries, and this chapter of the writings of Moses, as revealed to the Prophet Joseph Smith, restores some of them. The fact that precious things were left out is confirmed by verse 23, next.

23 **And now of this thing** [*Satan's tempting Moses and being commanded in the name of Jesus Christ to depart*] **Moses bore record; but because of**

wickedness it is not had among the children of men.

We might wonder why Satan would want this left out of the Bible. One of the obvious answers is that he is a loser here.

We are now about to be taught another important lesson. It is that obeying the commandments we have already received from God opens the door for additional light and knowledge from above.

Moses had been commanded that he should only worship God (verses 15 and 17, above). Then Satan came along and commanded Moses to worship him (verses 12 and 19). Moses remained faithful to God, refusing to give in to the devil's temptations. As a result, he was "filled with the Holy Ghost" (verse 24, next) and was taught many more things, as recorded in the next verses, including the following:

1. He learned prophetic details about his mission to free the children of Israel from Egypt (Egypt is often symbolic of Satan's kingdom in biblical symbolism), in verses 25–26.

2. He was taught more about the inhabitants of this earth, in verses 27–29.

3. He was privileged to again be transfigured and speak with Jehovah face-to-face, asking questions and receiving answers, in verses 30–41.

4. He was taught that there are other planets with people on them that exist now, in verses 33 and 35.

5. He learned that many earths have already "passed away," in verse 35.

6. He was taught that there is no limit to the number of worlds that the Father has created, in verses 33, 35, and 38.

7. He was shown that the highest satisfaction and glory of the Father consists in sending His spirit children to earths and helping them gain immortality (gaining a resurrected body of flesh and bones, thus living forever with physical bodies) and eternal life (exaltation), in verses 37–39.

8. He was told that many of his writings would be lost but that in the last days a prophet (Joseph Smith) would restore much of what he wrote (in Genesis through Deuteronomy).

Having seen the brief summary above of the rewards Moses received for obedience, is there any doubt that it is worth obeying the commandments in order to qualify for additional light and knowledge? We will now go through verses 24–41, using **bold** to point out the light and knowledge that Moses gained as a result of his obedience.

24 And it came to pass that when Satan had departed from the presence of **Moses**, that Moses lifted up his eyes unto heaven, being **filled with the Holy Ghost**, which beareth record of the Father and the Son [*the*

Holy Ghost testifies to us of the reality of Heavenly Father and Jesus Christ];

25 And calling upon the name of God, **he beheld his glory again**, for it was upon him; and **he heard a voice**, saying: Blessed art thou, Moses, for I, the Almighty, have chosen thee, and thou shalt be made stronger than many waters [*Moses will part the Red Sea—see Exodus 14:21*]; for **they shall obey thy command as if thou wert God**.

26 And lo, I am with thee, even unto the end of thy days; for **thou shalt deliver my people from bondage**, even Israel my chosen.

27 And it came to pass, as the voice was still speaking, **Moses** cast his eyes [*looked*] and **beheld the earth**, yea, even **all of it**; and **there was not a particle of it which he did not behold, discerning it by the spirit of God** [*seeing and comprehending by the power of the Holy Ghost far beyond the capacity of a mortal man*].

28 And he beheld also the inhabitants thereof, and **there was not a soul which he beheld not**; and **he discerned them by the Spirit of God** [*the Holy Ghost*]; and their numbers were great, even numberless as the sand upon the sea shore.

29 **And he beheld many lands**; and each land was called earth, and there were inhabitants on the face thereof.

> The fact that the Holy Ghost was with Moses, enabling him to see and comprehend the things in verses 27–29, above, answers a question that sometimes comes up in gospel discussions. The question is whether the Holy Ghost was upon the earth before the time of Christ. As you can see, the answer is yes. You may wish to read more on this subject in the Bible Dictionary (in the back of the Latter-day Saint Bible), under "Holy Ghost."
>
> Next, Moses asks Jehovah a broad question.

30 And it came to pass that Moses called upon God, saying: **Tell me, I pray thee, why these things are so, and by what thou madest them?**

31 And behold, **the glory of the Lord was upon Moses** [*he was transfigured—see verse 11*], so that **Moses stood in the presence of God, and talked with him face to face**. And the Lord God said unto Moses: For mine own purpose have I made these things. Here is wisdom and it remaineth in me.

> You will no doubt notice, in verses 32–35, that Jesus Christ is speaking here by way of divine investiture (see note following verse 3, above). In other words, He is speaking directly for the Father, as if He were the Father, without formally announcing that He is speaking the words of the Father. He is answering Moses's question, posed in verse 30.

32 And **by the word of my power** [*in other words, by Jesus Christ; Christ is the "Word"; see John 1:1–3*], **have I created them, which is mine Only**

Begotten Son, who is full of grace and truth.

33 And **worlds without number have I created**; and I also created them for mine own purpose [*which is explained in verse 39*]; and **by the Son I created them**, which is mine Only Begotten.

34 And **the first man** of all men have I called **Adam**, which is many.

> From Moses 3:7 we understand that verse 34, above, is referring to Adam being the first of all people on this earth (see Moses 1:34, footnote 34a; see also Bible Dictionary, under "Adam").
>
> Next, the Lord informs Moses that He will limit their discussion to this earth and its inhabitants, giving him just a bit more information about other earths and the people belonging to them.

35 But **only an account of this earth, and the inhabitants thereof, give I unto you**. For behold, **there are many worlds that have passed away by the word of my power** [*many worlds have already been created and have become celestialized, having been created and redeemed by the power of Jesus Christ—compare with Doctrine and Covenants 76:24*]. And **there are many that now stand** [*there are many planets now, in outer space, that have people like us on them; they too are children of God*], and **innumerable are they unto man; but all things are numbered unto me, for they are mine and I know them**.

> The last part of verse 35, above, contains a sweet and comforting insight into the power of God. We may sometimes feel tiny and insignificant among all His creations, but we are reminded above that, even though it appears impossible to us, He does know us individually. The same message is found at the end of verse 37.
>
> Next, in verse 36, Moses humbly responds to the Savior's statement at the beginning of verse 35 that He wishes to limit His instructions to Moses to this earth.

36 And it came to pass that **Moses spake unto the Lord**, saying: Be merciful unto thy servant, O God, and **tell me concerning this earth, and the inhabitants thereof, and also the heavens, and then thy servant will be content**.

37 And the Lord God spake unto Moses, saying: The heavens, they are many, and they cannot be numbered unto man [*a mortal can't possibly comprehend this*]; but **they are numbered unto me, for they are mine**.

38 And **as one earth shall pass away, and the heavens thereof even so shall another come**, and **there is no end to my works, neither to my words**.

> Verse 39, next, is one of the most often-quoted verses in all of the scriptures. You may wish to make sure it is marked in your own scriptures. It is

a brief and powerful statement of the Father's mission and goals for us.

39 For behold, this is my work and my glory—to bring to pass the immortality [*resurrection and living forever in a physical body of flesh and bone*] **and eternal life** [*exaltation, becoming like our Father in Heaven, becoming gods, having spirit offspring—see Acts 17:28–29, and living in family units forever*] **of man.**

Next, the Lord assigns Moses to record what he has been taught and will yet be taught. His writings are found today in the Bible, in Genesis, Exodus, Leviticus, Numbers, and Deuteronomy. However, as explained in verse 41, many of the "plain and precious things" (1 Nephi 13:28) he records will eventually be deleted by wicked men (see Moses 1:23).

40 And now, Moses, my son, **I will speak unto thee concerning this earth** upon which thou standest; and **thou shalt write the things which I shall speak.**

41 And **in a day when the children of men shall esteem my words as naught** [*do not consider the Bible to be of hardly any value*] and **take many of them from the book** [*the books of Moses, known today as Genesis through Deuteronomy, in the Old Testament*] **which thou shalt write**, behold, I will raise up another [*the Prophet Joseph Smith*] like unto thee; and **they shall be had again among the children of men—among as many as shall believe** [*in other words, among members of the Church; perhaps you've noticed that we don't generally give the Pearl of Great Price to anyone other than members, who have the capacity to appreciate and respect it; this is in harmony with the instructions given in verse 42*].

The taking of words "from the book," spoken of in verse 41, above, in addition to being literal, can also mean ignoring the Bible, considering it to be outdated and of no relevancy to modern society, even though it still exists and many people have copies of it.

As you are no doubt aware, many of the marvelous doctrines and insights given to us in this chapter would not be appropriate to share during a "first discussion" given by missionaries. Obviously, it would cause overload in people who do not already have a good foundation in the gospel. With this in mind, we see in verse 42, next, counsel from the Lord not to show these things to any except those who already believe and have a testimony of the restored gospel.

42 (These words were spoken unto Moses in the mount, the name of which shall not be known among the children of men. And now they are spoken unto you. **Show them not unto any except them that believe**. Even so. Amen.)

Having studied Moses, chapter 1, we will now study Abraham, chapter 3, which gives us many details and insights regarding our premortal existence and nicely leads up to the creation of the earth in preparation for our mortal existence, which is the topic of Genesis, chapter 1.

ABRAHAM 3

Background

We are taught many things in this chapter. Perhaps one of the most important is the fact that this life is a test (verse 25). Some people get a bit confused on this issue. They begin discussing God's foreknowledge and our agency and end up concluding that our future on Judgment Day is already determined because of His knowledge of the future. Regardless of discussions and debates on the subject, the revealed answer to the whole question is that this life is a test. We are indeed determining our future by whether we keep the commandments in this life (provided we are familiar with the gospel here).

One of the best-known doctrines in this chapter is the doctrine concerning the "noble and great" spirits, many of whom were reserved to come forth in this last dispensation. Also, a brief discussion of our "first estate" and "second estate" is presented here by Abraham. Among other things, Abraham will also teach us about intelligences and spirits and will give us a brief glimpse into the premortal councils during which Jesus was chosen to be the Redeemer and Satan was rejected.

Before teaching us these doctrines, however, Abraham will provide a background and setting for us, using the stars and planets as examples, emphasizing that they are well organized and that some of them govern the others. Using these examples, he will lead us to the fact that some spirits in premortality progressed more rapidly than others, becoming great and noble. He will also teach us that just as there are grand, governing planets, such as Kolob, so also is there a grand, governing being—namely, God.

Abraham tells us that through the Urim and Thummim (verse 1), he was taught much about the stars and planets. These lessons in astronomy took place before he journeyed to Egypt (see verse 15). Abraham uses Facsimile No. 2 to illustrate much of what he was taught about the relationships among the planets and much more. This reminds us that there was great revealed knowledge in ancient times about the stars and planets. Much of this was lost during periods of apostasy.

As we begin our study of chapter 3, we run into the term "Urim and Thummim." The Bible Dictionary informs us that "Urim and Thummim" is a Hebrew term that means "Lights and Perfections." It also tells us that there is more than one Urim and Thummim. Joseph Smith had the one used by the brother of Jared. Abraham had one and learned much, including the things he summarizes for us in this chapter. It is interesting that he received it while he lived in Ur (verse 1), which would mean that it was given to him relatively early in his life.

1 And **I, Abraham, had the Urim and Thummim**, which the Lord my God had given unto me, in Ur of the Chaldees;

2 And **I saw the stars**, that they were very great, and that **one of them** [*Kolob*] **was nearest unto the throne of God**; and there were many great ones which were near unto it;

Once in a while, members get Kolob confused with the actual planet on which Heavenly Father resides. They are not the same. As you saw in verse 2, above, Kolob is the planet nearest to the planet on which the Father lives.

As Abraham continues, he points out that some planets govern others. He is leading up to the point that some spirits progress more than others through their agency choices and thus become the "great and noble" whom God appoints to be rulers (verse 23).

3 And the Lord said unto me: **These are the governing ones**; and the name of **the great one is Kolob**, because it is near unto me, for I am the Lord thy God: I have set this one to govern all those which belong to the same order as that upon which thou standest.

We learn from verse 4, next, that the planet on which God resides has the same time system as Kolob. The Lord further informs us that one thousand years on our earth is one day on Kolob. You can see this same fact taught in the explanation of Fig. 1 provided for Facsimile No. 2. We are taught the same thing in 2 Peter 3:8.

4 And the Lord said unto me, by the Urim and Thummim, that **Kolob was after the manner of the Lord, according to its times and seasons in the revolutions thereof**; that one revolution was **a day unto the Lord**, after his manner of reckoning, it being **one thousand years** according to the time appointed unto that [*our earth*] whereon thou standest. **This is the reckoning of the Lord's time, according to the reckoning of Kolob**.

Next, Abraham teaches us about our moon, explaining that a day on the moon is longer than our earth days. It is worth noting that much of this knowledge about astronomy, which Abraham taught in ancient times, was lost during the dark ages.

5 And the Lord said unto me: **The planet which is the lesser light** [*the moon*], lesser than that which is to rule the day [*the sun*], even the night, is above or greater than that upon which thou standest in point of reckoning, for it **moveth in order** [*in its orbit*] **more slow**; this is in order because it standeth above the earth upon which thou standest, therefore **the reckoning of its time is not so many as to its number of days, and of months, and of years** [*compared to the earth; one day on the moon, from when the sun rises on one horizon to when it sets on the opposite horizon, is about twenty-nine days on earth*].

Abraham is now going to lead us to a major point he makes in verse 19; namely that there are various levels of intelligence and that God is the most intelligent of all.

As he teaches us, he will repeat a rather interesting phrase several times. It is "these two facts exist." He uses it (or something similar) in verses 6, 8, 16, 17, 18 (twice), and 19 (twice). We will use **bold** to point these out as we go along. His point will be that where you have two related things, there will always be something higher than they are. And as you pursue this "order," moving higher and higher, you will eventually come to God. In other words, God is the force behind the organization and order in the universe.

To put it simply, the order in the universe bears witness that there is a God.

Another way to put it might be that if we follow the simple teachings and commandments placed before us by the Lord, we will progress upward, seeing and understanding more and greater things. As we receive those things into our lives, we progress yet further and see more and yet greater things. If we continue this upward spiral, it leads to becoming like God (compare to D&C 88:49).

This process is illustrated in the example of the universe. First we see the earth, then we see the moon above it, and then we the sun above them both. Then we see larger stars beyond the sun, then the galaxy, then clusters of galaxies beyond it, and so forth, which ultimately leads to God. D&C 88:12–13 confirms this.

Let's sit down in Abraham's classroom now and listen carefully as this great prophet astronomer teaches us that all things in the universe have their order and proper relationship to each other. So, likewise, is there an "order of the gospel" as we move higher and higher, eventually keeping our second estate (verse 26) and becoming like God. Abraham will be quoting the Savior as he teaches us.

6 And the Lord said unto me: Now, Abraham, **these two facts exist** [*the sun rules the day, and the moon rules the night—see end of this verse*], behold thine eyes see it; it is given unto thee to know the times of reckoning, and the set time, yea, the set time of the earth upon which thou standest, and **the set time of the greater light** [*the sun*] **which is set to rule the day**, and **the set time of the lesser light** [*the moon*] **which is set to rule the night**.

7 Now the set time of the lesser light is a longer time as to its reckoning than the reckoning of the time of the earth upon which thou standest [*the moon has longer "days" than the earth*].

8 And **where these two facts exist**, there shall be **another fact above them**, that is, there shall be another planet whose reckoning of time shall be longer still [*there will be planets which have longer days than either the earth or the moon*];

> The Savior continues reasoning with Abraham, explaining that there are planets above other planets that have longer and longer days, until you arrive at Kolob, which has the longest days of all in this order of planets; namely, one thousand earth years to one of its days. The same time system is used on the planet upon which God lives.

9 And thus **there shall be the reckoning of the time of one planet**

above another, until thou come nigh unto Kolob**, which Kolob is after the reckoning of the Lord's time [*Kolob uses the same time system used by the celestial planet upon which God resides*]; which Kolob is set nigh [*near*] unto the throne of God, to govern all those planets which belong to the same order as that upon which thou standest.

> Perhaps one of the main implied messages in verse 10, next, is that just as Abraham is being taught about the orbits and time systems of the planets and stars leading up to Kolob and God's planet, so also will the Lord teach him the order of things, commandments, ordinances, and so forth leading up to his returning to the presence of God.

10 And **it is given unto thee to know the set time of all the stars that are set to give light, until thou come near unto the throne of God**.

> Abraham points out that he was instructed by the Savior Himself, face to face.

11 Thus **I, Abraham, talked with the Lord, face to face**, as one man talketh with another; and he told me of the works [*creations*] which his hands had made;

12 And **he said unto me: My son, my son** [*a term of closeness and endearment*] (and his hand was stretched out), behold I will show you all these. And he put his hand upon mine eyes, and **I saw those things which his hands had made**, which were many [*an understatement*]; and they multiplied before mine eyes, and **I could not see the end thereof**.

13 And he said unto me: This is Shinehah, which is the **sun**. And he said unto me: Kokob, which is star. And he said unto me: Olea, which is the **moon**. And he said unto me: Kokaubeam, which signifies **stars**, or all the great lights, which were in the firmament of heaven [*the night sky*].

> As the Savior teaches Abraham, he repeats His covenant and promise to Abraham that his posterity will be infinite in number.

14 And it was in the night time when the Lord spake these words unto me: **I will multiply thee, and thy seed after thee, like unto these; and if thou canst count the number of sands, so shall be the number of thy seeds**.

> We know from verse 15, next, that Abraham was taught all these things before he and Sarah went to Egypt. Thus, we understand that he taught the Egyptians much about astronomy.

15 And the Lord said unto me: **Abraham, I show these things unto thee before ye go into Egypt**, that ye may declare all these words.

> In verses 16–19, we see the transition from stars and planets to people and God. The main point of this part of the lesson is made in these verses.

16 **If two things exist**, and there be **one above the other, there shall be greater things above them**;

therefore Kolob is the greatest of all the Kokaubeam [*stars*] that thou hast seen, because it is nearest unto me [*the closer to God we come, the greater we become*].

17 Now, **if there be two things, one above the other**, and **the moon be above the earth**, then it may be that **a planet or a star may exist above it**; and there is nothing that the Lord thy God shall take in his heart to do but what he will do it—*"with God all things are possible" (Matthew 19:26).*

> We learn from verses 18–19, next, that, just as there are different magnitudes among stars and planets, so also there are differing degrees of intelligence and progression among spirits. Spirits progressed at different rates during premortality because of agency choices. Joseph Fielding Smith taught this. He said:
>
> "We know they were all innocent in the beginning; but the right of free agency which was given to them enabled some to outstrip others, and thus, through the eons of immortal existence, to become more intelligent, more faithful, for they were free to act for themselves, to think for themselves, to receive the truth or rebel against it" (*Doctrines of Salvation*, Vol. 1, page 59).

18 Howbeit that [*the fact of the matter is—see definition of "howbeit" in the 1828 Noah Webster Dictionary*] he made the greater star; as, **also, if there be two spirits, and one shall be more intelligent than the other**, yet **these two spirits**, notwithstanding [*even though*] one is more intelligent than the other, **have no beginning**; they existed before, they shall have **no end**, they shall exist after, for they are gnolaum, or eternal.

19 And the Lord said unto me: **These two facts do exist**, that there are **two spirits, one being more intelligent than the other; there shall be another more intelligent than they; I am the Lord thy God, I am more intelligent than they all** [*in other words, God is the central focus and supreme creative power of the universe*].

> At this point in the lesson, the Lord stops to remind Abraham that He is the one who sent the angel to free him from the sacrificial altar when he was about to be sacrificed. This appears to be a practical example given by the Savior at this point in the lesson to Abraham that He does, indeed, have power over all things.

20 **The Lord thy God sent his angel to deliver thee from the hands of the priest of Elkenah**.

> We will pause a moment here to clarify some gospel vocabulary. Abraham is using three words interchangeably in these verses to mean premortal spirits. They are intelligence, spirit, and soul. We will quote from the *Pearl of Great Price Student Manual* on this subject (**bold** added for emphasis):
>
> "Abraham learned that there are varying degrees of intelligence among Heavenly Father's spirit children. (**Abraham called the spirit children of our Heavenly Father 'spirits'** in Abraham 3:18–19, **'intelligences'** in

verse 22, and **'souls'** in verse 23.) He learned that God dwelled in the midst of all the spirits or intelligences and that God 'is more intelligent than they all' (v. 19)" (*Pearl of Great Price Student Manual,* page 37).

In other words, here in these verses we are taught about spirit children of the Father during our premortal existence. In many gospel discussions in our day, we differentiate between these three words as follows:

1. Intelligence: what we were before we were born to our Heavenly Parents as spirit children. This intelligence is eternal. It had no beginning. Joseph Smith taught this. He said (**bold** added for emphasis):

"I am dwelling on the immortality of the spirit of man. Is it logical to say that the intelligence of spirits is immortal, and yet that it has a beginning? **The intelligence of spirits had no beginning**, neither will it have an end. That is good logic" (*History of the Church,* Vol. 6, page 311).

Elder Smith taught (**bold** added for emphasis):

"Some of our writers have endeavored to explain what an intelligence is, but to do so is futile, for we have never been given any insight into this matter beyond what the Lord has fragmentarily revealed. We know, however, that **there is something called intelligence, which always existed. It is the real eternal part of man**, which was not created or made. **This intelligence combined with the spirit constitutes a spiritual** identity or **individual**.

"**The spirit of man, then, is a combination of the intelligence and the spirit,** which is an entity begotten of God" (*Progress of Man,* page 11).

2. Spirit: We were born to our Heavenly Parents as spirit sons and daughters. At that point, our intelligence was clothed in a spirit body. We became spirit beings. It is these spirits about which Abraham is teaching us. The spirit matter (D&C 131:7–8) from which our spirit bodies are created is eternal, but we began our life as spirits when we were born to our Heavenly Parents.

3. Soul: Technically speaking, in our modern gospel vocabulary, "soul" means the spirit and body combined (see D&C 88:15).

The Lord continues the lesson that God is more intelligent than all. If we did not understand and believe this, we would not be able to worship and obey Him with full faith. This is a vital lesson and reinforcement for Abraham, who came from a culture in which idol worshippers believed in gods who warred among themselves, sometimes winning and sometimes losing. Against this background of false gods and idol worship, the Savior bears witness to Abraham that He does have all power and all intelligence. As we continue, we will see the words "intelligences" and "souls" both used to mean premortal spirits.

21 **I dwell in the midst of them all**; I now, therefore, have come down unto thee to declare [*teach, explain, show*] unto thee the works which my hands have made, wherein **my**

wisdom excelleth them all, for **I rule in the heavens above, and in the earth beneath, in all wisdom and prudence, over all the intelligences** [*spirits—see verse 23*] thine eyes have seen from the beginning; I came down in the beginning in the midst of all the **intelligences** thou hast seen.

22 Now the Lord had shown unto me, Abraham, the **intelligences** [*spirits—see verse 23*] that were organized before the world was; and among all these there were many of the **noble and great ones**;

> We know from modern revelation that many of these "noble and great ones" have been reserved to come to earth in the last days. They are a major reason that the Church will not go into apostasy again, as has been the case with each preceding dispensation. In the October 1989 general conference of the Church, Elder Marvin J. Ashton quoted President Ezra Taft Benson on this subject as follows (**bold** added for emphasis):
>
> "I share with you a statement of President Benson made to a gathering of youth in Southern California after he became President of the Church: '**For nearly six thousand years, God has held you in reserve to make your appearance in the final days before the Second Coming**. Every previous gospel dispensation has drifted into apostasy, but ours will not. . . . **God has saved for the final inning some of his strongest children, who will help bear off the kingdom triumphantly**. And that is where you come in, for you are the generation that must be prepared to meet your God. . . . Make no mistake about it—you are a marked generation. There has never been more expected of the faithful in such a short period of time as there is of us. . . . Each day we personally make many decisions that show where our support will go. The final outcome is certain—the forces of righteousness will finally win. What remains to be seen is where each of us personally, now and in the future, will stand in this fight—and how tall we will stand. Will we be true to our last-days, foreordained mission?'" (Marvin J. Ashton, "'Stalwart and Brave We Stand,'" *Ensign,* November 1989, pages 36–37).

23 And God saw these **souls** [*spirits*] that they were good, and he stood in the midst of them, and he said: **These I will make my rulers**; for **he stood among those that were spirits**, and he saw that they were good; and he said unto me: **Abraham, thou art one of them; thou wast chosen before thou wast born** [*Abraham was foreordained to be a prophet while yet a spirit in premortality*].

> We understand from verse 24, next, in combination with verses 22–23, above, that many of the "noble and great" assisted with the creation of the earth. Elder Smith taught:
>
> "It is true that Adam helped to form this earth. He labored with our Savior Jesus Christ. I have a strong view or conviction that there were others also who assisted them. Perhaps Noah and Enoch; and why not Joseph Smith, and those who were

appointed to be rulers before the earth was formed?" (*Doctrines of Salvation,* Vol. 1, pages 74–75).

Note the use of the word "we" in verse 24, next, implying that many of the noble and great assisted the Savior in creating the world.

24 And there stood one among them [*the noble and great ones*] **that was like unto God** [*in other words, this was Jesus Christ*], **and he** [*Jesus*] **said unto those who were with him: We** will go down, for there is space there, and **we** will take of these materials, and **we** will make an earth whereon these may dwell;

Students sometimes ask why the first part of verse 24, above, doesn't just come right out and say "Jehovah" or "Jesus," instead of saying "one . . . like unto God." We see similar wording in other places in scripture. One example is found in 1 Nephi 1:8, wherein Nephi writes that his father "thought he saw God," rather than simply saying, "he saw God." Daniel 3:25 says that the king saw a fourth person in the fiery furnace with Shadrach, Meshach, and Abednego who was "like the Son of God," rather than saying he saw a fourth person, and it was Jesus. Yet another example is Revelation 1:13, where the Savior is standing in the midst of the seven candlesticks. The reference to Him, though, is indirect. It is "one like unto the Son of man." You will see another example in verse 27, near the end of this chapter.

What you are seeing here is the Old Testament custom of being careful not to use the name of God inappropriately. Rather than risk taking the name of God in vain, writers often referred to Him indirectly. Abraham is part of this culture of extreme care when using the name of God. Thus, we see the careful, indirect form of referring to Deity here in the Pearl of Great Price. Our world would be much different if such care existed today as part of our culture.

As mentioned in the introduction to this chapter, verse 25, next, contains an important doctrine. It is a revealed truth that lays to rest many false conclusions reached while discussing the foreknowledge of God and the agency of man. It states, simply and concisely, that we have been sent here to earth to be tested.

25 And we [*the Gods*] **will prove** [*test*] **them** [*the premortal spirits being sent to earth*] **herewith** [*by creating an earth and sending them to it*], **to see if they will do all things whatsoever the Lord their God shall command them**;

Many times over my years of teaching, students have come to class quite concerned that their agency here on earth is, in the eternal realities, of little or no consequence. For example, a student came to class on a Monday still somewhat shaken from a discussion in his Sunday School class the previous day. The topic of God's knowledge of the future had come up, and the conclusion of the class was that because God knows all things, past, present, and future, He could tell us all, right now, what our lot will be on the final

Day of Judgment. All we are doing here is proving to ourselves that God is right about us.

This was obviously disturbing to the young man because it made it sound as if what he does in this life really doesn't count. I told him that I don't understand all there is to know about God's foreknowledge and our use of agency. However, I know where the final answer is found that addresses this dilemma. It is in Abraham 3:25. We read it together in class, and he was relieved.

This is one of those cases in which the Lord has given us the final answer to the question without giving us all the information leading up to the answer. Perhaps we couldn't understand it all. But the answer is vital. It is that we are indeed determining our future by the agency choices we make here on earth, provided we have a knowledge and understanding of the gospel of Jesus Christ.

Next, we are taught about the "first estate" and the "second estate." The term "first estate" is used in Jude 1:6 in the New Testament. We will define these gospel terms:

First Estate

Our premortal life as spirits. The phrase "keep their first estate" means to earn the right to be born on earth and receive a physical body. Thus, those who didn't keep their first estate are the one-third who were cast out with Satan.

Second Estate

Our life on earth. Those who do not have a fair chance to hear and understand the gospel here on earth will get the opportunity in the postmortal spirit world. Those who "keep their second estate" are those who keep God's commandments and thus qualify to return to the presence of the Father and become like Him.

Remember that the scene Abraham is showing us here is taking place during our premortal life, where preparations are being made to create our earth and send the spirits to earth who have qualified for that next step in their progression.

26 And **they who keep their first estate shall be added upon** [*the spirits who are worthy will be allowed to continue their progression by going to earth to gain a physical body, gain knowledge and experience, and be tested*]; and **they who keep not their first estate** [*the spirits who joined Lucifer and rebelled against God*] **shall not have glory in the same kingdom with those who keep their first estate** [*including the fact that they will not attain telestial, terrestrial, or celestial glory; rather, they will go with Satan to outer darkness after things finish up on earth—see D&C 76:31–48; 88:114*]; and **they who keep their second estate** [*live the gospel on earth or in the spirit world if they didn't get a fair chance on earth*] **shall have glory added upon their heads for ever and ever** [*will attain exaltation*].

In verses 27–28, next, we are given a brief look at the choosing of Jesus Christ to be our Savior and also the rebellion of Lucifer. Additional information can be found in Moses 4:1–4.

27 And **the Lord** [*the Father*] **said: Whom shall I send? And one answered like unto the Son of Man** [*in other words, Jesus Christ—see note after verse 24, above*]: **Here am I, send me.** And **another** [*Lucifer*] **answered and said: Here am I, send me.** And the Lord said: **I will send the first** [*Christ*].

28 And **the second** [*Lucifer*] **was angry,** and **kept not his first estate** [*did not remain worthy to come to earth and gain a body*]; and, at that day, **many** [*one-third—see Revelation 12:4*] **followed after him**.

We will continue our study now with Genesis.

In Genesis, Moses records his account from the creation of the earth up to the time when Joseph (who was sold into Egypt) dies. There is much of great value within its pages. It is foundational to our understanding of other scriptures. However, over the ages, much has been changed or left out of Genesis as it stands in the Bible (see Moses 1:40–41). We will use the books of Moses and Abraham in the Pearl of Great Price to add these missing verses to this study guide as we go along. You will see that they add much from Genesis 1 to Genesis 6:13.

By the way, the missing verses found in the book of Moses, which was given to Joseph Smith by direct revelation (see heading to Moses in your Pearl of Great Price), are also found in the JST. There are some versification differences in the JST when compared to the book of Moses. There are also a few wording differences; for example, see JST Moses 4:4 compared to Moses 5:4.

One last comment before we start our verse-by-verse study of Genesis, chapter one. The *Old Testament Gospel Doctrine Teacher's Manual*, page 10, points out that there are some differences between the accounts of the Creation found in Genesis, Moses, and Abraham. We will quote from that manual: "How do the accounts of the Creation found in Genesis, Moses, and Abraham differ from each other? (Abraham and Moses saw in vision the organizing of this earth and then recorded their visions. Each included slightly different details. The account in Genesis was originally written by Moses, but some of the fulness of his account was lost. This fulness is restored in the book of Moses.)"

It goes on to say "The purpose of the Creation is to provide a place where Heavenly Father's spirit children can come to obtain a physical body and be tested or proven to see if they will obey him when they are away from his presence . . . although an account of the Creation is included in the book of Genesis, the purposes and importance of the Creation are explained only in latter-day revelation."

GENESIS 1

This chapter deals with the creation of our heaven and earth—in other words, the sun, moon, stars, solar system, sky, atmosphere, etc., that pertain to our earth. It gives an account in broad strokes, and leaves details to future revelation. As you can see, it does not tell us "How" God created these things but rather "that" He indeed did it. This is a very important testimony to us in our day, when so many do not believe in God, and thus, attribute the earth's coming into existence as a fortunate accident of nature.

In other words, this chapter of Genesis bears strong witness that we are not biological accidents careening through interstellar space on an accidental planet. Rather, God created this earth specifically for us, His children, for our continued education to become like Him.

We naturally have many questions about how God created the earth, how long it took, the place of dinosaurs, etc. We will get the answers to these questions and much more when the Savior comes to earth at the beginning of the Millennium. The Doctrine and Covenants tells us:

Doctrine and Covenants 101:32–34

32 Yea, verily I say unto you, **in that day when the Lord shall come, he shall reveal all things**—

33 Things which have passed, and hidden things which no man knew, **things of the earth, by which it was made**, and the purpose and the end thereof—

34 Things most precious, things that are above, and things that are beneath, things that are in the earth, and upon the earth, and in heaven.

For our purposes here, we will point out several places (over 40 times) in this chapter in which the Lord bears witness, in one way or another, that He created the earth. We will use underlined **bold** to point this out and will add a few notes as we go, plus the relevant verses from Moses.

1 In the beginning [*the beginning of our earth, solar system, atmosphere, sky, etc., see* OT Student Manual, Genesis–2 Samuel, *p 27*] **God created the heaven and the earth**.

Moses 2:1

1 AND it came to pass that the Lord spake unto Moses, saying: Behold, I reveal unto you concerning this heaven, and this earth; write the words which I speak. I am the Beginning and the End, the Almighty God; by mine Only Begotten I created these things [*Christ just quoted the Father here, which is often referred to as "divine investiture," in which Christ speaks for the Father without formally announcing that He is doing so*]; yea, in the beginning I created the heaven, and the earth upon which thou standest.

As you saw in Moses, above, we are informed that Jesus Christ is the "God" spoken of in these verses. He spoke for His Father, saying, "by mine Only Begotten I created these things." The premortal Christ is the Creator until it comes to the creation of man. At that point, the Father will take over. We will provide notes to that effect when we get to verse 26.

Also, Joseph Smith defined the word create for us. It is often misunderstood and thus taught that God created the earth out of nothing. This is not the case. The Prophet taught:

"You ask the learned doctors why they say the world was made out of nothing: and they will answer, 'Doesn't the Bible say He created the world?' And they infer, from the word create, that it must have been made out of nothing. Now, the word create came from the word baurau which does not mean to create out of nothing; it means 'to organize'; the same as a man would organize materials and build a ship. Hence, we infer that God had materials to organize the world out of chaos—chaotic matter, which is element, and in which dwells all the glory. Element had an existence from the time he had. The pure principles of element are principles which can never be destroyed; they may be organized and reorganized, but not destroyed. They had no beginning, and can have no end" (*Teachings of the Prophet Joseph Smith,* pages 350–52).

2 And the earth was without form, and void [*"empty and desolate"—see Abraham 4:2*]; and darkness *was* upon the face of the deep. And **the Spirit of God moved** [*the Hebrew word used here means "brooded" and is what a mother hen does as she incubates her eggs and then watches over her chicks*] upon the face of the waters.

Moses 2:2

2 And the earth was without form, and void; and I caused darkness to come up upon the face of the deep; and my Spirit moved upon the face of the water; for I am God.

3 And **God said**, Let there be light: and there was light.

4 And **God saw** the light, that *it was* good: and **God divided** the light from the darkness.

5 And **God called** the light Day, and the darkness **he called** Night. And the evening and the morning were **the first day**.

Moses 2:3–5

3 And I, God, said: Let there be light; and there was light.

4 And I, God, saw the light; and that light was good. And I, God, divided the light from the darkness.

5 And I, God, called the light Day; and the darkness, I called Night; and this I did by the word of my power, and it was done as I spake; and the evening and the morning were the first day.

Elder John Taylor, who later became president of the Church, taught that the light spoken of in verses 3–4, above, was not the sun. The sun will be created in verses 14–18. He said that God "caused light to shine upon [*the earth*] before the sun appeared in the firmament [*see Moses 2:3–4, 14–19*]; for God is light, and in him there is no darkness. He is the light of the sun and the power thereof by which it was made; he is also the light of the moon and the power by which it was made; he is the light of the stars and the power by which they are made" (in *Journal of Discourses,* Vol. 18, page 327; see also Revelation 21:23–25; Doctrine and Covenants 88:7–13).

There may be important symbolism here, namely, that the most important light of all is the light that comes into our lives from God—a light that enables us to distinguish between light from God and spiritual darkness.

Also, there are differing opinions as to the meaning of the word day, as used in verse 5, above and elsewhere in this chapter. Some believe it means 24 hours, some say it means one thousand years. The fact is, we do not know how long it took to create the earth, and neither do we know that each "day" was of the same length.

The *Old Testament Gospel Doctrine Teacher's Manual,* page 11, says: "The length of time required for the Creation is not known." It goes on to say "The term *day* in the scriptural account of the Creation does not represent a 24-hour period. The Hebrew word *yom* can be translated as 'day,' 'time,' or 'period.'"

Speaking of the "six days" required for creating the earth, President Brigham Young said that it "is a mere term, but it matters not whether it took six days, six months, six years, or six thousand years. The creation occupied certain periods of time. **We are not authorized to say what the duration of these days was** (bold added for emphasis), whether Moses penned these words as we have them, or whether the translators of the Bible have given the words their intended meaning. However, God created the world. God brought forth material out of which he formed this little terra firma upon which we roam. How long had this material been in existence? Forever and forever, in some shape, in some condition" (*Discourses of Brigham Young,* sel. John A. Widtsoe [1971], page 100).

Furthermore, Elder Bruce R. McConkie taught that a day, as used in the creation accounts, "is a specified time period; it is an age, an eon, a division of eternity; it is the time between two identifiable events. And each day, of whatever length, has the duration needed for its purposes. . . . There is no revealed recitation specifying that each of the 'six days' involved in the Creation was of the same duration" ("Christ and the Creation," *Ensign,* June 1982, page 11).

Abraham, who was an astronomer trained by the Lord (Abraham 3), did not use the term "day" in his account of the creation. Rather, he referred to each creative period as a "time" (see Abraham 4:8, 13, 19, 23, 31, and 5:2). That leaves things open as to how long it took.

6 ¶ And **God said**, Let there be a firmament [*the atmosphere surrounding the earth; the sky; the heavens we see as we look up from the earth*] in the midst of the waters, and let it divide the waters [*on the surface of the earth*] from the waters [*in the sky; the clouds, the dew, etc.*].

Moses 2:6

6 And again, I, God, said: Let there be a firmament in the midst of the water, and it was so, even as I spake; and I said: Let it divide the waters from the waters; and it was done;

7 And **God made** the firmament, and divided [*separated*] the waters which *were* under the firmament [*the waters on the earth's surface*] from the waters which *were* above the firmament [*the clouds, moisture in the atmosphere above us, etc.*]: and it was so.

Moses 2:7

7 And I, God, made the firmament and divided the waters, yea, the great waters under the firmament from the waters which were above the firmament, and it was so even as I spake.

Joseph Fielding Smith helped us understand verse 7, above. He taught:

"The waters above the firmament is a reference to the clouds and the waters which exist in the atmosphere above the earth" (*Answers to Gospel Questions,* Vol. 4, pages 116–17).

Bruce R. McConkie taught:

"'The waters' were 'divided' between the surface of the earth and the atmospheric heavens that surround it. A 'firmament' or an 'expanse' called 'Heaven' was created to divide 'the waters which were under the expanse from the waters which were above the expanse.' Thus, as the creative events unfold, provision seems to be made for clouds and rain and storms to give life to that which will yet grow and dwell upon the earth. (See Moses 2:6–8; Abraham 4:6–8.)" ("Christ and the Creation," *Ensign*, June 1982, page 11).

8 And **God called** the firmament Heaven. And the evening and the morning were **the second day**.

Moses 2:8

8 And I, God, called the firmament Heaven; and the evening and the morning were the second day.

Perhaps you've noticed that, in biblical cultures, the days go from sundown to sundown, as opposed to our system of midnight to midnight.

Next, the Lord organizes things such that, at this point in the creation, we have basically one ocean and one continent. They will be divided into several oceans and continents in the days of Peleg (Genesis 10:25).

9 ¶ And **God said**, Let the waters under the heaven [*those on the earth's surface*] be gathered together unto one place, and **let the dry *land* appear**: and it was so.

10 And **God called** the dry *land* Earth; and the gathering together of the waters **called he** Seas: and **God saw** that *it was* good.

Moses 2:9–10

9 And I, God, said: Let the waters under the heaven be gathered together unto one place, and it was so; and I, God, said: Let there be dry land; and it was so.

10 And I, God, called the dry land Earth; and the gathering together of the waters, called I the Sea; and I, God, saw that all things which I had made were good.

Did you notice, in verse 10 of Moses, above, the Lord used the word "Sea," singular, rather than "Seas," as in the Genesis version? It is an inspired reminder that at this time in creation there was just one ocean.

Next, in verses 11–12, as the third "day" continues, the Lord puts the eco systems in place that will be needed to sustain all forms of life on earth.

11 And **God said**, Let the earth bring forth **grass**, the **herb** yielding seed, *and* the **fruit tree** yielding fruit after his kind, whose seed *is* in itself [*such as apples, peaches, etc.*], upon the earth: and it was so.

12 And the earth brought forth grass, *and* herb yielding seed after his kind, and the tree yielding fruit, whose seed *was* in itself, after his kind: and **God saw** that *it was* good.

Moses 2:11–12

11 And I, God, said: Let the earth bring forth grass, the herb yielding seed, the fruit tree yielding fruit, after his kind, and the tree yielding fruit, whose seed should be in itself upon the earth, and it was so even as I spake.

12 And the earth brought forth grass, every herb yielding seed after his kind, and the tree yielding fruit, whose seed should be in itself, after his kind; and I, God, saw that all things which I had made were good;

Perhaps you noticed, in verses 11–12, above, that each plant was to procreate "after his kind." Regarding the importance of this phrase, Elder Boyd K. Packer taught:

"No lesson is more manifest in nature than that all living things do as the Lord commanded in the Creation. They reproduce 'after their own kind.' (See Moses 2:12, 24.) They follow the pattern of their parentage. . . . A bird will not become an animal nor a fish. A mammal will not beget reptiles, nor 'do men gather . . . figs of thistles' (Matthew 7:16.)" ("The Pattern of Our Parentage," *Ensign*, November 1984, page 67).

Elder Mark E. Petersen, of the Twelve, likewise taught the doctrinal significance of these words. He said:

"He commanded them to reproduce themselves. They too would bring forth only 'after their kind.' It could be in no other way. Each form of life was destined to bring forth after its own kind so that it would be perpetuated in the earth and avoid confusion.

"Man was always man, and always will be, for we are the offspring of God. The fact that we know of our own form and image and the further fact that we are God's offspring give us positive knowledge of the form and image of God, after whom we are made and of whom we are born as his children.

"God would not violate his own laws. When he decreed that all reproduction was to be 'after its kind,' he obeyed the same law. We are therefore of the race of God. To follow an opposite philosophy is to lead us into atheism" (*Moses: Man of Miracles* [Salt Lake City: Deseret Book, 1977], 163).

Moses 2:13 is the same as verse 13, next.

13 And the evening and the morning were **the third day** [*the "third time"—see Abraham 4:13*].

Next, the sun, moon, and stars are created.

14 ¶ And **God said**, Let there be lights in the firmament of the heaven [*in the sky*] to divide the day from the night; and let them be for signs, and for seasons, and for days, and years [*things that mortals can use for navigation and calendaring, etc.*]:

15 And let them be for lights in the firmament of the heaven to give light upon the earth: and it was so.

Moses 2:14–15

14 And I, God, said: Let there be lights in the firmament of the heaven, to divide the day from the night, and let them be for signs, and for seasons, and for days, and for years;

15 And let them be for lights in the firmament of the heaven to give light upon the earth; and it was so.

16 And **God made** two great lights; the greater light [*the sun*] to rule the day, and the lesser light [*the moon*] to rule the night: *he made* the stars also.

Moses 2:16

16 And I, God, made two great lights; the greater light to rule the day, and the lesser light to rule the night, and the greater light was the sun, and the lesser light was the moon; and the stars also were made even according to my word.

17 And **God set** them in the firmament of the heaven to give light upon the earth,

18 And to rule over the day and over the night, and to divide the light from the darkness: and **God saw** that *it was* good.

19 And the evening and the morning were **the fourth day**.

Moses 2:17–19

17 And I, God, set them in the firmament of the heaven to give light upon the earth,

18 And the sun to rule over the day, and the moon to rule over the night, and to divide the light from the darkness; and I, God, saw that all things which I had made were good;

19 And the evening and the morning were the fourth day.

Next, the fifth "day" of creation is briefly explained in verses 20–23. Creatures that live in water and birds of all kinds were created during this period. Once again, we see Moses emphasizing that they reproduce "after their kind" as he wrote his account.

20 And **God said**, Let the waters bring forth abundantly the moving creature that hath life, and fowl *that* may fly above the earth in the open firmament of heaven.

21 And **God created** great whales, and every living creature that moveth, which the waters brought forth abundantly, **after their kind**, and every winged fowl **after his kind**: and **God saw** that *it was* good.

22 And **God blessed** them, saying, Be fruitful, and multiply, and **fill** the waters in the seas, and let fowl multiply in the earth.

23 And the evening and the morning were **the fifth day**.

Moses 2:20–23

20 And I, God, said: Let the waters bring forth abundantly the moving creature that hath life, and fowl which may fly above the earth in the open firmament of heaven.

21 And I, God, created great whales, and every living creature that moveth, which the waters brought forth abundantly, after their kind, and every winged fowl after his kind; and I, God, saw that all things which I had created were good.

22 And I, God, blessed them, saying: Be fruitful, and multiply, and fill the waters in the sea; and let fowl multiply in the earth;

23 And the evening and the morning were the fifth day.

Did you notice the word "sea," in Moses, verse 22, above, as opposed to "seas" in Genesis? Another reminder that at this point there was one ocean.

The word "fill" in verse 22, above, will be especially helpful when we get to verse 28. In that verse, the word "replenish" will be used. Some people assume that "replenish" implies that Adam and Eve are to "refill" the earth, which in turn implies that it was once populated before Adam and Eve came on the scene. The revealed word of God teaches us that Adam "was the first man" (Doctrine and Covenants 84:16). The words "fill" and "replenish," as used in these verses, come from the same Hebrew word and both mean "to fill." See verse 28, footnote c in your Bible.

24 ¶ And **God said**, Let the earth bring forth the living creature **after his kind**, cattle [*this word generally refers to domesticated animals*], and creeping thing, and beast of the earth **after his kind**: and it was so.

25 And **God made** the beast of the earth after his kind, and cattle after their kind, and every thing that creepeth upon the earth after his kind: and **God saw** that *it was* good.

Moses 2:24–25

24 And I, God, said: Let the earth bring forth the living creature after his kind, cattle, and creeping things, and beasts of the earth after their kind, and it was so;

25 And I, God, made the beasts of the earth after their kind, and cattle after their kind, and everything which creepeth upon the earth after his kind; and I, God, saw that all these things were good.

Now, watch for a significant doctrine to be taught next, in verse 26, regarding the creation of mankind. There is a change in "Creators." At this point, when it comes to "creating" man, Heavenly Father takes over. This is because we are not "creations" of God, in the normal sense, like animals, trees, mountains, etc. Rather, we are the "offspring of God" (Acts 17:28), in other words, we are His literal spirit sons and daughters (see "The Family: A Proclamation to the World," *Ensign,* November 1995, page 102).

To put it another way, Christ is not our "creator," in the literal sense, rather, we are the "offspring" of our Heavenly Parents.

Bruce R. McConkie clearly taught that the Father took over when it came to the placement of man upon the earth. He said (**bold** added for emphasis):

"We know that Jehovah-Christ, assisted by 'many of the noble and great ones' (Abraham 3:22), of whom Michael is but the illustration, did in fact create the earth and all forms of plant and animal life on the face thereof. **But when it came to placing man on earth, there was a change in Creators. That is, the Father himself became personally involved.** All things were created by the Son, using the power delegated by the Father, except man. In the spirit and again in the flesh, man was created by the Father. There was no delegation of authority where the crowning creature of creation was concerned" (*The Promised Messiah,* page 62; see also *Doctrines of the Gospel Student Manual,* page 18).

26 ¶ And **God** [*the Father*] **said, Let us make** man in our image, after our likeness: and **let them have dominion** over the fish of the sea, and over the fowl of the air, and over the cattle, and over all the earth, and over every creeping thing that creepeth upon the earth.

Moses 2:26

26 And I, God, said unto mine Only Begotten, which was with me from the beginning: Let us make man in our image, after our likeness; and it was so. And I, God, said: Let them have dominion over the fishes of the sea, and over the fowl of the air, and over the cattle, and over all the earth, and over every creeping thing that creepeth upon the earth.

27 So **God created** man in his *own* image, in the image of **God created** he him; male and female **created he** them.

Concerning the creation of man and woman in verse 27, above, the First Presidency taught (**bold** added for emphasis):

"All **men and women are in the similitude of the universal Father and Mother**, and are literally the sons and daughters of Deity.

"'God created man in His own image.' This is just as true of the spirit as it is of the body, which is only the clothing of the spirit, its complement; the two together constituting the soul. The spirit of man is in the form of man, and the spirits of all creatures are in the likeness of their bodies. This was plainly taught by the Prophet Joseph Smith (Doctrine and Covenants, 77:2)" (The First Presidency [Joseph F. Smith, John R. Winder, and Anthon H. Lund], in James R. Clark, comp., *Messages of the First Presidency of The Church of Jesus Christ of Latter-day Saints,* 4:203).

Concerning how the physical bodies of Adam and Eve were formed, President Spencer W. Kimball taught (**bold** added for emphasis):

"Man became a living soul—mankind, male and female. The Creators breathed into their nostrils the breath of life and man and woman became living souls. **We don't know exactly how their coming into this world happened**, and when we're able to understand it the Lord will tell us" ("The Blessings and Responsibilities of Womanhood," *Ensign*, March 1976, page 72).

Our stewardship and responsibility for taking proper care of the earth and all things in it are summarized in verse 28, next.

28 And **God blessed** them, and **God said** unto them, Be fruitful, and multiply, and replenish [*see note after verse 22, explaining that "replenish" means "fill," not "refill"*] the earth, and **subdue it: and have dominion** over the fish of the sea, and over the fowl of the air, and over every living thing that moveth upon the earth.

29 ¶ And **God said**, Behold, **I have given** you every herb bearing seed, which *is* upon the face of all the earth, and every tree, in the which *is* the fruit of a tree yielding seed; to you it shall be **for meat** [*food*].

Moses 2:28–29

28 And I, God, blessed them, and said unto them: Be fruitful, and multiply, and replenish the earth, and subdue it, and have dominion over the fish of the sea, and over the fowl of the air, and over every living thing that moveth upon the earth.

29 And I, God, said unto man: Behold, I have given you every herb bearing seed, which is upon the face of all the earth, and every tree in the which shall be the fruit of a tree yielding seed; to you it shall be for meat.

You will find the word "meat" used many times in the scriptures. It helps to know that, in ancient times, "meat" was a general term for "food." If the writer was referring to what we call "meat" in our day, the word used was "flesh."

30 And to every beast of the earth, and to every fowl of the air, and to every thing that creepeth upon the earth, wherein *there is* life, *I have given* every green herb **for meat**: and it was so.

31 And **God saw** every thing that **he had made**, and, behold, *it was*

very good. And the evening and the morning were **the sixth day**.

Moses 2:30–31

30 And to every beast of the earth, and to every fowl of the air, and to everything that creepeth upon the earth, wherein I grant life, there shall be given every clean herb for meat; and it was so, even as I spake.

31 And I, God, saw everything that I had made, and, behold, all things which I had made were very good; and the evening and the morning were the sixth day.

As you can see in verses 1–31, above, there are many ways in which we are assured that God created the earth and everything in it. Thus, we know that it is not an accident of nature, nor is it a chance evolutionary happening. Elder John A. Widtsoe, of the Twelve, said:

"The earth came into being by the will and power of God. . . . Chance is ruled out. Latter-day Saints believe that the earth and the heavens and the manifold operations within the universe are products of intelligent action, of the mind of God" (Evidences and Reconciliations, page 150).

GENESIS 2

This chapter is a continuation of the Creation account. It points out that all things were created in spirit form (verse 5) before being placed on earth as physical entities. We learn of the creation of the Garden of Eden, the commandment not to partake of the tree of knowledge of good and evil (verse 17), the creation of Eve, and the importance of husband and wife being loyal to each other.

In verses 1–4, next, we find a summary of what we were taught in chapter 1. We will continue adding relevant verses from the Pearl of Great Price, Moses, so that you can readily see what was left out of this part of the Bible. For teaching purposes, we will continue to emphasize certain things with **bold.**

1 **Thus the heavens** [*JST, "heaven"*] **and the earth were finished, and all the host of them** [*everything that belongs in them*].

2 And **on the seventh day God** ended his work which he had made; and he **rested on the seventh day from all his work** which he had made.

Moses 3:1–2

1 THUS the heaven and the earth were finished, and all the host of them.

2 And on the seventh day I, God, ended my work, and all things which I had made; and I rested on the seventh day from all my work, and all things which I had made were finished, and I, God, saw that they were good;

In verse 3, we find that the Sabbath was made holy in the beginning of the earth's history. The sacred nature of the Sabbath was reemphasized by the Lord through Moses in the Ten Commandments (Exodus 20:8–11).

3 And **God blessed the seventh day, and sanctified it** [*made it a holy day*]: because that in it he had rested

from all his work which God created and made.

4 ¶ These *are* the generations of [*the story of*] the heavens and of the earth when they were created, in the day that **the Lord God** [*Jesus Christ—see footnote 4b in your Bible*] **made the earth and the heavens,**

Moses 3:3–4

3 And I, God, blessed the seventh day, and sanctified it; because that in it I had rested from all my work which I, God, had created and made.

4 And now, behold, I say unto you, that these are the generations of the heaven and of the earth, when they were created, in the day that I, the Lord God, made the heaven and the earth,

Verse 5, next, clarified by Moses 3:5, teaches us that all things were made in spirit form, before they were combined with the physical elements of the earth and became physical entities. As you are probably aware, there is very little written in the scriptures about our premortal existence. Most Christian churches do not even teach premortal life as a doctrine. Therefore, although brief, verse 5, next, is significant because it presents an opportunity to share the concept and doctrine of premortality with nonmember friends who believe the Bible.

5 And **every plant** of the field **before it was in the earth**, and every herb of the field before it grew: for the Lord God had not caused it to rain upon the earth, and *there was not* a man to till the ground.

Moses 3:5

5 And every plant of the field before it was in the earth, and every herb of the field before it grew. For **I, the Lord God, created all things, of which I have spoken, spiritually** [*in spirit form*], **before they were naturally** [*in physical form*] **upon the face of the earth**. For I, the Lord God, had not caused it to rain upon the face of the earth. And **I, the Lord God, had created all the children of men** [*those of us who were to come to this earth had all been born by that time as spirit children of our Heavenly Parents*]; and **not yet a man to till the ground**; for **in heaven created I them**; and there was not yet flesh upon the earth, neither in the water, neither in the air;

We inserted a note, in verse 5 of Moses, above, indicating that our group of spirits had all been born as spirit children to our heavenly parents before the physical creation of our earth. Elder James E. Talmage taught that there is a certain number of spirits assigned to this earth. He said:

"The population of the earth is fixed according to the number of spirits appointed to take tabernacles of flesh upon this planet; when these have all come forth in the order and time appointed, then, and not till then, shall the end come" (*Articles of Faith,* page 175).

Obviously, since our Heavenly Parents are exalted beings and have "a continuation of the seeds forever and ever" (Doctrine and Covenants 132:19), they will continue to have and rear spirit offspring forever, just as they did us, and will continue to create worlds to which these spirit offspring will be sent for their mortal experience and progression. Thus, this account of the creation which we are reading, written for us by Moses, is "only an account of this earth" (Moses 1:35) and our group of spirits.

6 But **there went up a mist from the earth, and watered the whole face of the ground** [*in preparation for the physical creation of all things to be placed upon the earth*].

Moses 3:6

6 But I, the Lord God, spake, and there went up a mist from the earth, and watered the whole face of the ground.

Are you noticing the extra emphasis we often see in Moses that God did indeed create the earth? This is a vital witness to us in our day when so many do not believe in a divine creation.

Next, we see the physical creation of man.

7 And **the Lord God** [*Heavenly Father*] **formed man** *of* **the dust of the ground** [*created a body from the physical elements of the earth*], **and breathed into his nostrils the breath of life** [*put into him his spirit—see Abraham 5:7*]; and man became a living soul [*spirit body plus physical body—compare with Doctrine and Covenants 88:15*].

Moses 3:7

7 And I, the Lord God, formed man from the dust of the ground, and breathed into his nostrils the breath of life; and man became a living soul, the first flesh upon the earth, the first man also; nevertheless, all things were before created; but spiritually were they created and made according to my word.

In verse 7 of Moses, above, we are taught that Adam was the "first man." The First Presidency explained this as follows:

"It is held by some that Adam was not the first man upon this earth, and that the original human being was a development from lower orders of the animal creation. These, however, are the theories of men. The word of the Lord declares that Adam was 'the first man of all men' (Moses 1:34), and we are therefore in duty bound to regard him as the primal [*original*] parent of our race" ("The Origin of Man," *Improvement Era*, November 1909, page 80).

In your Bible, you will notice a symbol at the beginning of verse 8, next, which looks like a fancy backward "P." Each time you see one of these in your King James Bible (the version the Church uses in English-speaking areas of the world), it means that it is going on to a new topic. In this case, we are moving on to the placement of Adam in the Garden of Eden.

8 ¶ And **the Lord God planted a garden eastward in Eden; and there he put the man** [*Adam*] **whom he had formed.**

Moses 3:8

8 And I, the Lord God, planted a garden eastward in Eden, and there I put the man whom I had formed.

The following two quotes tell us the location of the Garden of Eden (**bold** added for emphasis):

Brigham Young

"In the beginning, after this earth was prepared for man, the Lord commenced his work upon what is now called **the American continent, where the Garden of Eden was made**" (*Discourses of Brigham Young,* page 102).

Heber C. Kimball

"The spot chosen for the garden of Eden was **Jackson County**, in the State of **Missouri**, where [*the city of*] **Independence** now stands; it was occupied in the morn of creation by Adam" (in *Journal of Discourses,* Vol. 10, page 235).

In verse 9, next, Moses teaches us that there were two special trees in the Garden of Eden, and that they were in plain sight for Adam and Eve (when she comes along).

9 And out of the ground made the Lord God to grow every tree that is pleasant to the sight, and good for food; **the tree of life** also in the midst of the garden, and **the tree of knowledge of good and evil**.

Moses 3:9

9 And out of the ground made I, the Lord God, to grow every tree, naturally, that is pleasant to the sight of man; and man could behold it. And it became also a living soul. For it was spiritual [*in spirit form*] in the day that I created it; for it remaineth in the sphere in which I, God, created it, yea, even all things which I prepared for the use of man; and man saw that it was good for food. And I, the Lord God, planted the tree of life also in the midst of the garden, and also the tree of knowledge of good and evil.

Did you notice, in verse 9 of Moses, above, that "every tree . . . became also a living soul?" In other words, each spirit tree received a physical body during the physical creation, and thus became a "living soul." Understanding this doctrine should increase our appreciation and respect for the eco system created for us here on earth.

It is significant that the tree of knowledge of good and evil is placed "in the midst of the garden"; in other words, in plain sight, since, in verse 17, Adam will be commanded not to partake of it. As you know, agency choices form a vital part of the curriculum developed by the Lord for our education here on earth. Opposition is a necessary part of setting the stage of agency choices (2 Nephi 2:11–14). We will do more with this in a bit.

Bruce R. McConkie gave a brief insight about the two trees specifically mentioned in verse 9, above. He said (**bold** added for emphasis):

"The scriptures set forth that there were in the Garden of Eden two trees. One was **the tree of life**, which figuratively refers to eternal life; the other was **the tree of knowledge of good and evil**, which figuratively refers to how and why and in what manner mortality and all that appertains to it came into being" (*A New Witness for the Articles of Faith* [1985], 86).

We will not attempt to do anything with the geography described in verses 10–14, next, other than to suggest that there may be symbolic meaning in the fact that the four great rivers mentioned had their origin in the river that came out of the Garden of Eden. Symbolically, one message might be that all the world has greatly benefited from that which started in the Garden of Eden (Adam and Eve and the Fall).

10 And **a river went out of Eden** to water the garden; and from thence it was parted, and became into four heads.

11 The name of the first *is* Pison: that *is* it which compasseth the whole land of Havilah, where *there is* gold;

12 And the gold of that land *is* good: there *is* bdellium and the onyx stone.

13 And the name of the second river *is* Gihon: the same *is* it that compasseth the whole land of Ethiopia.

14 And the name of the third river *is* Hiddekel: that *is* it which goeth toward the east of Assyria. And the fourth river *is* Euphrates.

Moses 3:10–14

10 And I, the Lord God, caused a river to go out of Eden to water the garden; and from thence it was parted, and became into four heads.

11 And I, the Lord God, called the name of the first Pison, and it compasseth the whole land of Havilah, where I, the Lord God, created much gold;

12 And the gold of that land was good, and there was bdellium and the onyx stone.

13 And the name of the second river was called Gihon; the same that compasseth the whole land of Ethiopia.

14 And the name of the third river was Hiddekel; that which goeth toward the east of Assyria. And the fourth river was the Euphrates.

15 And **the Lord God took the man, and put him into the garden of Eden** to dress it [*cultivate it—see footnote 15c in your Bible*] and to keep it [*take good care of it*]

Moses 3:15

15 And I, the Lord God, took the man, and put him into the Garden of Eden, to dress it, and to keep it.

Before continuing with verses 16–17, next, it is helpful to remember what the first commandment given to Adam and Eve was. After creating them in Genesis 1:27, in verse 28, He told them to "be fruitful, and multiply, and replenish the earth"; in other words, He commanded them to have children. They cannot have children in their current condition in the Garden of Eden. Even though they have physical bodies, they are not yet mortal. The only way they can become mortal is to partake of the fruit of the tree of knowledge of good and evil. Next, in verses 16–17, He commands Adam not to partake of that tree. We will need additional information to help us with this, but first, let's look at the next two verses.

16 And **the Lord God commanded the man**, saying, **Of every tree of the garden thou mayest freely eat**:

Moses 3:16

16 And I, the Lord God, commanded the man, saying: Of every tree of the garden thou mayest freely eat,

17 **But of the tree of the knowledge of good and evil, thou shalt not eat of it**: for in the day that thou eatest thereof thou shalt surely die.

Moses 3:17 has important additional information. We will quote it here, **using bold for** the words that were left out of verse 17, above, in the Bible:

Moses 3:17

17 But of the tree of the knowledge of good and evil, thou shalt not eat of it**, nevertheless, thou mayest choose for thyself, for it is given unto thee; but, remember that I forbid it**, for in the day thou eatest thereof thou shalt surely die.

Do you see why the addition in Moses is so important? It is an invitation from the Lord for Adam and Eve to use their agency, and to own the consequences. Joseph Fielding Smith taught the significance of the additions to this verse in Moses. He said:

"Just why the Lord would say to Adam that he forbade him to partake of the fruit of that tree is not made clear in the Bible account, but in the original as it comes to us in the Book of Moses it is made definitely clear. It is that **the Lord said to Adam that if he wished to remain as he was in the garden, then he was not to eat the fruit, but if he desired to eat it and partake of death he was at liberty to do so**. So really it was not in the true sense a transgression of a divine commandment. Adam made the wise decision, in fact the only decision he could make" (*Answers to Gospel Questions,* Vol. 4, page 81).

Next, the topic changes to the creation of Eve. Many people misread this verse. The mistake they make is seeing, in their mind's eye, "helpmeet" rather than "help meet" (two separate words). We will say more about this in a moment.

18 ¶ And the Lord God said, *It is* not good that the man should be alone; I will make him an **help meet** for him.

Moses 3:18

18 And I, the Lord God, said unto mine Only Begotten, that it was not

good that the man should be alone; wherefore, I will make an help meet for him.

The additions in Moses make it very clear that Heavenly Father is doing the creating here.

The distinction between help meet and helpmeet (or helpmate, as it is sometimes referred to) is crucial to proper understanding of the roles of husband and wife. Helpmeet means "helper" or "assistant" and is often interpolated to mean "of lesser status." Help meet means "help that is vital for him." "Meet" means "necessary," "vital," "required" (compare with Doctrine and Covenants 58:26).

Thus, God created a vital help for Adam, a companion of equal status to work with him and he with her. The equality of husband and wife is clearly taught in the Proclamation on the Family. The First Presidency and the Quorum of the Twelve stated (**bold** added for emphasis):

"By divine design, fathers are to preside over their families in love and righteousness and are responsible to provide the necessities of life and protection for their families. Mothers are primarily responsible for the nurture of their children. In these sacred responsibilities, **fathers and mothers are** obligated to help one another as **equal partners**" (*Ensign*, November 1995, page 102).

President Howard W. Hunter taught the following about the proper relationship between husband and wife (**bold** added for emphasis):

"A man who holds the priesthood accepts his wife as a partner in the leadership of the home and family with full knowledge of and full participation in all decisions relating thereto. . . . The Lord intended that the wife be a help meet for man (**meet means equal**)—that is, **a companion equal and necessary in full partnership.**" ("Being a Righteous Husband and Father," *Ensign*, November 1994, pages 50–51)

Verse 19, next, and the first two thirds of verse 20 inform us that Adam was given the responsibility to name the creatures. This was a tremendous task and would require much inspiration. It also shows us the high intelligence and capability of Adam.

19 And out of the ground the Lord God formed every beast of the field, and every fowl of the air; and **brought *them* unto Adam to see what he would call them**: and whatsoever Adam called every living creature, that *was* the name thereof.

20 **And Adam gave names to all cattle** [*domesticated animals*]**, and to the fowl of the air, and to every beast of the field**; but for Adam there was not found an help meet for him.

We will add some notes to these same verses in Moses.

Moses 3:19–20

19 And out of the ground [*symbolic of the physical creation*] I, the Lord God, formed **every beast of the field, and every fowl of the air**; and commanded that they should

come unto Adam, to see what he would call them; and they **were also living souls**; for I, God, breathed into them the breath of life, and commanded that whatsoever Adam called every living creature, that should be the name thereof.

Did you notice that the creatures obeyed God's command and came to Adam to see what he would name them. Adam didn't have to chase down each one and name it. Also, did you notice that the animals are "living souls?" Their spirit bodies are combined with their physical bodies to make souls (compare with Doctrine and Covenants 88:15). Again, this simple doctrine teaches respect for animals.

20 And **Adam gave names to all cattle, and to the fowl of the air, and to every beast of the field**; but as for Adam, there was not found an help meet for him.

The last phrase of verse 20, above, sets the stage for the creation of Eve. Because the account given in verses 21–22, next, sounds literal, most people believe that a rib was actually taken from Adam from which to form Eve. The words of a modern prophet inform us that such was not the case. We will read these two verses first, and then read a quote from President Spencer W. Kimball.

21 And the Lord God caused a deep sleep to fall upon Adam, and he slept: and **he took one of his ribs, and closed up the flesh instead thereof** [*in place of the rib*];

22 And **the rib, which the Lord God had taken from man, made he a woman**, and brought her unto the man.

Moses 3:21–22

21 And I, the Lord God, caused a deep sleep to fall upon Adam; and he slept, and I took one of his ribs and closed up the flesh in the stead thereof;

22 And the rib which I, the Lord God, had taken from man, made I a woman, and brought her unto the man.

Among other things, the symbolism of the rib teaches that husband and wife walk side by side, as they follow the Lord's teachings about marriage.

President Spencer W. Kimball taught that the story of the rib is symbolic. He said:

"The story of the rib, of course, is figurative" ("The Blessings and Responsibilities of Womanhood," *Ensign*, March 1976, page 71).

In the Near Eastern culture in which Moses lived, the phrase "bone of my bone" and other similar phrases (see verse 23, next) mean, in effect, "We are family. We belong to each other." Thus, the imagery of taking a rib from Adam and forming Eve is a cultural way of symbolically saying that they are family.

Actually, we do the same thing in our language and culture. For example, we say, "He is a chip off the old block," meaning that he is just like his father. Someone learning English as a second language might wonder why we say he is a chip off the old block, when he is not a chip of wood and his father is not shaped like a block of wood.

All in all, this account lends feeling and intrigue to the all-important joining of Adam and Eve together as family, as parents of the human race on this earth. It gives much more than the fact that she came on the scene. It provides drama and focus, warmth and tenderness, belonging and protectiveness, unity and purpose to the account, far beyond the fact of Adam and Eve's coming forth to fulfill their role in the great "plan of happiness."

That Adam understood the symbolism is clear in his statement in verses 23–24, next.

23 And Adam said, This *is* now bone of my bones, and flesh of my flesh: she shall be called Woman, because she was taken out of Man.

24 Therefore shall a man leave his father and his mother, and shall cleave unto his wife: and they shall be one flesh.

Moses 3:23–24

23 And Adam said: This I know now is bone of my bones, and flesh of my flesh; she shall be called Woman, because she was taken out of man.

24 Therefore shall a man leave his father and his mother, and shall cleave unto his wife; and they shall be one flesh.

Did you notice that, in Moses, verse 23, above, the addition shows us that Adam, in effect, bears his testimony of Eve's importance? He says

"This I know now," which is stronger than the Genesis version.

Verse 25, next, reminds us that, at this point in the Creation, Adam and Eve were still in a state of innocence, not being embarrassed at being naked. Those feelings will come after the Fall (see Genesis 3:7). This verse in Moses is the same.

25 And **they were both naked, the man and his wife, and were not ashamed** [*embarrassed*].

Moses 3:25

25 And they were both naked, the man and his wife, and were not ashamed.

In addition to the simple literal meaning of verse 25, above, there may be an important symbolic meaning to the word, "naked." It could symbolize not hiding things from each other, being open and honest in our relationship with our spouse.

We will include Abraham, chapters 4 and 5 here, because they provide additional material to go along with Genesis 2, above.

ABRAHAM 4

Background

Abraham chapters 4 and 5 are accounts of the Creation. There are four major accounts of the Creation available to us. They are:

1. Genesis 1–2.
2. Moses 2–3.
3. Abraham 4–5
4. The account given in the temple.

By looking ahead to Abraham 5:3–4, we are given to understand that Abraham's account of the Creation, up to those verses (in other words, from 4:1–31 through 5:1–2), was primarily an account of the planning stages prior to the actual creation of the earth. This is reflected in the heading to chapter 4 in the Pearl of Great Price, which reads, *"The Gods plan the creation of the earth and all life thereon—Their plans for the six days of creation are set forth."* Therefore, we can easily refer to chapter 4 as a blueprint for the creation of our earth.

If we fail to understand this, we will become confused when we get to chapter 5 and begin reading about the actual Creation. We will likely say, "Wait a minute, I just read that. What's going on here?"

We need to be a bit careful, however, not to consider Abraham 4:1–31 through 5:1–2 to be exclusively a blueprint of creation, since it appears that, occasionally, Abraham refers to the planning and then jumps ahead and says, in effect, "This is what they actually did." It is quite common in ancient writings for the authors not to limit themselves to exact chronological order. Both Isaiah and Revelation are examples of scriptures that do not adhere to strict chronology.

This chapter is a continuation of Abraham 3:22–28, in which plans were being made to create our earth and send us to it. One of the unique contributions of Abraham is the fact that he uses the term "Gods" rather than the singular "God" in his account. Elder Mark E. Petersen commented on this as follows:

"The account of creation as given in the Book of Abraham is distinctive in that it says that great work was done by 'the Gods' in contrast to the belief that one God—one Almighty Being—made all things by himself, and out of nothing. There was a plurality of Gods engaged in creation. This fact is well corroborated in the Bible, including some passages in Genesis. . . .

"Who were these Gods?

"We believe in a Godhead of Father, Son, and Holy Ghost. Who else would have participated in the Creation?" (*Abraham, Friend of God*, pages 144–45).

Joseph Fielding Smith taught:

"It is true that Adam helped to form this earth. He labored with our Savior Jesus Christ. I have a strong view or conviction that there were others also who assisted them. Perhaps Noah and Enoch; and why not Joseph Smith, and those who were appointed to be rulers before the earth was formed? We know that Jesus our Savior was a Spirit when this great work was done. He did all of these mighty works before he tabernacled in the flesh" (*Doctrines of Salvation,* Vol. 1:74–75).

We will now proceed with our verse-by-verse study of Abraham 4 and 5.

1 And then the Lord said: Let us go down. And they went down at the beginning [*of the creation of our earth*], and they, that is **the Gods, organized and formed the heavens** [*the sky, our solar system, and so forth*] **and the earth.**

2 And the earth, after it was formed, was **empty and desolate** [*other accounts say "without form*

and void"], because they had not formed anything but the earth; and darkness reigned upon the face of the deep, and the Spirit of the Gods was **brooding** [*what a mother hen does when watching over her eggs and chicks*] upon the face of the waters.

3 And **they (the Gods)** said: Let there be light; and there was light.

4 And **they (the Gods)** comprehended the light, for it was bright; and they divided the light, or caused it to be divided, from the darkness.

5 And **the Gods** called the light **Day**, and the darkness they called **Night**. And it came to pass that from the evening until morning they called night; and from the morning until the evening they called day; and this was the first, or the beginning, of that which they called day and night.

6 And **the Gods** also said: Let there be an expanse [*atmosphere—see Bible Dictionary, under "Firmament"*] in the midst of the waters [*between the earth and the heavens*], and it shall divide the waters [*on earth*] from the waters [*clouds in the sky*].

7 And **the Gods** ordered [*organized, created*] the expanse, so that it divided the waters which were under the expanse from the waters which were above the expanse; and it was so, even as they ordered.

> Another unique contribution of Abraham's account of the Creation is that he refers to each "day" of creation as a "time." This leaves it open as to how long each creative period was. In the Gospel Doctrine manual for Old Testament classes, we read:
>
> "The length of time required for the Creation is not known" (*Old Testament Gospel Doctrine Teacher's Manual,* page 11).
>
> Speaking of the "six days" required for creating the earth, President Brigham Young said that it "is a mere term, but it matters not whether it took six days, six months, six years, or six thousand years. The Creation occupied certain periods of time. **We are not authorized to say what the duration of these days was** (**bold** added for emphasis), whether Moses penned these words as we have them, or whether the translators of the Bible have given the words their intended meaning. However, God created the world. God brought forth material out of which he formed this little terra firma upon which we roam. How long had this material been in existence? Forever and forever, in some shape, in some condition" (*Discourses of Brigham Young,* page 100).
>
> Furthermore, Elder Bruce R. McConkie taught that a day, as used in the creation accounts, "is a specified time period; it is an age, an eon, a division of eternity; it is the time between two identifiable events. And each day, of whatever length, has the duration needed for its purposes. . . . There is no revealed recitation specifying that each of the 'six days' involved in the Creation was of the same duration" ("Christ and the Creation," *Ensign,* June 1982, page 11).

We see this use of the word "time" at the end of verse 8, next. We will also see it in verses 13, 19, 23, 31, and in chapter 5, verse 2. We will denote these with **bold** as we go along.

8 And **the Gods** called the expanse, Heaven. And it came to pass that it was from evening until morning that they called night; and it came to pass that it was from morning until evening that they called day; and this was **the second time** that they called night and day.

> Next, the water on the earth is separated from the land, and the dry land is organized, preparatory to placing the earth's ecosystem upon it. As you can see, they initially planned for one ocean and one continent. Later, in the days of Peleg (Genesis 10:25), the continent and ocean will be broken up into several of each.

9 And **the Gods** ordered, saying: **Let the waters under the heaven be gathered together unto one place**, and **let the earth come up dry**; and it was so as they ordered;

10 And **the Gods** pronounced the dry land, Earth; and the gathering together of the waters, pronounced they, Great Waters; and **the Gods saw that they were obeyed**.

> The last phrase of verse 9 is interesting. We see a similar thing in verses 12, 18, and 25. It seems that the organization of elements to form the earth was not instantaneous; rather, it took some time for the elements to organize as commanded.

> Next, the ecosystem for the "dry land" is planned. The wording here in verses 11 and 12 is important. You will see that Abraham places an emphasis on each plant's reproducing after its "own" kind. The emphasis is especially strong in verse 12, where he says, "Whose seed could only bring forth the same in itself, after his kind." This tends to discredit theories in which God's creations evolve from one major species to another.

11 And **the Gods said: Let us prepare** [*implies that this is the planning stage of creation*] the earth to bring forth grass; the herb yielding seed; the fruit tree yielding fruit, **after his kind, whose seed in itself yieldeth its own likeness** upon the earth; and **it was so** [*it took place just as the Gods had planned it*], **even as they ordered** [*just as they had planned*].

12 And the Gods organized the earth to bring forth **grass from its own seed**, and **the herb to bring forth herb from its own seed**, yielding **seed after his kind**; and the earth to bring forth the tree **from its own seed**, yielding fruit, **whose seed could only bring forth the same in itself, after his kind**; and the Gods saw that they were obeyed.

13 And it came to pass that they numbered the days; from the evening until the morning they called night; and it came to pass, from the morning until the evening they called day; and it was **the third time**.

Next, we see the plan for creating the sun, moon, and stars. Abraham tells us that these will be used for navigation, calendaring, and so forth.

14 And the Gods organized the lights in the expanse of the heaven [*the sky*], and caused them to divide the day from the night; and **organized them to be for signs and for seasons, and for days and for years**;

15 And organized them to be for lights in the expanse of the heaven to give light upon the earth; and it was so.

16 And the Gods organized the two great lights, **the greater light** [*the sun*] to rule the day, and **the lesser light** [*the moon*] to rule the night; with the lesser light they set **the stars** also;

17 And the Gods set them in the expanse of the heavens [*the sky*], to give light upon the earth, and to rule over the day and over the night, and to cause to divide the light from the darkness.

As stated previously, verse 18 is one of Abraham's unique contributions to the story of the Creation. His statement here almost brings a grin to our faces.

18 **And the Gods watched those things which they had ordered until they obeyed**.

19 And it came to pass that it was from evening until morning that it was night; and it came to pass that it was from morning until evening that it was day; and it was **the fourth time**.

20 And the Gods said: **Let us prepare** [*the planning phase continued*] the waters to bring forth abundantly the moving creatures that have life; and the fowl, that they may fly above the earth in the open expanse of heaven [*the sky*].

21 And the Gods prepared the waters that they might bring forth great whales, and every living creature that moveth, which the waters were to bring forth abundantly **after their kind**; and every winged fowl **after their kind**. And the Gods saw that they **would be obeyed** [*in the future, when They implemented the plan*]**, and that their plan was good**.

22 And the Gods said: We will bless them, and cause them to be fruitful and multiply, and fill the waters in the seas or great waters; and cause the fowl to multiply in the earth.

23 And it came to pass that it was from evening until morning that they called night; and it came to pass that it was from morning until evening that they called day; and it was **the fifth time**.

24 And the Gods prepared the earth to bring forth the living creature **after his kind**, cattle and creeping things, and beasts of the earth **after their kind**; and it was so, as they had said [*planned*].

25 And the Gods organized the earth to bring forth the beasts after their kind, and cattle after their kind, and every thing that creepeth upon the earth after its kind; and **the Gods saw they would obey** [*when the plan was implemented*].

> Next, plans are made to place Adam and Eve on the earth.

26 **And the Gods took counsel** [*planned*] **among themselves** and said: Let us go down and form man in our image, after our likeness; and we will give them dominion over the fish of the sea, and over the fowl of the air, and over the cattle, and over all the earth, and over every creeping thing that creepeth upon the earth.

> It appears that in verse 27, next, Abraham is telling us that the plans made by the Gods were eventually carried out as discussed by Them.

27 **So the Gods went down to organize man** in their own image, in the image of the Gods to form they him, male and female to form they them.

> The wording in verses 28–31, next, indicates that Abraham is once again dealing with the planning, or blueprint, stage here.

28 And the Gods said: **We will bless** them. And the Gods said: **We will cause** them to be fruitful and multiply, and replenish [*"fill"—see Genesis 1:28, footnote c*] the earth, and subdue it, and to have dominion over the fish of the sea, and over the fowl of the air, and over every living thing that moveth upon the earth.

29 And the Gods said: Behold, **we will give** them every herb bearing seed **that shall come** upon the face of all the earth, and every tree **which shall have fruit** upon it; yea, the fruit of the tree yielding seed to them **we will give** it; it shall be for their meat [*food*].

30 And to every beast of the earth, and to every fowl of the air, and to every thing that creepeth upon the earth, behold, **we will give** them life, and also **we will give** to them every green herb for meat, and **all these things shall be thus organized** [*this will be the plan*].

31 And the Gods said: **We will do everything that we have said**, and organize them; and behold, **they shall be** very obedient. And it came to pass that it was from evening until morning they called night; and it came to pass that it was from morning until evening that they called day; and they numbered **the sixth time**.

ABRAHAM 5

Background

As you can see from the heading to Abraham, chapter 5, in your Pearl of Great Price, the Gods will finish planning the Creation (verses 1–3) and then proceed to carry it out in this chapter. One of the unique contributions of Abraham to our knowledge about the Creation is the fact that it was done on "Kolob standard time" (see verse 13).

Abraham was a trained astronomer, taught by the Lord (Abraham 3:1–17); thus, he noticed such things.

We will now proceed with our verse-by-verse study of Abraham 5. Verses 1–3 show us that Abraham's account of the Creation in chapter 4 was primarily that of the planning stages before the actual Creation.

1 And **thus** [*according to the plan We have made*] **we** [*the Gods*] **will finish the heavens and the earth, and all the hosts of them.**

2 And **the Gods said among themselves**: On **the seventh time we will end our work, which we have counseled** [*planned*]; and **we will rest** on the seventh time from all our work which we have counseled.

3 And the Gods concluded upon the seventh time, because that on the seventh time they would rest from all their works which they (the Gods) counseled among themselves to form [*organize, create*]; and sanctified it [*blessed it and made it holy*]. And **thus were their decisions at the time that they counseled among themselves to form the heavens and the earth.**

> Next, the Gods will begin the actual physical creation of the earth, sky, solar system, and so forth. The word "generations," in verse 4, may imply that there was considerable time involved and that there were several series of events leading up to the final preparation of the earth for the placement of man upon it. We will learn more details about the Creation and have all of our questions answered at the beginning of the Millennium according to the Doctrine and Covenants. We read:

D&C 101:32–34

32 Yea, verily I say unto you, in that day when the Lord shall come, he shall reveal all things—

33 Things which have passed, and hidden things which no man knew, **things of the earth, by which it was made**, and the purpose and the end thereof—

34 Things most precious, things that are above, and things that are beneath, things that are in the earth, and upon the earth, and in heaven.

4 And **the Gods came down and formed these the generations of the heavens and of the earth**, when they were formed in the day that **the Gods formed the earth and the heavens**,

> We are reminded in verse 5, next, that all things were created in spirit form before being placed on earth as physical creations. We will point this out with one of the phrases in verse 5.

5 **According to all that which they had said** [*according to their plan*] concerning every plant of the field before it was in the earth, and every herb of the field before it grew [*all things were created in spirit form, long before the earth was created physically*]; **for the Gods had not caused it**

to rain upon the earth when they counseled to do them, and had not formed a man to till the ground.

6 But there went up a mist from the earth, and watered the whole face of the ground.

> We find another one of Abraham's important contributions to our understanding of the Creation in verse 7. Genesis 2:7 and Moses 3:7 say that God "breathed into his [*Adam's*] nostrils the breath of life." Abraham says this also but explains this phrase by saying "took his spirit and put it into him."

7 And **the Gods formed man from the dust of the ground** [*formed his physical body from the elements of the earth*], **and took his spirit** (that is, the man's spirit), **and put it into him**; and breathed into his nostrils the breath of life, and man became a living soul.

8 **And the Gods planted a garden**, eastward in Eden, and **there they put the man**, whose spirit they had put into the body which they had formed.

> In verse 9, next, we see that the tree of knowledge of good and evil, of which Adam and Eve had been commanded not to partake, was placed in the midst of the garden in plain sight rather than in an obscure corner of Eden. So, likewise, was the tree of life placed in plain sight.

9 And out of the ground made the Gods to grow every tree that is pleasant to the sight and good for food; the tree of life, also, **in the midst of the garden**, and the tree of knowledge of good and evil.

> Elder Bruce R. McConkie explained the symbolic meaning of the two trees mentioned in verse 9, above. He said:
>
> "The scriptures set forth that there were in the Garden of Eden two trees. One was **the tree of life**, which figuratively refers to eternal life; the other was **the tree of knowledge of good and evil**, which figuratively refers to how and why and in what manner mortality and all that appertains to it came into being" (*A New Witness for the Articles of Faith,* page 86).

> With this in mind, one possible message for us, in verse 9, is that the Fall of Adam and Eve was absolutely essential in order for us to have eternal life (exaltation) available to us. Another possible message is that agency choices between good and evil are essential for gaining eternal life.

> Next, Abraham gives a bit more detail about Eden and then tells us about Adam in the Garden of Eden.

10 There was a river running out of Eden, to water the garden, and from thence it was parted and became into four heads.

11 And **the Gods took the man and put him in the Garden of Eden**, to dress it and to keep it [*to take care of it*].

> Next, Adam is commanded not to partake of the tree of knowledge of

good and evil. For more on this, see the notes following Moses 3:17 in this study guide.

12 And **the Gods commanded** the man, saying: **Of every tree of the garden thou mayest freely eat,**

13 **But of the tree of knowledge of good and evil, thou shalt not eat of it**; for in the time that thou eatest thereof, thou shalt surely die. **Now I, Abraham, saw that it was after the Lord's time, which was after the time of Kolob; for as yet the Gods had not appointed unto Adam his reckoning** [*the earth's time system*].

Based on Abraham's comment in the last half of verse 13, above, we understand that the earth was created in the presence of God and was still on the time system used by Kolob and the planet on which the Father resides. When Adam and Eve "fell," the earth "fell" with them and was brought to its current area of space and placed in this solar system. President Brigham Young explained a bit more about this. He said (**bold** used for emphasis):

"This earth is our home, it was framed expressly for the habitation of those who are faithful to God, and who prove themselves worthy to inherit the earth when the Lord shall have sanctified, purified and glorified it and brought it back into his presence, **from which it fell far into space**. Ask the astronomer how far we are from the nearest of those heavenly bodies that are called the fixed stars. Can he count the miles? It would be a task for him to tell us the distance. **When the earth was framed and brought into existence and man was placed upon it, it was near the throne of our Father in heaven**. And when man fell—though that was designed in the economy, there was nothing about it mysterious or unknown to the Gods, they understood it all, it was all planned—but **when man fell, the earth fell into space, and took up its abode in this planetary system, and the sun became our light**. When the Lord said—"Let there be light," there was light, for the earth was brought near the sun that it might reflect upon it so as to give us light by day, and the moon to give us light by night. This is the glory the earth came from, and **when it is glorified it will return again unto the presence of the Father**, and it will dwell there, and these intelligent beings that I am looking at, if they live worthy of it, will dwell upon this earth" (in *Journal of Discourses,* Vol. 7, page 143).

Joseph Smith taught that this earth will be taken back to where it came from. He said:

"This earth will be rolled back into the presence of God, and crowned with celestial glory" (*Teachings of the Prophet Joseph Smith,* page 181).

Having learned that our earth will be returned to the presence of God—as the celestial kingdom for the worthy who lived on it as mortals (see D&C 130:9–11)—we will take a moment and answer another question that sometimes arises. The question is whether other earths also become celestial planets for their worthy residents and are likewise moved through space into the presence of God. Orson Pratt tells us that the answer is yes. He said (**bold** added for emphasis):

"Inquires one—**'Do you mean to say that other worlds have fallen as well as ours?' Yes**, man is an agent; intelligence cannot exist on any other principle. All beings having intelligence must have their agency. Laws must be given, suited and adapted to this agency; and **when God sends inhabitants on various creations he sends them on the great and grand principle of giving them an opportunity to exercise that agency; and they have exercised it, and have fallen. . . . By and by, when each of these creations has fulfilled the measure and bounds set and the times given for this continuance in a temporal state, it and its inhabitants who are worthy will be made celestial and glorified together . . . they will all be in his presence** (in *Journal of Discourses,* Vol. 17, pages 332–33; the *Doctrine and Covenants Student Manual,* page 201, gives part of this quote from Elder Pratt).

Next, Abraham teaches us about the creation of Eve. Much ancient cultural symbolism is used to present emotion and feeling with the account.

First, though, we must look at the words "help meet" in verse 14. Many mistakenly read these words as one word, "helpmeet," which implies lesser status for Eve than for Adam. This is not true. The word "meet," as used in this type of context in the scriptures (such as D&C 58:26) means "essential, necessary, vital." Thus, Eve is a vital help for Adam, just as Adam is an essential help for Eve. Neither can attain exaltation and become a god without the other (D&C 131:1–4; 132:20).

14 And the Gods said: **Let us make an help meet for the man**, for **it is not good that the man should be alone**, therefore we will form an help meet for him.

15 **And the Gods caused a deep sleep to fall upon Adam**; and he slept, **and they took one of his ribs,** and closed up the flesh in the stead thereof;

16 **And of the rib which the Gods had taken from man, formed they a woman**, and brought her unto the man.

President Spencer W. Kimball taught that the Gods did not literally take a rib from Adam and make Eve; rather, the account is symbolical. He said:

"The story of the rib, of course, is figurative" ("The Blessings and Responsibilities of Womanhood," *Ensign,* March 1976, page 71).

We will read the next two verses and then say a bit more about the symbolism here.

17 And Adam said: **This was bone of my bones, and flesh of my flesh** [*we belong to each other, we are family*]; now she shall be called Woman, because she was taken out of man;

18 **Therefore shall a man leave his father and his mother, and shall cleave unto his wife, and they shall be one flesh**.

> Students often wonder why the account of the "rib" given here sounds so literal if it is just symbolic. Why the details about the "surgery," including putting Adam to sleep and closing up the flesh in place of the rib?
>
> The answer has to do with differences in cultures. Many Westerners are also "literalists." That is, they want the plain facts and don't want them embellished. Most Easterners, meaning people from cultures in the Middle East, tell a story with symbolism that provides the essential facts accompanied by words denoting feeling and emotion. In the case of the creation of Eve, we see descriptive words that provide emotion and tenderness, protectiveness and warmth, belonging and teamwork, unity and purpose, all carefully and tenderly crafted by the Gods, who attend to this union with personal focus. One can feel the caring of the Gods as they introduce Adam and Eve to each other, the culmination of Their creative endeavors, and the final step in carrying out their blueprint of creation.
>
> Some of my male students, thinking that this account of taking a rib from Adam and creating Eve was literal, have actually counted their ribs on both sides, thinking that they would find one less rib on the one side than on the other.

> Next, we are informed that Adam and Eve are innocent, as far as modesty is concerned.

19 And they were both naked, the man and his wife, **and were not ashamed** [*embarrassed*].

> Abraham now finishes his account of the Creation with a review of the things that had been done by the Gods in preparation for placing Adam and Eve on the earth. Then he tells us that Adam was given the responsibility to name the living creatures.
>
> Symbolically, this is a reminder that God delegates much to mortals for their growth and development.

20 And **out of the ground** [*the physical creation*] **the Gods formed every beast** of the field, and **every fowl** of the air, and **brought them unto Adam to see what he would call them**; and whatsoever Adam called every living creature, that should be the name thereof.

> Abraham finishes with the most important thing of all. Adam now has his eternal companion, Eve; and Eve now has her eternal companion, Adam.

21 **And Adam gave names to all cattle, to the fowl of the air, to every beast of the field**; and **for Adam, there was found an help meet** [*vital, essential*] **for him** [*Eve was an essential companion for Adam*].

> Having finished Abraham's account of the creation, we will now proceed with Genesis, chapter 3.

GENESIS 3

This chapter is basically the temptation scene in the Garden of Eden, which leads to the Fall of Adam and Eve. The Fall was good (see 2 Nephi 2:25). It was planned by the Lord as a vital step in preparing the way for us to be born on earth. One of the interesting things we learn from the Pearl of Great Price is that Satan did not know everything. Apparently, one of the things he did not know was that by tempting Eve, he would help to carry out God's plan of salvation. We read in Moses 4:6 that Satan, as he approached Eve to tempt her, "knew not the mind of God, wherefore he sought to destroy the world."

In this chapter, we will see the tempting by Satan, the partaking of the fruit by Eve and then by Adam, the results thereof, and the casting of them out of the Garden of Eden. Since there are many misconceptions about who and what got cursed here, we will add quite a few notes as we go.

You will also see that the book of Moses adds much to this chapter of Genesis. (Remember, the JST is the same as Moses in the Pearl of Great Price, but the versification of the JST is different.)

First, we will learn something important from the heading of this chapter (Genesis, chapter 3, in your Bible). It is that Lucifer is the one speaking to Eve, not a serpent. The heading says, "*The Serpent (Lucifer) deceives Eve.*"

Just as was the case with the story of the rib, in Genesis 2:21–24, so also in the depiction of a serpent speaking to Eve. Much cultural symbolism is used in the writing of these accounts that can make some things appear to be literal but that are in fact symbolic. When you go to the temple, you get the correct version of this scene. Satan has many names in scripture as well as in other writings. One of them is "serpent." We will quote from Revelation to demonstrate this and use **bold** to point it out:

Revelation 12:9

9 And the great **dragon** was cast out, that old **serpent**, called the **Devil**, and **Satan**, which deceiveth the whole world: he was cast out into the earth, and his angels were cast out with him.

We will now proceed with our study. First, we will examine very important additions from Moses, chapter 4:1-4. These verses are not found in the Bible. In fact, Genesis 3 in the Bible has twenty-four verses as compared to thirty-two verses in Moses 4.

These four verses give us insights about premortality and the Grand Council in Heaven that we all attended. We will be taught many important doctrines as we study these four verses.

In verse 1, we are informed that Lucifer wanted to be the Redeemer. (By the way, Lucifer means "the Shining One" or "Lightbringer"; see Bible Dictionary, under "Lucifer.") At the beginning of the verse, the Lord reminds Moses that he is already acquainted with Satan because of the confrontation he had with him in Moses 1:12–22. At the end of that tense confrontation, Lucifer was forced to depart after Moses commanded him to do so in the name of Jesus Christ. Now, the Lord tells Moses, in effect, that He is going to tell him how Lucifer became the devil. Pay close attention to how

Lucifer proposed to carry out our redemption.

Moses 4:1

1 And I, the Lord God, spake unto Moses, saying: **That Satan, whom thou hast commanded in the name of mine Only Begotten** [*in Moses 1:21*], **is the same which was from the beginning** [*perhaps meaning that he is the same character who caused trouble in the premortal councils*], and **he came before me** [*the Father*], saying—Behold, here am I, **send me** [*to be the Redeemer*], **I will be thy son**, and **I will redeem all mankind**, that **one soul shall not be lost**, and surely **I will do it**; wherefore **give me thine honor**.

Did you notice in verse 1 that Lucifer has "I" trouble? His focus is on himself. Not only that, but he claimed that he would "redeem all mankind," which means that no one would have had agency. Such would be impossible. Satan could not have delivered on that promise because compulsion in place of agency cannot lead to redemption and exaltation.

Did you also notice what Lucifer wanted in return for his proposed service? He wanted to replace the Father (Isaiah 14:14; Moses 4:3) and take the Father's "honor" for himself. In other words, he wanted the Father's power. We read this in the Doctrine and Covenants as follows (**bold** added for emphasis):

Doctrine and Covenants 29:36

36 And it came to pass that Adam, being tempted of the devil—for, behold, the devil was before Adam, for he rebelled against me [*in premortality*], saying, **Give me thine honor, which is my power**; and also a third part of the hosts of heaven turned he away from me because of their agency;

Next, in Moses 4:2, Jesus Christ humbly volunteers to be the Redeemer and to carry out the Father's plan, giving the Father the honor and glory.

Moses 4:2

2 But, behold, **my Beloved Son**, which was my Beloved and Chosen from the beginning, **said** unto me—**Father, thy will be done, and the glory be thine forever**.

Some people wonder whether it is permissible for members of the Church to think and come up with their own ideas about things as far as the gospel is concerned. Of course it is. The Lord encourages us to use our capacity to think and analyze (see Doctrine and Covenants 58:26–28). However, if we eventually find that our thinking goes against the revealed word and will of God, we would be wise to quickly change our thinking and to follow and support Him. Otherwise, we will find ourselves in the same situation as the devil—in open rebellion against God and the laws that govern the universe.

In summary, it is not a sin to think. But it is a sin to rebel. We learn this from Moses 4:3, next, as Moses is told what Lucifer did that led him to become the devil.

Moses 4:3

3 Wherefore, because that **Satan rebelled** against me, and **sought to destroy the agency of man**, which I, the Lord God, had given him [*in the premortal realm*], and **also, that I should give unto him mine own power**; by the power of mine Only Begotten, I caused that he should be cast down [*see Revelation 12:4, 7–9*];

There is an important issue to consider before we leave Moses 4:1–3, above. It is whether or not there were two plans presented in the Council in Heaven. We often hear that Jesus Christ presented his plan and Lucifer presented his plan. This is not true. Christ did not propose a separate plan of His own. The plan was already in place. It was the Father's plan, used countless times already on many worlds that had already become celestialized before our great premortal Council in Heaven was even held (see Moses 1:35).

Jesus supported the Father's plan. Lucifer proposed to change it—in effect, corrupting it. In a sense, it could be said that Lucifer came up with his own plan, but it is more accurate to say that he wanted to be the Savior in the Father's plan, proposing to eliminate agency so that all would be saved and desiring the glory for himself.

Guidelines for Church curriculum writers, reaffirmed in 2001 by the First Presidency and the Twelve, state that only one plan was presented, not two, that Jehovah (the premortal Jesus Christ) sustained Heavenly Father's plan, that Satan attempted to amend the Father's plan, and that Lucifer did not propose a separate plan of his own. Elder Bruce R. McConkie explained this. He taught:

"Although we sometimes hear it said that there were two plans—Christ's plan of freedom and agency, and Lucifer's plan of slavery and compulsion—such teaching does not conform to the revealed word. Christ did not present a plan of redemption and salvation, nor did Lucifer. There were not two plans up for consideration; there was only one; and that was the plan of the Father: originated, developed, presented, and put in force by him. Christ, however, made the Father's plan his own by his willing obedience to its terms and provisions" (Bruce R. McConkie, *Improvement Era,* May 1953, page 322).

Elder Neal A. Maxwell spoke of this. He said that it is "extremely important to get straight what happened in that premortal council. It was not an unstructured meeting, nor was it a discussion between plans, nor an idea-producing session, as to how to formulate the plan for salvation and carry it out. Our Father's plan was known, and the actual question put was whom the Father should send to carry out the plan" (*Deposition of a Disciple,* 11; see also John 7:16–18).

Moses 4:4, next, gives us a brief summary of Lucifer's motives and goals after he rebelled and became the devil.

Moses 4:4

4 **And he became Satan**, yea, even **the devil**, the **father** [*author*] **of all lies**, to **deceive** and to **blind** men, and to **lead** them **captive** at his will, even as many as would not hearken unto my voice.

We will now continue with the account in Genesis. As we read Genesis 3:1 and 5, we can almost feel the taunting in Satan's voice as he seeks to sow doubt in Eve's mind as to the intentions of God. In effect, he is saying to her that God is up to His old tricks, withholding important information from her.

Genesis 3

1 Now **the serpent** [*the devil—see footnote 1a in your Bible*] **was more subtil** [*cunning, tricky*] than any beast of the field which the Lord God had made. And **he** [*Satan*] **said unto the woman**, Yea, **hath God said, Ye shall not eat of every tree of the garden?**

Moses 4:5–7

5 And now the serpent was more subtle than any beast of the field which I, the Lord God, had made.

6 And Satan put it into the heart of the serpent, (for he had drawn away many after him,) and he sought also to beguile Eve, for he knew not the mind of God, wherefore he sought to destroy the world.

7 And he said unto the woman: Yea, hath God said—Ye shall not eat of every tree of the garden? (And he spake by the mouth of the serpent.)

2 And **the woman said** unto the serpent, **We may eat of the fruit of the trees of the garden**:

3 **But of the fruit of the tree which *is* in the midst of the garden, God hath said, Ye shall not eat of it, neither shall ye touch it, lest ye die**.

Moses 4:8–9

8 And the woman said unto the serpent: We may eat of the fruit of the trees of the garden;

9 But of the fruit of the tree which thou beholdest in the midst of the garden, God hath said—Ye shall not eat of it, neither shall ye touch it, lest ye die.

4 And **the serpent said** unto the woman, **Ye shall not surely die**:

5 **For God doth know that in the day ye eat thereof, then your eyes shall be opened, and ye shall be as gods, knowing good and evil.**

Moses 4:10–11

10 And the serpent said unto the woman: Ye shall not surely die;

11 For God doth know that in the day ye eat thereof, then your eyes shall be opened, and ye shall be as gods, knowing good and evil.

Did you notice how many lies Satan told Eve n Genesis 3:4–5? Answer: just one. He said that she would not die if she partook of the fruit. That is false. If she partakes, she will die a physical death. As a result, she will be resurrected and have a physical body eternally—a wonderful blessing! Everything else he said is true. It is typical of Satan to mix truth with falsehoods as a subtle means of trying to deceive us.

Next, in Genesis 3:6, Eve partakes and then gives it to Adam, and he partakes. If you read the verse carefully, you can see that Eve analyzed the situation quite thoroughly before partaking. The implication is that she made an intentional decision rather than simply falling into a trap set by Satan. We will do more with this in a moment.

6 And **when the woman saw that the tree *was* good for food**, and that it *was* **pleasant to the eyes, and** a tree to be **desired to make *one* wise**, she took of the fruit thereof, and did eat, and gave also unto her husband with her; and he did eat.

Moses 4:12

12 And when the woman saw that the tree was good for food, and that it became pleasant to the eyes, and a tree to be desired to make her wise, she took of the fruit thereof, and did eat, and also gave unto her husband with her, and he did eat.

Did you notice the change from "was pleasant" in Genesis to "became pleasant" in Moses? Certainly, one vital lesson we can learn from this change is that, over time, if we do not flee from temptation, it can "become" attractive and our ability to resist can become compromised.

In the Bible, this is all of this part of the story we get. As a result, many cultures have degraded Eve, and women in general, throughout history, blaming her for many of the troubles we endure as mortals. We are indebted to modern revelation for additional details that are vital to a correct understanding of Eve's role in the Fall.

We honor and revere both Eve and Adam for their roles in opening the door for us as spirit children of our Heavenly Parents, to come to earth. We will provide quotes here that support our respect and appreciation for Adam and Eve and that support the idea that Eve made an intentional choice, rather than naively making a blunder. We will use **bold** for emphasis.

"Satan was present to tempt Adam and Eve, much as he would try to thwart others in their divine missions: 'and he sought also to beguile Eve, for he knew not the mind of God, wherefore he sought to destroy the world' (Moses 4:6). **Eve faced the choice between selfish ease and unselfishly facing tribulation and death** (*Evidences and Reconciliations*, by Apostle John A. Widtsoe, page 193). As befit her calling, she realized that there was no other way and **deliberately chose mortal life so as to further the purpose of God and bring children into the world**" (*The Encyclopedia of Mormonism*, under "Eve").

Question: How could Eve "deliberately" choose, as indicated by Elder Widtsoe in the above quote, when she and Adam were "innocent" in the Garden of Eden? Where would she get the knowledge with which to make such an informed decision?

Elder Widtsoe answers this question in the following quote. He said:

"Such was the problem before our first parents: to remain forever at selfish ease in the Garden of Eden, or to face unselfishly tribulation and death, in bringing to pass the purposes of the Lord for a host of waiting spirit children. They chose the latter. . . . **This they did with open eyes and minds as to consequences**. The memory of their former estates [*including their premortal spirit existence*] may have been dimmed, **but the gospel had been taught them during their sojourn in the Garden of Eden** . . . the choice that they made raises Adam and Even to preeminence among all who have come on earth" (John A. Widtsoe, *Evidences and Reconciliations*, pages 193–194).

Elder George Albert Smith, who later became the President of the Church, also taught on this subject. He said:

"When God created the earth and placed our first parents upon it, **He did not leave them without knowledge concerning Himself**. It is true that there had been taken from them the remembrance of their pre-existent life, but in His tender mercy **He talked with** them and later He **sent His choice servants to instruct them in the things pertaining to eternal life**" (in Conference Report, October 1928, pages 90–91).

One last question before we move on. Why does Paul say that Eve was deceived? (See 1 Timothy 2:14.) No doubt she was, in some ways. But in the most important matters, she made an intelligent and wise choice. We will probably have to wait until we get a chance to talk to Eve, herself, perhaps during the Millennium, for the complete account. If you listen carefully to what she said, as the account is given in holy places, you will be reminded that she asked important and intelligent questions before partaking of the fruit, and she responded with unselfishness.

Yet, there could be many ways in which she was deceived. Perhaps in the sense of not believing that mortality would be so difficult at times. Perhaps she had no idea what it would be like to care for twenty or thirty sick children when they all had the flu! Maybe she was deceived into thinking that old age with its attendant pains and disabilities would not be at all difficult. Actually, she couldn't have understood these physical struggles because she had no basis on which to judge, since she and her husband were not yet mortal, even though they had physical bodies at this point.

Next, in verse 7, we see that Adam and Eve are already gaining knowledge and a sense of modesty.

7 And the eyes of them both were opened, and **they knew that they *were* naked**; and they sewed fig leaves together, and made themselves aprons.

Moses 4:13

13 And the eyes of them both were opened, and they knew that they had

been naked. And they sewed fig-leaves together and made themselves aprons.

As you know, from the above notes and commentary, Adam and Eve made a deliberate agency choice in partaking of the fruit. Part of having agency is owning the consequences of personal choices. We see this principle in action beginning with verse 8, next.

8 And **they heard the voice of the Lord God** [*the Father*] walking in the garden in the cool of the day [*in the evening—see footnote 8b, in your Bible*]: and **Adam and his wife hid themselves** from the presence of the Lord God amongst the trees of the garden.

Moses 4:14

14 And they heard the voice of the Lord God, as they were walking in the garden, in the cool of the day; and Adam and his wife went to hide themselves from the presence of the Lord God amongst the trees of the garden.

9 And **the Lord God called** unto Adam, and said unto him, **Where *art* thou?**

10 **And he** [*Adam*] **said, I heard thy voice** in the garden, **and I was afraid**, because I *was* naked; and I hid myself.

11 **And he** [*the Father*] **said, Who told thee that thou *wast* naked? Hast thou eaten of the tree**, whereof I commanded thee that thou shouldest not eat?

Moses 4:15–17

15 And I, the Lord God, called unto Adam, and said unto him: Where goest thou?

16 And he said: I heard thy voice in the garden, and I was afraid, because I beheld that I was naked, and I hid myself.

17 And I, the Lord God, said unto Adam: Who told thee thou wast naked? Hast thou eaten of the tree whereof I commanded thee that thou shouldst not eat, if so thou shouldst surely die?

Before we continue, we will remind you that we provided some notes following Genesis 2:15 and 17 in this study guide, which address the issue of the "two conflicting commandments." This issue often comes up again in people's minds at this point of reading Genesis. You may wish to read that note again now.

Next, we see that Adam is initially reluctant to take direct responsibility for his actions. We are all familiar with this feeling. All of us must eventually learn this lesson in accountability, which is inseparably connected with agency.

12 And **the man said, The woman whom thou gavest *to be* with me, she gave me of the tree, and I did eat**.

Moses 4:18

18 And the man said: The woman thou gavest me, and commandest that she should remain with me, she gave me of the fruit of the tree and I did eat.

Next, it is Eve's turn. She too is hesitant and attempts to divert attention from her to Satan.

13 And the Lord God [*the Father*] **said unto the woman, What** *is* **this** *that* **thou hast done? And the woman said, The serpent beguiled me, and I did eat.**

<u>Moses 4:19</u>

19 And I, the Lord God, said unto the woman: What is this thing which thou hast done? And the woman said: The serpent beguiled me, and I did eat.

We learn much about Satan and his status in verses 14–15, next. One of the most comforting doctrines is that he has less power than Christ. Thus, he will ultimately be defeated and cast out (see Doctrine and Covenants 88:111–14).

14 And the Lord God [*the Father*] **said unto the serpent, Because thou hast done this, thou** *art* **cursed above** [*limited more than*] **all cattle, and above every beast of the field** [*one aspect of this curse is that even "cattle" and "every beast of the field" get a physical body to go with their spirit; Satan will never get a physical body*]; **upon thy belly shalt thou go** [*Satan will be looked upon as the lowest of the low*], **and dust shalt thou eat all the days of thy life** [*perhaps meaning that he will always be behind the Savior, in effect, "eating the Savior's dust"; this could also be a play on words, saying, in effect, that Satan will be "eating dust"—in other words, associating with mortals, trying to swallow them up in* spiritual destruction, but never receive a mortal body himself, one made of the "dust of the ground"—see Moses 3:7]:

15 And **I will put enmity** [*a natural dislike, intense distrust, hatred*] **between thee** [*Satan*] **and the woman**, and **between thy seed** [*Satan's followers, including not only those evil spirits who followed him in premortality but also the wicked who follow him here on earth*] **and her seed** [*Jesus Christ*]; **it** [*Christ*] **shall bruise thy head** [*will triumph over Satan and his kingdom; will have power over Satan*], **and thou shalt bruise his heel** [*will cause suffering, including causing evil men to crucify the Savior, and also causing pain and sorrow by leading people away from Christ and His gospel*].

<u>Moses 4:20–21</u>

20 And I, the Lord God, said unto the serpent: Because thou hast done this thou shalt be cursed above all cattle, and above every beast of the field; upon thy belly shalt thou go, and dust shalt thou eat all the days of thy life;

21 And I will put enmity between thee and the woman, between thy seed and her seed; and he shall bruise thy head, and thou shalt bruise his heel.

Many of the notes supplied in verse 15, above, are taken from the *Old Testament Student Manual*. We will quote it here and add **bold** for teaching purposes.

"Since **Satan has no body** and therefore can have no literal children, **his seed are those who follow him**, both the one-third he led away in the premortal existence and those who follow his enticements in mortality until they come under his power. **The seed of the woman refers to Jesus Christ**, who was the only mortal born of an earthly mother and a Heavenly Father.

"President Joseph Fielding Smith referred to what the Apostle Paul wrote to the Roman Saints: 'Near the close of his epistle to the Roman saints, he said: "And the God of peace shall bruise Satan under your feet shortly. The grace of our Lord Jesus Christ be with you. Amen." [*Romans 16:20*.]

"The 'God of peace,' who according to the scriptures is to bruise Satan, is Jesus Christ (*Answers to Gospel Questions,* Vol. 1, page 3)."

"The promise concerning **the bruising of the heel and head** means that while Satan (as the serpent) will bruise the heel of the Savior by leading men to crucify him and seemingly destroy him, in actuality that very act of atonement will give Christ the power to overcome the power that Satan has over men and undo the effects of the Fall. Thus, **the seed of the woman (Christ) shall crush the head of the serpent (Satan and his kingdom) with the very heel that was bruised (the atoning sacrifice)**" (*Old Testament Student Manual: Genesis–2 Samuel,* page 41).

Before you read Genesis, verses 16–19, take a moment and answer the following question:

Question: **Who got the worst curse, Adam or Eve, in this scene in the Garden of Eden?** (By the way, the answer usually runs along gender lines.)

Now, go ahead and read the next four verses. We will give the answer after verse 19 (after we have quoted the equivalent verses from Moses).

16 Unto the woman he said, I will greatly multiply thy sorrow and thy conception; in sorrow thou shalt bring forth children; and thy desire *shall be* to thy husband, and he shall rule over thee.

17 And unto Adam he said, Because thou hast hearkened unto the voice of thy wife, and hast eaten of the tree, of which I commanded thee, saying, Thou shalt not eat of it: cursed *is* the ground for thy sake; in sorrow shalt thou eat *of* it all the days of thy life;

18 Thorns also and thistles shall it bring forth to thee; and thou shalt eat the herb of the field;

19 In the sweat of thy face shalt thou eat bread, till thou return unto the ground; for out of it wast thou taken [*your mortal body is made from the elements of the earth*]: for dust thou *art,* and unto dust shalt thou return.

Moses 4:22–25

22 Unto the woman, I, the Lord God, said: I will greatly multiply thy sorrow and thy conception. In sorrow thou shalt bring forth children, and thy desire shall be to thy husband, and he shall rule over thee.

23 And unto Adam, I, the Lord God, said: Because thou hast hearkened

unto the voice of thy wife, and hast eaten of the fruit of the tree of which I commanded thee, saying—Thou shalt not eat of it, cursed shall be the ground for thy sake; in sorrow shalt thou eat of it all the days of thy life.

24 Thorns also, and thistles shall it bring forth to thee, and thou shalt eat the herb of the field.

25 By the sweat of thy face shalt thou eat bread, until thou shalt return unto the ground—for thou shalt surely die—for out of it wast thou taken: for dust thou wast, and unto dust shalt thou return.

The answer to the question above, regarding Genesis, verses 16–19, is that neither Adam nor Eve was cursed. The devil was cursed (verse 14) and the ground was cursed (verse 17), which is a good thing for Adam's development. Verses 16–17 are often badly misunderstood. To those who misunderstand them, they make it sound like God is punishing Adam and Eve for partaking of the fruit. While the step to mortality and future parenthood is a very serious and sobering one, as reflected in the serious tone here, it should not be interpreted to be a punishment. It is not. We will provide notes in a moment that support the correct view.

The point is, again, that the Fall was good. It was good for Adam and Eve. It was good for us. It was the next step in our being given opportunities to become like our Father in Heaven. Lehi taught us about the need for the Fall and the blessings and opportunities that followed it. He said:

2 Nephi 2:22–25

22 And now, behold, **if Adam had not transgressed he would not have fallen**, but he **would have remained in the garden of Eden**. And **all things** which were created **must have** [*would have*] **remained in the same state** in which they were after they were created; and they must have remained **forever**, and had no end.

23 And they would have had **no children**; wherefore they would have remained in a state of **innocence**, having **no joy**, for they knew **no misery**; doing **no good**, for they knew **no sin**.

24 But behold, all things have been done in the wisdom of him [*God*] who knoweth all things [*in other words, the Fall was an intentional part of the Father's plan*].

25 **Adam fell that men might be; and men are, that they might have joy**.

With the above comments as background, we will repeat Genesis, verse 16. We will take considerable literary license as we add notes that first present it in a negative way, the way in which many read it when they take it out of the larger context of what we know about the plan of salvation and the great blessings which come to us through the Fall. After doing this, we will have President Spencer W. Kimball help us see it in a more positive way.

First, the negative approach. We will overdo it a bit.

Genesis 3:16 repeated

16 **Unto the woman he said**, [*shame, shame on you for disobeying Me. Because of your disobedience*] **I will greatly multiply thy sorrow and thy conception** [*I will make it hurt badly every time you have a child as a punishment for your disobedience*]; **in sorrow thou shalt bring forth children** [*as part of your punishment, you will have much of sadness and heartache because of your children*]; **and thy desire** *shall be* **to thy husband** [*you will have the basic status of a servant to your husband*], **and he shall rule over thee** [*because you started it all by your disobedience in the Garden of Eden, I will make you subject to your husband and he will be your superior*].

Now, we will quote Spencer W. Kimball. He was the President of the Church at the time he taught this; therefore, we can consider it doctrine. He will help us see this verse the way it should be understood:

"The Lord said to the woman: '. . . in sorrow thou shalt bring forth children.' I wonder if those who translated the Bible might have used the term distress instead of sorrow. It would mean much the same, except I think there is great gladness in most Latter-day Saint homes when there is to be a child there. As He concludes this statement he says, 'and thy desire shall be to thy husband, and he shall rule over thee.' (Gen. 3:16.) I have a question about the word rule. It gives the wrong impression. I would prefer to use the word preside because that's what he does. A righteous husband presides over his wife and family" ("The Blessings and Responsibilities of Womanhood," *Ensign*, March 1976, page 72).

Before we reread verse 16, we would also do well to consult with Eve as to her view of the Fall. After all, she was there and can give us an accurate view of the results, as she later thought back upon them. We can do so by reading her response to it in Moses 5:11:

Moses 5:11

11 And **Eve**, his wife, heard all these things and **was glad**, saying: **Were it not for our transgression we never should have** [*would have*] **had seed** [*children*], **and never should have known good and evil**, and the **joy** of our redemption, and the **eternal life** which God giveth unto all the obedient.

We will now reread verse 16 and include verses 17–19, adding notes that place our understanding of it into the greater context of the overall gospel and plan of salvation, including Eve's teachings and President Kimball's teaching, above, along with other helps, including the idea that "sorrow" can mean the trials and tribulations of mortality, or mortality itself.

Again, we may overdo it a bit, for purposes of emphasizing the

Genesis 3:16 (repeated) and verses 17–19

16 **Unto the woman he said** [*Thank you, thank you, thank you!*], **I will greatly multiply thy sorrow** [*because of your unselfish choice in the Garden of Eden, I can now give you many years in mortality*] **and thy conception** [*I can now send many of My spirit sons and daughters into your home to gain mortal bodies and learn the lessons of mortality*]; **in sorrow** [*in mortality, with the joys and sorrows, pains and distresses that attend it*] **thou shalt bring forth children**; and **thy desire** [*your highest loyalty, other than to God—compare with Moses 3:24, Doctrine and Covenants 42:22*] *shall be* **to thy husband, and he shall rule over** [*preside and serve you as the Savior does*] **thee**.

Notice, in verse 17, next, that "sorrow" is also used for Adam, as he begins the toil and labor that will be his responsibility and opportunity, as he also begins mortal life. This is perhaps another indicator that we can consider "sorrow" to be a term for mortality, rather than a description of punishment. The same Hebrew word is used in verse 17 as was used for Eve in verse 16, translated as "sorrow" in English.

One of the important lessons we can learn from verse 17, next, is that the ground was cursed for Adam's "sake"—in other words, for his blessing and benefit. It will be good for his growth and development to have to work for a living. We will add notes that emphasize this verse in the larger context of the plan of salvation.

17 **And unto Adam he said, Because thou hast hearkened unto the voice of thy wife** [*which was a very wise thing to do—see quote by Dallin H. Oaks, given after this verse*], **and hast eaten of the tree, of which I commanded thee, saying, Thou shalt not eat of it** [*unless you choose to become mortal and leave the Garden—see Moses 3:17 and the note that follows in this study guide*]: **cursed** *is* **the ground for thy sake** [*in order to bring blessings to you*]; **in sorrow** [*in an environment of work, toil, pain—in other words, in mortality*] **shalt thou eat** *of* **it** [*take your living from the soil*] **all the days of thy life;**

Elder Dallin H. Oaks spoke of the choices made by Adam and Eve that led to the Fall and spoke of Adam's wisdom in following the lead of his wife, Eve, on this matter. He said (**bold** added for emphasis):

"It was Eve who first transgressed the limits of Eden in order to initiate the conditions of mortality. Her act, whatever its nature, was formally a transgression but eternally a glorious necessity to open the doorway toward eternal life. **Adam showed his wisdom by doing the same**. And thus Eve and 'Adam fell that men might be' [*2 Nephi 2:25*]" (Dallin H. Oaks, "The Great Plan of Happiness," *Ensign*, November 1993).

The Lord continues to describe the conditions of "sorrow," or "mortality," in verses 24–25, next. Anyone who has seen the benefits of hard work can appreciate the blessings of such "sorrow."

18 **Thorns also and thistles** [*weeds, symbolic of the difficulties encountered in earning a living from the soil; symbolic of the trials and tribulations of mortal life*] **shall it bring forth to thee**; and thou shalt eat the herb [*produce*] of the field;

19 **In the sweat of thy face shalt thou eat bread**, till thou return unto the ground; for out of it wast thou taken [*your mortal body is made from the elements of the earth*]: for dust thou *art,* and unto dust shalt thou return.

Next, we are given the definition of the name "Eve."

20 And Adam called his wife's name Eve; because she was **the mother of all living**.

Moses 4:26

26 And Adam called his wife's name Eve, because she was the mother of all living; for thus have I, the Lord God, called the first of all women, which are many [*perhaps implying that there are many worlds (see Moses 1:35), each with their own "Adam" and "Eve," all of which have the same plan of salvation as is used on our earth*].

The Lord provides clothing for Adam and Eve as they leave the Garden of Eden.

21 Unto Adam also and to his wife did **the Lord God** make coats of skins, and **clothed them**.

Moses 4:27

27 Unto Adam, and also unto his wife, did I, the Lord God, make coats of skins, and clothed them.

Next, the Father summarizes the fact that Adam and Eve are now on their way into their mortal classroom, already having some understanding of good and evil. Thus, our first parents are on their way to continue their education and progress toward becoming like our Heavenly Parents.

22 ¶ And the Lord God said, **Behold, the man is become as one of us, to know good and evil**: and now, lest he put forth his hand, and take also of the tree of life, and eat, and live for ever:

23 Therefore **the Lord God sent him forth from the garden of Eden**, to till the ground from whence he was taken.

Moses 4:28–30

28 And I, the Lord God, said unto mine Only Begotten: Behold, the man is become as one of us to know good and evil; and now lest he put forth his hand and partake also of the tree of life, and eat and live forever,

29 Therefore I, the Lord God, will send him forth from the Garden of Eden, to till the ground from whence he was taken;

30 For as I, the Lord God, liveth, even so my words cannot return void, for as they go forth out of my mouth they must be fulfilled.

24 So he drove out the man; and **he placed at the east of the garden of Eden Cherubims** [*heavenly beings*], **and a flaming sword** which turned every way, **to keep** [*guard*] **the way of the tree of life** [*to prevent Adam and Eve from returning and partaking of the tree of life*].

Moses 4:31–32

31 So I drove out the man, and I placed at the east of the Garden of Eden, cherubim and a flaming sword, which turned every way to keep the way of the tree of life.

32 (And these are the words which I spake unto my servant Moses, and they are true even as I will; and I have spoken them unto you [*Joseph Smith*]. See thou show them unto no man, until I command you, except to them that believe. Amen.) [*This is a reminder that, as was the message in Moses 1:42, the book of Moses has some advanced doctrine that might overwhelm people with little or no understanding of gospel basics.*]

Genesis, verse 24, above, emphasizes the importance of the lessons to be had in mortality. In counseling and teaching his son Corianton regarding the plan of salvation, Alma spoke of what would have happened if Adam and Eve had returned and partaken of the tree of life. He said:

Alma 42:2–8

2 Now behold, my son, I will explain this thing unto thee. For behold, after the Lord God sent our first parents forth from the garden of Eden, to till the ground, from whence they were taken—yea, he drew out the man, and he placed at the east end of the garden of Eden, cherubim, and a flaming sword which turned every way, to keep the tree of life—

3 Now, we see that the man had become as God, knowing good and evil; and **lest he should put forth his hand, and take also of the tree of life, and eat and live forever, the Lord God placed cherubim and the flaming sword, that he should not partake of the fruit—**

4 And thus we see, that there was **a time granted unto man to repent**, yea, a probationary time, a time to repent and serve God.

5 For behold, **if Adam had put forth his hand immediately, and partaken of the tree of life, he would have lived forever**, according to the word of God, **having no space for repentance**; yea, and also **the word of God would have been void, and the great plan of salvation would have been frustrated**.

6 But behold, it was appointed unto man to die [*it is part of the plan for us to die*]—therefore, as they were cut off from the tree of life they should be cut off from the face of the earth—and man became lost forever, yea, they became fallen man.

7 And now, ye see by this that our first parents [*Adam and Eve*] were cut off both temporally [*physically*] and spiritually from the presence of the Lord; and thus we see they became subjects to follow after their own will [*they were now in a setting in which they could best exercise their agency*].

8 Now behold, **it was not expedient** [*wise, necessary*] **that man should be reclaimed from this temporal death** [*saved from mortality*]**, for that would destroy the great plan of happiness** [*the plan of salvation*].

GENESIS 4

There is much missing from the Bible that should be here in chapter 4. Moses 5, in the Pearl of Great Price, supplies the missing portions. For example, it provides fifteen verses leading up to what we see as verse 1 of Genesis, chapter 4.

The verses in Moses solve a problem encountered with the Bible, namely, that there is no indication that Adam and Eve had children before having Cain and Abel. A criticism leveled by some who challenge the validity of the Bible comes because Cain marries a wife (verse 17), after killing Abel. Where did his wife come from? The answer is simple. Moses 5:1–15 informs us that Adam and Eve had many children before having Cain and Abel. Problem solved!

A far more important issue is the concern that in the Bible account given here, it does not look like Cain is treated fairly. Why didn't the Lord accept Cain's offering (verse 5)? Did Cain have a fair chance? Was a sincere offering rejected unfairly? Did Cain know enough to deserve his punishment? Did he actually try to kill Abel, or did he hit him, not realizing that it was possible to kill a person?

The Pearl of Great Price supplies many answers. (See Moses 5:1–41, especially verses 16–38, along with the notes and commentary provided in this study guide.) For example, Adam and Eve taught the gospel of Jesus Christ to their family, including Cain and Abel. Cain held the Melchizedek Priesthood and had been taught the proper way to offer sacrifices, which was the blood sacrifice of a male firstling (firstborn) of the flock. Cain had a bad and arrogant attitude to begin with. Satan is the one who commanded Cain to offer sacrifice and encouraged him to mock God by offering a sacrifice of produce from his farm. Cain received repeated warnings from God, inviting him to do things right and receive the promised blessings. Cain rebelled against Adam and Eve and kept his evil doings from them. He surrounded himself with wicked peers, including a wicked wife. Satan taught Cain how to murder Abel. Cain gloried in his wickedness and murdered Abel in order to get his material possessions. Thus, we see clear evidence that Cain was extremely accountable for rebelling against God and making covenants with Satan. His punishment was completely fair according to the law of justice.

With this in mind, we will proceed with our study. First, we will look at the 15 verses of Moses missing from the Bible that originally led up to Genesis 4:1

Moses 5:1–15

1 And it came to pass that after I, the Lord God, had driven them out, that **Adam began to till the earth, and to have dominion over all the beasts of the field, and to eat his bread by the sweat of his brow**, as I the Lord had commanded him. And **Eve**, also, his wife, **did labor with him** [*a team*].

2 And **Adam knew his wife, and she bare unto him sons and daughters**, and **they began to multiply and to replenish the earth** [*as commanded in Moses 2:28; so we are already seeing that Adam and Eve had many children and grandchildren at this point*].

In order to again emphasize the value of the Lord's revealing the original writings of Moses to the Prophet Joseph Smith, we will make a partial list of the many additional things Moses, chapter 5 adds to the biblical account in Genesis 4. We will point out nine things added by way of verses 3–15, next. Remember, all of these things happened before Cain and Abel were born.

1. Their sons and daughters married and had children also.

2. Adam and Eve continued to pray and were taught by the Lord, even though they had been cast out of the Garden of Eden.

3. Adam and Eve were given commandments.

4. They offered sacrifices.

5. They were taught about the Atonement of Jesus Christ.

6. They faithfully taught the gospel of Jesus Christ to their children.

7. Satan came among them and spread his false doctrines and deceptions.

8. Apostasy followed disobedience.

9. The power of the Holy Ghost was manifest in the teaching of faith in Jesus Christ and repentance for the remission of sins.

3 And from that time forth, **the sons and daughters of Adam began to divide two and two** in the land [*in other words, they married and settled on places of their own*], and to till the land, and to tend flocks, and **they also begat sons and daughters** [*grandchildren for Adam and Eve*].

Adam will live to be 930 years old (see Moses 6:12), and so we consider that he and Eve would have had a great many children, thus fulfilling the promise of God, given to Eve in Moses 4:22, in which He said "I will greatly multiply thy . . . conception." We are not told how long Eve lived, but we assume it was to a ripe old age similar to Adam's. We understand that their years were the same as ours, based on the chronology given in Doctrine and Covenants 107:41–53. From this information, we see that Adam was still active and functioning in his priesthood eight generations down the line from him and Eve. Adam was 787 years old at this time, when he ordained Methuselah (Doctrine and Covenants 107:50).

By way of additional information, the Jewish historian Josephus, who lived at the time of Christ, indicated that the ancients did live that long and that their ages were measured in our type of years. He said (**bold** added for emphasis):

"Now when Noah had lived three hundred and fifty years after the Flood, and that all that time happily, he died, **having lived the number of nine hundred and fifty** years. But **let no one**, upon comparing the lives of the ancients with our lives, and with the few years which we now live, **think that what we have said of them is false** [*in other words, don't think that they didn't live that much longer than we do*]; or make the shortness of our lives at present an argument, that neither did they attain to so long a duration of life" (*Josephus, Antiquities of the Jews,* Book 1, chapter 3, verse 9).

President Wilford Woodruff commented on the fact that the ancients did live much longer than we do today. He said:

"The age of man is very short indeed in this day to what it was in ancient days. Men anciently lived to a very great age. When four or five hundred years old they took wives, begat children, and raised up posterity. Today our age is limited to something like three score years and ten [*seventy years*]" (Wilford Woodruff, in James R. Clark, *Messages of the First Presidency,* Vol. 3, page 319).

Next, in verse 4, we are informed that Adam and Eve communicated with God through prayer after being cast out of the Garden of Eden and that the Lord spoke with them from the direction of the Garden.

4 And **Adam and Eve, his wife, called upon the name of the Lord** [*they prayed*], and **they heard the voice of the Lord** from the way toward the Garden of Eden, **speaking unto them**, and they saw him not; for they were shut out from his presence [*this is similar to our general situation now*].

Next, Adam and Eve are commanded to offer sacrifices (Adam will officiate, using his priesthood, and Eve will participate, much the same as when we all participate in the sacrament as priesthood holders administer it to us). Commandments are instructions and invitations from God to us to help us qualify for additional knowledge and blessings, bringing us closer to God. We see this principle clearly taught in the next verses.

5 And he gave unto them commandments, that they should worship the Lord their God, and should offer the firstlings [*the firstborn males—see Deuteronomy 15:19*] of their flocks, for an offering unto the Lord. And Adam was obedient unto the commandments of the Lord.

At this point, we will be taught the value of obedience, even when we don't understand the reasons for the commandment or instruction. At first, Adam did not know the purpose of sacrificing the firstborn males of his flocks. All he knew was that he had been commanded by the Lord to do so, and so he did it. Often, such obedience has to persevere for quite some time before the Lord provides the reasons. As you can see from the first line of verse 6, next, such was the case for Adam and Eve.

6 And **after many days** an angel of the Lord appeared unto Adam, saying: Why dost thou offer sacrifices unto the Lord? And Adam said unto him: I know not, save the Lord commanded me.

Watch now as faith and obedience lead to additional knowledge. In fact, there seems to be a pattern here in which faith and obedience lead to additional revelation, which, when obeyed, leads to yet more blessings and revelation, which, when obeyed, lead to additional knowledge and understanding. And so, this wonderful upward spiral continues in the lives of the faithful. This is a principle and pattern that can continue to operate throughout our lives.

In verse 7, next, the reason for the commandment to sacrifice the firstlings (the firstborn males of the flocks) is given. An angel explains that the sacrificing of the firstborn male, which Adam has been doing as a matter of obedience, is symbolic of the sacrificing of the Son of God.

7 And then the angel spake, saying: **This thing is a similitude of** [*symbolic of*] **the sacrifice of the Only Begotten of the Father**, which is full of grace and truth [*who is full of ability and true doctrine to assist us in returning home to the Father*].

Next, Adam and Eve are taught the importance of worshipping in the name of Jesus Christ and are taught the doctrine of repentance and forgiveness. Again, they are receiving this additional instruction and doctrine because they were obedient to the initial commandments given them.

8 Wherefore, **thou shalt do all that thou doest in the name of the Son**, and **thou shalt repent and call upon God in the name of the Son forevermore**.

Next, one of the greatest blessings of all is given because of obedience. It is the witness of the Holy Ghost.

9 And in that day **the Holy Ghost fell upon Adam, which beareth record of the Father and the Son** [*one of the most important functions of the Holy Ghost*], saying: **I am the Only Begotten of the Father from the beginning** [*the Holy Ghost is bearing special witness that Jesus is the Christ, the Redeemer*], henceforth and forever, that as thou hast fallen **thou mayest be redeemed, and all mankind, even as many as will** [*in other words, all who exercise their agency to follow Christ by keeping His commandments may be redeemed and thus return to live with the Father forever*].

We have been watching as Adam progresses rapidly from simple obedience, without knowing why he was commanded to offer sacrifices, to receiving understanding, then to being given the help and witness of the Holy Ghost, which is a tremendous step forward. One of the lessons we learn is that, with the help of the Holy Ghost, one can move rapidly to a higher and much better understanding of the gospel.

Now, in verse 10, next, we will see the power of the Holy Ghost to expand our minds far beyond our normal capabilities, giving us knowledge and perspective that allow us to understand the true purposes of life and to maintain our direction toward exaltation.

One of the most significant teachings in verse 10 deals with the blessings that came as a result of the Fall. We are clearly taught that the Fall was good.

10 And in that day **Adam blessed** [*praised*] **God and was filled** [*with the Holy Ghost*], and **began to prophesy concerning all the families of the earth**, saying: Blessed be the name of God, for **because of my transgression my eyes are opened, and in this life I shall have joy, and again in the flesh I shall see God**.

We see in verse 11, next, that Eve also has been given great knowledge and powerful testimony because she likewise expresses gladness and joy for the blessings and opportunities that came as a result of the Fall. We also see that she is a great teacher!

11 And **Eve**, his wife, heard all these things and **was glad**, saying: **Were it not for our transgression we never should have had seed** [*we never would have had children*], and **never should have** [*never would have*] **known good and evil**, and the **joy of our redemption**, and the **eternal life** [*exaltation, attaining the highest degree of glory in the celestial kingdom, becoming* gods] **which God giveth unto all the obedient**.

Next, we see that Adam and Eve taught their children all that they had been taught.

12 And **Adam and Eve** blessed [*praised*] the name of God, and they **made all things known unto their sons and their daughters**.

Sadly, but not unexpectedly, Satan comes along as recorded in verse 13, next, and leads many of Adam and Eve's posterity astray. Even though we know that opposition is part of the plan, it still hurts to see people fall for the wiles of the devil.

13 And **Satan came among them**, saying: **I am also a son of God** [*perhaps meaning, "I, too, am righteous—see Moses 7:1, where "sons of God" means "the righteous." If so, he is lying. Another possibility is that he is saying that his ideas and doctrines are just as good as any others, that God's ways are not the only valid ways*]; and **he commanded them** [*he is counterfeiting God*], saying: **Believe it not** [*don't believe what their parents have taught them*]; and they believed it not, and **they loved Satan more than God. And men began from that time forth to be carnal** [*worldly*], **sensual** [*caught up in all forms of sexual immorality*], and **devilish** [*wicked*].

The phrase "they loved Satan more than God" in verse 13 is a pointed statement about any behavior that does not demonstrate loyalty to

God. One of the subtleties or traps that the devil uses successfully is that of convincing us that some of our intentional inappropriate behaviors are not all that dangerous. It can be helpful, when involved in such behaviors, to say to one's self, "At this moment, I love Satan more than God." While this may seem a bit strong, it can nevertheless be an effective way to pull us back from such behaviors. Perhaps it is the shock factor that makes this simple technique effective in steering us back onto the covenant path.

Have you noticed that we are being taught quite a bit about the role and function of the Holy Ghost in these verses from Moses? We will see more about Him in verse 14, next. By the way, this certainly answers the question, frequently asked, as to whether or not the Holy Ghost functioned on the earth before the mortal ministry of the Savior.

14 And **the Lord God called upon men by the Holy Ghost** everywhere and commanded them that they should repent;

We are taught in the Doctrine and Covenants that the Holy Ghost can play a major role in bearing witness to people that the gospel of Jesus Christ is true, whether or not they belong to the Church. If nonmembers do not heed the promptings and progress toward baptism, then the Holy Ghost withdraws. We read:

Doctrine and Covenants 130:23

23 A man may receive the Holy Ghost, and it may descend upon him and not tarry with him.

A simple and powerful summary of the gospel of Jesus Christ is given in Moses 5, verse 15, next. Such simplicity is difficult to misunderstand!

15 **And as many as believed in the Son, and repented of their sins, should be saved; and as many as believed not and repented not, should be damned** [*stopped in their progression*]; and the words went forth out of the mouth of God in a firm decree; wherefore they must be fulfilled.

We will now continue with the account as given in the Bible, starting with Genesis 4:1. Remember, Adam and Eve already had many children and grandchildren by this time.

1 And **Adam knew Eve his wife** [*they conceived a child*]; and **she conceived, and bare Cain**, and said, I have gotten a man from the Lord.

Moses 5:16

16 And Adam and Eve, his wife, ceased not to call upon God [*continued to be faithful in the gospel of Jesus Christ*]. And Adam knew Eve his wife, and she conceived and bare Cain, and said: I have gotten a man from the Lord; wherefore he may not reject his words [*as was the case with some of their previous children—see verse 13*]. But behold, Cain hearkened not, saying: Who is the Lord that I should know him? [*Cain has an arrogant, bad attitude.*]

We will pause here long enough to alert you to some steps of the pattern that Cain will follow and that will ultimately make him feel justified in slaying his brother. It is a clever series of steps in a trap set by Satan. The attitudes and rationalizations involved pose danger to all of us unless we avoid them or repent quickly upon realizing that we have begun following this path.

Some Steps in the Pattern of Cain's Deception

1. Having a cocky, arrogant attitude about God and His church, gospel, and so forth (see Moses 5:16).

2. Loving Satan more than God, enjoying evil more than the things of God (see Moses 5:18).

3. Making your own rules, in opposition to God's, and being angry at God for not accepting your rules for religion as being just as valid as those established by God (Moses 5:19–21).

4. Rejecting opportunities to understand and repent (Moses 5:22–25).

5. Being angry and rejecting God and His servants (Moses 5:26).

6. Surrounding yourself with friends and peers who enjoy evil just like you and who support you in your wickedness (Moses 5:27–28).

7. Making secret, dark, covenants with the devil and his evil representatives to destroy the righteous (Moses 5:29–30).

8. Glorying and rejoicing in wickedness (Moses 5:31).

9. Foolishly believing that you have attained true freedom by rejecting the laws of God (Moses 5:33).

10. Complaining bitterly and blaming others when you finally get caught; refusing to accept full accountability for your own actions (Moses 5:38–39).

Ultimately, the steps taken by Cain led him to become a son of perdition. You may wish to read Doctrine and Covenants 76:31–35 and compare the details given there to the path followed by Cain.

2 And **she again bare his brother Abel**. And Abel was a keeper of sheep [*a rancher*], but Cain was a tiller of the ground [*a farmer*].

Moses will add an important insight regarding Abel's attitude toward God to verse 2 and then add a verse (18) here that is completely missing from Genesis.

Moses 5:17–18

17 And she again conceived and bare his brother Abel. And Abel hearkened unto the voice of the Lord. And Abel was a keeper of sheep, but Cain was a tiller of the ground.

18 And **Cain loved Satan more than God** [*he loved evil more than righteousness*]. And **Satan commanded him**, saying: Make an offering unto the Lord.

There is something wrong and completely improper in verse 18 as far as Cain's situation is concerned. Did you catch it? It is that Cain's motive is that of following Satan rather than God. Satan commands Cain to worship God, to offer sacrifice.

The devil would never command us to do something that appears good unless he believed that it could ultimately bring us to him.

There is something else wrong with the situation, as reported in Genesis, verse 3, next, and Moses, verse 19. Can you see it?

3 And in process of time it came to pass, that **Cain brought of the fruit of the ground** [*some produce from his fields*] **an offering unto the Lord**.

Moses 5:19

19 And **in process of time** [*it apparently took time for Cain to decide to follow Satan's command*] it came to pass that **Cain brought of the fruit of the ground** [*he brought a harvest of crops, perhaps vegetables and grains*] **an offering unto the Lord**.

The problem is the type of sacrifice Cain is bringing. Adam's posterity had been commanded to offer the firstlings of the flock (verse 5, above)—in other words, the firstborn males, symbolizing the shedding of the blood of Christ as an atonement for our sins.

Under Satan's direction, Cain has made his own rules. While we don't know for sure, perhaps one of the things Satan said to Cain was that God discriminates against farmers and blesses ranchers unfairly. Of course, Cain's profession (farming) was just as honorable as Abel's (a rancher—see Genesis, 4:2, above). It is interesting that this verse emphasizes their two chosen careers, perhaps to prepare us for this scene in which Cain offers crops, which represent his livelihood, and in which Abel offers the firstlings of his flocks, representing his chosen livelihood. It may well be that Satan has already put it in Cain's mind that God is prejudiced against farmers, and he may have challenged Cain to offer crops as sacrifice to test God and see if He is fair.

Another important thing to realize here is the fact that Cain held the priesthood, which increased his accountability. Joseph Smith taught:

"The power, glory and blessings of the Priesthood could not continue with those who received ordination only [*except*] as their righteousness continued; for Cain also being authorized to offer sacrifice [*in other words, he held the priesthood*], but not offering it in righteousness, was cursed. It signifies, then, that the ordinances must be kept in the very way God has appointed; otherwise their Priesthood will prove a cursing instead of a blessing" (*Teachings of the Prophet Joseph Smith,* page 169).

4 And **Abel, he also brought of the firstlings of his flock** and of **the fat** [*best*] thereof. And the Lord had respect unto Abel and to his offering [*the Lord accepted Abel's offering*]:

5 **But unto Cain and to his offering he had not respect**. And Cain was very wroth [*angry*], and his countenance fell [*his face told the whole story*].

Moses 5:20–21

20 And **Abel,** he also **brought of the firstlings of his flock**, and **of the fat thereof**. And the Lord had respect unto Abel, and to his;

21 **But unto Cain, and to his offering, he had not respect.** Now Satan knew this, and it pleased him [*his plot to trap Cain was working well so far*]. And **Cain was very wroth,** and his countenance fell.

The Prophet Joseph Smith helped us understand the reasons that the Lord accepted Abel's sacrifice and rejected Cain's. He said:

"God, as before remarked, prepared a sacrifice in the gift of His own Son who should be sent in due time, to prepare a way, or open a door through which man might enter into the Lord's presence. . . . By faith in this atonement or plan of redemption, Abel offered to God a sacrifice that was accepted, which was the firstlings of the flock. Cain offered of the fruit of the ground, and was not accepted, because he could not do it in faith, he could have no faith, or could not exercise faith contrary to the plan of heaven. It must be shedding the blood of the Only Begotten to atone for man; for this was the plan of redemption; and without the shedding of blood was no remission; and as the sacrifice was instituted for a type [*a symbol*], by which man was to discern the great Sacrifice which God had prepared; to offer a sacrifice contrary to that, no faith could be exercised, because redemption was not purchased in that way, nor the power of atonement instituted after that order; consequently Cain could have no faith" (Teachings of the Prophet Joseph Smith, page 58).

6 And the **Lord said unto Cain, Why art thou wroth? and why is thy countenance fallen?**

Moses 5:22

22 **And the Lord said unto Cain: Why art thou wroth? Why is thy countenance fallen?**

Next, Cain is given a chance to repent.

7 **If thou doest well** [*if Cain follows the commandments rather than making his own rules*]**, shalt thou not be accepted? and if thou doest not well** [*if you do not repent*]**, sin lieth at the door** [*you are about to commit terrible sin*]. And unto thee *shall be* his desire [*Satan wants you—see Moses 5:23*], and thou shalt rule over him.

As you will see now, much has been left out between verses 7 and 8 in the Bible.

Moses 5:23–31

23 **If thou doest well, thou shalt be accepted. And if thou doest not well, sin lieth at the door, and Satan desireth to have thee;** and **except** [*unless*] **thou shalt hearken unto my commandments, I will deliver thee up** [*a basic rule of the law of justice; in other words, God cannot force us to obey Him and thus obtain mercy; if we choose to disobey, we must be "delivered up" to Satan and his punishments*], and it shall be unto thee according to his desire. And **thou shalt rule over him;**

It looks like we will have to wait for the final word from the Lord through the living prophet as to the exact meaning of the last phrase in verses 7 and 23, above. However, Joseph Smith did say that those with bodies have power over spirits who don't get bodies. He said (**bold** added for emphasis):

"We came to this earth that we might have a body and present it pure before God in the celestial kingdom. The great principle of happiness consists in having a body. **The devil has no body, and herein is his punishment**. He is pleased when he can obtain the tabernacle of man, and when cast out by the Savior he asked to go into the herd of swine, showing that he would prefer a swine's body to having none.

"All **beings who have bodies have power over those who have not**" (*Teachings of the Prophet Joseph Smith*, page 181).

Next, the Lord warns Cain that if he does not change course now, he will become a son of perdition, just like Satan. He will become the physical, mortal leader of Satan's work on earth. "Perdition" means "total loss," "destruction," "complete ruin."

24 For **from this time forth** thou shalt be the father [*author, sponsor*] of his [*Satan's*] lies; **thou shalt be called Perdition** [*if Cain does not repent and cease following Satan, he will become a son of perdition because his rebellion now would be just like Lucifer's rebellion against full and sure knowledge (see verses 22–23*]; for thou wast also before the world [*perhaps a reminder to Cain that he too lived in the premortal existence and was given opportunities there to know right from wrong; in fact, Cain had to have chosen right to the point of qualifying for mortal life, as opposed to the one-third who were cast out with the devil*].

Elder Bruce R. McConkie taught the meaning of "perdition." He said:

"Two persons, Cain and Satan, have received the awesome name-title Perdition. The name signifies that they have no hope whatever of any degree of salvation, that they have wholly given themselves up to iniquity, and that any feeling of righteousness whatever has been destroyed in their breasts" (*Mormon Doctrine*, 566).

The warning to Cain from the Lord continues, in verse 25, next, telling him that if he does not change course now, he will become known throughout the world as the one who committed the first murder and the one who started dark and terrible evil upon the earth.

25 And **it shall be said in time to come—That these abominations were had from Cain**; for **he rejected the greater counsel** [*the best counsel*] which was had from God; and this [*becoming "Perdition"*] is a cursing which I will put upon thee, **except thou repent** [*there is still time for Cain to repent*].

Next, in verse 26, Cain made an agency choice in the face of pure, complete knowledge between good and evil, which has eternal consequences for him.

26 And **Cain was wroth** [*angry*], and **listened not any more to the voice of the Lord, neither to Abel**, his brother, who walked in holiness before the Lord.

Moses chapter 5, verse 27, next, indicates that Cain had drawn others to follow him in his evil ways before he killed Abel. Verse 28 tells us, in effect, that he chose an evil woman to be his wife. In other words, he surrounded himself with evil friends and family who would support him in his evil ways. You no doubt have seen this type of behavior today among the intentionally wicked.

27 And Adam and his wife mourned before the Lord, because of Cain and his brethren.

28 And it came to pass that Cain took one of his brothers' daughters to wife, and they loved Satan more than God.

Adam and Eve's mourning because of Cain reminds us that many righteous parents find themselves in that situation. Elder Richard G. Scott gave counsel to those who mourn because a loved one has turned away from the Lord to pursue evil. He said:

"Many of you have heavy hearts because a son or daughter, husband or wife, has turned from righteousness to pursue evil. My message is for you.

"Your life is filled with anguish, pain, and, at times, despair. I will tell you how you can be comforted by the Lord.

"First, you must recognize two foundation principles:

"1. While there are many things you can do to help a loved one in need, there are some things that must be done by the Lord.

"2. No enduring improvement can occur without righteous exercise of agency. Do not attempt to override agency. The Lord himself would not do that. Forced obedience yields no blessings (see Doctrine and Covenants 58:26–33).

"I will suggest seven ways you can help. [*Elder Scott explained each of the following. You may wish to read the entire article in the May 1988 Ensign.*]

"First—Love without limitations.

"Second—Do not condone the transgressions, but extend every hope and support to the transgressor.

"Third—Teach truth.

"Fourth—Honestly forgive as often as is required.

"Fifth—Pray trustingly. "The . . . fervent prayer of a righteous man availeth much" (James 5:16).

"Sixth—Keep perspective. When you have done all that you can reasonably do, rest the burden in the hands of the Lord. . . . When the things you realistically can do to help are done, leave the matter in the hands of the Lord and worry no more. Do not feel guilty because you cannot do more. Do not waste your energy on useless worry. . . . In time, you will feel impressions and know how to give further help. You will find more peace and happiness, will not neglect others that need you, and will be able to give greater help because of that eternal perspective.

"One last suggestion—Never give up on a loved one, never!" ("To Help a Loved One in Need," *Ensign,* May 1988, pages 60–61).

Verse 29, next, gives an account of one of the most evil and blasphemous scenes of all time. In it, as you can see, Satan invites Cain to covenant with him by his own life (a most sacred type of covenant—see 1 Nephi 4:33) to put his wicked brethren under secret oath by their own lives, and, in the name of Jesus Christ, to keep their covenant from Adam. Satan, in turn, covenants that he will teach Cain how to murder Abel. In this verse, Satan is openly blaspheming and counterfeiting the most sacred covenants we make with God, in the name of Jesus Christ, as we enter into ordinances and covenants leading to exaltation.

29 And **Satan said unto Cain**: Swear [*covenant*] unto me by thy throat [*upon your life*], and if thou tell it thou shalt die [*this is to be done in secret*]; and **swear thy brethren by their heads** [*make your friends covenant upon their lives*], and **by the living God** [*a mockery of covenants we make in the name of the Father and in the name of Jesus Christ*], **that they tell it not** [*that they keep this dark secret of how to murder a secret*]; for if they tell it, they shall surely die; and this that thy father [*Adam*] may not know it; and **this day I will deliver thy brother Abel into thine hands** [*Satan will teach Cain how to kill Abel—see verse 31*].

Verse 30, next, is a reminder of how far Satan will go to deceive us into following him. He promises Cain, in effect, that he will be his servant. Mormon warned us against believing that the devil would keep his word. He said:

Alma 30:60

60 And thus we see the end of him who perverteth the ways of the Lord; and thus we see **that the devil will not support his children** [*followers*] **at the last day, but doth speedily drag them down to hell**.

30 And **Satan sware** [*promised, covenanted*] **unto Cain that he would do according to his commands**. And all these things were done in secret.

It is sad to note how far downward Cain has fallen since the last invitation from the Lord to repent, in verse 25. He turned completely from God and wholly embraced Satan. He now thinks like Satan and acts like Satan, glorying in wickedness, as we see in verse 31, next. All of this is a direct result of intentionally sinning against light.

31 And **Cain said: Truly I am Mahan** [*perhaps meaning "mind," "destroyer," "great one"; see Moses 5:31, footnote d*], **the master of this great secret, that I may murder and get gain** [*obtain others' possessions*]. Wherefore Cain was called **Master Mahan** and **he gloried in his wickedness**.

Having learned much from the verses in Moses, we can now continue with the next verse in Genesis 4, verse 8.

8 And Cain talked with Abel his brother: and it came to pass, when they were in the field, that **Cain rose up against Abel his brother, and slew him**.

Moses 5:32–33

32 And Cain went into the field, and Cain talked with Abel, his brother. And it came to pass that while they were in the field, Cain rose up against Abel, his brother, and slew him.

33 And Cain gloried in that which he had done, saying: I am free; surely the flocks of my brother falleth into my hands.

In verses 32–33, above, we see Cain kill Abel and then glory in what he has done as he considers that he is now "free" and will get all of Abel's possessions. He has intentionally followed Satan and will soon reap the whirlwind.

In the next verses, we note that Satan is significantly absent and provides no support for Cain as he attempts to lie his way out.

9 ¶ And **the Lord said unto Cain, Where** *is* **Abel thy brother? And he said, I know not:** *Am* **I my brother's keeper?**

10 And he said, **What hast thou done? the voice of thy brother's blood crieth unto me from the ground** [*you have killed Abel*].

Moses 5:34–35

34 And the Lord said unto Cain: Where is Abel, thy brother? And he said: I know not. Am I my brother's keeper?

35 And the Lord said: What hast thou done? The voice of thy brother's blood cries unto me from the ground.

Next, in verses 11–12, the Lord tells Cain what the two curses placed upon him are. These curses are not the same thing as the "mark" mentioned in verse 15. You can read Moses 5:40 and 7:22 for more about the mark.

11 And **now** *art* **thou cursed** from the earth, which hath opened her mouth to receive thy brother's blood from thy hand;

12 **When thou tillest the ground, it shall not henceforth yield unto thee her strength**; **a fugitive and a vagabond** [*wanderer*] **shalt thou be in the earth.**

Moses 5:36–37

36 And now thou shalt be cursed from the earth which hath opened her mouth to receive thy brother's blood from thy hand.

37 When thou tillest the ground it shall not henceforth yield unto thee her strength. A fugitive and a vagabond shalt thou be in the earth.

In the above verses, we see two curses placed upon Cain:

1. The earth will not bring forth abundant crops for him.

2. He will be a fugitive, running from enemies, real or perceived, and a vagabond, not having a permanent home.

Notice in the next verses that Cain expresses no remorse about his victim, Abel, nor about Adam and Eve's feelings at the loss of their choice son, nor about others who would miss Abel. This is typical of those who follow Satan's ways and have learned to think and feel like he does. We will use **bold** underlined to emphasize that Cain is concerned only with himself.

13 And Cain said unto the Lord, **My** punishment *is* greater than **I** can bear.

14 Behold, thou hast driven **me** out this day from the face of the earth; and from thy face shall **I** be hid; and I shall be a fugitive and a vagabond in the earth; and it shall come to pass, *that* every one that findeth **me** shall slay **me**.

Moses 5:38–39

38 And Cain said unto the Lord: Satan tempted me because of my brother's flocks. And I was wroth also; for his offering thou didst accept and not mine; my punishment is greater than I can bear.

39 Behold thou hast driven me out this day from the face of the Lord, and from thy face shall I be hid; and I shall be a fugitive and a vagabond in the earth; and it shall come to pass, that he that findeth me will slay me, because of mine iniquities, for these things are not hid from the Lord.

Did you notice, in the additions from Moses in verse 38, above, that Cain attempts to divert accountability from himself by blaming others? He specifically blames Satan and also the Lord.

Next, the Lord places a mark upon Cain to keep others from killing him.

15 And the Lord said unto him, Therefore whosoever slayeth Cain, vengeance shall be taken on him sevenfold. And **the Lord set a mark upon Cain** [*see Moses 7:8*], **lest any finding him should kill him**.

Moses 5:40

40 And I the Lord said unto him: Whosoever slayeth thee, vengeance shall be taken on him sevenfold. And I the Lord set a mark upon Cain, lest any finding him should kill him.

Later in Moses, Enoch explains the mark.

Moses 7:7–8

7 And the Lord said unto me: Prophesy; and I prophesied, saying: Behold the people of Canaan [*the descendants of Cain—see Moses 7:22*], which are numerous, shall go forth in battle array against the people of Shum, and shall slay them that they shall utterly be destroyed; and the people of Canaan shall divide themselves in the land, and the land shall be barren and unfruitful, and none other people shall dwell there but the people of Canaan;

8 For behold, the Lord shall curse the land with much heat, and the barrenness thereof shall go forth forever;

and there was a blackness came upon all the children of Canaan, that they were despised among all people.

16 ¶ And Cain went out from the presence of the Lord, and dwelt in the land of Nod, on the east of Eden.

Moses 5:41

41 And Cain was shut out from the presence of the Lord [*Cain has, in effect, been excommunicated*], and with his wife and many of his brethren dwelt in the land of Nod, on the east of Eden.

As we continue to the end of the chapter (Genesis 4 plus the Moses additions), we will see that gross wickedness and secret combinations spread from Cain and his wicked peers doing great individual and collective damage to society (summed up in verse 55 of Moses, chapter 5).

17 And **Cain knew his wife; and she conceived,** and **bare Enoch** [*not the "Enoch" who established the City of Enoch, which was taken up into heaven (Moses 7:69)*]: and he [*Cain*] builded a city, and called the name of the city, after the name of his son, Enoch.

18 And unto Enoch was born Irad [*Cain's grandson*]: and Irad begat Mehujael: and Mehujael begat Methusael: and Methusael begat Lamech [*Cain's great-great-great grandson*].

Moses 5:42–43

42 And **Cain knew his wife, and she conceived and bare Enoch**, and **he also begat many sons and daughters**. And he builded a city, and he called the name of the city after the name of his son, Enoch.

43 And unto Enoch was born Irad, **and other sons and daughters**. And Irad begat Mahujael, **and other sons and daughters**. And Mahujael begat Methusael, **and other sons and daughters**. And Methusael begat Lamech.

19 ¶ And Lamech took unto him two wives: the name of the one *was* Adah, and the name of the other Zillah.

20 And Adah bare Jabal: he was the father of such as dwell in tents, and *of such as have* cattle.

21 And his brother's name *was* Jubal: he was the father of all such as handle the harp and organ.

22 And Zillah, she also bare Tubal-cain, an instructer of every artificer in brass and iron: and the sister of Tubal-cain *was* Naamah.

Moses 5:44–46

44 And Lamech took unto himself two wives; the name of one **being** Adah, and the name of the other, Zillah.

45 And Adah bare Jabal; he was the father of such as dwell in tents, **and they were keepers of cattle**; and his brother's name was Jubal, **who** was the father of all such as handle the harp and organ.

46 And Zillah, she also bare Tubal Cain, an instructor of every artificer in brass and iron. And the sister of Tubal Cain was **called** Naamah.

23 And Lamech [*Cain's great-great-great grandson*] said unto his wives, Adah and Zillah, Hear my voice; ye wives of Lamech, hearken unto my speech: for **I have slain a man** [*Irad, Cain's grandson—see Genesis 4:18; see also Moses 5:49–50*] to my wounding, and a young man to my hurt [*in other words, "I'm in real trouble"*].

24 If Cain shall be avenged sevenfold, truly Lamech seventy and sevenfold [*if Cain was in trouble, then I am in real trouble*].

Moses 5:47–48

47 And Lamech said unto his wives, Adah and Zillah: Hear my voice, ye wives of Lamech, hearken unto my speech; for I have slain a man to my wounding, and a young man to my hurt.

48 If Cain shall be avenged sevenfold, truly Lamech **shall be** seventy and **seven fold**;

Next, we watch as secret combinations, including Satan worship, infiltrate and begin to destroy their society to the point where nobody can trust anybody. Lamech has killed Irad, Cain's grandson, and is afraid for his life. He asks his wives to keep his secret, but they tell everyone (see Moses 5:53, ahead), and he is forced to flee and live in hiding. The picture painted here is the exact opposite of a Zion society, where peace and safety prevail because of living the gospel of Jesus Christ.

As you will see, Moses adds many verses here between Genesis 4:24 and Genesis 4:25 that are missing from the biblical account:

Moses 5:49–55

49 For **Lamech having entered into a covenant with Satan**, after the manner of Cain [*just as Cain did*], wherein he became Master Mahan, master of that great secret which was administered unto Cain by Satan; and **Irad**, the son of Enoch [*Genesis 4:18, above*], having known their secret, **began to reveal it unto the sons of Adam**;

50 Wherefore **Lamech**, being angry, **slew him**, not like unto Cain, his brother Abel, for the sake of getting gain, but he slew him for the oath's sake [*because of the secret oath with Satan and fellow members of secret combinations not to reveal murders and plots against others*].

51 For, **from the days of Cain, there was a secret combination**, and **their works were in the dark**, and they knew every man his brother [*other members of the secret combination*].

You may wish to read more about secret combinations and their deadly effects on society as described in Helaman 6:21–30 and Ether 8:13–25.

52 Wherefore **the Lord cursed Lamech, and his house, and all them that had covenanted with Satan**; for they kept not the commandments of God, and it displeased God, and he ministered not unto them, and **their works were abominations**,

and began to spread among all the sons of men. And it was **among the sons of men.**

It is helpful to offer a bit of gospel vocabulary work here. The phrase "sons of men," as used in verse 52, above, means the wicked. But "sons of God," as used in Moses 8:13, were the righteous, covenant-keeping followers of God.

Next, in verses 53–54, we are told that Lamech violated his secret oath by telling his wives about his killing of Irad. Thus, he became a target of other members of his secret combination.

53 **And among the daughters of men these things were not spoken** [*apparently meaning that the wicked men who belonged to secret combinations kept it from their wives, as part of the oath they had taken to join the secret groups*], **because** that **Lamech had spoken the secret unto his wives**, and they rebelled against him, and declared these things abroad [*and they told everyone*], and had not compassion [*showed no mercy*];

54 **Wherefore** [*this is why*] **Lamech was despised, and cast out**, and **came not among the sons of men, lest he should die** [*for fear that they would find him and kill him*].

55 **And thus the works of darkness began to prevail among all the sons of men** [*among all the wicked*].

Verse 55, above, points out the importance of knowing that the phrase "sons of men" means the wicked and "sons of God" means the righteous (see Moses 7:1). Otherwise, at the end of verse 55, one would tend to believe that secret combinations had taken over everyone and that there were no righteous left. The fact is, there were still "sons of God" on earth at this time, including Adam and Eve (see Moses 6:1–4). In Moses 6:17, many of these righteous had to flee to a "land of promise," where they could worship God in peace.

56 And **God** cursed the earth with a sore curse, and **was angry with the wicked**, with **all the sons of men** whom he had made;

57 For **they would not hearken unto his voice, nor believe on his Only Begotten Son**, even him whom he declared should come in the meridian of time, **who was prepared from before the foundation of the world** [*in other words, Jesus Christ was called to be the Redeemer clear back in premortality*].

58 And thus **the Gospel began to be preached, from the beginning, being declared by holy angels sent forth from the presence of God, and by his own voice, and by the gift of the Holy Ghost.**

We are reminded that Adam and Eve had the gospel of Jesus Christ, including ordinances, in verse 59, next. We will see more of this in Moses 6:65–67.

59 And thus **all things were confirmed unto Adam, by an holy ordinance, and the Gospel preached**, and a decree sent forth, that **it should**

be in the world, until the end thereof; and thus it was. Amen.

We will quote Wilford Woodruff to help us understand the phrase "it [*the gospel*] should be in the world, until the end" in verse 59, above. He said:

"Now, any man acquainted with the Scriptures can clearly understand that there is but one true Gospel. There never was but one Gospel. Whenever that Gospel has been upon the earth it has been the same in every dispensation. **The ordinances of the Gospel have never been changed from the days of Adam to the present time**, and never will be to the end of time. While there were many sects and parties in existence in the early times, Jesus gave his disciples to understand that there was but one Gospel. He told them what it was. He declared unto them its ordinances. He commissioned them to preach the Gospel to every creature" (in *Journal of Discourses,* Vol. 24, pages 239–40).

A verse that is missing here between Genesis 4:24 and 25 in the Bible is added in the Moses account.

Moses 6:1

1 And Adam hearkened unto the voice of God [*was obedient to God's commandments*], and called upon his sons to repent.

The Lord sends Adam and Eve another son to fill the place of righteous Abel, as recorded in verse 25, next. We know that Abel went to his reward in paradise and was resurrected at the time of Christ's resurrection (see Doctrine and Covenants 133:54–55, which tells us that all the righteous, those worthy of celestial glory, from Adam down to the time of Christ, who had already died by that time, were resurrected with Him).

We continue with Genesis, chapter 4.

25 ¶ And **Adam knew his wife again** [*the biblical way of saying that Adam and Eve conceived again*]; and **she bare a son**, and called his name **Seth**: For God, *said she,* hath appointed me another seed instead of [*in the place of*] Abel, whom Cain slew.

26 And to Seth, to him also there was born a son; and he called his name Enos: **then began men to call upon the name of the Lord** [*there were many righteous people who worshipped the Father in the name of Jesus Christ*].

Moses 6:2–7

2 And Adam knew his wife again, and she bare a son, and he called his name Seth. And Adam glorified [*praised*] the name of God; for he said: God hath appointed me another seed, instead of Abel, whom Cain slew.

The Doctrine and Covenants tells us that Seth looked just like his father, Adam, and that the only way one could tell them apart was that Adam looked older. We read:

GENESIS 4

Doctrine and Covenants 107:43

43 Because he (Seth) was a perfect man, and his likeness was the express likeness of his father, insomuch that he seemed to be like unto his father in all things, and **could be distinguished from him only by his age**.

Next, in Moses 6:3, we are told that Seth was righteous and that he kept God's commandments, just as Abel had done.

3 And **God revealed himself unto Seth, and he rebelled not, but offered an acceptable sacrifice, like unto his brother Abel**. And to him also was born a son, and he called his name Enos.

4 And **then began these men to call upon the name of the Lord** [*in other words, they were righteous*], and the Lord blessed them;

The "book of remembrance" spoken of in verse 5, next, was a history of Adam and his righteous posterity. It was written under inspiration and is the type of record that later became scripture.

5 And **a book of remembrance** was kept, in the which was recorded, in the language of Adam, for **it was given unto as many as called upon God to write by the spirit of inspiration**;

The "language of Adam" is not in existence today as a complete spoken or written language. However, we do know at least one word because it was revealed to us in Doctrine and Covenants 78:20 and 95:17. The word is "Ahman," which is the name of Heavenly Father in the Adamic language. Elder Orson Pratt taught:

"There is one revelation that this people are not generally acquainted with. I think it has never been published, but probably it will be in the Church History. It is given in questions and answers. The first question is, 'What is the name of God in the pure language?' The answer says, 'Ahman.' 'What is the name of the Son of God?' Answer, 'Son Ahman—the greatest of all the parts of God excepting Ahman'" (in *Journal of Discourses,* Vol. 2, page 342).

Joseph Fielding Smith taught:

"We also learn from the closing verses of this revelation that Jesus Christ is also called Son Ahman. (See Doctrine and Covenants 95:17.) Therefore his name is connected with the name of the place where Adam dwelt. For that reason Elder Orson Pratt gives it the interpretation of 'The Valley of God'" (*Church History and Modern Revelation,* Vol. 1, page 310).

Elder Bruce R. McConkie explained this "book of remembrance." He said:

"Adam kept a written account of his faithful descendants in which he recorded their faith and works, their righteousness and devotion, their revelations and visions, and their adherence to the revealed plan of salvation. To signify the importance of honoring our worthy ancestors and of hearkening to the great truths revealed to them, Adam called his record a book of remembrance" (Mormon Doctrine, page 100).

Next, we are informed that Adam and Eve knew how to read and write and that they taught their children to do so also. This is a clear reminder that Adam and Eve were intelligent and well-educated.

6 And **by them their children were taught to read and write,** having a language which was pure and undefiled.

Next, Adam prophesies that the priesthood he holds (the Melchizedek Priesthood; he was a high priest—see note accompanying Moses 6:7, next) will be available to men upon the earth in the last days. In other words, Adam was a great prophet, and he prophesied about our day.

7 Now **this same Priesthood** [*which Adam and his righteous sons, grandsons, and so forth held*], which was in the beginning [*in Adam's day and also in premortality—see Alma 13:3*], **shall be in the end of the world also.**

Joseph Smith explained the topic of verse 7, above. He said (**bold** added for emphasis):

"The **Priesthood was first given to Adam**; he obtained the First Presidency, and held the keys of it from generation to generation. **He obtained it in the Creation, before the world was formed.** . . . The Priesthood is an everlasting principle, and existed with God from eternity, and will to eternity, without beginning of days or end of years. The keys have to be brought from heaven whenever the Gospel is sent. When they are revealed from heaven, it is by Adam's authority" (*Teachings of the Prophet Joseph Smith,* page 157).

The above quote from Joseph Smith reminds us of Adam's high position. It is important that we understand that Adam and Eve were two of the greatest and most valiant spirit children of our Heavenly Father, sent to earth to start things off right. They were highly intelligent, well-educated, married for time and eternity, and wonderful examples as parents who lived gospel-centered lives.

GENESIS 5

This chapter of the Bible contains the genealogy from Adam down to Noah. However, as you will see, a great many verses are added by the Moses version, which contribute greatly to our understanding, including Enoch and his great mission. (Note that the first seven verses of Moses, chapter 6, were given at the end of Genesis 4, above.)

1 **This** *is* **the book of the generations** [*genealogy*] **of Adam.** In the day that God created man, in the likeness of God made he him;

Moses 6:8

8 Now this prophecy [*"Now this same priesthood, which was in the beginning, shall be in the end of the world, also"—see Moses 6:7*] Adam spake, as he was moved upon by the Holy Ghost, and a genealogy was kept of the children of God. And this was the book of the generations of Adam, saying: In the day that God

created man, in the likeness of God made he him;

In Moses 6:8, above, we see that Adam and Eve and their righteous posterity kept their genealogy.

In order to understand the phrase "children of God" in Moses 6:8, it is helpful to remember, as we mentioned previously (note following Moses 5:55), that "sons of God" is a phrase referring to the righteous (see Moses 7:1), and "sons of men," or "daughters of men," means the wicked. Thus, the phrase "children of God," in verse 8, means the righteous men and women in Adam's day. The wicked generally do not keep their genealogy down through the ages. In fact, some governments have attempted to destroy all sense of family and belonging to extended family by mandating that people can have only one name, which eliminates family names and curtails a sense of belonging to a family unit.

Also in the next verses, we are given a brief review and reminder that we are created in the image of God. In other words, we are part of His family. He wants us to know this. We look like Him. He has a body of flesh and bones, just as we do, although His is a glorified, resurrected body (Doctrine and Covenants 130:22).

2 Male and female created he them; and blessed them, and **called their name Adam**, in the day when they were created.

Moses 6:9

9 In the image of his own body, male and female, created he them, and blessed them, and called their name Adam, in the day when they were created and became living souls [*spirits clothed in physical bodies—see Doctrine and Covenants 88:15*] in the land upon the footstool of God [*the earth*].

Did you notice something a bit unusual in the above verses with respect to the name Adam? As used here, it refers to both Adam and Eve. President Spencer W. Kimball gave a brief comment on this. He said:

"'Male and female created he them; and blessed them, and called their name Adam [*Mr. and Mrs. Adam, I suppose, or Brother and Sister Adam*], in the day when they were created.' (Genesis 5:1–2)" ("The Blessings and Responsibilities of Womanhood," *Ensign,* March 1976, page 71).

As we continue with the genealogy given in Genesis 5, you will notice that many of these men lived a long time. We understand that these people did actually live to be many hundreds of years old, and that their "years" were the same as ours.

The Jewish historian, Josephus, who lived at the time of Christ, indicated that the ancients did live that long and that their ages were measured in our type of years. He said (**bold** added for emphasis):

"Now when Noah had lived three hundred and fifty years after the Flood, and that all that time happily, he died, having lived the number of nine hundred and fifty years. But let no one, upon comparing the lives of the ancients with our lives, and with the few years which we now live, think that what we have said of them is false [*in other words, don't think that they didn't live that much longer than we do*]; or make the shortness of our lives at present an argument, that neither did they attain to so long a duration of life" (Josephus, Antiquities of the Jews, Book 1, chapter 3, verse 9).

President Wilford Woodruff commented on the fact that the ancients did live much longer than we do today. He said:

"The age of man is very short indeed in this day to what it was in ancient days. **Men anciently lived to a very great age**. When four or five hundred years old they took wives, begat children, and raised up posterity. Today our age is limited to something like three score years and ten [seventy years]" (in *Journal of Discourses,* Vol. 13, page 319).

After the Flood, the average life span decreased to under 200 years (Abraham lived to be 175, Isaac 180, Jacob 147, Joseph 110, Moses 120, Joshua 110), and then decreased further as the years went by.

We will use **bold** to highlight the fascinating statistics given here.

3 ¶ And Adam lived an hundred and thirty years, and begat *a son* in his own likeness, after his image; and called his name Seth:

4 And the days of Adam after he had begotten Seth were eight hundred years: and he begat sons and daughters:

5 And all the days that **Adam** lived were **nine hundred and thirty years**: and he died.

Moses 6:10–12

10 And Adam lived one hundred and thirty years, and begat a son in his own likeness, after his own image, and called his name Seth.

11 And the days of Adam, after he had begotten Seth, were eight hundred years, and he begat many sons and daughters;

12 And all the days that Adam lived were nine hundred and thirty years, and he died.

6 And Seth lived an hundred and five years, and begat Enos:

7 And Seth lived after he begat Enos eight hundred and seven years, and begat sons and daughters:

8 And all the days of **Seth** were **nine hundred and twelve years**: and he died.

You will see that the Moses verses here add significant content.

Moses 6:13–16

13 Seth lived one hundred and five years, and begat Enos, and prophesied in all his days, and taught his son Enos in the ways of God; wherefore Enos prophesied also.

14 And Seth lived, after he begat Enos, eight hundred and seven years, and begat many sons and daughters.

15 And the children of men were numerous upon all the face of the land.

And in those days Satan had great dominion among men, and raged in their hearts; and from thenceforth came wars and bloodshed; and a man's hand was against his own brother, in administering death, because of secret works, seeking for power.

16 All the days of Seth were nine hundred and twelve years, and he died.

9 ¶ And Enos lived ninety years, and begat Cainan:

10 And Enos lived after he begat Cainan eight hundred and fifteen years, and begat sons and daughters:

11 And all the days of **Enos** were **nine hundred and five years**: and he died.

Moses 6:17–18

17 And Enos lived ninety years, and begat Cainan. And Enos and the residue of the people of God came out from the land, which was called Shulon, and dwelt in a land of promise, which he called after his own son, whom he had named Cainan.

Throughout the scriptures, we see many groups of righteous people who are led away from lands filled with wickedness into a land of promise where they can worship God freely. Verse 17, above, contains the earliest mention of a "land of promise." In this case, Enos, Adam's grandson, and his people were the ones led to the promised land spoken of.

18 And Enos lived, after he begat Cainan, eight hundred and fifteen years, and begat many sons and daughters. And all the days of Enos were nine hundred and five years, and he died.

12 ¶ And Cainan lived seventy years, and begat Mahalaleel:

13 And Cainan lived after he begat Mahalaleel eight hundred and forty years, and begat sons and daughters:

14 And all the days of **Cainan** were **nine hundred and ten years**: and he died.

Moses 6:19

19 And Cainan lived seventy years, and begat Mahalaleel; and Cainan lived after he begat Mahalaleel eight hundred and forty years, and begat sons and daughters. And all the days of Cainan were nine hundred and ten years, and he died.

15 ¶ And Mahalaleel lived sixty and five years, and begat Jared:

16 And Mahalaleel lived after he begat Jared eight hundred and thirty years, and begat sons and daughters:

17 And all the days of **Mahalaleel** were **eight hundred and ninety and five years**: and he died.

Moses 6:20

20 And Mahalaleel lived sixty–five years, and begat Jared; and Mahalaleel lived, after he begat Jared, eight

hundred and thirty years, and begat sons and daughters. And all the days of Mahalaleel were eight hundred and ninety–five years, and he died.

Next, we see the birth of Enoch. He will be ordained by Adam at age twenty-five (Doctrine and Covenants 107:48) and called by the Lord to perform his special mission when he is sixty-five years old. As you will see, he considered himself "but a lad" (see Moses 6:31) at the time of his call. He will preach the gospel for 365 years before he and the City of Enoch are translated and taken up. Enoch will be 430 years old at the time of his translation (Moses 8:1). At the end of verse 21, you will see that Enoch had a righteous father, who taught him the gospel.

18 ¶ And Jared lived an hundred sixty and two years, and he begat Enoch:

19 And Jared lived after he begat Enoch eight hundred years, and begat sons and daughters:

20 And all the days of **Jared** were **nine hundred sixty and two years**: and he died.

Moses 6:21–24

21 And Jared lived one hundred and sixty–two years, and begat Enoch; and Jared lived, after he begat Enoch, eight hundred years, and begat sons and daughters. And Jared taught Enoch in all the ways of God.

22 And this is the genealogy of the sons of Adam, who was the son of God, with whom God, himself, conversed.

23 And they were preachers of righteousness, and spake and prophesied, and called upon all men, everywhere, to repent; and faith was taught unto the children of men.

24 And it came to pass that all the days of Jared were nine hundred and sixty–two years, and he died.

21 ¶ And Enoch lived sixty and five years, and begat Methuselah:

Moses 6:25

25 And Enoch lived sixty–five years, and begat Methuselah.

The book of Moses adds well over one hundred verses to this part of the Genesis account. We will add them here.

As you will no doubt see, there are many beautiful doctrines, precious gospel principles, and important pieces of information that were contained in Moses's original account that have been lost from the biblical account. Remember, these lost verses were restored through the Prophet Joseph Smith by direct revelation (see heading to the Book of Moses in the Pearl of Great Price).

Beginning with Moses 6:26, next, Moses writes about Enoch and his mission. From these inspired writings of Moses, revealed to the Prophet Joseph Smith, we learn many "plain and precious things" (1 Nephi 13:28) that were left out of Genesis, in the Bible. Moses's account of Enoch's mission and teachings will continue through Moses 8:2.

First, in verses 26–30, Enoch is called on his mission. He is sixty-five years old at this time (see verse 25, above). At this point, as previously mentioned, Adam is 687 years of age. Enoch was born about 625 years after the Fall of Adam and Eve. The only other references to him in the Bible, in addition to Genesis 5:19–24, are found in Luke 3:37, Hebrews 11:5, and Jude 1:14–15.

As you will sense, Enoch was not expecting this call and was quite reluctant to accept it. This must have been quite touching to Moses as he wrote this account because he went through similar concerns and feelings at the time of his own call to serve as a prophet (see Exodus 3–4, especially Exodus 3:11 and 4:1, 10).

Note how the Lord sets the stage with Enoch as to why it is so important that he accept this call to preach the gospel of Jesus Christ.

Moses 6:26-68

26 And it came to pass **that Enoch journeyed in the land**, among the people; and as he journeyed, **the Spirit of God descended out of heaven, and abode upon him**.

27 And **he heard a voice** from heaven, **saying: Enoch, my son, prophesy unto this people, and say unto them—Repent**, for thus saith the Lord: I am angry with this people, and my fierce anger is kindled against them; for **their hearts have waxed** [*grown*] **hard**, and **their ears are dull of hearing** [*they are spiritually deaf*], and **their eyes cannot see afar off** [*they lack wisdom; they cannot see the future consequences of their present actions and philosophies*];

28 And for these **many generations**, ever since the day that I created them, **have** they **gone astray**, and have **denied me**, and have **sought their own counsels** [*have left God and gone their own ways*] **in the dark** [*spiritual darkness*]; and in their own **abominations** [*extreme wickedness*] have they devised **murder**, and have **not kept the commandments**, which I gave unto their father [*ancestor*], Adam.

29 Wherefore, **they have foresworn themselves** [*made covenants with God and then broken them*], and, **by their oaths** [*including those made as they joined secret combinations—see Moses 5:51, 6:15*], **they have brought upon themselves death** [*spiritual and physical, in many cases*]; and a hell [*the spirit prison*] I have prepared for them, **if they repent not** [*they can still repent; it is not too late*];

30 And **this is a decree** [*an absolute*], which I have sent forth in the beginning of the world, from my own mouth, **from the foundation thereof** [*clear back in the premortal life; in other words, this is part of the plan of salvation*], and **by the mouths of my servants, thy fathers** [*ancestors*], **have I decreed it** [*the gospel of repentance and salvation, which Enoch is being called to preach*], even as **it shall be sent forth in the world, unto the ends**

thereof [*the gospel will ultimately be preached throughout the world*].

Next, we see Enoch's humility and concerns about his inadequacies.

31 And **when Enoch had heard these words, he bowed himself to the earth**, before the Lord, and spake before the Lord, saying: **Why is it that I have found favor in thy sight, and am but a lad** [*of sixty-five years of age; a "lad" compared to Adam and others still alive who were much older and more experienced in preaching*], and **all the people hate me**; for **I am slow of speech**; wherefore [*why*] am I thy servant [*why have You called me*]?

In addition to being relatively young and inexperienced, Enoch expressed two major concerns about his ability to be effective in carrying out this call from the Lord. They are:

1. "All the people hate me," which implies that, in such a wicked society, his life would be in danger if he started openly preaching the gospel.

2. "I am slow of speech," which implies that he had great difficulty speaking and was quite ineffective in communicating.

The Lord will address both of these concerns next, in verse 32, if Enoch is obedient and goes forth in faith to do the Lord's will.

32 And the Lord said unto Enoch: **Go forth** and do as I have commanded thee, and **no man shall pierce thee** [*he will be given physical protection*]. **Open thy mouth, and it shall be filled, and I will give thee utterance** [*his inability or disability in communicating will be healed*], for all flesh is in my hands [*I can do these things for you*], and I will do as seemeth me good.

Next, in this "MTC" conducted by the Lord for Enoch, he is instructed as to what to say. Furthermore, the Savior prophesies concerning the power over nature that He will give to Enoch.

33 **Say unto this people: Choose ye this day, to serve the Lord God who made you**.

34 Behold **my Spirit is upon you**, wherefore **all thy words will I justify** [*support*]; and the **mountains shall flee before you** [*the mountains will move at his command—see Moses 7:13*], and the **rivers shall turn from their course** [*Moses 7:13*]; and **thou shalt abide in me, and I in you** [*we will be a team*]; **therefore walk with me**.

Next, Enoch obeys a simple command that leads to his seeing a tremendous vision. This vision will give him the perspective that God has and will enable him to carry out his mission despite impossible odds.

35 And the Lord spake unto Enoch, and said unto him: **Anoint thine eyes with clay, and wash them, and thou shalt see**. And he did so.

The instruction of the Savior to put clay on his closed eyes and then wash it off and "see" reminds us of the blind man spoken of in John 9:6–7 who was healed of his blindness on the Sabbath day by the Master.

We will take a moment to read this account from the Bible:

John 9:6–7

6 When he [*the Savior*] had thus spoken, he spat on the ground, and made clay of the spittle, and **he anointed the eyes of the blind man with the clay**,

7 And said unto him, Go, wash in the pool of Siloam, (which is by interpretation, Sent.) [*"Sent," capitalized, is another name for Christ, the one "sent" by the Father to heal us from our "blindness"*] **He went his way therefore, and washed, and came seeing**.

Next, we are given a brief glimpse of what Enoch saw in this vision. From this time forth, his reputation begins to spread throughout the land.

36 And **he beheld the spirits that God had created; and he beheld also things which were not visible to the natural eye**; and from thenceforth came the saying abroad in the land: **A seer hath the Lord raised up unto his people**.

We will pause to take a closer look at the word "seer." It is an important gospel vocabulary word. Seers are vital to our salvation. We sustain the members of the First Presidency and the Quorum of the Twelve Apostles as "prophets, **seers**, and revelators." Elder John A. Widtsoe, of the Twelve, taught:

"A seer is one who sees with spiritual eyes. He perceives the meaning of that which seems obscure to others; therefore he is an interpreter and clarifier of eternal truth. He foresees the future from the past and the present (*Evidences and Reconciliations,* 258).

The Book of Mormon teaches us more about what seers do for us.

Mosiah 8:17

17 But a seer can know of things which are past, and also of things which are to come, and by them shall all things be revealed, or, rather, shall secret things be made manifest, and hidden things shall come to light, and things which are not known shall be made known by them, and also things shall be made known by them which otherwise could not be known.

Joseph Smith gave further instructions about the role of seers. He taught us what past seers **saw**, emphasizing that they saw into the future and prophesied about it. He said (**bold** added for teaching purposes):

"Wherefore, we again say, search the revelations of God; study the prophecies, and **rejoice that God grants unto the world Seers and Prophets**. They are **they who saw** the mysteries of godliness; **they saw** the flood before it came; **they saw** angels ascending and descending upon a ladder that reached from earth to heaven; **they saw** the stone cut out of the mountain, which filled the whole earth; **they saw** the Son of God come from the regions of bliss and dwell with men on earth; **they saw** the deliverer come out of Zion, and turn away ungodliness from Jacob; **they saw** the glory of the Lord when he showed the transfiguration of the earth on the mount;

they saw every mountain laid low and every valley exalted when the Lord was taking vengeance upon the wicked; **they saw** truth spring out of the earth, and righteousness look down from heaven in the last days, before the Lord came the second time to gather his elect; **they saw** the end of wickedness on earth, and the Sabbath of creation crowned with peace; **they saw** the end of the glorious thousand years, when Satan was loosed for a little season; **they saw** the day of judgment when all men received according to their works, and **they saw** the heaven and the earth flee away to make room for the city of God, when the righteous receive an inheritance in eternity" (*Teachings of the Prophet Joseph Smith,* pages 12–13).

We will continue now with Moses's account of Enoch's mission. As you will see, people have become curious as to who this "wild man" is (verse 38).

37 And it came to pass that **Enoch went forth** in the land, **among the people**, standing upon the hills and the high places, and cried with a loud voice, **testifying against their works**; and **all men were offended because of him** [*the wicked don't like to be told of their sins*].

38 And **they came forth to hear him**, upon the high places, saying unto the tent-keepers: Tarry ye here and keep the tents, while we go yonder to behold [*to see*] the seer, for he prophesieth, and **there is a strange thing in the land; a wild man hath come among us.**

Next, in verse 39, we see the Lord's promise to Enoch of physical protection (verse 32) in action.

39 And it came to pass when they heard him, **no man laid hands on him**; for fear came on all them that heard him; **for he walked with God** [*as invited to do so by the Lord—see end of verse 34*].

According to verse 40, next, there has been such commotion and curiosity about Enoch among these wicked people that they have selected one of their number to approach him directly and ask him who he really is. Perhaps this implies that they were so afraid of Enoch (verse 39, above) that they didn't dare get that close to him themselves.

40 And **there came a man unto him**, whose name was Mahijah, **and said** unto him: **Tell us plainly who thou art, and from whence thou comest?**

41 And he said unto them: **I came out from the land of Cainan** [*the "promised land" to which Enos and his righteous followers had been led; see verse 17*], the land of my fathers, **a land of righteousness** unto this day. And my father [*Jared; see verse 21*] taught me in all the ways of God [*a reminder of the powerful influence of righteous fathers*].

Next, in verses 42–46, Enoch continues to answer their question as to who he is and where he comes from. We feel the skillful flow and power of his words, and we see the promise of the Lord to him being fulfilled (verse 32), overcoming

Enoch's concern about being "slow of speech" (verse 31).

42 And it came to pass, **as I journeyed** from the land of Cainan, by the sea east, **I beheld a vision**; and lo, **the heavens I saw**, and **the Lord spake with me**, and gave me commandment; wherefore, for this cause, to keep the commandment, I speak forth these words.

One of the lessons we learn from verse 43, next, is the importance of having God be a part of our personal identity in our own minds.

43 And Enoch continued his speech, saying: The Lord which spake with me, the same is the God of heaven, and **he is my God** [*part of Enoch's identity*], and your God, and ye are my brethren, and why counsel ye yourselves, and deny the God of heaven [*why do you support each other in denying God*]?

One more comment about having our commitment to God be an integral part of our self-image. President Henry D. Moyle, counselor in the First Presidency, once told us as a group of missionaries serving in Austria that foremost in our minds should be the fact that we are members of the Lord's true church. He told us of his being on a train when a fellow passenger suddenly asked him, "What are you?" Without thinking, President Moyle immediately replied, "A Mormon." He could have told the man that he was a businessman, a civic leader, a philanthropist, a leader in The Church of Jesus Christ of Latter-day Saints, headquartered in Salt Lake City, Utah, or any one of several titles and positions he held. He told us that his response startled him at the time, but that, as he later thought about it, he was pleased with it because it was genuine. He was first and foremost "a Mormon."

As Enoch continues, he eloquently bears witness of God as the Creator, teaches about the Fall of Adam and Eve, reminds them all of the fact that they have been placed on earth by the God of heaven, points their minds to their living ancestors back to Adam, whom they know, and talks of their scriptures (the book of remembrance), which have been kept as commanded by the Lord.

44 **The heavens he made**; **the earth is his footstool** [*a scriptural phrase symbolizing that the earth and its contents are subject to God*]; and the foundation thereof is his. Behold, **he laid it** [*He created the earth*], **an host of men hath he brought** in upon the face thereof.

45 And **death hath come upon our fathers** [*our ancestors; in other words, all are subject to death because of the Fall*]; nevertheless **we know them**, and cannot deny, and even the first of all **we know**, even **Adam**.

Verse 45 is another reminder that the genealogy of man does not go back beyond Adam, who is the "first of all."

46 For **a book of remembrance we have written among us, according to the pattern given by the finger of God**; and it is given **in our own language** [*perhaps implying that it is readily accessible*

and easy for anyone to read, and that these people could and should read their scriptures, which explain the purposes of their being on earth].

Enoch has become a masterful teacher under the guidance and power of the Lord. As we study his sermon, which continues in verses 47–68, next, we will not only learn much more about Adam and what he was taught about the gospel, but we will also be taught much about the Fall and the Atonement of Jesus Christ.

Remember that many of the wicked people to whom Enoch preaches the gospel will repent and become a Zion people, ultimately being translated and taken up with the City of Enoch. We are watching the very beginnings of this great conversion of souls as we study these next verses. Pay close attention to the basics of the plan of salvation that can lead to such complete conversion.

47 And **as Enoch spake** forth the words of God, **the people trembled**, and could not stand in his presence.

A correct understanding of the Fall of Adam and Eve is essential to complete conversion. Next, Enoch teaches that the Fall was good. Mortality and the physical death that accompanies it are necessary if we want resurrected bodies. The trials and tribulations of mortality are part of the plan of salvation. Satan's opposition and temptation are necessary for the exercising of our agency.

48 And he said unto them: **Because that Adam fell, we are** [*Adam's Fall resulted in our being mortals upon the earth*]; and **by his fall came death**; and **we are made partakers of misery and woe.**

49 Behold **Satan hath come among the children of men, and tempteth them to worship him**; and **men have become carnal** [*worldly, materialistic, lacking in spirituality*], **sensual** [*involved in sexual immorality*], and **devilish** [*evil, wicked*], and are shut out from the presence of God.

The solution to the situations explained in verses 48–49 is given in simple, clear terms, beginning in verse 50. Adam will be used as an example.

50 But God hath made known unto our fathers that **all men must repent**.

51 And **he called upon our father** [*ancestor*] **Adam** by his own voice, saying: I am God; I made the world, and men before they were in the flesh [*a reference to our premortal life as spirit children of God; in other words, the Father has a plan for us*].

Next, Enoch explains that Adam was taught what we refer to as the "first principles and ordinances of the gospel" (fourth article of faith), namely, faith, repentance, baptism, and the gift of the Holy Ghost.

52 And he also said unto him: If thou wilt **turn unto me**, and **hearken unto** [*obey*] **my voice**, and **believe**, and **repent** of all thy transgressions,

and **be baptized**, even in water [*by immersion*], in the name of mine Only Begotten Son, who is full of grace and truth [*full of power to save us*], which is Jesus Christ, the only name which shall be given under heaven [*there is only one gospel with the power to save us*], whereby salvation shall come unto the children of men, ye shall receive **the gift of the Holy Ghost**, asking all things in his name [*the name of Jesus Christ*], and whatsoever ye shall ask, it shall be given you.

Next, in verse 53, Enoch explains that Adam had a question about why baptism is necessary, including why it was to be done by immersion. The Lord's answer will be given over several verses and summarized with beautiful symbolism in verses 59–60.

But before answering the question, the Lord puts Adam's mind at ease about his having partaken of the forbidden fruit in the Garden of Eden.

53 And our father Adam spake unto the Lord, and said: **Why is it that men must repent and be baptized in water?** And the Lord said unto Adam: Behold **I have forgiven thee thy transgression in the Garden of Eden.**

With that concern off his mind, the way is open for Adam to concentrate on the answer to his question about baptism. First, in verse 54, next, the Savior will address the issue of original sin, apparently a prevalent false doctrine spread by Satan in Adam's day. Those who believed in original sin (that children are born unclean because of Adam and Eve's transgression and fall) would believe that babies are unclean and must be baptized. The Savior will teach Adam that babies are not unclean and that they do not carry the sins of the parents, but that as they grow up and become accountable, they will need baptism. As stated in verse 54, this correct doctrine will spread throughout the land.

54 **Hence came the saying abroad among the people, that the Son of God hath atoned for original guilt** [*see second article of faith*], wherein **the sins of the parents cannot be answered upon the heads of the children,** for **they are whole** [*clean, pure*] from the foundation of the world.

What really happens to children and why they will eventually need to be baptized is clearly taught next, as the Lord continues to answer Adam's question about the need for baptism.

55 And the Lord spake unto Adam, saying: **Inasmuch as** [*since it is a fact that*] **thy children are conceived in sin** [*born into a world that contains much sin and wickedness*], even so **when they begin to grow up, sin conceiveth in their hearts** [*they begin to get sinful ideas and thoughts*], and **they taste the bitter, that they may know to prize the good** [*part of the plan for "opposition in all things"—see 2 Nephi 2:11*].

Elder McConkie taught the following about the phrase "conceived in sin," in verse 56, above:

"Conceived in sin" means "born into a world of sin" (*A New Witness for the Articles of Faith,* page 101).

Next, the doctrine of agency is taught as it relates to baptism. Children who are old enough to distinguish between right and wrong become accountable (at age eight—see Doctrine and Covenants 68:25–28). Thus, they become "agents unto themselves" (verse 56) and need baptism.

56 And **it is given unto them to know good from evil** [*they soon begin gaining the ability to differentiate between good and evil*]; **wherefore** [*this is the reason*] **they are agents unto themselves** [*thus, they can begin to exercise their moral agency*], and I have given unto you another law and commandment [*to teach repentance to your children, as described, beginning in verse 57, next*].

57 **Wherefore** [*therefore*] **teach** it unto **your children, that all men, everywhere, must repent, or they can in nowise inherit the kingdom of God** [*the celestial kingdom*], for no unclean thing can dwell there, or dwell in his [*the Father's*] presence; for, in the language of Adam, **Man of Holiness** is his name, and **the name of his Only Begotten is the Son of Man** [*of Holiness*], even Jesus Christ, a righteous Judge, who shall come in the meridian of time [*referring to the time of Christ's mortal mission on earth*].

The last half of verse 57 gives us an important clarification as to why Jesus is often referred to as the "Son of Man" in the scriptures. Over the years, students have often asked me why Jesus is referred to in this way, rather than as the "Son of God." They felt that calling Him the "Son of Man" did not represent who He was and that the phrase made it sound like He was the son of a mortal man rather than of the Father. An example of their concern is found in Matthew, where we read of the Savior's healing of the man with palsy (**bold** added for emphasis):

Matthew 9:6

6 But that ye may know that **the Son of man** hath power on earth to forgive sins, (then saith he to the sick of the palsy,) Arise, take up thy bed, and go unto thine house.

It was always a pleasure to point out to them that the answer is found in the last part of verse 57, above. The complete phrase is, in effect, that Jesus is the "Son of Man of Holiness." In other words, He is the Son of the Father.

Next, Adam was commanded to make sure that he and Eve surrounded their children with the gospel.

58 Therefore **I give unto you a commandment, to teach these things freely unto your children**, saying:

Next, Adam is told to teach his children about the Fall and the Atonement. Pay close attention in verse 59 to the words water, blood, and spirit. Note that they are given in a different order in the second half of verse 59 than in the first half. Note also that the second time they are given, the word spirit is capitalized. Significant symbolism is involved here. We will give verse 59, using **bold** to highlight these three words and their order. Then we will repeat verse 59, adding several notes.

59 That by reason of transgression cometh the fall, which fall bringeth death, and inasmuch as ye were born into the world by **water**, and **blood**, and the **spirit**, which I have made, and so became of dust a living soul, even so ye must be born again into the kingdom of heaven, of **water**, and of the **Spirit**, and be cleansed by **blood**, even the blood of mine Only Begotten; that ye might be sanctified from all sin, and enjoy the words of eternal life in this world, and eternal life in the world to come, even immortal glory;

As mentioned above, this verse points out the intentional symbolism between the process of physical birth and the process of spiritual rebirth, or being "born again," through the Atonement of Jesus Christ, with the help and guidance of the Holy Ghost. Water, blood, and spirit are involved in both. We will now add several notes to verse 59 as we go through it again.

Moses 6:59 (repeated)

59 That **by reason of** [*because of Adam and Eve's*] **transgression cometh the fall**, which fall **bringeth death** [*eventual physical death and spiritual death, meaning, being cut off from the direct presence of God*], and **inasmuch as** [*since*] **ye were born** [*physical birth*] **into the world by water** [*amniotic fluid*], and **blood** [*which accompanies physical birth*], and the **spirit** [*your premortal spirit, which is now in your physical body*], **which I have made** [*the Father is the father of our premortal spirits—see Hebrews 12:9*], **and so became of dust** [*the physical elements of the earth that form our mortal bodies*] **a living soul** [*the body and spirit combined together form a "soul"—see Doctrine and Covenants 88:15*], **even so ye must be born again** [*spiritually*] **into the kingdom of heaven** [*celestial glory*], of **water** [*baptism*], and of the **Spirit** [*the gift of the Holy Ghost*], and be cleansed by **blood** [*the Atonement of Christ*], even the blood of mine Only Begotten; **that ye might be sanctified** [*made pure, clean, fit to be in the presence of God*] **from all sin, and enjoy the words of eternal life** [*the gospel of Christ*] **in this world, and eternal life** [*exaltation*] **in the world to come, even immortal glory**;

Verse 60, next, is a brief review of what was taught in more detail in verse 59, above.

60 For by the **water** [*baptism*] ye keep the commandment; by the **Spirit** [*the Holy Ghost*] ye are justified, and by the **blood** [*of Christ—in other words, the Atonement*] ye are sanctified;

We will summarize what Adam was commanded to teach his children in verses 59–60:

1. The transgression of Adam and Eve brought the Fall (which was good—see 2 Nephi 2:22–25).

2. The Fall brought us the opportunity for mortal birth (and the experiences and trials of mortality)

and physical death (thus opening the door for resurrection).

3. The Fall also brought spiritual death (being cut off from the direct presence of God) and the need for spiritual rebirth, or being "born again" back into the presence of God.

4. By being baptized, we keep the commandment to be baptized (verse 60). But there is more to it than just being immersed in water by one holding proper authority.

5. After baptism, we are given the gift of the Holy Ghost. By following the teachings and promptings of the Holy Ghost, we are "justified"—in other words, lined up in harmony with God's laws and thus placed in a position to access the Atonement of Christ. The word "justified" as used here is similar to the word as used in computer language and word processing today. When we tell a computer to "justify" a margin, it lines things up in perfect harmony throughout the document. So it also is with the word "justified" here in verse 60. By our listening to and obeying the promptings of the Holy Ghost, we are gradually "lined up" in harmony with God, enabling the cleansing blood of Christ to cleanse us and "sanctify" us.

6. As we follow the guidance of the Holy Ghost, we access the cleansing blood of Christ in our lives and are made clean from sin and fit to be in the presence of God—in other words, we are "sanctified" (verse 60). Thus, we become worthy to dwell with God in celestial glory forever.

Next, in verse 61, we are taught the importance of having the Holy Ghost with us. We will point out several of the functions and attributes of the Holy Ghost with **bold**.

61 Therefore it [*the privilege of having the gift of the Holy Ghost*] is given to abide in you; **the record of heaven** [*the Holy Ghost, the source of our testimonies—see footnote 61a in your Pearl of Great Price*]; **the Comforter** [*the Holy Ghost*]; the **peaceable things of immortal glory**; the **truth of all things**; that which **quickeneth** [*gives life to*] **all things**, which **maketh alive all things**; that which **knoweth all things**, and **hath all power** according to **wisdom**, **mercy**, **truth**, **justice**, and **judgment**.

No wonder faithful Saints who have the gift of the Holy Ghost are said to have a special glow about them! They do!

Elder Parley P. Pratt taught about the functions of the Holy Ghost. He said:

"The gift of the Holy Spirit adapts itself to all these organs or attributes. It quickens all the intellectual faculties, increases, enlarges, expands and purifies all the natural passions and affections; and adapts them, by the gift of wisdom, to their lawful use. It inspires, develops, cultivates and matures all the fine-toned sympathies, joys, tastes, kindred feelings and affections of our nature. It inspires virtue, kindness, goodness, tenderness, gentleness and charity.

It develops beauty of person, form and features. It tends to health, vigor, animation and social feeling. It develops and invigorates all the faculties of the physical and intellectual man. It strengthens, invigorates, and gives tone to the nerves. In short, it is, as it were, marrow to the bone, joy to the heart, light to the eyes, music to the ears, and life to the whole being" (*Key to the Science of Theology/A Voice of Warning,* page 101).

Verse 62, next, clearly teaches that the Atonement of Jesus Christ is the central focus of the plan of salvation.

62 And now, behold, I say unto you: **This is the plan of salvation** unto all men, **through the blood of mine Only Begotten**, who shall come in the meridian of time.

Sometimes people wonder if we overdo it a bit on symbolism as we teach the gospel. Verse 63, next, indicates that there is probably far more symbolism of God's involvement in our lives than we realize. It is all around us and is constantly bearing witness to us that God exists, that we are His children, and that He has had this world created for us.

63 And behold, **all things have their likeness** [*symbolism*], and **all things are created and made to bear record of me**, both things which are **temporal** [*including physical creations*], and things which are **spiritual; things which are in the heavens above**, and things which are **on the earth**, and things which are **in the earth**, and things which are **under the earth**, both above and beneath: **all things bear record of me**.

As you can see, from the above verses, Adam and Eve were taught the gospel of Jesus Christ. They had a great knowledge of the plan of salvation, which they taught their children. Next, in verse 64, we see that Adam was baptized. Obviously, so was Eve.

(Remember, in context, that Enoch is teaching these things about Adam to the wicked people who are listening to him).

Adam Is Baptized

64 And it came to pass, **when the Lord had spoken with Adam**, our father [*ancestor; Enoch's great-great-great-great grandfather*], that **Adam** cried [*prayed*] unto the Lord, and he **was caught away by the Spirit of the Lord**, and was carried down into the water, and was **laid under the water**, and was **brought forth out of the water** [*in other words, Adam was baptized by immersion*].

65 And **thus he was baptized**, and the Spirit of God descended upon him, and thus he was born of the Spirit, and became quickened in the inner man.

Students sometimes ask who the "Spirit of the Lord" was in verse 64, above, and how a spirit could baptize a physical man. It is an interesting question, but we do not have the answer. It is one of the things for which we will have to wait. Perhaps we can ask Adam or Eve when we get to the other side. Or perhaps we will have to wait until the Savior reveals "all things" right after His Second Coming (Doctrine and Covenants 101:32–34).

Next, we are taught that Adam received the gift of the Holy Ghost.

Adam Receives the Gift of the Holy Ghost

66 And he heard a voice out of heaven, saying: Thou art **baptized with fire, and with the Holy Ghost**. This is the record [*the Holy Ghost is the one who testifies and bears witness*] of the Father, and the Son, from henceforth and forever;

Obviously, both Adam and Eve received the saving ordinances of the gospel. Elder McConkie taught (bold added for emphasis):

"Adam **and Eve**—our first parents, our common ancestors, the mother and father of all living—**had the fulness of the everlasting gospel**. They received the plan of salvation from God himself.... They saw God, knew his laws, entertained angels, received revelations, beheld visions, and were in tune with the Infinite. They exercised faith in the Lord Jesus Christ; repented of their sins; **were baptized** in similitude of the death, burial, and resurrection of the Promised Messiah; and **received the gift of the Holy Ghost**. They **were endowed** with power from on high, **were sealed** in the new and everlasting covenant of marriage, and **received the fulness of the ordinances of the**

house of the Lord" (*Mortal Messiah,* Vol. 1, pages 228–29).

Adam Is Given the Melchizedek Priesthood

67 And **thou art after the order of** [*you hold the same priesthood as*] **him** [*Jesus Christ*] **who was without beginning of days or end of years**, from all eternity to all eternity.

The "order," in verse 67, above, means high priest in the Melchizedek Priesthood. Wilford Woodruff taught that Adam held the keys of presidency in this priesthood. He quoted Joseph Smith, saying:

"The Prophet Joseph taught us that father Adam was the first man on the earth to whom God gave the keys of the everlasting priesthood. He held the keys of the presidency, and was the first man who did hold them" (*Discourses of Wilford Woodruff,* page 66).

Concerning the Melchizedek Priesthood and the keys of presidency given to Adam, the Doctrine and Covenants teaches:

Doctrine and Covenants 107:41

41 This order was instituted in the days of Adam.

Verse 68, next, summarizes the results of Adam's living the gospel, which was first preached on this earth to him and his wife, Eve. Through it, we can all be united again with God.

68 Behold, **thou art one in me**, a son of God; and thus [*through faith,*

repentance, baptism, and the gift of the Holy Ghost] may all become my sons [*becoming "sons and daughters unto God" (Doctrine and Covenants 76:24) is a scriptural phrase meaning to attain exaltation in the highest degree in the celestial kingdom*]. Amen.

As we begin Moses chapter 7, Enoch continues his speech to the people, begun in chapter 6 when they had a spokesman approach him and ask, "Tell us plainly who thou art, and from whence thou comest?" (Moses 6:40).

Having told them that he came from the righteous land of Cainan, a land of promise to which Enoch's great-great-grandfather Enos had led a group of righteous followers who were fleeing wickedness (Moses 6:17), Enoch then taught them that he was a prophet of God, and he told them about the gospel of Jesus Christ that had been preached to Adam and Eve. He taught them about the Fall and the Atonement and the necessity of faith, repentance, baptism, the gift of the Holy Ghost, and the Melchizedek Priesthood (Moses 6:44–68).

As we study chapter 7, we will learn much more about Enoch's mission as it continues. He will see a vision in which he will be shown "all things, even unto the end of the world" (verse 67). In studying this chapter, we will be given the advantage of seeing the big picture as it was shown to Enoch. It will strengthen our testimonies and give us the perspective of God on many issues. Among the many things we will learn about Enoch's mission are:

1. He will see the Savior and talk to Him face-to-face (verse 4).

2. He will see a vision in which the descendants of Cain destroy the people of Shum. He will see that Cain's descendants do not prosper (verses 5–8).

3. He will see many lands and peoples in vision and be told to go to them and preach the gospel (verses 9–11).

4. He will move mountains and change the course of rivers, in direct fulfillment of the Lord's promises to him in Moses 6:34 (verse 13).

5. He will be made a powerful preacher and teacher, in direct fulfillment of Moses 6:32 (verse 13).

6. Terrible wars and much bloodshed occurred during the time Enoch was preaching and gathering the righteous, but the faithful Saints who followed Enoch prospered and established a Zion people (verses 16–19).

7. He will see a vision in which he sees all of the inhabitants of the earth and the eventual taking of the City of Enoch up into heaven (verses 20–22).

8. As this vision continues, Enoch will see wickedness spread throughout the world before the Flood. He will see Satan and his angels laughing at the wickedness upon the earth and rejoicing in their evil success. He sees as the people of the world are warned of the destruction

that awaits them (the Flood) if they do not repent. He also sees many converted and caught up to join the righteous in the City of Enoch before the Flood cleanses the earth of wickedness (verses 23–27).

9. He will be perplexed when he sees God weeping because of the wickedness upon the earth, and we will listen carefully for the answer to Enoch's question, "How is it that thou canst weep?" (Verses 28–40).

10. We will be taught again about the relationship between knowledge and agency and be shown the reasons for the Flood (verses 32–34).

11. We will be told that our earth is the most wicked world (verse 36).

12. We will watch as Enoch, himself, weeps because of the wickedness he sees in the vision (verses 41–44).

13. Enoch will see the Savior's mortal ministry, including His crucifixion (verses 45–55).

14. Enoch will feel the pain of the earth because of the wickedness upon her, and we will feel to ask, with him, several times during the vision, "When shall the earth rest?" (verses 48–58). The answer will be given in verse 64. The earth will finally rest from wickedness during the Millennium.

15. Enoch will see the restoration of the gospel in the last days as it shines forth into the spiritual darkness and wickedness that beset the whole earth (verses 60–62).

16. Enoch will see the building of the New Jerusalem and will see his city, the City of Enoch, meet the Saints in the New Jerusalem as the Millennium begins (verses 62–65).

17. He will see some signs of the times in the last days, including natural disasters and the despair and gloom that is falling upon the wicked in our day (verse 66).

With the above outline of this chapter in mind, we will continue our verse-by-verse study. In verse 1, next, Enoch will continue his sermon, telling his listeners of the great blessings of being obedient to God's commandments and the awful consequences of ignoring the gospel message.

Moses 7:1–68

1 And it came to pass that **Enoch continued his speech**, saying: Behold, our father [*ancestor*] **Adam taught these things**, and **many have believed and become the sons of God** [*have become righteous followers of God, qualifying for salvation*], and **many have believed not, and have perished in their sins**, and are **looking forth with fear, in torment, for the fiery indignation of the wrath of God to be poured out upon them.**

As Enoch's mission continues, he is commanded to climb Mount Simeon. We do not know where that was.

As he obeys, the heavens open and he is transfigured (in order to withstand the presence of the Lord) and talks to the Savior face to face.

2 And from that time forth Enoch began to prophesy, saying unto the people, that: As I was journeying, and stood upon the place Mahujah, and cried [*prayed*] unto the Lord, there came a voice out of heaven, saying—**Turn ye, and get ye upon the mount Simeon**.

3 And it came to pass that I turned and went up on the mount; and as I stood upon the mount, **I beheld the heavens open**, and **I was clothed upon with glory** [*transfigured—see Moses 1:2, 11*];

4 And **I saw the Lord** [*Jesus Christ—see Moses 7:4, footnote a*]; and he stood before my face, and **he talked with me**, even as a man talketh one with another, **face to face; and he said unto me: Look, and I will show unto thee the world for the space of many generations**.

Next, in verses 5–8, Enoch sees in vision that the descendents of Cain destroy the people of Shum and take over their land. He sees also that the descendents of Cain do not prosper.

5 And it came to pass that **I beheld in the valley of Shum**, and lo, a great people which dwelt in tents, which were **the people of Shum**.

6 And again the Lord said unto me: Look; and **I looked towards the north, and I beheld the people of Canaan** [*Cain's descendents—see verses 8, 12, and 22; compare with Abraham 1:21, 24*], which dwelt in tents.

7 And the Lord said unto me: Prophesy; and **I prophesied, saying: Behold the people of Canaan, which are numerous, shall go forth in battle array against the people of Shum, and shall slay them that they shall utterly be destroyed**; and the people of Canaan shall divide themselves in the land, and **the land shall be barren and unfruitful**, and none other people shall dwell there but the people of Canaan;

8 For behold, **the Lord shall curse the land with much heat**, and the **barrenness** thereof shall go forth forever; and there was **a blackness** [*see also verse 22*] **came upon all the children of Canaan**, that they were despised among all people.

Next, Enoch sees many lands and peoples and is told to go to them and preach the gospel.

9 And it came to pass that **the Lord said unto me: Look; and I looked, and I beheld the land of Sharon**, and the land of **Enoch**, and the land of **Omner**, and the land of **Heni**, and the land of **Shem**, and the land of **Haner**, and the land of **Hanannihah**, and **all the inhabitants** thereof;

10 And the Lord said unto me: **Go to this people, and say unto them— Repent**, lest I come out and smite them with a curse, and they die.

In verse 11, next, Enoch is given wording that is reflected in the baptismal prayer we use today. We will quote it here before we continue to verse 11.

11 And he gave unto me a commandment that I should **baptize in the name of the Father**, and of the **Son**, which is full of grace and truth, and of the **Holy Ghost**, which beareth record of the Father and the Son.

Doctrine and Covenants 20:73

73 Having been commissioned of Jesus Christ, I baptize you **in the name of the Father**, and of the **Son**, and of the **Holy Ghost**. Amen.

At this point in the Lord's plan, the gospel was preached to all but the residents of the land of Canaan (verse 11, next). This may be a concern for some. It may be helpful to remember that during the Savior's mortal ministry, the gospel was to be taken only to the Israelites in the Holy Land. During the days of Moses and the children of Israel, the priesthood was held only by members of the tribe of Levi. The Lord has His reasons for what He does and we are wise to have complete faith in Him, knowing that the day will come when the righteous will have all of their questions answered.

We know that in the Lord's timetable, the gospel will be taught to all, whether on earth or in the spirit world mission field. Before the day of final judgment, everyone will be given the opportunity to hear and understand the pure gospel of Jesus Christ and then accept it or reject it according to their God-given agency. God is completely fair.

12 And it came to pass that **Enoch continued to call upon all the people, save it were** [*except*] **the people of Canaan, to repent**;

At the time of Enoch's call, he was promised by the Lord that he would be given power to move mountains and rivers (Moses 6:34). An example of this promise being fulfilled is recorded in verse 13, next. It will be fascinating to get more details someday. This advantage in battle must have been somewhat disturbing to the enemies of the people of God.

13 And so great was the faith of **Enoch** that he **led the people of God**, and **their enemies came to battle against them**; and **he spake** the word of the Lord, and **the earth trembled**, and **the mountains fled** [*moved*], **even according to his command**; and the **rivers of water were turned out of their course**; and the roar of the lions was heard out of the wilderness; and **all nations feared greatly, so powerful was the word of Enoch, and so great was the power of the language which God had given him** [*another fulfillment of the promise of the Lord—see Moses 6:32*].

We do not know anything about the land mentioned in verse 14, next, other than what is given here. It sounds, perhaps, as if their enemies were more afraid of Enoch and his Zion people than they were to venture out onto an unstable, new landmass in order to increase the distance between them.

14 **There also came up a land out of the depth of the sea, and so great was the fear of the enemies of the people of God, that they fled and stood afar off** and went upon the

land which came up out of the depth of the sea.

We presume that the "giants" mentioned in verse 15, next, were large men, perhaps like Goliath or even like many basketball players we see today. They would be formidable enemies in hand-to-hand combat. The Bible mentions giants, one of whom was King Og, of Bashan (spoken of in Deuteronomy), who was one of the last of a race of "giants." He used a bed that was thirteen and a half feet long by six feet wide (see Deuteronomy 3:11). The giants of Enoch's day were likewise afraid of Enoch and his people.

15 And **the giants of the land, also, stood afar off**; and there went forth a curse upon all people that fought against God;

Since we live in a day of "wars and rumors of wars" (Matthew 24:6), when the world is filled with wickedness and danger, verses 16–17, next, are especially helpful to us. They remind us that the thing that counts is having the Lord with us.

16 And from that time forth **there were wars and bloodshed among them**; but **the Lord came and dwelt with his people, and they dwelt in righteousness**.

17 The fear of the Lord was upon all nations, so great was the glory of the Lord, which was upon his people. And **the Lord blessed the land, and they were blessed upon the mountains, and upon the high places, and did flourish**.

You may wish to mark verse 18, next, in your own scriptures. It is one of the most-quoted definitions of a "Zion" people. It teaches us that we must be peacemakers, righteous, and generous if we desire to live in celestial glory.

18 And **the Lord called his people Zion**, because **they were of one heart and one mind**, and **dwelt in righteousness**; and there was **no poor among them**.

The only way to establish Zion among us is to live according to celestial law (Doctrine and Covenants 105:5). Such living requires that we become "pure in heart," as stated in Doctrine and Covenants 97:21.

Next, we are told that Enoch and his people built a city. It was called, among other names, the City of Enoch.

19 And Enoch continued his preaching in righteousness unto the people of God. And it came to pass in his days, that **he built a city that was called the City of Holiness, even Zion**.

President Spencer W. Kimball described the residents of this city. He said:

"Zion is a name given by the Lord to his covenant people, who are characterized by purity of heart and faithfulness in caring for the poor, the needy, and the distressed." (See Doctrine and Covenants 97:21.) ". . . This highest order of priesthood society is founded on the doctrines of love, service, work, self-reliance, and stewardship, all of which are circumscribed by the covenant of consecration" ("Welfare Services:

The Gospel in Action," *Ensign*, November 1977, page 78).

President Marion G. Romney, of the First Presidency, described a Zion society as follows:

"Always the aim has been unity, oneness, and equality among the members of the church of Christ. As an example, I call your attention to the record of Enoch, how he and his people reached a state of unity when the rest of the world was at war. [*Moses 7:15–17.*] 'And the Lord called his people Zion.' Why? 'Because they were of one heart and one mind, and dwelt in righteousness; and there was no poor among them'" ("Unity," *Ensign*, May 1983, page 17).

Next, in verses 20–21, we are given to understand that Enoch expected his City of Zion to remain permanently on the earth. The Lord explained to him that such would not be the case. Rather, because of increasing wickedness on earth, Enoch's city would eventually be translated and taken up into heaven (Moses 7:69). This translation took place 604 years before the Flood. In fact, Noah was born four years after Enoch and his city were taken up, and he was six hundred years old when he entered the ark (Genesis 7:6).

20 And it came to pass that **Enoch talked with the Lord; and he said unto the Lord: Surely Zion shall dwell in safety forever**. But the Lord said unto Enoch: Zion have I blessed, but **the residue** [*remainder*] **of the people have I cursed**.

If the word "cursed," as used at the end of verse 20, above, is misunderstood, it can make God look unfair and biased. Of course, He is not. When God "curses" people, it is generally another way of saying that He turns them over to the law of justice, which requires that they be punished for their sins and wickedness.

God operates according to the laws of mercy and justice. When people use their agency to obey the laws of the gospel, the law of mercy takes over in their behalf. They repent, are forgiven of their sins, reap the bountiful harvest of gospel living, and eventually return to live with the Father in celestial glory forever.

However, if they use their agency to choose evil and wickedness, they "curse" themselves in the sense that they subject themselves to the law of justice, which requires that those who do not access the Atonement of Christ become subject to the punishment of God.

Next, in verse 21, the Lord shows Enoch all the people on earth as well as the City of Enoch being translated and taken up to Heaven.

21 And it came to pass that the Lord showed unto Enoch all the inhabitants of the earth; and he beheld, and lo, **Zion** [*the City of Enoch*], **in process of time, was taken up into heaven**. And the Lord said unto Enoch: Behold mine abode forever.

Next, Enoch is shown that the posterity of Cain did not mix with the rest of the population during the time period depicted in this part of the vision.

22 And **Enoch also beheld** [*saw*] **the residue of** [*the rest of*] **the people** which were the sons [*descendants*] of Adam; and **they were a mixture of all the seed of Adam save** [*except*] **it was the seed of Cain,** for **the seed of Cain were black, and had not place among them**.

One of the great blessings of our day is that we live in the long-awaited time when the gospel is going forth into all the world. The priesthood is available to all worthy males. This is according to the revelation that President Spencer W. Kimball received in 1978 (see Official Declaration—2 at the end of your Doctrine and Covenants). Thus, the ordinances of exaltation are available to all Church members who choose to qualify for them. This is part of the fulfillment of the signs of the times—that the gospel will be preached to every nation, kindred, tongue, and people before the Second Coming (see Doctrine and Covenants 42:58).

Next, Enoch is shown what will take place on the earth between the time his city is taken up and the time of the Flood.

23 And after that Zion was taken up into heaven, **Enoch beheld, and lo, all the nations of the earth were before him** [*in the vision*];

24 And there came **generation upon generation**; and **Enoch was** high and lifted up, even **in the bosom of the Father, and of the Son of Man** [*Enoch was with the Father and the Son as he saw this part of the vision*]; and behold, **the power of Satan was upon all the face of the earth** [*which would lead to the cleansing of the earth by flood*].

25 And **he saw angels descending out of heaven**; and he heard a loud voice saying: **Wo, wo be unto the inhabitants of the earth** [*the inhabitants of the earth are being warned of the destruction that will come if they don't repent*].

26 And **he beheld Satan**; and he had **a great chain in his hand** [*symbolic of the captivity of sin and spiritual darkness*], and it veiled the whole face of the earth with [*spiritual*] darkness; and **he looked up and laughed, and his angels rejoiced**.

Verse 26, above, reminds us of the attitude of Satan and his angels as they laugh and rejoice at the destruction of the wicked in America at the time of the crucifixion of the Savior (3 Nephi 9:2).

Next, we see that the gospel was preached and there were many converts to the Church during this time, after the City of Enoch had been taken up and before the Flood. These righteous saints were translated and taken up to live in the City of Enoch.

27 And **Enoch beheld angels descending out of heaven, bearing testimony of the Father and Son**; and **the Holy Ghost fell on many** [*bringing true conversion and righteousness into their lives*], and **they were caught up** [*translated*] by the

powers of heaven **into Zion** [*the City of Enoch*].

Next in the vision, Enoch will be startled to see God and heaven weeping. He will ask some questions as a result.

28 And it came to pass that **the God of heaven** looked upon the residue of the people [*the wicked who remained on the earth*], and he **wept**; and Enoch bore record of it, saying: **How is it that the heavens weep, and shed forth their tears as the rain upon the mountains?**

29 And Enoch said unto the Lord: **How is it that thou canst weep, seeing thou art holy, and from all eternity to all eternity?**

As Enoch continues with his question, we are taught that there are countless earths that have already been created (compare with Moses 1:33, 35).

30 And were it possible that man could number the particles of the earth, yea, **millions of earths like this, it would not be a beginning to the number of thy creations**; and thy curtains are stretched out still [*God is still creating more earths*]; and yet thou art there, and thy bosom is there; and also thou art just; thou art merciful and kind forever;

31 And thou hast taken Zion to thine own bosom, from all thy creations, from all eternity to all eternity; and **naught** [*nothing*] **but peace, justice, and truth is the habitation of thy throne; and mercy shall go before thy face and have no end; how is it thou canst weep?**

Apparently, from what we see in the above verses, Enoch had thought that there was nothing but peace in being a god. He is surprised to see God weeping. There is an important insight for us in his response. It is that godhood is by far the happiest and most satisfying lifestyle in the universe (see last part of Doctrine and Covenants 132:16, 20), yet there is sadness and concern when children use their God-given agency to choose evil instead of good. Agency is a key principle and law in the universe. Knowledge and commandments enable people to use agency and be accountable for the outcome. This can bring happiness or sadness to parents. Gods are parents. The Lord will explain this to Enoch in verses 32–33, next.

32 **The Lord said unto Enoch: Behold** [*look at*] **these thy brethren** [*in other words, look at all these wicked people in the vision*]; **they are the workmanship of mine own hands** [*they are My children*], **and I gave unto them their knowledge**, in the day I created them; and in the Garden of Eden, gave I unto man his **agency**;

33 And **unto thy brethren have I said, and also given commandment, that they should love one another, and that they should choose me** [*be loyal to Me above all else*], **their Father; but behold** [*look*], **they are without affection, and they hate their own blood**;

Next, the Lord explains to Enoch that because of gross wickedness upon the earth, which he is being shown in the vision, He will flood the earth.

34 And **the fire of mine indignation** [*anger*] **is kindled against them**; and **in my hot displeasure will I send in the floods upon them**, for my fierce anger is kindled against them.

In verse 35, next, we are given several names for God. These name-titles reflect attributes of God.

35 Behold, I am God; **Man of Holiness** is my name; **Man of Counsel** is my name; and **Endless** and **Eternal** is my name, also.

Verse 36, next, is somewhat famous in the Church. It is the verse that tells us that we live on the most wicked earth God has created. We will do a bit more with the verse after reading it.

36 Wherefore, I can stretch forth mine hands and hold all the creations which I have made [*the Lord is fully aware of all His creations*]; and mine eye can pierce them [*see what is happening on them*] also, and **among all the workmanship of mine hands there has not been so great wickedness as among thy brethren**.

After reading verse 36, above, students often ask, "What did we do to deserve being sent to this earth?" They feel that they must have done something wrong in premortality to be sent here. I have responded that my feeling is that it is a great honor to be sent to this earth, the world to which the Savior was sent to gain His mortal body and serve His mortal mission, the earth upon which was performed the infinite Atonement of Jesus Christ, which blesses the inhabitants of all the Father's worlds—past, present, and future (Doctrine and Covenants 76:24). To me, they should be asking what they did right to deserve such an honor!

Next, in verse 37, the Lord summarizes the reason why the heavens weep over the wicked.

37 But behold, their sins shall be upon the heads of their fathers [*their wicked, rebellious ancestors*]; Satan shall be their father [*the author of their misery*], and **misery shall be their doom**; and the whole heavens shall weep over them, even all the workmanship of mine hands; wherefore **should not the heavens weep, seeing these shall suffer?**

38 But behold, **these which thine eyes are upon shall perish in the floods**; and behold, I will shut them up [*will lock them up*]; **a prison** [*the spirit prison—see 1 Peter 3:19–20*] **have I prepared for them**.

Note in verse 39, next, that two words are capitalized. They are "That" and "Chosen." Both refer to Jesus Christ. That is why they are capitalized.

Another thing, before we read verse 39. In this verse, Jesus is speaking directly for the Father in what is often referred to as "divine investiture" (see note following Moses 1:3). Perhaps you have noticed in the foregoing verses that He switches often between speaking for Himself and speaking as if He were the Father. This is common practice, and the context is the way we must determine whether it is Jesus speaking for Himself or quoting the Father. A helpful key is found in the writings of Joseph Fielding Smith. He said:

"All revelation since the fall has come through Jesus Christ, who is the Jehovah of the Old Testament. In all of the scriptures where God is mentioned and where he appeared, it was Jehovah who talked with Abraham, Noah, Enoch, Moses and all the prophets. He is the God of Israel, the Holy One of Israel; the one who led that nation out of Egyptian bondage, and who gave and fulfilled the law of Moses. The Father has never dealt with man directly and personally since the fall, and he has never appeared except to introduce and bear record of the Son. Thus the Inspired Version [*the Joseph Smith Translation of the Bible*] records that "no man hath seen God at any time, except he hath borne record of the Son."

"In giving revelations our Savior speaks at times for himself; at other times for the Father, and in the Father's name, as though he were the Father [*"divine investiture"*], and yet it is Jesus Christ, our Redeemer who gives the message. So, we see in Doctrine and Covenants 29:1 that he introduces himself as 'Jesus Christ, your Redeemer,' but in the closing part of the revelation [*example: verses 42 and 46*] he speaks for the Father, and in the Father's name as though he were the Father, and yet it is still Jesus who is speaking, for the Father has put his name on him for that purpose" (*Doctrines of Salvation,* Vol. 1, page 27).

As we read verse 39, now, we learn that there is hope for the spirits in prison, but these wicked will be in prison, tormented because of their wickedness, until Christ finishes His mortal mission. We know from Doctrine and Covenants 138 that He set up missionary work in the spirit prison between the time of His crucifixion and resurrection.

39 And **That** [*Jesus Christ*] **which I have chosen hath pled before my face** [*in other words, Jesus is our "advocate before the Father"— Doctrine and Covenants 45:3–5*]. Wherefore, **he suffereth for their sins** [*Christ atoned for the sins of all—see 2 Nephi 9:21*]; **inasmuch as** [*if*] **they will repent** in the day that my Chosen [*Jesus*] shall return unto me [*when the Savior has finished His mortal mission, and the preaching of the gospel is taken to the spirits in prison*], and **until that day** [*until they hear and accept the gospel in the spirit prison*] **they shall be in torment**;

40 Wherefore [*this is why*], **for this shall the heavens weep,** yea, and all the workmanship of mine hands.

Next, Enoch weeps also. He is growing much in understanding and perspective during the vision, and now he has the same feelings as the Lord has about wickedness among the people.

41 And it came to pass that the Lord spake unto Enoch, and told Enoch all the doings of the children

of men; wherefore **Enoch** knew, and looked upon their wickedness, and their misery, and **wept** and stretched forth his arms, and his heart swelled wide as eternity; and his bowels yearned [*every fiber of his being yearned for people to be righteous*]; and all eternity shook.

42 And **Enoch also saw Noah, and his family**; that the posterity of all the sons of Noah should be saved with a temporal [*physical*] salvation [*in other words, Enoch saw in the vision that Noah and his family would be saved from the flood, and would repopulate the earth*];

43 Wherefore **Enoch saw that Noah built an ark**; and that **the Lord smiled upon it, and held it in his own hand** [*protected it from the ravages of the Flood*]; **but upon the residue of the wicked** [*the rest of the people on earth, all of whom were wicked*] **the floods came and swallowed them up.**

At this point of the vision, we see Enoch discouraged and refusing to be comforted. Indeed, at this point, it can be depressing for all of us. But the Lord has a solution that will cause joy and happiness to enter our souls. He tells Enoch to cheer up at the end of verse 44, next. Watch for the reason in the next several verses.

44 And **as Enoch saw this, he had bitterness of soul, and wept over his brethren**, and said unto the heavens: **I will refuse to be comforted**; but the Lord said unto Enoch: **Lift up your heart, and be glad**; and **look.**

Elder Neal A. Maxwell spoke of Enoch's despair in verse 44, above. He said:

"If Enoch had not looked and been spiritually informed, he would have seen the human condition in isolation from the grand reality. If God were not there, Enoch's 'Why?' would have become an unanswered scream of despair!

"At first, Enoch refused 'to be comforted' (Moses 7:44). Finally, he saw God's plan, the later coming of the Messiah in the meridian of time, and the eventual triumph of God's purposes" (in Conference Report, October 1987, page 36; or "'Yet Thou Art There,'" *Ensign,* November 1987, pages 30–31).

Have you paid attention to the marvelous teaching techniques employed by the Master Teacher in this vision being given to Enoch? Have you felt the drama and tension building in the past few verses, preparing Enoch for the reason he can rejoice? When the mind is properly prepared, the lessons sink deep and become ingrained in the student. It is a privilege for us to also be taught by the Master as we study these "pearls of great price."

As Enoch "looks," the stage is set for the reason he can "lift up [*his*] heart, and be glad" (verse 44, above). He sees the future, from the time the Flood recedes and Noah and his family leave the ark. He sees God's plan unfold, with the Savior's mortal mission and Atonement as its center focus. This is the reason he can rejoice.

45 And it came to pass that **Enoch looked**; and **from Noah, he beheld all the families of the earth**; and he cried unto the Lord, saying: **When shall the day of the Lord come** [*when will the Savior come to earth*]? **When shall the blood of the Righteous** [*Christ*] **be shed** [*when will the Atonement be accomplished*], **that all they that mourn** [*for their sins; in other words, truly repent for their sins*] **may be sanctified** [*cleansed by the blood of Christ*] **and have eternal life** [*exaltation*]?

Next, the Lord answers Enoch's question as to when the Savior will come to earth for His mortal mission. It will be three thousand years in the future, from the time of Enoch.

46 And the Lord said: **It shall be in the meridian** [*the high point—see definition of "meridian" in various dictionaries*] **of time**, in the days of wickedness and vengeance [*when great wickedness is upon the earth*].

47 And behold, **Enoch saw the day of the coming of the Son of Man, even in the flesh** [*in a mortal body*]; **and his soul rejoiced** [*as the Lord said he could, at the end of verse 44, above*], saying: **The Righteous** [*Christ*] **is lifted up** [*crucified*], **and the Lamb** [*Christ*] **is slain** [*the Son of God will be sacrificed for the sins of the world*] **from the foundation of the world** [*planned and presented in the Father's plan for us, in the premortal councils*]; **and through faith** [*in Jesus Christ*] **I am in the bosom of the Father** [*I can return to live with the Father forever*], **and** behold, **Zion** [*Enoch's city and people*] **is with me**.

Next, in verses 48–49, Enoch hears the earth mourn because of the great wickedness upon her. He hears her ask when she will find relief and peace from the terrible wickedness on her. By the way, we know that the earth was baptized via the Flood and will be cleansed by fire at the Second Coming, symbolic of the Holy Ghost. It will then have a thousand years of peace during the Millennium, will die and be resurrected (Doctrine and Covenants 88:26), and will become the celestial kingdom (Doctrine and Covenants 130:9) for the righteous who have lived on it, including Christ.

48 And it came to pass that **Enoch looked upon the earth**; and he **heard a voice from the bowels thereof, saying: Wo, wo is me, the mother of men** [*the provider of nutrition, ecosystem, and so forth, which sustains mortal life*]; **I am pained**, I am **weary**, because of the wickedness of my children. **When shall I rest, and be cleansed from the filthiness** which is gone forth out of me? **When will my Creator sanctify me, that I may rest, and righteousness for a season abide upon my face?**

49 And **when Enoch heard the earth mourn, he wept**, and cried unto the Lord, saying: **O Lord, wilt thou not have compassion upon the earth?** Wilt thou not bless the children [*posterity*] of Noah?

Joseph Fielding Smith explained that the earth is a living thing. He said:

"The Lord here [*in Doctrine and Covenants 88*] informs us that the earth on which we dwell is a living thing, and that the time must come when it will be sanctified from all unrighteousness. In the Pearl of Great Price, when Enoch is conversing with the Lord, he hears the earth crying for deliverance from the iniquity upon her face. . . . It is not the fault of the earth that wickedness prevails upon her face, for she has been true to the law which she received and that law is the celestial law. Therefore the Lord says that the earth shall be sanctified from all unrighteousness" (*Church History and Modern Revelation,* Vol. 1, pages 366–67).

Next, Enoch pleads with the Lord to never flood the earth again. As you can feel, Enoch has become active in this vision. It is similar to the growth and increasing involvement of the servant in the allegory of the olive tree, given in Jacob 5, as the Master schools and teaches Enoch.

50 And it came to pass that **Enoch continued** his cry unto the Lord, **saying: I ask thee, O Lord, in the name of thine Only Begotten, even Jesus Christ, that thou wilt have mercy upon Noah and his seed** [*the descendants of Noah, which means all people after the Flood*]**, that the earth might never more be covered by the floods.**

51 And **the Lord** could not withhold [*hold back*]; and he **covenanted with Enoch**, and sware [*covenanted*] unto him with an oath [*the most solemn promise possible*], **that he would stay the floods** [*that there would not be another universal flood*]; **that he would call upon** [*preach the gospel to*] **the children** [*posterity*] **of Noah;**

52 And he sent forth an unalterable decree, that a remnant of his [*Noah's*] seed should always be found among all nations, while the earth should stand [*in other words, there would never be a complete destruction of the inhabitants of the earth*];

Next, in verse 53, Enoch is told that the Messiah will be a descendant of Noah. He is then given a brief summary of some of the name-titles of the Savior that describe His mission. Then he is taught that it takes work to access the blessings of the Atonement and that there is absolute security in building our lives on the "Rock" (Jesus Christ).

53 And the Lord said: Blessed is he [*Noah*] through whose seed Messiah shall come; for he saith—**I am Messiah** [*meaning "the anointed," "the King and Deliverer"—see Bible Dictionary, under "Messiah"*]**, the King of Zion** [*the King of the pure in heart—see Doctrine and Covenants 97:21*]**, the Rock of Heaven, which is broad as eternity** [*whose Atonement is infinite*]; **whoso** [*whoever*] **cometh in at the gate** [*repentance and baptism—see 2 Nephi 31:17–18*] **and climbeth up by me** [*continues to progress in the gospel of Jesus Christ*] **shall never fall**; wherefore, blessed are they of whom I have spoken, for **they shall come forth with songs of everlasting joy** [*they will receive exaltation*].

Enoch is still concerned about the earth and her feelings. In verse 54, next, he asks if the earth will obtain relief from wickedness when the Savior comes on earth to fulfill His mortal mission.

54 And it came to pass that Enoch cried unto the Lord, saying: **When the Son of Man cometh in the flesh, shall the earth rest?** I pray thee, show me these things.

In answer to Enoch's question, the Savior continues the vision, showing him that there will still be great wickedness upon the earth during His mission. In fact, He will be crucified. The earth will not yet be free of wickedness.

55 And **the Lord said unto Enoch: Look**, and **he looked and beheld the Son of Man lifted up on the cross** [*being crucified*], after the manner of men [*as was the common practice*];

56 And he heard a loud voice; and the heavens were veiled; and all the creations of God mourned; and **the earth groaned**; and the rocks were rent [*torn apart*]; and the saints arose [*were resurrected; this is the first part of the celestial resurrection, and it occurred at the time of Christ's resurrection*], and were crowned at the right hand of the Son of Man, with crowns of glory;

The Doctrine and Covenants tells us who the "saints" in verse 56, above, are. As you will see, they are all those, from Adam and Eve down to the Resurrection of Christ, who are worthy of celestial glory. This would include Enoch and the people in his city, as well as John the Baptist, who was beheaded by Herod near the end of the second year of the Savior's mortal mission (Matthew 14:10).

Doctrine and Covenants 133:54–55

54 Yea, and Enoch also, and they who were with him; the prophets who were before him [*including Adam*]; and Noah also, and they who were before him; and Moses also, and they who were before him;

55 And from Moses to Elijah, and from Elijah to John, who **were with Christ in his resurrection**, and the holy apostles, with Abraham, Isaac, and Jacob, shall be in the presence of the Lamb.

In verse 57, next, Enoch sees that many who die and enter spirit prison accept the gospel there and are saved (see Doctrine and Covenants 138:58–59). Those who don't accept it remain in spiritual darkness until the final judgment.

57 And as **many of the spirits** as were **in prison came forth, and stood on the right hand of God** [*symbolic of salvation; "right hand" symbolizes making and keeping covenants with God*]; and **the remainder were reserved in chains of darkness until the judgment of the great day** [*final Judgment Day*].

Enoch is still concerned about the earth's feelings, and he exercises the privilege of asking the Lord more questions.

58 And again **Enoch wept and cried unto the Lord, saying: When shall the earth rest?**

There seems to be a sense, in verse 59, next, that Enoch is a bit worried that he is asking too many questions. Thus, after seeing in vision the Savior's Ascension into heaven following His Resurrection, he explains to the Lord why he keeps asking questions.

59 And **Enoch beheld the Son of Man ascend up unto the Father**; and he called unto the Lord, saying: **Wilt thou not come again upon the earth?** Forasmuch as thou art God, and I know thee, and **thou hast sworn unto me** [*made covenants with me*], **and commanded me that I should ask** in the name of thine Only Begotten; thou hast made me, and given unto me a right to thy throne [*the Lord brought Enoch into His presence, where he could ask questions*], and not of myself, but through thine own grace; **wherefore** [*this is the reason*], **I ask thee if thou wilt not come again on the earth**.

The Savior answers Enoch's question, telling him that He will come again in the last days. He came to Joseph Smith in the First Vision and has come many times since. These "comings" of the Savior will culminate in the Second Coming.

60 And **the Lord said** unto Enoch: **As I live** [*the strongest type of promise or covenant in biblical culture*], **even so will I come in the last days** [*to restore the gospel, which will lead up to the Second Coming*], in the days of wickedness and vengeance [*when the earth is full of wickedness*], to fulfil the oath [*promise, covenant*] which I have made unto you concerning the children of Noah [*to preach the gospel to all the world—see end of verse 51, above*];

The Lord tells Enoch in verse 61, next, that the day will come when the earth will be freed from wickedness, but then He informs him of the final scenes before the Second Coming.

The earth's "rest" will begin with the thousand years of millennial peace. There will be a "little season" after the Millennium (Doctrine and Covenants 88:111–14) during which Satan will be let loose and wickedness will again rage on the earth. This final battle between good and evil will be called the Battle of Gog and Magog. After the devil and his evil followers are banished forever, the earth will be celestialized and finally "rest" as a celestial planet (see Doctrine and Covenants 130:9–11).

61 And **the day shall come that the earth shall rest** [*beginning with the Millennium*], **but before that day the heavens shall be darkened**, and **a veil of darkness** [*spiritual darkness*] **shall cover the earth**; and the heavens shall shake, and also the earth [*perhaps including natural disasters, earthquakes, and so forth*]; **and great tribulations shall be among the children of men**, but my people will I preserve [*a comforting promise for the Saints in the last days*];

Next, Enoch is told about the restoration of the gospel through Joseph Smith and the coming forth of the Book of Mormon.

62 And **righteousness will I send down out of heaven** [*the Restoration of the gospel through heavenly visions and manifestations*]; and **truth will I send forth out of the earth** [*the Book of Mormon*], **to bear testimony of mine Only Begotten** [*Jesus Christ*]; **his resurrection** from the dead; yea, and **also the resurrection of all men**; and **righteousness and truth will I cause to sweep the earth as with a flood** [*the gospel will be preached to every nation and people*], **to gather out mine elect** [*those who will accept the gospel and keep the commandments*] **from the four quarters of the earth** [*from the entire earth*], unto a place which I shall prepare, an Holy City [*the New Jerusalem*], that my people may gird up their loins [*prepare*], and be looking forth for the time of my coming; for there shall be my tabernacle [*Christ will visit the people in the New Jerusalem*], and it shall be called Zion, a New Jerusalem.

Next, Jesus tells Enoch that he and the people of his City of Enoch will meet the residents of the New Jerusalem (to be built in Independence, Jackson County, Missouri) and that it will be a joyous meeting.

63 And **the Lord said unto Enoch: Then shalt thou and all thy city** [*all the people in the City of Enoch*] **meet them** [*the inhabitants of the New Jerusalem*] there, and we will receive them into our bosom, and they shall see us; and we will fall upon their necks [*embrace, hug them*], and they shall fall upon our necks, and we will kiss each other;

Next, in verse 64, Enoch is finally told when the earth will rest.

64 And there shall be mine abode, and it shall be Zion, which shall come forth out of all the creations [*righteous, covenant-keeping converts from all nations will join Zion*] which I have made; **and for the space of a thousand years the earth shall rest** [*the earth will "rest" and have peace and freedom from wickedness during the Millennium*].

In verse 65, next, Enoch is shown in vision the Millennium. Then, in verse 66, he is shown the wickedness on earth before the Second Coming and that the sea will cause great devastations (compare with Doctrine and Covenants 88:90, which speaks of "the waves of the sea heaving themselves beyond their bounds.") He is also taught that there will be much despair and giving up hope, coupled with fear, in the last days.

65 And it came to pass that **Enoch saw the day of the coming of the Son of Man** [*the Second Coming*], in the last days, **to dwell on the earth in righteousness for the space of a thousand years**;

Joseph Fielding Smith explained who would remain on earth during the Millennium, after the destruction of the wicked at the Second Coming. He said:

"When the reign of Jesus Christ comes during the millennium, only those who have lived the telestial law will be removed. It is recorded in the Bible and other standard works of the Church that the earth will be cleansed of all its corruption and wickedness. Those who have lived virtuous lives, who have been honest in their dealings with their fellow man and have endeavored to do good to the best of their understanding, shall remain. . . .

"The gospel will be taught far more intensely and with greater power during the millennium until all the inhabitants of the earth shall embrace it. Satan shall be bound so that he cannot tempt any man. Should any man refuse to repent and accept the gospel under those conditions then he would be accursed [*Isaiah 65:20*]. Through the revelations given to the prophets we learn that during the reign of Jesus Christ for a thousand years, eventually all people will embrace the truth" (*Answers to Gospel Questions,* Vol. 1, page 108, 110–11).

66 But **before that day** he saw **great tribulations among the wicked**; and he also saw **the sea,** that it **was troubled,** and **men's hearts failing them** [*much discouragement, depression, gloom, and doom*], looking forth with fear for the judgments [*punishments*] of the Almighty God, which should come upon the wicked.

Next, Enoch, who has wept much during this vision, receives a "fulness of joy" as he sees the final results of the Atonement of Christ in the lives of the faithful.

67 And **the Lord showed Enoch all things, even unto the end of the world**; and **he** saw the day of the righteous [*the faithful Saints*], the hour of their redemption, and **received a fulness of joy**;

We now return to the Genesis account. You will see that the Moses account changes the order of some of the information. We will rearrange the Genesis verses to follow that order.

Genesis 5:23–32

23 And all the days of **Enoch** were three hundred sixty and five years [*actually, Enoch lived 430 years and was translated with the City of Enoch—see Moses 8:1*]:

Moses 7:68

68 And **all the days of Zion** [*the City of Enoch*], in the days of Enoch, **were three hundred and sixty-five years** [*the City of Enoch existed on earth for 365 years*].

We will repeat Genesis 5:21 here in order to help us return to the flow of the Genesis account and keep things straight regarding Enoch's son, Methuselah. We'll need this information in a bit.

21 And Enoch lived sixty and five years, and begat Methuselah:

22 And Enoch walked with God after he begat Methuselah three hundred years, and begat sons and daughters:

24 And Enoch walked with God: and he *was* not; for God took him [*he and*

his city were translated—see Moses 7:69, next; they were resurrected at the time of the Savior's resurrection—see Doctrine and Covenants 133:54–55, and will return to earth at the time of the Second Coming—see Moses 7:62–63].

Moses 7:69

69 And **Enoch and all his people walked with God, and he dwelt in the midst of Zion**; and it came to pass that Zion was not, for God received it up into his own bosom [*the City of Enoch was translated and taken up to heaven—see Doctrine and Covenants 107:49*]; and from thence [*from that time*] went forth the saying, Zion Is Fled.

President Brigham Young gave us a bit more information about the translation and taking up of Enoch and the City of Enoch. He taught that Enoch and his people were taken up "with the region they inhabited, their houses, gardens, fields, cattle and all their possessions" (*Discourses of Brigham Young,* page 105).

There are some verses from Moses, chapter 8, that fit here.

Moses 8:1–4

1 And all the days of Enoch were four hundred and thirty years [*and then he was translated*].

We learn from verse 2, next, that there were prophecies about Noah in the earliest times. In fact, God had covenanted with Enoch that Noah would be from his posterity. Therefore, Enoch's son Methuselah did not go up with his father in the City of Enoch when it was translated. Methuselah will be Noah's grandfather, and Enoch will be his great-grandfather.

2 And it came to pass that **Methuselah, the son of Enoch, was not taken** [*up with the City of Enoch*], that the covenants of **the Lord** might be fulfilled, which he made to Enoch; for he truly **covenanted with Enoch that Noah should be of the fruit of his loins** [*in other words, his descendant*].

It appears from the end of verse 3, next, that Methuselah became prideful about the fact that Noah was to be born through his posterity.

3 And it came to pass that **Methuselah** prophesied that from his loins should spring all the kingdoms of the earth (through Noah), and he **took glory unto himself**.

The information in verse 4, next, was also left out of the Bible.

4 And there came forth **a great famine** into the land, and **the Lord cursed the earth** with a sore [*severe*] curse, and **many** of the inhabitants thereof **died**.

25 And Methuselah lived an hundred eighty and seven years, and begat Lamech [*Noah's father*]:

26 And Methuselah lived after he begat Lamech seven hundred eighty and two years, and begat sons and daughters:

Moses 8:5–6

5 And it came to pass that Methuselah lived one hundred and eighty-seven years, and begat Lamech;

6 And Methuselah lived, after he begat Lamech, seven hundred and eighty-two years, and begat sons and daughters;

As you can see in verse 27, next, Methuselah lived 969 years, which is the longest of anyone on record. He died in the year that the Flood came.

27 And all the days of **Methuselah** were **nine hundred sixty and nine years**: and he died.

Moses 8:7

7 And **all the days of Methuselah were nine hundred and sixty-nine years**, and he died.

Next, Noah comes on the scene. He will preach the gospel for at least 120 years (Genesis 6:3), and his mission to preach the gospel to the wicked inhabitants of the earth, before the Flood, will be over when he enters the ark at age six hundred.

28 ¶ And Lamech lived an hundred eighty and two years, and begat a son:

29 And he called his name Noah, saying, This *same* shall comfort us concerning our work and toil of our hands, because of the ground which the Lord hath cursed.

30 And Lamech lived after he begat Noah five hundred ninety and five years, and begat sons and daughters:

31 And all the days of **Lamech** were **seven hundred seventy and seven years**: and he died.

Moses 8:8–11

8 And **Lamech lived one hundred and eighty-two years, and begat a son**,

9 And he called his name **Noah**, saying: This son shall comfort us concerning our work and toil of our hands, because of the ground which the Lord hath cursed [*probably a reference to the famine, mentioned in Moses 8:4*].

10 And Lamech lived, after he begat Noah, five hundred and ninety-five years, and begat sons and daughters;

11 And **all the days of Lamech were seven hundred and seventy-seven years**, and he died.

The three sons of Noah, mentioned in verse 32, next, were righteous (Moses 8:13, 27) and all held the Melchizedek Priesthood, according to the *Pearl of Great Price Student Manual,* used in our institutes of religion, which says:

"A list of the 'sons of God,' which began in Moses 5:8–25, continues in Moses 8 with the addition of Lamech (v. 5), Noah (v. 9), and Noah's three sons (v. 12). These brethren were all holders of the higher priesthood (see Doctrine and Covenants 107:40–52)" (Pearl of Great Price Student Manual, page 26).

32 And **Noah** was five hundred years old: and Noah begat Shem, Ham, and Japheth. [*Noah will live to be 950 years old—see Genesis 9:29.*]

Moses 8:12–13

12 And Noah was four hundred and fifty years old, and begat **Japheth**; and forty-two years afterward he begat **Shem** of her who was the mother of Japheth, and when he was five hundred years old he begat **Ham**.

13 And **Noah and his sons hearkened unto the Lord, and gave heed** [*and obeyed His commandments*]**, and they were called the sons of God** [*a term meaning that they were righteous followers of God*].

GENESIS 6

Chapters 6–9 deal with the Flood. Noah was called by the Lord to preach the gospel for 120 years before the Flood came. Thus, he began preaching when he was 480 years old and continued until he was 600, at which time he and his family entered the ark. He was Adam's great-great-great-great-great-great-great-great (eighth- great) grandson and was Enoch's great-grandson. He was born 126 years after Adam died (at age 930); thus, he was born 1056 years after the Fall and began preaching the gospel on this formal mission a little over 1500 years after the Fall of Adam and Eve. According to many Bible scholars, the Flood came between 2300 BC and 2400 BC.

We learn from the Prophet Joseph Smith that Noah was the angel Gabriel, who appeared to Mary and told her that she was to be the mother of the Son of God. He taught (**bold** added for emphasis):

"The Priesthood was first given to Adam; he obtained the First Presidency, and held the keys of it from generation to generation. He obtained it in the Creation, before the world was formed, as in Gen. 1:26, 27, 28. He had dominion given him over every living creature. He is Michael the Archangel, spoken of in the Scriptures. Then to **Noah, who is Gabriel**; he stands next in authority to Adam in the Priesthood; he was called of God to this office, and was the father of all living in his day, and to him was given the dominion. These men held keys first on earth, and then in heaven" (*History of the Church*, Vol. 3, page 386).

As stated earlier, Noah was called to preach the gospel for 120 years before the Flood finally came. Thus, the people had many years in which to repent and come unto Christ. But they refused (with the exception of those who were converted and caught up into the City of Enoch—see Moses 7:27). Thus, the wicked in the days of Noah had ample time to change their ways and be saved.

One of the important messages we learn from the account of Noah and the ark is the value of faith and obedience. For example, securing a year's supply of emergency food storage, as commanded by the Lord through our modern prophets, may be difficult during times of plenty because the need is not constantly pressed upon our minds by current circumstances. Therefore, it requires faith and obedience to gather food storage. Elder Spencer W. Kimball spoke of Noah and this principle. He taught:

"Paul, speaking to the Hebrews, said: 'By faith Noah being warned of God of things not seen as yet, moved with fear, prepared an ark to the saving of his house. . . .' (Hebrews 11:7).

"As yet there was no evidence of rain and flood. His people mocked and called him a fool. His preaching fell on deaf ears. His warnings were considered irrational. There was no precedent; never had it been known that a deluge could cover the earth. How foolish to build an ark on dry ground with the sun shining and life moving forward as usual! But time ran out. The ark was finished. The floods came. The disobedient and rebellious were drowned. The miracle of the ark followed the faith manifested in its building" (*Faith Precedes the Miracle*, 5).

Through the Flood, the earth itself was baptized. We will include two quotes that verify this doctrine:

ORSON PRATT

"The first ordinance instituted for the cleansing of the earth, was that of immersion in water; it was buried in the liquid element, and **all things sinful upon the face of the earth were washed away**. As it came forth from the ocean floor, like the new-born child, it was innocent; it rose to newness of life. It was its second birth from the womb of mighty waters—a new world issuing from the ruins of the old, clothed with all the innocence of this first creation" (Orson Pratt, in *Journal of Discourses*, Vol. 1, page 333).

BRIGHAM YOUNG

"The earth, in its present condition and situation, is not a fit habitation for the sanctified; but it abides the law of its creation, **has been baptized with water, will be baptized by fire** [*at the Second Coming*] and the Holy Ghost, and by-and-by will be prepared for the faithful to dwell upon [*it will be our celestial kingdom—see Doctrine and Covenants 130:9–11*]" (in *Journal of Discourses*, Vol. 8, page 83).

As we begin our study of chapter 6, we will briefly review the meanings of the phrases "sons of God," "sons of men," daughters of God," and "daughters of men." Basically, as used in this part of the Bible, "sons and daughters of God" means the righteous, and "sons and daughters of men" means the wicked.

Note that the Moses account replaces "sons of God" in verse 2 with "sons of men" (Moses 8:14), which completely changes the meaning. Additionally, "daughters of men" does not appear in the correct account. Rather, the Moses account shows that daughters of righteous men began to marry outside of the Church.

1 And it came to pass, when men began to multiply on the face of the earth, and daughters were born unto them,

2 That the sons of God saw the daughters of men that they were fair; and they took them wives of all which they chose.

Moses 8:14–15

14 And when these men [*the righteous sons of Noah—see Moses 8:13 above*] began to multiply on the face of the earth, and daughters were born unto them, the **sons of men** [*men who were not righteous, not loyal to God*] saw that those

daughters were fair, and they took them wives, even as they chose [*apparently these women were willing to marry outside the Church*].

15 And the Lord said unto Noah: **The daughters of thy sons have sold themselves** [*have intentionally distanced themselves from God*]; for behold mine anger is kindled against the **sons of men**, for they will not hearken to my voice.

Joseph Fielding Smith commented on the scriptural terminology mentioned above. He said:

"Because the daughters of Noah married the **sons of men** contrary to the teachings of the Lord, his anger was kindled, and this offense was one cause that brought to pass the universal flood. . . . The daughters who had been born, evidently under the covenant, and were the **daughters of the sons of God**, that is to say of those who held the priesthood, were transgressing the commandment of the Lord and were marrying out of the Church. Thus they were cutting themselves off from the blessings of the priesthood contrary to the teachings of Noah and the will of God. . . .

"Today there are foolish daughters of those who hold this same priesthood who are violating this commandment and marrying the sons of men; there are also some of the sons of those who hold the priesthood who are marrying the daughters of men. All of this is contrary to the will of God just as much as it was in the days of Noah"

(*Answers to Gospel Questions,* Vol. 1, pages 136–37).

The Moses account adds a verse here that is left out of the Bible. From it, we understand that Noah taught the gospel of Jesus Christ just as it was taught to Adam and Eve.

Moses 8:16

16 And it came to pass that **Noah prophesied, and taught the things of God, even as it was in the beginning**.

In Genesis 6:3, next, the Lord warns that these people have 120 years before He will send the Flood upon them.

We learn from verse 3 that there are limits as to how long the Spirit of the Lord will work with the wicked to get them to repent. After so long, the Spirit withdraws. While this is sad, it reminds us of the fact that agency is a supreme principle and that God will not violate it. We are indeed "free to choose liberty and eternal life, through the great Mediator of all men, or to choose captivity and death, according to the captivity and power of the devil" (2 Nephi 2:27).

Thus, this warning includes a 120-year grace period, with an invitation to repent, before the sending of the Flood.

3 And the Lord said, My spirit shall not always strive with man [*work with the rebellious and wicked*], for that he also *is* flesh: **yet his days shall be an hundred and twenty years**.

GENESIS 6

Moses 8:17

17 And the Lord said unto Noah: **My Spirit shall not always strive with man**, for he shall know that all flesh shall die; yet his days shall be an hundred and twenty years; **and if men do not repent, I will send in the floods upon them**.

4 There were giants in the earth in those days [*probably referring to extra tall and large families of people, perhaps similar to many basketball players today, or such as King Og of Bashan, spoken of in Deuteronomy 3:11*]; and also after that, when **the sons of God** came in unto the **daughters of men**, and they bare *children* to them, the same *became* mighty men which *were* of old, men of renown.

Moses 8:18

18 And in those days there were giants on the earth, and they sought Noah to take away his life; but the Lord was with Noah, and the power of the Lord was upon him.

Next, in the Moses account, we see that Noah was a high priest in the Melchizedek Priesthood. He was ordained to the priesthood at age ten by his grandfather, Methuselah, according to Doctrine and Covenants 107:52. Whether this was the ordination referred to in verse 19, next, or is a later ordination, we do not know. Whatever the case, Noah is now sent on his mission to preach the gospel.

Moses 8:19–21

19 And **the Lord** [*Jesus Christ*] **ordained Noah after his own order** [*gave him the same priesthood He holds; Christ is a high priest*], and **commanded him that he should go forth and declare his gospel unto the children of men**, even as it was given unto Enoch.

It must have been difficult for Noah to know and appreciate the gospel and its wonderful power to redeem and give sweet purpose and meaning to life and then see it rejected by the people (verses 20–21, next). Remember, though, that his mission was not without some success. Moses 7:27 informs us that many accepted the gospel and were taken up to join the City of Enoch.

20 And it came to pass that Noah called upon the **children of men** [*the wicked*] that they should repent; **but they hearkened not unto his words**;

21 And also, after that they had heard him, **they came up before him, saying**: Behold, **we are the sons of God** [*we are righteous*]; have we not taken unto ourselves the daughters of men? And **are we not eating and drinking, and marrying and giving in marriage?** And **our wives bear unto us children, and the same are mighty men**, which are like unto men of old, men of great renown. And **they hearkened not unto the words of Noah**.

As you saw in Moses, verses 20 and 21, above, not only did the people reject Noah's message, but they also taunted him, saying, in effect, that they were righteous and successful and didn't need the gospel he preached. This sounds very much like the arrogant statements of Nephi's brothers as they bore testimony to him that the wicked people of Jerusalem were righteous (1 Nephi 17:22).

The depth of depravity and degree of wickedness among the people in Noah's day are described in Genesis 6:5, next. They have become "ripe in iniquity," a phrase used often in the scriptures to describe individuals and societies that have become so wicked that they are like over-ripe fruit, gone rotten, and ready to fall and splatter upon the ground.

5 ¶ And God saw that the wickedness of man *was* great in the earth, and *that* **every imagination of the thoughts of his heart** *was* **only evil continually**.

Moses 8:22–24

22 And God saw that the wickedness of men had become great in the earth; and every man was lifted up in the imagination of the thoughts of his heart, being only evil continually.

23 And it came to pass that Noah continued his preaching unto the people, saying: Hearken, and give heed unto my words;

24 Believe and repent of your sins and be baptized in the name of Jesus Christ, the Son of God, even as our fathers, and ye shall receive the Holy Ghost, that ye may have all things made manifest; and if ye do not this, the floods will come in upon you; nevertheless they hearkened not.

Did you notice in verse 24, above, that Noah taught the same basic message that our missionaries teach today?

Verses 6–7, next, are places in which the Bible is not "translated correctly" (see the eighth article of faith). As they stand, they make it sound like God is repenting or changing His mind, having made a mistake by creating mankind. Such is not the case. Moses 8:25–26 will provide significant changes.

6 **And it repented the Lord that he had made man on the earth**, and it grieved him at his heart.

7 And the Lord said, I will destroy man whom I have created from the face of the earth; both man, and beast, and the creeping thing, and the fowls of the air; for **it repenteth me that I have made them**.

Moses 8:25–26

25 And it **repented Noah, and his heart was pained that the Lord had made man on the earth**, and it grieved him at the heart.

26 And the Lord said: I will destroy man whom I have created, from the face of the earth, both man and beast, and the creeping things, and the fowls of the air; for **it repenteth Noah that I have created them**, and that I have made them; and he hath called upon me; for they have sought his life.

As you can see, there is all the difference in the world between the incorrectly translated version in the Bible and the correct version.

8 But Noah found grace in the eyes of the Lord [*in other words, Noah was righteous and was found acceptable to the Lord*].

9 ¶ These *are* the generations of Noah [*this is Noah's family*]: **Noah was a just** [*righteous; lived the gospel with exactness*] **man** *and* perfect in his generations, *and* Noah walked with God.

10 And Noah begat three sons, Shem, Ham, and Japheth.

Moses 8:27

27 And thus Noah found grace in the eyes of the Lord; for Noah was a just man, and perfect in his generation; and he walked with God, as did also his three sons, Shem, Ham, and Japheth.

Since Jesus was the only perfect man to live on this earth, the phrase, "Noah was . . . perfect in his generations," in verse 9, above, needs a little explanation. Elder Mark E. Petersen, of the Quorum of the Twelve, explained that Noah was "near perfect." He said (**bold** added for emphasis):

"Noah, who built the ark, was one of God's greatest servants, chosen before he was born as were others of the prophets. He was no eccentric, as many have supposed. Neither was he a mythical figure created only in legend. Noah was real. . . .

"Let no one downgrade the life and mission of this great prophet. **Noah was so near perfect** in his day that he literally walked and talked with God. . . .

"Few men in any age were as great as Noah. In many respects he was like Adam, the first man. Both had served as ministering angels in the presence of God even after their mortal experience" (*Noah and the Flood* (Salt Lake City: Deseret Book, 1982), pages 1–2).

In verses 11–13, next, we see some of the problems that likewise afflict our world today. We will point them out with **bold**.

11 The earth also was **corrupt** before God, and the earth was **filled with violence**.

12 And God looked upon the earth, and, behold, it was **corrupt**; for all flesh had **corrupted** his way upon the earth.

13 And God said unto Noah, The end of all flesh is come before me; for **the earth is filled with violence** through them; and, behold, I will destroy them with the earth.

Moses 8:28–30

28 The earth was corrupt before God, and it was filled with violence.

29 And God looked upon the earth, and, behold, it was corrupt, for all flesh had corrupted its way upon the earth.

30 And God said unto Noah: The end of all flesh is come before me, for the earth is filled with violence, and behold I will destroy all flesh from off the earth.

Elder Parley P. Pratt taught that rampant sexual immorality was one of the chief reasons for the destruction of the wicked with the Flood. He said:

"The people before the flood, and also the Sodomites [*the residents of Sodom, who openly taught homosexuality*] and Canaanites [*after the flood*], had carried these corruptions and degeneracies so far that God, in mercy, destroyed them and thus put an end to the procreation of races so degenerate and abominable; while Noah, Abraham, Melchizedek, and others who were taught in the true laws of procreation [*the Lord's law, including the law of chastity*] 'were perfect in their generation,' and trained their children in the same laws" (Key to the Science of Theology, page 106).

Note

As mentioned earlier in this study guide, the book of Moses, in the Pearl of Great Price, covers up to Genesis 6:13. Therefore, from this point on in this study guide, we will use the JST (The Joseph Smith Translation of the Bible) as needed for additions and corrections to the Old Testament Bible text.

Next, Noah is instructed to build the ark. It is to be three stories high and about 450 feet long, 75 feet wide, and 45 feet tall. A "cubit" was about 18 inches long according to our English system of measurement.

14 ¶ Make thee an ark of gopher wood; rooms shalt thou make in the ark, and shalt pitch it within and without with pitch [*seal it inside and out*].

15 And this *is the fashion* which thou shalt make it *of:* The **length** of the ark *shall be* three hundred cubits [*about 450 feet*], the **breadth** of it fifty cubits [*about 75 feet*], and the **height** of it thirty cubits [*about 45 feet*].

16 A window [*JST: windows*] shalt thou make to the ark, and in a cubit shalt thou finish it above; and the door of the ark shalt thou set in the side thereof; **with lower, second, and third *stories*** shalt thou make it.

Next, the Lord tells Noah that He is going to destroy all flesh by sending the Flood.

17 And, behold, **I, even I, do bring a flood of waters upon the earth, to destroy all flesh**, wherein *is* the breath of life, from under heaven; *and* every thing that *is* in the earth shall die.

Some people wonder how a merciful and just God could send such a devastating flood upon "all flesh," including men, women, and children. The answer is that it was an act of love on the part of the Lord. It showed love toward the spirits who were waiting to be born on earth. If they were born to these wicked people, they would not stand a chance of being raised in righteousness. Also, it showed love to young children who were living at the time. Being swept off the earth by the Flood prevented their being corrupted by the wickedness in all facets of their society. Those under the age of accountability would be "saved in the celestial kingdom of heaven" (Doctrine and

Covenants 137:10), and others would have an opportunity to hear the gospel later, when the Savior organized its teaching in the spirit world (see Doctrine and Covenants 138:30), before they were completely corrupted.

John Taylor addressed this issue. He said:

"Now I will go back to show you how the Lord operates. He destroyed a whole world at one time save a few, whom he preserved for his own special purpose. And why? He had more than one reason for doing so. This antediluvian people [*the people who lived before the Flood*] were not only very wicked themselves, but having the power to propagate their species, they also transmitted their unrighteous natures and desires to their children, and brought them up to indulge in their own wicked practices. And the spirits that dwelt in the eternal worlds knew this, and they knew very well that to be born of such parentage would entail upon themselves an infinite amount of trouble, misery and sin. And supposing ourselves to be of the number of unborn spirits, would it not be fair to presume that we would appeal to the Lord, crying, 'Father, do not behold the condition of this people, how corrupt and wicked they are?' 'Yes.' 'Is it then just that we who are now pure should take of such bodies and thus subject ourselves to most bitter experiences before we can be redeemed, according to the plan of salvation?' 'No,' the Father would say, 'it is not in keeping with my justice.' 'Well, what will you do in the matter; man has his free agency and cannot be coerced, and while he lives he has the power of perpetuating his species?' 'I will first send them my word, offering them deliverance from sin, and warning them of my justice, which shall certainly overtake them if they reject it, and I will destroy them from off the face of the earth, thus preventing their increase, and I will raise up another seed.' Well, they did reject the preaching of Noah, the servant of God, who was sent to them, and consequently the Lord caused the rains of heaven to descend incessantly for forty days and nights, which flooded the land, and there being no means of escape, save for the eight souls who were obedient to the message, all the others were drowned. But, says the caviler [*one who quibbles or finds fault*], is it right that a just God should sweep off so many people? Is that in accordance with mercy? Yes, it was just to those spirits that had not received their bodies, and it was just and merciful too to those people guilty of the iniquity. Why? Because by taking away their earthly existence he prevented them from entailing their sins upon their posterity and degenerating them, and also prevented them from committing further acts of wickedness" (John Taylor, in *Journal of Discourses,* Vol. 19, pages 158–59).

Next, in verse 18, we see that Noah and his family would be the ones to reestablish the gospel of Jesus Christ with the covenants that go with it after the Flood. He is given some instruction about what he is to bring with him in the ark. More will be said in chapter 7.

18 But **with thee will I establish my covenant**; and thou shalt come into the ark, thou, and thy sons, and thy wife, and thy sons' wives with thee.

JST Genesis 8:23–24

23 But with thee will I establish my covenant, even as I have sworn unto thy father, Enoch, that of thy posterity shall come all nations.

24 And thou shalt come into the ark, thou and thy sons, and thy wife, and thy sons' wives with them.

19 And of every living thing of all flesh, **two of every sort** shalt thou bring into the ark, to keep *them* alive with thee; they shall **be male and female**.

20 Of fowls after their kind, and of cattle after their kind, of every creeping thing of the earth after his kind, two of every *sort* shall come unto thee, to keep *them* alive.

21 And take thou unto thee of all food that is eaten, and thou shalt gather *it* to thee; and it shall be for food for thee, and for them.

JST Genesis 8:27

27 And take thou unto thee of all food that is eaten, and thou shalt gather fruit of every kind unto thee in the ark, and it shall be for food for thee, and for them.

22 Thus did Noah; **according to all that God commanded him, so did he** [*he was completely obedient*].

GENESIS 7

In this chapter, Noah and his family, along with the animals and fowls, etc., enter the ark. There are a number of theories as to how long it kept raining and where all the water came from to completely flood the earth. We will mention one possibility as we go through this chapter. Also, there are many biblical scholars who do not believe that the waters of the Flood covered the earth completely. Rather, they speculate that it was a rather large-scale but local flood. We know from modern scripture and prophets that the Flood was universal. For example, the Book of Mormon speaks of the waters receding from "this land," meaning the land of the Book of Mormon. We read:

Ether 13:2

2 For behold, they rejected all the words of Ether; for he truly told them of all things, from the beginning of man; and that **after the waters** [*the Flood*] **had receded from off the face of this land** it became a choice land above all other lands, a chosen land of the Lord; wherefore the Lord would have that all men should serve him who dwell upon the face thereof;

President John Taylor, as the prophet and President of the Church, speaking of the Flood, said that the whole earth was covered with water. He taught:

President John Taylor

"The **earth was immersed**. It was **a period of baptism**" (John Taylor, in *Journal of Discourses,* Vol. 26, pages 74–75; quoted in the *Old Testament Student Manual: Genesis–2 Samuel,* page 55).

As we begin chapter 7, keep in mind that Noah has been preaching the gospel for 120 years now. No doubt, his righteous sons, Japheth, Shem, and Ham, have also done much preaching. They have been rejected and ridiculed. According to Moses 8:18, the "giants" mentioned in Genesis 6:4 tried to kill Noah. Imagine the mocking he and his family endured as they built the ark. It is likely that the wicked gathered around and mocked as Noah and his family, along with the animals, fowls, and "every creeping thing" (Genesis 6:20) entered it. With this picture in our minds, we will proceed.

1 And **the Lord said unto Noah, Come thou and all thy house** [*family*] **into the ark**; for thee have I seen righteous before me in this generation [*you are being saved from the Flood because of your righteousness*].

> Verse 2, next, mentions "clean" beasts and those that "are not clean." You can see a list of clean and unclean creatures in Leviticus 11.

> It would seem logical that the reason they take the clean "beasts" and "fowls" by sevens is that some of them will be used for food during the time spent on the ark. Also, some of the clean beasts and fowl will be used for sacrifices when Noah and his family leave the ark (Genesis 8:20). Obviously, they will preserve at least one male and one female of each species to repopulate the earth when they get off the ark.

> They only take two of the unclean beasts, one male and one female, because they are not allowed to eat the unclean. This law is later given to the children of Israel in considerable detail by Moses, for example (as previously mentioned), in Leviticus 11.

2 **Of every clean beast thou shalt take to thee by sevens**, the male and his female: and **of beasts that *are* not clean by two**, the male and his female.

3 Of **fowls** also of the air by sevens, the male and the female; **to keep seed alive** [*to propagate each species*] upon the face of all the earth.

> According to verse 4, next, the wicked have just seven days left in which to party and ridicule Noah and his family before the rain starts.

4 For **yet seven days, and I will cause it to rain upon the earth forty days and forty nights**; and **every living substance that I have made will I destroy from off the face of the earth**.

5 And Noah did according unto all that the Lord commanded him.

> Next, we learn that Noah was 600 years old when he entered the ark. As mentioned previously, he will be 950 years old when he dies (Genesis 9:29), having lived for about 349 more years after getting off the ark.

6 And **Noah *was* six hundred years old when the flood of waters was upon the earth**.

7 ¶ And **Noah went in, and his sons, and his wife, and his sons' wives with him, into the ark**, because of the waters of the flood.

8 Of clean beasts, and of beasts that *are* not clean, and of fowls, and of every thing that creepeth upon the earth,

> In verse 9, next, we get a clue that suggests that the animals came to Noah and entered the ark as commanded. This would have made it much easier for Noah.

9 **There went in two and two unto Noah** into the ark, the male and the female, as God had commanded Noah.

10 And it came to pass **after seven days**, that the waters of the flood were upon the earth.

> Verse 6 already told us and verse 11, next, affirms that Noah was six hundred years old when he and his family entered the ark. According to calculations made using this verse plus Genesis 8:13–18, especially verse 14, it appears that they spent between twelve and thirteen months on the ark.

11 ¶ In **the six hundredth year of Noah's life**, in the **second month, the seventeenth day of the month**, the same day were all the fountains of the great deep broken up, and the windows of heaven were opened.

> Verse 11, above, gives the impression that there was more than one source for the waters that caused the Flood. President John Taylor, as President of the Church, gave information on this. He said (**bold** added for emphasis).
>
> "I would like to know by what known law the immersion of the globe could be accomplished. It is explained here in a few words: '**The windows of heaven were opened**' that is, the waters that exist throughout the space surrounding the earth from whence come these clouds from which **the rain** descends. That was one cause. **Another cause was 'the fountains of the great deep were broken up'**—that is something beyond the oceans, something outside of the seas, **some reservoirs of which we have no knowledge**, were made to contribute to this event, and the waters were let loose by the hand and by the power of God; for God said He would bring a flood upon the earth and He brought it, but He had to let loose the fountains of the great deep, and pour out the waters from there, and when the flood commenced to subside, we are told 'that the fountains also of the deep and the windows of heaven were stopped, and the rain from heaven was restrained, and the waters returned from off the earth.' Where did they go to? From whence they came. Now, I will show you something else on the back of that. Some people talk very philosophically about tidal waves coming along. But the question is—How could you get a tidal wave out of the Pacific ocean, say, to cover the Sierra Nevadas? But the Bible does not tell us it was a tidal wave. It simply tells that '**all the high hills that were under the whole heaven were covered. Fifteen cubits upwards did the waters prevail; and the mountains were covered.**' That is, **the earth was immersed**. It was **a period of baptism**" (John Taylor, in *Journal of Discourses,* Vol. 26, pages 74–75; quoted in the *Old*

Testament Student Manual: Genesis–2 Samuel, page 55).

12 And **the rain was upon the earth forty days and forty nights**.

13 In the selfsame day [*probably referring to verses 7–10, above*] entered **Noah, and Shem, and Ham, and Japheth,** the sons of Noah, and **Noah's wife,** and the **three wives of his sons** with them, **into the ark;**

14 **They, and every beast** after his kind, and **all the cattle** after their kind, and **every creeping thing** that creepeth upon the earth after his kind, and **every fowl** after his kind, **every bird of every sort.**

15 And **they went in unto Noah into the ark,** two and two of all flesh, wherein *is* the breath of life [*that breathe air*].

16 And they that went in, went in male and female of all flesh, as God had commanded him: and the Lord shut him in [*shut the door*].

> It appears from verse 17, next, that it rained for forty days and the ark started floating.

17 And **the flood was forty days upon the earth; and the waters increased, and bare up the ark,** and it was lift up above the earth.

> It may be, based on verses 18–20, next, that the water continued to get deeper, after the initial 40 days of rain, until the depth was at least fifteen cubits (about 23 feet) above the highest hills.

18 And **the waters prevailed, and were increased greatly** upon the earth; and the ark went upon the face of the waters.

19 And **the waters prevailed exceedingly upon the earth; and all the high hills,** that *were* under the whole heaven, **were covered**.

20 **Fifteen cubits upward did the waters prevail; and the mountains were covered**.

> The JST adds the word, "and," to verse 20 here. This could be significant in that it could mean that the depth of the flood was well over fifteen cubits above the highest hills.
>
> **JST Genesis 8:41**
> 41 And the waters prevailed exceedingly upon the face of the earth, and all the high hills, under the whole heavens were covered. Fifteen cubits and upward did the waters prevail; and the mountains were covered.
>
> In verses 21–24, next, Moses emphasizes the complete destruction caused by the Flood, as prophesied by the Lord through his prophets.

21 And **all flesh died that moved upon the earth**, both of fowl, and of cattle, and of beast, and of every creeping thing that creepeth upon the earth, and every man [*in other words, all creatures, including man, who required air to breathe*]:

22 **All in whose nostrils** *was* **the breath of life, of all that** *was* **in the dry** *land***, died.**

23 And **every living substance** was destroyed which was **upon the face of the ground**, both **man**, and **cattle**, and the **creeping things**, and the **fowl** of the heaven; and they **were destroyed from** the earth: and **Noah only remained** *alive,* **and they that** *were* **with him in the ark**.

24 And the waters prevailed upon the earth an hundred and fifty days.

GENESIS 8

We mentioned in the note following chapter 7, verse 10, above, that Noah and his family were on the ark for a total of about twelve to thirteen months. We find out from verse 4, in this chapter, that it was about seven months from the time that the Flood began until the ark came to rest on the mountains of Ararat. At this point, the mountains were still under water, but the bottom of the ark apparently made contact with them.

Finally, about two and a half months later, they could see mountaintops (verse 5). Forty days later, Noah sent a raven out from the ark. Then he released a dove, which returned. Seven days later, he sent the dove out again. This time she returned with an olive leaf in her beak (verse 11). Seven days later, he released the dove again, and she did not return. After waiting several more weeks (verses 13–14), the ground was apparently sufficiently dry that they could leave the ark (verses 18–19).

We will use **bold** to outline the above information in verses 1–19. You may wish to underline or otherwise mark these **bolded** items in your scriptures.

This is one method of scripture marking used by some to, in effect, make brief sentences within the verses.

1 And **God remembered Noah, and every living thing**, and all the cattle that *was* with him **in the ark**: and God made a wind to pass over the earth, and the waters asswaged [*receded*];

2 The fountains also of the deep and the windows of heaven were stopped, and the rain from heaven was restrained;

3 And **the waters returned from off the earth continually**: and after the end of the hundred and fifty days the waters were abated [*decreased—see footnote 3c in your Bible*].

4 And **the ark rested in the seventh month**, on the **seventeenth day** of the month, **upon the mountains of Ararat**.

JST Genesis 8:47–49

47 And God remembered Noah, and all that were with him in the ark. And God made a wind to pass over the earth, and the waters assuaged.

48 The fountains also of the deep, and the windows of heaven were stopped, and the rain from heaven was restrained; and the waters returned from off the earth.

49 And after the end of the hundred and fifty days, the waters were abated. And the ark rested in the seventh month, on the seventeenth day of the month, upon the mountain of Ararat.

5 And **the waters decreased continually until the tenth month**: in the tenth *month,* on the first *day* of the month, were **the tops of the mountains seen**.

6 ¶ And it came to pass **at the end of forty days, that Noah opened the window** of the ark which he had made:

7 And **he sent forth a raven**, which went forth to and fro, until the waters were dried up from off the earth.

8 Also **he sent forth a dove** from him, to see if the waters were abated from off the face of the ground;

9 **But the dove found no rest** for the sole of her foot, and she **returned unto him** into the ark, for the waters *were* on the face of the whole earth: then he put forth his hand, and took her, and pulled her in unto him into the ark.

10 And he stayed **yet other seven days; and again he sent forth the dove** out of the ark;

11 And **the dove came in to him** in the evening; and, lo, **in her mouth** *was* **an olive leaf** pluckt off: so Noah knew that the waters were abated from off the earth.

12 And he stayed **yet other seven days**; and **sent forth the dove**; which **returned not** again unto him any more.

13 ¶ And it came to pass **in the six hundredth and first year**, in the first *month,* the first *day* of the month [*a little less than 11 months from the time they entered the ark—compare with Genesis 7:11*], the **waters were dried up** from off the earth: and **Noah removed the covering of the ark**, and looked, and, behold, the face of **the ground was dry**.

14 And in the **second month**, on the **seven and twentieth day of the month**, was the earth dried.

15 ¶ And **God spake unto Noah, saying**,

16 **Go forth of the ark** [*leave the ark*], thou, and thy wife, and thy sons, and thy sons' wives with thee.

17 **Bring forth with thee every living thing that** *is* **with thee**, of all flesh, *both* of fowl, and of cattle, and of every creeping thing that creepeth upon the earth; that they may breed abundantly in the earth, and be fruitful, and multiply upon the earth.

18 **And Noah went forth, and his sons, and his wife, and his sons' wives with him**:

19 **Every beast**, every **creeping thing**, and every **fowl**, *and* whatsoever creepeth upon the earth, after their kinds, **went forth out of the ark**.

Perhaps you have noticed that there is a lot of repetition in these verses. For example, in verse 13, it says "the waters were dried up from off the earth," and then near the end of the verse, it says "the face of the ground was dry." Verse 19 repeats some of verse 17. This is typical of writing styles in Old Testament times.

If you remember this fact, it will help you understand other Old Testament writings. It will be especially valuable when you study Isaiah. He uses much repetition in his teaching. Because of it, some people who are not familiar with this style decide that he can't be saying the same thing over and over that many times, therefore, he must be saying something else with each seeming repetition. Based upon this thinking, they try to find some other meaning to what he is saying and end up confused or drawing false conclusions. A brief example of this follows:

Isaiah 43:7

7 *Even* every one that is called by my name: for **I have created him** for my glory, **I have formed him**; yea, **I have made him**.

We will provide one more example from Isaiah's writings. It is a prophecy that the House of Israel (the faithful saints) will triumph over their enemies.

Isaiah 14:2

2 And the people shall take them, and bring them to their place: and **the house of Israel shall possess them** in the land of the Lord for servants and handmaids: and **they shall take them captives**, whose captives they were; and **they shall rule over their oppressors**.

We will now continue with the account of Noah as he and his family leave the ark. As a faithful servant of the Lord, one of the first things Noah does upon leaving the ark is build an altar and offer burnt offerings. Remember that he was commanded to bring seven pairs each of the "clean" animals and birds into the ark (Genesis 7:2–3). "Clean" meant those animals and birds that were approved by the Lord for eating and for use as sacrifices. A list of "clean" creatures was provided by Moses, and is found in Leviticus 11. Only "clean" animals and birds could be used for proper sacrifices. In Moses 5:6–7, Adam was taught that such sacrifices were symbolic of the sacrifice of the Son of God for our sins.

In verse 20, next, sacrifices are offered. We will read this verse as given here in Genesis and then read the equivalent verse in the JST, which gives additional information as to the purpose of these offerings.

20 ¶ And **Noah builded an altar unto the Lord**; and **took of every clean beast**, and of every **clean fowl**, and offered burnt offerings on the altar.

JST Genesis 9:4

4 And Noah builded an altar unto the Lord, and took of every clean beast, and of every clean fowl, and offered burnt offerings on the altar; and gave thanks unto the Lord, and rejoiced in his heart.

We will likewise read verses 21 and 22 as they stand in the Bible and then provide the Joseph Smith Translation of them so that you can appreciate the value of the Prophet Joseph Smith's inspired work on the Bible.

Among other things we learn in these verses is that there will never be another flood that covers the whole earth.

21 And the Lord smelled a sweet savour; and the Lord said in his heart, I will not again curse the ground any more for man's sake; for the imagination of man's heart *is* evil from his youth; neither will I again smite any more every thing living, as I have done.

22 While the earth remaineth, seedtime and harvest, and cold and heat, and summer and winter, and day and night shall not cease.

JST Genesis 9:5–7

5 And **the Lord spake unto Noah**, and he blessed him. And **Noah smelled a sweet savor, and he said in his heart**;

6 I **will call on the name of the Lord, that he will not again curse the ground** any more for man's sake, for the imagination of man's heart is evil from his youth; and he will not again smite any more every thing living, as he hath done [*by means of the Flood*], while the earth remaineth;

7 And, that seed-time and harvest, and cold and heat, and summer and winter, and day and night, may not cease with man.

GENESIS 9

Noah and his family are now the only people on earth. As commanded by the Lord in verse 1, next, it is their responsibility to begin the process of repopulating the earth.

1 And God blessed Noah and his sons, and said unto them, **Be fruitful, and multiply, and replenish the earth**.

In verses 2–3, next, the Lord says the same basic thing to Noah and his family that He said to Adam and Eve in Genesis 1:28–29, namely, that they are to have dominion over all the earth.

2 And the fear of you and the dread of you shall be upon every beast of the earth, and upon every fowl of the air, upon all that moveth *upon* the earth, and upon all the fishes of the sea; **into your hand are they delivered**.

3 Every moving thing that liveth shall be meat [*food*] for you; even as the green herb have I given you all things.

In verses 4–6, next, they are commanded not to eat blood and not to commit murder. We will read these verses first as they stand in the Bible, and will then quote the equivalent JST verses. Again, you will see the great value of the Joseph Smith Translation.

4 But flesh with the life thereof, *which is* the **blood** thereof, shall **ye not eat**.

5 And surely your blood of your lives will I require; at the hand of every beast will I require it, and at the hand of man; at the hand of every man's brother will I require the life of man.

6 **Whoso sheddeth man's blood, by man shall his blood be shed** [*capital punishment*]: for in the image of God made he man.

JST Genesis 9:10–13

10 **But, the blood** of all flesh which I have given you for meat, **shall be shed upon the ground** [*in other words, the animals are to be bled before being cooked and eaten*], which taketh life thereof, and **the blood ye shall not eat**.

11 And surely, blood shall not be shed, only [except] for meat [food], to save your lives [*to sustain your lives—compare to Doctrine and Covenants 49:18 and 59:18–20*]; and the blood of every beast will I require at your hands [*you are accountable for how you handle your "dominion" over the creatures of the earth*].

12 And **whoso sheddeth man's blood, by man shall his blood be shed** [*the law of capital punishment*]; for **man shall not shed the blood of man** [*in other words, "thou shalt not kill"—compare with Exodus 20:13*].

13 For a commandment I give, that **every man's brother shall preserve the life of man** [*we are to assist and protect each other*], for **in mine own image have I made man** [*man is in a different category than all of God's other creations; people are expected to exercise the virtues of God in their relationships with each other*].

We will now continue with Genesis. The instructions given in verse 1 of the Genesis account, above, are repeated in verse 7, next. We mentioned the practice of repeating things as a matter of culture and style in Old Testament writing (see note following Genesis 8:19 in this study guide). You will see the commandment to "have children" repeated four times within this next short verse. We will use **bold** to point them out.

7 And you, **be ye fruitful** [*have children*], and **multiply** [*have children*]; **bring forth abundantly** [*have children*] in the earth, and **multiply** [*have children*] therein.

Contrary to the cultures, laws, and philosophies of many people in our day, this commandment to have children is still in effect. As stated in *The Family: a Proclamation to the World,* given September 23, 1995, we read, "We declare that God's commandment for His children to multiply and replenish the earth remains in force."

As far as how many children to have and when to have them, one can go to "birth control" on the Church's web site, churchofjesuschrist.org, and find the current statement by the Church on this topic. At the time of this writing, the statement is, "Children are one of the greatest blessings in life, and their birth into loving and nurturing families is central to God's purposes for humanity. When husband and wife are physically able, they have the privilege and responsibility to bring children into the world and to nurture them. The decision of how many children to have and when to have them is a private matter for the husband and wife."

Next, in verses 8–17, we are taught about the covenant that the Lord made with Noah that He would not flood the earth again. As you will see, the rainbow is the "token" of this covenant. In other words, each time we see a rainbow, we can remember that there will never be another universal flood on this earth.

As we study the equivalent JST verses you will again see significant clarifications and additions made to these Bible verses by the Prophet Joseph Smith.

8 ¶ And God spake unto Noah, and to his sons with him, saying,

9 And I, behold, I establish my covenant with you, and with your seed after you;

JST Genesis 9:15

15 And God spake unto Noah, and to his sons with him, saying, And I, behold, **I will establish my covenant** with you, **which I made unto your father** [*ancestor; in this case, Noah's great-grandfather*] **Enoch**, concerning your seed [*posterity*] after you.

10 And with every living creature that *is* with you, of the fowl, of the cattle, and of every beast of the earth with you; from all that go out of the ark, to every beast of the earth.

The details of this covenant are spelled out in verse 11, next.

11 And I will establish my covenant with you; **neither shall all flesh be cut off any more by the waters of a flood**; neither shall there any more be a flood to destroy the earth.

JST Genesis 9:16–17

16 And it shall come to pass, that **every living creature** that is with you, of the fowl, and of the cattle, and of the beast of the earth that is with you, which shall go out of the ark, **shall not altogether perish**; neither shall all flesh be cut off any more **by the waters of a flood**; neither shall there any more be a flood to destroy the earth.

17 And **I will establish my covenant with you, which I made unto Enoch** [*as recorded in Moses 7:50–52*], concerning the remnants of your posterity.

Next, the Savior tells Noah that the rainbow will be the "token" or visible symbol of this covenant.

12 And God said, **This *is* the token of the covenant** [*the visual reminder of the covenant, namely, the rainbow—see verse 13, next*] **which I make between me and you and every living creature** that *is* with you, for perpetual generations:

13 **I do set my bow** [*the rainbow*] in the cloud, and **it shall be for a token of a covenant between me and the earth**.

14 And it shall come to pass, when I bring a cloud over the earth, that the bow shall be seen in the cloud:

15 And **I will remember** [*keep*] **my covenant, which** *is* **between me and you and every living creature** of all flesh; and **the waters shall no more become a flood to destroy all flesh**.

JST Genesis 9:18–20

18 And God made a covenant with Noah, and said, **This shall be the token of the covenant I make between me and you, and for every living creature with you**, and for perpetual generations;

19 I **will set my bow** [*rainbow*] **in the cloud; and it shall be for a token of a covenant between me and the earth**.

20 And it shall come to pass, when I bring a cloud over the earth, that the bow shall be seen in the cloud; and **I will remember** [*"remember" often means "keep" in such contexts in the scriptures*] **my covenant, which I have made between me and you**, for every living creature of all flesh. And **the waters shall no more become a flood to destroy all** flesh.

If we were not aware that the word "remember" usually means "keep" in such scriptural contexts as this, we could get into a bit of trouble because we might think, based on verse 16, next, that there is a possibility that God will forget His promises to us. Such is not the case (see Doctrine and Covenants 82:10, where the Lord says, "I, the Lord, am bound when ye do what I say").

16 And the bow shall be in the cloud; and I will look upon it, that I may remember the everlasting covenant between God and every living creature of all flesh that *is* upon the earth.

The words that we see in the last half of JST verse 21 through verse 24 are not found in Genesis. They are important additions provided by the Lord through the Prophet Joseph Smith.

JST Genesis 9:21–24

21 And the bow shall be in the cloud; and I will look upon it, that I may remember [*keep*] the everlasting covenant, which I made unto thy father Enoch; that, when men should keep all my commandments [*probably at about the time the Millennium begins*], Zion [*the City of Enoch—see end of this verse*] should again come on the earth [*as taught in Moses 7:62–63*], the city of Enoch which I have caught up unto myself [*which was taken up into heaven—see Moses 7:69*].

Next, in verses 22–23, we see more details of this covenant, made with Enoch and renewed with Noah. These details show us more about the City of Enoch, and its return to earth about the time of the beginning of the Millennium.

22 And this is mine everlasting covenant, that **when thy posterity shall embrace the truth**, and look upward, **then shall Zion** [*the City of Enoch*] **look downward** [*from heaven*], and all the heavens shall shake with gladness, and the earth shall tremble with joy;

23 And the general assembly of the church of the firstborn [*the righteous saints, living and dead, including those in the City of Enoch, who are worthy of exaltation—see Doctrine and Covenants 76:67–70*] **shall come down out of heaven**, and possess the earth, and shall have place until the end come. And **this is mine everlasting covenant, which I made with thy father Enoch**.

24 And **the bow** [*rainbow*] **shall be in the cloud**, and **I will establish my covenant unto thee**, which I have made between me and thee, **for every living creature of all flesh that shall be upon the earth**.

17 And God said unto Noah, **This** [*the rainbow*] **is the token** [*symbol*] **of the covenant**, which I have established between me and all flesh that *is* upon the earth.

JST Genesis 9:25

25 And God said unto Noah, **This** is **the token of the covenant** which I have established between me and thee; for all flesh that shall be upon the earth.

We will now continue with Genesis 9:18. By the way, the backwards "paragraph" mark at the beginning of verse 18, in your King James Version of the Bible, indicates that a new topic begins with this verse.

18 ¶ And the sons of Noah, that went forth of [*from*] the ark, were **Shem**, and **Ham**, and **Japheth**: and **Ham** *is* **the father of Canaan**.

19 These *are* the three sons of Noah: and of them [*through their posterity*] was the whole earth overspread [*populated*].

Next, we are told that grapes were among the crops that Noah planted.

20 And Noah began *to be* an husbandman [*a farmer, tiller of the soil*], and **he planted a vineyard** [*grape vines*]:

In verses 21–23, next, we see that Ham was disrespectful toward his father, Noah. From what little we have here, it appears that Ham, rather than covering Noah up to preserve his dignity, instead made light of the situation by calling Japheth and Shem to come look at their father in an embarrassing situation. Rather than joining Ham in showing disrespect, they politely cover Noah without looking at him.

21 And **he drank of the wine, and was drunken; and he was uncovered within his tent**.

JST Genesis 9:27

27 And Noah began to till the earth, and he was an husbandman; and he planted a vineyard, and he drank of the wine, and was drunken; and he was uncovered within his tent;

22 And **Ham**, the father of Canaan, **saw the nakedness of his father, and told his two brethren** without [*who were outside the tent*].

23 And **Shem and Japheth took a garment, and laid** *it* **upon both their shoulders, and went backward, and covered the nakedness of their father; and their faces** *were* **backward, and they saw not their father's nakedness**.

> There is a side issue that can be addressed because of the fact that Noah got drunk with wine (verse 21, above). In other words, the wine contained alcohol. Remember that the Word of Wisdom, which prohibits the drinking of alcoholic beverages (Doctrine and Covenants 89:7), was not given until 1833, in our day. Therefore, it was not against God's commandments for Noah to drink wine.
>
> Now, to another issue. Noah did not get drunk on fresh juice. Occasionally, well-meaning members of the Church teach that the "wine" mentioned in the Bible was all nonalcoholic. This is not the case. While they did have "new" wine—in other words, fresh juice—they also had fermented wine. Again, it was not "against the Word of Wisdom" because the Word of Wisdom had not yet been given.
>
> Next, we see more about Canaan, who was a descendant of Cain through his mother, Egyptus, who was Ham's wife—see Abraham 1:21–24.)

24 And **Noah** awoke from his wine, and knew what his younger son [*Ham*] had done unto him.

25 And he **said, Cursed** *be* **Canaan; a servant of servants shall he be** unto his brethren.

26 And he said, Blessed *be* the Lord God of Shem; and **Canaan shall be his servant**.

JST Genesis 9:30

30 And he said, Blessed be the Lord God of Shem; and Canaan shall be his servant, and a veil of darkness shall cover him, that he shall be known among all men.

27 God shall enlarge Japheth, and he shall dwell in the tents of Shem; and **Canaan shall be his servant**.

> Finally, we learn that Noah lived for 350 years after the Flood (actually closer to 349 years, since he was 600 years old when he entered the ark—see Genesis 7:6, and was on the ark for a little over a year—see Genesis 7:11 and 8:14). He died at age 950. As mentioned in the introductory notes to Genesis 6 in this study guide, he is the angel Gabriel, who told Mary she was to be the mother of Jesus. Truly, Noah is one of the greatest prophets who has ever lived.

28 ¶ And **Noah lived after the flood three hundred and fifty years**.

29 And **all the days of Noah were nine hundred and fifty years**: and he died.

GENESIS 10

This chapter provides a list of the descendants of Noah's three sons for several generations. Moses 8:12 tells us that Japheth was forty-two years older than Shem and that Shem was eight years older than Ham. Thus, in order of birth, Noah's three sons were Japheth, Shem, and Ham.

Using the information given in the heading to chapter 10 in your Bible, plus other sources in the scriptures, we understand that the descendants of Japheth were Gentiles, the descendants of Ham included the Canaanites, and the descendants of Shem will include Abraham, through whom the Lord will covenant to bless the whole earth with the gospel and its blessings, including the priesthood (see Genesis 12:2–3 and Abraham 2:9–11).

One of the interesting facts presented in this chapter is that in the days of Peleg, the earth was divided (verse 25). It is merely mentioned in passing, apparently because it was common knowledge in those days. We look forward to more information on this, but we understand from this brief mention that the landmass of the earth was divided into several continents and that the ocean became several oceans at this point.

We learn from the Doctrine and Covenants that the land and water on the earth will be moved back as they originally were before this division, in conjunction with the Second Coming of Christ. We read (**bold** added for emphasis):

Doctrine and Covenants 133:23–24

23 He shall command the great deep, and it shall be driven back into the north countries, and **the islands** [*continents*] **shall become one land**;

24 And the land of Jerusalem and the land of Zion shall be turned back into their own place, and **the earth shall be like as it was in the days before it was divided**.

We will now briefly study chapter 10. In verse 1 we see Noah's three sons listed as "Shem, Ham, and Japheth" even though Japheth is the oldest and Ham the youngest of the three (see note at the beginning of background, above). This same order is given elsewhere in scripture, including in Genesis 7:13 and Moses 8:27. It may be that the reason for listing Shem first is that he was the forefather of Abraham who is the grandfather of Jacob. Jacob, whose name was changed to "Israel" (Genesis 32:28), was the father of twelve sons. The descendants of these twelve sons became known as the "children of Israel" or "Israelites." The rest of the Bible, from Genesis 12 on, basically deals with Abraham and his descendants, specifically those known as Israelites. The two most prominent tribes in the scriptures, among the twelve tribes of Israel, are Judah (the Jews) and Joseph (Ephraim and Manasseh).

1 Now **these *are* the generations** [*descendants*] **of the sons of Noah, Shem, Ham, and Japheth**: and unto them were sons born **after the flood**.

The last phrase of verse 1, above, emphasizes that this chapter deals with children born to Shem, Ham, and Japheth, after the flood. Shem would have been about 108 years old when he and his wife entered the ark, Ham would have been about 100, and Japheth would have been about 150. It appears that these men may have had children born to them before the Flood, who joined the rest of the pre-Flood populace in wickedness. We will read a verse from the Pearl of Great Price that leads us to believe this.

Moses 8:15

15 And the Lord said unto Noah: **The daughters of thy sons have sold themselves** [*have joined in worldly wickedness*]; for behold mine anger is kindled against the sons of men, for they will not hearken to my voice.

The Bible continues with the descendants of these three sons of Noah, all three of whom were righteous (Moses 8:27).

2 **The sons of Japheth**; Gomer, and Magog, and Madai, and Javan, and Tubal, and Meshech, and Tiras.

3 And the sons of Gomer; Ashkenaz, and Riphath, and Togarmah.

4 And the sons of Javan; Elishah, and Tarshish, Kittim, and Dodanim.

5 By these were the isles of the Gentiles divided in their lands; every one after his tongue, after their families, in their nations.

6 ¶ And **the sons of Ham**; Cush, and Mizraim, and Phut, and Canaan.

7 And the sons of Cush; Seba, and Havilah, and Sabtah, and Raamah, and Sabtecha: and the sons of Raamah; Sheba, and Dedan.

8 And Cush begat **Nimrod**: he began to be a mighty one in the earth.

Once in a while you may have heard someone call someone else a "Nimrod." It is not a complementary term. Clarke's Bible Commentary indicates that Nimrod (verse 8, above) was a wicked man. We read:

"Though the words are not definite, it is very likely he was a very bad man. His name Nimrod comes from . . . marad, he rebelled; and the Targum [*ancient Jewish translations of the scriptures*], on 1 Chron. i. 10, says: Nimrod began to be a mighty man in sin, a murderer of innocent men, and a rebel before the Lord. The Jerusalem Targum says: 'He was mighty in hunting (or in prey) and in sin before God, for he was a hunter of the children of men in their languages; and he said unto them, Depart from the religion of Shem, and cleave to the institutes of Nimrod.' The Targum of Jonathan ben Uzziel says: 'From the foundation of the world none was ever found like Nimrod, powerful in hunting, and in rebellions against the Lord.' The Syriac calls him a warlike giant. The word . . . tsayid, which we render hunter, signifies prey; and is applied in the Scriptures to the hunting of men by persecution, oppression, and tyranny. Hence it is likely that Nimrod, having acquired power, used it in tyranny and oppression; and by rapine and violence founded that domination which was the first distinguished by the name of a kingdom on the face of the earth" (Vol. 1, page 86).

Verse 9, next, presents another example of where the Bible is not translated correctly. With the above quote from Clarke's Commentary in mind, let's read verse 9. Then we will look at the equivalent verse in the Joseph Smith Translation of the Bible—the JST).

9 **He was a mighty hunter before the Lord**: wherefore it is said, Even as Nimrod **the mighty hunter before the Lord**.

As you noticed, verse 9, above, says that Nimrod was "mighty . . . before the Lord." This wording implies that he was a righteous man. The JST changes this verse to read:

JST Genesis 10:5

5 And Cush begat Nimrod; he began to be a mighty one in the earth. **He was a mighty hunter in the land**. Wherefore, it is said; Even as Nimrod, **the mighty hunter in the land**.

Looking ahead to verse 10, we see that Nimrod founded what became the wicked kingdom of Babylon.

10 And **the beginning of his kingdom was Babel** [*which later became the wicked kingdom of Babylon—see Genesis 10:10, footnote a, in your Bible*], and Erech, and Accad, and Calneh, in the land of Shinar.

By the way, over time, "Babylon" became the generic term for gross wickedness and "Satan's kingdom" in the scriptures. See Isaiah 48:20, Revelation 14:8, Doctrine and Covenants 64:24; and 133:14.

11 Out of that land went forth Asshur, and builded **Nineveh** [*the wicked city that Jonah will visit as a missionary, in a little over 1200 years*], and the city Rehoboth, and Calah,

12 And Resen between Nineveh and Calah: the same *is* a great city.

13 And Mizraim begat Ludim, and Anamim, and Lehabim, and Naphtuhim,

14 And Pathrusim, and Casluhim, (out of whom came Philistim,) and Caphtorim.

15 ¶ And Canaan begat Sidon his firstborn, and Heth,

16 And the Jebusite, and the Amorite, and the Girgasite,

17 And the Hivite, and the Arkite, and the Sinite,

18 And the Arvadite, and the Zemarite, and the Hamathite: and afterward were the families of the Canaanites spread abroad.

19 And the border of the Canaanites was from Sidon, as thou comest to Gerar, unto Gaza; as thou goest, unto Sodom, and Gomorrah, and Admah, and Zeboim, even unto Lasha.

20 These *are* the sons of Ham, after their families, after their tongues, in their countries, *and* in their nations.

> Next, we see descendants of Shem. Note that special emphasis is given in verse 21 to Eber, even though he is a great grandson of Shem (see Genesis 11:10–14). Some Bible scholars believe that "Hebrew" is a form of the word "Eber." See Bible Dictionary, under "Hebrew." Whatever the case, Abraham is a direct descendant of Eber, and was the first man in the Bible to be referred to as a "Hebrew" (see Genesis 14:13).
>
> The Hebrews, well-known in the Bible, are direct descendants of Abraham. For example, the children of Israel are often referred to as "Hebrews" (see Genesis 41:12, where Joseph in Egypt is referred to as "an Hebrew." See also Exodus 1:15, where the midwives among the children of Israel are referred to as Hebrews).
>
> We will point out some of Abraham's genealogy with underlined bold (**bold**) in the next verses. This will take us down to Peleg, Abraham's great-great-great-grandfather. As mentioned in the background notes for this chapter in this study guide, Peleg is particularly significant because the earth was divided up into continents and oceans in his day.
>
> A complete genealogy from Abraham back to Shem will be given in Genesis 11.

21 ¶ Unto **Shem** also, **the father** [*ancestor*] **of all the children of Eber**, the brother of Japheth the elder [*Japheth was Shem's older brother—see Moses 8:12*], even to him were *children* born.

22 The children of Shem; Elam, and Asshur, and **Arphaxad**, and Lud, and Aram.

23 And the children of Aram; Uz, and Hul, and Gether, and Mash.

24 And Arphaxad begat **Salah**; and Salah begat **Eber**.

25 And unto Eber were born two sons: the name of one *was* **Peleg**; for **in his days was the earth divided**; and his brother's name *was* Joktan.

> Regarding the division of the earth, as mentioned in verse 25, above, perhaps you've noticed while looking at a world map that the eastern hemisphere and the western hemisphere look like they once fit together. Joseph Fielding Smith spoke of this. He said:
>
> "The dividing of the earth was not an act of division by the inhabitants of the earth by tribes and peoples, but a breaking asunder of the continents, thus dividing the land surface and creating the Eastern Hemisphere and Western Hemisphere. By looking at a wall map of the world, you will discover how the land surface along the northern and southern coast of the American Hemisphere and Europe and Africa has the appearance of having been together at one time. Of course, there have been many changes on the earth's surface since the beginning. We are informed by revelation that the time will come when this condition will be changed and that the land surface of the earth will come back again as

26 And Joktan begat Almodad, and Sheleph, and Hazarmaveth, and Jerah,

27 And Hadoram, and Uzal, and Diklah,

28 And Obal, and Abimael, and Sheba,

29 And Ophir, and Havilah, and Jobab: all these *were* the sons of Joktan.

> Remember that Moses is the author of Genesis. An indicator that someone is writing to us is evident in the phrase "as thou goest unto Sephar" in verse 30, next. Additional examples of this type of descriptive phrase are found in verse 19, above.

30 And their dwelling was from Mesha, **as thou goest unto Sephar** a mount of the east.

31 These *are* the sons of Shem, after their families, after their tongues, in their lands, after their nations.

32 **These** *are* **the families of the sons of Noah**, after their generations, in their nations: and by these were the nations divided in the earth **after the flood**.

GENESIS 11

Verses 1–9 give an account of the Tower of Babel. Up until this time, all people spoke the same language (see verse 1). As wickedness spread again after the Flood, the wicked undertook to build a tower that would reach to heaven (verse 4). In effect, these people were saying that they could bypass God and His rules for attaining heaven and get to heaven another way. Of course, the problem with this kind of thinking is that there is only one way to get to heaven, namely, through the gospel of Jesus Christ and His Atonement. This requires humility and personal righteousness along with compliance with God's commandments and the ordinances of the gospel. Thus, these wicked people were defying God.

Josephus mentions another likely problem with the building of the Tower of Babel. The writings of this Jewish historian are not in the same category as scripture, but he has proven to be quite accurate in many respects with regard to the Bible. He lived at the time of Christ and kept a meticulous history of the Jews and their ancestors, back to the beginning of the Bible. Josephus recounts that God had made a covenant with Noah that He would never again flood the earth (Genesis 9:8–11). Yet, according to his account, those working on the Tower of Babel defied God and, in effect, said that He was not trustworthy. They arrogantly claimed that they would build a tower high enough to be safe from another flood if God were to break His word and send one. We will include a quote here from the works of Flavius Josephus. He said:

Antiquities of the Jews, Book 1, chapter 4, verses 1–3

1 Now the sons of Noah were three,—Shem, Japhet, and Ham, born one hundred years before the

---

it was in the beginning and all be in one place. This is definitely stated in the Doctrine and Covenants. [Doctrine and Covenants 133:18–20 is then cited]" (*Answers to Gospel Questions*, Vol. 5, pages 73–74).

Deluge [*the Flood*]. These first of all [*immediately following the Flood*] descended from the mountains [*where the ark landed*] into the plains, and fixed their habitation there; and persuaded others who were greatly afraid of the lower grounds on account of the flood, and so were very loath to come down from the higher places, to venture to follow their examples. Now the plain in which they first dwelt was called Shinar. God also commanded them to send colonies abroad, for the thorough peopling of the earth, that they might not raise seditions among themselves, but might cultivate a great part of the earth, and enjoy its fruits after a plentiful manner. But they were so ill instructed that they did not obey God; for which reason they fell into calamities, and were made sensible, by experience, of what sin they had been guilty: for when they flourished with a numerous youth, God admonished them again to send out colonies; but they, imagining the prosperity they enjoyed was not derived from the favor of God, but supposing that their own power was the proper cause of the plentiful condition they were in, did not obey him. Nay, they added to this their disobedience to the Divine will, the suspicion that they were therefore ordered to send out separate colonies, that, being divided asunder, they might the more easily be Oppressed.

2 Now it was Nimrod who excited them to such an affront and contempt of God. He was the grandson of Ham, the son of Noah, a bold man, and of great strength of hand. He persuaded them not to ascribe it to God, as if it was through his means they were happy, but to believe that it was their own courage which procured that happiness. He also gradually changed the government into tyranny, seeing no other way of turning men from the fear of God, but to bring them into a constant dependence on his power. **He also said he would be revenged on God, if he should have a mind to drown the world again; for that he would build a tower too high for the waters to be able to reach!** and that he would avenge himself on God for destroying their forefathers!

3 Now the multitude were very ready to follow the determination of Nimrod, and to esteem it a piece of cowardice to submit to God; and they built a tower, neither sparing any pains, nor being in any degree negligent about the work: and, by reason of the multitude of hands employed in it, it grew very high, sooner than any one could expect; but the thickness of it was so great, and it was so strongly built, that thereby its great height seemed, upon the view, to be less than it really was. It was built of burnt brick, cemented together with mortar, made of bitumen, that it might not be liable to admit water. When God saw that they acted so madly, he did not resolve to destroy them utterly, since they were not grown wiser by the destruction of the former sinners; but he caused a tumult among them, by producing in them divers [*different, various*] languages, and causing that, through the multitude of those languages, they should not be able to understand one another. The place wherein they built

the tower is now called *Babylon* because of the confusion of that language which they readily understood before; for the Hebrews mean by the word *Babel,* confusion. The Sibyl also makes mention of this tower, and of the confusion of the language, when she says thus: **"When all men were of one language, some of them built a high tower, as if they would thereby ascend up to heaven**, but the gods sent storms of wind and overthrew the tower, and gave every one his peculiar language; and for this reason it was that the city was called *Babylon"* (Josephus, Flavius, *Antiquities of the Jews*, Book 1, chapter 4, verses 1–3).

As Latter-day Saints, we are acquainted with a specific group of people who lived in the region where the Tower of Babel was built. They became known as the Jaredites. Their history is found in the Book of Ether in the Book of Mormon and begins with the Tower of Babel, approximately 2243 BC (see "Gospel Dispensations" chart near the beginning of the Old Testament Student Manual).

Jared and his people must have been very concerned about the wickedness of the inhabitants of the area as they attempted to build a tower that would reach to heaven, in direct defiance of the Lord and His commandments. Ether 1 implies that this confusion of languages was prophesied. Thus, Jared and his brother, Mahonri Moriancumer, and their families were made aware that the Lord was going to confound the language (cause people to speak different languages so they could not communicate with each other in promoting their wicked goals).

Among other things, this confounding of languages would be an effective way to stop work on the Tower of Babel.

By the way, the name of Jared's brother, as mentioned above, is not specifically given in the Book of Mormon. We learned it from the Prophet Joseph Smith. George Reynolds told how the name was revealed to the Prophet. He said, "While residing in Kirtland, Elder Reynolds Cahoon had a son born to him. One day when President Joseph Smith was passing his door he called the Prophet in and asked him to bless and name the baby. Joseph did so and gave the boy the name of Mahonri Moriancumer. When he had finished the blessing he laid the child on the bed, and turning to Elder Cahoon he said, the name I have given your son is the name of the brother of Jared; the Lord has just shown it to me. Elder William F. Cahoon, who was standing near, heard the Prophet make this statement to his father; and this was the first time the name of the brother of Jared was known in the Church in this dispensation" ("The Jaredites," *Juvenile Instructor,* 1 May 1892, page 282).

The brother of Jared prayed to the Lord that He would not confound the language for him, his family, and their close friends (see Ether 1:33–37). The Lord promised that He would allow these righteous people to continue speaking a language that they would all understand and commanded them to depart for a land that was "choice above all the lands of the earth" (Ether 1:42). Thus, the Jaredites left at the time of the Tower of Babel and came to the Americas.

Also, since Noah lived another 349 years after he and his family departed from the ark, we understand that he was still alive at the time construction on the Tower of Babel was going on. No doubt he was concerned about it.

We will now read Genesis, chapter 11. Verses 1–9 give a brief account of the Tower of Babel. Verses 10–26 give a genealogy leading up to the birth of Abram (Abraham), and verses 27–32 give a brief introduction to Abram, his wife Sarai (Sarah), and their extended family. When we get to chapter 17, we will see that Abram's name changed to Abraham and Sarai's name changed to Sarah. We will say more about this at that time.

First, the Tower of Babel. In verse 1, next, we see that everyone was still speaking the same language at this time in the history of the world.

1 And **the whole earth was of one language, and of one speech**.

2 And it came to pass, **as they journeyed from the** *east* [*from the general region where the ark had landed*], that they found a plain in the land of Shinar; and they dwelt there.

JST Genesis 11:1

1 And the whole earth was of the same language, and of the same speech. And it came to pass, that many journeyed from the east, and as they journeyed from the east, they found a plain in the land of Shinar, and dwelt there in the plain of Shinar.

Above, we see a clue that many people gradually migrated westward after the ark landed and the earth began to be repopulated. (We understand from Genesis 8:4 that the ark landed on Mount Ararat, which is on the eastern border of modern Turkey.)

3 And they said one to another, Go to, let us make brick, and burn them thoroughly [*fire them in a brick kiln*]. And they had brick for stone, and slime had they for morter.

4 And they said, Go to, **let us build us a city and a tower, whose top** *may reach* **unto heaven**; and let us make us a name, lest we be scattered abroad upon the face of the whole earth.

Verse 4, above, presents another indicator of evil associated with the building of the Tower of Babel. The people had obviously been overcome by pride such that one of their objectives was to become well-known for building a tower so massive that they could reach heaven on their own, without God's help. Another apparent problem was that they defied the Lord's command to Noah and his sons to spread out and repopulate the earth. Rather than spreading out, these wicked people intentionally concentrated their population in one huge city.

In verse 5, next, we once again see the phrase, "the children of men." As used in the Bible, this phrase means "the wicked." The righteous in scripture are often referred to as "the children of God," the "sons of God," the "daughters of God," etc., and the wicked are often called the "sons of men," "daughters of men," etc. Examples are found, among other places, in Genesis 6:2 and Moses 8:14–15.

5 And the Lord came down to see the city and the tower, which the **children of men** builded.

6 And the Lord said, Behold, the people *is* one [*they are united, working together*], and they have all one language; and this [*the building of the Tower of Babel*] they begin to do: and now nothing will be restrained from them, which they have imagined to do [*there is no holding them back in carrying out the wicked desires of their hearts*].

7 Go to, **let us go down, and there confound** [*mix up, confuse*] **their language, that they may not understand one another's speech.**

8 So the Lord scattered them abroad from thence upon the face of all the earth: and they left off to build the city [*they stopped building the city and the Tower of Babel*].

JST Genesis 11:4–5

4 And the Lord came down, beholding the city and the tower which the children of men were building;

5 And the Lord said, Behold, the people are the same, and they all have the same language; and this tower they begin to build, and now, nothing will be restrained from them, which they have imagined, except I, the Lord, confound their language, that they may not understand one another's speech. So I, the Lord, will scatter them abroad from thence, upon all the face of the land, and unto every quarter of the earth.

As Moses tells us above (remember, Moses is the one who wrote Genesis and the JST reveals his writings that were left out of Genesis in the Bible), God caused the people to suddenly begin speaking different languages so that they could not understand each other. As you can well imagine, this would bring the work on the Tower to an immediate halt.

As we look at verse 9, next, we see that another aspect of the word "Babel" is associated with not being able to understand someone else's speech. It is interesting to note that we sometimes use the term "babbling" today in referring to someone whose speech we can't understand.

9 Therefore is [*this is the reason that*] **the name of it called Babel; because the Lord did there confound the language of all the earth:** and from thence did the Lord scatter them abroad upon the face of all the earth.

JST Genesis 11:6

6 And they were confounded, and left off to build the city, and they hearkened not unto the Lord, therefore, is the name of it called Babel, because the Lord was displeased with their works, and did there confound the language of all the earth; and from thence did the Lord scatter them abroad upon the face thereof.

Beginning with verse 10, next, we are given the genealogy of Abraham, who comes through Shem, Noah's middle son (see Moses 8:12). Moses, the writer of Genesis, is now narrowing the focus of his account of things after the Flood and pointing our minds toward Abraham, the great ancestor of covenant Israel. The covenants that God renewed with Abraham, when kept, lead one to exaltation, the highest degree of glory in the celestial kingdom.

We will note Abraham's direct ancestors through the use of underlined bold (**bold**). Notice that each of them had "sons and daughters" (likely a great many) who would also grow up, marry and have children. Thus, the population would increase very rapidly after the Flood.

10 ¶ These *are* the generations [*these are the descendants*] of **Shem**: Shem [*Noah's son*] *was* an hundred years old, and begat **Arphaxad** two years after the flood:

11 And Shem lived after he begat Arphaxad five hundred years, and begat sons and daughters.

12 And Arphaxad lived five and thirty years, and begat **Salah**:

13 And Arphaxad lived after he begat Salah four hundred and three years, and begat sons and daughters.

14 And Salah lived thirty years, and begat **Eber**:

15 And Salah lived after he begat Eber four hundred and three years, and begat sons and daughters.

16 And Eber lived four and thirty years, and begat **Peleg**:

17 And Eber lived after he begat Peleg four hundred and thirty years, and begat sons and daughters.

18 And Peleg lived thirty years, and begat **Reu**:

19 And Peleg lived after he begat Reu two hundred and nine years, and begat sons and daughters.

20 And Reu lived two and thirty years, and begat **Serug**:

21 And Reu lived after he begat Serug two hundred and seven years, and begat sons and daughters.

22 And Serug lived thirty years, and begat **Nahor**:

23 And Serug lived after he begat Nahor two hundred years, and begat sons and daughters.

24 And Nahor lived nine and twenty years, and begat **Terah** [*Abraham's father*]:

25 And Nahor lived after he begat Terah an hundred and nineteen years, and begat sons and daughters.

26 And Terah lived seventy years, and begat **Abram** [*Abraham*], Nahor, and Haran.

As an aside, it is interesting to see that after the Flood the life span of people became shorter and shorter. We will list the above men, and a few more, so that you can see this trend for yourself.

Life spans before and after the Flood (In years)

- Adam, 930
- Seth, 912
- Enos, 905
- Cainan, 910

- Mahalaleel, 895
- Jared, 962
- Enoch, translated at age 430
- Methuselah, 969
- Lamech, 777
- Noah, 950

The Flood

- Shem, born before the Flood, 610
- Arphaxad, 438
- Salah, 433
- Eber, 464
- Peleg, 239
- Reu, 239
- Serug, 230
- Nahor, 148
- Terah, 205
- Abraham, 175
- Isaac, 180
- Jacob, 147
- Joseph, 110

As you can see, Moses next focuses in on Abraham, who was to be a major player in the Father's plan for the salvation of His children here on earth. This is important for all of us because, as stated in our patriarchal blessings and the scriptures, we can have full access to the blessings of Abraham (Abraham 2:9–11), through our faithfulness to the gospel of Jesus Christ. Moses here points us to Abraham's father, two brothers, nephew, Lot, wife Sarai (Sarah), sister-in-law, Milcah, and Milcah's brother, Iscah.

27 ¶ Now these *are* the generations of [*this is the family of*] Terah: **Terah begat Abram** [*later changed to "Abraham" (see Genesis 17:5)*]**, Nahor, and Haran; and Haran begat Lot**.

28 And Haran died [*because of the famine in Ur—see Abraham 2:1*] before his father Terah in the land of his nativity, in Ur of the Chaldees.

29 And Abram and Nahor took them wives [*Haran's daughters— in other words, their nieces*]: the name of **Abram's wife** *was* **Sarai**; and the name of **Nahor's wife, Milcah**, the daughter of Haran [*Abraham's brother*], the father of Milcah, and the father of **Iscah**.

We will pause to provide a brief summary of Abraham's family at this point. It will be helpful as we proceed. The information is taken from Genesis 11:27–29, as confirmed in the chart provided in the *Old Testament Student Manual*, page 66.

The Family of Abraham

(At this point in time)

Terah (his father)
Terah's children: Abraham, Nahor, Haran
Abraham (wife, Sarah)
No children yet
Nahor (his brother, married Milcah)
No children yet
Haran (his brother)
Haran's children: Milcah, Lot, Iscah, Sarah (Sarai)

As you can see from the above information, Sarah is Abraham's niece. There is evidence to suggest that, after the death of Sarah's father, Haran (Abraham's youngest brother), Abraham's father, Terah (Sarah's grandfather) adopted her and her sister (see S. Kent Brown, "Biblical Egypt: Land of Refuge, Land of Bondage," *Ensign*, September 1980, pages 45, 47).

In their culture, this would have provided them more freedoms and privileges than would otherwise be accorded them. Legally, it would also make Sarah Abraham's sister. This information will be helpful when Abraham tells the Egyptians that Sarah is his sister, in order to keep them from killing him (Genesis 12:10–13).

Next, Moses mentions that Abraham and Sarah were not able to have children. This will become the background for a great miracle in the birth of Isaac, when Sarah is ninety years old and Abraham one hundred.

30 But **Sarai was barren** [*unable to have children*]; **she *had* no child**.

Abraham's home city of Ur is mentioned in verse 31, next. On a map in our day, Ur would be in Iraq, in the area of the modern town of Mugheir. It is about 150 miles inland to the northwest, from the Persian Gulf. The "Chaldees" (or "Chaldeans"), mentioned in verse 31, were residents of southern Babylon. Chaldea was another name for southern Babylon.

31 And Terah took Abram his son, and Lot the son of Haran his son's son [*in other words, Lot was Terah's grandson*], and Sarai his daughter in law [*Sarah was also his granddaughter through Haran*], his son Abram's wife; and they went forth with them from Ur of the Chaldees, to go into the land of Canaan [*basically what we call the Holy Land, today*]; and they came unto Haran [*near northern Syria or southern Turkey, today*], and dwelt there.

The Pearl of Great Price gives a different picture as to who led this expedition out of Ur to Haran. It was Abraham, not his father, who led out. Furthermore, it was the commandment of the Lord for Abraham to leave (see also Genesis 12:1).

Abraham 2:3–4

3 Now the Lord had said unto me: Abraham, get thee out of thy country, and from thy kindred, and from thy father's house, unto a land that I will show thee.

4 Therefore I left the land of Ur, of the Chaldees, to go into the land of Canaan; and I took Lot, my brother's son, and his wife, and Sarai my wife; and also my father followed after me, unto the land which we denominated Haran.

32 And the days of Terah were two hundred and five years: and Terah died in Haran.

Because Abraham plays such an important role in our understanding of Genesis, chapters 12–17, and because most patriarchal blessings include statements to the effect that our lineage is traced back to him and his pronounced blessings are to continue with and be fulfilled through us, we will include Abraham chapters 1 and 2 here.

ABRAHAM 1

Background

In this chapter, we will be given many details about Abraham's life that are not available elsewhere in scripture. As we begin, we see that Abraham lived in "the land of the Chaldeans" (verse

1). Genesis 11:28 tells us that "Ur of the Chaldees" is the "land of [Abraham's] nativity"; in other words, Abraham was born in Ur. On a map in our day, Ur would be in Iraq, in the area of the modern town of Mugheir. It is about 150 miles inland from the Persian Gulf, to the northwest. The "Chaldeans" were residents of southern Babylon. Chaldea was another name for southern Babylon.

Although Egypt was 875 miles west of Ur, it was influential in the lives of the citizens of Ur in Abraham's day. As we will see, beginning with verse 6, the religion of Egypt was a dominant influence in Ur. In fact, as depicted in Facsimile No. 1, one of Pharaoh's priests attempted to sacrifice Abraham on the altar. We will learn more about this from Abraham beginning with verse 12.

One of the things we learn about Abraham, in verse 1, is that he was gentle and modest. He gives the understatement of the ages in the last half of this verse. We know from this chapter that he was almost offered as a human sacrifice at the request of his relatives (verse 7), and that there was great anger against him when the priest of Pharaoh was struck dead by the Lord as he attempted to kill Abraham and when the temple of Pharaoh in Ur was destroyed. Thus, there was a public outcry against Abraham, the perceived cause of the destruction of the people's priest and shrine. With this as a setting, we read verse 1 (**bold** added for emphasis):

1 In the land of the Chaldeans, at the residence of my fathers [*in other words, in Abraham's home town*], **I, Abraham, saw that it was needful for me to obtain another place of residence;**

He will make another understatement at the end of Abraham 2:12. His quiet modesty of words is indeed exemplary.

As mentioned above, Abraham's father and extended family were apostates. They had once belonged to the true religion given from God through Noah and his righteous sons but had left it (see verse 5). They had turned to idol worship and the evil indulgences and practices that accompanied it. Verse 2, next, tells us that Abraham did not go with them in this departure from truth. Rather, he recognized the value of the gospel of Christ and stayed true to it. He gives his reasons for so doing in verses 2–4.

2 And, finding **there was greater happiness** and **peace** and **rest** for me, I sought for the blessings of the fathers, and the right [*of holding the Melchizedek Priesthood—see end of this verse*] whereunto I should be ordained to administer the same; having been myself a follower of righteousness, **desiring also to be one who possessed great knowledge**, and **to be a greater follower of righteousness**, and **to possess a greater knowledge** [*have on-going revelation and instruction*], and **to be a father of many nations** [*desiring to have a large posterity*], **a prince of peace**, and **desiring to receive instructions**, and **to keep the commandments of God, I became a** rightful heir, a **High Priest**, holding the right [*the Melchizedek Priesthood*] belonging to the fathers [*his righteous ancestors,*

including Shem, Noah, and so on back to Adam].

We see in verse 3, next, that Abraham was a high priest in the Melchizedek Priesthood.

3 **It** [*the office of high priest in the Melchizedek Priesthood*] **was conferred upon me from the fathers**; it came down from the fathers, from the beginning of time [*from the time of Adam—see note in this study guide for Moses 6:67, which tells us that Adam was a high priest in the Melchizedek Priesthood*], yea, **even from the beginning, or before the foundation of the earth** [*worthy men held this priesthood in premortality—compare with Alma 13:3*], down to the present time, even the right of the firstborn, or the first man, who is Adam, or first father, through the fathers unto me.

According to the Doctrine and Covenants, Abraham received his priesthood from Melchizedek. We read:

D&C 84:14

14 Which **Abraham received the priesthood from Melchizedek**, who received it through the lineage of his fathers, even till Noah;

Joseph Smith gave further detail about Abraham's meeting with Melchizedek and his subsequent ordination. He said:

"Abraham says to Melchizedek, I believe all that thou hast taught me concerning the priesthood and the coming of the Son of Man; so Melchizedek ordained Abraham and sent him away. Abraham rejoiced, saying, Now I have a priesthood" (*History of the Church,* Vol. 5, page 555).

4 **I sought for mine appointment unto the Priesthood** [*Abraham lived worthily and sought to be ordained a high priest in the Melchizedek Priesthood*] according to the appointment of God [*according to the pattern approved and established by the Lord*] unto the fathers concerning the seed [*perhaps meaning the pattern of father to son, established in the days of Adam*].

It may be that verse 4, above, is the introductory sentence of Abraham's explanation as to why he received the priesthood from Melchizedek (D&C 84:14) rather than from his father, Terah. It appears that he "sought" it from his "fathers" (direct ancestors), but they had apostatized and thus could not give it to him. This no doubt caused him much sorrow and heartache. He explains their apostasy, beginning in verse 5.

5 **My fathers having turned from their righteousness** [*they were once faithful to God*], **and from the holy commandments** which the Lord their God had given unto them, **unto the worshiping of the gods of the heathen** [*they had turned to idol worship*], **utterly refused to hearken to my voice**;

The four "gods," or idols, mentioned in verse 6, next, were Egyptian idols. You can see this by looking at Facsimile No. 1 and looking at

Figures 5–8, which are depicted as jars underneath the table-altar upon which Abraham has been placed in preparation for his sacrifice. As stated in verse 5, above, Abraham's father and other ancestors had joined the Egyptian religion in Ur, in which idols were worshipped and human sacrifice was practiced. If you look in the layers under the four jars (representing the four gods mentioned above), you will see a crocodile lurking. It represents Pharaoh as a god (see figure 9). The vital organs of the victim being sacrificed were placed in these jars and then poured out to a live crocodile as a part of worshipping Pharaoh as a god.

Human sacrifice is one of the worst of all blasphemies promoted by Satan. It is an abominable mockery of the sacrifice of the Son of God.

6 For **their hearts were set to do evil**, and were **wholly** [*completely*] **turned** to the god of **Elkenah**, and the god of **Libnah**, and the god of **Mahmackrah**, and the god of **Korash**, and **the god of Pharaoh**, king of Egypt;

7 Therefore **they turned their hearts to the sacrifice of the heathen in offering up their children unto these dumb idols** [*idols that are inanimate, deaf and dumb, having no capacity to hear or speak*], and **hearkened not unto my voice**, but **endeavored to take away my life by the hand of the priest of Elkenah** [*in other words, they attempted to murder Abraham, under the guise of religious worship, using the priest of Pharaoh as their executioner*].

The priest of Elkenah was also the priest of Pharaoh.

Next, Abraham explains that the Egyptian custom of sacrificing humans to their false gods had become firmly established in Chaldea, Abraham's homeland. He will mention specific instances of such sacrifices.

8 **Now, at this time it was the custom of the priest of Pharaoh**, the king of Egypt, **to offer up upon the altar** which was built in the land of Chaldea, for the offering unto these strange [*foreign*] gods, **men, women, and children**.

9 And it came to pass that **the priest made an offering unto the god of Pharaoh**, and **also unto the god of Shagreel**, even after the manner of the Egyptians. Now the god of Shagreel was the sun.

10 Even **the thank-offering of a child** did the priest of Pharaoh offer upon the altar which stood by the hill called Potiphar's Hill, at the head of the plain of Olishem.

In verse 11, next, we see another example, in addition to Abraham, of the practice among these wicked people of using human sacrifice to get rid of those who opposed them.

11 Now, **this priest had offered upon this altar three virgins at one time**, who were the daughters of Onitah, one of the royal descent directly from the loins of Ham. **These virgins were offered up because of their virtue; they would not bow**

down to worship gods of wood or of stone [*idols*], **therefore they were killed upon this altar,** and it was done after the manner of the Egyptians.

> Next, Abraham modestly gives us a few details of his almost being sacrificed. He tells us that he has included a drawing (Facsimile No. 1) that will help us understand what happened.

12 And it came to pass that **the priests laid violence upon me, that they might slay me also, as they did those virgins upon this altar**; and **that you may have a knowledge of this altar, I will refer you to the representation** [*drawing*] **at the commencement of this record.**

> Next, he tells us that the altar upon which victims were sacrificed looked like a bed.

13 **It** [*the altar*] **was made after the form of a bedstead** [*it was made like a bed*], such as was had among the Chaldeans, and **it stood before the gods of Elkenah, Libnah, Mahmackrah, Korash, and also a god like unto that of Pharaoh, king of Egypt.**

14 **That you may have an understanding of these gods, I have given you the fashion** [*a drawing*] **of them in the figures** [*figures 5–9*] **at the beginning, which manner of figures is called by the Chaldeans Rahleenos, which signifies hieroglyphics.**

> There is an important lesson for us in Facsimile No. 1. There is much symbolism in what Abraham did literally. It is that he was willing to put his "all" on the altar of sacrifice in order to remain true to God. In the facsimile, he is remaining loyal to the Lord at all costs. By doing so, he showed his great faith. Having such faith, he was enabled to pray fervently to be redeemed from the evil that was about to descend upon him. Figure 1 represents the "Angel of the Lord" who came and rescued Abraham. This "Angel" can represent Christ, who literally redeems us from the evils and sins of the world when we follow Him no matter what the cost.

> If you look at the facsimile again, you will see the knife held in the hand of the priest of Pharaoh, ready to sacrifice Abraham. In verse 15, Abraham tells us what happened next.

15 And **as they lifted up their hands upon me, that they might offer me up** and take away my life, behold, **I lifted up my voice** [*prayed*] **unto the Lord my God, and the Lord hearkened and heard, and he filled me with the vision of the Almighty** [*he saw the Savior—see verse 16*], **and the angel of his presence stood by me, and immediately unloosed my bands** [*untied him*];

16 And **his voice was unto me: Abraham, Abraham, behold, my name is Jehovah** [*the name of Christ in the Old Testament*], and **I have heard thee, and have come down to deliver thee,** and **to take thee away** from thy father's house, and

ABRAHAM 1

from all thy kinsfolk, into a strange land which thou knowest not of;

> One of the important messages we see in verse 16, above, and verse 17, next, is that in order to follow Christ, we must leave the worldly influences around us.

17 And this **because they have turned their hearts away from me**, to worship the god of Elkenah, and the god of Libnah, and the god of Mahmackrah, and the god of Korash, and the god of Pharaoh, king of Egypt; therefore I have come down to visit [*punish*] them, and to destroy him [*the priest*] who hath lifted up his hand against thee, Abraham, my son, to take away thy life.

> As you can see, in verse 18, next, when we leave the world and follow Christ, we are not alone.

> Verses 18–19 contain part of the Abrahamic covenant, the covenant that the Lord made with Abraham and through which the faithful in all ages since Abraham are blessed. This includes the faithful Saints in our day. We will speak in more detail about this when we get to Abraham 2:9–11. These are blessings and promises to us if we make covenants (which provide direction and security) and remain faithful.

18 Behold, **I will lead thee by my hand**, and **I will take thee, to put upon thee my name**, even **the Priesthood** of thy father, and **my power shall be over thee**.

19 As it was with Noah so shall it be with thee; but **through thy ministry my name shall be known in the earth forever**, for I am thy God.

> Next, Abraham gives a few more details as to what happened to the shrine of Egyptian gods in Ur, at which Abraham was nearly sacrificed.

20 Behold, Potiphar's Hill was in the land of Ur, of Chaldea. And **the Lord broke down the altar of Elkenah, and of the gods** [*the idols*] **of the land, and utterly destroyed them, and smote the priest that he died**; and **there was great mourning in Chaldea, and also in the court of Pharaoh** [*in other words, news of this destruction reached Egypt, almost nine hundred miles away*]; which Pharaoh signifies king by royal blood.

> Sadly, as you saw in verse 20, above, instead of repenting and turning to the true God, who obviously had great power over their "dumb" idols (verse 7) and false priests, these wicked people mourned the loss of their evil religious symbols and shrine. This is a reminder that wickedness does not promote rational thought.

> Next, in verses 21–27, Abraham gives us some detail explaining that the descendants of Cain were not allowed to hold the priesthood. One of the great blessings of our day is that all worthy men may now receive the priesthood, as revealed by the Lord to President Spencer W. Kimball in 1978 (see Doctrine and Covenants—Declaration 2, at the end of your Doctrine and

Covenants). Thus, the full gospel can now go to all the world in fulfillment of many prophecies to that effect, including Daniel 2:35, 44–45.

These next verses may not help us explain to those who do not believe in the Pearl of Great Price the fact that not all men have been allowed to hold the priesthood throughout most of the history of the world. However, they are helpful to us because they inform us that this practice did not originate in the early days of the restored gospel in this dispensation.

Abraham will explain that the king of Egypt in his day could not hold the priesthood. From what he says, we understand that Noah's son Ham, a righteous man (see Moses 8:13, 27), and his wife, Egyptus, came through the Flood with Noah and his wife, as well as with Ham's brothers, Japheth and Shem, and their wives—a total of eight people on the ark (see 1 Peter 3:20). Egyptus was a descendant of Cain. Thus, the restriction pertaining to the priesthood was preserved after the Flood through the posterity of Ham and Egyptus.

Ham's daughter, who was also named Egyptus, settled Egypt. Therefore, the Egyptians in Abraham's day could not hold the true priesthood.

21 Now **this king of Eg**ypt [*the Pharaoh mentioned at the end of verse 20, above*] **was a descendant from the loins of Ham, and was a partaker of the blood of the Canaanites** [*descendants of Cain*] **by birth.**

The word "Canaanites" is used both in verse 21, above, and in verse 22, next. According to Genesis 10:6, Ham and Egyptus named their fourth son Canaan. This is where the name Canaanites comes from. You can read more about this in your Bible Dictionary under "Canaan" and under "Canaanite."

22 **From this descent** [*from Ham and Egyptus*] **sprang all the Egyptians, and thus the blood of the Canaanites was preserved in the land.**

23 **The land of Egypt being first discovered by a woman, who was the daughter of Ham, and the daughter of Egyptus**, which in the Chaldean signifies Egypt, which signifies that which is forbidden;

24 When this woman discovered the land it was under water [*the waters of the Flood hadn't yet receded from it*], who afterward settled her sons in it; and **thus, from Ham, sprang that race which preserved the curse** [*of not holding the priesthood*] **in the land.**

From verses 25–27, we learn that the oldest son of Egyptus—in other words, a grandson of Ham and Egyptus and a great-grandson of Noah and his wife—became the first pharaoh. He was a righteous man and received a blessing from his great-grandfather, Noah.

25 Now **the first government of Egypt was established by Pharaoh, the eldest son of Egyptus, the daughter of Ham**, and it was

after the manner of [*patterned after*] the government of Ham, which was patriarchal [*passed down from father to son*].

26 **Pharaoh, being a righteous man,** established his kingdom and **judged his people wisely and justly all his days**, seeking earnestly to imitate that order [*the patriarchal order*] established by the fathers [*righteous men, back to Adam*] in the first generations, in the days of the first patriarchal reign, even in the reign of Adam, and also of **Noah**, his father [*great-grandfather*], who **blessed him with the blessings of the earth, and with the blessings of wisdom,** but **cursed him as pertaining to the Priesthood** [*in other words, he was not allowed to hold the priesthood*].

27 Now, **Pharaoh being of that lineage by which he could not have the right of Priesthood**, notwithstanding [*even though*] the Pharaohs would fain claim [*pretend to claim*] it from Noah, through Ham [*even though many later Pharaohs falsely claimed to have the true priesthood from Noah through Ham*], therefore **my father** [*Terah*] **was led away by their idolatry** [*their idol worship*];

28 But I shall endeavor, hereafter, to delineate [*to give and make notes about; to describe*] the chronology running back from myself to the beginning of the creation, for the records have come into my hands, which I hold unto this present time [*Abraham had scriptures and historical records in his possession; see also verse 31*].

Abraham now picks up the story of what happened after the shrine and the priest of Pharaoh were destroyed. Remember that this destruction took place at the time Abraham was freed from the sacrificial altar by the Lord.

29 Now, **after the priest of Elkenah** [*the one who had tried to sacrifice Abraham*] **was smitten that he died**, there came a fulfilment of those things which were said unto me concerning the land of Chaldea, that there should be **a famine in the land**.

One of the positive results of the famine initially was that Abraham's father repented and returned to God. Unfortunately, when things began going well for him again, he returned to his old ways (Abraham 2:5). This is one of the dangers of prosperity. Thus, Abraham is well acquainted with the joy and heartache that come and go when loved ones return to God when they are humbled but then leave again when prosperity and safety are once again theirs.

As we continue, Abraham tells us that because of the famine, his father repented of his evil plots against him.

30 Accordingly **a famine prevailed throughout all the land of Chaldea**, and **my father** was sorely [*severely*] tormented because of the

famine, and he **repented** of the evil which he had determined against me, to take away my life.

> Abraham will tell us more about the effects of the famine on him and his family in chapter 2. In the meantime, as Abraham closes chapter 1, we see that one of the main topics for him so far in these writings has been the importance of the priesthood and the blessings that flow to us from it. He emphasizes this again now.

31 But the records of the fathers, even the patriarchs, **concerning the right of Priesthood**, the Lord my God preserved in mine own hands; therefore a knowledge of the beginning of the creation, and also of the planets, and of the stars, as they were made known unto the fathers, have I kept even unto this day, and I shall endeavor to write some of these things upon this record, for the benefit of my posterity [*all of us*] that shall come after me.

ABRAHAM 2

Background

This chapter contains one of the most important matters in all of scripture for each of us. It concerns the blessings of Abraham, the Abrahamic covenant. Each of us who has had a patriarchal blessing has had our mind pointed to the "blessings of Abraham, Isaac, and Jacob." These are the blessings that make exaltation possible to us. This chapter contains a summary of these blessings in verses 9–11. We will discuss them when we get there.

But first, in verses 1–8, father Abraham tells us what happened to him and his family after they left Ur. We will do a quick bit of genealogy on Abraham's family at the time he leaves Ur, which will be helpful in the next verses. We will use Genesis 11:26–29 as our source.

> **Terah** (his father)
> **Abraham**
> **Nahor** (his brother)
> **Haran** (his brother)
> **Sarah** (his niece)
> **Lot** (his nephew)
> **Milcah** (his niece)

As you will see, Haran, Abraham's brother, will die because of the famine. Abraham will marry his niece, Sarai (Sarah), and Nahor will marry his niece, Milcah. To marry close relatives was not unusual in Abraham's day. Lot will travel with his uncles, Abraham and Nahor, and with his grandfather, Terah.

1 Now the Lord God caused the **famine** to wax sore [*grow severe*] in the land of Ur, insomuch that **Haran, my brother, died**; but Terah, my father, yet lived in the land of Ur, of the Chaldees.

> Next, Abraham tells us that he married his niece, Sarai (her name will be changed to Sarah in conjunction with the Lord's covenant with Abraham and Sarai that they will have a child—Isaac (see Genesis 17:15). It is interesting that a name change was often associated with covenant making in ancient times.

2 And it came to pass that **I, Abraham, took Sarai to wife**, and **Nahor, my brother, took Milcah to**

wife, who was the daughter of Haran.

3 Now **the Lord had said unto me: Abraham, get thee out of thy country**, and from thy kindred, and from thy father's house, unto a land that I will show thee.

> Next, Abraham tells us who went with him as he obeyed the Lord's commandment to leave.

4 **Therefore I left the land of Ur**, of the Chaldees, **to go into the land of Canaan**; and **I took Lot**, my brother's son, **and his wife**, **and Sarai my wife**; and **also my father followed after me**, unto the land which we denominated [*named*] Haran.

> From the wording in verse 4, above, it sounds as if Abraham's father, Terah, followed Abraham later. Of course, it could be that when Abraham determined to leave, as commanded by the Lord, Terah followed him. Whatever the case, they settled for a time in a place they named Haran, which was located far north and a bit east of what we know today as the Holy Land.
>
> Sadly, when things started going well in Haran, which they apparently did—when Abraham leaves Haran, they have "substance" and converts with them (verses 14–15)—his father apostatizes again and remains in Haran. He will die there at age 205 (Genesis 11:32).

5 And **the famine abated** [*ceased*]; and **my father tarried** [*remained*] **in Haran** and dwelt there, as there were **many flocks in Haran** [*prosperity*]; and **my father turned again unto his idolatry**, therefore he continued in Haran.

> Next, in verses 6–12, the Savior appears to Abraham and commands him to leave Haran with his family and followers. The Lord makes a covenant with him that is of vital interest to each of us. The details of the covenant are given in verses 9–11.

6 But **I, Abraham, and Lot**, my brother's son, **prayed unto the Lord**, and **the Lord appeared unto me, and said** unto me: Arise, and take Lot with thee; for **I have purposed to take thee away out of Haran, and to make of thee a minister to bear my name** in a strange land [*basically, the area of the Holy Land today*] **which I will give unto thy seed** [*posterity*] **after thee** for an everlasting possession, when they hearken to my voice.

> A very important matter, which is often misunderstood, is mentioned in verse 6, above. Did you notice to whom the "strange land" is to be given? The answer is to Abraham's "seed." And which of the major factions fighting over the Holy Land today are Abraham's seed? Answer: both Jews and Arabs. Abraham is a highly revered ancestor for both peoples.
>
> In an address given at Brigham Young University on February 4, 1979, President Howard W. Hunter reminded us that both the Jews and the Arabs are children of Abraham and thus, the promises given to Abraham apply to both (David

B. Galbraith, "President Howard W. Hunter, 1907–1995: A Man of Peace," *Brigham Young Magazine*, May 1995, page 5).

Next, the Savior identifies Himself to Abraham. As He does so, we see Him confirming Abraham's wisdom in rejecting idol worship. Idols can do none of the things Jehovah can. None of them is a god. He is!

7 For **I am the Lord thy God**; I dwell in heaven; the earth is my footstool; I stretch my hand over the sea, and it obeys my voice; I cause the wind and the fire to be my chariot; I say to the mountains—Depart hence—and behold, they are taken away by a whirlwind, in an instant, suddenly.

8 **My name is Jehovah**, and I know the end from the beginning; therefore **my hand shall be over thee** [*the Lord's blessings will be upon Abraham and his righteous posterity*].

> You may wish to bracket or put a box around verses 9–11 in your own scriptures, or otherwise mark them. They constitute a concise summary of the "blessings of Abraham, Isaac, and Jacob, as promised to faithful, covenant-keeping members of the Church. They are often referred to in patriarchal blessings. These verses contain the basics of the Abrahamic covenant.
>
> We will first go through verses 9–11, using **bold** to point out the basic elements of the covenant. Then, we will repeat the verses, adding notes and commentary.

9 And **I will make of thee a great nation**, and **I will bless thee above measure**, and **make thy name great among all nations**, and **thou shalt be a blessing unto thy seed after thee**, that **in their hands they shall bear this ministry and Priesthood unto all nations**;

10 And **I will bless them through thy name**; for **as many as receive this Gospel shall be called after thy name**, and **shall be accounted thy seed**, and **shall rise up and bless thee, as their father**;

11 And **I will bless them that bless thee, and curse them that curse thee**; and **in thee (that is, in thy Priesthood) and in thy seed (that is, thy Priesthood)**, for I give unto thee a promise that this right shall continue in thee, and **in thy seed after thee (that is to say, the literal seed, or the seed of the body) shall all the families of the earth be blessed**, even **with the blessings of the Gospel**, which are the blessings of **salvation**, even of **life eternal**.

> As mentioned above, we will now repeat verses 9–11, adding notes and commentary as we go. Remember that at the time Abraham was given these promises, he and Sarai had no children. He is sixty-two years old at this point, and she is fifty-two (see verse 14).
>
> Note how many different ways of saying "exaltation" (the highest degree of glory in the celestial kingdom) are used in these verses. Some of the blessings promised are

literal for Abraham here on earth; others are symbolic of exaltation for him as well as for the faithful in the eternities.

Verses 9–11, repeated

9 And **I will make of thee a great nation** [*literal for Abraham on earth; symbolic of exaltation*], and **I will bless thee above measure** [*exaltation; the blessings of exaltation are beyond measuring*], and **make thy name great among all nations** [*literal for Abraham; symbolic of exaltation for the faithful, wherein they become gods and their names become great among all the worlds they create*], and thou shalt be a blessing unto **thy seed after thee**, that in their hands they **shall bear this ministry and Priesthood unto all nations** [*through Abraham and his righteous posterity (the righteous of Israel), the gospel of Jesus Christ with the blessings of the priesthood will be taken throughout the world*];

10 And I will bless them through thy name; for **as many as receive this Gospel shall be called after thy name** [*all who accept the gospel and live it become "Abraham's seed"; whether they are literal descendants or are adopted in, it makes no difference; they too receive the promises made to Abraham*], **and shall be accounted thy seed** [*in other words, heirs to the promises and obligations of Abraham*], and shall rise up and bless [*praise*] thee, as their father [*ancestor*];

11 And **I will bless them that bless thee, and curse them that curse thee** [*in other words, the Lord will be on our side*]; and in thee (that is, **in thy Priesthood**) and in thy seed (that is, thy Priesthood), for I give unto thee a promise that this right shall continue in thee, and in thy seed after thee (that is to say, the literal seed, or the seed of the body) **shall all the families of the earth be blessed**, even **with the blessings of the Gospel**, which are the blessings of **salvation**, even of **life eternal** [*exaltation as gods, in the highest degree of glory of the celestial kingdom*].

As you can see, the main emphasis in the blessings and promises given to Abraham is exaltation. Thus, those who inherit the blessings of Abraham (through baptism and other covenants) and live worthy of them will be exalted.

The phrase "life eternal" in verse 11, above, is the same as "eternal life." As used in the scriptures, both phrases always mean "exaltation." Exaltation means becoming gods and living in the family unit forever. "Immortality," on the other hand, means being resurrected and living forever. All who have ever been born will be resurrected and live forever, whether in outer darkness or in telestial, terrestrial, or celestial glory. But only those who attain the highest glory in the celestial kingdom (D&C 131:1–4) receive "eternal life." An example of the use of "immortality" and "eternal life" as two separate scriptural concepts is found in Moses, as follows:

Moses 1:39

39 For behold, this is my work and my glory—to bring to pass the **immortality** [*resurrection*] and **eternal life** [*exaltation*] of man.

We will go through these verses one more time, this time pointing out our obligations as members of covenant Israel.

Verses 9–11, repeated again

9 And I will make of thee **a great nation** [*marry, and have children, where possible*], and I will bless thee above measure, and make thy name great among all nations, and **thou shalt be a blessing unto thy seed after thee** [*be a blessing and influence for good to our families*], that in their hands they shall **bear this ministry and Priesthood unto all nations** [*serve formal missions where possible, preach the gospel, and be missionaries under all circumstances, thus making the ordinances of the priesthood available to others*];

10 And I will bless them through thy name; for **as many as receive this Gospel shall be called after thy name** [*do all we can to ensure that our posterity are blessed by the gospel*], and shall be accounted thy seed, and shall rise up and bless thee, as their father [*do our best to pass the gospel of Jesus Christ on to our children, grandchildren, and so forth*];

11 And I will bless them that bless thee, and curse them that curse thee; and in thee (that is, in thy **Priesthood**) and in thy seed (that is, thy Priesthood), for I give unto thee a promise that this right shall continue in thee [*make sure we honor the priesthood and the priesthood ordinances we have received*], and in thy seed after thee (that is to say, the literal seed, or the seed of the body) **shall all the families of the earth be blessed** [*be a blessing for others constantly*], even with the blessings of the Gospel, which are the blessings of salvation, even of life eternal.

In verses 12–13, next, we see the gentle greatness and humility of Abraham as he once again uses an understatement (see also Abraham 1:1) to express his feelings. He has been saved from death on the altar. He has seen the Savior and, though still childless, has been told that his posterity will grow into nations and that his name will be honored and revered throughout the world. Not only that, but his posterity will also take the gospel and priesthood to all nations.

12 Now, after the Lord had withdrawn from speaking to me, and withdrawn his face from me, I said in my heart: **Thy servant has sought thee earnestly; now I have found thee**;

13 Thou didst send thine angel to deliver me from the gods of Elkenah, and **I will do well to hearken unto thy voice**, therefore let thy servant rise up and depart in peace.

14 So **I, Abraham, departed** as the Lord had said unto me, and Lot with me; and **I, Abraham, was sixty and two years old when I departed out of Haran**.

> As Abraham and his company depart, they will head southwest toward what we know today as the Holy Land. As stated in verse 14, above, he is now sixty-two years of age. That makes Sarai fifty-two years old. They have thirty-eight more years of trial of their faith ahead of them before the Lord's promise will be fulfilled that they will have a child. Abraham will be a hundred and Sarah will be ninety when Isaac is born.

15 And **I took Sarai** [*her name will be changed to Sarah in Genesis 17:15, which means "princess" in Hebrew, and "queen" in the Akkadian language*], whom I took to wife when I was in Ur, in Chaldea, **and Lot**, my brother's son, **and all our substance that we had gathered** [*it appears that by now Abraham has gathered considerable wealth*], **and the souls** [*converts*] **that we had won in Haran**, and came forth in the way to [*direction of*] the land of Canaan, and dwelt in tents as we came on our way;

16 Therefore, eternity was our covering and our rock and our salvation, as we journeyed from Haran by the way of Jershon, to come to the land of Canaan.

> Abraham informs us that he continued to worship God faithfully during his travels. In verse 17, next, we see the charity in Abraham's heart as he continues to pray for the blessings of the Lord upon his father and relatives who have been significant enemies to him.

17 Now **I, Abraham, built an altar** in the land of Jershon, and **made an offering unto the Lord**, and **prayed that the famine might be turned away from my father's house**, that they might not perish.

18 And then we passed from Jershon through the land unto the place of Sechem; it was situated in the plains of Moreh, and we had already come into the borders of the land of the Canaanites [*a land full of idol worship and attendant wickedness*], and **I offered sacrifice** there in the plains of Moreh, **and called on the Lord devoutly**, because we had already come into the land of **this idolatrous nation**.

> In verse 19, next, the Savior appears to Abraham and tells him that the land he is now traveling through will be given to his posterity.
>
> One thing you might take note of is that upon entering Canaan, which he refers to as "the land of this idolatrous nation," Abraham builds several altars. Perhaps an important message for us might be that when we are faced with increased opposition to our personal righteousness, it is wise to increase our time spent with the things of God.

19 And **the Lord appeared** unto me in answer to my prayers, **and said** unto me: **Unto thy seed will I give this land**.

20 And I, Abraham, arose from the place of the altar which I had built unto the Lord, and removed from thence unto a mountain on the east of Bethel, and pitched my tent there, Bethel on the west, and Hai on the east; and **there I built another altar unto the Lord**, and called again upon the name of the Lord.

> As Abraham informs us, the great famine that caused so much devastation in Ur is evident also in the land of the Canaanites. At this point in his journeying, Abraham determines to travel on to Egypt. This will pose a particular problem for Abraham and Sarai because she is a beautiful woman.
>
> By culture and tradition, the Egyptian pharaohs at this time in Egypt would never commit adultery. But they didn't hesitate to murder a man if they desired his wife. After the death of her husband, a wife would then be available. Thus, a pharaoh could then marry her and would not be committing adultery. We will quote from the *Old Testament Student Manual*:
>
> "The idea that Abraham, the great man of righteousness, seems to have told a deliberate lie in order to protect his own life has troubled many students of the Old Testament. That his life was in danger because of Sarah's beauty seems quite clear. It seems peculiar, but **whereas the Egyptian pharaohs had a strong aversion to committing adultery with another man's wife, they had no qualms about murdering the man to free his spouse for remarriage**.

> "'To kill the husband in order to possess himself of his wife seems to have been a common royal custom in those days. A papyrus tells of a Pharaoh who, acting on the advice of one of his princes, sent armed men to fetch a beautiful woman and make away with her husband. Another Pharaoh is promised by his priest on his tombstone that even after death he will kill Palestinian sheiks and include their wives in his harem' (Kasher, *Encyclopedia of Biblical Interpretation,* 2:128).
>
> "**Some scholars have noted that Abraham could validly state that Sarah was his sister. First of all, the Hebrew words brother and sister were often used for other blood relatives**. (See Genesis 14:14, in which Lot, Abraham's nephew, is called 'his brother.') Because Abraham and Haran, Sarah's father, were brothers, Sarah was Abraham's niece and thus could be called sister.
>
> "Another ancient custom permitted a woman to be adopted as a man's sister upon their marriage to give her greater legal and social status (see *Encyclopedia Judaica,* s.v. 'Sarah,' 14:866). Also, it is not unlikely that when Haran died Terah legally adopted Haran's children as his own, thus making Sarah Abraham's sister" (*Old Testament Student Manual: Genesis–2 Samuel, Religion 301,* page 66).

With the above explanations in mind, there is one more issue that is far more important than any other. It is the simple fact that the Lord told Abraham to ask Sarah to claim that she was his sister. Unfortunately, the Bible leaves this fact out (Genesis 12:10–13). We will see the Lord's counsel for solving the problem in verses 21–24, next.

21 And I, Abraham, journeyed, going on still towards the south; and there was a continuation of a famine in the land; and **I, Abraham, concluded to go down into Egypt**, to sojourn there, **for the famine became very grievous**.

22 And it came to pass **when I was come near to enter into Egypt, the Lord said unto me: Behold, Sarai, thy wife, is a very fair woman to look upon**;

23 Therefore it shall come to pass, **when the Egyptians shall see her, they will say—She is his wife; and they will kill you, but they will save her alive**; therefore see that ye do on this wise [*here is what you should do*]:

24 **Let her say unto the Egyptians, she is thy sister**, and thy soul shall live [*your body will remain alive*].

Next, in verse 25, Abraham brings up the subject with his wife.

25 And it came to pass that **I, Abraham, told Sarai, my wife, all that the Lord had said unto me**—Therefore **say unto them** [*the Egyptians*], I pray thee [*please*], **thou art my sister, that it may be well with me for thy sake** [*so that I can remain alive and also watch out for you*], **and my soul shall live because of thee** [*you can save my life*].

Elder Mark E. Petersen of the Quorum of the Twelve explained this situation as follows:

"To protect himself, Abraham had told Pharaoh that Sarah was his sister, which of course she was. Had he divulged that she was his wife, he might have been slain. But as his sister, Pharaoh was willing to buy her at a good price" (*Abraham, Friend of God,* page 69).

Elder Bruce R. McConkie taught:

"The Lord never sends apostles and prophets and righteous men to minister to his people without placing women of like spiritual stature at their sides. Adam stands as the great high priest, under Christ, to rule as a natural patriarch over all men of all ages, but he cannot rule alone; Eve, his wife, rules at his side, having like caliber and attainments to his own. Abraham is tested as few men have been when the Lord commands him to offer Isaac upon the altar (Gen. 22:1–19); and Sarah struggles with like problems when the Lord directs that she withhold from the Egyptians her status as Abraham's wife. . . . And so it goes, in all dispensations and at all times when there are holy men there are also holy women. Neither stands alone before the Lord. The exaltation of the one is dependent upon that of the other" (*Doctrinal New Testament Commentary,* Vol. 3, page 302).

Many Christians are quite critical of Abraham, claiming that it was out of character and disappointing that such an otherwise great man would lie to the Egyptians about his wife.

An *Ensign* article regarding this matter, written by S. Kent Brown, is helpful. Here is a quote from it:

"For Abraham and Sarah, Egypt constituted a place of refuge from the famine raging at the time of their arrival in Canaan (see Gen. 12:10). Interestingly, while Abraham and Sarah enjoyed respite from Canaan's drought, their visit to Egypt provided Sarah with one of her most difficult trials.

"Most are familiar with the story of Sarah posing as Abraham's sister (see Gen. 12:11–15). Even though Abraham later insisted that Sarah was his sister through his father, but not his mother (see Gen. 20:12), many students have felt confused with this explanation. It was not until the discovery of ancient Hurrian legal texts at the site of Nuzi, a city east of Ashur, the capital of ancient Assyria, that we obtained a clearer background for this incident.

"The Hurrians were people who flourished about the time of Abraham and later. Their kingdom included the land of Haran in which Abraham and Sarah lived for a number of years before moving to Canaan (see Gen. 11:31; Gen. 12:5). Interestingly, only in stories dealing with Sarah and Rebecca do we find the claim made that the wife was also a sister to her husband (see Gen. 12:10–20; Gen. 20:2–6; Gen. 26:1–11). Rebecca, like Sarah, spent her youth growing up in Haran, no doubt in contact with Hurrians.

"The contact is important when we learn that under Hurrian law women were frequently adopted as sisters by their husbands either before or during the marriage ceremony. Such a dual status, both wife and sister, had important consequences for a woman. It guaranteed to her special legal and social protections and opportunities which were simply not available to women in any other culture of the Near East. Because Sarah had lived within the Hurrian culture for a number of years, it is not unlikely that she enjoyed this status in her marriage, a status common among Hurrians. Therefore, Abraham's claim that Sarah was his sister upon their entry into the land of Egypt is not far-fetched in the least. Further, it is possible that Terah, Abraham's father, had adopted Sarah before her marriage to Abraham and that this is the meaning of the passage in Genesis 20:12. This particular practice, on the part of a prospective father-in-law, is documented from the Nuzi tablets. (See E. A. Speiser, 'The Wife-Sister Motif in the Patriarchal Narratives,' in *Biblical and Other Studies* [Cambridge, Mass.: Harvard Univ. Press, 1963], pp. 15–28.)

"In Genesis, Abraham is said to have insisted that Sarah was his sister because he feared for his life. The incident is clarified in the Book of Abraham where we learn it was revealed to Abraham that Sarah would maintain that she was his sister (see Abr. 2:21–25).

"This placed the burden on Sarah. Would she risk her own rights as wife in order to preserve the life of her husband as the Lord had asked? Indeed, Sarah's visit to Egypt became a period of intense trial for her. Even though the Lord protected her from the pharaoh's intent to make her his wife—and protected her virtue—the pharaoh was nevertheless allowed to take her into his household (Gen. 12:15–20). We see, then, that Egypt represented at the same time a haven from the famine and a place of testing for Sarah" ("Biblical Egypt: Land of Refuge, Land of Bondage," *Ensign,* September 1980, pages 45, 47).

When we get to Abraham and Sarah's stay in Egypt, in Genesis 12 in this study guide, we will learn some helpful background. Suffice it to say for now that Sarah was protected by the Lord, and Abraham was treated very well, perhaps in an attempt by Pharaoh to impress Sarah and gain her favor. Abraham was invited by Pharaoh to teach in his court (see Facsimile No. 3). We learn from Josephus, the Jewish historian, that Abraham was invited to teach mathematics and astronomy while there. This would, of course, be in addition to the gospel. It appears likely that they stayed twelve to thirteen years in Egypt, and Genesis 13:2 tells us that they were wealthy when they left.

GENESIS 12

Many things happen in this short chapter. Abraham and his group leave Ur, as commanded by Jehovah (the premortal Christ). Moses, the writer of Genesis, summarizes the basic Abrahamic covenant that the Lord made with Abraham at this point. Although Abraham and Sarah have not yet been able to have children, he is promised that large numbers of people will descend from him and Sarah, and that through him "shall all families of the earth be blessed" (verse 2).

After having left Ur, Abraham and those with him will settle for a time in Haran (in present-day Turkey, some 350–400 miles northeast of Jerusalem) and gather great wealth while there, as well as many converts to the gospel. Eventually, he and his followers will journey southwest, through Canaan (basically the Holy Land today) and, because of famine, will continue south and west into Egypt.

As he enters Egyptian territory, there will be much interest in Sarah shown by Egyptian princes, who will call Pharaoh's attention to her because of her great beauty. We will talk more about the Lord's instructions to Abraham and Sarah on this matter when we get to verses 11–13. Abraham will gain much additional wealth while in Egypt and then will be requested to leave when Pharaoh discovers that Sarah is not only his "sister" but also his wife, thus discovering why things went badly for Pharaoh whenever he attempted to make advances toward Sarah.

Note that Abram's name will be changed to "Abraham" in Genesis 17:5. We will say more about that when we get there.

We will now proceed with chapter 12.

1 Now **the Lord** had **said unto Abram, Get thee out of thy country** [*Haran, where he had apparently lived for some time now*], and from thy kindred [*relatives*], and from thy father's house [*his immediate family*], unto a land that I will shew thee:

In verses 2–3, next, we see a very basic summary of the Abrahamic covenant, which is the heritage of all faithful, baptized, covenant-keeping members of the Church. Such faithful members are often referred to as "Israel" because these covenants were renewed and reconfirmed through Jacob, Abraham's grandson, whose name was changed to "Israel" (see Genesis 32:28).

Keep in mind that the blessings of the Abrahamic covenant go far beyond this mortal life. In fact, they extend into the eternities. They are the blessings and covenants of the gospel of Jesus Christ that, when kept, lead to exaltation, becoming gods, and creating worlds for our own spirit children. In fact, we know through modern revelation that Abraham has already become a god (see Doctrine and Covenants 132:29, 37).

Note that one of the responsibilities of the Abrahamic covenant is that of missionary work, taking the gospel and priesthood blessings to others.

2 And **I will make of thee a great nation** [*Israel; symbolically, having innumerable spirit offspring as gods*], and **I will bless thee, and make thy name great** [*this has literally happened to Abraham on this world; symbolically, those who become gods will be "great" to the inhabitants of the worlds they create and fill with people*]; and **thou shalt be a blessing** [*Abraham will be a blessing to countless others*]:

3 And **I will bless them that bless thee, and curse him that curseth thee** [*Abraham will have the help of the Lord to eventually triumph over all things, whether in this life or in the life to come; so also with righteous saints in all ages*]: and **in thee shall all families of the earth be blessed** [*our responsibility, as was Abraham's, is to do all we can to spread the blessings of the gospel to all people*].

4 **So Abram departed** [*from Haran*], **as the Lord had spoken unto him; and Lot** [*his nephew*] **went with him**: and Abram *was* seventy and five years old when he departed out of Haran [*in the Pearl of Great Price, Abraham says that he was sixty-two years old when he departed—see Abraham 2:14*].

> In verse 1, above, Abraham was told to leave his extended family behind as he heads toward Canaan. In verse 4, above and 5, next, we see that the only family member he and Sarah took with them was Lot. We know that his father, Terah, had returned to idolatry while in Haran (Abraham 2:5), and it may be that other family members were also unwilling to follow the Lord. Whatever the case, Abraham knows what it is like to leave all in order to keep God's commandments.

5 And **Abram took Sarai his wife, and Lot his brother's son**, and all their substance that they had gathered [*he had gained great wealth while living in Haran*], and the souls [*we understand these to be converts—see Abraham 2:15*] that they had gotten in Haran; **and they went forth to go into the land of Canaan**; and into the land of Canaan they came.

6 And Abram passed through the land unto the place of Sichem, unto

the plain of Moreh. And the Canaanite [*descendants of Cain through Ham and Egypt—compare with Bible Dictionary, under "Canaanite"*] *was* then in the land.

> Next, the Savior appears to Abraham and promises to give the land of Canaan to his descendants. It will eventually become known basically as the land of Israel.

7 And **the Lord** [*Jehovah, the premortal Jesus Christ*] **appeared unto Abram, and said, Unto thy seed** [*descendants*] **will I give this land**: and **there builded he an altar** unto the Lord, who appeared unto him.

> In verse 7, above, and verse 8, next, Abraham builds altars to worship the Lord. From the time of Adam and Eve to the time of Christ, altars were built and firstborn, ritually clean, male animals, including lambs without blemish, were offered as sacrifices, symbolizing the coming sacrifice of the "Lamb of God"—in other words, the Only Begotten Son of God. As you have already observed, Abraham is a faithful follower of Jesus Christ and, as such, is faithful in his formal worship as well as in all other aspects of his life. He serves as an example of faithfulness and obedience to all of us.

8 And he removed from thence [*he moved from there*] unto a mountain on the east of Beth-el, and pitched his tent, *having* Beth-el on the west, and Hai on the east: **and there he builded an altar unto the Lord**, and called upon the name of the Lord.

9 And **Abram journeyed, going on still toward the south**.

> Next, because of the famine, Abraham heads toward Egypt. Because Sarah, his wife, is beautiful, it is highly likely that he will be killed so that the Pharaoh can marry her. Consequently, as they enter Egypt, Abraham introduces Sarah as his sister. Unfortunately, verses 10–13, next, in the Bible, do not mention that God told Abraham to tell the Egyptians that Sarah is his sister. This is a significant omission in the Bible, since it sheds a bad light on Abraham. We will first read these four verses in Genesis, then quote from Abraham's account of this situation from the Pearl of Great Price.

10 ¶ And **there was a famine in the land** [*of Canaan*]: and **Abram went down into Egypt** to sojourn [*stay for a time*] there; for the famine *was* grievous in the land.

11 And it came to pass, **when he was come near to enter into Egypt**, that **he said unto Sarai** his wife, Behold now, I know that **thou** *art* **a fair** [*beautiful*] **woman to look upon**:

12 **Therefore** it shall come to pass, **when the Egyptians shall see thee**, that **they shall say, This** *is* **his wife: and they will kill me, but they will save thee alive** [*to marry*].

13 **Say, I pray thee** [*please*], **thou** *art* **my sister: that it may be well with me for thy sake** [*so that I can remain alive to look out for you*]; **and my soul** [*body*] **shall live because of thee.**

We will now quote the equivalent verses from Abraham, in the Pearl of Great Price. Note especially that the Lord tells Abraham to tell the Egyptians that Sarah is his sister. Whatever the Lord commands becomes the righteous thing to do.

Abraham 2:21–25

21 And I, Abraham, journeyed, going on still towards the south; and there was a continuation of a famine in the land; and I, Abraham, concluded to go down into Egypt, to sojourn there, for the famine became very grievous.

22 And it came to pass when I was come near to enter into Egypt, **the Lord said unto me**: Behold, Sarai, thy wife, is a very fair woman to look upon;

23 Therefore it shall come to pass, when the Egyptians shall see her, they will say—She is his wife; and they will kill you, but they will save her alive; therefore see that ye do on this wise [*here is what you should do*]:

24 **Let her say unto the Egyptians, she is thy sister**, and thy soul shall live [*your body will remain alive*].

Next, in verse 25, Abraham brings the subject up with his wife.

25 And it came to pass that **I, Abraham, told Sarai, my wife, all that the Lord had said unto me**—Therefore **say unto them** [*the Egyptians*], I pray thee [*please*], **thou art my sister, that it may be well with me for thy sake** [*so that I can remain alive and also watch out for you*]**, and my soul shall live because of thee** [*you can save my life*].

Biblical scholars have indicated that it is highly likely that Sarah was legally Abraham's sister, in the culture of their day. We will say more about this in a minute. In the meantime, by culture and tradition, the Egyptian pharaohs at this time in Egypt would never commit adultery with another man's wife. But they didn't hesitate to murder a man if they desired his wife. After killing the man, his wife would then be "available." Thus, they could marry her and would not be committing adultery. We will quote from the *Old Testament Student Manual*, using **bold** for teaching emphasis:

"The idea that Abraham, the great man of righteousness, seems to have told a deliberate lie in order to protect his own life has troubled many students of the Old Testament. That his life was in danger because of Sarah's beauty seems quite clear. It seems peculiar, but **whereas the Egyptian pharaohs had a strong aversion to committing adultery with another man's wife, they had no qualms about murdering the man to free his spouse for remarriage**.

"'To kill the husband in order to possess himself of his wife seems to have been a common royal custom in those days. A papyrus tells of a Pharaoh who, acting on the advice of one of his princes, sent armed men to fetch a beautiful woman and make away with her husband. Another Pharaoh is promised by his priest on his tombstone, that even after death he will kill Palestinian sheiks and include their wives in his harem'" (Kasher, *Encyclopedia of Biblical Interpretation,* Vol. 2, page 128).

"Some **scholars have noted that Abraham could validly state that Sarah was his sister. First of all, the Hebrew words brother and sister were often used for other blood relatives**. (See Genesis 14:14, in which Lot, Abraham's nephew, is called 'his brother.') Because Abraham and Haran, Sarah's father, were brothers, Sarah was Abraham's niece and thus could be called "sister."

"Another ancient custom permitted a woman to be adopted as a man's sister upon their marriage to give her greater legal and social status (see *Encyclopedia Judaica,* s.v. 'Sarah,' 14:866). Also, it is not unlikely that when Haran died Terah legally adopted Haran's children as his own, thus making Sarah Abraham's sister" (*Old Testament Student Manual: Genesis–2 Samuel,* page 66).

Since this issue about Abraham's saying that Sarah was his sister is a rather big problem to many Christians, we will include more quotes here to help understand what he did.

Elder Mark E. Peterson, of the Twelve, explained this situation as follows:

"To protect himself, Abraham had told Pharaoh that Sarah was his sister, which of course she was. Had he divulged that she was his wife, he might have been slain. But as his sister, Pharaoh was willing to buy her at a good price" (*Abraham, Friend of God* (Salt Lake City: Deseret Book, 1979), page 69).

Bruce R. McConkie taught:

"The Lord never sends apostles and prophets and righteous men to minister to his people without placing women of like spiritual stature at their sides. Adam stands as the great high priest, under Christ, to rule as a natural patriarch over all men of all ages, but he cannot rule alone; Eve, his wife, rules at his side, having like caliber and attainments to his own. Abraham is tested as few men have been when the Lord commands him to offer Isaac upon the altar (Gen. 22:1–19); and Sarah struggles with like problems when the Lord directs that she withhold from the Egyptians her status as Abraham's wife. . . . And so it goes, in all dispensations and at all times when there are holy men there are also holy women. Neither stands alone before the Lord. The exaltation of the one is dependent upon that of the other" (*Doctrinal New Testament Commentary,* Vol. 3, page 302).

As already stated, many Christians are quite critical of Abraham, claiming that it was out of character and disappointing that such an otherwise great man would lie to the Egyptians about his wife. An *Ensign* article regarding this matter, written by S. Kent Brown, is helpful. Here is a quote from it:

"For Abraham and Sarah, Egypt constituted a place of refuge from the famine raging at the time of their arrival in Canaan (see Gen. 12:10). Interestingly, while Abraham and

Sarah enjoyed respite from Canaan's drought, their visit to Egypt provided Sarah with one of her most difficult trials.

"Most are familiar with the story of Sarah posing as Abraham's sister (see Gen. 12:11–15). Even though Abraham later insisted that Sarah was his sister through his father, but not his mother (see Gen. 20:12), many students have felt confused with this explanation. It was not until the discovery of ancient Hurrian legal texts at the site of Nuzi, a city east of Ashur, the capital of ancient Assyria, that we obtained a clearer background for this incident.

"The Hurrians were people who flourished about the time of Abraham, and later. Their kingdom included the land of Haran in which Abraham and Sarah lived for a number of years before moving to Canaan (see Gen. 11:31; Gen. 12:5). Interestingly, only in stories dealing with Sarah and Rebecca do we find the claim made that the wife was also a sister to her husband (see Gen. 12:10–20; Gen. 20:2–6; Gen. 26:1–11). Rebecca, like Sarah, spent her youth growing up in Haran, no doubt in contact with Hurrians.

"The contact is important when we learn that under Hurrian law women were frequently adopted as sisters by their husbands either before or during the marriage ceremony. Such a dual status, both wife and sister, had important consequences for a woman. It guaranteed to her special legal and social protections and opportunities which were simply not available to women in any other culture of the Near East. Because Sarah had lived within the Hurrian culture for a number of years, it is not unlikely that she enjoyed this status in her marriage, a status common among Hurrians. Therefore, Abraham's claim that Sarah was his sister upon their entry into the land of Egypt is not far-fetched in the least. Further, it is possible that Terah, Abraham's father, had adopted Sarah before her marriage to Abraham and that this is the meaning of the passage in Genesis 20:12. This particular practice on the part of a prospective father-in-law, is documented from the Nuzi tablets. (See E. A. Speiser, 'The Wife-Sister Motif in the Patriarchal Narratives,' in biblical and Other Studies, Cambridge, Mass.: Harvard Univ. Press, 1963, pages 15–28.)

"In Genesis Abraham is said to have insisted that Sarah was his sister because he feared for his life. The incident is clarified in the book of Abraham where we learn it was revealed to Abraham that Sarah would maintain that she was his sister (see Abraham 2:21–25).

"This placed the burden on Sarah. Would she risk her own rights as wife in order to preserve the life of her husband as the Lord had asked? Indeed, Sarah's visit to Egypt became a period of intense trial for her. Even though the Lord protected her from the pharaoh's intent to make her his wife—and protected her virtue—the pharaoh was nevertheless allowed to take her into his household (Genesis 12:15–20). We see, then, that Egypt represented at the same time a haven from the famine and a place of testing for Sarah" ("Biblical Egypt: Land of Refuge, Land of Bondage," *Ensign*, September 1980, pages 45, 47).

As we continue with Genesis 12, we see that, just as Abraham was told by the Lord, the Egyptians were quite taken by Sarah's beauty, and, in order to try to influence Sarah favorably, they treated Abraham, her "brother," very well (verse 16).

14 ¶ And it came to pass, that, when Abram was come into Egypt, **the Egyptians beheld the woman that she *was* very fair**.

15 **The princes** also **of Pharaoh saw her, and commended her before** [*recommended her to*] **Pharaoh: and the woman** [*Sarah*] **was taken into Pharaoh's house**.

It would appear at the end of verse 15, above, that Sarah is now in great danger, especially as far as the law of chastity is concerned. She is. However, the Lord protected her as reported in verse 17. In the meantime, verse 16, next, tells us that the Egyptian royalty treated Abraham very well in their attempts to win Sarah over.

16 And **he entreated Abram well for her sake** [*treated Abraham well in order to gain his favor as well as Sarah's*]: and he had **sheep**, and **oxen**, and **he asses**, and **menservants**, and **maidservants**, and **she asses**, and **camels**.

As previously mentioned, verse 17, next, says, in effect, that Pharaoh's advances toward Sarah were met with disaster after disaster. While this period of time in Egypt would have been a great trial for Sarah, her faith was no doubt strengthened as she saw the hand of the Lord protect her time after time.

17 And **the Lord plagued Pharaoh and his house with great plagues because of Sarai Abram's wife**.

When Pharaoh discovers that Sarah is Abraham's wife, he finds out the source of his unusual troubles and sends Abraham and his wife and company away from Egypt.

18 And **Pharaoh called Abram, and said, What *is* this *that* thou hast done unto me? why didst thou not tell me that she *was* thy wife?**

19 Why saidst thou, She *is* my sister? so I might have taken her to me to wife: now therefore behold thy wife, **take *her*, and go thy way**.

20 And Pharaoh commanded *his* men concerning him: and **they sent him away, and his wife, and all that he had**.

Josephus, the Jewish historian, tells of this time in Egypt for Abraham and Sarah. He misses the fact that the Lord instructed Abraham to introduce Sarah as his sister, but his account has some interesting information about the Pharaoh's problems (**bolded** for emphasis) while attempting to marry Sarah.

Antiquities of the Jews, Book 1, chapter 8, verses 1–2

1 Now, after this, when a famine had invaded the land of Canaan,

and Abram had discovered that the Egyptians were in a flourishing condition, he was disposed to go down to them. . . . Now, seeing he was to take Sarai with him, and was afraid of the madness of the Egyptians with regard to women, lest the king should kill him on occasion of his wife's great beauty, he contrived this device:—he pretended to be her brother, and directed her in a dissembling way to pretend the same, for he said it would be for their benefit. Now, as soon as he came into Egypt, it happened to Abram as he supposed it would; for the fame of his wife's beauty was greatly talked of; for which reason **Pharaoh**, the king of Egypt, would not be satisfied with what was reported of her, but would needs see her himself, and **was preparing to enjoy her; but God put a stop to his unjust inclinations, by sending upon him a distemper, and a sedition against his government**. And when he inquired of the priests how he might be freed from these calamities, they told him that this his miserable condition was derived from the wrath of God, upon account of his inclinations to abuse the stranger's wife. He then, out of fear, asked Sarai who she was, and who it was that she brought along with her. And when he had found out the truth, he excused himself to Abram, that supposing the woman to be his sister, and not his wife, he set his affections on her, as desiring an affinity with him by marrying her, but not as incited by lust to abuse her. He also made him a large present in money, and gave him leave to enter into conversation with the most learned among the Egyptians [*see Facsimile No. 3 in the Pearl of Great Price for a representation of this*]; from which conversation his virtue and his reputation became more conspicuous than they had been before.

In verse 2, next, of Josephus's account, we learn that, in addition to the gospel of Jesus Christ, Abraham also taught mathematics and astronomy to the Egyptians while he was there.

2 For whereas the Egyptians were formerly addicted to different customs, and despised one another's sacred and accustomed rites, and were very angry one with another on that account, Abram conferred with each of them, and, confuting the reasonings they made use of, every one for their own practices. demonstrated that such reasonings were vain and void of truth: whereupon he was admired by them in those conferences as a very wise man, and one of great sagacity, when he discoursed on any subject he undertook; and this not only in understanding it, but in persuading other men also to assent to him. **He communicated to them arithmetic, and delivered to them the science of astronomy**; for before Abram came into Egypt they were unacquainted with those parts of learning; for that science came from the Chaldeans into Egypt, and from thence to the Greeks also (Josephus, Flavius, *Antiquities of the Jews*, Book 1, chapter 8, verses 1–2).

GENESIS 13

As Abraham leaves Egypt, he is a very wealthy man. As we will see in this chapter, he is one who can handle great wealth without being corrupted by it. His nephew, Lot, has not progressed to that point in his personal growth. Even though Lot is out of line in his request to have the best land, Abraham gives it to him, thus demonstrating the generous nature of his heart.

1 And **Abram went up out of Egypt**, he, and his wife, and all that he had, and Lot with him, into the south [*the southern part of the Holy Land, today*].

2 And **Abram** *was* **very rich** in cattle, in silver, and in gold.

3 And he went on his journeys from the south even **to Beth-el** [*about ten to fifteen miles north of modern day Jerusalem*], unto the place where his tent had been at the beginning, between Beth-el and Hai;

4 **Unto the place of the altar** [*Genesis 12:8*], which he had made there at the first [*when he initially traveled southwest from Haran, through Canaan, and then to Egypt*]: and **there Abram called on the name of the Lord**.

> Next, in verses 5–11, we see Lot, who has been traveling with his Uncle Abraham for several years now, selfishly choose the best land for his herds and flocks. Abraham generously allows him to do so, even though Abraham, as leader of the clan, has every right to take the best for himself, according to his culture, and leave the leftovers to others in the group. Among other celestial attributes of Abraham evident here,
we see his strong desire to be a peacemaker.

5 ¶ And **Lot** [*Abraham's nephew*] also, which went with Abram, **had flocks, and herds, and tents**.

6 And **the land was not able to bear them** [*their herds, flocks, and followers were so numerous that there was not room for both to thrive in the same general area*], that they might dwell together: for **their substance was great, so that they could not dwell together**.

7 And there was a strife [*disagreement, trouble*] between the herdmen of Abram's cattle [*domesticated animals*] and the herdmen of Lot's cattle: and the Canaanite and the Perizzite dwelled then in the land.

8 And **Abram said unto Lot, Let there be no strife, I pray thee, between me and thee**, and between my herdmen and thy herdmen; for **we** *be* **brethren**.

9 *Is* **not the whole land before thee** [*can you see all this land before us*]? separate thyself, I pray thee, from me: **if** *thou wilt take* **the left hand, then I will go to the right**; or **if** *thou depart* **to the right hand, then I will go to the left**.

10 And **Lot** lifted up his eyes, and **beheld** [*looked at*] **all the plain of Jordan**, that it *was* **well watered every where**, before the Lord destroyed Sodom and Gomorrah [*Sodom and Gomorrah were thriving centers of wickedness at this time; we will read about*

their destruction in Genesis 19:24–25], **even as the garden of the Lord** [*the land that Lot was looking at was like the Garden of Eden*], like the land of Egypt, as thou comest unto Zoar.

11 Then Lot chose him all the plain of Jordan; and Lot journeyed east: and they separated themselves the one from the other.

> We see, in verse 12, next, that, in addition to choosing the best land, Lot also had a weakness for wanting to live on the edge as far as wickedness is concerned. He apparently felt that it would provide pleasure to be near Sodom.

12 Abram dwelled in the land of Canaan, and **Lot dwelled in the cities of the plain** [*which had a reputation for their wickedness*]**, and pitched *his* tent toward Sodom**.

> The phrase, "pitched his tent toward Sodom," in verse 12, above, seems to have more meaning than merely saying that he had the door of his tent facing Sodom. We see a similar phrase in the Book of Mormon. In Mosiah 2:6, King Benjamin's people pitched their tents with the doorways facing the temple. The phrase implies that their hearts were toward the temple, desiring God's word and instruction, being loyal to the gospel.
>
> Similarly, Lot's pitching his tent "toward Sodom" implies that Lot's heart was inclined toward the wickedness in Sodom. This unbridled yearning will later lead to the demise of his wife and the undoing of him and his family.

> Verse 13, next, leads us to understand the dangers of Lot's being a bystander, watching the doings of the Sodomites. One of the great sins of Sodom was homosexuality (see footnote 13b in your Bible). We see this evidenced in Genesis 19:5. Homosexuality was forbidden among covenant Israel as stated in Deuteronomy 23:17.

13 But the men of Sodom *were* wicked and sinners before the Lord exceedingly.

> One of the major messages Moses (the writer of Genesis) is pointing out to us here is the difference the thoughts and desires of our hearts make. He is emphasizing Lot as an example of one who may not participate directly in evil, but derives satisfaction in watching it.
>
> Abraham, on the other hand, is an example of one who diligently strives to be loyal to God in all ways. As a result, his personal righteousness and progress toward celestial character traits are constantly increasing. Next, in verses 14–17, the Lord (Jehovah) repeats a portion of the covenant He has previously discussed with Abraham (see Genesis 12:7, then 12:2–3; see also Genesis 17:2–8). One of the important messages for us in this repetition of the details of the covenant to Abraham is that we need repetition—thus, the importance of faithfully attending our church meetings, attending the temple, reading the scriptures, etc.

14 ¶ And the Lord said unto Abram, after that Lot was separated from him, **Lift up now thine eyes, and look** from the place where thou art **northward**, and **southward**, and **eastward**, and **westward**:

> The JST adds an entire verse here. It fits after verse 14, above, even though the verse numbering is different:

JST Genesis 13:13

> 13 And remember the covenant which I make with thee; for it shall be an everlasting covenant; and thou shalt remember the days of Enoch thy father [*ancestor*];

> One of the important things we are reminded of in this addition from the JST is the fact that the covenant made with Abraham was not a new covenant. It was a renewal of the covenants of exaltation for the faithful, previously made with Enoch (as pointed out above), as well as with Noah and the faithful back to Adam and Eve. The covenants of exaltation began with Adam and Eve, as far as this earth is concerned (see, for example, Moses 6:51–52, 64–68).

> Through making and keeping these covenants we can become like our Father in Heaven and enjoy the same fullness of eternal glory that He enjoys. These covenants, contained in the full gospel of Jesus Christ and administered by the priesthood, are the basic tools by which we may climb to the eternal heights already attained by our Father.

15 For **all the land which thou seest, to thee will I give it, and to thy seed for ever**.

16 **And I will make thy seed as the dust of the earth**: so that if a man can number the dust of the earth, *then* shall thy seed also be numbered.

> In verses 15–16, above, there is an implication regarding the Abrahamic covenant and the faithful Saints who participate in it that extends far beyond the land that Abraham could physically see with his eyes. You might ask how anyone could have this land "forever" (end of verse 15), since our lives are limited to a relatively few years. The answer is simple.

> This earth will become the celestial kingdom for the faithful Saints who live on it (see Doctrine and Covenants 130:9–11). Therefore, they will live on it forever. The posterity as numerous as the particles of "dust of the earth," spoken of in verse 16, above, is symbolic of having an infinite posterity of spirit children, as gods, after attaining exaltation. Exalted beings will have "a continuation of the seeds forever and ever" (see Doctrine and Covenants 132:19, end of verse).

17 Arise, walk through the land in the length of it and in the breadth of it; for I will give it unto thee.

18 Then Abram removed his tent, and came and dwelt in the plain of Mamre, which *is* in Hebron [*about twenty miles south of Jerusalem, as the crow flies*], and built there an altar unto the Lord.

GENESIS 14

With Lot and his people gone to settle in the area of Sodom, Abraham and his followers who have settled in Canaan still constitute a rather large population, with at least 318 men capable of serving as soldiers (see verse 14). We will see Abraham lead these soldiers to rescue Lot, who gets taken captive (verses 1–16).

One of the most important doctrines mentioned in this chapter is tithing (verse 20). This chapter shows us that Abraham paid tithing, and it allows us to teach nonmembers that the law of tithing is taught in the Bible.

Melchizedek is just barely mentioned here in the Bible, as Abraham pays tithing to him (verses 18–20) We will learn much more about him through modern revelation. But, for now, if you stop and look at these Bible verses carefully, some important insights begin to unfold. For example, why does such an important man as Abraham, who is the head of an entire gospel dispensation, pay tithing to Melchizedek? Is the "bread and wine" mentioned in verse 18 the sacrament? What position of authority is held by Melchizedek such that he would be the one to bless Abraham? As we come to Melchizedek in this chapter, we will point out several marvelous answers to these questions taken from modern revelation. By the way, Melchizedek is also briefly mentioned elsewhere in the Bible (Psalm 110:4; Hebrews 5:6; 10; 6:20; 7:1–28).

But first, a bit of background about the "kings" mentioned in these first several verses. When we think of kings today, we generally think of powerful monarchs ruling over vast empires. However, the kings who are battling each other in this chapter are kings over what we call "city-states." A city-state is basically a city and its surrounding territory ruled over by a king. These kings often made alliances with each other for protection and mutual advantage over other city-states. Thus, we are seeing several kings allied together fighting against other local kings. In the process, Lot and his group, who were living in Sodom (verse 12) near the southern end of the Dead Sea at the time, will be captured and taken some 180 miles north to Dan (about 25 miles north of the Sea of Galilee).

As we begin our study of this chapter, we see several of these kings mentioned who ruled over city-states.

1 And it came to pass in the days of **Amraphel** king of Shinar, **Arioch** king of Ellasar, **Chedorlaomer** king of Elam, and **Tidal** king of nations;

2 *That these* **made war with Bera** king of Sodom [*where Lot was living—see verse 12*], and with **Birsha** king of Gomorrah, **Shinab** king of Admah, and **Shemeber** king of Zeboiim, **and the king of Bela**, which is Zoar.

3 All these were joined together in the vale [*valley, lowlands area*] of Siddim, which is the salt sea [*the Dead Sea*].

4 Twelve years they served Chedorlaomer, and in the thirteenth year they rebelled.

5 And in the fourteenth year came Chedorlaomer, and the kings that *were* with him, and smote the

Rephaims in Ashteroth Karnaim, and the Zuzims in Ham, and the Emims in Shaveh Kiriathaim,

6 And the Horites in their mount Seir, unto El-paran, which *is* by the wilderness.

7 And they returned, and came to En-mishpat, which *is* Kadesh, and smote all the country of the Amalekites, and also the Amorites, that dwelt in Hazezon-tamar.

8 **And there went out the king of Sodom**, and **the king of Gomorrah**, and the king of **Admah**, and the king of **Zeboiim**, and the king of **Bela** (the same *is* Zoar;) and they **joined battle with them** in the vale of Siddim [*a valley or lowlands area by the Dead Sea*];

9 With Chedorlaomer the king of Elam, and with Tidal king of nations, and Amraphel king of Shinar, and Arioch king of Ellasar; four kings with five.

10 And the vale of Siddim *was full of* slimepits [*bitumen; asphalt pits*]; and **the kings of Sodom and Gomorrah fled, and fell there** [*were defeated*]; and they that remained fled to the mountain.

JST Genesis 14:9

9 And the vale of Siddim was filled with slime pits; and the kings of Sodom and Gomorrah fled and fell there; and they that remained fled to the mountain **which was called Hanabal.**

While the JST addition to Genesis, verse 10, above, is perhaps not a major change, it is nevertheless a reminder to us of the prophetic calling of Joseph Smith. Also, remember, as previously mentioned, that the verse numbering in the JST is quite often different than the Bible, as is the case here.

11 And they [*the victorious kings*] took all the goods of Sodom and Gomorrah, and all their victuals [*food supplies*], and went their way.

12 **And they took Lot**, Abram's brother's son, who dwelt in Sodom, **and his goods, and departed**.

Next, Abraham receives news that Lot has been captured and taken away.

It is significant to note that Abraham is referred to as a "Hebrew" in verse 13. This is the first time in Genesis that he is referred to as such. His descendants were commonly called "Hebrews" as well as "Israelites."

The JST addition here will emphasize Abraham's personal righteousness.

13 ¶ And there came one that had escaped, and told **Abram the Hebrew**; for he dwelt in the plain of Mamre [*a bit north of Hebron and west of the Dead Sea*] the Amorite, brother of Eschol, and brother of Aner: and these *were* confederate with [*allies of*] Abram.

JST Genesis 14:12

12 And there came one that had escaped, and told Abram the Hebrew, **the man of God**, for he dwelt in the plain of Mamre the Amorite, brother

of Eschol, and brother of Aner; and these were confederate with Abram.

14 And **when Abram heard that his brother** [*Lot*] **was taken captive, he armed his trained** *servants,* born in his own house, **three hundred and eighteen**, and pursued *them* unto Dan [*about twenty-five miles north of the Sea of Galilee*].

JST Genesis 14:13

13 And when Abram heard that **Lot, his brother's son,** was taken captive, he armed his **trained men**, and they which were born in his own house, three hundred and eighteen, and pursued unto Dan.

In verses 15–16, next, Abraham determines a military strategy to rescue Lot and succeeds.

15 And **he** [*Abraham*] **divided himself** [*deployed his soldiers in groups*] **against them** [*Lot's captors*], he and his servants, by night, **and smote them**, and pursued them unto Hobah, which *is* on the left hand of Damascus.

16 **And he** brought back all the goods, and also **brought again his brother Lot, and his goods, and the women also, and the people.**

One of the important lessons for us in the above verses is the fact that Abraham, a man of peace, did not hesitate to go to war when circumstances required it. This is especially helpful to us in our day, when many well-meaning people protest any and all wars. While their motives may be sincere, they fail to see the future. Captain Moroni, also a man of peace and mercy, rallied his armies in the cause of preserving "their liberty, their lands, their wives, and their children, and their peace" as well as their right to worship God (Alma 48:10–14).

17 ¶ **And the king of Sodom went out to meet him** after his return from the slaughter of Chedorlaomer, and of the kings that *were* with him, at the valley of Shaveh, which *is* the king's dale.

The JST changes next will be very significant because they show us that the sacrament was administered in ancient times when the full gospel was available on earth.

18 And Melchizedek king of Salem brought forth bread and wine: and he *was* the priest of the most high God.

JST Genesis 14:17

17 And **Melchizedek**, king of Salem, **brought forth bread and wine; and he break bread and blest it; and he blest the wine**, he being the priest of the most high God,

President John Taylor spoke of Melchizedek and the sacrament. He taught (**bold** added for emphasis):

"We will now turn to Melchizedek, of whom it is written in King James' translation:

"'And Melchizedek, king of Salem, brought forth bread and wine: and he was the priest of the most high God. And he blessed him, and said, Blessed be Abram of the most high God, possessor of heaven and earth: and blessed be the most high God, which hath delivered thine enemies into thy hand. And he gave him tithes of all.'—Gen., xiv, 18–20.

"This passage is given with greater completeness in the inspired translation [*the JST*], where it appears as follows:

"'And Melchizedek, King of Salem, brought forth bread and wine; and he brake bread and blessed it; and he blessed the wine, he being the priest of the Most High God; and he gave to Abram, and he blessed him, and said, Blessed Abram, thou art a man of the Most High God, possessor of heaven and of earth; and blessed is the name of the Most High God, which hath delivered thine enemies into thine hand. And Abram gave him tithes of all he had taken.'

"In **this action of Melchizedek, in administering the bread and wine**, by virtue of his priestly office, **is there not a representation of the body and blood of our Lord and Savior Jesus Christ**, as also indicated by the Messiah Himself when He partook of the passover [*Passover*] with His disciples? For Melchizedek was a great High Priest, of the same order and like Priesthood as was held by the Son of God. So great, indeed, that 'before his day it was called the Holy Priesthood, after the order of the Son of God; but out of respect or reverence to the name of the Supreme Being, to avoid the too frequent repetition of his name, they, the church, in ancient days, called that Priesthood after Melchizedek, or the Melchizedek Priesthood.'—Doctrine and Covenants, Sec. 107, Par. 3, 4, page 383" (*Mediation and Atonement* [Salt Lake City: *Deseret News*, 1882], 83–84).

As you know, in Old Testament times, animal sacrifices were administered by the priesthood as an ordinance that pointed the minds of the people forward to the coming sacrifice of the Son of God. It is interesting that the sacrament was administered here by Melchizedek. Perhaps it is a reminder to us that the full gospel of Jesus Christ was available to the righteous in ancient times.

19 And he blessed him, and said, Blessed *be* Abram of the most high God, possessor of heaven and earth:

20 And blessed be the most high God, which hath delivered thine enemies into thy hand. And he gave him tithes of all.

JST Genesis 14:18–20

18 And **he gave** [*the sacrament*] **to Abram**, and he blessed him, and said, Blessed Abram, thou art a man of the most high God, possessor of heaven and of earth;

19 And blessed is the name of the most high God, which hath delivered thine enemies into thine hand.

20 And **Abram gave him tithes of all he had taken** [*all he had added to his wealth, as a result of winning the battle and rescuing lot*].

As you can see, the last sentence of Genesis, verse 20, above, tells us that Abraham paid tithing to Melchizedek. This indicates that

Melchizedek was the presiding authority over the Church in that area.

The law of tithing is given in Doctrine and Covenants 119. Again, it is interesting that this law, which is a part of the gospel in our day, was also a part of the gospel in Abraham's day. It is another reminder that the full gospel of Jesus Christ has been available on earth whenever a people was willing to abide by it.

The fact that Abraham paid his tithing to Melchizedek is also an indicator that Melchizedek had the stewardship over the Lord's storehouse in that area (see JST, verse 37, below).

In verses 21–24, next, the King of Sodom expresses a desire to reward Abraham for what he has done. Abraham refuses anything other than repayment for expenses incurred. He does not impose his own unselfishness on some of the young men who fought along side of him and his soldiers. Rather, he allows them to take spoils of war if they so desire. We will read these verses now, using **bold** to point out the story line.

21 And **the king of Sodom said unto Abram, Give me the persons, and take the goods** [*the material things captured during the battle*] **to thyself.**

22 And **Abram said to the king of Sodom, I have lift up mine hand** [*covenanted*] **unto the Lord**, the most high God, the possessor of heaven and earth,

23 That I will not *take* from a thread even to a shoelatchet, and that I will not take any thing that *is* thine, lest thou shouldest say, I have made Abram rich:

Note that the Joseph Smith Translation of the Bible adds the phrase "And have sworn" to verse 23 denoting that Abraham had covenanted not to take anything at all from the king of Sodom. It may well be that he had covenanted to completely avoid anything that had to do with Sodom and its evil lifestyle.

JST Genesis 14:23

23 And have sworn that I will not take of thee from a thread even to a shoe-latchet, and that I will not take anything that is thine, (lest thou shouldest say, I have made Abram rich;)

24 Save only that which the young men [*Abraham's young soldiers*] have eaten, and the portion of the men which went with me, Aner, Eschol, and Mamre; let them take their portion.

This is the end of Genesis, chapter 14 in the Bible. The JST adds 16 verses here that were left out of the Bible.

JST Genesis 14:24–33

25 **And Melchizedek lifted up his voice and blessed Abram**.

Beginning with verse 26 in the JST, next, we are given some details of Melchizedek's youth.

26 Now **Melchizedek was a man of faith, who wrought righteousness**

[*who did works of righteousness*]; and **when a child he** feared God, and **stopped the mouths of lions, and quenched the violence of fire**.

27 And thus, having been approved of God, **he was ordained an high priest after the order of the covenant which God made with Enoch**,

28 **It being after the order of the son of God** [*it is the same priesthood that Jesus Christ holds*]; which order [*priesthood*] came, **not by man** [*not man-made*], nor the will of man; neither by father nor mother; neither by beginning of days nor end of years [*the priesthood is an eternal power*]; but of God;

29 And **it was delivered unto men by the calling of his** [*Christ's*] **own voice** [*men do not take it upon themselves, rather, must be properly called and ordained—see Hebrews 5:4*], according to his own will, **unto as many as believed on his name** [*in other words, the high priesthood is part of the full gospel of Jesus Christ*].

In verses 30–31, next, we are given a glimpse of the true power and potential of the Melchizedek Priesthood.

30 For God having sworn unto [*covenanted with*] Enoch and unto his seed [*posterity*] with an oath by himself [*as is the case with the "Oath and Covenant of the Priesthood," detailed in Doctrine and Covenants 84:33–41*]; that **every one being ordained after this order** [*the Melchizedek Priesthood*] and calling **should have power, by faith, to break mountains**, to **divide the seas**, to **dry up waters**, to **turn them out of their course**;

31 **To put at defiance the armies of nations**, to **divide the earth**, to **break every band**, to **stand in the presence of God**; to **do all things according to his will**, according to his command, **subdue principalities and powers**; and this by the will of the Son of God which was from before the foundation of the world [*who became the Redeemer in the premortal realm*].

32 And **men** [*such as Enoch*] **having this faith, coming up unto this order of God** [*having attained the office of high priest in the Melchizedek Priesthood*]**, were translated and taken up into heaven**.

33 And now, **Melchizedek was a priest of this order** [*a high priest*]; **therefore he obtained peace in Salem**, and was called the Prince of peace.

The Book of Mormon tells us more of Melchizedek's accomplishments as King over the land of Salem in establishing peace and righteousness among a wicked people. We will add **bold** for emphasis.

Alma 13:14–19

14 Yea, humble yourselves even as the people in the days of Melchizedek, who was also a high priest after this same order which I have spoken,

who also took upon him the high priesthood forever.

15 And **it was this same Melchizedek to whom Abraham paid tithes**; yea, even our father Abraham paid tithes of one-tenth part of all he possessed.

16 Now these ordinances were given after this manner, that thereby the people might look forward on the Son of God, it being a type of his order, or it being his order, and this that they might look forward to him for a remission of their sins, that they might enter into the rest of the Lord.

17 Now **this Melchizedek was a king over the land of Salem**; and **his people had waxed strong in iniquity and abomination; yea, they had all gone astray; they were full of all manner of wickedness**;

18 But **Melchizedek** having exercised mighty faith, and received the office of the high priesthood according to the holy order of God, **did preach repentance unto his people. And behold, they did repent**; and Melchizedek did establish peace in the land in his days; therefore he was called the prince of peace, for he was the king of Salem; and he did reign under his father.

19 Now, there were many before him, and also there were many afterwards, but none were greater; therefore, of him they have more particularly made mention.

As we continue now, with additions provided by the JST, verse 34, next, leads us to believe that Melchizedek and his people were translated and joined the City of Enoch, which had been taken up to heaven (Moses 7:69)

JST Genesis 14:34–40

34 And **his people** wrought righteousness [*became righteous, as shown by their good works*], and **obtained heaven**, and **sought for the city of Enoch** which God had before taken, separating it from the earth [*taking it up to heaven*], **having reserved it unto the latter days, or the end of the world** [*the time of the Second Coming, when it will return to earth to join Zion, the New Jerusalem—see Moses 7:62–63*];

35 And hath said, and sworn with an oath [*covenanted and promised*], that the heavens and the earth should come together [*perhaps a reference to the fact that the Church in heaven will join the Church on earth at the time of the Second Coming and Millennium—see Doctrine and Covenants 65:6*]; and the sons of God should be tried so as by fire.

36 And this **Melchizedek**, having thus established righteousness, was called the king of heaven by his people, or, in other words, **the King of peace** [*he was a "type" of Christ*].

37 And he lifted up his voice, **and he blessed Abram, being the high priest, and the keeper of the storehouse of God;**

38 Him whom God had appointed **to receive tithes for the poor.**

39 Wherefore [*this is why*], Abram paid unto him tithes of all that he had, of all the riches which he possessed, which God had given

him more than that which he had need.

40 And it came to pass, that **God blessed Abram, and gave unto him riches, and honor, and lands for an everlasting possession** [*the earth will become the celestial kingdom for the worthy Saints who have lived on it (see Doctrine and Covenants 130:9–11); thus, Abraham and those who enter faithfully into the Abrahamic covenant will literally have it for "an everlasting possession"*]; **according to the covenant which he had made** [*the Abrahamic covenant*], and according to the blessing wherewith Melchizedek had blessed him.

By way of a few final notes here regarding Melchizedek, we mention that his name literally means "king of righteousness." "Melchi" means "king," and "zedek" means "righteousness."

Also, according to Doctrine and Covenants 84:14, "Abraham received the priesthood from Melchizedek."

Another interesting question occasionally comes up as to whether or not Melchizedek is Shem, Noah's son. Some have speculated that Melchizedek could be Shem because of so many scriptural similarities between the two. However, Doctrine and Covenants 84:14 appears to put considerable distance between Melchizedek and Noah. We will quote it here:

Doctrine and Covenants 84:14

14 Which Abraham received the priesthood from **Melchizedek**, who **received it through the lineage of his fathers** [*ancestors*]**, even till Noah**;

Doctrine and Covenants 84:14, though, can be read two different ways. It can say, in effect, that Melchizedek received the priesthood through the lineage of his ancestors, from Adam down to his father, Noah. Or, it can be understood to say that Melchizedek received the priesthood through the lineage of his ancestors back to Noah. Someday we will find out which is correct.

In conclusion, we will add a quote from an article in the November 1973 *Ensign*, which explores the question as to whether Melchizedek is Shem.

"Let us examine first what we know about Shem. Although the Bible names Shem as the eldest son of Noah (Gen. 5:32), modern-day revelation places Japheth as the eldest (Moses 8:12). Both reports, however, are harmonious in naming Shem as the progenitor of Israel and in the fact that the priesthood descended through Shem to all the great patriarchs after Noah. (1 Chron. 1:24–27.) In this patriarchal order of priesthood, Shem stands next to Noah. He held the keys to the priesthood and was the great high priest of his day.

"Living contemporary with Shem was a man known as Melchizedek, who was also known as the great high priest. The scriptures give us the details of Shem's birth and ancestry but are silent as to his ministry and later life. Of Melchizedek, however, the opposite is true. Nothing is recorded about his birth or ancestry, even though the Book of Mormon states that he did have a father. (Al. 13:17–18.) Concerning his ministry and life we have several interesting and important facts. (Gen. 14:18–20; Heb. 7:1–4; Al. 13:17–18.)

"All of this provokes some questions and calls for answers. Were there two high priests presiding at the same time? Why is the record silent concerning Shem's ministry? Why is nothing known concerning Melchizedek's ancestry?

"Because of this state of knowledge on our part, many Saints and gospel scholars have wondered if these men were the same person. The truth is, we do not know the answer. But an examination of the scriptures is fascinating because it seems to indicate that these men may have been one and the same. For example, here is the case for their oneness:

"1. The inheritance given to Shem included the land of Salem. Melchizedek appears in scripture as the king of Salem, who reigns over this area.

"2. Shem, according to later revelation, reigned in righteousness and the priesthood came through him. Melchizedek appears on the scene with a title that means 'king of righteousness.'

"3. Shem was the great high priest of his day. Abraham honored the high priest Melchizedek by seeking a blessing at his hands and paying him tithes.

"4. Abraham stands next to Shem in the patriarchal order of the priesthood and would surely have received the priesthood from Shem; but Doctrine and Covenants 84:5–17 says Abraham received the priesthood from Melchizedek.

"5. Jewish tradition identifies Shem as Melchizedek.

"6. President Joseph F. Smith's remarkable vision names Shem among the great patriarchs, but no mention is made of Melchizedek.

"7. *Times and Seasons* (15 December 1844, page 746) speaks of 'Shem, who was Melchizedek. . . .'

"On the other hand, there is a case for their being two distinct personalities. Many persons believe Doctrine and Covenants 84:14 is proof that there are perhaps several generations between Melchizedek and Noah. The scripture says, 'Which Abraham received the priesthood from Melchizedek, who received it through the lineage of his fathers, even till Noah.'

"If it does turn out that Shem and Melchizedek are the same person, this scripture should prove no stumbling block, because it could be interpreted to mean that priesthood authority commenced with Adam and came through the fathers, even till Noah, and then to Shem" (Alma E. Gygi, "Is It Possible That Shem and Melchizedek Are the Same Person?" *Ensign*, November 1973, pages 15–16).

It will be most interesting to meet Melchizedek in the next life or during the Millennium and find out much more about this great high priest.

GENESIS 15

Time is marching on and Abraham and Sarah are still childless. With great faith in the Lord's promise of numerous descendants for him (Genesis 13:16), Abraham is now wondering if this promise might be fulfilled in a way other than how he had originally thought. In this chapter, Abraham asks the Lord for permission to designate the son of his foreman, Eliezer, to be his heir (verses 1–3)—in other words, to be the one through whom the promise of posterity for Abraham and Sarah might be fulfilled. Since he was born in Abraham's household, he could thus qualify as a "son" according to the laws and customs of the day. You will see the Lord's answer to this proposal in verses 4–6.

Also, in this chapter (verses 13–14) we will see the prophecy that Abraham's posterity will be afflicted in a strange land for four hundred years (the children of Israel in Egypt).

The Joseph Smith Translation will add four important verses between verses 5 and 6 of the account in Genesis.

As we proceed, we see Abraham, in humble sincerity, propose an alternative plan for an heir.

1 After these things [*the events in Genesis 14*] the word of the Lord came unto Abram in **a vision**, saying, Fear not, Abram: I *am* thy shield, *and* thy exceeding great reward [*including the promise of numerous posterity*].

2 And **Abram said, Lord God, what wilt thou give me, seeing I go childless**, and the steward [*foreman*] of my house *is* this Eliezer of Damascus?

3 And Abram said, Behold, **to me thou hast given no seed** [*Sarah and I have not been able to have children*]: and, lo, **one born in my house is mine heir** [*please let the son of Eliezer (verse 2) be my heir and the one through whom Thy promises to us may be fulfilled*].

The Lord answers Abraham's suggestion very clearly, in verse 4, next.

4 And, behold, the word of the Lord *came* unto him, saying, **This** [*Eliezer's son*] **shall not be thine heir; but he that shall come forth out of thine own bowels** [*the offspring of your own body*] **shall be thine heir.**

Next, the Savior reaffirms His promise of countless posterity to Abraham by having him come out of his tent and gaze up at the stars at night.

5 And **he** [*Jehovah*] **brought him** [*Abraham*] **forth abroad**, and said, **Look now toward heaven, and tell the stars** [*try counting the stars*], **if thou be able to number them** [*if you can count them*]: and he said unto him, **So shall thy seed be** [*you will get an idea of how many posterity you will have*].

As mentioned in the background above, the JST adds four verses between verses 5 and 6 in the Genesis account. We will include them here. As we read them, it becomes obvious that these early Saints knew far more about the Savior, His gospel, and mortal mission than the Old Testament indicates. Abraham asks another question, gets an answer from the Savior, and receives peace.

JST Genesis 15:9–12

9 And **Abram said**, Lord God, **how wilt thou give me this land for an everlasting inheritance?**

10 And the Lord said, **Though thou wast dead, yet am I not able to give it thee** [*is anything impossible with God*]?

In verse 11 of the JST, next, we are given an important eternal perspective. It is that some blessings we expect and hope to receive here in mortality can be received in the next life instead. The end result in eternity is the same.

In being taught this lesson, Abraham will also be taught about the Savior's mortal mission and resurrection.

11 And **if thou shalt die, yet thou shalt possess it** [*as a resurrected being when the earth becomes our celestial planet—see Doctrine and Covenants 130:9–11*], **for the day cometh, that the Son of man** [*Jesus Christ*] **shall live; but how can he live if he be not dead? he must first be quickened** [*resurrected*].

12 And it came to pass, that **Abram looked forth and saw the days of the Son of man** [*Abraham saw the mortal ministry of Christ in vision*], **and was glad, and his soul found rest**, and **he believed in the Lord** [*he had faith in Jesus Christ*]; and the Lord counted it unto him for righteousness.

We now continue with the account as given in Genesis, in the Bible. The first phrase in verse 6, next, gives the key to peace for us, as well as for Abraham.

6 **And he** [*Abraham*] **believed in the Lord**; and he [*the Lord*] counted [*credited*] it to him for righteousness.

7 And **he said unto him, I *am* the Lord that brought thee out of Ur of the Chaldees** [*Abraham's homeland*]**, to give thee this land** [*Canaan*] **to inherit it**.

8 And **he said, Lord God, whereby shall I know that I shall inherit it?**

9 And **he** [*Jehovah*] **said unto him, Take me an heifer** [*a young cow*] of three years old, **and a she goat** of three years old, **and a ram** of three years old, and **a turtledove, and a young pigeon**.

JST Genesis 15:14

14 And Abram said, Lord, whereby shall I know that I shall inherit it? **yet he believed God.** And the Lord said unto him, Take me a heifer of three years old, and a she goat of three years old, and a ram of three years old, and a turtle-dove, and a young pigeon.

In Genesis, verse 9, above, and 10, next, the Lord has Abraham do things that signify making a covenant in his culture (see Jeremiah

34:17–19 for another example of this type of covenant making).

10 **And he** [*Abraham*] **took unto him all these, and divided them in the midst** [*slaughtered them and cut them in half*], **and laid each piece one against another: but the birds divided he not.**

11 And when the fowls [*probably referring to carrion birds like vultures, magpies, etc.*] came down upon the carcases, Abram drove them away.

> In verse 12, next, Abraham has a rather frightening dream or vision in which he is shown that his posterity (the main subject of the events in this chapter) will indeed come along, and, in fact, they will spend some difficult days in bondage in a foreign land (Egypt).

12 And when the sun was going down, **a deep sleep fell upon Abram**; and, lo, **an horror of great darkness fell upon him** [*he saw the misery of Egyptian bondage that would come upon his posterity, the children of Israel*].

13 **And he** [*the Lord*] **said unto Abram**, Know of a surety that **thy seed shall be a stranger in a land** *that is* **not theirs** [*Egypt*], **and shall serve them** [*they will be slaves*]; and they [*their Egyptian taskmasters*] shall afflict them **four hundred years;**

14 And also **that nation, whom they shall serve, will I judge** [*Egypt will get their deserved punishment for how they treated the Hebrew slaves*]: and **afterward shall they** [*the children of Israel*] **come out** [*escape from Egypt*] **with great substance** [*wealth*].

> Abraham is being shown the future of his posterity for many hundreds of years and his own peaceful passing. At this point he is somewhere near seventy-five years old and will live another hundred years.

15 **And thou shalt go to thy fathers** [*die*] **in peace**; thou shalt be buried in a good old age [*for him, this will be 175 years old—see Genesis 25:7*].

> In verse 16, next, Abraham is told that his posterity will eventually inherit the land of Canaan (the promised land, which is in Palestine today), which the Lord has promised to his descendants. When they do, they will destroy the Canaanites of the land (see Deuteronomy 7:1–2, 20:16–18) as Joshua leads them across the Jordan River into the promised land. But the Lord explains to Abraham that the inhabitants of the land are not yet wicked enough to qualify for destruction.

16 But **in the fourth generation** [*after four hundred years in Egypt*] **they** [*Abraham's posterity, the children of Israel*] **shall come hither** [*to the land of Canaan*] **again: for the iniquity of the Amorites** *is* **not yet full** [*the current inhabitants of Canaan are not yet ripe in iniquity—in other words, not yet completely wicked, ready to be destroyed*].

17 And it came to pass, that, when the sun went down, and it was dark, behold a smoking furnace, and a burning lamp that passed between

those pieces [*the pieces of carcasses spoken of in verses 9–10, above*].

As you will have noticed by now, the Lord has restated and reconfirmed portions of His covenant with Abraham, many times. A portion of it is repeated again in verse 18, next. As previously stated, this is a reminder to us of the importance of constantly renewing and being reminded of our covenants with the Lord, through our faithful activity in the Church, temple attendance, scripture reading, and so forth.

Also, in verses 18–21, next, we see that the promise made to Abraham concerning the land to be inherited by his posterity includes the Arab nations as well as the Israelites.

18 **In the same day the Lord made a covenant with Abram**, saying, **Unto thy seed have I given this land**, from the river of Egypt [*the Nile River*] unto the great river, the river Euphrates:

19 **The Kenites, and the Kenizzites, and the Kadmonites**,

20 And **the Hittites, and the Perizzites, and the Rephaims**,

21 And **the Amorites, and the Canaanites, and the Girgashites, and the Jebusites**.

GENESIS 16

Abraham is now eighty-five years old, and Sarah is very concerned that she has not yet been able to bear any children. Being childless in her society was not only a terrible disappointment but also carried with it a social stigma. Thus, it was not only the custom but also the expectation of her culture that she ask her husband to marry one of her servants and have children by her for them (see Clarke, *Bible Commentary,* Vol. 1, pages 109–11). Since Sarah owned her servant, the child of such a marriage would legally belong to Sarah.

Consequently, she will request Abraham to marry her servant, Hagar, which he will do (verse 3). Later, when Hagar discovers that she is expecting a child, an unfortunate conflict develops between her and Sarah as she flaunts the fact that she can bear children but Sarah cannot.

We see human emotions displayed as the conflict heightens to the point that Sarah evicts Hagar. Later, after she has fled from Sarah, Hagar is told by a heavenly messenger that she will have innumerable posterity (verse 10). She is also told to humble herself and return to Sarah. He tells her that she is to name her child "Ishmael," which means "God hears" (verse 11; see also footnote 11a in your Bible).

We will now proceed with this chapter.

1 Now **Sarai Abram's wife bare him no children**: and **she had an handmaid** [*a female servant or attendant*], an Egyptian, whose name *was* **Hagar**.

2 And **Sarai said unto Abram, Behold now, the Lord hath restrained me from bearing: I pray thee, go in unto my maid; it may be that I may obtain children by her.** And **Abram hearkened to the voice of Sarai.**

At this point, Abraham and Sarah have lived in Canaan for ten years. Sarah is seventy-five years old and Abraham is eighty-five. He will be eighty-six when Ishmael is born (see verse 16). It is important to note that Abraham and Hagar will be legally married, as stated at the end of verse 3, next.

3 And Sarai Abram's wife **took Hagar her maid the Egyptian**, after Abram had dwelt ten years in the land of Canaan, **and gave her to her husband Abram to be his wife**.

4 ¶ And he went in unto **Hagar**, and she **conceived**: and **when she saw that she had conceived, her mistress** [Sarah] **was despised in her eyes** [she flaunted it before Sarah].

In verses 5–6, Sarah asks Abraham to solve the problem. He turns it over to her to solve.

5 And **Sarai said unto Abram, My wrong** *be* **upon thee** [I have brought trouble upon myself; please provide a solution for me]: **I have given my maid into thy bosom; and when she saw that she had conceived, I was despised in her eyes**: the Lord judge between me and thee.

6 **But Abram said unto Sarai, Behold, thy maid** *is* **in thy hand** [she is your servant]; **do to her as it pleaseth thee** [you solve it however you want to]. **And when Sarai dealt hardly with her** [dealt severely with her], **she** [Hagar] **fled from her face**.

Hagar has run away from Sarah and is now in the wilderness by a spring of water. An angel appears to her and gives counsel and blessing.

7 ¶ And **the angel of the Lord found her by a fountain of water in the wilderness**, by the fountain in the way to Shur.

8 And **he said**, Hagar, Sarai's maid, **whence camest thou? and whither wilt thou go** [where did you come from and where do you plan on going]? And she said, **I flee from the face of my mistress Sarai**.

9 And **the angel** of the Lord **said** unto her, **Return to thy mistress**, and **submit thyself under her hands** [humble yourself and be obedient to Sarah].

10 And **the angel** of the Lord **said** unto her, **I will multiply thy seed exceedingly,** that it shall not be numbered for multitude.

JST Genesis 16:11

11 And the angel of the Lord said unto her, **The Lord** will multiply thy seed exceedingly, so that it shall not be numbered for multitude.

11 And the angel of the Lord said unto her, Behold, **thou** *art* with child, and **shalt bear a son**, and shalt **call his name Ishmael** [which means "God hears"]; because the Lord hath heard thy affliction.

Next we see a prophetic description of the personality of Ishmael and his descendants, among whom are the Arabs today.

12 And **he will be a wild man** [*one who loves his freedom and is fiercely independent; see also footnote 12a in your Bible*]; **his hand** *will be* **against every man, and every man's hand against him** [*there will be much in-fighting among his descendants; also, his descendants will be involved in much fighting against all other people*]; **and he shall dwell in the presence of all his brethren** [*Ishmael's descendants will dwell with all of Abraham's posterity, including Israelites, in the land given to Abraham by the Lord; in other words, the Arabs have their rightful place in the Middle East, along with the Jews and other descendants of Abraham*].

13 And she called the name of the Lord that spake unto her, Thou God seest me: for she said, Have I also here looked after him that seeth me?

The JST helps us understand verse 13, above.

JST Genesis 16:14–16

14 And she called the name of the angel of the Lord.

15 And he spake unto her, saying, Knowest thou that God seest thee?

16 And she said, I know that God seest me, for I have also here looked after him.

14 Wherefore the well was called Beer-lahai-roi; behold, *it is* between Kadesh and Bered.

JST Genesis 16:17–18

17 And there was a well between Kadesh and Bered, near where Hagar saw the angel.

18 And the name of the angel was Beer-la-hai-roi; wherefore the well was called Beer-la-hai-roi for a memorial.

15 ¶ **And Hagar bare Abram a son: and Abram called his son's name**, which Hagar bare, **Ishmael**.

16 And **Abram** *was* **fourscore and six** [*eighty-six*] **years old, when Hagar bare Ishmael** to Abram.

GENESIS 17

As we begin chapter 17, Abraham is ninety-nine years old; Sarah is eighty-nine. Ishmael, who was born when Abraham was eighty-six, is now about thirteen years old. Abraham and Sarah are still childless, but the Lord will assure them again that they will have a son (Isaac) through whom the promises and covenants, including ordinances of the gospel of Jesus Christ, will go forth to all the earth. Sarah is well past the age when a woman could bear children. The miracle birth of a covenant son will be symbolic of the miraculous birth of the Son of God, through whose birth and mortal mission the promises of the Father will be kept to His children on earth.

Now that the promised miraculous conception and birth are about to take place, we will see Abram's name changed to Abraham (verse 5) and Sarai's name changed to Sarah (verse 15). Having a name change, or getting a new name, is often associated in the scriptures with covenant making and promised blessings. The blessings would not otherwise be available without the associated covenants.

Jacob is another example of a name change made in conjunction with covenant making. His name will be changed to Israel (Genesis 32:26–28). Yet another example is found with King Benjamin's people. He will promise them a new name, in conjunction with covenant making. It will be "a name, that thereby they may be distinguished above all the people" (Mosiah 1:11). The name will be the name of Jesus Christ (Mosiah 5:8). It is, in effect, a new name, symbolizing that they are new people, born again through the principles of the gospel and the Atonement of Christ, given new opportunities for growth and progression that would not be available to them without making covenants with God and keeping them.

Also in this chapter, we will see the law of circumcision instituted as a token of the covenant.

The Joseph Smith Translation will provide much help in understanding this chapter.

1 And **when Abram was ninety years old and nine, the Lord appeared** to Abram, **and said** unto him, I *am* the Almighty God; walk before me, and **be thou perfect**.

JST Genesis 17:1

1 And when Abram was ninety and nine years old, the Lord appeared to Abram, and said unto him, I, the Almighty God, give unto thee a commandment; that **thou shalt walk uprightly before me, and be perfect**.

The commandment to "be perfect" is repeated in one form or another in several places in the scriptures. For example, it is seen in Deuteronomy 18:13, Matthew 5:48, 3 Nephi 12:48, 27:27, and Doctrine and Covenants 67:13. At first, becoming perfect may seem impossible. However, we are not expected to accomplish it during mortality. In fact, the commandment to "be perfect" is another way of saying, in effect, "become gods." We know from modern revelation that it is possible to literally become gods (for example, Doctrine and Covenants 132:20). Joseph Fielding Smith spoke of the commandment to become perfect. He said:

"Salvation does not come all at once; we are commanded to be perfect even as our Father in heaven is perfect. It will take us ages to accomplish this end, for there will be greater progress beyond the grave, and it will be there that the faithful will overcome all things, and receive all things, even the fulness of the Father's glory.

"I believe the Lord meant just what he said: that we should be perfect, as our Father in heaven is perfect. That will not come all at once, but line upon line, and precept upon precept, example upon example, and even then not as long as we live in this mortal life, for we will have to go even beyond the grave before we reach that perfection and shall be like God.

"But here we lay the foundation. Here is where we are taught these simple truths of the gospel of Jesus Christ, in this probationary state, to prepare us for that perfection. It is our duty to be better today than we were yesterday, and better tomorrow than we are today. Why? Because we are on that road, if we are keeping the commandments of the Lord, we are on that road to perfection, and that can only come through obedience and the desire in our hearts to overcome the world" (*Doctrines of Salvation*, Vol. 2, page 18–19).

Elder Dallin H. Oaks (now President Dallin H. Oaks) counseled us not to become too discouraged about our imperfections during mortality. He said:

"Another idea that is powerful to lift us from discouragement is that the work of the Church . . . is an eternal work. Not all problems . . . are fixed in mortality. The work of salvation goes on beyond the veil of death, and we should not be too apprehensive about incompleteness within the limits of mortality" ("Powerful Ideas," *Ensign,* November 1995, page 26).

Next, in verses 2–3 and the JST verses that follow, we see Jehovah reconfirm the fact that Abraham will be the head of a gospel dispensation. It is, in effect, a restoration of the gospel through Abraham. The need for this is evident as we see the accompanying JST verses tell us that apostasy and wickedness were rampant in Abraham's day. Among other wicked deviations from the true gospel, Abel had been substituted for Christ as the Redeemer.

2 And **I will make my covenant between me and thee, and will multiply thee exceedingly**.

3 And Abram fell on his face [*a sign of humility in his culture*]: and God talked with him, saying,

JST Genesis 17:3–7

3 And it came to pass, that Abram fell on his face, and called upon the name of the Lord.

4 And God talked with him, saying, My people have gone astray from my precepts, and have not kept mine ordinances, which I gave unto their fathers [*ancestors*];

5 And **they have not observed** mine anointing [*perhaps meaning Christ's mortal mission—see Bible Dictionary under "Anointed One"*], and the burial, or **baptism** wherewith I commanded them;

In JST, verse 5, above, we are taught that baptism was practiced in ancient times, as part of the gospel of Jesus Christ. Another example of baptism anciently is Adam, who was baptized and received the gift of the Holy Ghost (see Moses 6:64–66).

JST verses 6–7, next, inform us that apostates in Abraham's day had begun baptizing infants, sprinkling blood, which they taught was in remembrance of Abel's blood that was shed for our sins, and had substituted Abel (whom Cain killed) for Christ in their worship services, claiming that Abel performed the Atonement.

6 But **have turned from the commandment**, and **taken unto**

themselves the washing of children, and the blood of sprinkling;

7 And have said that the blood of the righteous Abel was shed for sins; and have not known wherein they are accountable before me.

We now continue with the Genesis account.

4 As for me, behold, my covenant *is* with thee, and thou shalt be a father of many nations.

JST Genesis 17:8

8 But as for thee, behold, I will make my covenant with thee, and thou shalt be a father of many nations.

Next, Abram's name is changed to "Abraham."

5 Neither shall thy name any more be called Abram, but **thy name shall be Abraham** [*"father of a multitude"*]; for a father of many nations have I made thee.

JST Genesis 17:9

9 And this covenant I make, that thy children [*descendants*] may be known among all nations. Neither shall thy name any more be called Abram, but thy name shall be called Abraham; for, a father of many nations have I made thee.

Perhaps you've noticed that a change of name, in the scriptures, is often associated with making covenants with God. Jacob's name will be changed to "Israel" in Genesis 32:28 in conjunction with promised blessings. A "new name," as discussed by King Benjamin with his people (Mosiah 1:11), implies that through making and keeping covenants, we become new people, born again, with new opportunities for growth and progress toward exaltation. The "new name" that Benjamin gave his people was the name of Christ (see Mosiah 5:8). "New name" is mentioned in Revelation 2:17 as well as in Doctrine and Covenants 130:11, where it is mentioned in conjunction with qualifying for celestial glory.

6 And I will make thee exceeding fruitful [*you will have numerous descendants*], and **I will make nations of thee**, and **kings shall come out of thee**.

The phrase "kings shall come out of thee" in verse 6, above, can have at least two meanings. One is that leaders of nations will come through Abraham's lineage. Another is that "kings," meaning exalted men (Revelation 1:6), will achieve exaltation through the blessings of the gospel that Abraham and his posterity bring to the world.

Bruce R. McConkie reminds us that the above explanation of "kings" and exaltation also applies to righteous women in the Church. He taught: "If righteous men have power through the gospel and its crowning ordinance of celestial marriage to become kings and priests to rule in exaltation forever, it follows that the women by their side (without whom they cannot attain exaltation) will be queens and priestesses. (Rev. 1:6; 5:10.) Exaltation grows out of the eternal union of a man and his wife. Of those whose marriage endures in eternity, the Lord says, 'Then shall they be gods' (Doctrine and Covenants 132:20); that is, each of them, the man and the woman, will be a god. As such they will rule over their dominions forever." (Bruce R. McConkie, Mormon Doctrine, 2nd ed. Salt Lake City: Bookcraft, 1966, 613.)

Next, in verse 7, Jehovah continues to explain the covenant, emphasizing again that Abraham will have posterity (through Sarah, see verse 16).

7 And **I will establish my covenant between me and thee and thy seed after thee** in their generations for an everlasting covenant, to be a God unto thee, and to thy seed after thee.

The JST adds significantly to the Genesis verse 7, above. Through Joseph Smith's inspired work on the Bible, we find that verse 7 deals with the covenant of circumcision, that age eight was taught in ancient times as the age at which children begin to become accountable, and that the covenants spoken of as the Abrahamic covenant did not originate with Abraham, rather, with the "fathers," which would include Adam, Seth, Enoch, Noah, and so forth.

JST Genesis 17:11–12

11 And **I will establish a covenant of circumcision** with thee, and it shall be my covenant between me and thee, and thy seed after thee, in their generations; that thou mayest know for ever that **children are not accountable before me until they are eight years old** [*compare with D&C 68:27*].

12 And **thou shalt observe to keep all my covenants wherein I covenanted with thy fathers** [*ancestors*]; and thou shalt keep the commandments which I have given thee with mine own mouth, and I will be a God unto thee and thy seed after thee.

8 **And I will give unto thee, and to thy seed** after thee, the land wherein thou art a stranger, **all the land of Canaan**, for an everlasting possession; **and I will be their God**.

Next, Abraham is taught more about circumcision as a token (symbol) of the covenant. We will provide a quote from the *Old Testament Student Manual*, which summarizes this topic, then move ahead with Genesis account, verse 9. First, the quote:

"The word circumcision comes from the Latin words meaning 'to cut around.' It was instituted by revelation as a sign or token that one was of the covenant seed of Abraham. To better understand why the Lord chose this particular sign or token, read the account in the Joseph Smith Translation:

'And it came to pass, that Abram fell on his face, and called upon the name of the Lord.

'And God talked with him, saying, My people have gone astray from my precepts, and have not kept mine ordinances, which I gave unto their fathers;

'And they have not observed mine anointing, and the burial, or baptism wherewith I commanded them;

'But have turned from the commandment, and taken unto themselves the washing of children, and the blood of sprinkling;

'And have said that the blood of the righteous Abel was shed for sins; and have not known wherein they are accountable before me. . . .

'And I will establish a covenant of circumcision with thee, and it shall be my covenant between me and thee, and thy seed after thee, in their generations; that thou mayest know for ever that children are not accountable before me until they are eight years old" (JST Genesis 17:3–7, 11).

"Much additional information is given in this account.

"1. Before instituting the law of circumcision, the Lord explained why he was establishing this token of the covenant.

  a. The people had left correct principles and forsaken the true ordinances.
  b. Baptism was one ordinance being incorrectly observed.
  c. The people were washing their children and sprinkling blood in remembrance of Abel's blood, which they taught was shed for sins.
  d. They misunderstood the relationship between accountability of children and the atonement of Jesus Christ.

"2. Because of this apostasy, circumcision was instituted.

  a. It was a covenant token.
  b. It was for the seed of Abraham.
  c. It signified that children were not accountable until they were eight years old.

"Other scriptures make it clear that it was not the act itself but rather what it stood for that gave circumcision its greatest significance.

"In many places the Lord speaks of true circumcision as being the circumcision of the heart. The heart that is 'circumcised' is one that loves God and is obedient to the Spirit. The 'uncircumcised in heart' are wicked, proud, and rebellious (Ezekiel 44:7; see also Deuteronomy 10:16; 30:6; Jeremiah 4:4; Ezekiel 44:7; Acts 7:51; Romans 2:25–29; Colossians 2:11).

"Though a person may have had the token of circumcision in the flesh, unless he was righteous the covenant was invalidated and the circumcision became profitless. Thus, circumcision was only a sign or token of what needed to happen to the inward man. If the inward change had not taken place, then circumcision was virtually meaningless. (See Jeremiah 9:25–26; Romans 2:25–29; 1 Corinthians 7:19; Galatians 5:1–6; 6:12–15; Philippians 3:3–4.)

"With the fulfillment of the Mosaic law under Jesus, the token of circumcision was no longer required of God's covenant people (see Acts 15:22–29; Galatians 5:1–6; 6:12–15).

"The Abrahamic covenant makes frequent reference to one's seed (see Genesis 17:6–12). The organ of the body that produces seed and brings about physical birth is the organ on which the token of the covenant was made. The organ of spiritual rebirth, however, is the heart (see 3 Nephi 9:20). Thus, when a person was circumcised, it signified that while he had been born into the covenant, he need not be baptized until he became accountable before the Lord. But spiritual circumcision, or the circumcision of the heart, must take place once one becomes accountable or one is not considered as true Israel. As Paul said so aptly, 'For he is not a Jew, which is one outwardly; neither is that circumcision, which is outward in the flesh: but he is a Jew, which is one inwardly; and circumcision is that of the heart, in the spirit, and not in the letter; whose praise is not of men, but of God' (Romans 2:28–29)." (*Old Testament Student Manual, Genesis–2 Samuel*, 1981, p 69)

With the above information and clarifications in mind, we will now continue with the Genesis account.

9 ¶ And **God said unto Abraham, Thou shalt keep my covenant** therefore, thou, and thy seed after thee in their generations.

10 This *is* my covenant, which ye shall keep, between me and you and thy seed after thee; **Every man child among you shall be circumcised**.

11 And ye shall circumcise the flesh of your foreskin; and **it shall be a token of the covenant betwixt me and you**.

12 And **he that is eight days old shall be circumcised** among you, every man child in your generations, he that is born in the house, or bought with money of any stranger, which *is* not of thy seed [*who is not one of your direct descendants*].

13 He that is born in thy house, and he that is bought with thy money, must needs be circumcised: **and my covenant shall be in your flesh for an everlasting covenant**.

14 And **the uncircumcised man child** whose flesh of his foreskin is not circumcised, that soul **shall be cut off from his people**; he hath broken my covenant.

Next, in verse 15, Sarai's name is changed to Sarah.

15 ¶ And God said unto Abraham, **As for Sarai thy wife, thou shalt not call her name Sarai, but Sarah** [*"princess"—see Bible Dictionary under "Sarah"*] *shall* her name *be*.

In verse 16, Abraham is told that Sarah will bear a son.

16 And **I will bless her, and give thee a son also of her**: yea, I will bless her, and **she shall be *a mother* of nations; kings of people shall be of her** [*the same blessing given to Abraham in verse 6, above*].

The Joseph Smith Translation makes a very important change in wording for verse 17, next. Whereas the Genesis account uses the word "laughed" for Abraham's response to the news that Sarah would have a son, the JST uses the word "rejoiced." The JST also changes the two questions at the end of verse 17 to a statement. Thus, in fact, Abraham is faithfully confirming what the Lord has just told him, rather than questioning it.

17 **Then Abraham fell upon his face** [*a sign of humility and submission in his culture*], **and laughed**, and said in his heart, **Shall *a child* be born unto him that is an hundred years old?** and **shall Sarah, that is ninety years old, bear?**

JST Genesis 17:23

23 **Then Abraham fell upon his face and rejoiced**, and said in his heart, **There shall a child be born unto him that is an hundred years old, and Sarah that is ninety years old shall bear.**

The JST also sheds helpful light on verse 18, next. We will first read it as it stands in the Genesis account and then read the change in the JST.

18 And Abraham said unto God, **O that Ishmael might live before thee!**

JST Genesis 17:24

24 And Abraham said unto God, Oh that Ishmael might live uprightly before thee!

19 And God said, **Sarah thy wife shall bear thee a son indeed; and thou shalt call his name Isaac: and I will establish my covenant with him for an everlasting covenant,** *and* **with his seed after him.**

The word *also*, as added in the JST by the Prophet Joseph Smith to verse 19, above, may seem somewhat insignificant. But it is very important because it reminds us that the same covenant (comprising the blessings and promises contained in the gospel of Jesus Christ) that was made with Adam and others, such as Enoch, Noah, and Abraham, will also be made with Isaac. Furthermore, it is also that same "covenant" by which all worthy Saints will eventually return to the presence of the Father to live with Him in eternal exaltation, as gods.

JST Genesis 17:25

25 And God said, Sarah thy wife shall bare thee a son, and thou shalt call his name Isaac; and I will establish my covenant with him **also**, for an everlasting covenant with his seed after him.

20 And **as for Ishmael**, I have heard thee [*the name, "Ishmael," means "God heareth"—see Bible Dictionary, under "Ishmael"*]: Behold, **I have blessed him, and will make him fruitful**, and will multiply him exceedingly; twelve princes [*twelve sons, heads of tribes or peoples—the ancestors of the Arabs today*] shall he beget, and I will make him a great nation.

21 **But my covenant** [*the Abrahamic covenant, including the responsibility of taking the gospel of Christ to all the world*] **will I establish with Isaac, which Sarah shall bear unto thee at this set time in the next year.**

22 And he left off talking with him, and God went up from Abraham.

> Ever faithful and obedient, Abraham immediately carries out the commandment regarding circumcision for him and the males in his household.

23 ¶ And Abraham took Ishmael his son, and all that were born in his house, and all that were bought with his money, every male among the men of Abraham's house; and circumcised the flesh of their foreskin **in the selfsame day**, as God had said unto him.

24 **And Abraham** *was* **ninety years old and nine, when he was circumcised** in the flesh of his foreskin.

25 And **Ishmael his son** *was* **thirteen years old, when he was circumcised** in the flesh of his foreskin.

> Again, Moses (the writer of Genesis) emphasizes to us that Abraham obeyed immediately. This simple, faith-based obedience is obviously an important part of the lesson he has in mind for us here. It is an essential attribute for all who desire to be counted among those who reap the full blessings of the Abrahamic covenant.

26 **In the selfsame day** was Abraham circumcised, and Ishmael his son.

27 And all the men of his house, born in the house, and bought with money of the stranger [*unbelievers; foreigners*], were circumcised with him.

GENESIS 18

There are two main things going on in this chapter. First, Abraham hosts three messengers, sent by the Lord to confirm to him that Sarah will indeed have a son. Second, Abraham, upon finding out that Sodom and Gomorrah are going to be destroyed, asks the Lord if the righteous people in the cities will be destroyed also. It will basically come down to the proposal that if Abraham can find at least ten righteous people in Sodom, the city will not be destroyed.

Once again, the JST will prove to be important in correctly understanding many things in this chapter.

Remember, after Abraham and his followers returned from Egypt, he and Lot separated. Abraham generously allowed Lot to choose where he wanted to settle with his herds and flocks, and Abraham took what was left (Genesis 13:5–12). Lot selfishly selected the best lands and chose also to live in Sodom (Genesis 14:12). Abraham settled in Canaan, on the plains of Mamre, west of the Dead Sea.

As we begin, verse 1 deals with two completely separate events. First, the Lord appears to Abraham. Later, still in verse 1, Abraham is sitting in the door of his tent. As the account continues in verse 2, he sees three holy men (see heading to this chapter in your Bible) standing not far from him. We don't know who these men were, but JST Genesis 18:23 speaks of them as "angels which were holy men, and were sent forth after the order of God."

1 And **the Lord appeared unto him** in the plains of Mamre: **and he**

sat in the tent door in the heat of the day;

2 **And he lift up his eyes and looked, and, lo, three men stood by him**: and when he saw *them,* **he ran to meet them from the tent door, and bowed himself toward the ground**,

> Joseph Fielding Smith explained the above verses as follows:
>
> "We are not justified in teaching that our Heavenly Father, with other heavenly persons, came down, dusty and weary, and ate with Abraham. This is not taught in the 18th chapter of Genesis. The first verse of that chapter should read as follows: 'And the Lord appeared unto him in the plains of Mamre.' That is a complete thought. The second part of this paragraph has nothing to do with the Lord's appearing to Abraham. . . . : 'And he sat in the tent door in the heat of the day; and he lifted up his eyes and looked, and, lo, three men stood by him.' These three men were mortals. They had bodies and were able to eat, to bathe, and sit and rest from their weariness. Not one of these three was the Lord" (*Doctrines of Salvation,* Vol. 1, page 16).
>
> As you can see, the JST for verse 3, next, clarifies that Abraham is speaking to the three messengers from God, rather than to the Lord Himself, as it reads in the Genesis account.

3 And said, **My Lord**, if now I have found favour in thy sight, pass not away, I pray thee, from thy servant:

JST Genesis 18:3

3 **My brethren**, if now I have found favor in your sight, pass not away I pray you from thy servant.

Verses 4–8, next, of the Genesis account inform us that Abraham graciously saw to the needs for refreshment and food for his guests, with Sarah making bread and a servant preparing meat for the occasion. We see another wonderful character trait of Abraham as we watch him hurry to provide for the needs of these men. Here, again, Abraham is a "type" of Christ. In the scriptures, we see the word "succor" describing what the Lord does for us (Alma 7:12). "Succor" means "to run to the aid of." Abraham was "running to the aid of" his guests.

4 Let a little water, I pray you, be fetched, and **wash your feet**, and **rest yourselves under the tree**:

5 And **I will fetch a morsel of bread**, and comfort ye your hearts; after that ye shall pass on: for therefore are ye come to your servant. And they said, So do, as thou hast said.

6 And **Abraham hastened into the tent unto Sarah, and said, Make ready quickly three measures of fine meal, knead *it,* and make cakes upon the hearth**.

7 And **Abraham ran unto the herd, and fetcht a calf tender and good, and gave *it* unto a young man; and he hasted to dress it** [*prepare it for eating*].

8 **And he took butter, and milk, and the calf which he had dressed, and set** *it* [*JST, "them"*] **before them**; and he stood by them under the tree, and they did eat.

> Next, in verses 9–14, these holy men reconfirm that Sarah will have a son (Isaac).

9 ¶ And **they said unto him, Where** *is* **Sarah thy wife? And he said, Behold, in the tent.**

10 **And he said**, I will certainly return unto thee according to the time of life; and, lo, **Sarah thy wife shall have a son**. And Sarah heard *it* in the tent door, which *was* behind him.

JST Genesis 18:9

> 9 And one of them blessed Abraham, and he said, I will certainly return unto thee from my journey, and lo, according to the time of life, Sarah thy wife shall have a son.

11 **Now Abraham and Sarah** *were* **old** *and* **well stricken in age**; *and* **it ceased to be with Sarah after the manner of women** [*Sarah was past the age when she could have children*].

> Next, we see that Sarah is astonished as she overhears this news. It appears that Abraham has not yet told her that she is going to have a child, even though he has been told it by the Lord (Genesis 17:16). Perhaps he had not yet determined how to go about telling her. This may be one of the important reasons as to why the Lord sent these three holy men to visit Abraham and Sarah's household.

12 **Therefore Sarah laughed within herself, saying, After I am waxed old shall I have pleasure** [*how could one as old as I have a baby*]**, my lord being old also** [*it's not just me, Abraham is also ancient*]**?**

> We should be cautious about being critical of Sarah for laughing within herself at this astounding news. We might find ourselves doing the same thing under similar circumstances. She is embarrassed about it later, as indicated in verse 15.

13 And the Lord said unto Abraham, **Wherefore** [*why*] **did Sarah laugh**, saying, Shall I of a surety bear a child, which am old?

14 **Is any thing too hard for the Lord?** At the time appointed I will return unto thee, according to the time of life, and **Sarah shall have a son**.

JST Genesis 18:13–14

> 13 And the **angel of the Lord** said unto Abraham, Wherefore did Sarah laugh, saying, Shall I of a surety bear a child, which am old? Is anything too hard for the Lord?
>
> 14 At the time appointed, behold, I will return unto thee from my journey, which the Lord hath sent me; and according to the time of life thou mayest know that Sarah shall have a son.

15 **Then Sarah denied, saying, I laughed not; for she was afraid.**

And he said, **Nay; but thou didst laugh.**

> Next, the attention of these holy men turns toward Sodom. Remember, as stated previously, that Lot settled his family in Sodom. Abraham is obviously concerned as he comes to understand that Sodom and Gomorrah are ripe for destruction.

16 ¶ **And the men** [*JST, "angels"*] **rose up from thence, and looked toward Sodom: and Abraham went with them** to bring them on the way.

17 And the Lord said, Shall I hide from Abraham that thing which I do;

18 Seeing that **Abraham shall surely become a great and mighty nation**, and all the nations of the earth shall be blessed in him?

JST Genesis 18:17

> 17 And the angel of the Lord, said, Shall I hide from Abraham that thing which the Lord will do for him; seeing that Abraham shall surely become a great and mighty nation, and all the nations of the earth shall be blessed in him?

> Have you noticed how many times the Lord is reassuring Abraham that he will indeed become the father of a great nation? We saw it again in verse 18, above. This constant reassurance is a reminder of the mercy and kindness of the Lord.

> Next, Abraham is complimented for teaching his family and household the ways of the Lord.

19 For I know him, that **he will command his children and his household after him, and they shall keep the way of the Lord, to do justice and judgment** [*to do that which is right and just*]; **that the Lord may bring upon Abraham that which he hath spoken of him.**

> President Spencer W. Kimball spoke of Abraham's righteous teaching of his family. He said:
>
> "Abraham's desire to do God's will in all things led him to preside over his family in righteousness. Despite all his other responsibilities, he knew that if he failed to teach and exemplify the gospel to his children he would have failed to fulfill the most important stewardship he had received" ("The Example of Abraham," *Ensign*, June 1975, page 5).

> From verse 20 to the end of the chapter, the topic turns to the wickedness of Sodom and Gomorrah and their impending destruction. Not only was their society steeped in sexual immorality, including homosexuality, but their citizens were also completely caught up in pursuing their own selfish interests to the exclusion of others. Ezekiel described this. He said:

Ezekiel 16:49–50

> 49 Behold, this was the iniquity of thy sister Sodom, pride, fulness of

bread, and abundance of idleness was in her and in her daughters, neither did she strengthen the hand of the poor and needy.

50 And they were haughty, and committed abomination before me: therefore I took them away as I saw *good*.

Returning to Genesis now, the JST will give us a correct understanding of verses 20–21. First, the Genesis account.

20 And **the Lord** said, Because the cry of Sodom and Gomorrah is great, and because their sin is very grievous;

21 **I will go down now**, and see whether they have done altogether according to the cry of it, which is come unto me; and if not, I will know.

JST Genesis 18:19–22

19 And **the angel of the Lord said unto Abraham**, The Lord said unto us, Because the cry of Sodom and Gomorrah is great, and because their sin is very grievous, I will destroy them.

20 And **I will send you** [*the messengers in verse 19*], **and ye shall go down now**, and see that their iniquities are rewarded unto them.

21 And ye shall have all things done altogether according to the cry of it, which is come unto me.

22 And if ye do it not, it shall be upon your heads; for I will destroy them, and you shall know that I will do it, for it shall be before your eyes.

Again, we will see the great value of the JST as we first read verses 22–23 in the Genesis account and then read the JST additions and corrections.

As we continue, we feel Abraham's concern and compassion for others.

22 And **the men** turned their faces from thence, and went toward Sodom: but Abraham stood yet before the Lord.

23 ¶ And **Abraham drew near**, and said, Wilt thou also destroy the righteous with the wicked?

JST Genesis 18:23–25

23 And **the angels which were holy men, and were sent forth after the order of God**, turned their faces from thence and went toward Sodom.

24 But Abraham stood yet before the Lord, **remembering the things which had been told him**.

25 And **Abraham drew near to Sodom**, and said unto the Lord, calling upon his name, saying, Wilt thou destroy the righteous with the wicked? **Wilt thou not spare them?**

Next, Abraham ventures to bargain with the Lord, asking, in effect, if the Lord would spare the city if any righteous people could be found living in Sodom. Again, the JST will help us as we see from it that Abraham is the one who is invited to find righteous people in Sodom, rather than the Lord.

24 **Peradventure there be** [*what if there are*] **fifty righteous within the**

city: wilt thou also destroy and not spare the place for the fifty righteous that *are* therein?

JST Genesis 18:26

26 Peradventure there may be fifty righteous within the city, wilt thou also destroy and not spare the place for the fifty righteous that may be therein?

25 **That be far from thee** to do after this manner, **to slay the righteous with the wicked**: and that the righteous should be as the wicked, that be far from thee: Shall not the Judge of all the earth do right?

JST Genesis 18:27–28

27 O may that be far from thee to do after this manner, to slay the righteous with the wicked; and that the righteous should be as the wicked.

28 O God, may that be far from thee, for shall not the Judge of all the earth do right?

We are seeing Abraham in the same situation as the servant in the allegory of the tame and wild olive trees (Jacob 5). In both cases, these great servants of the Lord become very compassionate and involved in pleading that the wicked might be spared a little longer in order that more might be converted and saved. In other words, they have become Christlike in this respect.

26 And the Lord said, **If I find** in Sodom fifty righteous within the city, then I will spare all the place for their sakes.

JST Genesis 18:29

29 And the Lord said unto Abraham, If thou findest in Sodom, fifty righteous within the city, then I will spare all the place for their sakes.

The JST of verse 27, next, is very different than the Genesis version.

27 And Abraham answered and said, Behold now, **I have taken upon me to speak unto the Lord, which *am but* dust and ashes**:

JST Genesis 18:30

30 And Abraham answered and said, Behold, now, **I have taken upon me to speak unto the Lord, which is able to destroy the city, and lay all the people in dust and ashes**;

Next, in verses 28–32, Abraham pleads that if the number he could find were smaller and smaller, would the Lord still spare the city. The Lord says yes, He would not destroy the city.

One of the major messages we are being taught here is that the Lord is very patient and merciful.

28 **Peradventure there shall lack five of the fifty righteous**: wilt thou destroy all the city for *lack of* five? And he said, If I find there forty and five, I will not destroy *it*.

29 And he spake unto him yet again, and said, **Peradventure there shall be forty** found there. And he said, I will not do *it* for forty's sake.

30 And he said *unto him,* Oh let not the Lord be angry, and I will speak:

Peradventure there shall thirty be found there. And he said, I will not do *it,* if I find [*JST, "if thou shalt find"*] thirty there.

31 And he said, Behold now, I have taken upon me to speak unto the Lord: **Peradventure there shall be twenty found there**. And he said, I will not destroy *it* for twenty's sake.

32 And he said, Oh let not the Lord be angry, and I will speak yet but this once: **Peradventure ten** shall be found there. And **he said, I will not destroy *it* for ten's sake** [*if ten righteous can be found*].

33 **And the Lord went his way, as soon as he had left communing with Abraham**: and Abraham returned unto his place.

JST Genesis 18:41–42

41 **And as soon as he had left communing with the Lord, Abraham went his way**.

42 **An**d it came to pass that Abraham returned unto his tent.

GENESIS 19

This is a sad chapter. Perhaps one of the major messages Moses had in mind for us as he included this account of the demise of Lot's family in his record is that it does not pay to intentionally live near the edge of evil and gross wickedness—in other words, being excited by watching it but foolishly thinking that it is not all that dangerous and sinful since we are not participating directly in it.

Lot will be visited in Sodom by three holy men. They are referred to in verse 15 as "angels of God, which were holy men." We do not know who these men were, nor do we know where they came from. One possibility is that they might have come from Melchizedek's righteous community. Or, they could possibly have come down from the City of Enoch (which had been translated and taken up—see Genesis 5:24 and Moses 7:69) to minister. We simply don't know. The Prophet Joseph Smith taught that translated beings can serve as ministers for God to other people. He taught (**bold** added for emphasis):

"Many have supposed that the doctrine of translation was a doctrine whereby men were taken immediately into the presence of God, and into an eternal fullness, but this is a mistaken idea. Their place of habitation is that of the terrestrial order, and a place prepared for such characters He held in reserve to be **ministering angels** unto many planets, and who as yet have not entered into so great a fullness as those who are resurrected from the dead" (*Teachings,* page 170).

We will watch as these three holy men (likely the same three who spoke with Abraham in chapter 18) come to Sodom to destroy it and the other wicked cities of the plain, including Gomorrah. They will be hosted overnight by Lot. Wicked men of the city will gather and request that Lot send his guests out onto the street, along with his two unmarried daughters, in order that they might "know them" (verse 5). According to footnote 5a in your Bible, "know," in this context, means to engage in sexual activities with them. Since Sodom was a famous center for homosexuality, as well as all other forms of sexual perversion and debauchery, it is obvious what these citizens had in mind to do with the three holy men as well as with Lot's two daughters. The three holy men smite the mob with blindness and the problem is solved.

The next day, the three messengers from the Lord counsel Lot to encourage his sons-in-law and grandsons to leave the city before they call upon the powers of heaven to destroy it. Sadly, these family members scoff at Lot and refuse to leave. Thus, Lot and his wife, with their two unmarried daughters, flee the city. They are told not to even look back. Lot's wife disobeys and is destroyed, leaving Lot and his two daughters.

They end up living in a cave, and the daughters, fearing that they will never marry, get their father drunk and intentionally engage in an incestuous relationship with him in order to conceive.

As mentioned at the beginning of these background notes, this is a sad and depressing chapter, no doubt intended to be a warning concerning the end result of lives in which intentional compromise of gospel principles is the lifestyle of choice.

With this background in mind, we will now proceed with chapter 19.

1 And **there came** two angels [*Hebrew: "messengers"*] at even; and Lot sat in the gate of Sodom: and **Lot seeing *them* rose up to meet them**; and he bowed himself with his face toward the ground;

JST Genesis 19:1–2

1 And it came to pass, that there came **three angels** to Sodom in the evening; and Lot sat in the door of his house, in the city of Sodom.

2 And Lot, seeing the angels, rose up to meet them; and he bowed himself with his face toward the ground;

2 And **he said**, Behold now, my lords, **turn in, I pray you, into your servant's house**, and tarry all night, and wash your feet [*a common part of hospitality offered in hot, dusty climates of the Near East*], and ye shall rise up early, and go on your ways. And **they said, Nay; but we will abide** [*stay*] **in the street all night**.

3 **And he pressed upon them greatly** [*he put pressure on them to accept his hospitality*]; **and they** turned in unto him, and **entered into his house**; and he made them a feast, and did bake unleavened bread, and they did eat.

> Next, the wicked men of Sodom surround Lot's house and demand that he send his guests out for them to be sexually abused.

4 ¶ But before they lay down [*JST, "to rest"*], **the men** of the city, *even* the men **of Sodom**, **compassed** [*surrounded*] **the house round**, both old and young, all the people from every quarter:

5 **And they called unto Lot**, and said unto him, **Where *are* the men which came in to thee this night? bring them out unto us, that we may know them** [*engage in sexual conduct with them*].

> Next, Lot goes out and begs the mob to leave them alone.

6 And **Lot went out** at the door unto them, and shut the door after him,

7 **And said, I pray you, brethren, do not so wickedly**.

> Verse 8, next, is badly mistranslated. It makes it appear that Lot is offering his virgin daughters to the mob, if they will just leave the three holy men alone. The JST gives us the correct version.

8 Behold now, **I have two daughters** which have not known man [*who are virgins*]; **let me, I pray you, bring them out unto you, and do ye to them as** *is* **good in your eyes**: only unto these men do nothing; for therefore came they under the shadow of my roof [*under my protection*].

JST Genesis 19:13–14

> 13 And Lot said, Behold now, I have two daughters which have not known man; **let me, I pray you, plead with my brethren that I may not bring them out unto you; and ye shall not do unto them as seemeth good in your eyes**;
>
> 14 For God will not justify his servant in this thing; wherefore, let me plead with my brethren, this once only, that unto these men ye do nothing, that they may have peace in my house; for therefore came they under the shadow of my roof.

The mob refuses his efforts to stop them and accuses him of coming to stay in their city and now trying to take over and rule them.

9 And they said, Stand back. And **they said** *again,* **This one** *fellow* [*Lot*] **came in to sojourn** [*to stay with them in their city*], **and he will needs be a judge** [*now he wants to take over*]: **now will we deal worse with thee, than with them**. And they pressed sore upon the man, *even* Lot, and came near to break the door.

JST Genesis 19:9–10

> 9 And they said unto him, Stand back. And they were angry with him.
>
> 10 And they said **among themselves**, This one man came in to sojourn among us, and he will needs now make himself to be a judge; now we will deal worse with him than with them.

10 **But the men** [*the three holy men*] put **forth their hand, and pulled Lot into the house** to them, and shut to the door.

11 **And they smote the men that** *were* **at the door of the house with blindness**, both small and great: so that they wearied themselves to find the door.

> Next, the holy men instruct Lot to gather his family members from the city and flee. The JST informs us that he had more than one son-in-law as well as grandsons.

12 ¶ And the men said unto Lot, Hast thou here any besides? son in law, and thy sons, and thy daughters, and **whatsoever thou hast in the city, bring** *them* **out of this place**:

13 For **we will destroy this place**, because the cry of them is waxen great [*has grown very large*] before the face of the Lord; and **the Lord hath sent us to destroy it.**

JST Genesis 19:18–19

> 18 And these holy men said unto Lot, Hast thou any here besides thy sons-in-law, and thy son's sons and thy daughters?
>
> 19 And they commanded Lot, saying, Whatsoever thou hast in the city, thou shalt bring out of this place, for we will destroy this place;

> As Lot attempts to get his married daughters and their sons and husbands to leave, he is ignored by his sons-in-law. Their living in a wicked environment has taken its sad toll.

14 And **Lot went out, and spake unto his sons in law**, which married his daughters, and said, **Up, get you out of this place;** for the Lord will destroy this city. **But he seemed as one that mocked unto his sons in law**.

> It appears that Lot, himself, is in no great hurry to leave the city, as instructed by the holy men. Verse 15, next, indicates that they had to "hasten" his efforts to get him on his way. And verse 16 says that he "lingered" such that the messengers had to take him, his wife and daughters by the hand and lead them to the outskirts of the city.

15 ¶ And when the morning arose, then **the angels hastened Lot**, saying, Arise, take thy wife, and thy two daughters, which are here; lest thou be consumed in the iniquity of the city.

16 And **while he lingered, the men** [*JST: the angels*] **laid hold upon his hand, and upon the hand of his wife, and upon the hand of his two daughters**; the Lord being merciful unto him: **and they brought him forth, and set him without** [*outside of*] **the city**.

> In verse 17, next, we see the command not to look back, as they flee the city. Some Bible scholars suggest that this phrase, in the language of the day, means "don't return." We will say a bit more about this possibility after verse 26.

17 ¶ And it came to pass, **when they had brought them forth** abroad, that he [*JST: "they"*] **said**, Escape for thy life; **look not behind thee**, neither stay thou in all the plain; escape to the mountain, lest thou be consumed.

> Even at this point, Lot is haggling with those who are trying to save his life. In verses 18–22, he requests that they allow him to stay in Zoar (verse 22), one of the five cities (including Sodom and Gomorrah) of the plain of Jordan, rather than fleeing to the mountain as instructed in verse 17, above.

18 And **Lot said unto them, Oh, not so**, my Lord:

19 Behold now, thy servant hath found grace in thy sight, and thou hast magnified thy mercy, which

thou hast shewed unto me in saving my life; and **I cannot escape to the mountain**, lest some evil take me, and I die:

JST Genesis 19:26

26 And Lot said unto **one of them**, Oh, not so my Lord! behold now, thy servant has found grace in thy sight, and thou hast magnified thy mercy which thou hast showed unto me in saving my life; and I cannot escape to the mountain, lest some evil overtake me, and I die.

20 Behold now, **this city** *is* **near** to flee unto, and it *is* a little one: **Oh, let me escape thither**, (*is* it not a little one?) and my soul shall live.

21 And he said unto him, See, I have accepted thee concerning this thing also, that I will not overthrow this city, for the which thou hast spoken.

22 Haste thee, escape thither; for I cannot do any thing till thou be come thither. Therefore the name of the city was called Zoar.

23 ¶ The sun was risen upon the earth when Lot entered into Zoar.

JST Genesis 19:27–30

27 Behold now, here is another city, and this is near to flee unto and it is a little one; oh, let me escape thither, and may the Lord not destroy it, and my soul shall live.

28 And the angel said unto him, See, I have accepted thee concerning this thing also, that I will not overthrow this city, for the which thou hast spoken; haste thee, escape thither, for I cannot do anything until thou be come thither.

29 And the name of the city was called Zoar. Therefore the sun was risen upon the earth when Lot entered into Zoar.

30 And the Lord did not destroy Sodom until Lot had entered into Zoar.

Next, Sodom and Gomorrah are destroyed with fire, along with some other wicked cities of the plain. This might be considered symbolic of the destruction of the wicked by fire, at the time of the Second Coming. At that time, however, the "fire" will be the glory of the coming Lord (Doctrine and Covenants 5:19).

24 Then **the Lord rained upon Sodom and upon Gomorrah brimstone and fire** from the Lord out of heaven;

JST Genesis 19:31

31 And then, when Lot had entered into Zoar, the Lord rained upon Sodom, and upon Gomorrah; for the angels called upon the name of the Lord for brimstone and fire from the Lord out of heaven.

25 And **he overthrew those cities, and all the plain, and all the inhabitants of the cities**, and that which grew upon the ground.

26 ¶ **But his wife looked back from behind him**, and she became a pillar of salt.

JST Genesis 19:33

33 But it came to pass, when Lot fled, his wife looked back from behind him, and became a pillar of salt.

As mentioned, a few moments ago, there is some thought among scriptural scholars that the phrase, "looked back" might indicate that Lot's wife returned to Sodom. We will quote from the *Old Testament Student Manual* on this.

"The account of Lot's wife being turned into a pillar of salt has puzzled many commentators. Was this event a literal thing, or was it figurative? There are two indications in the scriptures that the phrase "looked back" was an idiomatic way of saying "she turned back" or "returned to Sodom." When warning the disciples of the destruction that was going to come upon Jerusalem, the Savior warned them to flee without delay, not even going into the house to get their possessions. Jesus said, 'And he that is in the field, let him likewise not return back. Remember Lot's wife' (Luke 17:31–32; emphasis added). He then admonished them that he who seeks to save his life will lose it, and he who loses his life will find it. Elder Bruce R. McConkie paraphrased those verses in these words.

'Look not back to Sodom and the wealth and luxury you are leaving. Stay not in the burning house, in the hope of salvaging your treasures, lest the flame destroy you; but flee, flee to the mountains.

'Seek temporal things and lose eternal life; sacrifice the things of this life and gain eternal life.' (*Doctrinal New Testament Commentary,* Vol. 1, page 645.)

"The implication is that Lot's wife started back to Sodom, perhaps to save some possessions, and was caught in the destruction.

"In the Doctrine and Covenants is a scripture that uses the same terminology as Genesis 19:26. After warning the Saints to flee spiritual Babylon, which is wickedness, the Lord says, 'He that goeth, let him not look back lest sudden destruction shall come upon him' (Doctrine and Covenants 133:15; emphasis added). Again, the implication is that of a return to wickedness.

"Most scholars agree that the most probable site of Sodom is now covered by the southern part of the Dead Sea, a body of water with a high salt content. If Lot's wife returned to Sodom, she would have been caught in the destruction. Her becoming a pillar of salt could be a figurative way of expressing this outcome.

"But whatever it was that happened to Lot's wife, it is clear that she perished" (*Old Testament Student Manual: Genesis–2 Samuel,* page 77).

Next, Abraham gets up early in the morning and views the destruction.

27 ¶ And **Abraham gat up early in the morning** to the place where he stood before the Lord:

28 **And he looked toward Sodom and Gomorrah**, and toward all the land of the plain, and beheld, **and,**

lo, the smoke of the country went up as the smoke of a furnace.

We will use the JST to clear up some confusion in verse 29, next.

29 ¶ And it came to pass, when God destroyed the cities of the plain, that **God remembered Abraham**, and sent Lot out of the midst of the overthrow, when he overthrew the cities in the which Lot dwelt.

JST Genesis 19:35

35 And it came to pass, when God had destroyed the cities of the plain, that **God spake unto Abraham, saying, I have remembered Lot**, and sent him out of the midst of the overthrow, that thy brother might not be destroyed, when I overthrew the city in the which thy brother Lot dwelt.

Next, in verses 30–38, we see the sad conclusion to Lot's family. As you have no doubt noticed, there is a definite contrast between Lot and Abraham. Lot has compromised and lived on the edge, whereas, Abraham has always done his best to live the gospel with exactness. We are being taught a lesson by studying this contrast, as presented by Moses, the writer of Genesis.

Lot and his daughters end up living in a cave in the mountain. Why they left Zoar is not clear. But, for whatever reason, his daughters despair of ever marrying and having children. They come up with an evil plot in order to each bear a child.

30 **And Lot went up out of Zoar, and dwelt in the mountain, and his two daughters with him**; for he feared to dwell in Zoar: and **he dwelt in a cave**, he and his two daughters.

31 And **the firstborn said unto the younger,** Our father *is* old, and *there is* not a man in the earth to come in unto us after the manner of all the earth [*in other words, there is not a man to marry us so that we can have children*]:

JST Genesis 19:37

37 **And the firstborn dealt wickedly, and said unto the younger**, Our father has become old, and we have not a man on the earth to come in unto us, to live with us after the manner of all that live on the earth;

In the culture of the day, there was a very strong desire to carry on one's family line into the future. Lot's wife had perished and all his married children and grandchildren had died also in the destruction of Sodom. Thus, the family line of Lot was about to come to a close. This is apparently the thinking in the older daughter's mind as she proposes an incestuous relationship with their father in order that they may have posterity that would carry on the family line (end of verse 32).

32 **Come, let us make our father drink wine, and we will lie with him** [*have sexual relations with him*]**, that we may preserve seed of** [*posterity for*] **our father.**

33 **And they made their father drink wine** that night: **and the firstborn went in, and lay with her father**; and he perceived not [*was so*

drunk that he didn't realize what was happening] when she lay down, nor when she arose.

JST Genesis 19:39

39 **And they did wickedly,** and made their father drink wine that night; and the firstborn went in and lay with her father; and he perceived not when she lay down, nor when she arose.

34 And it came to pass on the morrow, that the firstborn said unto the younger, Behold, I lay yesternight with my father: let us make him drink wine this night also; and go thou in, *and* lie with him, that we may preserve seed of our father [*so that our father has posterity through us*].

35 And **they made their father drink wine that night also: and the younger arose, and lay with him**; and he perceived not when she lay down, nor when she arose.

36 **Thus were both the daughters of Lot with child** [*were pregnant*] **by their father**.

As stated next, the Moabites and the Ammonites of southern Israel were the people who descended from these two sons of Lot by his daughters.

37 And the firstborn bare a son, and called his name Moab: the same *is* the father [*the ancestor*] of the **Moabites** [*who lived east of the Dead Sea*] unto this day.

38 And the younger, she also bare a son, and called his name Benammi: the same *is* the father of the **children of Ammon** [*the Ammonites, who lived east of Jerusalem, across the Jordan River*] unto this day.

GENESIS 20

From verse 1 of this chapter, it appears that Abraham left Hebron shortly after the destruction of Sodom and Gomorrah and traveled west toward the Mediterranean Sea, settling for a time in Gerar, which was Philistine territory.

Abraham is faced with the same problem he had upon entering Egypt, namely, the likelihood that he would be killed so that the local king could marry Sarah. It is a great tribute to Sarah's beauty that, even at this age (she will live to be 127 years old—see Genesis 23:1), she is still very attractive. Abraham uses the same solution given him by the Lord in Egypt. He introduces Sarah as his sister. You may wish to review the notes provided in Genesis 12 of this study guide for more about Sarah as his "sister."

Sure enough, Abimelech, king of the Philistines, desires her for a wife and sends for her, taking her into his household. It appears that she was there for some time. As was the case in Egypt, the Lord protected her, much to the distress of Abimelech. Among other things, once Sarah had been brought into the king's palace, no children at all were born in his household (verse 18). This, of course, was a major disaster in his culture and a most puzzling problem.

Upon being told in a dream what the problem was, the king called Abraham to come to him, apologizing and giving gifts to him as well as inviting him to settle anywhere he desired.

1 **And Abraham journeyed from thence** [*Hebron*] toward the south country, and dwelled between Kadesh and Shur, **and sojourned** [*stayed*] **in Gerar.**

> Next, Abraham introduces Sarah as his sister. Remember that Sarah is his niece, having been born to Abraham's brother, Haran. And in his culture, there was not generally a separate word for "niece" or "nephew," "aunt" or "uncle." Rather, they were simply referred to as "sister" or "brother" (for example, see verse 16 in this chapter, where Abimelech refers to Abraham as Sarah's "brother").

2 **And Abraham said of Sarah his wife, She** *is* **my sister: and Abimelech** king of Gerar sent, and **took Sarah.**

3 But **God came to Abimelech in a dream** by night, **and said to him**, Behold, thou *art but* a dead man, for **the woman which thou hast taken;** for she *is* **a man's wife.**

JST Genesis 20:2–4

2 And Abraham said again of Sarah his wife, She is my sister.

3 And Abimelech, king of Gerar, sent and took Sarah. But God came to Abimelech in a dream by night, and said unto him, Behold, thou hast taken a woman which is not thine own, for she is Abraham's wife.

4 And the Lord said unto him, Thou shalt return her unto Abraham, for if thou do it not thou shalt die.

4 **But Abimelech had not come near her** [*had not become involved sexually with her*]: and **he said, Lord, wilt thou slay also a righteous nation?**

5 **Said he** [*Abraham*] **not unto me, She** *is* **my sister?** and she, even **she herself said, He** *is* **my brother**: in the integrity of my heart and innocency of my hands have I done this [*in other words, "this was an honest mistake"*].

JST Genesis 20:5–6

5 And Abimelech had not come near her: **for the Lord had not suffered him** [*allowed him to*].

6 And he said, Lord, wilt thou slay me, and also a righteous nation? Behold, said he not unto me, She is my sister? And she, even she herself said, He is my brother; and in the integrity of my heart and innocency of my hands have I done this.

6 And **God said** unto him in a dream, Yea, **I know that thou didst this in the integrity of thy heart** [*I know this was an honest mistake*]; for **I also withheld** [*protected*] **thee from sinning against me: therefore suffered I thee not** [*this is the reason why I did not allow you*] **to touch her.**

> Next, beginning with verse 7, the Lord tells Abimelech what to do about the whole situation.

7 Now therefore **restore the man *his* wife**; for **he *is* a prophet, and he shall pray for thee, and thou shalt live**: and if thou restore *her* not [*JST, "to him"*], know thou that thou shalt surely die, thou, and all that *are* thine.

8 Therefore Abimelech rose early in the morning, and called all his servants, and told all these things in their ears: and the men were sore afraid.

> Next, in verses 9–10, King Abimelech scolds Abraham. In verses 11–13, Abraham explains his reason for introducing Sarah as his sister.

9 **Then Abimelech called Abraham, and said unto him, What hast thou done unto us?** and what have I offended thee, that thou hast brought on me and on my kingdom a great sin? thou hast done deeds unto me that ought not to be done.

10 And Abimelech said unto Abraham, **What sawest thou, that thou hast done this thing?**

11 And **Abraham said, Because I thought, Surely the fear of God *is* not in this place** [*these people do not know the true God and they don't know and keep His commandments, including not to murder husbands of beautiful wives*]; **and they will slay me for my wife's sake**.

> In verse 12, next, in what could easily appear to us as a riddle, Abraham clarifies the issue, according to his culture.

12 And yet **indeed *she is* my sister**; she *is* **the daughter of my father, but not the daughter of my mother**; and **she became my wife**.

> What Abraham is saying, in verse 12, above, is that his wife, Sarah, is his "sister" (in a normal use of the word in his society) because she is his father's granddaughter. In other words, Abraham's father was Terah. Abraham's brother was Haran. Haran and his wife had a daughter named Sarah (Abraham's niece). And, in their culture, a granddaughter was referred to as a "daughter."

13 And it came to pass, **when God caused me to wander from my father's house, that I said unto her** [*his wife, Sarah*], This *is* thy kindness which thou shalt shew unto me; **at every place whither we shall come, say of me, He *is* my brother**.

> Next, King Abimelech gives Abraham expensive gifts, gives Sarah back to him, and invites him to stay anywhere in his kingdom.

14 And **Abimelech took sheep, and oxen, and menservants, and womenservants, and gave *them* unto Abraham, and restored him Sarah his wife**.

15 And Abimelech said, Behold, my land *is* before thee: **dwell where it pleaseth thee**.

> The JST helps us understand what the last half of verse 16, next, is saying.

16 And **unto Sarah he said, Behold, I have given thy brother** [*Abraham*] **a thousand** *pieces* **of silver**: behold, **he** *is* **to thee a covering of the eyes**, unto all that *are* with thee, and with all *other:* thus she was reproved.

JST Genesis 20:17

17 And unto Sarah he said, Behold, I have given thy brother a thousand pieces of silver; behold, **he shall give unto thee a covering of the eyes, and it shall be a token unto all that thou mayest not be taken again from Abraham thy husband**. And thus she was reproved.

It appears, from the JST corrections above, that Abimelech suggested that hereafter, when Abraham and Sarah were traveling in areas where they were not known, Sarah should veil her face to hide her beauty and thus avoid such problems in the future.

Next, we are told one of the major problems encountered by Abimelech during the time he was attempting to take Sarah as a wife.

17 ¶ So Abraham prayed unto God: and **God healed Abimelech, and his wife, and his maidservants; and they bare** *children*.

18 **For the Lord had fast** [*tightly*] **closed up all the wombs of the house of Abimelech, because of Sarah Abraham's wife** [*no children were born to Abimelech during the time he was attempting to get Sarah to join his harem*].

GENESIS 21

This chapter deals with three main events: the birth and first years of Isaac, the evicting of Hagar and Ishmael from Abraham's camp, and a dispute over water between the herdsmen of Abraham and some of King Abimelech's servants.

First, in verses 1–8, we see the birth of Isaac, his circumcision, as commanded by the Lord of all Abraham's posterity in Old Testament times, and the celebration at the time he was weaned. The emphasis in verse 1, next, is that the Lord keeps His promises.

1 And **the Lord visited** [*blessed*] **Sarah as he had said**, and the Lord did unto Sarah as he had spoken.

2 For **Sarah conceived, and bare Abraham a son** in his old age, at the set time of which God had spoken to him [*in other words, as promised*].

JST Genesis 21:1

1 And the Lord visited Sarah as he had said, and the Lord did unto Sarah as he had spoken **by the mouth of his angels**; for Sarah conceived and bear Abraham a son in his old age, at the set time of which the angels of God had spoken to him.

3 And **Abraham called the name of his son** that was born unto him, whom Sarah bare to him, **Isaac**.

4 And **Abraham circumcised his son Isaac being eight days old**, as God had commanded him.

5 And **Abraham was an hundred years old, when his son Isaac was born unto him**.

6 ¶ And **Sarah said, God hath made me to laugh**, *so that* all that hear will laugh with me.

JST Genesis 21:5

5 And Sarah said, God has made me to **rejoice**; and also all that know me will **rejoice** with me.

The JST makes some changes to the Genesis verse 7, next. Note especially that Sarah bears witness that God keeps His promises (in the JST version).

7 And **she said**, Who would have said unto Abraham, that Sarah should have given children suck [*would be blessed to nurse her own child*]? for I have born *him* a son in his old age.

JST Genesis 21:6

6 And **she said unto Abraham**, Who would have said that Sarah should have given children suck? **For I was barren, but the Lord promised, and I have borne unto Abraham a son in his old age**.

The JST combines verses 8–9, next, into one verse. This is significant because it leads us to understand that Ishmael was mocking Isaac during the celebration, rather than his disrespect being demonstrated at a later date. Ishmael would have been somewhere around sixteen years old at this time.

Just a reminder that the backward "P" at the beginning of verse 9 in the King James version of the Bible indicates the beginning of a new topic.

8 And **the child grew, and was weaned: and Abraham made a great feast the *same* day that Isaac was weaned**.

9 ¶ And Sarah saw the son [*Ishmael*] of Hagar the Egyptian, which she had born unto Abraham, mocking.

JST Genesis 21:7

7 And the child grew, and was weaned. **And the day that Isaac was weaned**, Abraham made a great feast, and Sarah saw the son of Hagar the Egyptian, which Hagar had borne unto Abraham, mocking; **and she was troubled**.

Remember that Hagar had mocked Sarah (see Genesis 16:4) when she discovered that she was expecting. She was, in effect, taunting Sarah because she could not bear children and Hagar could. Now it seems that Hagar's attitude and disrespect had rubbed off on her son, Ishmael, who was likewise mocking Isaac. As a result, Sarah asks Abraham to send Hagar and Ishmael away. As stated in verse 11, this was hard on Abraham because he loved Ishmael.

10 **Wherefore** [*as a result*] **she** [*Sarah*] **said unto Abraham, Cast out this bondwoman** [*Hagar*] **and her son** [*Ishmael*]: for the son of this bondwoman shall not be heir with my son, *even* with Isaac.

11 And **the thing was very grievous in Abraham's sight because of his son**.

Next, in verses 12–13, the Lord comforts Abraham and tells him to grant Sarah's request, assuring him that Isaac is the covenant son through whom the Abrahamic covenant will be fulfilled. In addition, He reaffirms that the promise to Abraham of a numerous posterity will be partially fulfilled through Ishmael.

12 ¶ And **God said** unto Abraham, **Let it not be grievous in thy sight** because of the lad, and because of thy bondwoman; **in all that Sarah hath said unto thee, hearken unto her voice; for in Isaac shall thy seed be called**.

13 And **also of the son of the bondwoman** [*Ishmael*] **will I make a nation, because he** *is* **thy seed**.

With a heavy heart, Abraham obeys the Lord. The angel of the Lord provides assistance for Hagar and Ishmael in the wilderness.

14 And **Abraham rose up early in the morning, and took bread, and a bottle of water, and gave** *it* **unto Hagar, putting** *it* **on her shoulder, and the child, and sent her away**: and she departed, and wandered in the wilderness of Beer-sheba.

15 And the water was spent in the bottle, and she cast the child under one of the shrubs [*in the shade*].

16 And she went, and sat her down over against *him* [*German Bible, "across from him"*] a good way off, as it were a bowshot: for she said, Let me not see the death of the child. And she sat over against *him,* and lift up her voice, and wept.

17 And God heard the voice of the lad; and **the angel of God called to Hagar out of heaven**, and said unto her, What aileth thee, Hagar? **fear not; for God hath heard the voice of the lad** where he *is*.

Next, in verse 18, Hagar is promised that Ishmael will live and from him will come a large posterity (the Arab nations today).

18 Arise, lift up the lad, and hold him in thine hand; for **I will make him a great nation**.

19 And God opened her eyes, and she saw a well of water [*she was made aware of a spring of water nearby*]; and she went, and filled the bottle with water, and gave the lad drink.

20 And **God was with the lad; and he grew, and dwelt in the wilderness, and became an archer**.

21 And he dwelt in the wilderness of Paran: and **his mother took him a wife** out of the land of Egypt.

JST Genesis 21:19

19 And **he took him a wife** out of the land of Egypt.

Next, in verses 22–34, we are reminded how precious sources of water are in the arid climates where Abraham lived. A well had been commandeered away from Abraham's herdsmen by some of King Abimelech's men. The dispute is settled peacefully by Abraham and Abimelech. King Abimelech was the one who desired to have Sarah for a wife and took her away from Abraham for a time, believing that she was his sister, and had great difficulties as a result (see Genesis 20).

22 ¶ And it came to pass at that time, that **Abimelech and Phichol the chief captain of his host spake unto Abraham**, saying, God *is* with thee in all that thou doest [*you seem to prosper no matter what happens*]:

23 Now therefore swear [*covenant, promise*] unto me here by God that thou wilt not deal falsely with me, nor with my son, nor with my son's son: *but* according to the kindness that I have done unto thee, thou shalt do unto me, and to the land wherein thou hast sojourned [*lived in the land in King Abimelech's domain on which Abraham and his people were still living*].

24 And Abraham said, I will swear.

25 And **Abraham reproved** [*scolded*] **Abimelech because of a well of water, which Abimelech's servants had violently taken away**.

Next, in verse 26, we see that King Abimelech was unaware that the incident had taken place until Abraham made him aware of it.

26 And **Abimelech said**, I wot [*know*] not who hath done this thing: neither didst thou tell me, **neither yet heard I** *of it,* **but to day**.

We have seen Abraham's great character as a peacemaker on many occasions thus far, and we see it again now. Rather than fighting to ensure access to a well he dug, he takes the peaceful approach. He presents gifts to Abimelech as a witness that the well belongs to Abraham. They make a peaceful covenant to that effect, and the problem is solved.

27 And **Abraham took sheep and oxen, and gave them unto Abimelech; and both of them made a covenant**.

28 And Abraham set seven ewe lambs of the flock by themselves [*he separated out seven female lambs from his flock*].

Abraham is obviously a master of intrigue and getting someone's attention. Apparently, without saying anything, he has separated out the seven lambs from his flock, as mentioned in verse 28, above. Now he has Abimelech's full attention, and Abimelech, out of curiosity, asks Abraham what he is doing.

29 **And Abimelech said unto Abraham, What** *mean* **these seven ewe lambs** which thou hast set by themselves?

30 And **he** [*Abraham*] **said, For** *these* **seven ewe lambs shalt thou take of my hand** [*accept from me*]**, that they may be a witness unto me, that I have digged this well**.

31 Wherefore he called that place Beer-sheba [*"the well of the oath"*]; because there they sware [*made an agreement, a covenant*] both of them.

32 **Thus they made a covenant at Beer-sheba**: then Abimelech rose

up, and Phichol the chief captain of his host, and they returned into the land of the Philistines [*in other words, they went home*].

The JST considerably changes verse 33, next.

33 ¶ And *Abraham* planted a grove in Beer-sheba, and called there on the name of the Lord, the everlasting God.

JST Genesis 21:31

31 Then Abimelech, and Phicol, the chief captain of his hosts, rose up, and they planted a grove in Beer-sheba, and called there on the name of the Lord; and they returned unto the land of the Philistines.

34 And Abraham sojourned [*remained*] in the Philistines' land many days.

GENESIS 22

This is one of the most significant chapters in Genesis, and in all the scriptures, for that matter. In it, Abraham will be asked by the Lord to sacrifice his covenant son, Isaac. It is probably impossible for us to imagine the feelings in Abraham's heart as he obediently made preparations and traveled the three days' journey to Mount Moriah, a major hill of Jerusalem, with Isaac and two young male servants. Perhaps, among mortals, only Abraham can fully appreciate the feelings of Heavenly Father as He sacrificed His Only Begotten Son.

To make matters even more difficult for this great prophet, the memory of his own near sacrifice on the altar in the pagan temple in Ur (see Pearl of Great Price, Abraham, Facsimile No. 1) must have vividly returned to his mind upon being commanded to sacrifice Isaac. He himself had been bound upon the altar and had not been rescued by the Lord until the knife was raised to sacrifice him.

We must not overlook Isaac's role in this test of faith. Isaac would have been strong and vigorous, probably into his thirties at this time, while Abraham would have been quite elderly, unable to carry out this command of the Lord without Isaac's willing cooperation. We will quote from the *Old Testament Student Manual* on this:

"Isaac voluntarily submitted to Abraham. This important parallel is often overlooked. The Old Testament does not give enough detail to indicate exactly how old Isaac was at the time of this event, but it is very likely that he was an adult. Immediately following the account of the sacrifice on Mount Moriah is recorded the statement that Sarah died at the age of 127 (see Genesis 23:1). Thus, Isaac would have been 37 at the time of her death. Even if the journey to Moriah had happened several years before Sarah's death, Isaac would have been in his thirties, as was the Savior at the time of his crucifixion. Nevertheless, the exact age is not really important. What is significant is that Abraham was well over a hundred years old and Isaac was most likely a strong young man who could have put up a fierce resistance had he chosen to do so. In fact, Isaac submitted willingly to what his father intended, just as the Savior would do" (*Old Testament Student Manual,* page 78).

There is much symbolism in this chapter. For example, Abraham is a "type" of Heavenly Father, meaning that he symbolizes the Father. Isaac is a "type" of the Savior, the Son of God. We will make a brief chart of some of the "types" involved in the account of Abraham and the commandment to sacrifice Isaac.

TYPES (SYMBOLS)

Abraham and Isaac

1. THE FATHER: Sacrificed His Only Begotten Son.

    ABRAHAM: Called upon to sacrifice his only covenant son, Isaac.

2. THE SAVIOR'S BIRTH: Was miraculous.

    ISAAC'S BIRTH: Was miraculous.

3. THE SAVIOR: Voluntarily gave His life (John 10:18).

    ISAAC: Voluntarily submitted to his father, Abraham.

4. THE SAVIOR: Was in the tomb for three days.

    ABRAHAM AND ISAAC: Took three days to journey to Moriah.

5. THE SAVIOR: Carried His own cross on which He was sacrificed.

    ISAAC: Carried the wood for his sacrifice.

6. THE SAVIOR: Was sacrificed on Golgotha.

    ISAAC: Was placed on the altar on Moriah, part of the same set of hills in Jerusalem as Golgotha.

We will see more "types" or parallels as we now study this chapter.

1 And it came to pass after these things [*the things in chapter 21*], that **God did tempt** [*test, prove his faithfulness—see footnote 1a, in your Bible*] **Abraham,** and said unto him, Abraham: and he said, Behold, *here* I *am.*

> The JST makes an important change in verse 2, next. As you can see, it leaves out "son." This is important since Abraham had another son, Ishmael, at this time.

2 And he said, **Take now thy son, thine only** *son* **Isaac, whom thou lovest, and get thee into the land of Moriah** [*part of a hill or ridge system in the Jerusalem area*]; **and offer him there for a burnt offering upon one of the mountains which I will tell thee of.**

JST Genesis 22:2

> 2 And the Lord said, Take now thy son, **thine only Isaac,** whom thou lovest, and get thee into the land of Moriah; and offer him there for a burnt offering, upon one of the mountains of which I will tell thee.

3 ¶ And **Abraham** rose up early in the morning, and saddled his ass, and **took two of his young men with him, and Isaac his son,** and **clave** [*cut*] **the wood for the burnt offering,** and rose up, and went unto the place of which God had told him.

4 Then **on the third day** Abraham lifted up his eyes, and saw the place afar off.

5 And **Abraham said** unto his young men, Abide ye here with the ass; and **I and the lad will go yonder and worship, and come again to you**.

> The word "lad" in verse 5, above, has made many people think that Isaac was a young boy at this time. As noted in the background material for this chapter, above, most scholars believe that Isaac was a man in his thirties at the time of this test. Remember that Enoch was sixty-five years old (Moses 6:25) at the time of his calling to be a prophet, and he considered himself to be "but a lad" (Moses 6:31).
>
> Next, in verse 6, Abraham is a "type" of the Father as he lays the symbol of sacrifice upon his son, Isaac. Similarly, the Father laid the burden of the Atonement upon His Son, who had volunteered to be the supreme sacrifice for us all.

6 And **Abraham** [*symbolic of the Father*] **took the wood of the burnt offering** [*symbolic of the cross*]**, and laid** *it* **upon Isaac his son**; and he took the fire [*the vessel containing hot coals for the fire*] in his hand, and a knife; and they went both of them together [*symbolic of the Father and the Son working together for the salvation of souls*].

JST Genesis 22:7

7 And Abraham took the wood of the burnt offering, and **laid it upon his back** [*symbolic of the cross that Jesus carried on His back*]; and he took the fire in his hand, and a knife, and Isaac his son [*symbolic of Christ*]; and they went both of them together.

> Isaac's question in verse 7, next, must have pierced Abraham's heart to the core. Perhaps there is a similarity between this and the effect of the Savior's plea, "O my father, if it be possible, let this cup pass from me" (Matthew 26:39) upon our Heavenly Father.

7 And **Isaac spake unto Abraham his father, and said, My father**: and he said, Here *am* I, my son. And he said, **Behold the fire and the wood: but where** *is* **the lamb for a burnt offering?**

> Abraham's answer to his son was filled with faith, developed over long years of exacting obedience to God's commandments and instructions.

8 And **Abraham said, My son, God will provide himself a lamb for a burnt offering**: so they went both of them together [*symbolic of the perfect unity between the Father and the Son in carrying out the Atonement for us*].

9 And **they came to the place which God had told him of** [*on Mount Moriah*]; and **Abraham built an altar there** [*symbolic of the "altar cross" upon which the Son of God was sacrificed*], **and laid the wood in order, and bound Isaac his son, and laid him on the altar upon the wood** [*Isaac had voluntarily submitted completely to the will of his father, assisting his father carry out the will of God*].

10 And **Abraham stretched forth his hand, and took the knife to slay his son**.

> Imagine the relief in Abraham's whole soul as the angel of the Lord stops him (verses 11–12, next) and tells him he has passed the test! Imagine, also, being the angel who was privileged to deliver such a sweet message!

11 **And the angel of the Lord called unto him out of heaven**, and said, Abraham, Abraham: and he said, Here *am* I.

12 And he said, **Lay not thine hand upon the lad**, neither do thou any thing unto him: for **now I know that thou fearest God, seeing thou hast not withheld thy son, thine only** *son* **from me**.

> There is also symbolism in verse 13, next. Just as a ram was provided to be sacrificed in place of Isaac, so also was the Son of God sacrificed for our sins so that we could be spared for them, if we repent (Doctrine and Covenants 19:15–19).

13 **And Abraham lifted up his eyes, and looked, and behold** behind *him* **a ram caught in a thicket by his horns**: and **Abraham went and took the ram, and offered him up for a burnt offering in the stead of** [*in the place of*] **his son**.

> The Apostle Paul added an important insight to the account of Abraham and Isaac here. As a testimony to the great faith possessed by Abraham, Paul said that he had faith that the Lord would restore Isaac to life if he were required to actually sacrifice him. Paul taught (**bold** added for emphasis):

Hebrews 11:17–19

17 By faith Abraham, when he was tried [*tested*], offered up Isaac: and he that had received the promises offered up his only begotten *son*,

18 Of whom it was said, That in Isaac shall thy seed be called:

19 **Accounting that God** *was* **able to raise** *him* **up, even from the dead**; from whence also he received him in a figure [*figuratively speaking*].

14 And Abraham called the name of that place Jehovah-jireh: as it is said *to* this day, In the mount of the Lord it shall be seen [*in other words, "in this mount Jesus Christ will be seen"—see footnote 14b in your Bible, implying that the Savior will be crucified in this same area*].

> Next, an angel speaks for the Lord and repeats the basic elements of the Abrahamic covenant, which will be carried through Isaac. The JST will be helpful in understanding verses 15–16 in the Genesis account.

15 ¶ And the angel of the Lord called unto Abraham out of heaven the second time,

16 And said, **By myself have I sworn**, saith the Lord, **for because thou hast done this thing**, and hast not withheld thy son, thine only *son*:

JST Genesis 22:19–20

19 And the angel of the Lord called unto Abraham out of heaven the second time, and said,

20 Thus saith the Lord, **I have sworn by myself, that because thou hast done this thing**, and hast not withheld thy son, thine only Isaac from me;

To promise by the living God or by one's own life was the strongest possible promise or oath in the Old Testament world. The phrase, "I have sworn by myself," in JST verse 20, above, is such a promise, in this case being given by the Lord, Himself. We see a similar oath given to Zoram by Nephi in 1 Nephi 4:32.

The angel continues, reconfirming Jehovah's promises to Abraham.

17 **That in blessing I will bless thee, and in multiplying I will multiply thy seed** [*posterity*] **as the stars of the heaven, and as the sand which** *is* **upon the sea shore**; and thy seed shall possess the gate of his enemies [*among other things, this means that the righteous descendants of Abraham will triumph over all obstacles that stand in the way of exaltation*];

18 **And in thy seed shall all the nations of the earth be blessed**; because thou hast obeyed my voice.

Next, in verse 19, Abraham and Isaac return with the young men to their home in Beer-sheba. No doubt there was a great sense of relief in their hearts along with a wonderful feeling of having passed the most difficult of tests. This would be a very strong bond between them forever.

19 **So Abraham returned** unto his young men, and they rose up and went together **to Beer-sheba**; and Abraham dwelt at Beer-sheba.

In verses 20–24, the stage is set for Isaac to find Rebekah and marry her. It will be a sweet love story. Remember that Nahor is Abraham's brother and that he remained behind in Haran (see Genesis 11:31 and 12:1, 4) when Abraham was commanded by the Lord to depart and go southwest (to Canaan and then to Egypt). Thus, we see that Abraham has many relatives in the area of Haran. Of the eight children of Nahor, Moses (the writer of Genesis) focuses on Bethuel and Rebekah, his daughter. Isaac will marry his niece, Rebekah, just as Abraham married his niece, Sarah. He will be forty years old when he marries Rebekah (Genesis 25:20). We will read the story in Genesis 24.

20 ¶ And it came to pass after these things, that **it was told Abraham**, saying, Behold, **Milcah** [*Sarah's sister*], she **hath also born children unto thy brother Nahor**;

21 **Huz** his firstborn, and **Buz** his brother, and **Kemuel** the father of Aram,

22 And **Chesed**, and **Hazo**, and **Pildash**, and **Jidlaph**, and **Bethuel**.

23 And **Bethuel begat Rebekah**: these eight Milcah did bear to Nahor, Abraham's brother.

24 And his concubine [*servant wife*], whose name *was* Reumah, she bare also Tebah, and Gaham, and Thahash, and Maachah.

GENESIS 23

In this chapter, Sarah will die and be buried in a cave in Hebron, west of the Dead Sea. She was one of the great women in the scriptures. Isaiah spoke of her when he counseled the people to look to their noble ancestors as an example of righteous living (Isaiah 51:1–2). No doubt she has become a god, along with her husband, Abraham, who has already become a god (see Doctrine and Covenants 132:29, 37). The Doctrine and Covenants teaches us that righteous husbands and wives serve together as gods in eternity. We read (**bold** added for emphasis):

Doctrine and Covenants 132:19–20

19 And again, verily I say unto you, **if a man marry a wife by my word**, which is my law, and **by the new and everlasting covenant, and it is sealed unto them by the Holy Spirit of promise**, by him who is anointed, unto whom I have appointed this power and the keys of this priesthood; and it shall be said unto them—Ye shall come forth in the first resurrection; and if it be after the first resurrection, in the next resurrection; and shall inherit thrones, kingdoms, principalities, and powers, dominions, all heights and depths—then shall it be written in the Lamb's Book of Life, that he shall commit no murder whereby to shed innocent blood, and if ye abide in my covenant, and commit no murder whereby to shed innocent blood, it shall be done unto them in all things whatsoever my servant hath put upon them, in time, and through all eternity; and shall be of full force when they are out of the world; and **they shall pass by the angels, and the gods**, which are set there, **to their exaltation** and glory in all things, as hath been sealed upon their heads, which glory shall be a fulness and a continuation of the seeds forever and ever.

20 **Then shall they be gods**, because they have no end; therefore shall they be from everlasting to everlasting, because they continue; then shall they be above all, because all things are subject unto them. Then shall they be gods, because **they have all power**, and the angels are subject unto them.

Next, in this chapter, Abraham will negotiate with some residents of the area for a cave in which to bury Sarah. For this chapter, we will **bold** a few key statements in the narrative and then move on to chapter 24.

1 And **Sarah was an hundred and seven and twenty years old**: *these were* the years of the life of Sarah.

> At this point, then, Abraham was 137 years old, Isaac was 37, and Ishmael was about 51 years of age.

2 And **Sarah died in** Kirjath-arba; the same is **Hebron** in the land of Canaan: and **Abraham came to mourn for Sarah, and to weep for her.**

3 ¶ And **Abraham** stood up from before his dead [Sarah], and **spake unto the sons of Heth, saying**,

4 I *am* a stranger and a sojourner with you: **give me a possession of a buryingplace with you, that I may bury my dead** out of my sight.

5 And **the children of Heth answered** Abraham, saying unto him,

6 Hear us, my lord: thou *art* a mighty prince among us: **in the choice of our sepulchres bury thy dead** [*choose any one you want*]; none of us shall withhold from thee his sepulchre, but that thou mayest bury thy dead.

7 And Abraham stood up, and bowed himself to the people of the land, *even* to the children of Heth.

8 And **he communed with them, saying**, If it be your mind that I should bury my dead out of my sight; hear me, and **intreat for me to Ephron** the son of Zohar [*please negotiate with Ephron for the cave of Machpelah for me*],

9 **That he may give me the cave of Machpelah**, which he hath, which *is* in the end of his field; **for as much money as it is worth** he shall give it me for a possession of a buryingplace amongst you.

10 And Ephron dwelt among the children of Heth: and Ephron the Hittite answered Abraham in the audience of the children of Heth, *even* of all that went in at the gate of his city, saying,

11 **Nay, my lord, hear me: the field give I thee, and the cave that** *is* **therein, I give it thee**; in the presence of the sons of my people give I it thee: bury thy dead.

12 And **Abraham** bowed down himself before the people of the land.

13 And he **spake unto Ephron** in the audience of the people of the land, saying, **But if thou** *wilt give it*, **I pray thee, hear me: I will give thee money for the field; take** *it* **of me, and I will bury my dead there**.

14 And **Ephron answered** Abraham, saying unto him,

15 My lord, hearken unto me: **the land** *is worth* **four hundred shekels of silver; what** *is* **that betwixt me and thee? bury therefore thy dead**.

16 And Abraham hearkened unto Ephron; and **Abraham weighed to Ephron the silver** [*weighed out 400 sheckels of silver and gave it to him*], which he had named in the audience of the sons of Heth, four hundred shekels of silver, current *money* with the merchant.

> Verse 17, next, contains a description of the ground that Abraham purchased as a burial place for Sarah.

17 ¶ And the field of Ephron, which *was* in Machpelah, which *was* before Mamre, **the field, and the cave** which *was* therein, **and all the trees that** *were* **in the field**, that *were* in all the borders round about, were made sure [*were secured in the transaction*]

18 Unto Abraham for a possession in the presence of the children of Heth, before all that went in at the gate of his city.

19 And after this, **Abraham buried Sarah his wife in the cave of the field of Machpelah** before Mamre: **the same** *is* **Hebron** in the land of Canaan.

> As previously mentioned, repetition is a common literary technique among ancient writers. Isaiah makes constant use of this technique for emphasis. Moses did the same as he wrote Genesis. A good example of repetition is found in verse 20, next.

20 And the field, and the cave that *is* therein, were made sure unto Abraham for a possession of a buryingplace by the sons of Heth.

GENESIS 24

This chapter contains one of the greatest love stories of all time. It is tender and sweet. It is the story of finding a wife for Isaac.

By now, Isaac is nearing forty years of age. He was born about 1900 BC and is the one through whom the Abrahamic covenant (Genesis 12:2–3; 17:1–8; Abraham 2:9–11) is to be perpetuated. Since this covenant involves the priesthood and taking the blessings and ordinances performed by worthy priesthood holders to all the world, Abraham is naturally concerned that Isaac not marry a wife whose lineage would prevent his posterity from holding the priesthood.

During this time, Abraham is living among the Philistines (Genesis 21:34) in the land of Canaan among people who are descendants of Cain (see Bible Dictionary, under "Canaan" and under "Canaanite"), coming through the lineage of Ham (Noah's son) and his wife, Egyptus. At that time, the descendants of Ham and Egyptus were not permitted to hold the priesthood (see Abraham 1:21–26).

Thus, Abraham is very concerned that Isaac not marry a Canaanite woman. Later, Isaac will have the same concern about his son, Jacob (see Genesis 28:1).

Abraham's inspired solution to this concern is to have his "eldest servant" (the foreman over all of his properties and concerns) travel to Haran to find a wife for Isaac among his own extended family members. Haran was near the headwaters of the Euphrates River, some 450 miles northwest of Abraham's current home among the Canaanites. Abraham and Sarah had relatives still living in Haran.

Abraham and Sarah had spent many years in Haran, after leaving Ur approximately ninety years before. Seventy-eight years before, they, with Lot and others, had left Haran, as commanded by the Lord (Abraham 2:6). From Haran, they had traveled southwest through Canaan and eventually into Egypt.

Other members of Abraham's family had remained in Haran. These relatives included Abraham's brother and sister-in-law, Nahor and Milcah. Milcah, by the way, was Sarah's sister. As mentioned in Genesis 22:20–23, Nahor and Milcah have had eight children by now, and among their grandchildren is a young woman named Rebekah. Abraham's loyal and trusted servant is to look for a wife for Isaac in Haran.

As we begin our study of this chapter, we see Abraham ask his foreman to covenant with him that he will try to find a wife for Isaac among Abraham's relatives in Haran. You will see the servant put his hand under Abraham's hand (the JST version) as a token of making a covenant. This was apparently according to a custom in Abraham's day for making serious promises. As usual, we will use **bold** to point out the story line and for teaching emphasis.

1 And **Abraham was old**, *and* well stricken in age [*had become quite old*]: and the Lord had blessed Abraham in all things.

2 And Abraham said unto his eldest servant of his house, that ruled over all that he had [*in other words, his chief steward or foreman*], Put, I pray thee, thy hand **under my thigh**:

3 And I will make thee **swear** [*promise, covenant*] by the Lord, the God of heaven, and the God of the earth, **that thou shalt not take a wife unto my son of the daughters of the Canaanites**, among whom I dwell:

4 But thou shalt go unto my country, and to my kindred [*in Haran*], and take a wife unto my son Isaac.

JST Genesis 24:2

2 And Abraham said unto his eldest servant of his house, that ruled over all that he had; Put forth I pray thee thy hand **under my hand**, and I will make thee swear before the Lord, the God of heaven, and the God of the earth, that thou shalt not take a wife unto my son, of the daughters of the Canaanites among whom I dwell; but thou shalt go unto my country, and to my kindred and take a wife unto my son Isaac.

Next, in verse 5, the servant is worried that Isaac's future wife might not be willing to leave home and come to Abraham's place. Thus, he asks if he should take Isaac to her if she is unwilling to come to him.

5 And the servant said unto him, **Peradventure** [*what if*] **the woman will not be willing to follow me unto this land**: must I needs bring thy son again unto the land from whence thou camest? [*should I take Isaac to Haran*]?

6 And Abraham said unto him, Beware thou that thou **bring not my son thither** again [*in other words, "absolutely not"*].

Next, in verse 7, Abraham, who has developed tremendous faith over years of trial and testing, expresses his faith and confidence that the Lord will send angelic help for the servant as he does his best to carry out this daunting task. There is great power in Abraham's faith.

7 ¶ **The Lord** God of heaven, which took me from my father's house, and from the land of my kindred, and which spake unto me, and that sware unto me [*covenanted with me*], saying, Unto thy seed will I give this

land; he **shall send his angel before thee,** and thou shalt take a wife unto my son from thence [*from Haran*].

> The servant, being a man of great honesty and integrity himself, is concerned about making a promise that he might not be able to fulfill. Abraham, seeing his concern, takes pressure off of him in verse 8, next.

8 And if the woman will not be willing to follow thee, then thou shalt be clear from this my oath: only bring not my son thither again [*just don't take Isaac to Haran under any circumstances*].

> We are led to wonder why Abraham would be so against allowing Isaac to go to his relatives in Haran, as expressed in the above verses. We do not know. But one possibility might be the fact that Abraham's father apostatized again while dwelling in Haran (Abraham 2:5), and perhaps Abraham was worried that his influence might have carried on among other members of the family there.
>
> Whatever the case, the servant makes the sign of the promise in verse 9, next, and covenants with Abraham to do as he has been instructed.

9 And the servant put his hand under the **thigh** of Abraham his master, and sware [*covenanted*] to him concerning that matter.

JST Genesis 24:8

> 8 And the servant put his hand under the **hand** of Abraham his master, and sware to him concerning that matter.

> As we follow the account, you will see that this chief servant of Abraham is a mighty man of God himself, full of faith, humility, and commitment to duty.

10 ¶ And the servant took ten camels of the camels of his master, and departed; for all the goods of his master were in his hand [*Abraham had placed him in charge of everything he had*]: and he arose, and went to Mesopotamia, unto the city of Nahor [*by now, there was a city named after Abraham's brother in the region of Haran*].

11 And he made his camels to kneel down without [*outside of*] the city by a well of water at the time of the evening, even the time that women go out to draw water.

12 And he said [*he prayed*], O Lord God of my master Abraham, I pray thee, send me good speed this day [*help me accomplish my task*], and shew [*pronounced "show"*] kindness unto my master Abraham.

13 Behold, I stand here by the well of water; and the daughters of the men of the city come out to draw water:

> In effect, the servant applies the principles taught in Doctrine and Covenants 9:7–9 in verse 14, next. He comes up with a possible plan and proposes it to the Lord. We will quote these verses from the Doctrine and Covenants here:

Doctrine and Covenants 9:7–9

> 7 Behold, you have not understood; you have supposed that I would

give it unto you, when you took no thought save it was to ask me.

8 But, behold, I say unto you, that **you must study it out in your mind; then you must ask me if it be right**, and if it is right I will cause that your bosom shall burn within you; therefore, you shall feel that it is right.

9 But if it be not right you shall have no such feelings, but you shall have a stupor of thought that shall cause you to forget the thing which is wrong; therefore, you cannot write that which is sacred save it be given you from me.

Watch, now, as the servant prays and proposes his plan to the Lord.

14 And let it come to pass, that the damsel to whom I shall say, Let down thy pitcher, I pray thee, that I may drink; and she shall say, Drink, and I will give thy camels drink also: let the same be she that thou hast appointed for thy servant Isaac; and thereby shall I know that thou hast shewed kindness unto my master.

15 ¶ And it came to pass, before he had done speaking, that, behold, Rebekah came out, who was born to Bethuel, son of Milcah, the wife of Nahor, Abraham's brother [*in other words, Rebekah is Abraham's niece*], with her pitcher upon her shoulder.

The JST adds helpful correction to the Genesis account in verse 16, next. From it, we find that the servant had never before seen anyone so beautiful.

16 And the damsel was very fair to look upon, a virgin, **neither had any man known her** [*a way of saying that she was a virgin*]: and she went down to the well, and filled her pitcher, and came up.

JST Genesis 24:16

16 And the damsel being a virgin, very fair to look upon, **such as the servant of Abraham had not seen, neither had any man known the like unto her;** and she went down to the well, and filled her pitcher, and came up.

17 And the servant ran to meet her, and said, Let me, I pray thee, drink a little water of [*from*] thy pitcher.

18 And she said, Drink, my lord: and she hasted, and let down her pitcher upon her hand, and gave him drink.

19 And when she had done giving him drink, she said, I will draw water for thy camels also, until they have done drinking [*a formidable task, since ten thirsty camels would drink a lot of water!*].

20 And she hasted, and emptied her pitcher into the trough, and ran again unto the well to draw water, and drew for all his camels.

21 And the man wondering at her held his peace [*did not say anything*], **to wit** whether the Lord had made his journey prosperous or not [*whether this was the answer to his prayer; according to verse 22, next, he obviously quickly decided that it was*].

JST Genesis 24:21

21 And the man, wondering at her, held his peace, **pondering in his heart** whether the Lord had made his journey prosperous or not.

22 And it came to pass, as the camels had done drinking, that the man took a golden earring of half a shekel weight [*NIV, "about one fifth ounce"*], and two bracelets for her hands of ten shekels [*NIV, "about 4 ounces"*] weight of gold;

23 And said, Whose daughter art thou? tell me, I pray thee: is there room in thy father's house for us to lodge in?

24 And she said unto him, I am the daughter of Bethuel the son of Milcah, which she bare unto Nahor [*in other words, I am Nahor's granddaughter*].

25 She said moreover unto him, We have both straw and provender [*food, hay*] enough, and room to lodge in.

> Next, we see that this great servant of Abraham (and the Lord) was quick to express gratitude to God. We do well to follow his example.

26 And the man bowed down his head, and worshipped [*thanked*] the Lord.

27 And he said, Blessed [*praised*] be the Lord God of my master Abraham, who hath not left destitute my master of his mercy and his truth: I being in the way [*not knowing for sure where I should go once I got here*], the Lord led me to the house of my master's brethren [*relatives*].

28 And the damsel ran, and **told them of her mother's house** these things.

JST Genesis 24:27

27 **And the damsel ran to the house, and told her mother** these things.

29 ¶ And Rebekah had a brother, and his name was Laban: and Laban ran out unto the man, unto the well.

> We will pause a moment here and talk a bit more about Rebekah's brother, Laban, introduced in verse 29, above. In several years, Jacob, who will be born to Isaac and Rebekah twenty years after they are married, will travel to Haran in search of a wife. There, he will work seven years for Laban (his uncle) in order to marry his daughter, Rachel. Laban will deceive him by having him marry his older daughter, Leah. Jacob will marry Rachel a week later with the agreement that he must work another seven years to pay her father for the privilege of marrying her. She will be his cousin. We will read about this in Genesis 29.
>
> Now back to Laban, as he hurries to meet Abraham's servant.

30 And it came to pass, when he saw the earring and bracelets upon his sister's hands, and when he heard the words of Rebekah his sister, saying, Thus spake the man unto me; that he came unto the man; and, behold, he [*Abraham's*

servant] stood by the camels at the well.

31 And he [*Laban*] said, Come in, thou blessed of the Lord; wherefore standest thou without [*why are you still standing outside*]? for I have prepared the house, and room for the camels.

> Next, Laban extends the best of mid-Eastern hospitality to the weary travelers.

32 ¶ And the man [*Abraham's servant*] came into the house: and he [*Laban*] ungirded [*JST: "unburdened"*] his camels, and gave straw and provender for the camels, and water to wash his feet, and the men's feet that were with him.

> Next, Abraham's servant refuses to eat until he has delivered his message from Abraham.

33 And **there was set** *meat* [*food*] **before him to eat: but he said, I will not eat, until I have told mine errand**. And he said [*JST: "Laban said"*]**, Speak on.**

34 And **he said, I** *am* **Abraham's servant**.

35 And **the Lord hath blessed my master greatly**; and **he is become great** [*he has become a very prosperous and prominent man*]: and he hath given him flocks, and herds, and silver, and gold, and menservants, and maidservants, and camels, and asses.

36 And **Sarah my master's wife bare a son** to my master **when she was old: and unto him hath he given all that he hath** [*Isaac will inherit all that Abraham has*].

37 And **my master made me swear** [*promise with an oath*]**, saying, Thou shalt not take a wife to my son of the daughters of the Canaanites**, in whose land I dwell:

38 But **thou shalt go unto my father's house** [*to the descendants of Terah (Abraham's father)*]**, and to my kindred** [*relatives*]**, and take a wife unto my son.**

39 And **I said unto my master, Peradventure** [*JST: "perhaps"*] **the woman will not follow me.**

40 **And he said** unto me, **The Lord**, before whom I walk [*whom I worship*]**, will send his angel with thee, and prosper thy way** [*bless you with success*]**; and thou shalt take a wife for my son of my kindred**, and of my father's house:

41 **Then shalt thou be clear** [*freed*] **from** *this* **my oath, when thou comest to my kindred**; and **if they give not thee** *one* [*JST: "a wife for my son"*]**, thou shalt be clear from my oath.**

42 And **I came this day unto the well, and said, O Lord** God of my master Abraham, if now thou do prosper my way which I go:

> As Abraham's servant continues explaining his mission to them, he

rehearses the plan he proposed to the Lord in silent prayer for discerning who should become Isaac's wife.

43 Behold, I stand by the well of water; and it shall come to pass, that when the virgin cometh forth to draw *water,* **and I say to her, Give me, I pray thee, a little water of thy pitcher to drink**;

44 And she say to me, Both drink thou, and I will also draw for thy camels: *let* **the same** *be* **the woman whom the Lord hath appointed out for my master's son**.

45 And before I had done speaking in mine heart, behold, **Rebekah came** forth **with her pitcher on her shoulder; and she went down unto the well, and drew** *water:* **and I said unto her, Let me drink, I pray thee**.

46 And she made haste, and let down her pitcher from her *shoulder,* **and said, Drink, and I will give thy camels drink also**: so I drank, and she made the camels drink also.

47 And I asked her, and said, Whose daughter *art* **thou?** And **she said, The daughter of Bethuel**, Nahor's son, whom Milcah bare unto him: **and I put the earring upon her face**, and the bracelets upon her hands.

The JST makes helpful corrections to the last part of verse 47, above.

JST Genesis 24:51

51 And I gave the earrings unto her, to put into her ears, and the bracelets upon her hands.

48 And I bowed down my head, and worshipped [*thanked*] **the Lord**, and blessed [*praised*] the Lord God of my master Abraham, which had led me in the right way to take my master's brother's daughter [*Nahor's granddaughter, Rebekah*] unto his son [*Isaac*].

Next, the servant requests an answer to the proposal from Rebekah's brother and father. It is proper, according to the custom of the day, to first request permission from the family. We will see that Rebekah was also in agreement when we get to verses 57–58.

49 And now if ye will deal kindly and truly with my master [*in other words, if the answer is yes*], **tell me**: and **if not, tell me; that I may turn to the right hand, or to the left** [*so that I know which direction this is going to go*].

50 Then Laban [*Rebekah's brother*] **and Bethuel** [*her father*] **answered** and said, **The thing proceedeth from the Lord: we cannot speak unto thee bad or good** [*in other words, this thing comes from the Lord; we would not dare to take it upon ourselves to interfere*].

51 Behold, **Rebekah** *is* **before thee, take** *her,* **and go, and let her be thy master's son's wife, as the Lord hath spoken**.

52 And it came to pass, that, **when Abraham's servant heard their words, he worshipped** [*thanked*] **the Lord**, *bowing himself* to the earth.

53 And **the servant brought forth jewels of silver, and jewels of gold, and raiment** [*clothing*], **and gave *them* to Rebekah: he gave also to her brother and to her mother precious things.**

As you can see, in verse 54, next, the servant is anxious to get on his way back to Abraham. It is likely that part of the reason for this hurrying on his part is a desire to give the good news to Abraham as quickly as possible.

54 And **they did eat and drink, he and the men that *were* with him, and tarried all night** [*stayed through the night*]; **and they rose up in the morning, and he said, Send me away unto my master** [*Abraham*].

55 **And her brother and her mother said, Let the damsel abide with us *a few* days, at the least ten; after that she shall go.**

The servant is very insistent about leaving immediately. Rebekah will cast the deciding vote.

56 And **he said unto them, Hinder me not**, seeing the Lord hath prospered my way [*blessed my mission with success*]; **send me away that I may go to my master.**

57 And **they said, We will call the damsel, and enquire at her mouth** [*ask her to tell us what she desires*].

58 And **they called Rebekah, and said unto her, Wilt thou go with this man? And she said, I will go.**

59 And **they sent away Rebekah their sister, and her nurse, and Abraham's servant, and his men.**

Next, as Rebekah prepares, the family leaves a blessing with her, one very typical of mid-Eastern culture, and one that reflects Rebekah's role as the future mother of Israel (Jacob).

60 And **they blessed Rebekah, and said** unto her, Thou *art* our sister, **be thou *the mother* of thousands of millions,** and let thy seed possess the gate of those which hate them [*may you triumph over all your enemies*].

61 ¶ **And Rebekah arose, and her damsels** [*woman servants*]**, and they rode upon the camels, and followed the man: and the servant took Rebekah, and went his way.**

One can imagine that Isaac was somewhat nervous about the results of his father's servant's mission, since his future happiness depended on the outcome. Beginning with verse 62, next, we see him in the evening, thinking about things in the quiet solitude of a field. Perhaps he had made calculations as to about how long it would take the servant's camel train to travel to Haran and back and was anxiously keeping a watch out for their return.

Whatever the case, he sees them coming in the distance, and then meets Rebekah and falls instantly in love.

62 And **Isaac came from the way of the well** Lahai-roi; for he dwelt in the south country.

63 **And** Isaac **went out to meditate in the field at the eventide:** and he **lifted up his eyes, and saw, and, behold, the camels** *were* **coming.**

64 And **Rebekah lifted up her eyes, and when she saw Isaac, she lighted off** [*got off*] **the camel.**

65 **For** she *had* **said unto the servant, What man** *is* **this that walketh in the field to meet us? And the servant** *had* **said, It** *is* **my master:** therefore she took a vail, and covered herself.

66 And **the servant told Isaac all things that he had done.**

67 And **Isaac brought her into his mother Sarah's tent, and took Rebekah, and she became his wife**; and **he loved her**: and Isaac was comforted after his mother's *death* [*see Genesis 23:1–2*].

> As stated previously, Isaac is forty years old when he and Rebekah are married. She will not be able to have children for twenty years, which will be a severe trial for her and Isaac. We will feel her greatness and closeness to the Lord in chapter 25 when we see her pray to Him concerning her inability to bear children. We will also hear His direct revelation to her on the matter.

GENESIS 25

In this chapter, Abraham, who is now approximately 140 years old (he will die at age 175—see verse 7), will marry a woman by the name of Keturah and will have six sons by her. It is, of course, likely that he had some daughters also, but if so, they are not mentioned in the account. It is also reasonable to suppose that each of these sons, if worthy, received the Melchizedek Priesthood from their father. If we are guessing correctly, Moses's line of priesthood authority will come through one of these sons, namely, Midian.

According to footnote 2b, in your King James version of the Bible, Midian will establish a family in the land of Midian (east of the Sinai Peninsula and across the Gulf of Aqaba, about 100 miles south of the Dead Sea). In roughly 500 years, Moses will flee to this land when he is forced to leave Egypt. Jethro, the priest of Midian (Exodus 2:16), will become Moses's father-in-law when he marries Zipporah (Exodus 2:21). According to Doctrine and Covenants 84:6, Moses will receive the Melchizedek Priesthood from Jethro (Reuel—Exodus 2:18).

Also in this chapter, we will read of Ishmael's posterity, of the birth of twins to Isaac and Rebekah (Esau and Jacob), and of Esau's disdain for the birthright blessing and the responsibility to live the gospel and carry on the heritage and blessings of Abraham and Isaac to all the world (Abraham 2:9–11). Therefore, he will sell his birthright to Jacob for a meal of bread and lentil soup (verses 33–34).

First, in verses 1–10, Abraham remarries, has children, dies at age 175, and is buried near Sarah's grave in Hebron (about 25 miles south southwest of Jerusalem).

1 Then **again Abraham took a wife, and her name** *was* **Keturah.**

2 And **she bare him Zimran**, and **Jokshan**, and **Medan**, and **Midian** [*who is possibly in the direct line of Moses's Melchizedek Priesthood—see background notes above*], and **Ishbak**, and **Shuah**.

3 And Jokshan begat Sheba, and Dedan. And the sons of Dedan were Asshurim, and Letushim, and Leummim.

4 And **the sons of Midian**; Ephah, and Epher, and Hanoch, and Abida, and Eldaah. All these *were* the children of Keturah.

5 ¶ And **Abraham gave all that he had unto Isaac**.

> It appears from verse 6, next, that Abraham's flocks and herds were so large that there was not sufficient grazing to support all of his sons and their families and herds. Therefore, he gave them gifts to give them a good start on their own and sent them away to establish families and grazing lands of their own. Isaac, the birthright son, remained to inherit Abraham's territory and properties.

6 But **unto the sons of the concubines** [*second class wives, according to the social structure of the day, perhaps meaning Hagar and Keturah*], **which Abraham had, Abraham gave gifts, and sent them away from Isaac his son**, while he yet lived, eastward, unto the east country.

> Next, in verse 7, Moses tells us that Abraham lived to be 175 years of age.

7 And **these** *are* **the days of the years** [*JST, "the number of the years"*] **of Abraham's life** which he lived, **an hundred threescore and fifteen years** [*175 years*].

8 **Then Abraham gave up the ghost**, and died in a good old age, an old man, and full *of years;* **and was gathered to his people** [*went to the postmortal spirit world, where he joined Sarah and his righteous ancestors back to Adam and Eve; he was resurrected at the time of the Savior's resurrection—see Doctrine and Covenants 133:55*].

9 And **his sons Isaac and Ishmael buried him in the cave of Machpelah** [*where Sarah had been buried forty-eight years earlier*], in the field of Ephron the son of Zohar the Hittite, which *is* before Mamre;

10 The field which Abraham purchased of the sons of Heth: **there was Abraham buried, and Sarah his wife.**

11 ¶ And it came to pass after the death of Abraham, that God blessed his son Isaac; and Isaac dwelt by the well Lahai-roi [*in southern Israel, about fifty to sixty miles south of Jerusalem*].

> Next, we see that Ishmael, Abraham's son by Hagar, had twelve

sons. His descendants became the Arab nations today. We know that he also had daughters. Esau, twin brother of Jacob, will marry one of Ishmael's daughters (Genesis 28:9).

12 ¶ Now **these** *are* **the generations** [*descendants*] **of Ishmael**, Abraham's son, whom Hagar the Egyptian, Sarah's handmaid, bare unto Abraham:

13 And these *are* the names of the sons of Ishmael, by their names, according to their generations: the firstborn of Ishmael, **Nebajoth**; and **Kedar**, and **Adbeel**, and **Mibsam**,

14 And **Mishma**, and **Dumah**, and **Massa**,

15 **Hadar**, and **Tema**, **Jetur**, **Naphish**, and **Kedemah**:

16 These *are* the sons of Ishmael, and these *are* their names, by their towns, and by their castles; **twelve princes** [*leaders of tribes or nations*] according to their nations.

17 And **these** *are* **the years of the life of Ishmael**, an hundred and thirty and seven years [*Ishmael lived to be 137 years old*]: and he gave up the ghost and died; and was gathered unto his people.

> Next, Moses informs us that the descendants of Ishmael settled in a large geographical area, basically from Egypt to Assyria.

18 And **they dwelt from Havilah unto Shur, that** *is* **before Egypt, as thou goest toward Assyria**: *and* he died in the presence of all his brethren.

> Next, Moses gives us an account of Isaac and Rebekah and their twins, Esau and Jacob.

19 ¶ And **these** *are* **the generations** [*descendants*] **of Isaac**, Abraham's son: Abraham begat Isaac:

20 And **Isaac was forty years old when he took Rebekah to wife**, the daughter of Bethuel the Syrian of Padan-aram [*Haran*], the sister to Laban the Syrian [*Haran was near the northern border of Syria*].

> We learn from verse 21, next, that Rebekah was barren (could not have children) for twenty years. In a culture that valued children and posterity, this was a very deep and painful problem for Isaac and Rebekah. He prayed fervently to the Lord, and they were blessed with twins.

21 And **Isaac intreated** [*prayed fervently to*] **the Lord for his wife, because she** *was* **barren**: and the Lord was intreated of him [*the Lord answered his prayers*], and **Rebekah his wife conceived**.

JST Genesis 25:21

21 And Isaac entreated the Lord for his wife, **that she might bare children**, because she was barren. And the Lord was entreated of him, and Rebekah his wife conceived.

Next, Rebekah feels trouble of some sort within her womb. We see her great faith and closeness to the Lord as she prays to find out what the situation is.

22 And **the children** [*twins*] **struggled together within her; and she said, If** *it be* **so, why** *am* **I thus** [*what am I feeling inside me*]**? And she went to enquire of the Lord.**

JST Genesis 25:22

> 22 And the children struggled together **within her womb**; and she said, **If I am with child, why is it thus with me**? And she went to inquire of the Lord.

Next, in verse 23, the Lord gives Rebekah a very specific revelation concerning her twins. She is, in effect, given the gift of prophecy (see Doctrine and Covenants 46:22) and sees the future.

23 And the Lord said unto her, **Two nations** *are* **in thy womb** [*you are going to have twins who will become heads of two nations*]**, and two manner of people shall be separated from thy bowels** [*there will be great differences between the personalities of your two sons and their descendants*]**; and** *the one* **people shall be stronger than** *the other* **people** [*the descendants of Jacob will be stronger than the descendants of Esau*]**; and the elder shall serve the younger** [*in other words, the younger will have the birthright blessings*]**.**

> It will be very helpful for us to keep in mind what Rebekah now knows about her two sons by direct revelation from God when we get to chapter 27. There, Rebekah will instruct Jacob in getting the birthright blessing from his father, Isaac, in the place of Esau. Without this prophetic knowledge of the will of God concerning Jacob, we might be quite disturbed at what goes on to secure the birthright blessing from Isaac for Jacob. Knowing it was God's will makes all the difference in how we view Rebekah's actions at the time.

24 ¶ And **when her days to be delivered were fulfilled** [*when she gave birth*]**, behold,** *there were* **twins in her womb.**

25 And the first came out red, all over like an hairy garment; and they called his name Esau [*a word that means "hairy"—see Bible Dictionary under "Esau"*].

26 And after that came his brother out, and his hand took hold on Esau's heel; and his name was called Jacob [*meaning "supplanter"—in other words, "one who takes another's place"*]: and Isaac *was* threescore years old [*sixty years old*] when she bare them.

> Verse 27, next, needs a bit of explanation in order to be correctly understood. The basic meaning of "plain," as used to describe Jacob, is that he was well-rounded, whole, and complete (see footnote 27b, in your Bible), whereas, Esau was not. He tended toward one main interest in life, namely, hunting.

27 And **the boys grew**: and **Esau was a cunning hunter, a man of**

the field; and **Jacob *was* a plain man, dwelling in tents**.

The word "loved" as used in verse 28, next, means "favored" or "preferred." In other words, Isaac tended to favor Esau because he enjoyed the benefits of fresh meat from Esau's hunting skills, whereas, Rebekah got along best with Jacob. As any parent will tell you, it is not uncommon for one parent in a family to get along best with some of the children and the other parent to get along better with other children.

28 And **Isaac loved Esau, because he did eat of *his* venison: but Rebekah loved Jacob**.

Next, in verses 29–34, we read about the famous "mess of pottage," or "bowl of lentil soup." At issue here is the Abrahamic covenant. It is to be perpetuated through Isaac's posterity. As you will clearly see in these verses, Esau is using his agency to distance himself from the birthright responsibilities, which, in this case, include the responsibility of carrying the gospel and the blessings of the priesthood to all the world (in other words, the "Abrahamic covenant"—see Abraham 2:9–11).

We will see another indicator that Esau has little interest in living a life worthy of being a man of God as we get to Genesis 26:34–35, when he marries "out of covenant Israel."

29 ¶ And **Jacob sod pottage** [*planted and grew a crop of lentils*]: and **Esau came from the field** [*from hunting—see verse 27, above*]**, and he *was* faint** [*was very hungry*]:

30 And **Esau said to Jacob, Feed me**, I pray thee, **with that** same **red *pottage;* for I *am* faint**: therefore was his name called Edom [*"red"—in other words, Esau, whose name meant "hairy," was also called "Edom," which means "red"—see verse 25, above*].

It is obvious from verse 31, next, that Jacob is aware that he is to be the birthright son, and to carry on the responsibilities of the Abrahamic covenant. It is highly likely that his mother had shared her revelation from God (verse 23, above) with him and taught him what his role in God's work was to be.

In the culture of the day, the firstborn son would normally be the one who received the birthright, which included a double portion of land and the responsibility to watch over the family. Therefore, Jacob would naturally be looking for opportunities to properly obtain the birthright from Esau. Without knowing about the Lord's revelation to Rebekah, we could easily misunderstand what Jacob does in these next verses and consider it to merely be a selfish act on his part. As you will see, Esau has no real interest in the birthright.

31 And **Jacob said, Sell me this day thy birthright**.

32 And **Esau said, Behold, I *am* at the point to die: and what profit shall this birthright do to me** [*what good does the birthright do me when I am this hungry*]?

33 And **Jacob said, Swear to me this day** [*covenant with me now that the birthright will come to me*]; **and he**

sware unto him: and **he sold his birthright unto Jacob**.

Moses points out specifically to us at the end of verse 34, next, that Esau has no interest in the birthright, which, as noted above, normally included the responsibility of running the family business and making sure that other family members were adequately taken care of. In this case, as previously mentioned, the birthright also involved living righteously, exercising the priesthood, doing missionary work, and passing on the blessings and covenants of the gospel of Jesus Christ made to Adam and passed down through the ages to Abraham.

You may have noticed that the phrase "the blessings of Abraham, Isaac, and Jacob," or wording to that effect, is mentioned in our patriarchal blessings today. It is a reminder to us that we are capable of attaining exaltation and that we have the responsibility to take the blessings of the gospel and the priesthood to all within our sphere of influence.

34 **Then Jacob gave Esau bread and pottage of lentiles; and he did eat and drink**, and rose up, and went his way: **thus Esau despised** [*rejected; did not care about*] ***his* birthright**.

GENESIS 26

In this chapter, we will see that the Abrahamic covenant is renewed with Isaac (verse 3). Because of a new famine plaguing his area, Isaac determines to move, perhaps thinking to go to Egypt as his father, Abraham, had done years before. He travels west toward Egypt with his family as far as Gerar. This is the domain of King Abimelech, who had become a great friend of Abraham after some initial troubles when the king had attempted to marry Sarah (Genesis 20). The Lord commands Isaac not to continue to Egypt but to remain in Abimelech's country.

We will mention just a bit more about the trouble King Abimelech had initially with Abraham and Sarah. In Genesis 20, we read that as Abraham and Sarah settled temporarily in Gerar, Abraham requested that she be introduced as his sister (as he had done earlier in Egypt). King Abimelech, thinking that Sarah was only Abraham's sister, had sent for her and taken her to his palace, where he tried unsuccessfully to persuade her to marry him. The Lord sent trouble upon him and his household during the time of these attempts. Finally, the king discovered that Sarah was not only Abraham's "sister" (meaning his niece, in the language of his culture) but also his wife. He scolded Abraham (Genesis 20:9–10), and then Abraham told him that he had done it to avoid being killed (Genesis 20:11). Having settled the issue, Abraham and Abimelech became great friends.

Now, many years later, Isaac, the covenant son of Abraham and Sarah, is in King Abimelech's domain, and Rebekah is also a stunningly beautiful woman. Isaac is also aware, as was his father, of the custom of a king's killing a husband in order to marry his wife. As mentioned in the notes and commentary for Genesis 12 in this study guide, kings in this culture would not think of committing adultery with another man's wife. But they had no problem with murdering her husband so that she would become a widow, and once more be eligible for marriage.

With this in mind, Isaac will introduce Rebekah as his sister for mutual protection (see verse 7). But later, when King Abimelech sees Isaac and Rebekah together, he suspects that she is his wife (verses 8–10), having had experience already with Abraham and Sarah. When Isaac confirms the fact, the king immediately issues an edict that no one is to make advances toward Rebekah. Thus, the problem is solved, and Isaac prospers as Abimelech's guest and becomes immensely wealthy.

At the end of this chapter (verses 34–35), Esau confirms his disregard for the gospel and the Abrahamic covenant by marrying Canaanite wives, which makes it so that his descendants by them cannot hold the priesthood (see note after verse 33, in this chapter).

We will now proceed with chapter 26.

1 And **there was a famine in the land**, beside the first famine that was in the days of Abraham. And **Isaac went unto Abimelech king of the Philistines unto Gerar**.

2 And **the Lord appeared unto him, and said, Go not down into Egypt**; dwell in the land which I shall tell thee of:

> In verses 3–5, next, the Lord confirms the Abrahamic covenant to Isaac.

3 **Sojourn in this land** [*stay in King Abimelech's land*], **and I will be with thee, and will bless thee**; for unto thee, and **unto thy seed, I will give all these countries, and I will perform the oath which I sware unto Abraham thy father**;

4 And **I will make thy seed to multiply as the stars of heaven**, and **will give unto thy seed all these countries**; and **in thy seed shall all the nations of the earth be blessed** [*compare with Abraham 2:9–11, Genesis 12:2–3*];

5 **Because that Abraham obeyed my voice, and kept my charge, my commandments, my statutes, and my laws**.

> Next, in verse 6, we see that Isaac, like his father, Abraham, was obedient.

6 ¶ **And Isaac dwelt in Gerar**:

7 **And the men of the place asked** *him* **of his wife; and he said, She** *is* **my sister**: for he feared to say, *She is* my wife; lest, *said he,* the men of the place should kill me for Rebekah; because she *was* fair to look upon.

8 And it came to pass, **when he had been there a long time**, that **Abimelech** king of the Philistines **looked out at a window, and saw**, and, behold, **Isaac** *was* **sporting with Rebekah his wife** [*NIV, "caressing his wife Rebekah"*].

9 And **Abimelech called Isaac, and said, Behold, of a surety she** *is* **thy wife**: and how [*why*] saidst thou, **She** *is* **my sister?** And **Isaac said** unto him, Because I said, **Lest I die**

for her [*in other words, I was afraid someone would kill me so he could marry her*].

10 And **Abimelech said, What** *is* **this thou hast done unto us? one of the people might lightly have lien** [*laid; committed adultery*] **with thy wife**, and thou shouldest have brought guiltiness upon us.

11 And **Abimelech charged** [*issued an edict to*] **all** *his* **people, saying, He that toucheth this man or his wife shall surely be put to death.**

> Next, we see that temporal blessings follow Isaac just as they did Abraham.

12 **Then Isaac sowed** [*planted crops*] in that land, **and received in the same year an hundredfold** [*an extraordinarily large harvest*]: and **the Lord blessed him.**

13 And **the man waxed** [*grew*] **great, and went forward, and grew until he became very great** [*wealthy and prominent*]:

14 For **he had** possession of **flocks**, and possession of **herds**, and great store of **servants**: and **the Philistines** [*King Abimelech's subjects*] **envied him.**

> At the end of verse 14, above, and in verse 15, next, we see that envy and jealousy begin to take a toll as jealous citizens vandalize and sabotage Isaac's wells.

15 For **all the wells** which his father's servants had digged in the days of Abraham his father, **the Philistines had stopped them, and filled them with earth.**

16 And **Abimelech said unto Isaac, Go from us; for thou art much mightier than we.**

17 ¶ And **Isaac departed** thence, and **pitched his tent in the valley of Gerar** [*about 45 miles southwest of Jerusalem; about 10 miles southeast of Gaza*], and dwelt there.

18 And **Isaac digged again the wells of water,** which they had digged in the days of Abraham his father; for the Philistines had stopped them after the death of Abraham: and he called their names after the names by which his father had called them.

19 And **Isaac's servants digged in the valley, and found there a well of springing water.**

> Trouble over water rights comes up again in verses 20–22, next. We see that Isaac was a peaceful man and would rather move on than fight.

20 **And the herdmen of Gerar did strive with Isaac's herdmen, saying, The water** *is* **ours**: and he called the name of the well Esek; because they strove with him.

21 And **they digged another well, and strove for that also**: and he called the name of it Sitnah.

22 And **he removed from thence** [*he moved*], **and digged another well**; and for that they strove not: and he called the name of it Rehoboth; and

he said, For now the Lord hath made room for us, and we shall be fruitful in the land.

23 And he went up from thence to Beer-sheba [*about 15 miles southeast of Gerar*].

> Once again, the Lord reaffirms the Abrahamic covenant upon Isaac in verse 24, next.

24 And **the Lord appeared unto him** the same night, **and said,** I *am* the God of Abraham thy father: fear not, for **I *am* with thee, and will bless thee, and multiply thy seed for my servant Abraham's sake**.

25 And **he builded an altar there**, and called upon the name of the Lord and pitched his tent there: and there Isaac's servants digged a well.

> In verses 26–33, next, we see a peace treaty made between King Abimelech and Isaac. Apparently Isaac's wealth and growing prosperity, along with an increasing number of servants and followers, made him a potentially serious enemy for the Philistines of King Abimelech's kingdom. Therefore, the king and his leading men approached Isaac with a request that they make a peace pact.

26 ¶ Then **Abimelech went to him** from Gerar, and Ahuzzath one of his friends, and Phichol the chief captain of his army.

27 And **Isaac said unto them, Wherefore** [*why*] **come ye to me, seeing ye hate me, and have sent me away from you?**

28 And **they said, We saw certainly that the Lord was with thee** [*in other words, you keep prospering and growing in strength and military capability*]: **and we said, Let there be now an oath betwixt us,** *even* betwixt us and thee, and let us make a covenant with thee;

29 **That thou wilt do us no hurt**, as we have not touched thee, and as we have done unto thee nothing but good, and have sent thee away in peace: thou *art* now the blessed of the Lord.

> Isaac, a man of peace, graciously hosts these worried men and agrees to peace.

30 And **he** [*Isaac*] **made them a feast**, and they did eat and drink.

31 And **they rose up betimes** [*got up early*] **in the morning, and sware one to another** [*gave their word; made a covenant of peace*]: and Isaac sent them away, **and they departed from him in peace**.

> Isaac's servants bring him good news on the same day, shortly after Abimelech and his party had gone. Keep in mind that this was arid country where water meant everything. Thus, this new well was a great blessing from the Lord.

32 And it came to pass **the same day, that Isaac's servants came, and told him concerning the well** which they had digged, and said unto him, **We have found water.**

33 And **he called it Shebah**: therefore [*this is the reason why*] **the name of the city** *is* **Beer-sheba** [*meaning "wells of an oath"*] unto this day.

Next, in verses 34–35, we see that Esau's actions bring great sorrow to Isaac and Rebekah. He has married two wives who are of Canaanite descent. Thus, his descendants from them will not be able to hold the priesthood (see Bible Dictionary, under "Canaan" and under "Canaanite." Also, read Abraham 1:21–26). The Abrahamic covenant cannot continue with Esau's posterity by them.

34 ¶ And **Esau was forty years old when he took to wife Judith** the daughter of Beeri **the Hittite**, and **Bashemath** the daughter of Elon **the Hittite**:

35 **Which were a grief of mind unto Isaac and to Rebekah**.

GENESIS 27

This chapter has long troubled Bible scholars and readers alike. A quick, superficial reading of it leaves one with the understanding that Rebekah and Jacob dishonestly obtained the status of covenant son for Jacob, and that Isaac was deceived, thus giving Esau's blessing to Jacob. Ultimately, such conclusions would invalidate the sacredness of the Abrahamic covenant and lead to the cheapening of the work of God.

While there are many things we do not understand, there are some we do.

1. Rebekah was clearly told, years ago, by direct revelation from the Lord that Jacob was to be the covenant son (Genesis 25:22–23).

2. Esau did not respect or prove worthy of the birthright and the responsibility of perpetuating the Abrahamic covenant. He "despised" his birthright (Genesis 25:34) and sold it to Jacob for a mess of pottage (Genesis 25:29–33). Furthermore, Esau married Canaanite wives (Genesis 26:34–35), who were not worshippers of God and whose ancestry came through Ham and Egypt and thus could not hold the priesthood (Abraham 1:21–26). Therefore, his posterity could not have perpetuated the Abrahamic covenant, which includes the priesthood blessings and ordinances of the gospel of Jesus Christ.

3. Once the blessing had been given to Jacob by Isaac and Isaac had discovered the deception, he confirmed that the blessing belonged to Jacob by saying, "And he shall be blessed" (Genesis 27:33). If this had not been the case, he could have used his priesthood keys to revoke the blessing given to Jacob and pronounced it, instead, upon Esau. Such is the right of authorized servants of God (see Matthew 16:19).

4. It appears that Esau was not disputing the fact that Jacob had validly obtained the birthright from him (Genesis 27:36) but was disturbed that he had "taken

away [*his*] blessing" also (Genesis 27:36). The fact is that Esau had long since "taken away" the blessings of the Abrahamic covenant from himself by his apostate behavior.

5. We know from modern revelation that Isaac and Jacob have become gods (Doctrine and Covenants 132:37). Thus, Rebekah has also become a god (Doctrine and Covenants 132:20).

6. One of the interesting things about the Old Testament is that it presents people as they are. Thus, we are often shown the human weaknesses of great people in its pages. This should be comforting to us, knowing as we do that if they could make it to exaltation despite their human frailties, so can we, through the Atonement of Jesus Christ.

7. We have seen a great many examples of places in the Old Testament in which the Joseph Smith Translation corrections have completely changed the story. It may be that we simply do not have the correct version of all that went on here in this chapter. Since the Prophet Joseph Smith did not make any changes to it, we are left to wonder if it didn't need any or if it was something he planned to do thoroughly at a later date but did not get back to it.

Whatever the case, items 1–5 above are certainties and can be very helpful here. We will have to wait for a future time for other clarifications. We know that Jacob became the father of twelve sons, the twelve tribes of Israel, and that the blessings of Abraham, Isaac, and Jacob are being carried to all the world now through this lineage by worthy members of the Church whose patriarchal blessings emphasize to each, individually, their role in carrying the Abrahamic covenant to all the world.

Using the above background, we will now proceed with chapter 27. As we do so, verse 1 informs us that Isaac is blind and advanced in years. He would like a good meal of fresh venison before he dies. Esau and Jacob were born when Isaac was sixty years old (Genesis 25:26), and Esau was forty years old when he married the Hittite women (Genesis 26:34). Thus, Isaac was one hundred at that time and could be much older as we begin this chapter. It appears from the context that he expected to die soon. We know that he lived to be 180 years of age (see Genesis 35:28).

1 And it came to pass, that **when Isaac was old, and his eyes were dim, so that he could not see, he called Esau his eldest son**, and said unto him, My son: and he said unto him, Behold, *here am* I.

2 **And he said**, Behold now, **I am old, I know not the day of my death**:

3 Now therefore **take**, I pray thee, thy weapons, **thy quiver and thy bow, and go out to the field, and take me** *some* **venison**;

4 And **make me savoury meat**, such as I love, and bring *it* to me, **that I may eat; that my soul may bless thee before I die.**

From verse 4, above, we understand that Isaac is planning to give Esau a blessing before he dies. Next, beginning with verse 5, Rebekah is alarmed, fearing that her elderly husband may give Esau the blessing that rightfully belongs to Jacob. As we discussed in the background notes to this chapter, Rebekah was very close to God and knew by direct revelation to her that Jacob was to be the covenant son. Thus, according to this account, she takes action to assure that this is the case.

There is perhaps a major message here for us. In a healthy eternal marriage, the husband and wife serve together as "equal partners" (see "The Family: A Proclamation to the World," paragraph 7, *Ensign*, November 1995, page 102). Thus, in matters pertaining to the family, sometimes the husband leads out, and sometimes the wife leads out.

Eve led the way in the Garden of Eden, and Adam followed, when it came time to move ahead with the Father's plan to send His spirit children to earth. Once out of the Garden of Eden, Adam led in offering sacrifices by the authority of his priesthood, and Eve followed.

In the case of Isaac and Rebekah, Isaac had led out in many instances and Rebekah had followed. But in this case, Rebekah, knowing what she does about Jacob and Esau, leads out, and Isaac will confirm it. You may wish to read ahead in Genesis 28:3–4, where Isaac confirms again that Jacob is the covenant son.

5 And **Rebekah heard when Isaac spake to Esau his son**. And Esau went to the field to hunt *for* venison, *and* to bring *it*.

6 ¶ And **Rebekah spake unto Jacob her son, saying, Behold, I heard thy father speak unto Esau thy brother, saying**,

7 **Bring me venison**, and make me savoury meat, **that I may eat, and bless thee before the Lord before my death**.

> Next, Rebekah uses very strong terminology, including exercising her position in their culture to command her son.

8 Now **therefore, my son, obey my voice according to that which I command thee**.

9 **Go now to the flock**, and **fetch** me from thence **two good kids** of the goats [*in other words, young, tender goats*]; **and I will make them savoury meat for thy father, such as he loveth**:

10 **And thou shalt bring** *it* **to thy father, that he may eat, and that he may bless thee before his death**.

> Jacob immediately sees some technical problems with Rebekah's proposed action, and points them out to her.

11 And **Jacob said to Rebekah** his mother, Behold, **Esau** my brother *is* **a hairy man, and I** *am* **a smooth man**:

12 **My father peradventure** [*perhaps*] **will feel me, and I shall seem**

to him as a deceiver; and **I shall bring a curse upon me, and not a blessing**.

> Next, in verse 13, Rebekah tells Jacob that she will take full responsibility for what happens.

13 And his mother said unto him, **Upon me** *be* **thy curse, my son: only obey my voice**, and go fetch me *them*.

14 And **he went, and fetched, and brought** *them* **to his mother: and his mother made savoury meat, such as his father loved.**

15 And **Rebekah took goodly raiment** [*fine clothing*] **of her eldest son Esau**, which *were* with her in the house, **and put them upon Jacob** her younger son:

> From what Rebekah does next, we see that the statement about Esau upon his birth, that he was very hairy (Genesis 25:25), was apparently not an exaggeration.

16 And **she put the skins of the kids of the goats upon his hands, and upon the smooth of his neck** [*to make Jacob's skin feel like Esau's*]:

17 And **she gave the savoury meat and the bread, which she had prepared, into the hand of her son Jacob.**

18 ¶ And **he came unto his father, and said, My father**: and **he said**, Here *am* I; **who** *art* **thou, my son?**

19 And **Jacob said** unto his father, **I** *am* **Esau thy firstborn; I have done** according as thou badest [*asked*] **me: arise, I pray thee, sit and eat of my venison, that thy soul may bless me.**

20 And **Isaac said unto his son, How** *is it* **that thou hast found** *it* **so quickly**, my son? And he said, **Because the Lord** thy God **brought** *it* to me.

21 And **Isaac said** unto Jacob, **Come near**, I pray thee, **that I may feel thee**, my son, **whether thou** *be* **my very son Esau or not.**

22 And **Jacob went near unto Isaac his father; and he felt him, and said, The voice** *is* **Jacob's voice, but the hands** *are* **the hands of Esau.**

23 And **he discerned him not** [*he didn't discover that it was Jacob*], **because his hands were hairy, as his brother Esau's hands: so he blessed him.**

24 And **he said,** *Art* **thou my very son Esau? And he said, I** *am*.

25 And **he said, Bring** *it* **near to me, and I will eat of my son's venison, that my soul may bless thee. And he brought** *it* **near to him, and he did eat: and he brought him wine, and he drank.**

26 **And his father Isaac said unto him, Come near now, and kiss me, my son.**

> As you can see, according to this account, Isaac is still suspicious. But Rebekah has done a skillful job

of making Jacob not only feel like Esau but also smell like him.

27 And he came near, and kissed him: and **he smelled the smell of his raiment** [*clothing*]**, and** blessed him, **and said, See, the smell of my son** *is* **as the smell of a field** which the Lord hath blessed [*in other words, you smell like you have been out hunting and have had success*]:

> Next, in verses 28–29, Isaac proceeds with the blessing.

28 Therefore **God give thee of the dew of heaven, and the fatness** [*bounty, goodness*] **of the earth, and plenty of corn and wine**:

29 **Let people serve thee, and nations bow down to thee** [*Jacob's descendants will be leaders among their people*]**: be lord over thy brethren, and let thy mother's sons bow down to thee: cursed** *be* **every one that curseth thee, and blessed** *be* **he that blesseth thee.**

> Next, Esau comes home from a successful hunt and prepares a meal of fresh venison for his father, as requested.

30 ¶ And it came to pass, **as soon as Isaac had made an end of blessing Jacob, and Jacob was yet scarce gone out from the presence of Isaac** his father, that **Esau his brother came in from his hunting**.

31 And **he also had made savoury meat, and brought it unto his father**, and said unto his father, **Let my father arise, and eat of his son's venison, that thy soul may bless me**.

32 And **Isaac his father said unto him, Who** *art* **thou?** And **he said, I** *am* **thy son, thy firstborn Esau**.

33 And **Isaac trembled** very exceedingly, **and said, Who?** where *is* he that hath taken venison, and brought *it* me, and I have eaten of all before thou camest, and have blessed him? yea, *and* **he shall be blessed**.

> As mentioned previously, the last words of verse 33, above, "and he shall be blessed," confirm that Jacob rightfully received the blessing, which comes from heaven. If it had not been right, the blessing would not have been confirmed as valid, since heaven cannot be deceived.
>
> Esau is, of course, very upset at this point. As with many of us, now that he has lost something through neglect, it suddenly becomes precious to him, whereas, in times past, he cared little or none at all about it. He pleads for a blessing and will get one in verses 39–40.

34 And **when Esau heard the words of his father, he cried with a great and exceeding bitter cry**, and said unto his father, **Bless me,** *even* **me also, O my father**.

35 And **he said, Thy brother came with subtilty, and hath taken away thy blessing**.

36 And **he** [*Esau*] said, **Is not he rightly named Jacob** [*the name means "the supplanter"—in other*

words, "one who takes the place of another"]? **for he hath supplanted me** these **two times: he took away my birthright** [*Esau is not being honest here; he willingly sold it to Jacob because he didn't want it—see Genesis 25:29–34*]; **and**, behold, **now he hath taken away my blessing.** And he said, **Hast thou not reserved a blessing for me?**

37 **And Isaac answered** and said unto Esau, Behold, **I have made him thy lord, and all his brethren have I given to him for servants; and with corn and wine have I sustained him: and what shall I do now unto thee, my son?**

> Even though Esau has earned what is happening to him now, it still tugs at the heart as we see his anguish. In a way, this might remind us of the fate of the wicked on the day of final judgment and the feelings of the righteous as they weep for them.
>
> On the brighter side, perhaps there is also a parallel to be considered here. It is that Isaac will still have a lesser blessing for Esau. This may be similar in principle to the terrestrial and telestial kingdoms, which still represent great blessings for those who enter them (see Doctrine and Covenants 76:88–89), despite the fact that these degrees of glory are far less than the rewards to the righteous in celestial glory.

38 **And Esau said unto his father, Hast thou but one blessing, my father? bless me,** *even* **me also, O my father.** And **Esau** lifted up his voice, and **wept.**

> Next, in verses 39–40, Isaac gives Esau a blessing.

39 And Isaac his father answered and said unto him, **Behold, thy dwelling shall be the fatness** [*the best*] **of the earth, and of the dew of heaven from above**;

40 And **by thy sword shalt thou live, and shalt serve thy brother; and it shall come to pass when thou shalt have the dominion, that thou shalt break his yoke from off thy neck**.

> Next, in verse 41, we catch a glimpse of Esau's true personality, developed and strengthened over many years of failure to control his passions and yield to the gospel. He is caught up in bitterness and self-pity, and vows, after Isaac dies, to murder Jacob.

41 ¶ And **Esau hated Jacob because of the blessing wherewith his father blessed him**: and **Esau said in his heart, The days of mourning for my father are at hand** [*my father will soon die*]; **then will I slay** my brother **Jacob**.

> Wisely, Rebekah, who has heard of Esau's threats against Jacob, takes charge again and sends her covenant son to live with relatives in Haran (would be in southern Turkey today) in hopes that Esau's hatred will cool off after a while. Jacob is to go to her brother, Laban, who lives there with his family. There are many other relatives in the area also. Incidentally, Laban has a cute daughter named Rachel.

42 And **these words of Esau her elder son were told to Rebekah:** and she sent and called Jacob her younger son, **and said unto him, Behold, thy brother Esau, as touching thee, doth comfort himself,** *purposing* **to kill thee.**

43 **Now therefore, my son,** obey my voice; and arise, **flee thou to Laban my brother to Haran**;

44 And **tarry with him a few days, until thy brother's fury turn away**;

45 Until thy brother's anger turn away from thee, and he forget *that* which thou hast done to him: **then I will send, and fetch thee from thence: why should I be deprived also of you both in one day?**

> The last phrase of verse 45, above, bears explaining. If Esau murders Jacob, then, according to the law, he will be found and executed. Thus, Rebekah and Isaac would lose both their sons.
>
> Rebekah has another concern that is much on her mind. We see it in verse 46, next. Jacob has not yet married, and she is very worried that he may choose to marry a Canaanite wife, as was the case with Esau. Isaac will follow her lead and take over, commanding Jacob not to marry a Canaanite. We will see this at the beginning of chapter 28.

46 And **Rebekah said to Isaac, I am weary of my life** [*I am worried to death*] **because of the daughters of Heth** [*Canaanites—see Genesis 28:1*]: **if Jacob take a wife of the daughters of Heth, such as these** *which are* **of the daughters of the land, what good shall my life do me?**

GENESIS 28

Though relatively short, this chapter is packed with information. First, Isaac will command Jacob not to marry a Canaanite. Then he will support Rebekah's strong instruction (Genesis 27:43) to Jacob to go to Haran, adding that he should seek a wife from Rebekah's relatives who live there.

A very important part of the chapter is found in verses 3–4, wherein Isaac blesses Jacob with the blessings of Abraham, confirming again that Jacob is the covenant son.

In verses 6–9, Esau will choose one of Ishmael's daughters as a wife, yet again marrying one through whom the priesthood could not be perpetuated. (Ishmael's mother, Hagar, was an Egyptian. The Egyptians' lineage came through Ham (Noah's son) and Egypt. Her lineage was not allowed to bear the priesthood (see Abraham 1:21–26).

During Jacob's travels toward Haran, he will have a vision of a ladder reaching up into heaven. Modern revelation will be a great help to us as we study this vision (verses 12–15). In it, the Lord will reconfirm the blessings of Abraham and Isaac upon Jacob.

Finally, Jacob will commit to pay tithing (verse 22).

We will now go ahead with the chapter as Isaac follows through with what Rebekah started with Jacob.

1 And **Isaac called Jacob, and blessed him, and charged** [*commanded*] **him, and said** unto him, **Thou shalt not take a wife of the daughters of Canaan.**

2 Arise, **go to Padan-aram**, [*Haran*] **to the house of Bethuel thy mother's father; and take thee a wife from thence of the daughters of Laban thy mother's brother.**

> Verses 3–4, next, are the blessings of Abraham—in other words, the blessings and responsibilities of the Abrahamic covenant are being pronounced and reconfirmed again (see Genesis 27:28–29) upon Jacob by Isaac. In a way, perhaps, this repetition might be similar to each time we partake of the sacrament, wherein our baptismal covenants are renewed.

3 And **God Almighty bless thee, and make thee fruitful, and multiply thee, that thou mayest be a multitude of people;**

4 **And give thee the blessing of Abraham,** to thee, and to thy seed with thee; that thou mayest inherit the land wherein thou art a stranger, which God gave unto Abraham.

5 And **Isaac sent away Jacob**: and he went to Padan-aram [*Haran*] unto Laban, son of Bethuel the Syrian, the brother of Rebekah, Jacob's and Esau's mother.

6 ¶ **When Esau saw that Isaac had blessed Jacob, and sent him away** to Padan-aram, to take him a wife from thence; and that as he blessed him he gave him a charge, saying, Thou shalt not take a wife of the daughters of Canaan;

7 And that Jacob obeyed his father and his mother, and was gone to Padan-aram;

8 And Esau **seeing that the daughters of Canaan pleased not Isaac his father;**

9 **Then went Esau unto Ishmael, and took** unto [*added to*] the wives which he had **Mahalath** the daughter of Ishmael Abraham's son, the sister of Nebajoth, **to be his wife.**

> Next, we will see the rather well-known vision known as "Jacob's ladder." As mentioned in the background notes, above, for this chapter, we will get much help on this from modern prophets.
>
> We will first read it, noting that the blessings of Abraham and Isaac (the Abrahamic covenant) are being reconfirmed upon Jacob by Jehovah, and then we will bring in the modern helps.

10 ¶ And **Jacob went out from Beer-sheba** [*Isaac's home*], **and went toward Haran** [*about 500 miles to the northeast*].

11 And **he lighted upon** [*stopped at*] **a certain place, and tarried there all night,** because the sun was set; and he took of the stones of that place, and put *them for* his pillows, and lay down in that place to sleep.

12 And **he dreamed, and behold a ladder set up on the earth, and the**

top of it reached to heaven: and behold the angels of God ascending and descending on it**.

13 And, **behold, the Lord stood above it** [*the Savior waits at the top of the ladder (symbolically, in other words, in celestial glory) to welcome us into His Father's house*]**, and said, I *am* the Lord God of Abraham thy father, and the God of Isaac: the land whereon thou liest, to thee will I give it, and to thy seed;**

14 And **thy seed shall be as the dust of the earth, and thou shalt spread abroad to the west, and to the east, and to the north, and to the south: and in thee and in thy seed shall all the families of the earth be blessed**.

15 And, behold, I *am* with thee, and will keep thee in all *places* whither thou goest, and will bring thee again into this land [*the Holy Land*]; for I will not leave thee, until I have done *that* which I have spoken to thee of.

> The Prophet Joseph Smith taught that the rungs on the ladder in Jacob's dream represent the telestial, terrestrial, and celestial kingdoms. He taught (**bold** added for emphasis):
>
> "Paul ascended into the third heavens, and he could **understand the three principal rounds of Jacob's ladder—the telestial, the terrestrial, and the celestial glories or kingdoms**, where Paul saw and heard things which were not lawful for him to utter. I could explain a hundred fold more than I ever have of the glories of the kingdoms manifested to me in the vision, were I permitted, and were the people prepared to receive them" (*Teachings of the Prophet Joseph Smith*, 304–5).

President Marion G. Romney of the First Presidency, in an article about temples and covenant-making, spoke of additional symbolism in this dream (**bold** added for emphasis):

"When Jacob traveled from Beersheba toward Haran, he had a dream in which he saw himself on the earth at the foot of a ladder that reached to heaven where the Lord stood above it. He beheld angels ascending and descending thereon, and **Jacob realized that the covenants he made with the Lord there were the rungs on the ladder that he himself would have to climb in order to obtain the promised blessings—blessings that would entitle him to enter heaven and associate with the Lord**.

"Because he had met the Lord and entered into covenants with him there, Jacob considered the site so sacred that he named the place Bethel, a contraction of Beth-Elohim, which means literally 'the House of the Lord.' He said of it: '. . . this is none other but the house of God, and this is the gate of heaven.' (Gen. 28:17.)

"Jacob not only passed through the gate of heaven, but by living up to every covenant he also went all the way in. Of him and his forebears Abraham and Isaac, the Lord has said: '. . . because they did none other things than that which they were commanded, they have entered into their exaltation, according to the promises, and sit upon thrones, and are not angels but are gods.' (Doctrine and Covenants 132:37.)

"Temples are to us all what Bethel was to Jacob. Even more, they are also the gates to heaven for all of our unendowed kindred dead. We should all do our duty in bringing our loved ones through them" ("Temples—The Gates to Heaven," *Ensign*, March 1971, page 16; emphasis added).

As Jacob awakes from the dream, he takes steps to make this a sacred site thereafter.

16 ¶ And **Jacob awaked out of his sleep, and he said, Surely the Lord is in this place**; and I knew *it* not.

17 And he was afraid [*filled with reverent awe*], and said, How dreadful [*wonderful*] *is* this place! **this *is* none other but the house of God, and this *is* the gate of heaven** [*just as covenants are the gateway to heaven for us, helping us stay on the covenant path*].

18 And **Jacob** rose up early in the morning, and **took the stone** that he had put *for* his pillows, **and set it up *for* a pillar**, and **poured oil upon the top of it** [*consecrated it as a sacred place*].

19 And he called the name of that place Beth-el: but the name of that city *was called* Luz at the first.

Next, Jacob makes a covenant with the Lord, including to pay tithing.

20 And **Jacob vowed a vow**, saying, **If God will be with me**, and will keep me in this way that I go, and will give me bread to eat, and raiment [*clothing*] to put on,

21 So that I come again to my father's house in peace; then shall the Lord be my God:

22 And this stone, which I have set *for* a pillar, **shall be God's house**: and of all that thou shalt give me **I will surely give the tenth unto thee.**

The JST makes a change to verse 22, above.

JST Genesis 28:22

22 **And the place of this stone which I have set for a pillar, shall be the place of God's house**; and of all that thou shalt give me I will surely give the tenth unto thee.

GENESIS 29

Once again, a descendant of Abraham has come to Haran, where Abraham lived for several years after being instructed by the Lord to leave Ur. Haran was located in present-day Turkey, near the northern border of today's Syria. Jacob has come to get away from his twin brother, Esau (Genesis 27:41), and to find a wife, as instructed by his mother and father, Rebekah and Isaac.

While staying with his Uncle Laban, his mother's brother, Jacob will fall in love with his cousin, Rachel. Striking an agreement with Laban, Jacob will work seven years in return for Laban's consent for him to marry Rachel. But at the end of the seven years (which fly by because he is in love—see verse 20)—Laban deceives him, and Jacob finds that he is married to Rachel's older sister, Leah, instead. He complains to Laban, who quickly explains that local customs dictate that a younger sister is not to be married off until any older sisters are married.

No doubt seeking to avoid trouble with Jacob, Laban quickly seeks to appease his nephew by proposing that he wait a week and then marry Rachel also and pay for her over the next seven years. Jacob, a man of peace like his father (Isaac) and his grandfather (Abraham), agrees and settles into married life.

Remember that Jacob has been promised that his "seed shall be as the dust of the earth" (Genesis 28:14). Before he is through having children, he will have twelve sons and a number of daughters.

As we begin this chapter, Jacob arrives in the land of his relatives, stops by a well, and asks the men at the well where they are from. They answer that they are from Haran, which is exactly what he is looking for.

1 Then **Jacob went on his journey, and came into the land of the people of the east.**

2 And **he looked, and behold a well in the field**, and, lo, there *were* three flocks of sheep lying by it; for out of that well they watered the flocks: **and a great** [*large, heavy*] **stone** *was* **upon the well's mouth.**

> Moses provides an editorial comment here in verse 3, next, informing us that this was a centrally located well, and that when enough men were there, they worked together to roll the large stone from the mouth of the well, watered the flocks, and then put the stone back in place.
>
> In telling us this, Moses is setting the stage for Jacob to impress Rachel by removing the stone by himself.

3 And **thither** [*there*] **were all the flocks gathered**: and **they** [*several men*] **rolled the stone from the well's mouth, and watered the sheep, and put the stone again upon the well's mouth in his place.**

4 And **Jacob said unto them**, My brethren, **whence** *be* ye [*where do you come from*]? And **they said**, Of **Haran** *are* we.

5 And **he said** unto them, **Know ye Laban** the son [*the grandson*] of Nahor? **And they said, We know** *him*.

6 And he said unto them, *Is* he well? **And they said,** *He is* well: and, behold, **Rachel his daughter** [*Jacob's cousin*] **cometh with the sheep.**

> Next, it appears that Jacob is attempting to get the men who have gathered at the well to water their flocks, to get on with the business of taking them away to graze. Perhaps he has seen Rachel and would like time to meet her without interference from them. First, he tells the herdsmen that there is still much daylight left and they should not bunch the flocks together yet.

7 And **he said, Lo,** *it is* **yet high day, neither** *is it* **time that the**

cattle [*domesticated animals, such as sheep and goats*] **should be gathered together: water ye the sheep, and go** *and* **feed** *them*.

> According to verse 8, next, it appears that the men are waiting for other men to come along who are strong enough to move the heavy stone.

8 And they said, **We cannot**, until all the flocks be gathered together, and *till* **they roll the stone from the well's mouth**; then we water the sheep.

9 ¶ And **while he yet spake with them, Rachel came with her father's sheep**: for she kept [*took care of*] them.

> Next, with Rachel looking on, Jacob rolls the stone away from the well by himself.

10 And it came to pass, **when Jacob saw Rachel the daughter of Laban his mother's brother** [*in other words, his first cousin*], and the sheep of Laban his mother's brother, that **Jacob went near, and rolled the stone from the well's mouth, and watered the flock of Laban his mother's brother**.

11 **And Jacob kissed Rachel** [*no doubt the customary kiss of greeting common in that culture rather than a romantic kiss*]**, and lifted up his voice** [*probably meaning in thanks to God*]**, and wept**.

> The reason that we suggest that Jacob "lifted up his voice" in thanks to the Lord, verse 11 above, is that he had made a vow (Genesis 28:20–21) to be loyal to God if He would guide him to his father's relatives in Haran. The Lord had guided him directly to a member of his mother's brother's family (Rachel), which was no small miracle. And so, he had great cause to express gratitude.
>
> Next, in verse 12, Rachel is very excited when she finds out who he is and runs to tell her father, Laban (Rebekah's brother, Jacob's uncle).

12 And **Jacob told Rachel that he** *was* **her father's brother** [*nephew*]**, and that he** *was* **Rebekah's son: and she ran and told her father**.

13 And it came to pass, **when Laban heard the tidings** [*the news*] of Jacob his sister's son, that **he ran to meet him, and embraced him, and kissed him, and brought him to his house**. And he told Laban all these things.

14 And **Laban said to him, Surely thou** *art* **my bone and my flesh** [*you are family; you are welcome to stay here*]**. And he abode with him the space of a month**.

> Based on the context, starting with verse 15, next, we understand that Jacob worked on Laban's ranch during the month that followed with no payment by way of wages. Laban approaches him, suggesting that it is time to make an agreement concerning wages for Jacob. According to local custom, Jacob will propose that he work for Rachel's hand in marriage. A deal is made for him to work seven years for her.

15 ¶ And **Laban said unto Jacob, Because thou** *art* **my brother** [*nephew*]**, shouldest thou therefore serve me for nought** [*is it fair, just because you are family, for you to work for nothing*]**? tell me, what** *shall* **thy wages** *be?*

16 And **Laban had two daughters**: the name of the elder *was* **Leah**, and the name of the younger *was* **Rachel**.

17 **Leah** *was* **tender eyed** [*had lovely, soft, delicate eyes*]; **but Rachel** *was* **beautiful and well favoured** [*was well-endowed with beauty in every respect*].

18 And **Jacob loved Rachel**; and said, **I will serve thee seven years for Rachel thy younger daughter**.

> Perhaps you've noticed that Moses (remember, he is the author of the first five books of the Old Testament) has been depicting Laban as a bit of a smooth operator almost every time we've come across him in recent chapters. Verse 19, next, seems to confirm this, that Laban is not to be trusted.

19 And **Laban said,** *It is* **better that I give her to thee, than that I should give her to another man**: abide with me [*it's a deal*].

> Time flies by and soon the agreed-upon time is up.

20 **And Jacob served seven years for Rachel; and they seemed unto him** *but* **a few days, for the love he had to her**.

> The JST renders verse 21, next, a bit different than the Genesis account,
> as is the case also with verses 22 and 23.

21 ¶ And **Jacob said unto Laban, Give** *me* **my wife** [*let me marry her*]**, for my days are fulfilled** [*the seven years are up and I have kept my part of the bargain*]**, that I may go in unto her**.

JST Genesis 29:21

21 And Jacob said unto Laban, **Give unto me my wife, that I may go and take her, for my days of serving thee are fulfilled.**

22 And **Laban gathered together all the men of the place, and made a feast** [*a marriage feast for Jacob and Rachel*].

JST Genesis 29:22

22 **And Laban gave her to Jacob**, and gathered together all the men of the place, and made a feast.

23 And it came to pass in the evening, that he took Leah his daughter, and brought her to him; **and he went in unto her**.

JST Genesis 29:23

23 And it came to pass in the evening, that he took Leah his daughter, and brought her to Jacob, **and she went in and slept with him.**

24 **And Laban gave unto his daughter Leah Zilpah his maid** *for* **an handmaid.**

> The statements in verse 24, above, as well as in verse 29 are important for our understanding as Leah and Rachel later give their maid servants

to Jacob for wives (Genesis 30:3, 4, 9). We will quote from the *Old Testament Student Manual* for commentary on this:

"The gift of the handmaidens to each daughter made the servants the direct property of each wife, not of Jacob. Thus, later, when the handmaids had children, the children were viewed legally as the children of Rachel and Leah" (*Old Testament Student Manual*, page 87).

According to verse 25, next, Jacob woke up to a surprise the next morning. He had been married to Leah! Perhaps she had worn a heavy veil (such as mentioned in Genesis 24:65) during the marriage ceremony and it was dark in the tent when they retired for the night. Perhaps Leah and Rachel, as sisters, were similar in height and weight. Perhaps Laban had told her not to speak above a whisper so Jacob would not recognize a different voice. Whatever the case, he was not married to Rachel!

25 And **it came to pass, that in the morning, behold, it *was* Leah: and he said to Laban, What *is* this thou hast done unto me? did not I serve with thee for Rachel? Wherefore** [*why*] then **hast thou beguiled** [*deceived, tricked*] **me?**

Laban, acting rather innocent, has a ready answer for his irritated son-in-law. He follows it with a proposed solution to the concern.

26 **And Laban said, It must not be so done in our country, to give the younger before the firstborn.**

27 **Fulfil her week** [*wait a week, for Leah's sake, during which the customary seven days of wedding feasts would take place*], **and we will give thee this** [*Rachel*] **also for the service which thou shalt serve with me yet seven other years** [*in other words, a "buy now, pay later" plan*].

28 And **Jacob did so, and fulfilled her week: and he gave him Rachel his daughter to wife also.**

29 And **Laban gave to Rachel his daughter Bilhah his handmaid to be her maid.**

The JST makes a change to verse 30, next, giving us the sense that, while Jacob loved Leah, he naturally loved Rachel more.

30 And **he went in also unto Rachel**, and **he loved also Rachel more than Leah**, and served with him [*Laban*] yet seven other years.

JST Genesis 29:30

30 And **he went in also and slept with Rachel**, and **he loved Rachel also, more than Leah**, and served with Laban yet seven other years.

The word "hated" in verse 31, next, is harsh and is not a good translation. We will again quote from the *Old Testament Student Manual:*

"The Hebrew word *sahnay* does not mean 'hate' as the term is used today, but rather conveys the idea of 'loving less.' A better translation would be, 'when the Lord saw that Leah was loved less or was not as favored,' he opened her womb" (*Old Testament Student Manual,* page 87).

Much time has passed as we get to verse 31, and it will continue to move quickly through the rest of this chapter and chapter 30.

31 ¶ And **when the Lord saw that Leah** *was* **hated, he opened her womb**: but **Rachel** *was* **barren** [*had not had any children yet*].

Through the rest of this chapter, and up to Genesis 30:24, we will see eleven of the twelve sons of Jacob born. The twelfth son, Benjamin, will be born years later, as recorded in Genesis 35:16–18. These sons will become the heads of the twelve tribes of Israel (Jacob's name was changed to "Israel"—see Genesis 32:28) and are underlined in the next several verses. Jacob will also have daughters. However, only one of them will be mentioned by name, Dinah, who causes serious trouble for the family (see Genesis 34). Others are evident in Genesis 46:7.

Leah will have four sons in rapid succession, during which time Rachel will have no children. As you will see, each son is given a name which has meaning to the mother.

32 And Leah conceived, and bare a son, and she called his name **Reuben**: for she said, Surely the Lord hath looked upon my affliction; now therefore my husband will love me.

33 And she conceived again, and bare a son; and said, Because the Lord hath heard that I *was* hated [*loved less than Rachel*], he hath therefore given me this *son* also: and she called his name **Simeon**.

34 And she conceived again, and bare a son; and said, Now this time will my husband be joined unto me, because I have born him three sons: therefore was his name called **Levi**.

35 And she conceived again, and bare a son: and she said, Now will I praise the Lord: therefore she called his name **Judah**; and left bearing [*no more children came for a while*].

GENESIS 30

In this chapter, Jacob will end up with a total of four wives. Rachel will request that he marry her handmaid, Bilhah, in order for Rachel to have children through her. As previously mentioned, this was in harmony with the customs of the day. Leah will follow suit, giving her servant, Zilpah, to Jacob for a wife since it has been a considerable time since Leah has born any more children.

We will see some things in this chapter that will seem strange to us because of differences between our culture and Jacob's culture. Some of these differences will come because of superstitions and local customs and beliefs in Haran.

We will continue to use underlined bold (**bold**) to point out the names of Jacob's sons and will use bold as usual to add a bit of commentary as we proceed with this chapter.

1 And **when Rachel saw that she bare Jacob no children, Rachel envied her sister** [Leah]**; and said unto Jacob, Give me children, or else I die.**

Jacob is obviously frustrated by Rachel's request, and shows it in verse 2, next.

2 And **Jacob's anger was kindled against Rachel: and he said,** *Am* **I in God's stead, who hath withheld from thee the fruit of the womb?** [*In other words, am I God? Have I caused you not to have children? I am not God and have no power to do anything about it.*]

3 And **she said, Behold my maid Bilhah, go in unto her** [*have children by her*]**; and she shall bear upon my knees** [*local custom, meaning that any children Bilhah has would belong to Rachel*] **that I may also have children by her.**

4 And she gave him Bilhah her handmaid **to wife**: and Jacob went in unto her.

JST Genesis 30:3–4

3 And she said, Behold my maid Bilhah, **go in and lie with her**; and she shall bear upon my knees, that I may also have children by her.

4 And she gave him Bilhah her handmaid to wife [*they were married*]; and Jacob **went and lay with her**.

It is important to understand that his wives' servants, Bilhah and Zilpah, were legally married to Jacob, as pointed out in verses 4 and 9.

We will point out the seven additional sons who will now be born to Jacob. Benjamin, the twelfth son and Rachel's youngest, will not be born for several years.

5 And Bilhah conceived, and bare Jacob a son.

6 And Rachel said, God hath judged me, and hath also heard my voice, and hath given me a son: therefore called she his name **Dan**.

7 And Bilhah Rachel's maid conceived again, and bare Jacob a second son.

8 And Rachel said, With great wrestlings have I wrestled with my sister, and I have prevailed: and she called his name **Naphtali**.

9 When **Leah** saw that she had left bearing [*she was not having any more children*], she **took Zilpah her maid, and gave her Jacob to wife.**

10 And Zilpah Leah's maid bare Jacob a son.

11 And Leah said, A troop cometh: and she called his name **Gad**.

12 And Zilpah Leah's maid bare Jacob a second son.

13 And Leah said, Happy am I, for the daughters will call me blessed: and she called his name **Asher**.

> The mandrakes spoken of in verses 14–16 [*next*] seem to have something to do with local superstition and folklore. Apparently, they were thought to assist in fertility. It appears that Reuben was concerned about his mother's worries and disappointment about not bearing more children, and so he sought to do something for her by bringing her mandrakes.
>
> Upon seeing the mandrakes, Rachel will beg her sister to give her some of them.

14 ¶ And **Reuben** [*Leah's oldest son*] went in the days of wheat harvest [*in the fall*], and **found mandrakes in the field, and brought them unto his mother Leah**. Then **Rachel said to Leah, Give me, I pray thee, of thy son's mandrakes**.

> Leah's response to Rachel's request in verse 15, next, indicates that she is bitter about the fact that Jacob loves Rachel more than he loves her. She refuses Rachel's request. Rachel makes a counteroffer, saying that she will encourage Jacob to sleep with Leah that night if she can have the mandrakes herself. Leah agrees to the offer and tells Jacob as he comes in from the fields that evening (verse 16).
>
> As you have noticed, this is one of the places in which the Old Testament tells it like it is.

15 And **she** [*Leah*] **said** unto her [*Rachel*], **Is it a small matter that thou hast taken my husband** [*that you have taken my husband's heart*]? and **wouldest thou take away my son's mandrakes also? And Rachel said, Therefore** [*if you let me have the mandrakes*] **he shall lie with thee** [*I will encourage Jacob to sleep in your tent with you*] **to night for thy son's mandrakes** [*in exchange for your mandrakes*].

> One can easily feel a bit sorry for Jacob while all this fierce rivalry is going on between Leah and Rachel.

16 **And Jacob came out of the field in the evening, and Leah went out to meet him, and said, Thou must come in unto me; for surely I have hired thee with my son's mandrakes** [*I have given Rachel my mandrakes in exchange for having you spend the night with me*]. **And he lay with her that night**.

JST Genesis 30:16

> 16 And Jacob came out of the field in the evening, and Leah went out to meet him, and said, **Thou must come in and lie with me**; for surely I have hired thee with my son's mandrakes. And he lay with her that night.

17 And God hearkened unto **Leah, and she conceived, and bare Jacob the fifth son** [*Leah's fifth son*].

18 And Leah said, God hath given me my hire [*reward*], because I have given my maiden to my husband: and she called his name **Issachar**.

19 And Leah conceived again, and bare Jacob the sixth son.

20 And Leah said, God hath endued me *with* a good dowry; now will my husband dwell with me, because I have born him six sons: and she called his name **Zebulun**.

21 And afterwards she bare a daughter, and called her name **Dinah**.

> We will include a quote from the *Old Testament Student Manual* about mandrakes:
>
> "Although Bible scholars are not sure exactly what plant is meant by the word mandrake, the significance of this plant to Rachel and Leah is clear. 'The Hebrew name denotes love fruit. The fruit had a pleasant taste and odor, and was supposed to ensure conception.' (Bible dictionary, s.v. "mandrakes.") In other words, the mandrakes were thought to enhance a woman's fertility and ability to have children. Knowledge of this belief helps explain the interchange between Rachel and Leah. Rachel desired the mandrakes so that she could at last bear children of her own. As has already been seen, there was a fierce competition between the sisters in this regard. Leah's response was, therefore, equally natural. She indicated that Rachel had already taken her husband, which probably meant only that Rachel had the first place in his affections. (Some scholars, however, believe that this passage means that Jacob actually lived in Rachel's tent rather than in Leah's tent.) The one advantage Leah had was her ability to bear children, while Rachel could not. In essence she told Rachel that it would be foolish for her to give Rachel her mandrakes and help her have children, for this would only lessen Leah's one advantage (vs. 15). So Rachel made a counter offer. She promised that she would encourage Jacob to go to Leah that night if she, Rachel, could have the mandrakes (vs. 15). Leah agreed and told Jacob. Out of the agreement Leah conceived and bore Jacob a fifth son (vss. 17–18). She later bore another son and Jacob's first daughter (vss. 19–21).
>
> "Although not stated specifically, the record implies that the mandrakes did nothing for Rachel. Finally, Rachel did conceive, but it was not because of mandrakes. Rather, 'God hearkened to her, and opened her womb' (vs. 22)" (*Old Testament Student Manual,* page 88).

Next, Rachel will finally be blessed with a child of her own. His name will be Joseph. He will be the birthright son. Reuben, Leah's oldest son, who normally would have obtained the birthright (double property inheritance and the responsibility to run the ranch), lost the birthright by committing adultery with Bilhah (Genesis 35:22). Joseph will be the one through whom the Abrahamic covenant is perpetuated.

In about seventeen years, his jealous brothers will sell Joseph into slavery and he will end up in Egypt.

22 ¶ And **God remembered Rachel**, and God hearkened to her, **and opened her womb**.

23 **And she conceived, and bare a son**; and said, God hath taken away my reproach [*the stigma, in her culture, of not having children*]:

24 And she called his name **Joseph**; and said, The Lord shall add to me another son.

> By now, Jacob has finished the additional seven years of work for Rachel. Beginning with verse 25, next, Jacob notifies Laban of this and desires to depart and take his family back to Canaan, in the southern part of Israel, to his homeland where his mother and father still live. As a businessman, Laban is reluctant to let him go because he has noticed that when Jacob is around, everything on the ranch prospers.

25 ¶ And it came to pass, **when Rachel had born Joseph, that Jacob said unto Laban, Send me away, that I may go unto mine own place, and to my country**.

26 **Give** *me* **my wives and my children, for whom I have served thee, and let me go**: for thou knowest my service which I have done thee [*you know that I have paid off my debts to you*].

27 And **Laban said** unto him, I pray thee, if I have found favour in thine eyes, *tarry: for* **I have learned by experience that the Lord hath blessed me for thy sake** [*because of you*].

Next, Laban basically says, "Whatever you want me to pay you to stay around, just tell me and I will pay it."

28 And he said, **Appoint me thy wages, and I will give** *it*.

29 And **he** [*Jacob*] **said unto him**, Thou knowest how I have served thee, and how thy cattle was with me.

30 For *it was* little which thou hadst before I *came,* and it is *now* increased unto a multitude [*you didn't have much when I first came, but now you have large flocks*]; and **the Lord hath blessed thee since my coming**: and now when shall I provide for mine own house also [*when do I get my own flocks and herds to provide for my own household*]?

31 And he said, What shall I give thee? And Jacob said, **Thou shalt not give me any thing: if thou wilt do this thing for me** [*if you will do one thing for me*]**, I will again feed** *and* **keep thy flock** [*I will stay and continue to take care of your flocks too*].

> No doubt, Laban is paying very close attention as Jacob spells out the details of his proposed deal with him in verses 32–33, next.

32 **I will pass through all thy flock** to day, **removing** from thence **all the speckled and spotted cattle** [*"sheep"—see footnote 32a in your Bible*]**, and all the brown cattle among the sheep, and the spotted and speckled among the goats**:

and ***of such*** **shall be my hire** [*these sheep and goats will become my pay*].

> Next, Jacob continues explaining the deal, reminding Laban that his integrity is such that Laban needn't worry about getting cheated.

33 **So shall my righteousness** [*integrity*] **answer for me** in time to come, **when it shall come for my hire before thy face** [*you can trust me*]: **every one** [*each sheep or goat born*] **that** *is* **not speckled and spotted among the goats, and brown among the sheep**, that **shall be counted stolen with me** [*I will give back to you (Laban)*].

> Next, Laban agrees to the deal.

34 And **Laban said, Behold, I would it might be according to thy word**.

> Next, Laban separates out the specified sheep and goats and gives them to Jacob and his sons.

35 **And he** [*Laban*] **removed that day the he goats** [*male goats*] **that were ringstraked** [*had spots or blotches of different colors*] **and spotted, and all the she goats that were speckled and spotted,** *and* **every one that had** *some* **white in it, and all the brown among the sheep**, and **gave** *them* **into the hand of his sons** [*Jacob and his sons*].

> Next, distance is provided between Laban's remaining flocks and Jacob's new flocks so that there is no danger of getting the offspring of the two groups mixed up.

36 And he [*Laban*] **set three days' journey betwixt himself and Jacob**: and Jacob fed the rest of Laban's flocks.

> What Jacob does next must have had something to do with local superstition. It appears that there was a belief that what the mother animal sees at the time of conception will influence the color of her offspring. The real reason for Jacob's success was that the Lord blessed him.

37 ¶ And **Jacob took him rods of green poplar, and of the hazel and chesnut tree; and pilled** [*peeled*] **white strakes** [*streaks*] **in them, and made the white appear which** *was* **in the rods** [*revealing the white wood under the bark of the sticks*].

38 And **he set the rods which he had pilled before the flocks in the gutters in the watering troughs when the flocks came to drink, that they should conceive when they came to drink**.

39 And **the flocks conceived before** [*looking at*] **the rods, and brought forth cattle ringstraked, speckled, and spotted**.

> In the last verses of this chapter, we see Jacob using methods of animal husbandry that in his day were considered to be valid. The end result, as told in verse 43, is that he grew greatly in wealth and prosperity.

40 And Jacob did separate the lambs [*kept his own growing flock separate from Laban's*], and set the faces of the

flocks toward the ringstraked, and all the brown in the flock of Laban; and he put his own flocks by themselves, and put them not unto Laban's cattle.

41 And it came to pass, whensoever the stronger cattle did conceive, that Jacob laid the rods before the eyes of the cattle in the gutters, that they might conceive among the rods [*believing that they would then have multicolored offspring, which, according to his bargain with Laban, would become his property*].

42 But when the cattle were feeble, he put *them* [*the sticks with the bark peeled in streaks*] not in: so the feebler were Laban's, and the stronger [*multicolored offspring*] Jacob's.

> Looking ahead to Genesis 31:7–8, it appears that there is much that is left out of the story here. Laban kept changing his mind and changing the terms of the agreement. Despite his efforts to cheat Jacob, the Lord blessed Jacob. These blessings are summarized in verse 43, next.

43 And **the man increased exceedingly, and had much cattle, and maidservants, and menservants, and camels, and asses**.

GENESIS 31

Jacob has now been living in Laban's household for twenty years (verse 38). Laban has done everything he could to cheat Jacob, but Jacob has still prospered. Among other things, Laban has taken and squandered his daughters' dowries (verse 15). The proceeds of the work that Jacob did for each of his wives (seven years for Leah and seven years for Rachel) were to have been the personal property of each wife and should have been set aside to provide security for each of them as they started their new families.

The Lord commands Jacob to return to his own country, where Isaac and Rebekah still live and where Esau and his wives and families live. Laban does not like Jacob and will be unwilling to let him go in peace; therefore, Jacob departs in secret. Before doing so, however, he holds a family council with Rachel and Leah and asks their opinion about what they should do (verses 4–16). They counsel with him and then give their approval for leaving.

As we pick up the story in verse 1, we see that Laban's own sons are murmuring about Jacob and his prosperity as compared to Laban and his failures. As is typically the case with the wicked, they tend to blame the righteous for their problems. Jacob overhears their complaints, which confirm his concerns about his father-in-law. Laban's sons are probably worried that they won't have much by way of inheritance when their father dies.

1 And **he heard the words of Laban's sons, saying, Jacob hath taken away all that *was* our father's**; and of *that* which *was* our father's hath he gotten all this glory [*Jacob has taken away everything he now has from our father, which should be our inheritance*].

2 And Jacob beheld the countenance of Laban, and, behold, it *was* not toward him as before [*Laban's attitude toward him had changed for the worse*].

3 And **the Lord said unto Jacob, Return unto the land of thy fathers, and to thy kindred; and I will be with thee.**

4 And **Jacob sent and called Rachel and Leah to the field** unto his flock,

5 **And said unto them, I see your father's countenance, that it** *is* **not toward me** as before; but the God of my father [*in other words, Jehovah, the true God*] hath been with me.

6 And **ye know that with all my power I have served your father.**

7 And **your father hath deceived me, and changed my wages ten times**; but God suffered him not to hurt me [*did not permit Laban to prevent my prosperity*].

> Next, Jacob bears testimony to his wives of the blessings and protection he has received from the Lord, despite Laban's crafty attempts to cheat him.

8 **If he said** thus, **The speckled shall be thy wages; then all the cattle bare speckled**: and **if he said** thus, **The ringstraked shall be thy hire; then bare all the cattle ringstraked.**

9 **Thus God hath taken away the cattle of your father, and given** *them* **to me.**

> Jacob continues to bear testimony to Rachel and Leah of the Lord's intervention in his behalf.

10 And it came to pass **at the time that the cattle conceived, that I lifted up mine eyes, and saw in a dream,** and, behold, **the rams which leaped upon the cattle** *were* **ringstraked, speckled, and grisled.**

11 And **the angel of God spake unto me in a dream,** *saying,* Jacob: And I said, Here *am* I.

12 And he said, Lift up now thine eyes, and **see, all the rams which leap upon the cattle** *are* **ringstraked, speckled, and grisled** [*in other words, only male sheep and goats whose coloring would favor Jacob's increase were involved in producing offspring among Laban's flocks*]**: for I have seen all that Laban doeth unto thee.**

13 I *am* the God of Beth-el, where thou anointedst the pillar [*as he traveled from Canaan to Haran twenty years ago—see Genesis 28:18*], *and* where thou vowedst a vow unto me: **now arise, get thee out from this land, and return unto the land of thy kindred.**

> Next, as Rachel and Leah consider leaving their father, they discuss reasons as to why they should leave. Among other things, Laban has used up all their dowry, himself, leaving nothing for them.

14 And **Rachel and Leah** answered and **said** unto him, *Is there* **yet any portion or inheritance for us in our father's house?** [*The answer is no.*]

15 Are we not counted of him strangers [*aren't we just the same as strangers, rather than family members, as far*

as our personal financial status and dowries are concerned]? for **he hath sold us, and** hath quite **devoured also our money.**

The following quote will help you understand the seriousness of what Laban has done to his daughters:

"The dowry was an important part of marriage. We meet it first in Jacob, who worked seven years for Laban to earn a dowry for Rachel (Gen. 29:18). The pay for this service belonged to the bride as her dowry, and Rachel and Leah could indignantly speak of themselves as having been 'sold' by their father, because he had withheld from them their dowry (Gen. 31:14, 15). It was the family capital; it represented the wife's security, in case of divorce where the husband was at fault. If she were at fault, she forfeited it. She could not alienate it from her children. There are indications that the normal dowry was about three years' wages. The dowry thus represented funds provided by the father of the groom, or by the groom through work, used to further the economic life of the new family. If the father of the bride added to this, it was his privilege, and customary, but the basic dowry was from the groom or his family. The dowry was thus the father's blessing on his son's marriage, or a test of the young man's character in working for it" (Rushdoony, *Institutes of Biblical Law,* pages 176–77).

Next, in verse 16, Rachel and Leah give their consent to Jacob to follow God's commandment to take them and leave Laban. They reason that all that the Lord has taken from Laban and given to Jacob in terms of increase in flocks and so forth, are, in effect, their dowry too.

16 For **all the riches which God hath taken from our father, that** *is* **ours** [*is, in effect, our inheritance*]**, and our children's**: now then, **whatsoever God hath said unto thee, do**.

Having participated in a family counsel with his wives and having their approval, Jacob gathers them and the family possessions and leaves.

17 ¶ Then **Jacob rose up, and set his sons and his wives upon camels;**

18 And **he carried away all his cattle, and all his goods which he had gotten,** the cattle of his getting, which he had gotten in Padan-aram [*Haran*], for **to go to Isaac his father in the land of Canaan.**

Verse 19, next, poses some problems. Rachel took some images belonging to her father as she departed with Jacob and the family. We will first read the verse and then provide a helpful quote.

19 And Laban went to shear his sheep: and **Rachel had stolen the images that** *were* **her father's.**

"There is much debate among scholars about what the images were that were stolen by Rachel and what they represented. The Hebrew word that is sometimes used for small images of false gods is teraphim. Some translators render the word as 'household gods.'

Was Laban an idolator? If so, why did Jacob go all the way back to Haran to find a wife if they were idolators like the Canaanites? Others believe they were astrological devices used for telling the future. But this suggestion raises the same question. One scholar theorized that these images were somehow tied in with the legal rights of inheritance (see Guthrie, *New Bible Commentary,* page 104). If this theory is correct, the possessor of the teraphim had the right to inherit the father's property. This circumstance would explain why Rachel stole the images, since her father had 'stolen' her inheritance (see Genesis 31:14–16). It would also explain Laban's extreme agitation over their loss and Jacob's severe penalty offered against the guilty party (see Genesis 31:31)" (*Old Testament Student Manual,* page 89).

As the story continues to unfold, Jacob and his procession are underway. Laban will not discover that they have left until three days later (verse 22). This makes us think that Jacob and his herds had been living some distance from Laban. This would be logical since only a limited number of animals can graze in a given area of grassland.

20 And **Jacob stole away unawares to Laban** the Syrian, in **that he told him not that he fled.**

21 So **he fled with all that he had**; and he rose up, and passed over the river, and set his face *toward* [headed toward] the mount Gilead.

22 And **it was told Laban on the third day that Jacob was fled.**

23 And **he** took his brethren with him, and pursued after him seven days' journey; and they **overtook him in the mount Gilead**.

> Whatever Laban's plans were regarding Jacob, they probably changed because of the warning in a dream, mentioned in verse 24, next.

24 And **God came to Laban** the Syrian **in a dream** by night, and said unto him, **Take heed that thou speak not to Jacob either good or bad** [*don't try to influence Jacob in any way*].

25 ¶ Then **Laban overtook Jacob**. Now Jacob had pitched his tent in the mount: and Laban with his brethren pitched in the mount of Gilead.

> At first, Laban doesn't seem to pay much attention to the warning he received in the dream. However, except for the matter of the images taken by Rachel, he will finally abide by God's counsel in verse 29 and beyond.

26 And **Laban said to Jacob, What hast thou done, that thou hast stolen away unawares to me, and carried away my daughters, as captives *taken* with the sword** [*why are you treating my daughters like captives*]?

27 **Wherefore** [*why*] **didst thou flee away secretly**, and steal away from me; **and didst not tell me, that I**

might have sent thee away with mirth, and with songs, with tabret, and with harp?

> We know from the context here that what Laban claimed he would have done (verse 27, above) had he known they were leaving is not true.

> Laban continues, laying all the blame on Jacob.

28 **And hast not suffered me** [*given me the chance*] **to kiss my sons and my daughters** [*grandchildren and Leah and Rachel*]**? thou hast now done foolishly in** *so* **doing.**

29 **It is in the power of my hand to do you hurt: but the God of your father spake unto me yesternight, saying, Take thou heed that thou speak not to Jacob either good or bad.**

> Having calmed down and indicated that he is no longer planning to harm Jacob, Laban does bring up the matter of the stolen images. If, indeed, the images carried with them the right to inheritance for his daughters (see note after verse 19, above) and he was desperate to retrieve them, we can easily understand his concern, even though it would be dishonest and morally wrong on his part to claim their rightful personal property back.

30 **And now,** *though* **thou wouldest needs be gone, because thou sore longedst after thy father's house,** *yet* **wherefore hast thou stolen my gods?**

In verse 31, next, Jacob answers Laban's previous question as to why he left secretly. Then, in verse 32, we see that Jacob is caught completely off guard by this accusation and strongly denies that anyone in his company has Laban's images. He is so certain that this is the case that he says that if anyone in his group stole them, they should be executed. He does not know that Rachel took them.

31 And **Jacob answered and said to Laban, Because I was afraid**: for I said, **Peradventure** [*what if*] **thou wouldest take by force thy daughters from me.**

32 **With whomsoever thou findest thy gods, let him not live** [*let him be executed*]: **before our brethren discern thou what** *is* **thine with me, and take** *it* **to thee** [*in other words, search everyone and everything in our camp, and if you find any stolen property, take it back*]. For **Jacob knew not that Rachel had stolen them.**

33 And **Laban went into Jacob's tent,** and into **Leah's tent,** and into **the two maidservants' tents**; but he **found** *them* **not.** Then went he out of Leah's tent, and **entered into Rachel's tent.**

> Verses 34–35, next, tell us that Rachel had indeed stolen the images and had hidden them inside a chair upon which she was sitting as her father searched her belongings. She cunningly claims that because it is her time of the month, she cannot appropriately stand up. It works and Laban leaves without them.

34 Now **Rachel had taken the images, and put them in the camel's furniture, and sat upon them**. And **Laban searched all the tent, but found** *them* **not**.

35 And she said to her father, Let it not displease my lord that **I cannot rise up before thee; for the custom of women** *is* **upon me**. And he searched, but found not the images.

> By now, Jacob is thoroughly angry with Laban, and for the next seven verses, he will take Laban to task for his behavior toward him over the past many years.

36 ¶ And **Jacob was wroth** [*angry*], **and chode with** [*chastised*] **Laban**: and Jacob answered and said to Laban, **What** *is* **my trespass? what** *is* **my sin, that thou hast so hotly pursued after me?**

37 Whereas thou hast searched all my stuff, **what hast thou found of all thy household stuff? set** *it* **here before my brethren and thy brethren, that they may judge betwixt us both.**

38 **This twenty years** *have* **I** *been* **with thee**; **thy ewes and thy she goats have not cast their young** [*have not failed to bear young*], and **the rams of thy flock have I not eaten.**

39 **That which was torn** *of beasts* [*the sheep and goats that were killed by wild animals*] **I brought not unto thee; I bare the loss of it**; of my hand didst thou require it [*you made me bear those losses*], *whether* stolen by day, or stolen by night.

40 *Thus* I was; **in** the day the **drought** consumed me, and the **frost** by night; and **my sleep departed from mine eyes** [*I lost a lot of sleep taking good care of your property and business affairs*].

41 Thus have I been twenty years in thy house; **I served thee fourteen years for thy two daughters**, and **six years for thy cattle: and thou hast changed my wages ten times**.

42 **Except the God of my father, the God of Abraham, and the fear of Isaac, had been with me, surely thou hadst sent me away now empty** [*if it hadn't been that everything I touched was blessed by God, you would have sent me away empty-handed long ago*]. **God hath seen mine affliction and the labour of my hands, and rebuked** *thee* **yesternight**.

> Next, it is Laban's turn to respond. Either he is a slick talker, or his heart has truly been touched by Jacob's rebuke. We will choose to think that his heart has been touched.

43 ¶ And **Laban answered** and said unto Jacob, *These* **daughters** *are* **my daughters, and** *these* **children** *are* **my children**, and *these* cattle *are* my cattle, and all that thou seest *is* mine [*everything here came to you from me*]: and **what can I do this day** unto these my daughters, or unto their children which they have born [*what can I do but make peace with you*]?

> Next, Laban proposes that they make peace, and that they do it in the form of a covenant so that it is binding upon them and their people.

44 Now therefore **come thou, let us make a covenant**, I and thou; and let it be for a witness between me and thee.

45 And **Jacob took a stone, and set it up** *for* **a pillar**.

46 And Jacob said unto his brethren, **Gather stones; and they took stones, and made an heap: and they did eat there upon the heap** [*part of the covenant making process in their culture*].

47 And **Laban called it Jegar-sahadutha** [*the pile of stones that bear witness of a covenant*]: but Jacob called it Galeed [*"heap of witness"*].

48 And Laban said, **This heap** *is* **a witness between me and thee this day**. Therefore was the name of it called Galeed;

49 And Mizpah [*the lookout point*]; for he said, **The Lord watch between me and thee, when we are absent one from another**.

50 **If thou shalt afflict my daughters, or if thou shalt take** *other* **wives** beside my daughters, no man *is* with us [*even though there may be no formal witnesses*]; see, **God** *is* **witness** betwixt me and thee.

51 And Laban said to Jacob, Behold this heap, and behold *this* pillar, which I have cast betwixt me and thee;

52 **This heap** *be* **witness**, and *this* pillar *be* witness, **that I will not pass over this heap to thee, and that thou shalt not pass over this heap and this pillar unto me, for harm** [*for the purpose of doing harm to each other*].

53 The God of Abraham, and the God of Nahor, the God of their father, judge betwixt us [*be our witness*]. **And Jacob sware** [*made an oath or covenant*] by the fear [*respect*] of his father Isaac.

54 Then **Jacob offered sacrifice** upon the mount, and called his brethren to eat bread: and they did eat bread, and tarried all night in the mount.

55 And **early in the morning Laban rose up, and kissed his sons and his daughters, and blessed them: and Laban departed, and returned unto his place**.

GENESIS 32

The main topic of this chapter is Jacob's concern about meeting Esau again after some twenty years. Esau had vowed to kill Jacob (Genesis 27:41), and Jacob had fled to Haran to get away from him and to find a wife. Now, after all these years, he is returning as a wealthy man to his original home in Canaan.

Is Esau still angry? Does he still want to kill Jacob? Will he accept gifts from Jacob? Is peace possible? All these questions and more were undoubtably on Jacob's mind as he traveled southwest toward his destiny.

One of the most important things, doctrinally, in this chapter is the changing of Jacob's name to "Israel" (verse 28).

As the chapter begins, some messengers of God meet him. We know nothing more about this than what is recorded in verses 1–2, next.

1 And Jacob went on his way [*after the meeting with Laban in chapter 31*], and **the angels of God met him**.

2 And **when Jacob saw them, he said, This** *is* **God's host**: and he called the name of that place Mahanaim.

Next, beginning with verse 3, Jacob sets up a strategy to attempt to make peace with Esau before he and his people arrive in Canaan.

3 And **Jacob sent messengers before him to Esau his brother unto the land of Seir, the country of Edom** [*the country south of the Dead Sea where Esau had settled*].

4 And **he commanded them, saying, Thus shall ye speak unto my lord Esau; Thy servant Jacob saith thus, I have sojourned** [*lived*] **with Laban, and stayed there until now**:

5 And **I have oxen, and asses, flocks, and menservants, and womenservants** [*I have wealth and can take care of myself*]: and **I have sent to tell my lord, that I may find grace in thy sight** [*I come seeking to make peace with you*].

The news that Jacob's messengers bring back after speaking with Esau sounds rather threatening.

6 ¶ And **the messengers returned to Jacob, saying, We came to thy brother Esau, and also he cometh to meet thee, and four hundred men** with him.

Fearing the worst, Jacob divides his people and possessions into two groups.

7 Then **Jacob was greatly afraid and distressed**: and **he divided the people** that *was* with him, **and the flocks, and herds, and the camels, into two bands**;

8 And said, **If Esau come to the one company, and smite it, then the other company which is left shall escape**.

Next, Jacob appeals to the Lord to protect him and his people from Esau. He calls upon the Lord to keep the promises made to him when He commanded him to leave Haran and return to Canaan (Genesis 31:3), humbly expressing that he is not worthy of all the promised blessings but would be grateful for them.

9 ¶ And **Jacob said, O God** of my father Abraham, and God of my father Isaac, the Lord **which saidst unto me, Return unto thy country, and to thy kindred, and I will deal well with thee**:

10 **I am not worthy of the least of all the mercies**, and of all the truth, which thou hast shewed unto thy servant; for with my staff I passed over this Jordan; and now I am become two bands.

11 **Deliver me, I pray thee, from the hand of my brother**, from the

hand of Esau: **for I fear him, lest he will come and smite me,** *and* **the mother with the children.**

12 And **thou saidst, I will surely do thee good, and make thy seed as the sand of the sea, which cannot be numbered for multitude** [*he is humbly reminding the Lord of the Abrahamic covenant, with its attendant blessings and promises, He had conferred upon him, see Genesis 28:14*].

Next, Jacob will prepare and send a very large gift to Esau.

13 ¶ **And he** lodged there that same night; and **took** of that which came to his hand **a present for Esau his brother**;

14 **Two hundred she goats**, and **twenty he goats, two hundred ewes**, and **twenty rams**,

15 **Thirty milch** [*milk*] **camels with their colts, forty kine** [*cows*], and **ten bulls, twenty she asses, and ten foals** [*A total of about 580 animals*].

16 And **he delivered** *them* **into the hand of his servants, every drove** [*herd*] **by themselves** [*each type of animal being in a separate herd*]; **and said unto his servants, Pass over before me** [*go on ahead of me*], **and put a space betwixt drove and drove** [*put some space between each herd*].

17 And **he commanded the foremost** [*the group that was to be out in front*], saying, **When Esau my brother meeteth thee, and asketh thee, saying, Whose** *art* **thou? and whither goest thou? and whose** *are* **these before thee?**

18 Then **thou shalt say,** *They be* **thy servant Jacob's; it** *is* **a present sent unto my lord Esau**: and, behold, also **he** *is* **behind us**.

19 And **so commanded he the second, and the third, and all that followed the droves, saying, On this manner shall ye speak unto Esau, when ye find him.**

20 And **say ye moreover** [*in addition, say*], Behold, thy servant **Jacob** *is* **behind us**. For he said, I will appease him with the present that goeth before me, and afterward I will see his face; peradventure [*perhaps*] he will accept of me [*in other words, tell Esau that Jacob is coming and desires to make peace*].

21 **So went the present over before him**: and himself lodged that night in the company.

22 And **he rose up that night, and took his two wives, and his two womenservants, and his eleven sons, and passed over the ford Jabbok** [*the River Jabbok, a little less than half way between the Dead Sea and the Sea of Galilee, to the east of the Jordan River*].

23 And he took them, and sent them over the brook, and sent over that he had [*sent everyone on ahead*].

We have no definite information as to who the messenger was spoken of in verses 24–28, next. However, Joseph Fielding Smith did have some definite counsel regarding him. He taught:

"Who wrestled with Jacob on Mount Peniel? The scriptures say it was a man. The Bible interpreters say it was an angel. More than likely it was a messenger sent to Jacob to give him the blessing. To think he wrestled and held an angel who couldn't get away, is out of the question. The term angel as used in the scriptures, at times, refers to messengers who are sent with some important instruction. Later in this chapter when Jacob said he had beheld the Lord, that did not have reference to his wrestling" (*Doctrines of Salvation*, Vol. 1, page 17).

24 ¶ **And Jacob was left alone; and there wrestled a man with him until the breaking of the day.**

25 And when he [*the man*] saw that he prevailed not against him [*Jacob*], he touched the hollow of his thigh [*he touched his hip*]; and the hollow of Jacob's thigh was out of joint [*his hip was out of joint*], as he wrestled with him.

26 And he said, Let me go, for the day breaketh. And **he** [*Jacob*] **said, I will not let thee go, except thou bless me**.

Next, in verses 27–28, Jacob's name is changed to Israel, meaning "He perseveres with God" (see footnote 28b, in your Bible). Also, in the October 2020 general conference of the Church, President Russell M. Nelson defined "Israel" as meaning "let God prevail" (in our lives).

27 And **he said unto him, What** *is* **thy name?** And he said, **Jacob**.

28 And he said, **Thy name shall be called no more Jacob, but Israel**: for as a prince hast thou power with God and with men, and hast prevailed.

As mentioned previously (see note after Genesis 17:5 in this study guide), in Biblical culture, a name change was often associated with the making of covenants with God and the promised blessings associated with the covenants. Such name changes can symbolize becoming a new person with greatly expanded opportunities for progress and growth toward becoming like God.

29 And **Jacob asked** *him,* **and said, Tell** *me,* I pray thee, **thy name**. And **he said, Wherefore** [*why*] *is* it *that* thou dost ask after my name? **And he blessed him there**.

As stated by Apostle Joseph Fielding Smith in the quote above, Jacob's seeing God face to face in verse 30, next, is not associated with his wrestling in verses 24–26. It was a separate occurrence.

30 And Jacob called the name of the place Peniel: for **I have seen God face to face**, and my life is preserved.

31 And as he passed over Penuel the sun rose upon him, and he halted upon his thigh [*he was limping because of the injury to his hip*].

32 Therefore the children of Israel eat not *of* the sinew [*tendon*] which

shrank, which *is* upon the hollow of the thigh [*which is attached to the hip socket*], unto this day: because he touched the hollow of Jacob's thigh in the sinew that shrank.

GENESIS 33

This is a chapter that shows the power of making peace when both parties desire it. As you know, there was extreme hatred on Esau's part toward Jacob. But time softened his anger, and Jacob did everything he could think of and followed his own efforts with prayer to God for help (Genesis 32:11). It worked. We will rejoice with these two brothers as they make peace, as we now study this chapter.

In verses 1–3, Jacob sees Esau coming with the four hundred men reported previously to him by his advance party of messengers (see Genesis 32:6). Not knowing yet whether that means war or peace, Jacob organizes his family according to wives and children. Then he, himself, goes in front of them all and approaches Esau, humbly bowing to the earth seven times as he goes. In his culture, the number seven represents completeness, and it may be that this gesture on his part is meant to signal Esau that he has done all he possibly can to make peace.

1 And **Jacob lifted up his eyes, and looked, and, behold, Esau came**, and **with** him **four hundred men**. And **he divided** [*separated*] **the children unto Leah**, and unto **Rachel**, and unto **the two handmaids** [*Zilpah and Bilhah*].

2 And **he put the handmaids and their children foremost** [*in front*], and **Leah and her children after**, and **Rachel and Joseph hindermost** [*the farthest back*].

3 And **he passed over before them** [*then Jacob went ahead of them all*], **and bowed himself to the ground seven times, until he came near to his brother**.

> Can you imagine the relief and joy that swept over Jacob as Esau ran to him and greeted him with great affection!

4 And **Esau ran to meet him, and embraced him, and fell on his neck**, and **kissed him: and they wept**.

5 **And he** [*Esau*] **lifted up his eyes, and saw the women and the children; and said, Who** *are* **those with thee?** And he [*Jacob*] said, **The children which God hath graciously given thy servant** [*has graciously given me*].

> What follows now is a very tender scene as each of Jacob's families come forward and greet Esau.

6 **Then the handmaidens came near, they and their children, and they bowed themselves**.

7 And **Leah also with her children came near, and bowed** themselves: **and after came Joseph near and Rachel, and they bowed** themselves.

8 **And he** [*Esau*] **said, What *meanest* thou by all this drove** [*the 500 plus animals that Jacob had organized into groups and sent in advance to Esau—see Genesis 32:13-21*] **which I met?** And he said, *These are* **to find grace in the sight of my lord** [*these are a peace offering to you*].

9 And **Esau said, I have enough, my brother; keep that thou hast unto thyself**.

10 And **Jacob said, Nay**, I pray thee, if now I have found grace in thy sight, then **receive my present** at my hand: **for therefore** [*because of these gifts*] **I have seen thy face, as though I had seen the face of God** [*I have seen a great change in your feelings toward me*], and **thou wast pleased with me**.

11 Take, I pray thee, my blessing that is brought to thee [*please accept my gesture of peace*]; because God hath dealt graciously with me [*because God has answered my prayers*], and because I have enough [*I have plenty*]. And he urged him, **and he took *It*** [*Esau accepted the gift*].

> Next, Esau says, in effect, "Let's go home together. I will go in front of you" (perhaps to protect Jacob and his families from any dangers along the way). But Jacob suggests that since he has young children and many flocks with him, he will need to travel more slowly than Esau, who has only his men accompanying him.

12 **And he** [*Esau*] **said, Let us take our journey, and let us go**, and **I will go before** [*out in front of*] thee.

13 **And he** [*Jacob*] **said** unto him, My lord knoweth that **the children *are* tender** [*young*], and **the flocks and herds with young *are* with me**: and **if men should overdrive them** [*push them too hard*] one day, **all the flock will die**.

14 **Let my lord, I pray thee, pass over before his servant** [*you go on ahead*]: **and I will lead on softly** [*I will be gentle with those who travel with me and move slowly*], **according as the cattle that goeth before me and the children be able to endure**, until I come unto my lord unto Seir [*I will catch up with you at your home in Seir (the area that Esau had settled on, south of the Dead Sea)*].

15 **And Esau said, Let me now leave with thee *some* of the folk that *are* with me** [*let me leave some of my men with you to assist as needed*]. And **he** [*Jacob*] **said, What needeth it?** [*That won't be necessary.*] **let me find grace in the sight of my lord** [*just give your blessing to us and we will be fine*].

16 ¶ **So Esau returned** that day on his way **unto Seir**.

> As stated, Jacob will move slowly, stopping as needed for his family and flocks to rest up.

17 And **Jacob journeyed to Succoth**, and built him an house, and made booths for his cattle: therefore the

name of the place is called Succoth [*about thirty miles north of the Dead Sea, just east of the Jordan River*].

18 ¶ And Jacob **came to Shalem**, a city of Shechem [*across the Jordan River and about twenty miles west of Succoth and 35 miles north of Jerusalem*], which *is* **in the land of Canaan**, when he came from Padanaram; and pitched his tent before [*outside of*] the city.

> While Jacob and his family will eventually end up in southern Canaan, in Hebron, he will settle for a while in Shechem.

19 And **he bought a parcel of a field, where he had spread his tent**, at the hand of the children of Hamor [*he bought the piece of land from the children of Hamor*], Shechem's father, **for an hundred pieces of money**.

20 And **he erected there an altar**, and called it El-elohe-Israel [*meaning "God is the God of Israel"*].

GENESIS 34

This chapter is not a particularly pleasant one. While Jacob and his people are temporarily living in Shechem, Dinah, one of Jacob and Leah's daughters, is abducted and raped. Simeon and Levi get revenge by inviting all the men of the area to join their religion, which requires that they be circumcised. In an attempt to restore peace between them and Jacob's people, they agree to this. Then, while the men are incapacitated because of the surgery, Simeon and Levi go to the city and kill all of them (verse 25). They then plunder the city. This was not what Jacob wanted and he told them so, adding that his sons had made him "to stink among the inhabitants of the land" (verse 30).

Again, this is one of those chapters in which the Old Testament tells it like it is. One thing we can do with it, however, is use it as a lesson manual of sorts, to better learn the language of the Old Testament. We will add a number of notes as we go along to help with this.

1 And **Dinah the daughter of Leah**, which she bare unto Jacob, **went out to see the daughters of the land** [*went out to visit some of the women who lived there*].

2 And **when Shechem** the son of Hamor the Hivite, prince of the country, **saw her, he took her, and lay with her, and defiled her** [*took away her chastity*].

> One commentator on the Bible suggests that the word "took" in verse 2, above, means to take by force. He said:
>
> "The Hebrew word that is translated 'took' in the phrase 'he took her' can mean 'to take away, sometimes with violence and force; to take possession, to capture, to seize upon.'" (Wilson, *Old Testament Word Studies,* s.v. "take," page 435).

Verse 3, next, indicates that after the evil deed was done, Shechem tried to gain Dinah's affection and win her heart, despite what he had done to her. In fact, he eventually asks his father to obtain permission for him to marry her.

3 And **his soul clave unto Dinah the daughter of Jacob, and he loved the damsel, and spake kindly unto the damsel.**

4 **And Shechem spake unto his father Hamor, saying, Get me this damsel to wife.**

Next, after Jacob hears the bad news, he waits until his sons come in from the fields, then tells them what has happened.

5 And **Jacob heard that he had defiled Dinah his daughter**: now his sons were with his cattle in the field: and **Jacob held his peace until they were come.**

6 ¶ And **Hamor the father of Shechem went out unto Jacob to commune with him** [*to ask for Dinah's hand in marriage for his son as he had requested above*].

7 And **the sons of Jacob** came out of the field **when they heard** *it:* and the men were grieved [*saddened*], and they **were very wroth** [*livid with rage*], because he [*Shechem*] had wrought folly in Israel [*had brought dishonor to the family of Jacob*] in lying with Jacob's daughter; which thing ought not to be done.

8 And **Hamor** [*Shechem's father*] **communed with them**, saying, The soul of my son **Shechem longeth for your daughter: I pray you give her him to wife.**

9 And **make ye marriages with us,** *and* **give your daughters unto us, and take our daughters unto you.**

Hamor, the "prince of the country" (verse 2), continues, inviting Jacob and his sons to settle permanently in his city-state.

10 And **ye shall dwell with us: and the land shall be before you; dwell and trade ye therein, and get you possessions therein.**

Even Shechem, himself, the one who violated Dinah (verse 2), is bargaining unashamedly with Jacob and Dinah's brothers for her hand in marriage, offering to provide whatever dowry they request in exchange for the privilege of marrying their sister. Her brothers immediately see their opportunity and cunningly set a trap.

11 And **Shechem said unto her father and unto her brethren**, Let me find grace in your eyes [*please look upon me with favor*], and **what ye shall say unto me I will give.**

12 **Ask me never so much dowry and gift, and I will give according as ye shall say unto me: but give me the damsel to wife.**

13 And **the sons of Jacob answered** Shechem and Hamor his father **deceitfully** [*without exposing their true motive*], **and said, because he had defiled Dinah their sister**:

14 And they said unto them, **We cannot** do this thing, to **give our sister to one that is uncircumcised;**

for that *were* a reproach unto us [*that would be against our religion*]:

15 But in this will we consent unto you [*this is what we require in order to give permission*]**: If ye will be as we be, that every male of you be circumcised**;

16 Then will we give our daughters unto you, and we will take your daughters to us, and we will dwell with you, and we will become one people.

17 But if ye will not hearken unto us, to **be circumcised; then will we take our daughter** [*sister*]**, and we will be gone** [*we will leave the country*].

18 And their words pleased Hamor, and Shechem Hamor's son.

19 And **the young man** [*Shechem*] **deferred not to do the thing** [*did not hesitate to be circumcised*], because he had delight in Jacob's daughter [*because he really liked Dinah*]: and he *was* more honourable than all the house of his father.

> Next, Hamor and Shechem tell the men of their city what they have agreed to, reminding them that it will make it possible for them also to marry the young women of Jacob's company. They agree to go along with it. The trap is now in place.

20 ¶ And Hamor and Shechem his son **came unto** the gate of **their city, and communed with the men of their city, saying,**

21 These men *are* **peaceable with us** [*want to live peaceably with us*]; therefore let them dwell in the land, and trade therein; for the land, behold, *it is* large enough for them; **let us take their daughters to us for wives, and let us give them our daughters.**

> Next, in verse 22, Hamor and Shechem explain to their men that there is just one catch.

22 Only herein will the men consent unto us for to dwell with us, to be one people, **if every male among us be circumcised**, as they *are* circumcised.

23 *Shall* not their cattle and their substance and every beast of theirs *be* ours? only **let us consent unto them, and they will dwell with us**.

> The men agree that it would be worth it.

24 And unto Hamor and unto Shechem his son hearkened all that went out of the gate of his city; and **every male was circumcised**, all that went out of the gate of his city.

> Now the trap is ready to be sprung. Simeon and Levi carry out their plot for revenge. It is excessive.

25 ¶ And it came to pass **on the third day, when they were sore** [*the men of the city were laid up because of the surgery*], that two of the sons of Jacob, **Simeon and Levi**, Dinah's brethren, took each man his sword, and **came upon the city boldly, and slew all the males.**

26 **And they slew Hamor and Shechem** his son with the edge of the sword, **and took Dinah out of Shechem's house, and went out** [*of the city*].

> Next, Simeon and Levi, having taken Dinah to safety, take some of their brothers and return to the city and plunder it.

27 **The sons of Jacob came upon the slain, and spoiled** [*plundered*] **the city**, because they had defiled their sister.

28 **They took their sheep, and their oxen, and their asses, and that which** *was* **in the city, and that which** *was* **in the field**,

29 **And all their wealth, and all their little ones, and their wives took they captive**, and spoiled even all that *was* in the house.

> Jacob strongly disapproves of what his sons have done and tells them so in verse 30, next.

30 And Jacob said to Simeon and Levi, **Ye have troubled me to make me to stink among the inhabitants of the land**, among the Canaanites and the Perizzites: and I *being* few in number, they shall gather themselves together against me, and slay me; and I shall be destroyed, I and my house.

> His sons retort with their justification for what they have done.

31 And they said, **Should he deal with our sister as with an harlot?**

GENESIS 35

The Lord now commands Jacob to move with his family to the south and up to Beth-el, the place where he had camped years ago on his way to Haran to escape from Esau. While camped at that spot, he had the vision of the ladder reaching into heaven (see Genesis 28:10–19).

Beth-el means "house of God," and this sacred spot will now take on the aspect of a temple for Jacob and his family. In fact, Jacob commands his family members to make specific preparations to enter holy ground, much the same way we prepare to go to the temple today (verses 2–3).

Also, in this chapter we will see an emphasis placed upon the changing of Jacob's name to "Israel" in conjunction with the Abrahamic covenant, which is reconfirmed by the Lord upon him here (verses 10–13). A "new name," as mentioned in Revelation 2:17 and Doctrine and Covenants 130:11, is often mentioned in association with making or renewing covenants with the Lord. Receiving another name, as discussed by King Benjamin with his people (Mosiah 1:11), implies that through making and keeping covenants, we become new people, born again, with new opportunities for growth and progress toward exaltation. The "new name" that King Benjamin gave his people was the name of Christ (see Mosiah 5:8).

In this chapter, Rachel will finally have another child. It will be a son who will be named Benjamin (verses 16–19). Sadly, Rachel will die during childbirth.

Reuben, the oldest son of Leah and, thus, the firstborn of Jacob, will lose the right to the birthright by committing adultery with Bilhah (verse 22), Rachel's servant woman and his father's fourth wife.

And, at the end of the chapter, Isaac will die at age 180.

As we begin, Jacob is commanded to move his family from Shechem and go southward in the mountains, back to the sacred spot of ground that he named Beth-el over twenty years ago.

1 And **God said unto Jacob, Arise, go up to Beth-el, and dwell there**: and **make there an altar unto God**, that appeared unto thee when thou fleddest from the face of Esau thy brother.

> It appears from verse 2, next, that some of Jacob's family might already have become tainted by the idol worshipping practices of people around them. He calls upon them to repent and dress appropriately and prepare to enter upon holy ground.

2 Then **Jacob said unto his household**, and to all that *were* with him, **Put away the strange gods that** *are* **among you, and be clean, and change your garments** [*put on clean clothing*]:

3 And **let us arise, and go up to Beth-el; and I will make there an altar unto God**, who answered me in the day of my distress, and was with me in the way which I went.

4 And they gave unto Jacob all the strange gods [*idols*] which *were* in their hand, and *all their* earrings [*perhaps they had pagan inscriptions on them and were a part of idol worship*] which *were* in their ears; and Jacob hid them under the oak which *was* by Shechem.

> Next, in verse 5, we see that God protected them as they journeyed to their "temple."

5 And they journeyed: and **the terror of God was upon the cities that** *were* **round about them, and they did not pursue after the sons of Jacob**.

6 ¶ So **Jacob came to** Luz, which *is* in the land of Canaan, that *is,* **Beth-el**, he and all the people that *were* with him.

7 **And he built there an altar**, and called the place El-beth-el: because there God appeared unto him, when he fled from the face of his brother.

8 But **Deborah Rebekah's nurse died, and** she **was buried** beneath Beth-el under an oak: and the name of it was called Allon-bachuth.

> Next, in verses 9–12, Jehovah appears to Jacob and reconfirms the Abrahamic covenant upon him. You may wish to compare these verses with Abraham 2:9–11 in the Pearl of Great Price.

9 ¶ And **God appeared unto Jacob again**, when he came out of Padan-aram [*Haran*], **and blessed him**.

10 And God said unto him, Thy name *is* Jacob: **thy name shall not be called any more Jacob, but Israel** [*a name change associated with*

making a covenant] shall be thy name: and he called his name Israel.

11 And God said unto him, I *am* God Almighty: **be fruitful and multiply; a nation and a company of nations shall be of thee, and kings shall come out of thy loins**;

12 And **the land which I gave Abraham and Isaac, to thee I will give it, and to thy seed** [*posterity*] **after thee will I give the land.**

13 And God went up from him in the place where he talked with him.

14 And **Jacob set up a pillar in the place where he talked with him**, *even* a pillar of stone: and he poured a drink offering thereon, and he poured oil thereon.

15 And **Jacob called the name of the place** where God spake with him, **Beth-el**.

> Rachel is expecting her second child, and, as they approach Ephrath (the location of modern Bethlehem), she goes into labor.

16 ¶ And **they journeyed from Beth-el; and there was but a little way to come to Ephrath** [*as they were just outside of town*]: and **Rachel travailed** [*went into labor*], and **she had hard labour.**

17 And it came to pass, when she was in hard labour, that **the midwife said unto her, Fear not; thou shalt have this son also.**

18 And it came to pass, **as her soul was** in **departing**, (for she died) that **she called his name Ben-oni**: but **his father called him Benjamin.**

19 And **Rachel died, and was buried in the way to Ephrath, which** *is* **Beth-lehem.**

20 And **Jacob set a pillar upon her grave: that** *is* **the pillar of Rachel's grave unto this day** [*one can still visit Rachel's Tomb there, today*];

> On a personal note, my wife, Janette, and I have had the privilege of visiting Rachel's tomb, which is just one mile north of Bethlehem. We had a tender feeling of reverence there.
>
> After mourning Rachel's death, Israel (Jacob) continues his journey toward his final destination of Hebron in Canaan. He will stop temporarily somewhere past the tower of Edar.
>
> While there, his son, Reuben, the first son of the first wife, Leah, will commit a terrible sin that involves incest. As a result, he will lose his birthright. Joseph is the next in line, since he is the first son of the second wife, Rachel. Thus, Joseph will receive the birthright.

21 ¶ And **Israel** [*Jacob*] **journeyed, and spread his tent beyond the tower of Edar.**

22 And it came to pass, when Israel dwelt in that land, that **Reuben went and lay with** [*committed adultery with*] **Bilhah his father's concubine**:

and Israel heard *it*. Now the sons of Jacob were twelve:

> Next, a brief summary is given of the sons of Israel. They will become the twelve tribes of Israel. We will use underlining plus bold to point this out.

23 **The sons of Leah**; **Reuben**, Jacob's firstborn, and **Simeon**, and **Levi**, and **Judah**, and **Issachar**, and **Zebulun**:

24 **The sons of Rachel**; **Joseph**, and **Benjamin**:

25 And **the sons of Bilhah**, Rachel's handmaid; **Dan**, and **Naphtali**:

26 And **the sons of Zilpah**, Leah's handmaid; **Gad**, and **Asher**: these *are* the sons of Jacob, which were born to him in Padan-aram.

> Finally, after more than twenty years, Jacob has returned to Hebron.

27 ¶ **And Jacob came unto Isaac his father** unto Mamre, **unto** the city of Arbah, which *is* **Hebron**, where Abraham and Isaac sojourned [*lived*].

28 **And the days of Isaac were an hundred and fourscore years** [*Isaac was 180 years old*].

29 And **Isaac gave up the ghost, and died**, and **was gathered unto his people** [*went to the postmortal spirit world*], *being* old and full of days: and **his sons Esau and Jacob buried him**.

GENESIS 36

This chapter is primarily a record of the posterity of Esau, who was also known as "Edom."

1 Now **these** *are* **the generations** [*descendants*] **of Esau**, who *is* Edom.

2 **Esau took his wives of the daughters of Canaan** [*whose posterity could not hold the priesthood*]; **Adah** the daughter of Elon the Hittite, and **Aholibamah** the daughter of Anah the daughter of Zibeon the Hivite;

3 And **Bashemath** Ishmael's daughter, sister of Nebajoth.

4 And **Adah bare** to Esau **Eliphaz**; and **Bashemath bare Reuel**;

5 And **Aholibamah bare Jeush**, and **Jaalam**, and **Korah**: these *are* the sons of Esau, which were born unto him in the land of Canaan.

6 And **Esau** took his wives, and his sons, and his daughters, and all the persons of his house, and his cattle, and all his beasts, and all his substance, which he had got in the land of Canaan; and **went into the country from the face of his brother Jacob**.

7 For **their riches were more than that they might dwell together**; and **the land wherein they were strangers could not bear** [*support*] **them because of their cattle** [*flocks*].

8 **Thus dwelt Esau in mount Seir**: Esau *is* Edom.

The rest of the chapter gives a detailed record of Esau's descendants.

9 ¶ And these *are* the generations [*descendants*] of Esau the father of the Edomites in mount Seir:

10 These *are* the names of Esau's sons; Eliphaz the son of Adah the wife of Esau, Reuel the son of Bashemath the wife of Esau.

11 And the sons of Eliphaz were Teman, Omar, Zepho, and Gatam, and Kenaz.

12 And Timna was concubine to Eliphaz Esau's son; and she bare to Eliphaz Amalek: these *were* the sons of Adah Esau's wife.

13 And these *are* the sons of Reuel; Nahath, and Zerah, Shammah, and Mizzah: these were the sons of Bashemath Esau's wife.

14 ¶ And these were the sons of Aholibamah, the daughter of Anah the daughter of Zibeon, Esau's wife: and she bare to Esau Jeush, and Jaalam, and Korah.

15 ¶ These *were* dukes of the sons of Esau: the sons of Eliphaz the firstborn *son* of Esau; duke Teman, duke Omar, duke Zepho, duke Kenaz,

16 Duke Korah, duke Gatam, *and* duke Amalek: these *are* the dukes *that came* of Eliphaz in the land of Edom; these *were* the sons of Adah.

17 ¶ And these *are* the sons of Reuel Esau's son; duke Nahath, duke Zerah, duke Shammah, duke Mizzah: these *are* the dukes *that came* of Reuel in the land of Edom; these *are* the sons of Bashemath Esau's wife.

18 ¶ And these *are* the sons of Aholibamah Esau's wife; duke Jeush, duke Jaalam, duke Korah: these *were* the dukes *that came* of Aholibamah the daughter of Anah, Esau's wife.

19 These *are* the sons of Esau, who *is* Edom, and these *are* their dukes.

20 ¶ These *are* the sons of Seir the Horite, who inhabited the land; Lotan, and Shobal, and Zibeon, and Anah,

21 And Dishon, and Ezer, and Dishan: these *are* the dukes of the Horites, the children of Seir in the land of Edom.

22 And the children of Lotan were Hori and Hemam; and Lotan's sister *was* Timna.

23 And the children of Shobal *were* these; Alvan, and Manahath, and Ebal, Shepho, and Onam.

24 And these *are* the children of Zibeon; both Ajah, and Anah: this *was that* Anah that found the mules in the wilderness, as he fed the asses of Zibeon his father.

25 And the children of Anah *were* these; Dishon, and Aholibamah the daughter of Anah.

26 And these *are* the children of Dishon; Hemdan, and Eshban, and Ithran, and Cheran.

27 The children of Ezer *are* these; Bilhan, and Zaavan, and Akan.

28 The children of Dishan *are* these; Uz, and Aran.

29 These *are* the dukes *that came* of the Horites; duke Lotan, duke Shobal, duke Zibeon, duke Anah,

30 Duke Dishon, duke Ezer, duke Dishan: these *are* the dukes *that came* of Hori, among their dukes in the land of Seir.

31 ¶ And these *are* the kings that reigned in the land of Edom, before there reigned any king over the children of Israel.

32 And Bela the son of Beor reigned in Edom: and the name of his city *was* Dinhabah.

33 And Bela died, and Jobab the son of Zerah of Bozrah reigned in his stead.

34 And Jobab died, and Husham of the land of Temani reigned in his stead.

35 And Husham died, and Hadad the son of Bedad, who smote Midian in the field of Moab, reigned in his stead: and the name of his city *was* Avith.

36 And Hadad died, and Samlah of Masrekah reigned in his stead.

37 And Samlah died, and Saul of Rehoboth *by* the river reigned in his stead.

38 And Saul died, and Baal-hanan the son of Achbor reigned in his stead.

39 And Baal-hanan the son of Achbor died, and Hadar reigned in his stead: and the name of his city *was* Pau; and his wife's name *was* Mehetabel, the daughter of Matred, the daughter of Mezahab.

40 And these *are* the names of the dukes *that came* of Esau, according to their families, after their places, by their names; duke Timnah, duke Alvah, duke Jetheth,

41 Duke Aholibamah, duke Elah, duke Pinon,

42 Duke Kenaz, duke Teman, duke Mibzar,

43 Duke Magdiel, duke Iram: these *be* the dukes of Edom, according to their habitations in the land of their possession: he *is* Esau the father of the Edomites.

GENESIS 37

This is probably one of the best-known chapters in the Old Testament. It is the chapter in which Joseph is sold into Egypt. He is one of the greatest examples in scripture of a man of integrity, one who lives the gospel and honors his covenants and commitments to God, no matter what the consequences.

Joseph will become a great prophet. In 2 Nephi 3:4–22, Lehi quotes many of Joseph's prophecies as he gives his last counsel to his youngest son, also named Joseph, his last born in the wilderness. We will quote these verses from the Book of Mormon here, adding some notes and commentary so that you can feel the greatness of Joseph, who was sold into Egypt. Remember, Lehi is talking to his own son, Joseph, Nephi's youngest brother.

2 Nephi 3:4–22

4 For behold, thou art the fruit of my loins [*you are my offspring*]; and **I am a descendant of Joseph who was carried captive into Egypt**. And great were the covenants of the Lord which he made unto Joseph.

5 Wherefore, **Joseph** [*who was sold into Egypt*] **truly saw our day**. And he obtained a promise of the Lord, that out of the fruit of his loins [*out of his posterity*] the Lord God would raise up a righteous branch unto [*a righteous leader for*] the house of Israel; not the Messiah, but a branch which was to be broken off [*scattered*], nevertheless, to be remembered in the covenants of the Lord that the Messiah should be made manifest unto them in the latter days, in the spirit of power, unto the bringing of them out of darkness unto light—yea, out of hidden darkness [*many who are in spiritual darkness think they are "enlightened" or living in the light; therefore, their spiritual darkness is "hidden" to them*] and out of captivity unto freedom [*the restoration of the gospel*].

6 For Joseph [*in Egypt*] truly testified, saying: A seer [*Joseph Smith Jr.*] shall the Lord my God raise up, who shall be a choice seer unto the fruit of my loins [*my posterity; both Ephraim and Manasseh*]).

7 Yea, Joseph [*in Egypt*] truly said: Thus saith the Lord unto me: A choice seer [*Joseph Smith Jr.*] will I raise up out of the fruit of thy loins; and he shall be esteemed highly among the fruit of thy loins [*highly respected among your posterity*]. And unto him will I give commandment that he shall do a work [*restoration of the gospel in the last days*] for the fruit of thy loins, his brethren [*his fellow Israelites*], which shall be of great worth unto them, even to the bringing of them to the knowledge of the covenants which I have made with thy fathers [*Abraham, Isaac, and Jacob*].

8 And I will give unto him [*Joseph Smith Jr.*] a commandment that he shall do none other work, save the work which I shall command him [*Joseph Smith Jr. will not prosper in things other than his work in the gospel; see Doctrine and Covenants 24:9*]. And I will make him great in mine eyes; for he shall do my work.

9 And he [*Joseph Smith Jr.*] shall be great like unto Moses, whom I have said I would raise up unto you [*the children of Israel in Egypt*], to deliver my people, O house of Israel.

10 And Moses will I raise up, to deliver thy people out of the land of Egypt.

11 But a seer [*Joseph Smith Jr.*] will I raise up out of the fruit of thy [*Joseph in Egypt*] loins; and unto him [*Joseph Smith Jr.*] will I give power to bring forth my word unto the seed of thy loins [*Ephraim and Manasseh*]—and not to the bringing forth my word only, saith the Lord, but to the convincing them of my word, which shall have already gone forth among them [*by way of the Bible*].

12 Wherefore, the fruit of thy [*Joseph in Egypt*] loins shall write [*the Book of Mormon*]; and the fruit of the loins of Judah shall write [*the Bible*]; and that which shall be written by the fruit of thy loins [*the Book of Mormon*], and also that which shall be written by the fruit of the loins of Judah [*the Bible*], shall grow together, unto the confounding [*stopping*] of false doctrines and laying down of contentions, and establishing peace among the fruit of thy loins, and bringing them to the knowledge of their fathers [*ancestors*] in the latter days, and also to the knowledge of my covenants, saith the Lord.

13 And out of weakness he [*Joseph Smith Jr.*] shall be made strong, in that day when my work shall commence among all my people, unto the restoring thee, O house of Israel, saith the Lord.

14 And thus prophesied Joseph [*in Egypt*], saying: Behold, that seer [*Joseph Smith Jr.*] will the Lord bless; and they that seek to destroy him [*seek to stop him from accomplishing the Lord's work*] shall be confounded [*unsuccessful*]; for this promise, which I have obtained of the Lord, of the fruit of my loins, shall be fulfilled. Behold, I [*Joseph in Egypt*] am sure of the fulfilling of this promise;

15 And his name [*Joseph Smith, Jr.*] shall be called after me; and it shall be after the name of his father [*he will be named after his father*]. And he shall be like unto me [*a prophet and seer*]; for the thing, which the Lord shall bring forth by his hand, by the power of the Lord shall bring my people unto salvation.

16 Yea, thus prophesied Joseph [*in Egypt*]: I am sure of this thing, even as I am sure of the promise of Moses; for the Lord hath said unto me, I will preserve thy seed forever.

17 And the Lord hath said: I will raise up a Moses; and I will give power unto him in a rod [*he will be a great leader with authority*]; and I will give judgment unto him in writing [*Moses will be a skilled writer—he wrote Genesis, Exodus, Leviticus, Numbers, and Deuteronomy*]. Yet I will not loose his tongue [*Moses won't be a great speaker—see Exodus 4:10*], that he shall speak much, for I will not make him mighty in speaking. But I [*Jehovah, Jesus*] will write unto him my law, by the finger of mine own hand [*the stone tablets containing the commandments*]; and I will make a

spokesman for him [*Aaron—see Exodus 4:14–16*].

18 And the Lord said unto me [*Joseph in Egypt*] also: I will raise up unto the fruit of thy loins [*your posterity*]; and I will make for him [*Joseph Smith Jr.*] a spokesman [*perhaps meaning Sidney Rigdon—see Doctrine and Covenants 100:9*]. And I, behold, I [*the Lord*] will give unto him [*Joseph Smith Jr.*] that he shall write [*translate*] the writing of the fruit of thy loins [*the Book of Mormon plates*], unto the fruit of thy loins [*so that My gospel can come to your descendants*]; and the spokesman of thy loins shall declare it.

19 And the words [*from the golden plates*] which he [*Joseph Smith Jr.*] shall write [*translate*] shall be the words which are expedient [*essential*] in my wisdom should go forth unto the fruit of thy loins. And it shall be as if the fruit of thy loins [*the Book of Mormon prophets and people*] had cried unto them from the dust; for I know their faith.

20 And they [*the Book of Mormon prophets*] shall cry from the dust [*shall speak from the past*]; yea, even repentance unto their brethren, even after many generations have gone by them. And it shall come to pass that their cry shall go, even according to the simpleness of their words. [*The Book of Mormon will be instrumental in restoring the gospel's "plain and precious" truths.*]

21 Because of their [*prophets of the Book of Mormon*] faith their words shall proceed forth out of my [*the Lord's*] mouth unto their brethren who are the fruit of thy loins [*descendants of Joseph in Egypt*]; and the weakness of their words will I make strong in their faith, unto the remembering of my covenant [*keeping of my promise*] which I made unto thy [*Joseph in Egypt*] fathers [*ancestors*].

In verse 22, next, Lehi tells his son, Joseph, that the prophecies he has just quoted are typical of the prophecies of Joseph in Egypt.

22 And now, behold, my son Joseph [*Lehi's son*], after this manner did my father [*my ancestor, Joseph in Egypt*] of old prophesy.

The above verses from the Book of Mormon bear clear testimony that Joseph in Egypt was a mighty prophet of God. We will mention one more important thing about him regarding symbolism and then continue with the account of his early years given in Genesis 37.

In the notes for Genesis 22 in this study guide, we mentioned that Abraham was a "type" for the Father, meaning that Abraham was a symbolic representation of Heavenly Father. Isaac was a "type" of Christ, meaning that Isaac symbolically represented the Son of God, for example, as he carried the wood to the place of sacrifice (similar to Jesus' carrying His own cross) and as he voluntarily cooperated with Abraham in preparation for his being sacrificed.

Joseph, Jacob's son, was also a "type" of Christ. For example:

JOSEPH AS A TYPE OF CHRIST

1. THE SAVIOR was hated by His people.

    JOSEPH was hated by his brothers.

2. THE SAVIOR knew at an early age that He had a special mission to perform.

    JOSEPH knew at an early age (through dreams) that he would be instrumental in saving his brethren.

3. THE SAVIOR was thirty years old when He began His mission to save us.

    JOSEPH was thirty years old when he became the prime minister of Egypt, thus, in a position to save his people.

4. THE SAVIOR took seven ìdaysî to create the earth and prepare it for us.

    JOSEPH, as prime minister, took seven years to prepare Egypt against the coming famine and thus provided physical salvation for his own brothers when they came.

5. THE SAVIOR mercifully forgave those who crucified Him.

    JOSEPH mercifully forgave those who brutally sold him into slavery.

6. THE SAVIOR was sold for the price of a common slave, thirty pieces of silver in His day (Matthew 26:15).

    JOSEPH was sold for the price of a common slave, twenty pieces of silver in his day (Genesis 37:28).

We will now return to our preparations to study chapter 37. Jacob has been home for some time now, having made peace with Esau and returned to the land of Canaan, where his father and mother, Isaac and Rebekah, had settled. His father has died. He was 180 years old. Life has settled down into a routine, and things appear to have been going rather well for Jacob (Israel).

As mentioned previously, Joseph is the birthright son (Reuben having lost the right when he committed adultery with Bilhah, one of his father's wives—see Genesis 35:22). Joseph has been given a coat of many colors by his father, which many Bible scholars believe was a special coat indicating that he was the birthright son. Unfortunately, his brothers were jealous of him.

As Moses (the writer of Genesis) begins the account in chapter 37, here, he points out that Jacob is a "stranger, in the land of Canaan." The term "stranger" means "foreigner," as used in King James English (we are studying the King James version of the Bible). Thus, we are to understand that Jacob and his family are still considered to be foreigners among the Canaanites.

1 And **Jacob** dwelt in the land wherein his father **was a stranger** [*he was a "foreigner," not a Canaanite*], **in the land of Canaan**.

Verse 2, next, tells us that Joseph is now seventeen years old. He had gone out to help some of his brothers tend the flocks. Upon returning home, he informs his father about some things that are out of order. His very strong sense of right and wrong is already making itself felt, and it will cause trouble between him and his brothers.

2 These *are* the generations of Jacob [*this is an account of the descendants of Jacob*]. **Joseph, *being* seventeen years old, was feeding the flock with his brethren**; and the lad *was* with the sons of Bilhah, and with the sons of Zilpah, his father's wives: and **Joseph brought unto his father their evil report** [*Joseph told his father about some mischief they were involved in*].

Next, we see that Joseph was indeed Jacob's favorite son. As stated in verse 3, Jacob was quite old when Joseph was born to Rachel, his first love. His extra love for Joseph may also have had to do with the fact that he was the birthright son, which means that Joseph would eventually inherit a double portion of his father's wealth to enable him to carry on with the family business and take care of other family members as needed.

It may also have been because he was the only one, except for little Benjamin, who had not caused serious trouble for him already. Whatever the case, Joseph has been given a "coat of many colours," and his brothers are jealous of him.

3 Now **Israel** [*Jacob*] **loved Joseph more than all his children, because he *was* the son of his old age: and he made him a coat of *many* colours**.

4 And **when his brethren saw that their father loved him more than all his brethren, they hated him, and could not speak peaceably unto him**.

Next, we see that the gift of prophecy (Doctrine and Covenants 46:22) is already being manifest with Joseph. The prophetic dreams that Joseph had (verses 5–11) did not go over well with his brothers.

5 ¶ And **Joseph dreamed a dream, and he told *it* his brethren: and they hated him yet the more**.

6 And he said unto them, **Hear, I pray you, this dream which I have dreamed**:

7 For, behold, **we *were* binding sheaves in the field** [*making bundles of grain stocks*], and, lo, **my sheaf arose, and** also **stood upright**; and, behold, **your sheaves stood round about, and made obeisance** [*bowed down*] **to my sheaf**.

The above dream was indeed prophetic. It foretold the day when Joseph's brothers would bow down to him in Egypt, where he would become the prime minister (see Genesis 42:6). Even though his brothers knew that Joseph was going to receive the birthright and thus would someday rule over them in many matters, they scoffed at this dream and their hatred toward him grew stronger.

Another aspect of the fulfillment of the prophecy in verse 7, above, might well be found in Doctrine and Covenants 133:32. It foretells of the latter days when the lost ten tribes will return and receive the blessings of the gospel and the temple at the hands of "the children of Ephraim," who was Joseph's birthright son.

Doctrine and Covenants 133:32

32 And **there shall they fall down and be crowned with glory** [*receive their temple blessings*], even in Zion, by the hands of the servants of the Lord, even the children of Ephraim.

Thus, Joseph's descendants are gathered to the gospel first in the last days and prepare the way for the other tribes of Israel to receive the restored gospel and the ensuing blessings of the temple and exaltation.

We will continue with the account of Joseph in Genesis.

8 And **his brethren said to him, Shalt thou indeed reign over us? or shalt thou indeed have dominion over us?** And **they hated him yet the more for** [*because of*] **his dreams, and for his words**.

9 ¶ And **he dreamed yet another dream**, and told it his brethren, and said, Behold, I have dreamed a dream more; and, **behold, the sun** [*symbolic of his father—see verse 10, next*] **and the moon** [*symbolic of his mother*] **and the eleven stars** [*his brothers*] **made obeisance** [*bowed down*] **to me.**

10 And **he told** *it* **to his father, and to his brethren: and his father rebuked him**, and said unto him, What *is* this dream that thou hast dreamed? Shall I and thy mother and thy brethren indeed come to bow down ourselves to thee to the earth?

11 And his brethren envied him; but **his father observed the saying** [*kept it in the back of his mind*].

One of the things we see, based on verse 12, next, is that these people took their flocks rather long distances to find good grazing for them. In this case, Joseph's brothers have worked their way about fifty miles north of Jacob's main headquarters for their flocks to feed in the area around Shechem. By the way, this was the area where the brothers had stirred up trouble with the locals when their sister, Dinah, was abducted (see Genesis 33:18; 34). Perhaps Jacob was worried about their safety, and thus sent Joseph to see if all was well with them.

12 ¶ And **his brethren went to feed their father's flock in Shechem**.

13 And **Israel** [*Jacob*] **said unto Joseph**, Do not thy brethren feed *the flock* in Shechem? **come, and I will send thee unto them.** And he said to him, Here *am I* [*I am ready to do as you ask*].

14 And he said to him, **Go, I pray thee, see whether it be well with thy brethren, and well with the flocks; and bring me word again. So he sent him** out of the vale

[*shallow valley, flatlands*] of Hebron, **and he came to Shechem**.

> When Joseph arrived in Shechem, he couldn't find his brothers. They had moved the flocks another fifteen to twenty miles north to Dothan.

15 ¶ And **a certain man found him**, and, behold, *he was* wandering in the field: **and** the man **asked him**, saying, **What seekest thou?**

16 And **he said, I seek my brethren: tell me, I pray thee, where they feed *their flocks*.**

17 And **the man said, They are departed hence** [*they have gone away from here*]; for **I heard them say, Let us go to Dothan.** And **Joseph** went after his brethren, and **found them in Dothan.**

> Next, we see the depth of hatred that Joseph's brothers had for him. In fact, in this sense, his brothers are "types" of the people who conspired to crucify the Savior.

18 And **when they saw him afar off, even before he came near unto them, they conspired against him to slay him.**

19 And they said one to another, **Behold, this dreamer cometh** [*they are still extremely angry with Joseph because of the two dreams he had*].

20 Come now therefore, and **let us slay him, and cast him into some pit**, and **we will say, Some evil beast hath devoured him**: and we shall see what will become of his dreams [*then we will see whether his dreams about ruling over us come true*].

> Next, we see Reuben, Jacob's firstborn and Joseph's oldest brother stop them from killing Joseph. Remember that Reuben was the one to whom the birthright would have belonged, according to tradition, if he had not committed grievous sin with Bilhah (see Genesis 35:22). There is perhaps a reminder in this for us that there is good in almost all people.

> In fact, verse 21 implies that Reuben was not actively involved in the plot to kill Joseph. Rather, he listened as the others discussed it and took steps to prevent it.

21 And **Reuben heard it** [*the plot*], and he **delivered** [*rescued*] **him out of their hands; and said, Let us not kill him**.

> Verse 22, next, informs us that Reuben was stalling for time with the intent of saving Joseph's life and then secretly pulling him out of the pit and getting him safely on his way back to their home in Hebron.

22 And **Reuben said unto them, Shed no blood,** *but* **cast him into this pit that** *is* **in the wilderness, and lay no hand upon him**; that [*in order that*] **he might rid him out of their hands** [*get Joseph away from them*], **to deliver him to his father again.**

23 ¶ And it came to pass, **when Joseph was come unto his brethren**, that **they stript Joseph out of his coat**, *his* coat of *many* colours that *was* on him;

24 And they **took him, and cast him into a pit** [*apparently a dry well*]: and the pit *was* empty, *there was* no water in it.

> In verses 25–28, we will see Judah (the direct ancestor of the Jews) propose a plan to profit from the deal. They see a camel train of Ishmeelite merchants coming, obviously heading for Egypt, and Judah says, in effect, "We will be missing an opportunity to make money if we kill him. Let's sell him as a slave instead." The brothers agree.
>
> While we don't know, we might be justified in thinking that Judah also did not want to kill Joseph and was trying to come up with an alternative plan. Someday we will find out.

25 And **they sat down to eat bread** [*to eat their meal*]: and **they lifted up their eyes and looked, and, behold, a company of Ishmeelites** came from Gilead with their camels **bearing spicery and balm and myrrh, going to carry** *it* **down to Egypt**.

26 **And Judah said** unto his brethren, **What profit** *is it* **if we slay our brother, and conceal his blood?**

> There is certainly an element of hypocrisy in what Judah says next (unless he was also trying to stall for time) as he suggests that since Joseph is their own flesh and blood, they shouldn't do something as terrible as killing him. Rather, it would be much kinder to merely sell him into Egyptian slavery.

27 **Come, and let us sell him to the Ishmeelites**, and **let not our hand be upon him; for he** *is* **our brother** *and* **our flesh**. And his brethren were content.

> The dry well into which they had dropped Joseph was apparently far enough away from their camp that his brothers did not hear another group of travelers as they came by. While they were finalizing their scheme to sell Joseph as a slave to the Ishmeelite merchants, some Midianite businessmen came along, discovered Joseph, pulled him out of the well, and sold him to the Ishmeelites themselves for twenty pieces of silver, the going price for a young slave.

28 **Then there passed by Midianites merchantmen**; and **they drew** and lifted up **Joseph out of the pit, and sold Joseph to the Ishmeelites for twenty** *pieces* **of silver**: and they brought Joseph into Egypt [*to sell him there on the slave market*].

> Imagine Reuben's surprise and dismay as he later, secretly, returned to the pit and found that Joseph was gone!

29 ¶ And **Reuben returned unto the pit; and, behold, Joseph** *was* **not in the pit**; and **he rent his clothes** [*he tore his clothes, a sign of extreme anguish and mourning in his culture*].

30 And **he returned unto his brethren, and said, The child** *is* **not**; and I, whither shall I go?

> Having been foiled in their plan to sell Joseph, the brothers now face the reality of bringing the news to their father, Jacob. They come up

with a plot to deceive him and deflect guilt from themselves.

31 And **they took Joseph's coat, and killed a kid of the goats** [*a young goat*], **and dipped the coat in the blood**;

> Having returned to their father with the bloody coat of many colors, they innocently ask Jacob if he recognizes it and whether it might be the coat of his son (they use language that distances themselves from Joseph as their brother).

32 And **they sent the coat of *many* colours, and** they **brought *it* to their father**; and said, **This have we found: know now whether it *be* thy son's coat or no.**

> Their evil and dishonest plot worked, breaking their father's heart.

33 And **he knew** [*recognized*] **it**, and said, ***It is* my son's coat; an evil beast hath devoured him; Joseph is without doubt rent** [*torn*] **in pieces.**

34 And **Jacob rent** [*tore*] **his clothes, and put sackcloth upon his loins** [*dressed in rough, coarse clothing, which represented mourning in his culture*], **and mourned for his son many days.**

> As a side issue, verse 35, next, reminds us that Jacob had daughters as well as his twelve sons, even though none of the daughters is mentioned in the Bible except for Dinah (Genesis 34).

35 And **all his sons and all his daughters rose up to comfort him**; but **he refused to be comforted**; and he said, For I will go down into the grave unto my son mourning. Thus his father wept for him.

> Verse 36, next, tells us that the result of the Midianites' selling Joseph to the Ishmeelite merchants (verse 28, above) was that Joseph ended up as a slave in Egypt, purchased by Potiphar, a powerful official in Pharaoh's court.

36 And **the Midianites sold him into Egypt** [*by way of the Ishmeelite traders—see Genesis 39:1*] **unto Potiphar, an officer of Pharaoh's, *and* captain of the guard**.

GENESIS 38

Chapter 38 is an unpleasant chapter. In typical Old Testament honesty, it reports "the sordid tale of Judah's incestuous relationship with his daughter-in-law" (see Old Testament Student Manual, page 94).

This chapter includes hypocrisy, lying, breaking covenants, adultery, marrying out of the covenant, selfishness, and more. As a result, it provides a stark contrast between Joseph, who is honorable, no matter what, and who is at this time a slave in Egypt, and Judah and others, who appear in this chapter as the complete opposites of Joseph.

Judah is the direct ancestor of the Savior. Therefore, one of the lessons we can learn here is that ancestry does not necessarily determine righteousness, nor limit potential in attaining celestial glory and exaltation.

Another lesson is that breaking covenants and intentionally engaging in wickedness leads to trouble and lack of peace, right here in mortality. Honesty and righteousness are, indeed, the best policy!

We will now proceed.

1 And it came to pass at that time [*after they had sold Joseph into slavery*], that Judah went down from his brethren, and turned in to a certain Adullamite, whose name *was* Hirah [*Judah stayed with a man named Hirah*].

Next, Judah marries out of the covenant and has three children by a Canaanite wife.

2 And **Judah saw there a daughter of a certain Canaanite**, whose name *was* Shuah; and **he took her** [*married her*], **and** went in unto her.

JST Genesis 38:2

2 And Judah saw there a daughter of a certain Canaanite, whose name was Shuah; and he took her, and **went in and lay with her.**

3 And **she conceived, and bare a son**; and he called his name Er.

4 And **she conceived again, and bare a son**; and she called his name Onan.

5 And **she yet again conceived, and bare a son**; and called his name Shelah: and he was at Chezib, when she bare him.

Many years are passing by in these verses. By verse 6, Er, the son of Judah mentioned in verse 3, has grown up and marries a girl named Tamar. Tamar will be an important player in the intrigue of the next several verses.

6 And **Judah took a wife for Er** his firstborn, whose name *was* **Tamar**.

7 And **Er**, Judah's firstborn, **was wicked** in the sight of the Lord; **and the Lord slew him**.

8 And **Judah said unto Onan** [*Er's brother, Judah's second son by Shuah (verses 2 and 4)*], Go in unto thy brother's wife, and marry her, and raise up seed to thy brother [*a common practice in that day, required by the law of Moses (Deuteronomy 25:5; Matthew 22:24)*].

JST Genesis 38:8

8 And Judah said unto Onan, **Go and marry thy brother's wife, and raise up seed unto thy brother.**

9 And **Onan knew that the seed** [*the offspring of his marriage to Shuah*] **should not be his** [*would belong to his dead brother, Er, rather than to him*]; and it came to pass, when he went in unto his brother's wife, that he spilled *it* [*his seed*] on the ground, lest that he should give seed to his brother.

In order to better understand what is going on here, and in the next verses, we will say a bit more about the culture in which this is taking place. We will quote from the *Old Testament Student Manual* for help:

"Ancient customs of the Middle East provided that a brother of a deceased man should marry his widow. Under Moses this custom became law (see Deuteronomy 25:5–10). The purpose of such a marriage was to produce a male heir for the dead man and thus perpetuate his name and memory. It was regarded as a great calamity to die without a son, for then the man's lineage did not continue and also the man's property reverted to someone else's family (through daughters, if he had any, or through other relatives). It may be that Onan, who by virtue of the death of his older brother would have been next in line for the inheritance of Judah, refused to raise up seed through Tamar because the inheritance would have stayed with the elder son's family. He went through the outward show of taking Tamar to wife, but refused to let her have children. Thus, when Judah failed to keep his promise to send the youngest son to her, Tamar resorted to deception in order to bear children" (*Old Testament Student Manual*, pages 94–95).

10 And the thing which he did displeased **the Lord**: wherefore he **slew him also**.

> Next, in verse 11, Judah tells Tamar to wait for a few years until the next brother in line who would be obligated to marry her (Judah's youngest son, Shelah—verse 5, above), grows up and he will have him marry Tamar so she can have children for her and her deceased husband, Er.

11 **Then said Judah to Tamar his daughter in law, Remain a widow** at thy father's house [*in the meantime, live with your father*], **till Shelah my son be grown**: for he said, Lest peradventure he die also [*let's hope he doesn't die too*], as his brethren *did*. And Tamar went and dwelt in her father's house.

> It appears that many years have now passed and Judah has not kept his promise to Tamar that when Shelah got old enough, he would see to it that Shelah would marry her. As a result, Tamar determines a strategy to make sure she has offspring.
>
> In verse 12, next, we are told that Judah had had a daughter by Shuah and that this daughter died. After the days of mourning were over, he went to visit his sheepshearers in Timnath, accompanied by his old friend Hirah (see verse 1). Tamar finds out where her dishonest father-in-law is staying and travels to work her plan.

12 ¶ And **in process of time** [*over the years*] **the daughter** of Shuah Judah's wife **died**; and **Judah was comforted, and went** up unto his sheepshearers **to Timnath**, he and his friend Hirah the Adullamite.

13 And **it was told Tamar**, saying, Behold thy father in law [*Judah*] goeth up to Timnath to shear his sheep.

> Next, in verse 14, Tamar disguises herself as a prostitute and sits along the road to Timnath in an area where harlots typically waited for customers. Judah's youngest son, Shelah, was grown up, and Judah had not given him to her for a husband as promised.

14 And **she put her widow's garments off** from her [*she took off her black clothing that designated her as a widow*], and **covered her with a vail** [*a signal, in that setting, that she was a prostitute—see verse 15*], and wrapped herself, **and sat in an open place**, which *is* by the way to Timnath; **for** [*because*] **she saw that Shelah was grown, and she was not given unto him to wife**.

> We are watching Judah's eroding lifestyle as he travels down the wide path to personal spiritual destruction (see 3 Nephi 14:13). Next, in verses 15–16, he stops to become involved with this harlot, not realizing that it is Tamar, his daughter-in-law.

15 **When Judah saw her, he thought her** *to be* **an harlot**; because she had covered her face.

16 And **he turned unto her** by the way [*as she waited along the side of the road*], **and said, Go to** [*go into your place of business*], I pray thee, **let me come in unto thee**; (for he knew not that she *was* his daughter in law.) And **she said, What wilt thou give me, that thou mayest come in unto me** [*what will you pay to become involved with me*]?

JST Genesis 38:16

> 16 And he turned unto her by the way, and said, Go to, I pray thee, let me come in **and lie with thee**; (for he knew not that she was his daughter-in-law;) and she said, What wilt thou give me, that thou mayest come in **and lie with me**?

17 And **he said, I will send** *thee* **a kid** [*a young goat*] from the flock. And **she said, Wilt thou give** *me* **a pledge** [*something as security that I may keep until you send the payment*], **till thou send** *it*?

18 And **he said, What pledge shall I give thee? And she said, Thy signet** [*his seal, used in signing or sealing business documents*]**, and thy bracelets, and thy staff** that *is* in thine hand. And **he gave** *it* **her, and came in unto her, and she conceived by him**.

JST Genesis 38:18

> 18 And he said, What pledge shall I give thee? And she said, Thy signet, and thy bracelets, and thy staff that is in thine hand. And he gave it her, and came in **and slept with her**, and she conceived by him.

19 And **she arose, and went away**, and laid by her vail from her [*took off her harlot's disguise*], and put on the garments of her widowhood.

> Next, Judah sends his friend, Hira, the Adullamite, with a young goat to pay the harlot and retrieve the articles he left as collateral. Much to Hira's dismay, the prostitute is gone and none of the local men who know the habits and places of business of the local harlots are aware of this other temptress.

20 And **Judah sent the kid by the hand of his friend the Adullamite, to receive** *his* **pledge** [*to retrieve the signet, bracelets, and staff*] from the

woman's hand: **but he found her not**.

21 **Then he asked the men of that place**, saying, **Where** *is* **the harlot, that** *was* **openly by the way side?** And **they said, There was no harlot in this** *place*.

22 And **he returned to Judah, and said, I cannot find her; and also the men of the place said,** *that* **there was no harlot in this** *place*.

23 And Judah said, Let her take *it* to her, lest we be shamed: behold, I sent this kid, and thou hast not found her [*in other words, let her keep the items lest we be embarrassed by continuing to try to find her*].

> Next, we are reminded that one of the worst forms of wickedness is hypocrisy. In fact, as you read and study the New Testament, you will find that one of the only categories of wickedness that the Savior came down very hard on was the category of hypocrisy. You may wish to read Matthew 23 as a reminder of this fact.
>
> Judah now becomes a terribly perfect example of pure hypocrisy and a strong reminder to us that the truly wicked are no longer capable of thinking like honest people. He finds out that Tamar is expecting a child and that it is the result of sexual immorality on her part. He commands that she be executed for her immorality by being burned to death.

24 ¶ And it came to pass **about three months after**, that **it was told Judah**, saying, **Tamar thy daughter in law hath played the harlot**; and also, behold, **she** *is* **with child by whoredom**. And **Judah said, Bring her forth, and let her be burnt**.

> Imagine Judah's feelings when Tamar shows him the "pledge" items, including his signet seal and staff, which he left with her in payment for using her as a harlot.

25 When she *was* brought forth, **she sent to her father in law** [*Judah*], **saying, By the man, whose these are, am I with child**: and she said, **Discern** [*you tell us*]**, I pray thee, whose** *are* **these, the signet, and bracelets, and staff**.

> Judah is embarrassed and humbled, and we see a spark of honesty still surviving in his soul.

26 And **Judah acknowledged** *them,* **and said, She hath been more righteous than I**; because that I gave her not to Shelah my son. And he knew her again no more [*he did not repeat his adultery with her again*].

> Next, Tamar gives birth to twins.

27 ¶ And it came to pass **in the time of her travail** [*when she went into labor*], that, behold, **twins** *were* **in her womb**.

> During the birth of twins, the midwife tied a scarlet thread on the hand of the firstborn. This was very important in their culture because the firstborn would have legal rights and responsibilities that the other children would not have.

28 And it came to pass, **when she travailed, that** *the one* **put out** *his*

hand: and the midwife took and bound upon his hand a scarlet thread, saying, **This came out first**.

29 And it came to pass, as **he drew back his hand**, that, behold, **his brother came out**: and she said, How hast thou broken forth? *this* breach *be* upon thee: therefore his name was called **Pharez** [*meaning "breach" or "rule breaker, one who causes contention." Ruth traced her genealogy through Pharez (Ruth 4:18); thus Jesse and David and, consequently, the Savior came through this line*].

30 And afterward came out his brother, that had the scarlet thread upon his hand: and his name was called Zarah.

> We will pause here for a moment and point out what could be a very important lesson for us regarding the principle of repentance. As we leave Judah now, he is deeply entrapped in grievous sin. However, as we see him years later bowing down before Joseph in Pharaoh's court and offering to be put in slavery in place of Benjamin, we see that a rather significant change of heart has taken place.
>
> The lesson is that, given sufficient time, many people change. The Atonement finally reaches them. They repent and move closer to the Savior in their actions. Thus, given time and sufficient humbling experiences, Judah changed for the better. There is hope for him.

GENESIS 39

As stated in the background notes for Genesis 37 in this study guide, Joseph is one of the greatest examples of honesty and absolute integrity. He keeps the commandments of the Lord under any and all circumstances. We will see much of this as we now follow him to Egypt and watch him as he is sold as a slave.

He is sold to a man named Potiphar, who, according to many Bible Scholars, was the commanding officer of Pharaoh's royal body guard and was thus the executioner of Pharaoh's enemies as occasion required (see *Old Testament Student Manual*, page 94).

As we begin with verse 1, we see that Potiphar purchased Joseph as a slave from the Ishmeelite camel train merchants who had bought him from the Midianite merchant men mentioned in Genesis 37:28.

Imagine the misery, loneliness, and worry in the heart of seventeen-year-old Joseph as all his plans and hopes seem to vanish upon being taken as a slave to Egypt. No doubt, his faith in God was a saving strength to him. He will be thirty years old when he is made the second in command, directly under Pharaoh, in all Egypt. Thus, we know that he has about twelve or thirteen years of slavery or imprisonment ahead of him at this point (Genesis 41:40, 46).

1 And **Joseph was brought down to Egypt**; and **Potiphar**, an officer of Pharaoh, **captain of the guard**, an Egyptian, **bought him** of [*from*] the hands of the Ishmeelites, which had brought him down thither.

Moses (the writer of Genesis) immediately assures us that Joseph is blessed by the Lord in all that he does, and Potiphar, observing this, soon puts Joseph in charge of everything in his household. Joseph's integrity and righteousness is already paying off, even under normally abject circumstances.

2 And **the Lord was with Joseph**, and **he was a prosperous man**; and he was in the house of his master the Egyptian.

3 And **his master saw that the Lord *was* with him, and that the Lord made all that he did to prosper in his hand**.

4 And Joseph found grace [*favor*] in his sight, and he served him: **and he made him overseer over his house, and all *that* he had he put into his hand**.

5 And it came to pass from the time *that* he had made him overseer in his house, and over all that he had, that **the Lord blessed the Egyptian's house for Joseph's sake; and the blessing of the Lord was upon all that he had in the house, and in the field**.

6 And **he** [*Potiphar*] **left all that he had in Joseph's hand**; and **he knew not ought he had** [*he did not have the slightest idea or worry as to what was going on in his business affairs and his household matters because he trusted Joseph completely*], save the bread [*food*] which he did eat. **And Joseph was *a* goodly *person*, and well favoured** [*Joseph was well-built and handsome*].

We are now coming to one of the best-known stories in all of the Bible. It is the account of Potiphar's wife as she attempts to persuade Joseph to violate the law of chastity with her.

7 ¶ **And it came to pass after these things** [*after Joseph had been promoted to be overseer over all Potiphar's concerns*], that **his master's wife cast her eyes upon Joseph** [*looked with lust upon Joseph*]; and **she said, Lie with me** [*commit adultery with me*].

Joseph's simple reply teaches volumes by way of counsel and example to all.

8 But **he refused, and said** unto his master's wife, Behold, **my master wotteth not** [*does not know*] **what *is* with me in the house**, and **he hath committed all that he hath to my hand** [*he trusts me completely*];

You may wish to especially mark the last part of verse 9, next, in your own scriptures. It contains great counsel.

9 *There is* none greater in this house than I; **neither hath he kept back any thing from me but thee**, because thou *art* his wife: **how then can I do this great wickedness, and sin against God?**

According to verse 10, next, Potiphar's wife did not give up at this point. Rather, she continued day after day in her attempts to persuade Joseph to give in to her lustful desires. Joseph continued to refuse her advances.

10 And it came to pass, as **she spake to Joseph day by day**, that **he hearkened not unto her**, to lie by her, *or to be with her.*

> Finally, in desperation, Potiphar's wife watched for an opportunity when Joseph was in the house alone taking care of business in Potiphar's office. Perhaps arranging for all the servants to leave the house, she desperately made another attempt for Joseph.

11 And it came to pass about this time, that ***Joseph* went into the house to do his business** [*to take care of running his master's business affairs, according to the NIV*]; and ***there was none of the men of the house there within.***

12 And **she caught** [*grabbed*] **him by his garment** [*his cloak*], saying, **Lie with me**: and **he left his garment in her hand**, and fled, and got him out.

> The lase phrase of verse 12, above, "fled and got him out," provides excellent advice for any who find themselves confronted with temptation. There was no hesitation, no analyzing, no wondering if now was the time for action. He simply fled away from the circumstance. He would deal with the consequences later with a clear conscience.
>
> In Joseph's case, the consequence will be years in prison. Yet, better to be in a miserable physical prison with a clear conscience than to be in comfortable physical circumstances with a guilty conscience.

> Potiphar's wife has been spurned and rejected, and her anger now knows no bounds. No doubt, one of her first concerns is whether or not Joseph will tell Potiphar. As you will see, she immediately sets up a plausible alibi, designed to protect herself at Joseph's expense.

13 And it came to pass, **when she saw that he had left his garment** [*cloak*] **in her hand, and was fled forth** [*and had fled out of the house*],

14 That **she called** [*no doubt screamed*] **unto the men of her house**, and spake unto them, **saying, See, he** [*my husband*] **hath brought in an Hebrew** [*Joseph was "an Hebrew"—in other words a direct descendant of Abraham through Isaac and Jacob*] **unto us to mock us; he came in unto me to lie with me, and I cried with a loud voice** [*I had to scream to scare him away*]:

> Next, Potiphar's wife continues her lying and keeps Joseph's cloak so that she can show the incriminating evidence to her husband when he comes home.

15 And it came to pass, when he heard that I lifted up my voice and cried, that he left his garment [*cloak*] with me, and fled, and got him out.

16 And she laid up his garment by her, until his lord [*Joseph's master, Potiphar*] came home.

> Next, she repeats the lie to her husband when he returns home. Imagine his disappointment and then his anger with Joseph!

17 And **she spake unto him** according to these words, **saying, The Hebrew servant, which thou hast brought unto us, came in unto me to mock me**:

18 And it came to pass, **as I lifted up my voice and cried, that he left his garment with me, and fled ou**t.

19 And it came to pass, **when his master heard the words of his wife**, which she spake unto him, saying, After this manner did thy servant to me; that **his wrath** [*anger*] **was kindled**.

20 And **Joseph's master took him, and put him into the prison**, a place where the king's prisoners *were* bound: and he was there in the prison.

> It is amazing that Joseph was not executed immediately. One tends to wonder whether, after his initial anger cooled, Potiphar suspected that his wife might not be telling the truth and thus sent Joseph to prison rather than to his death. We do not know. We do know that the Lord had a major mission for his young prophet—that of saving his people, the covenant people of Abraham, Isaac, and Jacob, although many of them were not that worthy at the moment.
>
> Next, Moses tells us that the blessings of the Lord continued to go with Joseph, even though it appeared initially that he had suffered a major setback. In time, the chief officer in charge of the prison will turn everything over to Joseph. In other words, Joseph will end up running the prison.
>
> Again, one of the major messages we can learn from this is that the blessings of the Lord, no matter what the circumstances, are better than the pangs of a guilty conscience.

21 ¶ **But the Lord was with Joseph**, and shewed him mercy, and **gave him favour in the sight of the keeper of the prison**.

22 And **the keeper of the prison committed to Joseph's hand all the prisoners that** *were* **in the prison; and whatsoever they did there, he was the doer** *of it*.

JST Genesis 39:22

22 And the keeper of the prison committed to Joseph's hand all the prisoners that were in the prison; and whatsoever they did there, he was **the overseer** of it.

23 **The keeper of the prison looked not to any thing** *that was* **under his hand** [*in other words, he did not check up on Joseph*]; **because the Lord was with him, and** *that* **which he did, the Lord made** *it* **to prosper**.

GENESIS 40

Joseph has probably been in prison for a number of years by now. As mentioned at the end of Genesis 39, Joseph is the overseer or supervisor of the whole prison. He no doubt was the one who made arrangements for the "hosting" of the butler and the baker of Pharaoh as the angry king of Egypt sent them to his special prison. These two men, who had somehow incurred the wrath of Pharaoh, will both dream strange dreams in the course of their imprisonment. Joseph will interpret them for them. And eventually, this will lead to his being brought before Pharaoh to interpret his troubling dreams (chapter 41).

In verses 1–4, Moses informs us that these two high-ranking servants of the king have offended him and are thus placed in the special prison. One wonders if this prison might have been extra secure, used mainly for political prisoners. We don't know.

1 And it came to pass after these things [*after Joseph had been blessed by the Lord to become overseer of the Pharaoh's special prison*], that **the butler of the king of Egypt and *his* baker had offended their lord the king of Egyp**t.

2 And **Pharaoh was wroth** [*very angry*] **against two *of* his officers**, against the chief of the butlers, and against the chief of the bakers.

> Did you notice the repetition in verses 1 and 2 above? Such repetition is very typical of Old Testament writers. Among other things, they do it to emphasize a point.

3 **And he put them in ward** [*confinement*] in the house of the captain of the guard, **into the prison, the place where Joseph *was* bound.**

4 **And the captain of the guard** [*probably Potiphar—see Genesis 37:36*] **charged Joseph with them** [*it sounds like Potiphar personally turned them over to Joseph*], **and he served them** [*Joseph personally saw to their needs in prison*]: and they continued a season in ward [*they remained in prison for a while*].

> Next, we learn that the two dreams were very confusing and troubling to the butler and the baker. Joseph sees their fallen faces the next morning and asks them what is wrong.

5 ¶ And **they dreamed a dream both of them**, each man his dream **in one night**, each man according to the interpretation of his dream, the butler and the baker of the king of Egypt, which *were* bound in the prison.

6 And **Joseph came in unto them in the morning, and looked upon them, and, behold, they *were* sad**.

7 **And he asked** Pharaoh's officers that *were* with him in the ward of his lord's house, saying, **Wherefore look ye *so* sadly to day?**

8 And **they said** unto him, **We have dreamed a dream, and *there is* no interpreter of it. And Joseph said unto them, *Do* not interpretations *belong* to God?** [*In other words, God can interpret dreams.*] **tell me *them*,** I pray you.

9 And **the chief butler told his dream** to Joseph, and said to him, **In my dream**, behold, **a vine *was* before** [*in front of*] **me;**

10 And **in the vine *were* three branches**: and it *was* as though it

budded, *and* her blossoms shot forth; and **the clusters thereof brought forth ripe grapes:**

11 And **Pharaoh's cup** *was* **in my hand: and I took the grapes, and pressed them into Pharaoh's cup, and I gave the cup into Pharaoh's hand.**

> Next, Joseph, with the help of God, interprets the butler's dream. It is a prophecy with a happy outcome.

12 And **Joseph said unto him, This** *is* **the interpretation** of it: **The three branches** *are* **three days:**

13 Yet **within three days shall Pharaoh** lift up thine head, and **restore thee unto thy place** [*as chief of Pharaoh's butlers*]: and thou shalt deliver Pharaoh's cup into his hand, after the former manner when thou wast his butler.

> Next, in verses 14–15, Joseph asks the butler to put in a good word for him to the Pharaoh, when he is restored to his former position.

14 But **think on me when it shall be well with thee**, and shew kindness, I pray thee, unto me, **and make mention of me unto Pharaoh, and bring me out of this house:**

15 For indeed **I was stolen away out of the land of the Hebrews: and here also have I done nothing that they should put me into the dungeon.**

> The baker is encouraged by the good news received by the butler through the interpretation of his dream by Joseph. He likewise requests that Joseph interpret his dream. Sadly, the outcome for him will be opposite the butler's.

16 **When the chief baker saw that the interpretation was good, he said** unto Joseph, **I also** *was* **in my dream** [*I also had a dream*], and, behold, *I had* **three white baskets on my head:**

17 And **in the uppermost basket** *there was* **of all manner of bakemeats** [*baked goods*] **for Pharaoh; and the birds did eat them out of the basket upon my head.**

18 And **Joseph answered** and said, **This** *is* **the interpretation** thereof: **The three baskets** *are* **three days:**

19 Yet **within three days shall Pharaoh lift up thy head from off thee, and shall hang thee on a tree; and the birds shall eat thy flesh from off thee.**

> In three days, both prophetic dreams are fulfilled.

20 ¶ And it came to pass **the third day,** *which was* **Pharaoh's birthday**, that **he made a feast** unto all his servants: and he lifted up the head of the chief butler and of the chief baker among his servants [*he brought both the butler and the baker from the prison and had them stand in front of his other servants*].

21 And **he restored the chief butler unto his butlership again**; and he gave the cup into Pharaoh's hand:

22 But he hanged the chief baker: as Joseph had interpreted to them.

Next, we see that the butler forgot to put in a good word for Joseph. Joseph will remain in prison for another two years until the king has two disturbing dreams. Then, the butler will remember him.

23 **Yet did not the chief butler remember Joseph, but forgat him**.

GENESIS 41

In this chapter, Joseph's situation changes completely. When Pharaoh has two disturbing dreams, the butler will remember Joseph's ability to interpret dreams. The king will send for him, and he will interpret them. Pharaoh believes Joseph and appoints him second in command, under him, for all of Egypt.

Joseph is now in a position to save his father's family from the severe drought that is coming in about seven years.

Joseph will marry and have two sons, Manasseh and Ephraim.

First, we see that it was not until two years later that the butler remembered to say something to Pharaoh about Joseph. As mentioned above, the occasion was two disturbing dreams had by the king.

1 And **it came to pass at the end of two full years, that Pharaoh dreamed**: and, behold, **he stood by the river**.

2 And, behold, **there came up out of the river seven well favoured kine** and **fatfleshed** [*fat, healthy cows*]; and **they fed in a meadow**.

3 And, behold, **seven other kine came up after them out of the river, ill favoured and leanfleshed** [*doing poorly and undernourished*]; **and stood by the** *other* **kine upon the brink of the river**.

4 And **the ill favoured and leanfleshed kine did eat up the seven well favoured and fat kine**. So Pharaoh awoke.

5 And **he slept and dreamed the second time**: and, behold, **seven ears of corn** [*grain*] **came up upon one stalk, rank and good** [*full and well-formed*].

6 And, behold, **seven thin ears and blasted with the east wind sprung up after them**.

The "east wind" spoken of in verse 6, above, was a sign of coming destruction and famine. In that climate, the hot east wind came in off the hot desert sands and blew upon the crops, sometimes drying up plants and gardens and destroying them in a matter of hours.

7 **And the seven thin ears devoured the seven rank and full ears**. And **Pharaoh awoke, and, behold,** *it was* **a dream**.

8 And it came to pass **in the morning that his spirit was troubled**; and **he sent** and called **for all the magicians of Egypt, and all the wise men** thereof: and Pharaoh told them his dream; but *there was* **none that could interpret them unto Pharaoh**.

Imagine the pressure upon the magicians and wise men who are unable to interpret the dream for the distraught king. At this point, the butler is very embarrassed. He had completely forgotten his promise two years ago to talk to Pharaoh about Joseph's unjust imprisonment. Now he is suddenly reminded about Joseph because of the Pharaoh's dreams and the need for one who can interpret them.

9 ¶ **Then spake the chief butler unto Pharaoh, saying, I do remember my faults this day** [*I have made a serious mistake*]:

10 [*Two years ago*] **Pharaoh was wroth with his servants, and put me in ward** [*prison*] in the captain of the guard's house, ***both* me and the chief baker**:

11 And **we dreamed a dream in one night, I and he**; we dreamed each man according to the interpretation of his dream.

12 And ***there was* there with us a young man, an Hebrew, servant** to the captain of the guard; and **we told him, and he interpreted to us our dreams**; to each man according to his dream he did interpret.

13 And it came to pass, **as he interpreted to us, so it was**; me he restored unto mine office, and him he hanged.

In verse 14, next, we catch a glimpse of another of Joseph's virtues. While some prisoners might have gone straight into the King's court, tattered and ragged, in an attempt to elicit sympathy, Joseph takes the time to shave and put on clean, neat clothing.

14 ¶ **Then Pharaoh sent and called Joseph**, and they brought him hastily out of the dungeon: and **he shaved *himself,* and changed his raiment** [*clothes*]**, and came in unto Pharaoh**.

15 And **Pharaoh said** unto Joseph, **I have dreamed a dream**, and ***there is* none that can interpret it**: and **I have heard say of thee, *that* thou canst understand a dream to interpret it**.

Joseph is quick to take no credit to himself. Rather, he specifically tells the king that he cannot interpret dreams. The answer will come from the true God.

16 And **Joseph answered Pharaoh, saying, *It is* not in me: God shall give Pharaoh an answer of peace**.

As Pharaoh retells his dreams to Joseph, we get a few additional details that we did not get in verses 2–7, above.

17 And **Pharaoh said** unto Joseph, In my dream, behold, I stood upon the bank of the river:

18 And, behold, there came up out of the river seven kine, fatfleshed and well favoured; and they fed in a meadow:

19 And, behold, seven other kine came up after them, poor and very ill favoured and leanfleshed, **such as**

I never saw in all the land of Egypt for badness:

20 And the lean and the ill favoured kine did eat up the first seven fat kine:

21 And **when they had eaten them up, it could not be known that they had eaten them; but they** *were* **still ill favoured, as at the beginning.** So I awoke.

22 And I saw in my dream, and, behold, seven ears came up in one stalk, full and good:

23 And, behold, seven ears, **withered**, thin, *and* blasted with the east wind, sprung up after them:

24 And the thin ears devoured the seven good ears: and I told *this* unto the magicians; but *there was* none that could declare *it* to me.

> Next, through the inspiration of God, Joseph interprets the dreams.

25 ¶ And **Joseph said unto Pharaoh, The dream of Pharaoh** *is* **one** [*both dreams mean the same thing*]: **God hath shewed Pharaoh what he** *is* **about to do.**

26 **The seven good kine** *are* **seven years**; and **the seven good ears** *are* **seven years**: the dream *is* one.

27 And **the seven thin and ill favoured kine** that came up after them *are* **seven years**; and **the seven empty ears** blasted with the east wind **shall be seven years of famine.**

28 This *is* the thing which I have spoken unto Pharaoh: **What God** *is* **about to do he sheweth unto Pharaoh.**

29 Behold, **there come seven years of great plenty throughout all the land of Egypt:**

30 **And there shall arise after them seven years of famine**; and all the plenty shall be forgotten in the land of Egypt; and **the famine shall consume the land;**

31 And **the plenty shall not be known in the land by reason of that famine following**; for it *shall be* very grievous [*it will be a severe famine*].

> Next, in effect, Joseph tells Pharaoh that the fact that he had two dreams was in accordance with the law of witnesses (Deuteronomy 19:15). We see the same thing in 2 Corinthians 13:1 where we read: "In the mouth of two or three witnesses shall every word be established."

32 And **for that the dream was doubled unto Pharaoh twice;** *it is* **because the thing** *is* **established by God**, and God will shortly bring it to pass.

> Next, Joseph suggests that Pharaoh find a wise man and give him authority to prepare for the coming famine.

33 **Now therefore let Pharaoh look out a man discreet and wise, and set him over the land of Egypt.**

34 Let Pharaoh do *this,* and **let him appoint officers over the land, and take up the fifth part of the land of Egypt** [save one-fifth of the bounteous crops per year] **in the seven plenteous years.**

35 And **let them gather all the food of those good years** that come, and lay up corn [grain] under the hand of Pharaoh, and let them keep food in the cities.

36 And **that food shall be for store to the land against the seven years of famine,** which shall be in the land of Egypt; that the land perish not through the famine.

37 ¶ **And the thing was good in the eyes of Pharaoh, and in the eyes of all his servants.**

38 And **Pharaoh said unto his servants, Can we find** *such a one* **as this** *is* [can you think of anyone better qualified for the job than Joseph], **a man in whom the Spirit of God** *is?*

39 And **Pharaoh said unto Joseph,** Forasmuch as God hath shewed thee all this, *there is* **none so discreet and wise as thou** *art:*

> Next, Joseph is promoted to be second in command in Egypt.

40 **Thou shalt be over my house, and according unto thy word shall all my people be ruled: only in the throne will I be greater than thou.**

41 And Pharaoh said unto Joseph, See, I have set thee over all the land of Egypt.

42 And **Pharaoh took off his ring** [the signet ring of authority] **from his hand, and put it upon Joseph's hand,** and **arrayed him in vestures of fine linen, and put a gold chain about his neck;**

43 And **he made him to ride in the second chariot** which he had; **and they cried before him** [the king's servants ran ahead of Joseph's royal chariot with loud voices, saying], **Bow the knee: and he made him** *ruler* **over all the land of Egypt.**

> Next, in verse 44, Pharaoh emphasizes once more that he truly has given this power and authority to Joseph.

44 And **Pharaoh said unto Joseph, I** *am* **Pharaoh, and without thee shall no man lift up his hand or foot in all the land of Egypt** [no one can make a move without your permission].

45 And **Pharaoh called Joseph's name Zaphnath-paaneah** [the one who furnishes the sustenance of the land]; **and he gave him to wife Asenath the daughter of Potipherah priest of On**. And Joseph went out over *all* the land of Egypt.

> The question often comes up at this point as to where Joseph's wife came from. It would be logical to assume that she was an Egyptian. But this cannot be the case since their son, Ephraim, received the birthright, which included the Abrahamic covenant and the responsibility to take the blessings of the priesthood to all the world (see Genesis 48:14–16). Therefore, we conclude that

the priest of On (verse 45) and his wife and daughter, Asenath, were Noah's descendants through Shem or Japheth, rather than Ham.

Next, we are told that Joseph was thirty years old when he began his mission to save the Egyptians. In the process of living among unbelievers, he was also in a position to save his own family from the famine. Perhaps you can sense an important parallel here. Jesus came to earth and lived mainly among unbelievers in order to save His "family," meaning the righteous who "are born of him and have become his sons and his daughters" (see Mosiah 5:7).

46 ¶ And **Joseph** *was* **thirty years old when he stood before Pharaoh king of Egypt** [*when he became second in command of all Egypt*]. **And Joseph** went out from the presence of Pharaoh [*went out from Pharaoh, authorized with his authority*], and **went throughout all the land of Egypt.**

47 **And in the seven plenteous years the earth brought forth by handfuls** [*in abundance*].

48 **And he gathered up all the food of the seven years**, which were in the land of Egypt, **and laid up** [*stored*] **the food in the cities**: the food of the field, which *was* round about every city, laid he up in the same.

49 And **Joseph gathered corn** [*grain*] **as the sand of the sea, very much**, until he left numbering [*stopped trying to keep an accurate record of how much they had stored up*]; for *it was* without number.

50 And **unto Joseph were born two sons before the years of famine came**, which Asenath the daughter of Potipherah priest of On bare unto him.

51 And Joseph called the name of the firstborn **Manasseh**: For God, *said he,* hath made me forget all my toil, and all my father's house.

52 And the name of the second called he **Ephraim**: For God hath caused me to be fruitful in the land of my affliction.

As mentioned earlier, Ephraim will be the birthright son (see Genesis 48:13–19.) Many members of the Church today trace their Abrahamic blessings through Ephraim and Manasseh, as stated in their patriarchal blessings.

Finally, the years of plenty came to an end, and a severe famine gripped Egypt, as well as many lands and countries around them. It will likewise afflict Jacob and Joseph's eleven brothers in the land of Canaan. They will soon be forced to come to Egypt seeking to purchase food to sustain them and their families during the famine.

53 ¶ And **the seven years of plenteousness, that was in the land of Egypt, were ended.**

54 And **the seven years of dearth** [*drought; famine*] **began to come**, according as Joseph had said: and **the dearth was in all lands; but in all**

the land of Egypt there was bread [*food, because of the food storage program supervised by Joseph*].

55 And when all the land of Egypt was famished [*when they had consumed all their own available food*], **the people cried to Pharaoh for bread** [*food*]: **and Pharaoh said** unto all the Egyptians, **Go unto Joseph; what he saith to you, do**.

> We see one of the major principles of our welfare system today at work as Joseph distributes food supplies in Egypt. Rather than merely giving the grain out, which promotes waste, he still had the people pay for it, which helps eliminate waste and lack of appreciation.

56 And the famine was over all the face of the earth [*meaning the whole surrounding area, not the whole earth*]: And **Joseph** opened all the storehouses, and **sold** unto the Egyptians; and the famine waxed sore [*grew severe*] in the land of Egypt.

57 And all countries came into Egypt to Joseph for to buy *corn* [*grain*]; because that the famine was *so* sore in all lands.

GENESIS 42

By now, the famine has become so severe that Jacob and his family, still living in Canaan, cannot survive.

We get some idea of how old Jacob is at this time by doing a bit of math. Genesis 47:28 tells us that he lived for seventeen years in Egypt and that he died at age 147. Therefore, he would have traveled to Egypt at about age 130. He is probably pretty close to that age as this chapter begins.

Ten of his sons will journey to Egypt to buy grain. Benjamin stays home. Jacob's heart was already broken over twenty years before when, as far as he knows, Joseph was killed by a wild beast (Genesis 37:33). He could not stand to lose Benjamin in addition to losing Joseph.

When the ten brothers arrive in Egypt and are taken to Joseph to negotiate the purchase of some grain, he recognizes them but they do not recognize him. He intentionally treats them roughly, accusing them of being spies and lying to him about it. In the course of the conversation, they tell them they have a youngest brother named Benjamin. Joseph demands that they prove that they are not lying by bringing their youngest brother, Benjamin, to Egypt. In the course of all this, he sees that his brothers have mellowed and that their hearts have softened over the years.

Nevertheless, he still demands that they bring Benjamin. They do so, leaving Simeon behind as a hostage and bringing Benjamin back with them.

As we begin, verses 1–2 inform us that Jacob, having heard that there is grain in Egypt, requests his sons go and buy some and bring it back so they can survive the famine. Remember that the word "corn," as used in the Bible, means "grain."

1 Now when Jacob saw that there was corn in Egypt, Jacob said unto

his sons, Why do ye look one upon another [*why are you standing around looking at each other, doing nothing*]?

2 And he said, **Behold, I have heard that there is corn in Egypt: get you down thither, and buy for us** from thence; that we may live, and not die.

3 ¶ And **Joseph's ten brethren went down to buy corn in Egypt.**

4 But **Benjamin,** Joseph's brother, **Jacob sent not with his brethren;** for he said, Lest peradventure [*for fear that*] mischief befall him.

5 **And the sons of Israel** [*Jacob*] **came to buy** *corn* **among those that came** [*came to Egypt along with others who came for the same purpose*]: for the famine was in the land of Canaan [*the "promised land," to which Moses led the children of Israel after escaping Egyptian bondage; Joshua led the Israelites across the Jordan River into the land*].

> Imagine Joseph's feelings when he saw his brothers kneeling to him as had been prophesied in his dreams so long ago! (Genesis 37:7 and 9.)

6 And **Joseph** *was* **the governor over the land,** *and* **he** *it was* **that sold to all the people of the land**: and **Joseph's brethren came, and bowed down themselves before him** *with* **their faces to the earth.**

7 And **Joseph** saw his brethren, and he **knew them, but made himself strange unto them** [*did his best to keep them from recognizing him,* *including speaking to them through an interpreter—see verse 23*], and spake roughly unto them; and he said unto them, **Whence come ye?** And they said, From the land of Canaan to buy food.

8 And **Joseph knew** [*recognized*] **his brethren, but they knew not him**.

> Next, Joseph, remembering his dreams about them, determines not to reveal his identity to them just yet. Instead, he tests them by accusing them of being spies.

9 And **Joseph remembered the dreams which he dreamed of them**, and **said unto them, Ye** *are* **spies**; to see the nakedness of the land ye are come.

10 And **they said** unto him, **Nay, my lord, but to buy food are thy servants come**.

11 **We** *are* **all one man's sons;** we *are* true [*honest*] *men,* **thy servants are no spies.**

12 And **he said unto them, Nay, but to see the nakedness of the land ye are come** [*you have come to see if we have become vulnerable because of the famine*].

> Next, they explain that there are twelve brothers, and that the reason there are only ten in Egypt is that one of them stayed home with their father and one (Joseph) had passed away.

13 And **they said, Thy servants** *are* **twelve brethren, the sons of one man in** the land of **Canaan;** and,

behold, **the youngest *is* this day with our father**, and **one *is* not**.

14 And **Joseph said** unto them, **That *is it*** that I spake unto you, saying [*like I said*], **Ye *are* spies**:

15 **Hereby ye shall be proved** [*this is how I will find out if you are lying or not*]: By the life of Pharaoh **ye shall not go forth hence, except your youngest brother come hither** [*I will not let you go home unless your youngest brother comes here to prove that you are not lying*].

16 **Send one of you, and let him fetch your brother, and ye** [*the rest of you*] **shall be kept in prison**, that your words may be proved, whether there be any truth in you: or else by the life of Pharaoh surely ye *are* spies.

17 And **he put them all** together **into ward** [*into prison*] three days.

> Three days later, Joseph tells them that he has reconsidered and has a different plan.

18 And **Joseph said** unto them the third day, **This do, and live; *for* I fear God** [*I want to be sure I do what is right before God*]:

19 **If ye *be* true** [*honest*] **men, let one of your brethren be bound in the house of your prison** [*be kept as a hostage in the same prison you have all been in for the past three days*]: go ye [*the rest of you*], carry corn [*grain*] for the famine of your houses:

20 **But bring your youngest brother unto me; so shall your words be verified**, and ye shall not die. And they did so.

> Next, we see Joseph's brothers talking among themselves about what they did to Joseph so many years ago and deciding that they are being punished by God for ignoring his pleadings at the time. They are now going through the same basic thing they put him through. They do not realize that Joseph understands every word they are saying.

21 ¶ And **they said one to another, We *are* verily** [*truly*] **guilty concerning our brother**, in that **we saw the anguish of his soul, when he besought us** [*when he pled with us*], and **we would not hear; therefore** [*that is why*] **is this distress come upon us**.

22 And **Reuben answered them, saying, Spake I not unto you** [*didn't I tell you*], saying, **Do not sin against the child** [*young Joseph*]; **and ye would not hear?** therefore, behold, also **his blood is required** [*we are guilty of getting him killed and are going to pay for it now*].

23 And **they knew not that Joseph understood *them;* for he spake unto them by an interpreter**.

> Because of his tender feelings toward them, Joseph has to leave the room until he gets control over his emotions.

24 And **he turned himself about from them, and wept; and returned to them again**, and communed with

them, and **took from them Simeon, and bound him before their eyes.**

> Next, Joseph secretly returns the money they paid for the grain and has it placed in each of their sacks. In addition, he provides supplies for their journey back to their father so that they will not have to get into the grain bags until they are well on their way home. When they discover it, they are afraid because it looks like they have been framed to look like thieves.

25 ¶ **Then Joseph commanded to fill their sacks with corn, and to restore every man's money into his sack, and to give them provision for the way**: and thus did he unto them.

26 And they laded their asses with the corn, and departed thence [*for home*].

27 And **as one of them opened his sack to give his ass provender** [*feed*] **in the inn, he espied his money; for, behold, it** *was* **in his sack's mouth** [*it was at the top of his bag of grain*].

28 And he said unto his brethren, **My money is restored**; and, lo, *it is* **even in my sack**: and their heart failed *them,* and **they were afraid**, saying one to another, **What** *is* **this** *that* **God hath done unto us?**

29 ¶ And **they came unto Jacob** their father unto the land of Canaan, **and told him all that befell unto them**; saying,

30 **The man,** *who is* **the lord of the land** [*Joseph*], **spake roughly to us, and took us for spies** of the country.

31 And **we said** unto him, We *are* true *men;* **we are no spies**:

32 **We** *be* **twelve brethren**, sons of our father; **one** *is* **not, and the youngest** *is* **this day with our father** in the land of Canaan.

33 And **the man**, the lord of the country, **said** unto us, **Hereby shall I know that ye** *are* **true** [*honest*] *men;* **leave one of your brethren here** with me, and **take** *food for* **the famine of your households, and be gone**:

34 And **bring your youngest brother unto me: then shall I know that ye** *are* **no spies**, but *that* ye *are* true *men: so* will I deliver you your brother [*then I will free Simeon—see verse 24*], and ye shall traffick in the land [*buy whatever you need in Egypt*].

35 ¶ And it came to pass **as they emptied their sacks, that, behold, every man's bundle of money** *was* **in his sack**: and when *both* they and their father saw the bundles of money, **they were afraid.**

36 **And Jacob their father said** unto them, Me have ye bereaved *of my children* [*you have taken my children from me*]: Joseph *is* not, and Simeon *is* not, and ye will take Benjamin *away:* all these things are against me.

Next, in a desperate attempt to get Jacob to let them take Benjamin back to Egypt with them, Reuben attempts to make a terribly difficult bargain with his father in order to convince him how careful he would be with Benjamin.

37 And **Reuben spake unto his father,** saying, Slay my two sons, if I bring him not to thee: deliver him into my hand [*turn Benjamin over to me*], and I will bring him to thee again.

38 **And he** [*Jacob*] **said, My son shall not go down with you**; for his brother is dead, and he is left alone: if mischief befall him by the way in the which ye go, then shall ye bring down my gray hairs with sorrow to the grave [*in other words, if you took Benjamin and something happened to him, it would kill me*].

GENESIS 43

With Jacob's refusal to let them take Benjamin back to Egypt, they survive for a while on the provisions that they brought back. But soon, their food is once again running out.

1 And the famine *was* sore [*severe*] in the land.

2 And it came to pass, **when they had eaten up the corn** [*grain*] **which they had brought out of Egypt, their father said unto them, Go again, buy us a little food.**

Next, we see Judah, the one who suggested that they sell Joseph as a slave (Genesis 37:27), pleading to his father, sincerely offering to take full responsibility for the safety of Benjamin. As you can see, we are watching a deep change of heart taking place in Judah.

3 And **Judah spake unto him**, saying, The man [*Joseph, in Egypt*] did solemnly protest unto us, saying, Ye shall not see my face [*I will refuse to see you*], except [*unless*] your brother *be* with you.

4 **If thou wilt send our brother with us, we will go down and buy thee food**:

5 **But if thou wilt not send** *him,* **we will not go** down: for the man said unto us, Ye shall not see my face, except your brother *be* with you.

6 And **Israel** [*Jacob*] **said, Wherefore dealt ye** *so* **ill with me,** *as* **to tell the man whether ye had yet a brother** [*why did you have to go and tell him that you had another brother*]?

7 And **they said, The man asked us straitly** [*straightforward*] of our state, and of our kindred, **saying,** *Is* **your father yet alive? have ye** *another* **brother?** and we told him according to the tenor of these words [*and we simply answered his questions*]: could we certainly know [*how were we to know*] that he would say, Bring your brother down?

8 And **Judah said unto Israel his father, Send the lad with me**, and we will arise and go; that we may live, and not die, both we, and thou, *and* also our little ones [*let us go or you and we and all of our families will die from the famine*].

9 **I will be surety** [*security*] **for him**; of my hand shalt thou require him: **if I bring him not unto thee**, and set him before thee, then **let me bear the blame for ever**:

10 For except we had lingered [*if we hadn't stayed here at home so long*], surely now we had returned this second time [*we would already be back in Egypt now*].

> Finally, Israel is convinced that his sons must return and take Benjamin with them.

11 And **their father Israel said unto them, If** *it must be* **so now**, do this; **take of the best fruits** of the land in your vessels, and **carry down the man a present**, a little **balm**, and a little **honey, spices**, and **myrrh, nuts**, and **almonds**:

12 And **take double money** in your hand; and the money that was brought again in the mouth of your sacks, carry *it* again in your hand; peradventure it *was* an oversight [*in case the Egyptians made a mistake in leaving your previous payment in your grain sacks*]:

13 **Take also your brother** [*Benjamin*], and arise, go again unto the man:

14 And **God Almighty give you mercy before the man**, that he may send away your other brother [*Simeon*], and Benjamin. If I be bereaved *of my children,* I am bereaved [*if I lose my children, I lose them*].

15 ¶ And **the men took that present, and they took double money** in their hand, **and Benjamin**; and rose up, **and went down to Egypt, and stood before Joseph**.

> Imagine Joseph's joy when he saw his brothers finally come in with Benjamin! He had no doubt worried when so much time had passed and they had still not returned.
>
> Also, imagine the surprise and concern of the brothers when they were invited to come to Joseph's home for a meal. They feared that it was a trap and that they somehow would be framed again.

16 And **when Joseph saw Benjamin with them, he said to the ruler of his house, Bring** *these* **men home**, and slay [*kill an animal for a feast*], and **make ready; for** *these* **men shall dine with me at noon**.

17 And the man did as Joseph bade; and the man brought the men into Joseph's house.

18 And **the men were afraid**, because they were brought into Joseph's house; and they said, Because of the money that was returned in our sacks at the first time are we brought in; that he may seek occasion [*evidence*] against us, and fall

upon us [*and arrest us all*], and take us for bondmen [*slaves*], and our asses.

Because of their concern and fear, the brothers attempt to explain to Joseph's chief servant what happened the first time they came to Egypt to buy grain.

19 And **they came near to the steward of Joseph's house**, and they communed with him at the door of the house,

20 **And said**, O **sir, we came indeed down at the first time to buy food**:

21 And it came to pass, **when we came to the inn** [*as we traveled back toward our home*], that **we opened our sacks, and, behold,** *every* **man's money** *was* **in the mouth of his sack**, our money in full weight: and **we have brought it again** in our hand.

22 And **other money have we brought down in our hands to buy food**: we cannot tell [*we have no idea*] who put our money in our sacks.

This must have been a pleasant duty for Joseph's chief steward. We sense from verse 23, next, that he was an honest, sincere man himself. He puts their minds at ease about the money they found in their bags of grain and extends hospitality to them.

23 And **he said**, Peace *be* to you, **fear not: your God**, and the God of your father, **hath given you treasure in your sacks: I had your money** [*I received your money, personally, when you paid it, last time you were here*]. And **he brought Simeon out unto them**.

24 **And the man brought the men into Joseph's house**, and **gave** *them* **water**, and they washed their feet; and he **gave their asses provender** [*he fed their donkeys*].

25 And they made ready the present [*spoken of in verse 11, above*] against Joseph came at noon [*in preparation for Joseph's arrival at noon*]: for they heard that they should eat bread [*a meal*] there.

26 ¶ And **when Joseph came** home, **they brought him the present** which *was* in their hand into the house, and **bowed themselves to him to the earth** [*another fulfillment of his dreams that his family would bow down to him*].

27 And **he asked them** of *their* welfare, and said, *Is* **your father well**, the old man of whom ye spake? *Is* **he yet alive?** [*Jacob is now somewhere near 130 years old*]

28 And **they answered**, Thy servant **our father** *is* **in good health, he** *is* **yet alive**. And they bowed down their heads, and made obeisance [*showed him respect and honor*].

29 And **he lifted up his eyes, and saw his brother Benjamin**, his mother's son [*his full brother*], **and said,** *Is* **this your younger brother**, of whom ye spake unto me? And he said, God be gracious unto thee, my son.

Once again, Joseph has to leave the room because his emotions are running so close to the surface. After a while, he regains control and enters the room again and proceeds with the meal.

30 And **Joseph made haste** [*left the room*]; **for his bowels did yearn upon his brother** [*his whole being wanted to hug Benjamin*]: and **he sought** *where* **to weep; and he entered into** *his* **chamber, and wept there**.

31 And **he washed his face**, and **went out, and refrained himself** [*kept his emotions under control*], and said, Set on bread [*start the meal*].

> It is interesting to note the racial prejudice against the Hebrews on the part of the Egyptians, as mentioned in verse 32, next. It says much about the very high regard held for Joseph by the Egyptians that he was such a successful leader there.

32 And they set on for him by himself, and for them by themselves, and for the Egyptians, which did eat with him, by themselves: because **the Egyptians might not eat bread with the Hebrews; for that** *is* **an abomination unto the Egyptians**.

> Joseph had arranged in advance to have his brothers seated according to age, causing them to wonder how he could possibly know to do this.

33 And they sat before him, the firstborn according to his birthright, and the youngest according to his youth: and **the men marvelled one at another** [*the brothers were astonished*].

34 And he took *and sent* messes [*servings, portions of food*] unto them from before him [*from his table*]: but Benjamin's mess was five times so much as any of theirs. And **they drank, and were merry with him**.

GENESIS 44

As mentioned in the background notes at the beginning of Genesis 37, Joseph was a "type" of Christ. This means that his life and mission were representative in many ways of the life and mission of the Savior.

Perhaps you've noticed many ways, in chapters 41–43, in which Joseph is symbolic of Christ, in addition to the six parallels we noted in chapter 37. Some examples are:

1. **The Savior** is second only to the Father and has been put in charge of all things, under His direction.

    Joseph was second only to the king and was put in charge of all things, under him.

2. Under the direction of **the Savior**, we are being tested during our sojourn here on earth.

    Under the direction of **Joseph**, his brothers were tested during their sojourn in Egypt.

3. **Jesus** is the "bread of life," and we come to Him for nourishment and eternal life.

Joseph has an abundance of grain, and his brothers have come to him to sustain their lives.

4. **The Savior** waits patiently with deepest love and tender emotion for us as we grow and mature spiritually.

   Joseph is waiting patiently with deep love and tender emotion as his brothers grow and mature spiritually.

5. Although **the Savior** is often in our midst (Doctrine and Covenants 38:7), we usually don't see Him.

   Joseph is in the midst of his brothers, but they do not recognize him.

6. **The Savior** speaks to us through His prophets and has His faithful servants (bishops, stake presidents, teachers, and so forth) do much of the direct work with us.

   Joseph spoke to his brothers through an interpreter (Genesis 42:23) and had his faithful servants do much of the direct work with them.

And so, the parallels or "types" go on and on. According to the Pearl of Great Price, many such "types" are deliberately planned by the Lord to bear witness of Him to us. We read:

Moses 6:63

63 And behold, all things have their likeness, and all things are created and made to bear record of me, both things which are temporal, and things which are spiritual; things which are in the heavens above, and things which are on the earth, and things which are in the earth, and things which are under the earth, both above and beneath: all things bear record of me.

As Moses continues the account of Joseph and his brothers in Egypt, we will see yet another test designed by Joseph for them. It promotes growth and humility in the brothers, especially in Judah, whose heart was originally hard and bitter against Joseph (Genesis 37:26–27). As mentioned previously, this earth life is designed (among other things, including joy and happiness) to provide us with tests and difficulties that can lead to our developing Christlike character traits, including humility and compassion.

Benjamin will be "caught stealing," and the brothers will be brought back to Egypt to "face the judge" (Joseph). Benjamin will face being kept in Egypt. In humility and sincerity, Judah will offer himself to suffer in place of Benjamin and to remain in Egypt as a slave to Joseph. His compassion is both for his youngest brother, Benjamin, and for his father, Jacob.

We will now proceed with the chapter. In the first verses, we see the test designed by Joseph to "prove" his brothers to see if their hearts have truly softened over time. His test is accompanied by generous blessings of food and wealth.

1 And **he commanded the steward of his house,** saying, **Fill the men's sacks *with* food, as much as they can carry, and put every man's money in his sack's mouth.**

2 And **put my cup**, the silver cup [*perhaps symbolic of the "bitter cup" that the Savior endured for us*], **in the sack's mouth of the youngest** [*Benjamin*], **and his corn money. And he did according to the word that Joseph had spoken.**

3 As soon as the morning was light, the men were sent away, they and their asses.

4 *And* **when they were gone out of the city,** *and* **not** *yet* **far off, Joseph said unto his steward,** Up, **follow after the men; and when thou dost overtake them, say unto them, Wherefore have ye rewarded evil for good** [*why have you returned evil to us for the good we did for you*]?

5 *Is* not this [*Joseph's silver cup*] *it* in which my lord drinketh, and whereby indeed he divineth? ye have done evil in so doing.

6 ¶ And **he overtook them, and** he **spake** unto them **these** same **words**.

7 And **they said** unto him, **Wherefore saith my lord these words? God forbid that thy servants should do according to this thing** [*in other words, we are innocent*]:

8 Behold, the money, which we found in our sacks' mouths, we brought again unto thee out of the land of Canaan: how then should we [*why would we*] steal out of thy lord's house silver or gold?

Next, the brothers are so sure of everybody's innocence that they tell Joseph's steward that he is welcome to execute whoever has the silver cup. They are in for a surprise.

By the way, have you noticed that one of the most difficult tests in our lives is when things go terribly wrong through no fault of our own, and most especially when we are falsely accused? It is this type of test through which Joseph's brothers are now about to be taken.

9 **With whomsoever of thy servants it be found, both let him die**, and we also will be my lord's bondmen [*and the rest of us will return to Egypt as slaves*].

Next, the steward rejects their offer for him to execute the guilty one, if such there be, and to all become bondmen in Egypt. Instead, he indicates that the guilty party will return with him to Egypt and the rest can go free.

10 And **he** [*Joseph's steward*] **said**, Now also *let* it *be* according unto your words: **he with whom it is found shall be my servant; and ye shall be blameless.**

11 **Then they speedily took down every man his sack to the ground, and opened every man his sack.**

12 **And he** [*the steward*] **searched,** *and* began at the eldest, and left at the youngest: and **the cup was found in Benjamin's sack.**

13 **Then they** [*Joseph's brothers*] **rent** [*tore*] **their clothes** [*a demonstration of deepest anguish and distress, in their*

culture], and laded [*loaded*] every man his ass, and returned to the city.

> Note that, whereas Reuben and Simeon (the oldest brothers) have previously taken the lead in matters, this time Judah seems to be leading out. According to Genesis 38, he has been a very wicked man. Yet, as you will see next, his heart has become especially softened as he goes through the repentance process and he will demonstrate some sincere, Christlike qualities. This is a sweet reminder that there is hope for grievous sinners because of the Atonement of Jesus Christ (compare with Jacob 6:4–5).

14 ¶ And **Judah and his brethren came to Joseph's house**; for he *was* yet there: and they fell before him on the ground.

15 And **Joseph said** unto them, **What deed *is* this that ye have done?** wot ye not [*did you not know*] that such a man as I can certainly divine [*that I have special powers to discover secrets*]?

16 And **Judah said**, What shall we say unto my lord? what shall we speak? or **how shall we clear ourselves? God hath found out the iniquity of thy servants** [*God knows that we have done wicked things in the past*]: behold, we *are* my lord's servants, both we, and *he* also with whom the cup is found.

17 And **he** [*Joseph*] **said, God forbid that I should do so** [*it would not be right for me to keep the innocent with the guilty*]: but **the man in whose hand the cup is found, he shall be my servant; and as for you, get you up in peace unto your father**.

> Next, Judah asks if he might be permitted to whisper something in Joseph's ear.

18 ¶ **Then Judah came near** unto him, and said, Oh my lord, **let thy servant, I pray thee, speak a word in my lord's ears**, and let not thine anger burn against thy servant: for thou *art* even as Pharaoh.

19 **My lord asked** his servants [*you asked us*], saying, **Have ye a father, or a brother?**

20 And **we said** [*we answered*] unto my lord, **We have a father, an old man, and a child of his old age, a little one** [*Benjamin*]; **and his brother** [*Joseph*] **is dead, and he alone is left of his mother** [*Benjamin is Rachel's only remaining son*], **and his father loveth him.**

21 And **thou saidst** unto thy servants, **Bring him down unto me, that I may set mine eyes upon him**.

22 And **we said** unto my lord, The lad cannot leave his father: for *if* he should leave his father, *his father* would die.

23 And **thou saidst** unto thy servants, **Except your youngest brother come down with you, ye shall see my face no more**.

> Verse 23, above, is yet another example of Joseph as a "type" of Christ. We are told many times in

the scriptures by the Savior that unless we keep His commandments, we cannot return to Him and see His face. Here, in this verse, Joseph, in effect, says that unless his brothers keep his commandment, they will see his face no more.

24 And it came to pass **when we came up** [*returned home*] **unto** thy servant **my father** [*Jacob*]**, we told him the words of my lord** [*we told him what you said*].

25 And our **father said, Go again,** *and* **buy us a little food.**

26 And **we said**, We cannot go down: **if our youngest brother be with us, then will we go** down: for we may not see the man's face, except our youngest brother *be* with us.

27 And thy servant my **father said** unto us, **Ye know that my wife bare me two** *sons:*

28 And the **one** went out from me, and I said, Surely he **is torn in pieces** [*was killed by a wild animal*]; and I saw him not since:

29 **And if ye take this** [*Benjamin*] **also** from me, **and mischief** [*harm*] **befall him**, ye shall bring down my gray hairs with sorrow to the grave [*it will kill me*].

> Having given Joseph the above background information, Judah now pleads that he be kept as a slave in place of Benjamin. In effect, he is volunteering to be sacrificed in place of Benjamin in order that Benjamin might go home to his father.

Do you see the parallels here? The Savior pleads our case before the Father (Doctrine and Covenants 45:3–5). He volunteered to be sacrificed in order that we might be freed from deserved punishment and return to live with our Father.

We will watch as Judah tenderly and sincerely pleads for the welfare of his Father and for the well-being of Benjamin.

30 Now **therefore when I come to** thy servant **my father, and the lad** *be* **not with us** [*if I go home without Benjamin*]; **seeing that his life is bound up in the lad's life** [*my fathers "work and his glory" (compare with Moses 1:39) is completely tied in with the life of his child*];

31 **It shall come to pass, when he seeth that the lad** *is* **not** *with us,* **that he will die**: and thy servants shall bring down the gray hairs of thy servant our father with sorrow to the grave.

32 For **thy servant** [*I, Judah*] **became surety for the lad** [*I guaranteed his safety*] unto my father, saying, **If I bring him not unto thee, then I shall bear the blame to my father for ever.**

33 Now therefore, I pray thee, **let thy servant abide instead of the lad a bondman to my lord** [*let me be punished in the place of Benjamin, thus remaining in Egypt and becoming your servant*]; and **let the lad go up with his brethren.**

34 For **how shall I go up to my father, and the lad** *be* **not with me?**

lest peradventure I see the evil that shall come on my father [*in other words, I couldn't stand to see this happen to my father*].

> Remember that Judah said all of this privately to Joseph, out of his brothers' hearing (verse 18, above). It is evident that he does not want glory for himself, nor to impress anyone else. He just wants what is best for his father and his brother. The contrast between Judah's tender feelings about his father now and the cruel, callous lack of feeling he had exhibited before as he and his brothers took Joseph's blood-stained cloak to him is truly remarkable. Again, it is a reminder that one of the major purposes of this life for us is to be molded and shaped in the Master's hand and allowed to progress toward exaltation through His Atonement.

GENESIS 45

After Judah finishes whispering his pleadings in Joseph's ear, Joseph can no longer control his tender emotions. He will command that all his servants and others leave the room so that he can be alone with his brothers. Still, all in Pharaoh's palace could hear his joyful sobbing.

Imagine his brothers' great surprise when they finally recognize him as Joseph.

1 **Then Joseph could not refrain himself** before all them that stood by him; **and he cried, Cause every man to go out from me**. And there stood no man [*servants or officers*] with him, while **Joseph made himself known unto his brethren**.

2 And **he wept aloud**: and the Egyptians and the house of Pharaoh heard.

3 And **Joseph said unto his brethren, I *am* Joseph**; doth my father yet live? And **his brethren could not answer him; for they were troubled at his presence** [*they still didn't recognize him and were confused and worried about what was going on*].

4 And **Joseph said unto his brethren, Come near to me**, I pray you. And **they came near. And he said, I *am* Joseph your brother, whom ye sold into Egypt**.

> Next, Joseph shows his Christlike mercy as he gently puts his brothers at ease. The scene reminds us of many incidents in the scriptures where the Savior says "fear not."

5 Now therefore **be not grieved, nor angry with yourselves, that ye sold me hither** [*into Egypt*]: for **God did send me before** [*ahead of*] **you to preserve life** [*it was God's way of sending me on this mission to save many lives from the famine*].

> There is yet another parallel or "type" in verse 5, above. "Egypt" is often used in the scriptures to symbolize the earth and its wicked inhabitants. It is similar to the use of the word "Babylon." Just as Joseph was sent to Egypt to save many lives from the famine, so also was the Savior sent to a wicked world to save many from

the "famine of hearing the word of the Lord" (Amos 8:11).

Next, in verses 6–8, Joseph continues putting his brothers' minds at ease as he explains more about the famine.

6 For these two years *hath* the famine *been* in the land [*the famine has been going on for two years so far*]: and yet *there are* five years [*and there are five years to go*], in the which *there shall* neither *be* earing [*the grain crops will fail to form ears of grain*] nor harvest.

7 And **God sent me before you to preserve you a posterity in the earth, and to save your lives by a great deliverance** [*in other words, Joseph is, in effect, their redeemer*].

8 So now *it was* **not you *that* sent me hither, but God**: and he hath made me a father to Pharaoh, and lord of all his house, and a ruler throughout all the land of Egypt.

Next, Joseph instructs his brothers to hurry home to their father and tell him the good news, bringing him and the whole family to live near Joseph (their "redeemer").

9 **Haste ye, and go up to my father, and say unto him, Thus saith thy son Joseph, God hath made me lord of all Egypt: come down unto me, tarry not**:

10 And **thou shalt dwell in the land of Goshen**, and thou shalt **be near unto me**, thou, and thy children, and thy children's children, and thy flocks, and thy herds, and all that thou hast:

11 And **there will I nourish thee**; for yet *there are* five years of famine; lest thou, and thy household, and all that thou hast, come to poverty.

12 And, **behold**, your eyes see, and the eyes of my brother Benjamin, that *it is* **my mouth that speaketh unto you**.

13 And **ye shall tell my father of all my glory in Egypt, and of all that ye have seen**: and ye shall **haste** [*hurry*] and bring down my father hither.

ßNext, Joseph shows great affection for Benjamin and his brothers.

14 And **he fell upon his brother Benjamin's neck** [*he embraced Benjamin*], **and wept**; and Benjamin wept upon his neck.

15 **Moreover he kissed all his brethren, and wept upon them**: and after that his brethren talked with him.

Word spread fast about the great reunion of Joseph and his brothers.

16 ¶ And **the fame thereof was heard in Pharaoh's house, saying, Joseph's brethren are come**: and **it pleased Pharaoh** well, and his servants.

17 And **Pharaoh said unto Joseph, Say unto thy brethren, This do ye; lade** [*load*] **your beasts, and go**, get you **unto the land of Canaan**;

18 And **take your father and your households, and come unto me**: and I will give you the good of the land of Egypt, and ye shall eat the fat [*best*] of the land.

19 Now thou art commanded, this do ye; **take** you **wagons out of the land of Egypt for your little ones, and for your wives, and bring your father, and come**.

20 Also regard not your stuff [*don't worry about bringing all your belongings from home*]; for the good of all the land of Egypt *is* yours.

21 **And the children of Israel** [*Jacob*] **did so**: and **Joseph gave them wagons**, according to the commandment of Pharaoh, and gave them **provision** for the way [*for the journey*].

22 To all of them he gave each man **changes of raiment** [*clothing*]; but **to Benjamin** he gave **three hundred** *pieces* **of silver**, and **five changes of raiment**.

23 And **to his father** he sent after this *manner;* ten asses laden with **the good things of Egypt**, and ten she asses laden with **corn** [*grain*] and **bread** and **meat** [*food*] for his father by the way [*as he traveled back to Egypt*].

> Just a reminder that the word "meat" as used in verse 23, above, means "food." When the Bible speaks of beef, venison, chicken, lamb, goat, and so forth, it uses the word "flesh."

> As Joseph sends his brothers off to go get their father and families, he gives them some very important advice at the end of verse 24, next.

24 So **he sent his brethren away**, and they departed: and he said unto them, **See that ye fall not out by the way** [*don't get caught up in quarreling or arguing as you go*].

25 ¶ And **they went up out of Egypt, and came into the land of Canaan unto Jacob their father**,

> As seen in verse 26, next, it was more than Jacob could possibly believe when they told him about Joseph and his status in Egypt.

26 **And told him**, saying, **Joseph** *is* **yet alive, and he** *is* **governor over all the land of Egypt**. And **Jacob's heart fainted, for he believed them not**.

27 **And they told him all the words of Joseph, which he had said unto them**: and **when he saw the wagons** which Joseph had sent to carry him, **the spirit of Jacob their father revived**:

28 And **Israel said,** *It is* **enough; Joseph my son** *is* **yet alive: I will go and see him before I die** [*Jacob will spend the last seventeen years of his life in Egypt before dying at age 147—see Genesis 47:28*].

GENESIS 46

As you can well imagine, it must have been very difficult for Jacob, at his age, to relocate to Egypt. As he travels, he faithfully worships the Lord by building an altar (verse 1), and the Lord appears to him and reassures him that going to Egypt is the right thing to do (verses 2–4).

Imagine also how anxiously Joseph waited to see his father again.

1 And **Israel** [*Jacob*] **took his journey with all that he had**, and came to Beer-sheba, **and offered sacrifices unto the God of his father Isaac.**

2 And **God** [*Jehovah, the premortal Jesus Christ*] **spake unto Israel in the visions of the night**, and said, Jacob, Jacob. And he said, Here *am* I.

3 And he said, I *am* God, the God of thy father: **fear not to go down into Egypt; for I will there make of thee a great nation** [*they will become known as the children of Israel*]:

4 **I will go down with thee into Egypt; and I will also surely bring thee up** *again:* and Joseph shall put his hand upon thine eyes [*Joseph's own hand will close your eyelids when you die*].

5 And Jacob rose up from Beer-sheba: and **the sons of Israel carried Jacob their father, and their little ones, and their wives, in the wagons** which Pharaoh had sent to carry him.

6 And they took their cattle, and their goods, which they had gotten in the land of Canaan, and came into Egypt, Jacob, and **all his seed** [*about sixty-six people in all—see verse 26*] **with him**:

Counting Joseph, his wife, and two sons, Jacob will have a total of seventy family members living now in Egypt (see verse 27). Next, Moses provides a list of Jacob's family members.

7 **His sons, and his sons' sons with him, his daughters, and his sons' daughters**, and **all his seed** [*posterity*] **brought he with him into Egypt.**

8 ¶ And **these** *are* **the names of the children of Israel, which came into Egypt**, Jacob and his sons: Reuben, Jacob's firstborn.

9 And the sons of Reuben; Hanoch, and Phallu, and Hezron, and Carmi.

10 ¶ And the sons of Simeon; Jemuel, and Jamin, and Ohad, and Jachin, and Zohar, and Shaul the son of a Canaanitish woman.

11 ¶ And the sons of Levi; Gershon, Kohath, and Merari.

12 ¶ And the sons of Judah; Er, and Onan, and Shelah, and Pharez, and Zerah: but Er and Onan died in the land of Canaan. And the sons of Pharez were Hezron and Hamul.

13 ¶ And the sons of Issachar; Tola, and Phuvah, and Job, and Shimron.

14 ¶ And the sons of Zebulun; Sered, and Elon, and Jahleel.

15 These *be* the sons of Leah, which she bare unto Jacob in Padan-aram, with his daughter Dinah: all the souls of his sons and his daughters *were* thirty and three.

16 ¶ And the sons of Gad; Ziphion, and Haggi, Shuni, and Ezbon, Eri, and Arodi, and Areli.

17 ¶ And the sons of Asher; Jimnah, and Ishuah, and Isui, and Beriah, and Serah their sister: and the sons of Beriah; Heber, and Malchiel.

18 These *are* the sons of Zilpah, whom Laban gave to Leah his daughter, and these she bare unto Jacob, *even* sixteen souls.

19 The sons of Rachel Jacob's wife; Joseph, and Benjamin.

20 ¶ And **unto Joseph in the land of Egypt were born Manasseh and Ephraim**, which Asenath the daughter of Poti-pherah priest of On bare unto him.

21 ¶ And the sons of Benjamin *were* Belah, and Becher, and Ashbel, Gera, and Naaman, Ehi, and Rosh, Muppim, and Huppim, and Ard.

22 These *are* the sons of Rachel, which were born to Jacob: all the souls *were* fourteen.

23 ¶ And the sons of Dan; Hushim.

24 ¶ And the sons of Naphtali; Jahzeel, and Guni, and Jezer, and Shillem.

25 These *are* the sons of Bilhah, which Laban gave unto Rachel his daughter, and she bare these unto Jacob: all the souls *were* seven.

26 **All the souls that came with Jacob into Egypt**, which came out of his loins, besides Jacob's sons' wives, all the souls *were* **threescore and six** [*66*];

27 And **the sons of Joseph, which were born him in Egypt,** *were* **two** souls: **all the souls of the house of Jacob, which came into Egypt,** *were* **threescore and ten** [*70*].

> As Jacob and his procession arrive in Egypt, Jacob assigns Judah to go on ahead of them to Joseph to get directions for traveling to the land of Goshen, which Pharaoh has given them to live on.

28 ¶ And **he sent Judah before him unto Joseph, to direct his face unto Goshen**; and they came into the land of Goshen.

29 And **Joseph made ready his chariot, and went up to meet Israel his father**, to Goshen, **and presented himself unto him; and he fell on his neck, and wept on his neck a good while**.

30 And **Israel said unto Joseph, Now let me die** [*now, I am content to die*], **since I have seen thy face, because thou** *art* **yet alive**.

> In verses 31–34, next, we are given to understand that the Egyptians are very prejudiced against shepherds, the occupation of Jacob and his sons. Thus, Joseph gives his brothers counsel and instruction about settling in Goshen, in spite of being looked down upon by their Egyptian hosts.

31 And **Joseph said unto his brethren**, and unto his father's house, **I will go up, and shew** [*show*] **Pharaoh, and say** unto him, **My**

brethren, and my father's house, which *were* in the land of Canaan, are come unto me;

32 **And the men *are* shepherds**, for their trade hath been to feed cattle; and they have brought their flocks, and their herds, and all that they have.

33 And it shall come to pass, **when Pharaoh shall call you, and shall say, What *is* your occupation?**

34 That ye shall **say, Thy servants' trade hath been about cattle** [*NIV, "we have tended livestock"*] from our youth even until now, both we, *and* also our fathers: **that ye may dwell in the land of Goshen; for every shepherd *is* an abomination unto the Egyptians**.

> A clue as to why the Egyptians looked down on shepherds is found in the *Old Testament Student Manual*, page 96. We read:
>
> "Several Egyptian deities were represented by cattle, especially female cattle. Since the Hebrews were herdsmen who slaughtered and ate cattle, regardless of sex, this practice would have been viewed by the Egyptians as a terrible abomination" (see Keil and Delitzsch, Commentary, Vol 1, page 362; Clarke, Bible Commentary, Vol. 1, page 245; cf. Genesis 43:34).

GENESIS 47

We will see several things in this chapter. Jacob and his family will settle in Egypt, in the land of Goshen (in northern Egypt on the Nile River Delta). Joseph will personally introduce some of his brothers and his father to Pharaoh. His father will leave a blessing with Pharaoh.

We will watch and learn from Joseph as he applies principles of self-reliance in the distribution of food storage among his people.

And, finally, we will see the "children of Israel" (the posterity of Jacob) begin to increase in number and prosper in the land.

In verse 1, next, Joseph reports to Pharaoh that his family has successfully settled in Goshen.

1 Then **Joseph came and told Pharaoh**, and said, **My father and my brethren, and their flocks, and their herds, and all that they have**, are come out of the land of Canaan; and, behold, they *are* **in the land of Goshen**.

> Next, Joseph selects five of his brothers to be introduced to Pharaoh. He had previously coached them as to what they should say when asked by the king what they do for an occupation (Genesis 46:33–34). They will do exactly as Joseph has instructed them. They have learned an important lesson.

2 And **he took some of his brethren**, *even* **five men, and presented them unto Pharaoh**.

3 And **Pharaoh said** unto his brethren, **What *is* your occupation?** And **they said** unto Pharaoh, Thy servants *are* **shepherds**, both we, *and*

also our fathers [*as were our ancestors*].

4 **They said** moreover [*in addition*] unto Pharaoh, **For to sojourn** [*live*] **in the land are we come**; for thy servants have no pasture for their flocks; for **the famine** *is* **sore** [*severe*] **in the land of Canaan**: now therefore, we pray thee [*please*], **let thy servants dwell in the land of Goshen**.

> Next, we see the esteem and respect that Pharaoh has for Joseph as he generously tells Joseph to let his father's family settle in the most fertile part of the land.

5 And **Pharaoh spake unto Joseph**, saying, Thy father and thy brethren are come unto thee:

6 The land of Egypt *is* before thee; **in the best of the land make thy father and brethren to dwell**; in the land of Goshen let them dwell: **and if thou knowest** *any* **men of activity** [*with special skill*] among them, then **make them rulers over my cattle** [*put them in charge of my flocks also*].

7 And **Joseph brought in Jacob his father, and set him before Pharaoh: and Jacob blessed Pharaoh**.

8 And **Pharaoh said** unto Jacob, **How old** *art* **thou?**

9 And **Jacob said** unto Pharaoh, The days of the years of my pilgrimage [*my life so far on earth*] *are* **an hundred and thirty years**: few and evil [*unpleasant—see footnote 9b in your Bible*] have the days of the years of my life been, and have not attained unto the days of the years of the life of my fathers [*ancestors*] in the days of their pilgrimage [*he has lived few years, compared to Adam (930), Methuselah (969), Noah (950), and others*].

10 And **Jacob blessed Pharaoh, and went out** from before Pharaoh.

11 ¶ And **Joseph placed his father and his brethren**, and gave them a possession in the land of Egypt, **in the best of the land**, in the land of Rameses, as Pharaoh had commanded.

12 And **Joseph nourished his father, and his brethren, and all his father's household, with bread, according to** *their* **families** [*according to their family size and needs*].

> Next, in verses 13–26, we will observe how Joseph administers the welfare system he has established in Egypt. By this time, the severe drought (Genesis 41:54) has made it so that hardly any crops in Egypt will grow. Therefore, the people must live off of the food storage, saved up during the seven years of plenty (Genesis 41:29).

13 ¶ And *there was* **no bread in all the land; for the famine** *was* **very sore**, so that the land of Egypt and *all* the land of Canaan fainted by reason of [*struggled because of*] the famine.

> First of all, since the people generally still have money but no food, Joseph

avoids the dole by having them buy grain from the supplies in storage. This makes them careful with what they receive because they have to pay for it themselves. The welfare principle involved here is to have people earn what they receive from the storehouse.

14 And **Joseph gathered up all the money that was found in the land of Egypt, and in the land of Canaan, for the corn which they bought**: and Joseph brought the money into Pharaoh's house.

Next, when the people no longer have money with which to buy welfare goods, Joseph requires them to use their other resources in payment for grain. The principle here is that they should exhaust their other available resources before they receive handouts.

15 And **when money failed** [*ran out*] in the land of Egypt, and in the land of Canaan, all the Egyptians came unto Joseph, and said, Give us bread: for why should we die in thy presence? for the money faileth.

16 And **Joseph said, Give your cattle; and I will give you** [*grain in exchange*] **for your cattle**, if money fail.

17 And **they brought their cattle unto Joseph: and Joseph gave them bread *in exchange*** for horses, and for the flocks, and for the cattle of the herds, and for the asses: and **he fed them with bread for** [*in exchange for*] **all their cattle for that year.**

As you are no doubt noticing, we are being shown by Joseph (and Moses, the writer of Genesis) that the dole is to be avoided at all costs. There is a principle here. Among other things, we do not appreciate that for which we have not sacrificed. Also, personal dignity is preserved when we are able to give something in exchange for welfare goods.

18 When that year was ended, they came unto him **the second year**, and said unto him, We will not hide *it* from my lord, how that our money is spent; my lord [*Joseph*] also hath our herds of cattle; **there is not ought** [*nothing*] **left** in the sight of my lord, **but our bodies, and our lands** [*in other words, all we have left are ourselves and the land that we own*]:

These Egyptians seem to understand the principles of proper welfare distribution very well. Certainly, during the seven years of plenty, Joseph had not only gathered food storage, but had also taught the people correct principles of administering a welfare program. We see this in verse 19, next, as the people suggest that they could sell themselves as slaves as well as their land to Joseph in exchange for grain. Joseph rejects buying them, but agrees with buying their land.

19 Wherefore [*why*] shall we die before thine eyes, both we and our land? **buy us and our land for bread**, and we and our land will be servants unto Pharaoh: and give *us* seed, that we may live, and not die, that the land be not desolate.

20 And **Joseph bought all the land of Egypt for Pharaoh**; for the Egyptians sold every man his field, because the famine prevailed over them: **so the land became Pharaoh's**.

> Joseph did relocate people, as needed, in order to make best possible use of available resources. Also, as a matter of wisdom and common sense, he did not disturb the priests of Pharaoh.

21 And **as for the people, he removed them to cities from** *one* **end of the borders of Egypt even to the** *other* **end** thereof.

22 **Only the land of the priests bought he not**; for the priests had a portion *assigned them* of Pharaoh, and did eat their portion which Pharaoh gave them: wherefore they sold not their lands.

> An overriding principle of welfare administration is that of self-reliance. Next, we see Joseph applying this principle as he gives people seed to plant on the land that now belongs to Pharaoh. They are required to give Pharaoh 20 percent of their produce, but they are to keep 80 percent for themselves.

23 Then **Joseph said** unto the people, Behold, **I have bought you this day and your land for Pharaoh**: lo, *here is* **seed for you**, and ye shall sow the land [*plant the ground*].

24 And it shall come to pass **in the increase**, that **ye shall give the fifth** *part* **unto Pharaoh**, and **four parts shall be your own**, for seed of the field, and for your food, and for them of your households, and for food for your little ones.

> Because of the way Joseph has administered the plan, the people have appreciation in their hearts. This is one of the opposites of greed. Proper principles of welfare are designed to preserve and foster gratitude.

25 And **they said, Thou hast saved our lives**: let us find grace in the sight of my lord, and we will be Pharaoh's servants.

26 And Joseph made it a law over the land of Egypt unto this day, *that* Pharaoh should have the fifth *part;* except the land of the priests only, *which* became not Pharaoh's.

> We now return to Israel and his people. As we see, in verse 27, next, over the years they prosper and increase greatly in population.

27 ¶ And **Israel** [*Jacob's sons and their families*] **dwelt in the land of Egypt**, in the country of Goshen; **and they** had possessions therein, and **grew, and multiplied exceedingly**.

28 And **Jacob lived in the land of Egypt seventeen years:** so the whole age of Jacob was an hundred forty and seven years [*Jacob lived a total of 147 years*].

> Next, as Jacob realizes that his life is drawing to a close, he calls Joseph to him and makes him

covenant with him that he will carry his bones out of Egypt and bury him with his ancestors.

29 And **the time drew nigh that Israel must die: and he called his son Joseph**, and said unto him, If now I have found grace in thy sight, put, I pray thee, thy hand under my thigh [*the JST changed the word "thigh" to "hand" in Genesis 24:2; perhaps that change applies here also*], and deal kindly and truly with me; **bury me not, I pray thee, in Egypt**:

30 But **I will lie with my fathers**, and thou shalt carry me out of Egypt, and **bury me in their buryingplace**. And he [*Joseph*] said, I will do as thou hast said.

31 And he said, Swear [*make an oath; promise*] unto me. And **he sware unto him**. And Israel bowed himself upon the bed's head [*at the head of the bed—see footnote 31b, in your Bible*].

GENESIS 48

In this chapter, Jacob, in effect, gives patriarchal blessings to Joseph's two sons, Manasseh and Ephraim. Manasseh was his firstborn and Ephraim the second born. Joseph brings them both to Jacob at the same time and positions his sons so that the oldest will be under his father's right hand (in order to receive the birthright blessing, according to their culture) and the youngest under the left.

However, much to Joseph's surprise and concern, Jacob crosses his right hand over to the head of Ephraim and his left to the head of Manasseh (verse 14). In order to understand why Joseph was concerned, we need to understand something about his culture.

In biblical culture, the right hand was the covenant hand—in other words, the hand with which covenants were made. The right hand also symbolized the best, including the birthright blessings and privileges. Joseph had obviously planned on having Manasseh, his firstborn, receive the birthright blessing and was thus startled at first when Jacob, under inspiration, changed things around.

As we start this chapter, we understand that Jacob (Israel) is getting close to 147, the age at which he will die. In verse 1, he sends for Joseph, who brings his two sons to visit their grandfather.

1 *And it came to pass after these things, that one* told Joseph, **Behold, thy father *is* sick**: and **he took with him his two sons, Manasseh and Ephraim**.

2 And *one* **told Jacob**, and said, Behold, **thy son Joseph cometh unto thee**: and **Israel** strengthened himself [*gathered his strength with great effort*], and **sat upon the bed**.

Next, Jacob retells to Joseph and Joseph's sons his dream of the ladder reaching up to heaven (Genesis 28:12–15) at a place in Canaan, which was originally named "Luz," but which Jacob renamed "Beth-el" (see Genesis 28:19). "Beth-el" means "house of God." In so doing, he is reviewing the Abrahamic covenant with Joseph and his sons. Before the meeting is over, Jacob will bestow it upon Ephraim.

3 And **Jacob said unto Joseph, God Almighty appeared unto me at Luz in the land of Canaan, and blessed me**,

Verse 4, next, contains a portion of the Abrahamic covenant. You may wish to read Abraham 2:9–11, in the Pearl of Great Price, which contains a more complete version of it.

4 And said unto me, **Behold, I will make thee fruitful, and multiply thee, and I will make of thee a multitude of people; and will give this land to thy seed after thee *for* an everlasting possession.**

In verse 5, next, Jacob adopts Ephraim and Manasseh as his own. This, in effect, provides Joseph with a double portion of inheritance from his father (see verse 22). Thus, in many lists of lineage used in relation to patriarchal blessings, showing the tribes of Israel, we see thirteen names. The name, Joseph, has been replaced with his sons, Ephraim and Manasseh.

5 ¶ And **now thy two sons, Ephraim and Manasseh**, which were born unto thee in the land of Egypt before I came unto thee into Egypt, *are* **mine**; as Reuben and Simeon, they shall be mine.

The JST adds to verse 5, above, as follows:

JST Genesis 48:5

5 And now, of thy two sons, Ephraim and Manasseh, which were born unto thee in the land of Egypt, before I came unto thee into Egypt; behold, they are mine; and the God of my fathers shall bless them; even as Reuben and Simeon they shall be blessed, for they are mine; wherefore they shall be called after my name. (Therefore they were called Israel.)

In summary, there are generally thirteen possible lineages that could be given in patriarchal blessings in conjunction with the blessings of Abraham, Isaac, and Jacob. They are

1. Reuben
2. Simeon
3. Levi
4. Judah
5. Dan
6. Naphtali
7. Gad
8. Asher
9. Issachar
10. Zebulun
11. Ephraim
12. Manasseh
13. Benjamin

The JST also adds to verse 6, next, and adds five verses between the Genesis version of verses 6 and 7.

6 And **thy issue, which thou begettest after them** [*any children you have after Ephraim and Manasseh*], **shall be thine,** *and* shall be called after the name of their brethren in their inheritance [*in other words, Ephraim and Manasseh will each receive a land inheritance, just like Jacob's other eleven sons, Reuben through Benjamin; any other children born to Joseph would receive inheritances through Ephraim and Manasseh*].

JST Genesis 48:6–11

6 And thy issue which thou begettest after them, shall be thine, and shall be called after the name of their brethren in their inheritance, **in the tribes; therefore they were called the tribes of Manasseh and of Ephraim**.

7 And Jacob said unto Joseph, When the God of my fathers appeared unto me in Luz, in the land of Canaan; he sware unto me, that he would give unto me, and unto my seed, the land for an everlasting possession.

8 Therefore, O my son, he hath blessed me in raising thee up to be a servant unto me, in saving my house from death;

9 In delivering my people, thy brethren, from famine which was sore in the land; wherefore the God of thy fathers shall bless thee, and the fruit of thy loins [*Ephraim and Manasseh, Genesis 48:5*], that they shall be blessed above thy brethren, and above thy father's house;

10 For thou hast prevailed, and thy father's house hath bowed down unto thee, even as it was shown unto thee, before thou wast sold into Egypt by the hands of thy brethren; wherefore thy brethren shall bow down unto thee, from generation to generation, unto the fruit of thy loins forever;

In the JST version, verse 11, next, we see a major responsibility given by the Lord to descendants of Ephraim and Manasseh.

11 For **thou shalt be a light unto my people, to deliver them in the days of their captivity, from bondage; and to bring salvation unto them, when they are altogether** [*completely*] **bowed down under sin.**

We will now continue with the Genesis version, as of verse 7, next.

7 And **as for me** [*Jacob*], when I came from Padan, **Rachel died by me in the land of Canaan** [*near Bethlehem*] in the way [*as we were traveling*], when yet *there was* but a little way to come unto Ephrath: **and I buried her there** in the way of Ephrath; the same *is* Bethlehem.

Next, Jacob turns his attention directly to Ephraim and Manasseh. As many grandfathers do, he asks Joseph, in effect, "and who might these two fine young men be?"

8 **And Israel beheld** [*saw*] **Joseph's sons, and said, Who** *are* **these?**

9 And **Joseph said** unto his father, **They** *are* **my sons**, whom God hath given me in this *place* [*in Egypt*]. **And he** [*Jacob*] **said, Bring them**, I pray thee, **unto me** [*in other words, bring them closer*], **and I will bless them**.

10 Now **the eyes of Israel were dim for** [*because of*] **age, so that** he could not see. And he [*Joseph*] brought them near unto him; and he [*Jacob*] kissed them, and embraced them.

JST Genesis 48:16

16 Now the eyes of Israel were dim for age, so that **he could not see well**. And he brought them near unto him; and he kissed them, and embraced them.

11 And Israel said unto Joseph, **I had not thought to see thy face: and, lo, God hath shewed me also thy seed** [*in other words, I did not think I would ever see you again, and now I have not only seen you but also your children*].

12 And **Joseph brought them out from between his knees** [*the NIV version of the Bible says, in effect, that Joseph took them down off Grandpa Jacob's knees*], and he [*Joseph*] bowed himself with his face to the earth [*with his face pointing down toward the ground*].

> Next, we will see the Lord intervene to make sure that the correct son receives the birthright blessing.

13 And **Joseph took** them both, **Ephraim in his right hand toward Israel's left hand**, and **Manasseh in his left hand toward Israel's right hand**, and brought *them* near unto him.

14 And **Israel stretched out his right hand, and laid** *it* **upon Ephraim's head**, who *was* the younger, **and his left hand upon Manasseh's head, guiding his hands wittingly** [*knowingly*]; for [*NIV, "even though"*] Manasseh *was* the firstborn [*and thus would normally have received the birthright blessing*].

> Note that both sons will receive the blessings of Abraham and Isaac in verse 16, which are the blessings of exaltation, contingent upon their remaining worthy. These blessings include the responsibility to take the gospel and priesthood blessings to all the world.
>
> Such is the case with all who receive patriarchal blessings today. They are blessed with the blessings of Abraham, Isaac, and Jacob, which are the blessings of exaltation, provided that they live worthy of them. Thus, they are assured that they have the basic capability of attaining all the blessings that the Father has attained. They are likewise blessed with the responsibility to take the gospel and the blessings of the priesthood to all within their sphere of influence.

15 ¶ **And he blessed Joseph**, and said, God, before whom my fathers Abraham and Isaac did walk, the God which fed me all my life long unto this day.

16 The Angel which redeemed me from all evil, **bless the lads; and let my name be named on them, and the name of my fathers Abraham and Isaac; and let them grow into a multitude in the midst of the earth**.

17 And **when Joseph saw that his father laid his right hand upon the head of Ephraim, it displeased him**: and he held up his father's hand, to remove it from Ephraim's head unto Manasseh's head.

18 And **Joseph said unto his father, Not so, my father: for this** *is* **the firstborn; put thy right hand upon his head.**

19 And **his father refused**, and said, I know *it,* my son, I know *it:* he [*Manasseh*] **also shall become a people**, and he also shall be great: **but truly his younger brother** [*Ephraim*] **shall be greater than he** [*will have more posterity than he*], and his seed [*descendants*] shall become a multitude of nations.

> In verse 20, next, Moses reviews for us what has just taken place.

20 **And he** [*Jacob*] **blessed them that day, saying**, In thee shall Israel bless, saying, [*throughout the ages, fathers in Israel will bless their posterity, saying*], God make thee as Ephraim and as Manasseh: and he set Ephraim before Manasseh [*he gave Ephraim the birthright blessing and indicated that Ephraim would be even more prominent than Manasseh*].

> Indeed, Ephraim has been given the leading role in the last days of gathering the rest of Israel and taking the gospel to all the world.

> According to verse 21, next, Jacob knows he is about to die.

21 And **Israel said unto Joseph, Behold, I die**: but God shall be with you, and bring you again unto the land of your fathers.

22 **Moreover** [*in addition*] **I have given to thee one portion above thy brethren** [*I have given you a double inheritance, through adopting your sons—see verse 5, above*], which I took out of the hand of the Amorite with my sword and with my bow.

Joseph Fielding Smith explained much of what took place in the above verses. He said:

"Joseph, son of Jacob, because of his faithfulness and integrity to the purposes of the Lord, was rewarded with the birthright in Israel. It was the custom in early times to bestow upon the firstborn son special privileges and blessings, and these were looked upon as belonging to him by right of birth. Reuben, the first of Jacob's sons, lost the birthright through transgression, and it was bestowed upon Joseph, who was the most worthy of all the sons of Jacob [1 Chronicles 5:1–2].

"When Jacob blessed Joseph, he gave him a double portion, or an inheritance among his brethren in Palestine and also the blessing of the land of Zion—'the utmost bound of the everlasting hills.' He also blessed him with the blessings of heaven above, of the deep which lieth under, and of posterity [*Genesis 49:22–26*]. **Jacob also blessed the two sons of Joseph with the blessings of their father, which they inherited, and he placed Ephraim, the younger, before Manasseh, the elder, and by inspiration of the Lord conferred upon Ephraim the birthright in Israel**" (Smith, *Doctrines of Salvation*, Vol. 3, pages 250–51).

GENESIS 49

In this chapter, Jacob gives each of his twelve sons a father's blessing. Each blessing contains prophecy about that son and his descendants. The blessings given to Judah and Joseph stand out from the rest and are considerably longer than the others. It appears from verse 33 that Jacob gave these blessings during the final hours of his life.

Among other things, Jacob identified some character traits of each son and the direction these would take them in their lives. Thus, the blessings contain warnings for some of them.

As we proceed, we will use underlined bold (**bold**) to identify each of Jacob's twelve sons.

1 And **Jacob called unto his sons, and said, Gather yourselves together, that I may tell you** *that* **which shall befall you in the last days**.

2 Gather yourselves together, and hear, ye sons of Jacob; and hearken unto Israel your father.

3 ¶ **Reuben**, thou *art* my firstborn, my might, and the beginning of my strength [*the beginning of my posterity*], the excellency of dignity, and the excellency of power:

> The incident referred to in verse 4, next, is described in Genesis 35:22. Reuben committed adultery with his father's wife, Bilhah.

4 Unstable as water, thou shalt not excel; because thou wentest up to thy father's bed; then defiledst thou *it:* he went up to my couch.

5 ¶ **Simeon** and **Levi** *are* brethren; instruments of cruelty *are in* their habitations.

> These two sons caused much grief for Jacob. One such incident is described in Genesis 34:25–26.

Their sister, Dinah, had been taken by force and robbed of her chastity by a man from a certain city. Simeon and Levi helped talk the men of that city into being circumcised in order to make peace. The men agreed to do it. When they were incapacitated because of the surgery, Simeon and Levi killed them all. Of them, Jacob said, "Ye have troubled me to make me to stink among the inhabitants of the land" (Genesis 34:30). In other words, they had brought dishonor to their father.

6 O my soul, come not thou into their secret; unto their assembly, mine honour, be not thou united: for in their anger they slew a man, and in their selfwill they digged down a wall.

7 Cursed *be* their anger, for *it was* fierce; and their wrath, for it was cruel: I will divide them in Jacob, and scatter them in Israel.

> Judah, the fourth son of Jacob and Leah, is next to be blessed. The Savior will come through his lineage. Among other things, this is prophesied in verse 10 by the phrases, "the sceptre shall not depart from Judah," and "until Shiloh (Christ) come." The "sceptre" is also symbolic of many kings who came from the tribe of Judah.

> Verse 8, next, foreshadows the fact that the Jews will become a mighty military power in the last days and will "be in the neck of [*her*] enemies."

8 ¶ **Judah**, thou *art he* whom thy brethren shall praise: thy hand *shall be* in the neck of thine enemies; thy

father's children shall bow down before thee.

9 Judah *is* a lion's whelp: from the prey, my son, thou art gone up: he stooped down, he couched as a lion, and as an old lion; who shall rouse him up?

10 The sceptre shall not depart from Judah, nor a lawgiver from between his feet, until Shiloh come; and unto him *shall* the gathering of the people *be*.

11 Binding his foal unto the vine, and his ass's colt unto the choice vine; he washed his garments in wine, and his clothes in the blood of grapes:

12 His eyes *shall be* red with wine, and his teeth white with milk.

> Elder Ezra Taft Benson spoke of the blessing given to Judah. He said:
>
> "The great blessing to Judah is that it contemplated the coming of Shiloh who would gather his people to him. This prophecy concerning Shiloh has been subject to several rabbinic and Christian interpretations and the object of considerable controversy. The interpretation given this passage by the Mormon Church is one based on revelation to modern prophets, not on scholarly commentary. It was revealed to Joseph Smith that Shiloh is the Messiah. (See Gen. 50:24, JST)" ("A Message to Judah from Joseph," *Ensign*, December 1976, page 71).

13 ¶ **Zebulun** shall dwell at the haven of the sea; and he *shall be* for an haven of ships; and his border *shall be* unto Zidon.

14 ¶ **Issachar** *is* a strong ass couching down between two burdens:

15 And he saw that rest *was* good, and the land that *it was* pleasant; and bowed his shoulder to bear, and became a servant unto tribute.

16 ¶ **Dan** shall judge his people, as one of the tribes of Israel.

17 Dan shall be a serpent by the way, an adder in the path, that biteth the horse heels, so that his rider shall fall backward.

18 I have waited for thy salvation, O Lord.

19 ¶ **Gad**, a troop shall overcome him: but he shall overcome at the last.

20 ¶ Out of **Asher** his bread *shall be* fat, and he shall yield royal dainties.

21 ¶ **Naphtali** *is* a hind [*a deer, specifically, a doe*] let loose: he giveth goodly words.

22 ¶ **Joseph** *is* a fruitful bough [*will have a large posterity*], *even* a fruitful bough by a well; *whose* branches run over the wall [*Joseph's posterity will come over the ocean; this prophecy was fulfilled, at least in part, by the coming of Lehi and his people to America—see 3 Nephi 15:12*]:

23 The archers have sorely grieved him, and shot *at him,* and hated him:

24 But his bow abode in strength, and the arms [*arm is symbolic of power in Biblical symbolism*] of his hands were made strong by the hands of the mighty *God* of Jacob [*Jehovah, Christ*]; (from thence *is* the shepherd [*Jehovah, Christ*], the stone of Israel [*Jehovah, Christ*]:)

25 *Even* by the God of thy father, who shall help thee; and by the Almighty, who shall bless thee with blessings of heaven above, blessings of the deep that lieth under, blessings of the breasts, and of the womb:

26 The blessings of thy father have prevailed above the blessings of my progenitors [*Joseph is promised blessings even greater than his ancestors*] unto the utmost bound of the everlasting hills [*his posterity will reach to the Rocky Mountains*]: they shall be on the head of Joseph, and on the crown of the head of him that was separate from his brethren.

27 ¶ **Benjamin** shall ravin *as* a wolf [*will be a ravenous wolf*]: in the morning he shall devour the prey, and at night he shall divide the spoil.

28 ¶ **All these** *are* **the twelve tribes of Israel**: and this *is it* that their father spake unto them, and blessed them; every one according to his blessing he blessed them.

After giving each son a prophetic blessing, Jacob now gives them specific instructions that they are to bury him in the same cave in Hebron in which his father and mother, Isaac and Rebekah, are buried, along with his first wife, Leah, and with Abraham and Sarah.

29 And **he charged them, and said unto them, I am to be gathered unto my people: bury me with my fathers in the cave that** *is* **in the field of Ephron the Hittite**,

30 In the cave that *is* in the field of Machpelah, which *is* before Mamre, in the land of Canaan, **which Abraham bought** with the field of Ephron the Hittite for a possession of a buryingplace.

31 **There they buried Abraham and Sarah** his wife; **there they buried Isaac and Rebekah** his wife; and **there I buried Leah**.

32 The purchase of the field and of the cave that *is* therein *was* from the children of Heth.

Finally, Jacob dies.

33 And **when Jacob had made an end of commanding his sons, he gathered up his feet into the bed, and yielded up the ghost**, and was gathered unto his people.

We know from modern revelation that Jacob has already become a god. In the Doctrine and Covenants we read:

Doctrine and Covenants 132:37

37 **Abraham** received concubines, and they bore him children; and it was accounted unto him for righteousness, because they were given unto him, and he abode in my law; as **Isaac** also and **Jacob** did none other things than that which they were commanded; and because they did none other things than that which they were commanded, they **have entered into their exaltation**, according to the promises, and sit upon thrones, **and are not angels but are gods**.

GENESIS 50

The book of Genesis now draws to a close. It is foundational to the understanding of the rest of the scriptures. Many terms and phrases used in other books of scripture have their origins in Genesis. Having studied it, you will now be in a much better position to understand other books in the Old Testament, as well as the New Testament, Book of Mormon, Doctrine and Covenants, and Pearl of Great Price. Not only that, but you will be better prepared to understand gospel lessons in classes and quorums, Come, Follow Me lessons, as well as the sermons and writings of the leaders of the Church.

At the conclusion of Genesis 49, Joseph's father, Jacob (Israel) passed away. In verse 1, next, Joseph gently closes his father's eyelids (as promised by the Lord in Genesis 46:4), and bids farewell to him.

1 And **Joseph fell upon his father's face**, and **wept** upon him, **and kissed him**.

2 And **Joseph commanded his servants the physicians to embalm his father**: and the physicians embalmed Israel.

> The process of embalming took forty days and was followed by thirty days of mourning for those of high rank and station in Egypt. Thus, they mourned for a total of seventy days for Jacob (see verse 3, next).

3 And **forty days** were fulfilled for him; for so are fulfilled the days of those which are **embalmed**: and **the Egyptians mourned for him threescore and ten days** [*a total of 70 days*].

> Jacob had requested that he not be buried in Egypt, but rather in the same cave as his wife, Leah, and his parents, Isaac and Rebekah, along with his grandparents, Abraham and Sarah (see Genesis 49:29–31). Therefore, Joseph now requests permission from Pharaoh to take his father and grant his request.

4 And **when the days of his mourning were past, Joseph spake unto the house of Pharaoh, saying,** If now I have found grace in your eyes, speak, I pray you, in the ears of Pharaoh, saying,

5 **My father made me swear** [*promise*], saying, Lo, I die: in my grave which I have digged for me **in the land of Canaan, there shalt thou**

bury me. Now **therefore let me go up, I pray thee, and bury my father**, and I will come again.

6 And **Pharaoh said, Go up, and bury thy father, according as he made thee swear**.

> From the size of the procession of Egyptian dignitaries described in verse 7, next, we gain an idea of the high esteem in which Joseph was held by Pharaoh.

7 ¶ And **Joseph went up** [*to Hebron, in southern Palestine today, a distance of some 200 miles*] **to bury his father**: and **with him went up all the servants of Pharaoh**, the **elders of his house** [*the leading servants and officers of Joseph's headquarters in Egypt*], and all the elders [*the statesman and leaders*] of the land of Egypt,

8 **And all the house of Joseph, and his brethren, and his father's house**: only their little ones, and their flocks, and their herds, they left in the land of Goshen [*in the Nile River Delta*].

9 And there went up with him both **chariots** and **horsemen**: and **it was a very great company**.

10 And **they came to the threshing floor of Atad**, which *is* beyond Jordan [*near the Jordan River*], and **there they mourned** with a great and very sore lamentation: and he made a mourning **for his father seven days**.

11 **And when the** inhabitants of the land, the **Canaanites, saw the mourning** in the floor of Atad, **they said, This** *is* **a grievous mourning to the Egyptians** [*some important person has died among the Egyptians*]: wherefore the name of it was called Abel-mizraim, which *is* beyond Jordan.

12 And his [*Jacob's*] sons did unto him according as he commanded them:

13 For **his sons carried him into the land of Canaan, and buried him in the cave of the field of Machpelah** [*where Leah, Isaac, Rebekah, Abraham, and Sarah were buried*], which Abraham bought with the field for a possession of a buryingplace of Ephron the Hittite, before Mamre.

14 ¶ And **Joseph returned into Egypt, he, and his brethren, and all that went up with him to bury his father**, after he had buried his father.

> Now that their father has died, Joseph's brothers fear that Joseph will get revenge for all the evil things they did to him. They forget that Joseph is Christlike in his mercy and desire to forgive them. This is another sense in which Joseph is a "type" of Christ.
>
> Also, as you will see, the brothers themselves have changed much, repenting of former wickedness and humbly asking for forgiveness.

15 ¶ And **when Joseph's brethren saw that their father was dead, they said, Joseph will peradventure** [*perhaps*] **hate us, and will certainly requite us** [*get even with*

us for] **all the evil which we did unto him**.

16 **And they sent a messenger unto Joseph, saying, Thy father did command before he died, saying,**

17 So shall ye **say unto Joseph, Forgive, I pray thee now, the trespass of thy brethren, and their sin**; for they did unto thee evil: and now, **we pray thee, forgive the trespass of the servants of the God of thy father** [*in other words, please forgive us*]. **And Joseph wept when they spake unto him**.

18 And his brethren also went and fell down before his face; and they said, Behold, we *be* thy servants.

Next, Joseph gently scolds them for bowing down to him (verse 18, above) and reminds them that he is not God. Then, he puts their minds at ease, much the same as the Savior does time and again as He speaks to His righteous followers who still worry about their sins even though they have repented.

19 And **Joseph said unto them, Fear not**: for *am* I in the place of God [*do you think I am God*]?

20 **But as for you, ye thought evil against me**; *but* **God meant it unto good, to bring to pass, as** *it is* **this day, to save much people alive**.

21 Now therefore **fear ye not**: I will nourish you, and your little ones. And **he comforted them, and spake kindly unto them**.

Next, we learn that Joseph lived to be 110 years old. As he is about to die, his posterity visit him and he prophesies that the children of Israel will someday be brought out of Egypt and be given the land of Canaan (basically the Holy Land, today), as promised by the Lord.

22 ¶ And Joseph dwelt in Egypt, he, and his father's house: and **Joseph lived an hundred and ten years**.

23 And **Joseph saw Ephraim's children of the third** *generation:* **the children also of Machir the son of Manasseh were brought up upon Joseph's knees**.

24 And **Joseph said** unto his brethren, **I die**: and **God will surely visit** [*bless*] **you, and bring you out of this land unto the land which he sware** [*promised*] **to Abraham, to Isaac, and to Jacob**.

The JST adds much to the Genesis account, beginning with verse 24, above. It adds 11 new verses between Genesis verses 24 and 25, adding considerably to Genesis verses 24, 25, and 26. We will include these additions here. As you study these verses, you will see much prophecy, and be reminded that Joseph in Egypt was indeed a great prophet of God.

JST Genesis 50:24–35

24 And Joseph said unto his brethren, I die, and go unto my fathers; and I go down to my grave with joy. The God of father Jacob be with you, to deliver you out of affliction in the days of your bondage; for the Lord hath visited me, and I have

obtained a promise of the Lord, that out of the fruit of my loins, the Lord God will raise up a righteous branch out of my loins; and unto thee, whom my father Jacob hath named Israel, a prophet; (not the Messiah who is called Shilo;) and this prophet [*Moses*] shall deliver my people out of Egypt in the days of thy bondage.

25 And it shall come to pass that they shall be scattered again; and a branch shall be broken off, and shall be carried into a far country; nevertheless they shall be remembered in the covenants of the Lord, when the Messiah cometh; for he shall be made manifest unto them in the latter days, in the Spirit of power; and shall bring them out of darkness into light; out of hidden darkness, and out of captivity unto freedom.

26 A seer shall the Lord my God raise up, who shall be a choice seer unto the fruit of my loins.

27 Thus saith the Lord God of my fathers unto me, A choice seer [*Joseph Smith*] will I raise up out of the fruit of thy loins, and he shall be esteemed highly among the fruit of thy loins; and unto him will I give commandment that he shall do a work for the fruit of thy loins, his brethren.

28 And he shall bring them to the knowledge of the covenants which I have made with thy fathers [*the ancestors of Joseph in Egypt, including Abraham, Isaac, and Jacob*]; and he [*Joseph Smith*] shall do whatsoever work I shall command him.

29 And I will make him [*Joseph Smith*] great in mine eyes, for he shall do my work; and he shall be great like unto him [*Moses*] whom I have said I would raise up unto you, to deliver my people, O house of Israel, out of the land of Egypt; for a seer [*Moses*] will I raise up to deliver my people out of the land of Egypt; and he shall be called Moses. And by this name he shall know that he is of thy house; for he shall be nursed by the king's daughter, and shall be called her son.

30 And again, a seer [*Joseph Smith*] will I raise up out of the fruit of thy loins [*Joseph Smith will be a descendant of Joseph in Egypt*], and unto him will I give power to bring forth my word unto the seed of thy loins; and not to the bringing forth of my word only, saith the Lord, but to the convincing them of my word [*the Bible*], which shall have already gone forth among them in the last days;

31 Wherefore the fruit of thy loins shall write [*the Book of Mormon*], and the fruit of the loins of Judah shall write [*the Bible*]; and that which shall be written by the fruit of thy loins, and also that which shall be written by the fruit of the loins of Judah [*the Book of Mormon and the Bible*], shall grow together unto the confounding of false doctrines, and laying down of contentions, and establishing peace among the fruit of thy loins, and bringing them to a knowledge of their fathers in the latter days; and

also to the knowledge of my covenants, saith the Lord.

32 And out of weakness shall he [*Joseph Smith*] be made strong, in that day when my work shall go forth among all my people, which shall restore them, who are of the house of Israel, in the last days.

33 And that seer [*Joseph Smith Jr.*] will I bless, and they that seek to destroy him shall be confounded [*those who seek to destroy his work will not succeed*]; for this promise I give unto you; for I will remember you from generation to generation; and his name shall be called Joseph [*Joseph Smith Jr.*], and it shall be after the name of his father [*his father will also be named Joseph*]; and he shall be like unto you [*Joseph in Egypt*]; for the thing which the Lord shall bring forth by his hand shall bring my people unto salvation.

34 And the Lord sware unto [*covenanted with*] Joseph that he would preserve his seed for ever, saying, I will raise up Moses, and a rod shall be in his hand, and he shall gather together my people, and he shall lead them as a flock, and he shall smite the waters of the Red Sea with his rod.

35 And he shall have judgment, and shall write the word of the Lord [*Genesis, Exodus, Leviticus, Numbers, Deuteronomy*]. And he shall not speak many words, for I will write unto him my law by the finger of mine own hand [*the Ten Commandments tablets*]. And I will make a spokesman for him, and his name shall be called Aaron.

We will now return to the Genesis version of chapter 50, as of verse 25, next. We will also provide the JST changes for verses 25 and 26.

25 And Joseph took an oath of the children of Israel, saying, God will surely visit you [*you will someday be brought out of Egypt by the Lord*], and ye shall carry up my bones from hence.

JST Genesis 50:37

37 And Joseph confirmed many other things unto his brethren, and took an oath of the children of Israel, saying unto them, God will surely visit you, and ye shall carry up my bones from hence [*and when you leave, take my remains with you*].

26 **So Joseph died**, *being* **an hundred and ten years old**: and **they embalmed him, and he was put in a coffin in Egypt.**

JST Genesis 50:38

38 So Joseph died when he was an hundred and ten years old; and they embalmed him, and they put him in a coffin in Egypt; and he was kept from burial by the children of Israel, that he might be carried up and laid in the sepulchre with his father. And thus they remembered the oath which they sware unto him.

Exodus

As noted in the full title of Exodus (the second book of Moses called Exodus), as given in the King James Version of the Bible (the version we use in the English-speaking areas of the Church), Moses is the writer of Exodus. In fact, Moses wrote the first five books of the Old Testament—Genesis, Exodus, Leviticus, Numbers, and Deuteronomy.

In the book of Exodus, we are introduced to Moses and his ministry, which continues through Deuteronomy. He was the great "law giver," and the "law of Moses" is referred to time and time again in the scriptures, including the Book of Mormon. As you will see, much of Old Testament ritual and practice, given by the Lord through His prophet Moses was designed to point the minds of the Old Testament people toward Christ and His mission and atoning sacrifice for us. We will point this out many times as we go along, especially when we get to Leviticus 14:1–20.

Moses was born somewhere around 1500 BC (the few chronologies we have vary considerably, so we can't be exact on this). He lived on earth for 120 years and then was translated (see Bible Dictionary under "Moses"); in other words, he was taken up into heaven without dying. He was resurrected at the time of Christ's resurrection (see Doctrine and Covenants 133:54–55).

His life can be divided into three periods of forty years each

1. Forty years as a prince in Egypt.
2. Forty years as a shepherd.
3. Forty years as a prophet, leading the children of Israel from Egyptian bondage.

Moses's First Forty Years

According to the respected Jewish historian Flavius Josephus, who lived around the time of Christ, Moses was a handsome and prominent prince in Egypt during the first forty years of his life. He had an excellent education and was a highly successful military leader for the Egyptians during this period of time (see Josephus, *Antiquities of the Jews*, Book 2, chapter 9, paragraph 7; chapter 10, paragraphs 1–2).

In the New Testament, Stephen teaches us that Moses was "learned in all the wisdom of the Egyptians, and was mighty in words and in deeds" during this first forty years of his life (see Acts 7:22–23).

Moses's Second Forty Years

At the age of forty, Moses defended a Hebrew slave, and in the process, killed an Egyptian taskmaster (Exodus 2:11–12, Acts 7:24). As a result, he was forced to flee from Egypt and came to the land of Midian, where he met and married a daughter of Jethro (Reuel), who was the priest of Midian (see Exodus 2:15–21, 3:1). He lived the quiet life of a shepherd for the next forty years.

Moses's Third Forty Years

At age eighty, Moses was called by the Lord (at the burning bush; see Exodus 3:2) to serve as a prophet. Thus, during the next forty years of his life, he served as the prophet of God who led the children of Israel out of Egyptian slavery and worked to prepare them for entrance into the promised land. We will learn much detail about this forty-year period as we study Exodus, Leviticus, Numbers, and Deuteronomy. At the end of this forty years, Moses was 120 years old and was translated (see Bible Dictionary, under "Moses").

As a translated being, he ministered to the Savior on the Mount of Transfiguration some months before the Lord's crucifixion (see Matthew 17:1–3). As mentioned above, he was resurrected at the time of the Savior's resurrection (see Doctrine and Covenants 133:54–55).

On April 3, 1836, the resurrected Moses appeared to Joseph Smith and Oliver Cowdery in the Kirtland Temple and conferred upon them "the keys of the gathering of Israel . . . and the leading of the ten tribes from the land of the north" (Doctrine and Covenants 110:11).

Moses was considered by the Jews to be one of the greatest prophets to have ever lived. And indeed, he was. His ministry was prophesied by, among others, Joseph who was sold into Egypt, as recorded in the JST, Genesis 50, as follows (**bold** added for emphasis):

JST Genesis 50:24, 29, 34–35

24 And **Joseph** [*who was sold into Egypt*] **said unto his brethren**, I die, and go unto my fathers; and I go down to my grave with joy. The God of father Jacob be with you, to deliver you out of affliction in the days of your bondage; for the Lord hath visited me, and I have obtained a promise of the Lord, that out of the fruit of my loins, **the Lord God will raise up** a righteous branch out of my loins; and unto thee, whom my father Jacob hath named Israel, **a prophet**; (not the Messiah who is called Shilo;) **and this prophet** [*Moses*] **shall deliver my people out of Egypt in the days of thy bondage**.

Next, Joseph in Egypt prophesies concerning Joseph Smith, comparing him to Moses.

29 And I will make him [*Joseph Smith*] great in mine eyes, for he shall do my work; and he shall be great like unto him [*Moses*] whom I have said I would raise up unto you, to deliver my people, O house of Israel, out of the land of Egypt; for **a seer** [*Moses*] **will I raise up to deliver my people out of the land of Egypt; and he shall be called Moses**. And by this name he shall know that he is of thy house; for **he shall be nursed by the king's daughter, and shall be called her son**.

34 And **the Lord sware unto** [*covenanted with*] **Joseph** that he would preserve his seed for ever, saying, **I will raise up Moses**, and a rod shall be in his hand, **and he shall gather together my people** [*the children of Israel*], **and he shall lead them as a flock, and he shall smite the waters of the Red Sea with his rod.**

35 And **he shall** have judgment, and shall **write the word of the Lord** [*Genesis, Exodus, Leviticus, Numbers, Deuteronomy*]. And he shall not speak many words, for I will write unto him my law by the finger of mine own hand [*the Ten Commandments tablets*]. **And I will**

make a spokesman for him, and his name shall be called Aaron.**

We will now learn of Moses's birth and ministry, as we study selections from Exodus, Leviticus, Numbers and Deuteronomy.

EXODUS 1

To better understand the setting for this first chapter of Exodus, let's take a brief look in the Old Testament at the background leading up to it. Genesis is the first of the five books written by Moses. It covers the Creation and the approximately 2000 years from the Fall of Adam and Eve to the death of Joseph who was sold into Egypt (see Genesis 50:26).

In Genesis, Moses taught us that God created the earth, that Adam and Eve were placed in the Garden of Eden, partook of the forbidden fruit and became mortal (which was good), that Satan began promoting his evil work among the descendants of Adam and Eve, that Enoch preached, Noah preached, the Flood came, evil men built the Tower of Babel after the Flood, the Lord restored the gospel through Abraham and established the Abrahamic Covenant, and that Isaac continued the covenant, as did Jacob, who had twelve sons.

As Genesis continues, Moses records that several of Jacob's sons sold their younger brother, Joseph, into slavery when he was seventeen years old. He was taken to Egypt and sold as a slave there but was blessed by the Lord to eventually become second in command to the pharaoh. He prepared the Egyptians for a severe famine that had been prophesied, gathering grain and supplies during seven years of plenty. When the famine came to Egypt, it also plagued the area where Joseph's father and brothers lived in the southwestern part of Palestine. Thus, Joseph's brothers were forced to travel to Egypt to obtain provisions to sustain their lives and the lives of their families. Eventually, they (a total of seventy individuals) moved to Egypt, where they were welcomed by the pharaoh and Joseph and were given land on which to settle. Over the years, these Israelites multiplied and flourished as a separate people in Egypt. We know them as the children of Israel, or the descendants of Jacob and his twelve sons.

Elder Mark E. Petersen informs us that it was about 430 years from the time that Joseph's father ("Israel," or "Jacob") and brothers moved their families to Egypt to the time when Moses led their descendants out of Egypt. He said (**bold** added for emphasis):

"The fulfillment of God's promises to Abraham required that Israel should become numerous. To accomplish this, the little family, numbering only 70 persons (Genesis 46:26–27), needed sufficient time and a peaceful place in which to grow. Egypt was that place. . . .

"Palestine was a battleground for warring nations that moved back and forth in their conquests between the Nile and the Euphrates. Israel would have found no peace there. They required stable conditions for their eventual growth and development. . . .

"**At the end of 430 years**, the Lord now decreed that the time had arrived for Israel to occupy her own land and there become that 'peculiar people' who would await the coming of their

Messiah" (Petersen, Moses, pages 27–30).

As Moses picks up the history at the beginning of Exodus, chapter 1, he informs us that the Egyptians eventually came to fear the children of Israel because of their rapid growth and, as a result, placed them in bondage, making them serve them as slaves. By the time Moses comes on the scene, it is likely that the Israelites have been slaves for two to three hundred years.

In chapter 1, Moses begins with a brief review of the names of the twelve sons of Jacob (whose name was changed to Israel—Genesis 32:28) and reminds us how these direct descendants of Abraham, Isaac, and Jacob came to be in Egypt in the first place.

As we proceed now with our study of Exodus, we will routinely use **bold** to emphasize and point things out. You may wish to underline or otherwise mark some of these **bolded** items in your own scriptures. You might also consider writing some of the brief notes in your own scriptures that we add within and between the verses in this study guide.

1 *Now* **these** *are* **the names of the children of Israel** [*the twelve sons of Jacob*], **which came into Egypt**; every man and his household [*his family, servants, and so forth*] came **with Jacob**.

2 **Reuben, Simeon, Levi,** and **Judah,**

3 **Issachar, Zebulun,** and **Benjamin,**

4 **Dan,** and **Naphtali, Gad,** and **Asher.**

5 And all the souls that came out of the loins of Jacob [*Jacob's descendants*] were **seventy souls**: for **Joseph was in Egypt** *already*.

You may wonder whether Jacob had any daughters since none is mentioned above. He did. The only one whose name we know was Dinah (Genesis 34:1). However, we know that he had daughters (plural) because they are referred to in Genesis 46:6–7.

Next, in verse 6, Moses covers more than one hundred years by simply telling us that Joseph and his brothers passed away.

6 And Joseph died, and all his brethren, and all that generation.

Just a brief study note: The backward "P" at the beginning of verse 7, next, informs us that a new topic or paragraph is now being addressed. This symbol is used throughout the King James Version of the Bible. Each time you see it, you will know that there is a change of topic.

In this case the new topic is the fact that the Israelites had large families and thus multiplied rapidly in Egypt.

7 ¶ And **the children of Israel were fruitful, and increased abundantly**, and multiplied, and waxed [*grew*] exceeding mighty; and **the land was filled with them**.

Did you notice how many times Moses said, in one way or another, that the population of the children of Israel grew rapidly in verse 7, above? We count at least five. We will repeat verse 7 here and underline each of these repetitions:

Verse 7, repeated

And the children of Israel were fruitful, and increased abundantly, and multiplied, and waxed [*grew*] exceeding mighty; and the land was filled with them.

The reason we point this out is that this type of repetition for emphasis is common in Old Testament times. It will be very helpful for you to know this, for example, when it comes to studying the writings and teachings of Isaiah. Otherwise, you might conclude that Isaiah is saying many different things in a particular passage when in reality he is simply repeating the same thing in different ways for emphasis.

An example of this is found in Isaiah 34:11–15, where he employs many different images, including owls and lonely beasts of the desert, to say over and over that there will be no wicked left on earth after the Second Coming.

Moving on, beginning with verse 8, next, we see that eventually a new pharaoh came to power in Egypt who did not have the love and respect for Joseph and his people, the Israelites, which the old king had shown. This new king feared the rapid growth of the children of Israel and determined to do something about it.

Some Bible scholars point out that the pharaoh who was in power at the time that Joseph was sold as a slave in Egypt, as well as later when his father and brothers moved to Egypt, may not have been Egyptian. Thus, the new king, referred to in verse 8, may well have been an Egyptian who came into power after the overthrow of the previous ruling party. We will quote from the *Old Testament Student Manual* for a bit more on this possibility.

"Many scholars speculate that Joseph came to power in Egypt while the nation was under the domination of the Hyksos people. The ancient historian Manetho called the Hyksos the shepherd-kings and told how their conquest and dominion were bitterly hated by the Egyptians. The Hyksos were Semitic peoples from the lands north and east of Egypt. Since Jacob and his family were also Semitic, it is easy to understand how Joseph would be viewed with favor by the Hyksos and also how, when the Hyksos were finally overthrown and driven out of Egypt, the Israelites would suddenly fall from favor with the native Egyptians.

"Many people have wondered how Joseph could be vice-regent [*in Egypt*] for so many years without having his name in any of the records or monuments of Egypt. If the theory of Hyksos domination is correct, then Joseph's name would have been purged from records and monuments along with those of the other Hyksos rulers. Nevertheless, one scholar claimed that he found the Egyptian name Yufni, which would be the equivalent in Egyptian of the Hebrew Yosef (see Donovan Courville, 'My Search for Joseph,' *Signs of the Times*, October 1977, pp. 5–8). While the evidence is not positively conclusive, at least it can be said that there may be extra-biblical evidence [*evidence outside* of the Bible] of Joseph's existence" (Old Testament Student Manual: Genesis–2 Samuel, p. 103).

You can also read more about these Hyksos, or shepherd kings, in our Bible Dictionary, under "Egypt." We will now continue with the story as told by Moses.

8 Now **there arose up a new king over Egypt, which knew not Joseph.**

9 And **he said** unto his people, Behold, **the people of the children of Israel** are **more and mightier than we:**

> As you can see, in verse 10, next, one of the main fears of the Egyptians was that, in the event of war, the Israelites might join with the enemies of Egypt and help overpower Egypt.

10 Come on, **let us deal wisely with them**; **lest** they multiply, and it come to pass, that, when there falleth out any war [*if we go to war against outside enemies*], **they join also unto our enemies**, and fight against us, and *so* get them up out of the land.

> As a result of this concern, the Egyptians put the Israelites in bondage. While in slavery, the children of Israel built a number of treasure cities for Pharaoh.

11 **Therefore they did set over them taskmasters to afflict them with their burdens.** And **they built** for Pharaoh **treasure cities**, Pithom and Raamses.

> This plan to curtail the growth of the Israelites didn't work.

12 But **the more they afflicted them, the more they multiplied** and grew. And they [*the Egyptians*] were grieved [*were worried, apprehensive*] because of the children of Israel.

13 And the Egyptians made the children of Israel to serve with rigour [*they put heavier burdens upon them*]:

14 And **they made their lives bitter with hard bondage**, in morter, and in brick, and in all manner of service in the field: all their service, wherein **they made them serve**, *was* **with rigour**.

> Because their plan to curtail growth among the Israelites with brutal work did not work, the Pharaoh ordered the Israelite midwives to kill baby Israelite boys as they were born.

> Remember that the Israelites were also commonly referred to as Hebrews, as seen in verse 15, next.

15 ¶ And **the king of Egypt spake to the Hebrew midwives**, of which the name of the one *was* Shiphrah, and the name of the other Puah:

16 **And he said, When ye do the office of a** [*when you serve as a*] **midwife to the Hebrew women**, and see *them* upon the stools [*upon special structures for birthing*]; **if it** *be* **a son, then ye shall kill him**: but if it *be* a daughter, then she shall live.

17 **But the midwives feared God, and did not as the king of Egypt commanded them, but saved the men children alive.**

18 And **the king of Egypt called for the midwives, and said** unto them, **Why have ye done this thing**, and have saved the men children alive?

19 And **the midwives said** unto Pharaoh, **Because the Hebrew women** *are* not as the Egyptian women; for they *are* lively, and **are delivered ere the midwives come in unto them**. [*In other words, the Hebrew women are so robust that they have their babies before we get there.*]

> As a result, the rapid growth among the Israelites continued unchecked. Moses is setting the stage and emotional climate for us in preparation for telling us about his own birth and preservation from death as a male Israelite baby (in the first verses of chapter 2).

20 Therefore God dealt well with [*blessed*] the midwives: and the people multiplied, and waxed [*grew*] very mighty.

21 And it came to pass, because the midwives feared [*respected and honored*] God, that he made them houses [*blessed them with families of their own—see footnote 21b in your Bible*].

> The environment of fear and worry for expectant Israelite parents was greatly increased by Pharaoh's next edict, as explained in verse 22.

22 And **Pharaoh charged** [*commanded*] **all his people**, saying, **Every son that is born** [*to the Israelites*] **ye shall cast into the river**, and every daughter ye shall save alive.

EXODUS 2

In this chapter, Moses is born. He was a pure descendant of Levi, one of the original twelve sons of Jacob (see Exodus 1:2). One of the reasons we emphasize this genealogy is that it was the men of the tribe of Levi who administered the rites and rituals of the Levitical or Aaronic Priesthood among the Israelites from the time they wandered in the wilderness to the time of John the Baptist.

Moses's father, Amram, was a grandson of Levi. Thus, Moses was a great-grandson of Levi. Moses's mother was Jochebed, also a direct descendant of Levi (see Exodus 6:16–20).

It is interesting to note that Levi lived 137 years (see Exodus 6:16); his son, Kohath, lived 133 years (Exodus 6:18); and his son, Amram (Moses's father), lived 137 years (see Exodus 6:20). Thus, the lives of these three men spanned 407 years.

Moses had an older sister, Miriam (who will keep watch over the tiny ark in which Moses is placed in the bulrushes), and an older brother, Aaron.

As we proceed now with this chapter, Moses is born. Remember that his birth and mission had been previously prophesied by Joseph in Egypt (see JST Genesis 50:24, 29, 34–35, as quoted in the introduction to Exodus in this study guide). Moses was one of the "noble and great" spirits spoken of in Abraham 3:22. Imagine how he felt as his time came to bid farewell to his premortal associates and pass through the veil of forgetfulness into mortality!

1 And **there went a man** [*Amram, Moses's father*] **of the house of Levi**

[*a direct descendant of Levi*], **and took** *to wife* **a daughter of Levi** [*Jochebed*].

2 And **the woman conceived, and bare a son** [*Moses*]: and when she saw him that he *was a* goodly *child,* **she hid him three months.**

> This must have been a very tense and difficult three months for Moses's parents, knowing that Egyptian spies on every side were on the lookout for newborn Israelite baby boys.

3 And **when she could not longer hide him, she took for him an ark of bulrushes** [*a papyrus basket made of reeds*], and daubed it with slime [*tar*] and with pitch [*to make it watertight*], and **put the child therein**; **and** she **laid** *it* **in the flags** [*bulrushes, reeds*] **by the river's brink** [*edge*].

4 **And his sister** [*Miriam*] **stood afar off, to wit what would be done to him** [*to see what would happen to him*].

> We see the hand of the Lord in what happens next.

5 ¶ And **the daughter of Pharaoh came down to wash** *herself* **at the river**; and her maidens walked along by the river's side; **and when she saw the ark among the flags, she sent her maid to fetch it.**

6 And **when she had opened** *it*, **she saw the child: and, behold, the babe wept. And she had compassion on him**, and said, **This** *is one* **of the Hebrews' children.**

What happens next is truly miraculous. Miriam comes out of hiding and addresses Pharaoh's daughter. Within a brief period of time, Moses's mother, Jochebed has been summoned, and a deal is struck for her to nurse the infant Moses and to be paid wages while raising him for Pharaoh's daughter.

Thus, in one quick turn of events, inspired by heaven, Moses will be raised by his own mother and father, under the protection of Pharaoh's daughter. He will no doubt be taught the gospel by his righteous parents, including the prophecies that the children of Israel will someday be led out of Egyptian captivity. By the time he is turned over to Pharaoh's daughter to live as her son, in the king's court and be taught the ways of the Egyptians, he will have a firm foundation in the true gospel and the Abrahamic covenant. Among other things, it is highly likely that he will quietly understand that he is the one who will someday be called by God to lead his people out of Egypt. We suspect this to be the case because of the teachings of Stephen in Acts 7. We will quote Stephen's words here, as he tells of Moses, at age forty, slaying an Egyptian taskmaster to protect a Hebrew slave, and the surprisingly negative reaction of some Israelites to the incident:

Acts 7:25

25 For he [*Moses*] supposed his brethren would have understood how that God by his hand would deliver them: but they understood not.

We will continue now with the narrative as given by Moses.

7 Then said his sister [*Miriam*] **to Pharaoh's daughter, Shall I go and call to thee a nurse of the Hebrew women, that she may nurse the child for thee?**

8 And Pharaoh's daughter said to her, **Go. And the maid went and called the child's mother.**

9 And **Pharaoh's daughter said unto her, Take this child away, and nurse it for me, and I will give** *thee* **thy wages.** And the woman [*Moses's mother, Jochebed*] took the child, and nursed it.

10 **And the child grew, and she brought him unto Pharaoh's daughter, and he became her son**. And **she called his name Moses** [*a direct fulfillment of prophecy; see JST Genesis 50:29*]: and she said, Because I drew him out of the water.

> We will pause here and quote from Josephus, the Jewish historian. While his writings are not in the same category as scripture, they are often interesting and helpful. In fact, they are occasionally quoted in the *Old Testament Student Manual,* published by the Church Educational System. Among other things in this passage from his writings, Josephus tells of a vision given to Moses's father, Amram. In it, Amram is told that his son (Moses), yet to be born, will lead the Israelites from Egyptian bondage. We will use bold for emphasis as we go along. Josephus wrote:
>
> "3. A man whose name was **Amram**, one of the nobler sort of the Hebrews, was afraid for his whole nation, lest it should fail, by the want of young men to be brought up hereafter, and was very uneasy at it, his wife being then with child, and he knew not what to do. Hereupon he **betook himself to prayer to God**; and entreated him to have compassion on those men who had nowise transgressed the laws of his worship, and to afford them deliverance from the miseries they at that time endured, and to render abortive their enemies' hopes of the destruction of their nation. **Accordingly God had mercy on him**, and was moved by his supplication. **He stood by him in his sleep, and exhorted him not to despair** of his future favors. He said further, that he did not forget their piety towards him, and would always reward them for it, as he had formerly granted his favor to their forefathers, and made them increase from a few to so great a multitude. He put him in mind, that when Abraham was come alone out of Mesopotamia into Canaan, he had been made happy, not only in other respects, but that when his wife was at first barren, she was afterwards by him enabled to conceive seed, and bare him sons. That he left to Ismael and to his posterity the country of Arabia; as also to his sons by Ketura, Troglodytis; and to Isaac, Canaan. That by my assistance, said he, he did great exploits in war, which, unless you be yourselves impious, you must still remember. As for Jacob, he became well known to strangers also, by the greatness of that prosperity in which he lived, and left to his sons, who came into Egypt with no more than seventy souls,

while you are now become above six hundred thousand. Know therefore that I shall provide for you all in common what is for your good, and particularly for thyself what shall make thee famous; for that child, out of dread of whose nativity the Egyptians have doomed the Israelite children to destruction, shall be **this child of thine**, and shall be concealed from those who watch to destroy him: and when he is brought up in a surprising way, he **shall deliver the Hebrew nation from the distress they are under from the Egyptians**. His memory shall be famous while the world lasts; and this not only among the Hebrews, but foreigners also:—all which shall be the effect of my favor to thee, and to thy posterity. He shall also have such a brother, that he shall himself obtain my priesthood, and his posterity shall have it after him to the end of the world.

"4. **When the vision had informed him of these things, Amram awaked and told it to Jochebed who was his wife**. And now the fear increased upon them on account of the prediction in Amram's dream; for they were under concern, not only for the child, but on account of the great happiness that was to come to him also. However, the mother's labor was such as afforded a confirmation to what was foretold by God; for it was not known to those that watched her, by the easiness of her pains, and because the throes of her delivery did not fall upon her with violence. And now they nourished the child at home privately for three months; but after that time Amram, fearing he should be discovered, and, by falling under the king's displeasure, both he and his child should perish, and so he should make the promise of God of none effect, he determined rather to trust the safety and care of the child to God, than to depend on his own concealment of him, which he looked upon as a thing uncertain, and whereby both the child, so privately to be nourished, and himself should be in imminent danger; but he believed that God would some way for certain procure the safety of the child, in order to secure the truth of his own predictions. When they had thus determined, they made an ark of bulrushes, after the manner of a cradle, and of a bigness sufficient for an infant to be laid in, without being too straitened: they then daubed it over with slime, which would naturally keep out the water from entering between the bulrushes, and put the infant into it, and setting it afloat upon the river, they left its preservation to God; so the river received the child, and carried him along. But Miriam, the child's sister, passed along upon the bank over against him, as her mother had bid her, to see whither the ark would be carried, where God demonstrated that human wisdom was nothing, but that the Supreme Being is able to do whatsoever he pleases: that those who, in order to their own security, condemn others to destruction, and use great endeavors about it, fail of their purpose; but that others are in a surprising manner preserved, and obtain a prosperous condition almost from the very midst of their calamities; those, I mean, whose dangers arise by the appointment of God. And, indeed, such a providence was exercised in the case of this child, as showed the power of God.

"5. **Thermuthis was the king's daughter. She was now diverting herself by the banks of the river; and seeing a cradle borne along by the current, she sent some that could swim, and bid them bring the cradle to her.** When those that were sent on this errand came to her with the cradle, and she saw the little child, she was greatly in love with it, on account of its largeness and beauty; for God had taken such great care in the formation of Moses, that he caused him to be thought worthy of bringing up, and providing for, by all those that had taken the most fatal resolutions, on account of the dread of his nativity, for the destruction of the rest of the Hebrew nation. Thermuthis bid them bring her a woman that might afford her breast to the child; yet would not the child admit of her breast, but turned away from it, and did the like to many other women. Now Miriam was by when this happened, not to appear to be there on purpose, but only as staying to see the child; and she said, "It is in vain that thou, O queen, callest for these women for the nourishing of the child, who are no way of kin to it; but still, if thou wilt order one of the Hebrew women to be brought, perhaps it may admit the breast of one of its own nation." Now since she seemed to speak well, Thermuthis bid her procure such a one, and to bring one of those Hebrew women that gave suck. So when she had such authority given her, she came back and brought the mother, who was known to nobody there. And now the child gladly admitted the breast, and seemed to stick close to it; and so it was, that, at the queen's desire, the nursing of the child was entirely intrusted to the mother.

"6. Hereupon it was that **Thermuthis imposed this name *Mouses* upon him, from what had happened when he was put into the river; for the Egyptians call water by the name of *Mo*, and such as are saved out of it, by the name of *Uses:* so by putting these two words together, they imposed this name upon him**. And he was, by the confession of all, according to God's prediction, as well for his greatness of mind as for his contempt of difficulties, the best of all the Hebrews, for Abraham was his ancestor of the seventh generation. For Moses was the son of Amram, who was the son of Caath, whose father Levi was the son of Jacob, who was the son of Isaac, who was the son of Abraham. Now **Moses's understanding became superior to his age, nay, far beyond that standard; and when he was taught, he discovered greater quickness of apprehension than was usual at his age**, and his actions at that time promised greater, when he should come to the age of a man. God did also give him that tallness, when he was but three years old, as was wonderful. And as for his beauty, there was nobody so unpolite as, when they saw Moses, they were not greatly surprised at the beauty of his countenance; nay, it happened frequently, that those that met him as he was carried along the road, were obliged to turn again upon seeing the child;

that they left what they were about, and stood still a great while to look on him; for the beauty of the child was so remarkable and natural to him on many accounts, that it detained the spectators, and made them stay longer to look upon him" (*Antiquities of the Jews,* Book 2, chapter 9, paragraphs 3–6).

Having included this rather lengthy but interesting quote from Josephus, we will now return to the account in Exodus. As we move on to verse 11, keep in mind that forty years have now passed since his birth. His life as a prince in Egypt is about to come to an abrupt close.

11 ¶ And it came to pass in those days, **when Moses was grown** [*when he was forty years old—see Acts 7:23*], that **he went out unto his brethren** [*the Hebrews; the children of Israel*], and looked on their burdens: **and he spied an Egyptian smiting an Hebrew**, one of his brethren.

12 And **he looked this way and that way, and when he saw that** *there was* **no man, he slew the Egyptian, and hid him in the sand.**

13 And **when he went out the second day** [*the next day*], behold, **two men of the Hebrews strove** [*fought*] together: and **he said to him that did the wrong, Wherefore smitest thou thy fellow** [*why are you hitting one of your own people*]?

The answer Moses received from his fellow Hebrew, who he expected to be grateful for what he did yesterday for his people, shocked him. He had supposed that the Israelites would protect him by keeping quiet about his killing the day before, of an Egyptian who had been beating a Hebrew slave. Such was not the case.

14 And **he said, Who made thee a prince and a judge over us? intendest thou to kill me, as thou killedst the Egyptian?** And **Moses feared, and said, Surely this thing is known** [*the Hebrews were spreading it around and the Pharaoh would find out, putting Moses in danger of being executed*].

15 Now **when Pharaoh heard this thing, he sought to slay Moses. But Moses fled** from the face of Pharaoh, **and dwelt in the land of Midian**: and he sat down by a well.

If you look at a map depicting the ancient world of the Old Testament, you will see that Moses fled over some very hostile desert terrain, from Egypt across the Sinai Peninsula to the Land of Midian, which is located on the western edge of the Arabian Peninsula and on the east side of the Gulf of Aqaba (the northeastern tip of the Red Sea). It is likely that he thus traveled four hundred to five hundred miles to escape from Egypt.

When Moses arrived, he found a well that was used by local shepherds to water their flocks. He also found his wife. The priest of Midian (who will soon be his father-in-law) spoken of in verse 16, next, was Jethro (see Exodus 3:1). Doctrine and Covenants 84:6 informs us that Moses received the Melchizedek Priesthood from his future father-in-law, Jethro (also known as Reuel—see vs 18).

Thus, his coming to Midian, marrying one of Jethro's daughters, receiving the Melchizedek Priesthood, and living forty years as a shepherd was significant preparation for his future call as a prophet.

His introduction to his future wife, verses 16–17, next, is the kind of material that makes good movies.

16 Now **the priest of Midian** [*Jethro*] **had seven daughters: and they came and drew** *water,* **and filled the troughs to water their father's flock.**

17 And the **shepherds came and drove them away: but Moses stood up and helped them** [*this is probably quite an understatement*]**, and watered their flock.**

The understatement mentioned in verse 17, above, reminds us of the modesty and humility of Moses. Remember, he is the author of Exodus.

We can imagine the excited chatter of the seven daughters as they hurried to their father to report the events at the well. It may well be that Moses was grinning as they forgot their manners and left him at the well, knowing that their father would likely send them back to get him.

18 And **when they came to Reuel** [*Jethro—see Exodus 3:1*] their father, **he said, How** *is it that* **ye are come so soon to day?**

19 And **they said, An Egyptian** [*Moses was apparently still dressed like an Egyptian when he arrived at the well*] **delivered us out of the hand of the shepherds, and also drew** *water* **enough for us, and watered the flock.**

20 And **he said** unto his daughters, And **where** *is* **he? why** *is* **it** *that* **ye have left the man? call him, that he may eat bread** [*so that he can come and have a meal with us*].

Verses 21–22, next, obviously summarize a considerable period of time. In fact, they briefly introduce the next forty years of Moses's life, during which time he was a family man and shepherd.

21 And **Moses was content to dwell with the man** [*Jethro*]**: and he gave Moses Zipporah his daughter.**

22 And **she bare** *him* **a son**, and he called his name Gershom: for he said, I have been a stranger in a strange land.

We suspect that these forty years spent with Jethro and his family would have been valuable time for Moses as he prepared for his calling to be a prophet at age eighty. Since Jethro conferred the Melchizedek Priesthood upon Moses (see Doctrine and Covenants 84:6), as previously mentioned, it is highly likely that Jethro also taught Moses many things over the course of these forty years, which would serve him well as a prophet and the leader of the Israelite exodus from Egypt. We will quote from the Bible Dictionary concerning Jethro:

Bible Dictionary: Jethro

"Also called Jether and Reuel, a prince and priest of Midian who gave Moses a home after his flight from Egypt, and afterward became his father-in-law (Ex. 3:1; 4:18; 18:1–12). It was from Jethro that Moses received the Melchizedek Priesthood (Doctrine and Covenants 84:6–7). He also gave Moses some practical advice about administrative delegation of responsibility (Exodus 18:13–27)."

Verses 23–25, next, set the stage for Moses to return to Egypt as the prophet and leader of the Exodus. The pharaoh who sought Moses's life (verse 15, above) has died, and the time for bringing the Israelite slaves out of Egyptian bondage is drawing near.

Also, under the current pharaoh, the bondage and slavery of the children of Israel has become much more abusive and severe. You may wish to read more about this in the Bible Dictionary, under "Egypt."

23 ¶ And it came to pass **in process of time**, that **the king of Egypt** [*the pharaoh*] **died**: and **the children of Israel sighed by reason of** [*because of*] **the bondage**, and they cried, and their cry came up unto God by reason of the bondage.

24 And **God heard their groaning, and** God **remembered** [*determined that it was time to fulfill*] **his covenant with Abraham, with Isaac, and with Jacob**.

Verse 24, above, presents an opportunity to study Old Testament vocabulary and language. We will focus on "remembered" and "his covenants." The "covenant" made with Abraham (see Abraham 2:9–11), and likewise confirmed upon Isaac and Jacob represents the gospel of Jesus Christ, which has the power to free us completely from the bondage of sin. This Abrahamic covenant, when kept by mortals, brings exaltation, which is life in the family unit in the highest degree of glory in the celestial kingdom (see Doctrine and Covenants 131:1–4; 132:19–20).

In Bible imagery, Egypt is sometimes used to symbolize Satan's kingdom, with all of its evils and false doctrines and philosophies (see for example Revelation 11:8). Thus, the covenants between God and man provide the way to escape "spiritual Egypt."

When God "remembers" His covenants, it is another way of saying, in effect, that the time has come to fulfill the promises made to Abraham, Isaac, and Jacob that their posterity would be led out of captivity. These promises are reiterated in a prophesy given by Joseph in Egypt, as found in JST Genesis 50. He prophesied:

JST Genesis 50:29, 34

29 And I will make him [*Joseph Smith*] great in mine eyes, for he shall do my work; and he shall be great like unto him [*Moses*] whom I have said I would raise up unto you, to deliver my people, O house of Israel, out of the land of Egypt; for **a seer** [*Moses*] **will I raise up to deliver my people out of the land of Egypt; and he shall be called Moses**. And by this name he shall know that he is of thy house; for **he shall be nursed by the king's daughter, and shall be called her son.**

34 And **the Lord sware unto** [*covenanted with*] **Joseph** that he would preserve his seed for ever, saying, **I will raise up Moses**, and a rod shall be in his hand, **and he shall gather together my people** [*the children of Israel*]**, and he shall lead them as a flock, and he shall smite the waters of the Red Sea with his rod.**

25 And God looked upon the children of Israel, and **God had respect unto *them*** [*was aware of their plight, see footnote 25a in your Bible*].

EXODUS 3

In this chapter, Moses, who is now eighty years old, receives his call to return to Egypt and lead the children of Israel out of bondage. This call comes when the Lord appears to him in the burning bush (verse 2). Moses will now serve forty years as a prophet before he is translated and taken up to heaven at age 120 (see Bible Dictionary, under "Moses").

Latter-day Saints are at a great advantage compared to others who study the Bible when it comes to this chapter and the ones that follow. For example, because of the Joseph Smith Translation of the Bible (the JST), we know that it was the Lord Himself—Jehovah, the premortal Christ—who appeared to Moses rather than "the angel of the Lord," as stated in verse 2 in the Bible.

As we begin with verse 1, Moses has been a shepherd for about forty years and has no doubt led a comparatively tranquil and peaceful existence during those years. His life will be drastically changed as he leads the flock to graze near Sinai.

1 Now **Moses kept the flock of Jethro his father in law**, the priest of Midian: **and he led the flock** to the backside of the desert, **and came to the mountain of God,** *even* **to Horeb** [*Sinai—see Bible Dictionary, under "Horeb"*].

We will first read verse 2, next, as it stands in the Bible and then include the Joseph Smith Translation (the JST) right after it. We will use **bold** to point out the JST changes. You will see that there is a significant difference between the two renderings.

2 And **the angel of the LORD** appeared unto him in a flame of fire **out of the midst** of a bush: and he looked, and, behold, the bush burned with fire, and the bush *was* not consumed.

JST Exodus 3:2

2 And **again, the presence of the Lord** appeared unto him, in a flame of fire **in the midst** of a bush; and he looked, and, behold, the bush burned with fire, and the bush was not consumed.

As you can see, there is quite a difference. In the JST, we are informed that it was the Lord Himself who appeared to Moses in the burning bush, rather than one of God's angels. Thus, Moses was in the presence of the premortal Savior, who was the God of the Old Testament. It was Christ who called to him from the burning bush. We will say more about this in a moment.

As we continue, we feel Moses's awe and wonder at the fact that the bush appears to be burning but is not consumed by the fire.

3 And Moses said, I will now turn aside, and see this great sight, why the bush is not burnt.

4 And when the LORD saw that he turned aside to see, **God called unto him out of the midst of the bush, and said, Moses, Moses.** And he said, Here *am* I.

> Did you notice that the word LORD in verse 4, above, is all capital letters? Spelled this way, it means "Jehovah," who is the premortal Jesus Christ. We mentioned above that we would say more about the fact that He is the God of the Old Testament. We are often told in church classes and sermons that the Savior is the God of the Old Testament, but why isn't it more obvious in the Bible? The answer is rather simple. "Jehovah" is His Old Testament name.
>
> The Bible Dictionary informs us that "Jehovah is the premortal Jesus Christ." It also says that Jehovah is the "proper name of the God of Israel" (see Bible Dictionary, under "Jehovah"). In other words, the name for Jesus Christ in the Old Testament is Jehovah. So, why don't we see the name Jehovah more often in English versions of the Old Testament? Again, the answer is simple but important.
>
> In the original Hebrew text of the Old Testament, the Savior's Old Testament name, Jehovah, appears more than five thousand times. So, what happened in the King James English translation (the Bible we use)? We will answer with another question.
>
> You will see LORD in all capitals again in verse 7 and in chapter 4, verses 1, 2, 4, 6, 10, 11 (twice), and on and on. The translators of the King James Version of the Bible chose to use the word LORD in place of Jehovah. When you realize this, you begin to see Jesus Christ constantly throughout the Old Testament!
>
> We will get even more technical for a moment. If you look at the above-mentioned verses (and countless others) in your King James Bible, you will notice that LORD is actually spelled with a large capital L followed by small capitals—ORD—making the word "LORD."
>
> In summary, the premortal Jesus Christ in the Hebrew Old Testament was referred to as Jehovah. "Lord" was substituted for "Jehovah" in the King James Version of the English Bible. For an excellent explanation of this subject, see Keith H. Meservy, 'LORD = Jehovah," *Ensign*, June 2002, page 29.
>
> We will now continue with Exodus, chapter 3, as the Savior asks Moses to remove his sandals and then introduces Himself to him.

5 And he [*Jehovah, the Savior before He received His mortal body—see, for example, Ether 3:16*] **said, Draw not nigh hither: put off thy shoes from off thy feet, for the place whereon thou standest** *is* **holy ground.**

6 Moreover he said, **I *am* the God of thy father, the God of Abraham, the God of Isaac, and the God of Jacob**. And Moses hid his face; for he was afraid to look upon God.

> In verses 7–10, next, Jesus gives Moses some background as to the need for his service as a prophet and then tells him he will be sent to Egypt.

7 ¶ And the LORD said, **I have surely seen the affliction of my people** which *are* in Egypt, **and have heard their cry** by reason of [*because of*] their taskmasters [*slave drivers*]; for I know their sorrows;

8 And **I am come down to deliver them** out of the hand of the Egyptians, and to bring them up out of that land unto a good land and a large, unto a land flowing with milk and honey; unto the place of the Canaanites, and the Hittites, and the Amorites, and the Perizzites, and the Hivites, and the Jebusites [*the inhabitants of Palestine at the time of Moses*].

9 Now therefore, behold, **the cry of the children of Israel is come unto me**: and I have also seen the oppression wherewith the Egyptians oppress them.

10 Come now **therefore**, and **I will send thee unto Pharaoh, that thou mayest bring forth my people the children of Israel out of Egypt**.

> In verse 11, next, Moses humbly asks, in effect, "Why me?" Watch how the Lord reassures him in the first part of verse 12. It is similar in principle to the assurances given to each of us as we are set apart to various callings in the Church.

11 ¶ **And Moses said unto God, Who *am* I**, that I should go unto Pharaoh, and that I should bring forth the children of Israel out of Egypt?

12 And he [*Jesus*] said, **Certainly I will be with thee**; and **this *shall be* a token** [*a sign*] **unto thee**, that I have sent thee: When thou hast brought forth the people out of Egypt, **ye shall serve God upon this mountain** [*Mount Sinai; in other words, the Lord will meet Moses again on Sinai, after he has led the Israelites out of Egypt; at that time, he will receive the Ten Commandments*].

> In verse 13, next, Moses asks another question. He is obviously worried about the reaction of the Israelites in Egypt when he suddenly arrives among them and informs them that he has been called by the Lord to lead them out of the country and thus free them from bondage. A specific concern he has is what he should say if they ask for the name of the god who sent him.
>
> This may sound strange to us because we know about the true God. But remember that these Hebrew slaves have spent many generations in Egypt, and it is highly likely that they have been thoroughly influenced over the years by the false doctrine that there are many gods,

13 And Moses said unto God, Behold, *when* **I come unto the children of Israel, and** shall **say** unto them, **The God of your fathers hath sent me** unto you; **and they** shall **say** to me, **What** *is* **his name? What shall I say unto them?**

> The Savior responds to Moses's question by instructing him to tell the Israelites that Jehovah sent him. Another name for Jehovah is "I AM." Doctrine and Covenants 29:1 informs us that this is the case. We will quote it here:
>
> **Doctrine and Covenants 29:1**
>
> 1 Listen to the voice of **Jesus Christ,** your Redeemer, **the Great I AM,** whose arm of mercy hath atoned for your sins. [*You may also wish to read John 8:58, footnote b, in your Bible, which likewise identifies "I AM" as Jehovah.*]

14 And God said unto Moses, I AM THAT I AM [*perhaps meaning "I, Jehovah, am the 'I AM' they have heard of"*]: and he said, **Thus shalt thou say unto the children of Israel, I AM hath sent me unto you.**

> In the context of Exodus 3:13–14 here, it is obvious that I AM is a name for Jehovah that the children of Israel in Egypt would recognize.
>
> The Lord next instructs Moses to remind the Israelite slaves that He, Jehovah, is the God of Abraham, Isaac, and Jacob. Among other things, this is a strong reminder that, as descendants of Abraham, Isaac, and Jacob, they are still the Lord's covenant people and they can assume that role in the Lord's work if they will repent, follow Moses and live the gospel.

15 And God said moreover unto Moses, **Thus shalt thou say unto the children of Israel, The LORD God** [*Jehovah*] **of your fathers, the God of Abraham, the God of Isaac, and the God of Jacob, hath sent me unto you**: this [*Jehovah, I AM*] *is* my name for ever, and this *is* my memorial unto all generations.

> Next, Jehovah gives Moses specific instructions as to what to do when he arrives in Egypt.

16 **Go, and gather the elders of Israel together** [*the leaders among the Israelites in Egyptian bondage*], **and say** unto them, **The LORD God** [*Jehovah*] **of your fathers, the God of Abraham, of Isaac, and of Jacob, appeared unto me, saying, I have surely visited you,** and *seen* that which is done to you in Egypt [*in effect, the Lord is aware of your cries and is ready to bless you with freedom*]:

> As the Savior continues to instruct Moses, He tells him to tell the Israelites that the time has come for the Lord to bring them out of Egypt and into Palestine, the promised land. There is symbolism here. If we faithfully follow the living prophet, we will successfully come into the "promised land," in other words, heaven.

17 **And I have said, I will bring you up out of the affliction of Egypt**

unto the land of the Canaanites, and the Hittites, and the Amorites, and the Perizzites, and the Hivites, and the Jebusites, **unto a land flowing with milk and honey** [*a good land where prosperity can abound*].

18 And they shall hearken to thy voice: and thou shalt come, thou and the elders of Israel, unto the king of Egypt [*Pharaoh*], and ye shall say unto him, The LORD God of the Hebrews hath met with us: and now let us go, we beseech thee, three days' journey into the wilderness, that we may sacrifice to the LORD our God.

> Next, in verses 19–22, the Lord prophesies what will happen when Moses goes to Egypt and talks to the elders, or leaders of the Israelites, and then predicts Pharaoh's initial reaction and what will happen after the ten plagues. Thus, Moses knows beforehand what is going to happen. The Savior also gives him specific instructions for the gathering of wealth before they leave Egypt.

19 ¶ And I am sure that **the king of Egypt will not let you go**, no, not by a mighty hand.

20 And **I will stretch out my hand, and smite Egypt with all my wonders** [*the ten plagues*] which I will do in the midst thereof: and **after that he will let you go**.

21 And **I will give this people favour in the sight of the Egyptians** [*they will be especially anxious to see you go after the plagues*]: and it shall come to pass, that, **when ye go, ye shall not go empty**:

22 But **every woman shall borrow** of her neighbour, and of her that sojourneth in her house, jewels of **silver**, and jewels of **gold**, and **raiment** [*clothing*]: and ye shall put *them* upon your sons, and upon your daughters; and **ye shall spoil** [*take great wealth from*] **the Egyptians**.

EXODUS 4

As we study this chapter we will see that Moses is still very concerned that the children of Israel in Egypt will not believe him. The Lord gives him confidence through some rather spectacular miracles, which he will be allowed to repeat in front of the Israelites when the time is right. And if they still don't believe Moses has been called of God, he can perform yet another miracle to convince them, namely, pour water from the Nile River upon the sand and it will become blood.

You will see that Moses still has a major concern. He considers himself to be a poor communicator and perhaps has a speech impediment of some sort. Despite the marvelous signs he has just been given, he is still somewhat lacking in faith that he can fulfill the calling that the Lord has given him. You will see the righteous anger of the Lord at this continued reluctance on his part. Aaron, who is an excellent speaker and skilled communicator, is given to Moses as a spokesman.

Despite this humble beginning and evidence of human weakness in Moses, you will see him become a mighty servant of God. In Ether 12:27, Moroni teaches us that we are given weaknesses in order to become strong. Moses is a living testimony of this principle at work.

As we proceed with verse one, you can sense Moses's deep feelings of inadequacy.

1 AND Moses answered and said, **But**, behold, **they** [*the children of Israel*] **will not believe me**, nor hearken unto my voice: for **they will say, The LORD hath not appeared unto thee**.

> Moses is in for quite a scare as the Lord teaches him that with God, nothing is impossible (Luke 1:37).

2 And **the LORD said unto him, What is that in thine hand?** And he said, **A rod**.

3 And he said, **Cast it on the ground**. And he cast it on the ground, and **it became a serpent; and Moses fled from before it**.

4 And **the LORD said** unto Moses, Put forth thine hand, and **take it by the tail**. And **he** put forth his hand, and **caught it, and it became a rod in his hand:**

5 **That they may believe** that the LORD God of their fathers, the God of Abraham, the God of Isaac, and the God of Jacob, hath appeared unto thee.

> Do you sense that these demonstrations of Jehovah's power are perhaps not just for the Israelites but also for Moses?

6 ¶ And **the LORD said furthermore** unto him, **Put now thine hand into thy bosom.** And he put his hand into his bosom: **and when he took it out, behold, his hand was leprous as snow** [*was completely white with leprosy*].

7 **And he said, Put thine hand into thy bosom again.** And he put his hand into his bosom again; and **plucked it out of his bosom, and, behold, it was turned again as his other flesh**.

8 And it shall come to pass, **if they will not believe thee, neither hearken to the voice of the first sign, that they will believe the voice of the latter sign.**

9 And it shall come to pass, **if they will not believe also these two signs, neither hearken unto thy voice,** that thou shalt **take of the water of the river, and pour it upon the dry land: and the water which thou takest out of the river shall become blood** upon the dry land.

> Moses has yet another concern. He is not a gifted communicator. In fact, he is "slow of speech."

10 ¶ **And Moses said unto the LORD**, O my Lord, **I am not eloquent** [*not good at speaking*], neither heretofore, nor since thou hast spoken unto thy servant: but **I am slow of speech, and of a slow tongue**.

11 **And the LORD said** unto him, **Who hath made man's mouth? or who maketh the dumb, or deaf, or the seeing, or the blind? have not I the LORD?**

Jesus assures him that He will cure him of his slowness of speech.

12 Now therefore go, and **I will be with thy mouth, and teach thee what thou shalt say**.

> But Moses still demonstrates lack of faith in the Lord's reassurances and thus incurs a small portion of Jehovah's righteous anger. This, too, is an important part of Moses's training to be a prophet.

13 And **he said, O my Lord, send, I pray thee, by the hand of him whom thou wilt send** [*in other words, could You send someone else? (See footnote 13a in your Bible*].

14 And the **anger of the LORD was kindled against Moses**, and he said, Is not **Aaron** the Levite thy brother? I know that he can speak well. And also, behold, he **cometh forth to meet thee:** and when he seeth thee, he will be glad in his heart.

15 And **thou shalt speak unto him, and put words in his mouth: and I will be with thy mouth, and with his mouth, and will teach you what ye shall do** [*I will inspire you*].

> Next, the Lord defines the roles Moses and Aaron, his brother, will play respectively in redeeming Israel from Egyptian bondage.

16 And **he shall be thy spokesman** unto the people [*Aaron will deliver your messages*]: and he shall be, even he shall be to thee instead of a mouth [*he will be your mouthpiece*], and **thou shalt be to him instead of God** [*you will preside over him in this work*].

17 And **thou shalt take this rod in thine hand, wherewith thou shalt do signs** [*perform miracles*].

> This is the end of the calling and instructing of Moses by Jehovah from the burning bush, which began in Exodus 3:2.
>
> Moses, chapter 1, in the Pearl of Great Price fits here, between Exodus 4:17 and Exodus 4:18. You may wish to read or review Moses, chapter 1, with notes and commentary, at the beginning of Genesis in this study guide so that you can better understand the perspectives Moses has been given by Jehovah in order to continue on from here in his calling as a prophet. We learn from Moses 1:17, 25–26, that these revelations were given to Moses between the time of his calling at the burning bush and the time he actually went back to Egypt near the end of Exodus 4. You will see that Moses received tremendous revelations and experiences that are not recorded in the Bible.
>
> First, we will summarize a number of these revelations and perspectives given to Moses (in Moses, chapter one, in the Pearl of Great Price) by the Lord, and then we will continue with Exodus 4:18.
>
> 1. Moses is taken up to a high mountain, where he is shown things from God's perspective (verse 1).
> 2. He talks with the Savior face to face (verse 2).

3. The Savior personally introduces Himself to Moses (verse 3) and shows him many of the things He has already created (verse 4).

4. Moses is told that he is a son of God (verse 4).

5. He is told that he has a role, similar to the Savior's role, as he leads the children of Israel out of Egypt (verse 6).

6. Moses is shown the whole earth and all the inhabitants (verse 8).

7. Moses discovers firsthand that the accomplishments of the mighty kings of Egypt and other powerful rulers of nations and kingdoms on earth are nothing compared to God (verses 9–10).

8. Moses personally experiences being transfigured by the Holy Ghost, in order to survive being in the direct presence of God (verse 11).

9. He gains firsthand experience with Satan and now knows that Satan is a real being who skillfully opposes God and His purposes and goals for His children (verse 12).

10. Moses personally sees the difference between the glory that rests upon God and the lack of glory upon Satan (verses 13–15).

11. Moses discovers that he cannot overcome Satan without God's help and without keeping the commandments (verses 16–22).

12. He learns that Satan attempts to counterfeit being Christ (verse 19).

13. Moses learns that obedience to God's commandments brings more light and knowledge (verses 24–41).

14. He learns prophetic details about his mission to free the Hebrews from Egypt, including that he will be given power to part the Red Sea (verses 25–26).

15. He is transfigured again and is privileged to speak with Jehovah face-to-face, asking questions and receiving answers (verses 30–41).

16. He is taught that worlds without number have already been created by the Savior, that many have already finished up, and that there are other planets in outer space that have people on them, just like this earth (verses 33 and 35). Thus, Moses can understand that the plan of salvation is a tried and proven plan, not a new experiment.

17. Moses is taught that there is no limit to the number of worlds being created, that it is an ongoing and eternal work (verse 38).

18. Above all, Moses is taught that the Father's whole goal and purpose is to "bring to pass the immortality and eternal life" (exaltation) of His children (verse 39). And Moses will be assisting our Father in Heaven in this as he carries out his call to return to Egypt.

19. Moses is told that many of his writings will be lost but that in the last days on this earth, a prophet (Joseph Smith) would

restore much of what Moses will write (in Genesis through Deuteronomy).

Is there any question in your mind that Moses was well-prepared to return to Egypt as a prophet? What a tremendous understanding and perspective he received! It will be vital to his personal survival and his overall persistence in leading an often rebellious and fickle people to the land of promise.

Perhaps you have already noticed that there is considerable symbolism in what Moses was called to do.

Remember, he was told by the Savior, who was speaking for the Father at the time, that his role and calling was "in the similitude of mine Only Begotten" (Moses 1:6). In other words, the Savior's role is to lead us from the bondage of sin and Satan's kingdom through the waters of baptism, to the kingdom of heaven. Moses's role was to lead his people from Egypt (symbolic of sin and Satan's kingdom) through the waters of the Red Sea (symbolic of the waters of baptism) and into the promised land (symbolic of heaven).

We will now go back, as previously mentioned, and pick things up with Exodus, chapter 4, verse 18, where Moses begins preparations to return to Egypt, as instructed by the Lord.

18 ¶ And **Moses went and returned to Jethro his father in law, and said unto him, Let me go, I pray thee, and return unto my brethren which are in Egypt**, and see whether they be yet alive. And Jethro said to Moses, Go in peace.

19 **And the LORD said unto Moses** in Midian, Go, return into Egypt: for **all the men are dead which sought thy life**.

20 And **Moses took his wife and his sons**, and set them upon an ass, **and** he **returned to the land of Egypt**: and **Moses took the rod of God in his hand** [*a rod or staff was symbolic of power and authority in that culture*].

> The JST makes a vital change in verse 21, next. God does not harden peoples' hearts. It would be a violation of their agency.

21 And the LORD said unto Moses, When thou goest to return into Egypt, see that thou do all those wonders before Pharaoh, which I have put in thine hand: but **I will harden his heart,** that he shall not let the people go.

JST Exodus 4:21

21 And the Lord said unto Moses, When thou goest to return into Egypt, see that thou do all those wonders before Pharaoh, which I have put in thine hand, and I will prosper thee; **but Pharaoh will harden his heart**, and he will not let the people go.

Next, in verses 22–23, Moses is instructed to tell Pharaoh that the Israelites are the Lord's covenant people and must be set free in order to serve Him. A severe warning to Pharaoh accompanies the instruction.

22 And **thou shalt say unto Pharaoh, Thus saith the LORD, Israel is my son, even my firstborn:**

23 And I say unto thee, **Let my son go, that he may serve me:** and **if thou refuse to let him go,** behold, **I will slay thy son, even thy firstborn.**

> Verses 24–26, next, are a bit difficult to understand. We will read them as they stand in the Bible, in the JST, and then quote from the Old Testament Student Manual.

24 ¶ And it came to pass by the way in the inn, that the LORD met him, and sought to kill him.

25 Then Zipporah took a sharp stone [*NIV: "a flint knife"*], and cut off the foreskin of her son [*circumcised her son*], and cast it at his feet, and said, Surely a bloody husband art thou to me.

26 So he let him go: then she said, A bloody husband thou art, because of the circumcision [*NIV: "bridegroom of blood," likely meaning "as my husband, you are now in compliance with the law of circumcision"*].

JST Exodus 4:24–26

> 24 And it came to pass, that **the Lord appeared unto him as he was in the way, by the inn. The Lord was angry with Moses, and his hand was about to fall upon him to kill him; for he had not circumcised his son.**
>
> 25 Then Zipporah took a sharp stone and circumcised her son, **and cast the stone at his feet,** and said, Surely thou art a bloody husband unto me.
>
> 26 And **the Lord spared Moses and let him go, because Zipporah, his wife, circumcised the child.** And she said, Thou art a bloody husband. And **Moses was ashamed** [*perhaps because he had not circumcised his son himself*], **and hid his face from the Lord, and said, I have sinned before the Lord.**

A quote from the Old Testament Student manual is helpful here.

"The King James Version lacks detail in this account. The Joseph Smith Translation indicates that the Lord was angry with Moses for failing to circumcise his son. It appears that Zipporah had not wanted to circumcise Gershom but relented when the Lord expressed His anger to Moses." (*Old Testament Student Manual, Genesis–2 Samuel*, p 106)

Remember that the law of circumcision was given to Abraham in Genesis 17:10–14 and that his posterity were to keep this law throughout the Old Testament. Moses had failed to keep the law as was required of the Lord's covenant people, and thus he incurred the Lord's anger. Have you noticed that Moses's "learning curve" is rather steep?

Next, Moses's older brother, Aaron, is inspired to go meet Moses in the wilderness.

27 ¶ And **the LORD said to Aaron, Go into the wilderness to meet Moses.** And he went, and met him in the mount of God, and kissed him.

28 And **Moses told Aaron all the words of the LORD who had sent**

him, and all the signs which he had commanded him**.

29 ¶ And **Moses and Aaron** went and **gathered together all the elders** [*leaders*] **of the children of Israel:**

> Next, we see Aaron stepping into his role as a spokesman for Moses (Exodus 4:16). The results indicate that he was very effective in his calling.

30 And **Aaron spake all the words** which the LORD had spoken unto Moses, **and did the signs** in the sight of the people.

31 And **the people believed:** and when they heard that the LORD had visited the children of Israel, and that he had looked upon their affliction, **then they bowed their heads and worshipped.**

EXODUS 5

As you read this chapter, you will see that Moses and Aaron ask Pharaoh to free Israel, but he refuses. You will find a number of important applications for us in our lives. For example, conversion through signs and wonders is often shallow.

Note the shallowness of the commitment of the Israelites to the Lord and His prophet, Moses, when their burdens are increased (they now are required by their slave drivers to get their own straw and still keep up with their daily quota of bricks). They were "converted" through the miracles performed at the end of Exodus 4. Note in 5:21, for example, that the elders of Israel complain, saying in effect that Moses and Aaron have made them "stink" in the eyes of Pharaoh and his officers.

Application: The patience of the Lord is wonderful.

Watch for the continuing growth that comes to Moses as he expresses honest concerns to the Lord when he obeys, but his expectations are not met. Pay attention to the Lord's patient responses and encouragement. It is much the same as when He is dealing with us. He gives us commandments and counsel, we obey, but things sometimes don't go the way we expect, and we find ourselves discouraged, disappointed, and perhaps even a bit irritated on occasion.

1 AND **afterward** [*after the miracles and conversions in 4:30–31*] **Moses and Aaron went in, and told Pharaoh, Thus saith the LORD God of Israel, Let my people go,** that they may hold a feast unto me in the wilderness.

2 And **Pharaoh said, Who is the LORD,** that I should obey his voice to let Israel go? **I know not the LORD, neither will I let Israel go.**

3 And **they said, The God of the Hebrews** hath met with us: let us go, we pray thee, three days' journey into the desert, and sacrifice unto the LORD our God; lest he fall upon us with pestilence, or with the sword.

4 And **the king of Egypt said** unto them, **Wherefore do ye, Moses and Aaron, let the people from their works** [*what do you think you are doing, relieving the people from their work*

as *slaves*]? **get you unto your burdens** [*get back to work*].

> Pharaoh will now retaliate, increasing the burdens on the Israelite slaves who make bricks for Pharaoh's building projects by making them gather their own straw, which was provided them up to this point.
>
> This can remind us of the principle that promised blessings generally do not come until after the trial of our faith.

Doctrine and Covenants 58:4

4 For after much tribulation come the blessings.

5 And **Pharaoh said**, Behold, the people of the land now are many, and **ye make them rest from their burdens**.

6 And **Pharaoh commanded the same day the taskmasters** [*the Egyptian overseers*] **of the people**, and their officers, saying,

7 **Ye shall no more give the people straw to make brick**, as heretofore: **let them go and gather straw for themselves**.

8 **And the tale** [*quota, see footnote 5a in your Bible*] of the bricks, which they did make heretofore, **ye shall lay upon them; ye shall not diminish ought thereof: for they be idle; therefore they cry, saying, Let us go and sacrifice to our God**.

9 **Let there more work be laid upon the men**, that they may labour therein; and let them not regard vain words.

10 ¶ And **the taskmasters** of the people went out, and their officers, and they **spake to the people**, saying, **Thus saith Pharaoh, I will not give you straw**.

11 Go ye, **get you straw where ye can find it:** yet **not ought** [*not a bit*] **of your work shall be diminished**.

12 **So the people were scattered abroad** throughout all the land of Egypt **to gather stubble** [*what's left after the stalks of straw are harvested*] **instead of straw**.

13 **And the taskmasters hasted them**, saying, Fulfil your works, your daily tasks, as when there was straw.

> As you might well suspect, the task of meeting their daily quota of bricks just got much more difficult. In fact, in verse 14, next, the Israelite foremen appointed by Pharaoh's slave drivers are beaten because their people are falling short of their daily quotas now.

14 And **the officers of the children of Israel**, which Pharaoh's taskmasters had set over them, **were beaten**, and demanded, Wherefore have ye not fulfilled your task in making brick both yesterday and to day, as heretofore?

> The Israelite foremen take their complaints directly to Pharaoh.

15 ¶ **Then the officers of the children of Israel came and cried unto Pharaoh,** saying, **Wherefore dealest thou thus with thy servants?**

16 **There is no straw given unto thy servants,** and they [*your slave drivers*] **say to us, Make brick:** and, behold, **thy servants are beaten; but the fault is in thine own people.**

17 But **he said, Ye are idle, ye are idle** [*NIV: "you are just being lazy"*]: **therefore ye say, Let us go and do sacrifice to the LORD.**

18 **Go** therefore now, **and work**; for **there shall no straw be given you, yet shall ye deliver the tale** [*quota*] **of bricks.**

19 And **the officers of the children of Israel did see that they were in evil case** [*in big trouble*], after it was said, Ye shall not minish ought from your bricks of your daily task.

> The Israelite foremen now complain bitterly to Moses and Aaron and blame them for their new troubles. As indicated, previously, their conversion by miracles has little depth.

20 ¶ And **they met Moses and Aaron,** who stood in the way, as they came forth from Pharaoh:

21 **And** they **said** unto them, **The LORD look upon you, and judge** [*may the Lord condemn you for what you have done*]; **because ye have made our savour to be abhorred** [*you have made us stink*] **in the eyes of Pharaoh, and in the eyes of his servants, to put a sword in their hand to slay us** [*you are going to get us killed*].

> Now Moses turns to the Lord and complains. He is still learning, himself, but will yet grow and become one of the most faithful and powerful prophets of all time. Right now, his learning curve is still quite steep.

22 **And Moses returned unto the LORD, and said,** Lord, **wherefore hast thou so evil entreated this people** [*why are You treating us so badly*]? **why is it that thou hast sent me** [*what is the purpose in sending me if this is the way it is going to be*]?

23 For **since I came to Pharaoh** to speak **in thy name, he hath done evil to this people; neither hast thou delivered thy people at all.**

> As you can tell, Moses is very frustrated!

EXODUS 6

Next, the Lord responds to Moses's complaint in the last verses of chapter 5, above. He reassures Moses that He will support him. Perhaps you've noticed that our idea of how the Lord will fulfill His promises and how He actually does it are often not the same. We often end up having to be much more patient and persevering than we anticipated, and thus end up growing more than we otherwise would have.

Another important insight in this chapter is that righteous and faithful people in ancient times were well acquainted with the fact that Jesus Christ was the God of the Old Testament.

1 THEN the LORD said unto Moses, Now shalt thou see what I will do to Pharaoh: for with a strong hand shall he let them go, and with a strong hand shall he drive them out of his land.

2 And **God spake unto Moses, and said** unto him, **I am the LORD:**

3 And I appeared unto Abraham, unto Isaac, and unto Jacob, by *the name of* God Almighty, but **by my name JEHOVAH was I not known to them**.

> The JST makes a very important doctrinal change to verse 3, above.
>
> **JST Exodus 6:3**
>
> 3 And I appeared unto Abraham, unto Isaac, and unto Jacob. **I am the Lord God Almighty; the Lord JEHOVAH. And was not my name known unto them?**
>
> The answer to the question posed at the end of the JST verse, above, is a resounding yes! One of the main things we learn from this verse in its correct form is that faithful people in Old Testament times clearly knew that Jesus Christ was the God of the Old Testament, working under the direction of the Father.
>
> Perhaps this is a good place to add a reminder that will help you better distinguish whether Heavenly Father or Jesus Christ is speaking, appearing, and so forth, in the scriptures. A general rule of thumb is that until the Fall of Adam and Eve, it was Heavenly Father appearing and speaking in scripture, often accompanied by the Son. After the Fall, it is almost always the Savior who is speaking and appearing, except when the Father introduces the Son. Joseph Fielding Smith explained this. He said:
>
> "All revelation since the fall has come through Jesus Christ, who is the Jehovah of the Old Testament. In all of the scriptures, where God is mentioned and where he has appeared, it was Jehovah who talked with Abraham, with Noah, Enoch, Moses and all the prophets. He is the God of Israel, the Holy One of Israel; the one who led that nation out of Egyptian bondage, and who gave and fulfilled the law of Moses. The Father has never dealt with man directly and personally since the fall, and he has never appeared except to introduce and bear record of the Son. Thus the Inspired Version [*the Joseph Smith Translation, John 1:19*] records that "no man hath seen God at any time, except he hath borne record of the Son" (*Doctrines of Salvation, v*ol. 1, page 27).
>
> We will continue now with Exodus, chapter 6, as Jehovah continues reassuring Moses that he will be supported in his calling to free the Israelites from Egyptian bondage.

4 And **I have also established my covenant with them,** to give them the land of Canaan, the land of their pilgrimage, wherein they were strangers.

5 And **I have also heard the groaning of the children of Israel,** whom the Egyptians keep in bondage; and

I have remembered my covenant [*I will fulfill My promises*].

6 Wherefore **say unto the children of Israel, I am the LORD, and I will bring you out from under the burdens of the Egyptians,** and I will rid you out of their bondage, and I will redeem you with a stretched out arm, and with great judgments:

> Did you notice the Atonement symbolism in verse 6, above? In the scriptures, Egyptian bondage was sometimes used to symbolize the captivity of Satan (example: Revelation 11:8). The Lord has power to redeem us from our sins and thus free us from "the burdens of the Egyptians," or, in other words, the bondage of sin.

7 And I will take you to me for a people, and I will be to you a God: and **ye shall know that I am the LORD your God, which bringeth you out from under the burdens of the Egyptians.**

8 And **I will bring you in unto the land, concerning the which I did swear** [*covenant*] **to give it to Abraham, to Isaac, and to Jacob;** and I will give it you for an heritage: I am the LORD.

JST Exodus 6:8

> 8 And I will bring you in unto the land, concerning the which I did swear to give it to Abraham, to Isaac, and to Jacob; and I will give it you for a heritage; I the Lord will do it.

9 ¶ And **Moses spake so unto the children of Israel: but they hearkened not** unto Moses for anguish of spirit [*because of discouragement*], and for cruel bondage.

10 And the **LORD spake unto Moses, saying,**

11 Go in, **speak unto Pharaoh king of Egypt, that he let the children of Israel go out of his land.**

> Have you noticed that Moses is still learning to trust the Lord completely? Rather than going forward with faith, he pushes back a bit.

12 **And Moses spake before the LORD,** saying, **Behold, the children of Israel have not hearkened unto me; how then shall Pharaoh hear me,** who am of uncircumcised lips [*inability to communicate effectively (see the JST for verse 29, later in this chapter)*]?

> The premortal Christ is very patient and simply reaffirms the instruction to do as He has said.

13 And **the LORD spake unto Moses and unto Aaron,** and gave them a charge unto the children of Israel, and unto Pharaoh king of Egypt, to **bring the children of Israel out of the land of Egypt.**

> Next, we are given some family history for Moses and Aaron.

14 ¶ These be the heads of their fathers' houses: The sons of Reuben the firstborn of Israel; Hanoch, and Pallu, Hezron, and Carmi: these be the families of Reuben.

15 And the sons of Simeon; Jemuel, and Jamin, and Ohad, and Jachin,

and Zohar, and Shaul the son of a Canaanitish woman: these are the families of Simeon.

16 ¶ And these are the names of the sons of Levi according to their generations; Gershon, and Kohath, and Merari: and the years of the life of Levi were an hundred thirty and seven years.

17 The sons of Gershon; Libni, and Shimi, according to their families.

18 And the sons of Kohath; Amram, and Izhar, and Hebron, and Uzziel: and the years of the life of Kohath were an hundred thirty and three years.

19 And the sons of Merari; Mahali and Mushi: these are the families of Levi according to their generations.

20 And Amram took him Jochebed his father's sister to wife; and she bare him **Aaron and Moses:** and the years of the life of Amram were an hundred and thirty and seven years.

21 ¶ And the sons of Izhar; Korah, and Nepheg, and Zichri.

22 And the sons of Uzziel; Mishael, and Elzaphan, and Zithri.

23 And Aaron took him Elisheba, daughter of Amminadab, sister of Naashon, to wife; and she bare him Nadab, and Abihu, Eleazar, and Ithamar.

24 And the sons of Korah; Assir, and Elkanah, and Abiasaph: these are the families of the Korhites.

25 And Eleazar Aaron's son took him one of the daughters of Putiel to wife; and she bare him Phinehas: these are the heads of the fathers of the Levites according to their families.

The JST adds much that is missing from the next verses.

26 **These are that Aaron and Moses, to whom the LORD said, Bring out the children of Israel from the land of Egypt** according to their armies.

JST Exodus 6:26

26 **These are the sons of Aaron, according to their families. And all these are the names of the children of Israel according to the heads of their families, that the Lord said unto Aaron and Moses, they should bring up out of the land of Egypt,** according to their armies [*NIV, "clan by clan"*].

27 **These are they which spake to Pharaoh king of Egypt**, to bring out the children of Israel from Egypt: these are that Moses and Aaron.

JST Exodus 6:27

27 **These are they concerning whom the Lord spake to Pharaoh, king of Egypt, that he should let them go. And he sent Moses and Aaron to bring out the children of Israel from Egypt.**

28 ¶ And it came to pass **on the day when the LORD spake unto Moses** in the land of Egypt,

29 That the LORD spake unto Moses, **saying, I am the LORD: speak**

thou unto Pharaoh king of Egypt all that I say unto thee.

JST Exodus 6:28

28 And it came to pass, on the day the Lord spake unto Moses, in the land of Egypt, that **the Lord commanded Moses** that he should speak unto Pharaoh, king of Egypt, saying, **I, the Lord, will do unto Pharaoh, king of Egypt,** all that I say unto thee.

30 And Moses said before the LORD, Behold, **I am of uncircumcised lips,** and how shall Pharaoh hearken unto me [*what is going to make Pharaoh even listen to me*]?

JST Exodus 6:29

29 And Moses said, before the Lord, Behold, **I am of stammering lips, and slow of speech;** how shall Pharaoh hearken unto me?

EXODUS 7–11
THE TEN PLAGUES

The general purpose of the ten plagues and pestilences

In the course of chapters 7–11, the ten plagues fall upon Pharaoh and his people, with the tenth plague finally persuading Pharaoh to let the Israelites go. There are different ways to count the plagues, but the most common way comes up with ten. We will use this approach. (Boils and blains are usually counted together as one plague, and hail and fire, since they came together, are usually counted as one as well. If each of these were counted separately, we would have twelve plagues.)

In general, the purpose of large-scale plagues and pestilences is to punish wickedness and serve as a wake-up call to the people involved. We see this time and time again in the Book of Mormon, in times of apostasy and wickedness. The devastations sent by the Lord upon the wicked usually led to humility, repentance, and a return to God and personal righteousness. We often refer to these recurring cycles in the Book of Mormon as the "cycle of apostasy." Such plagues and pestilences have been prophesied for our day, the last days. (See, for example, Doctrine and Covenants 84:96–97, 87:6, 88:86–91.)

In the case of the ten plagues in Egypt, in addition to convincing Pharaoh and the Egyptians to let the Lord's people go, they served as a wake-up call to the Israelites to listen to God and His prophet. The fact that these disasters fell upon the Egyptians but not the Israelites served also as a testimony to the children of Israel that theirs was the true God and Moses was His prophet. We will list these plagues here, along with the main verses in which they appear.

1. WATER TURNS TO BLOOD
Exodus 7:14–25

2. FROGS
Exodus 8:1–15

3. LICE
Exodus 8:16–19

4. FLIES
Exodus 8:20–32

5. DEATH OF EGYPTIAN CATTLE
Exodus 9:3 and 6

6. BOILS AND BLAINS
Exodus 9:8–12

Boils and blains seem to go together. Blains were blisters, small inflammations of the skin that were filled with pus.

7. HAIL AND FIRE
Exodus 9:13–35

8. LOCUSTS
Exodus 10:1–20

9. THICK DARKNESS
Exodus 10:21–29

Have you noticed that the three days of darkness that came upon the Egyptians as a plague had similarities with the three days of darkness the Nephites experienced at the time of the Savior's crucifixion? For example, it was a "thick darkness" which could be felt (Exodus 10:21–22; 3 Nephi 8:20).

There is symbolism here. When we ignore God or cast Him out of our lives, spiritual darkness fills in where His light was. This darkness can be felt. In fact, no doubt you have literally "felt" evil, when you have approached it, considered participating in it, or while it was being practiced by others, or when approached by individuals and groups engaged in gross evil.

Before we go on to the tenth plague, we will ask a quick question. Did you know that, in a way, the ten plagues are to be repeated again in the last days? Revelation 16, which contains prophecies to be fulfilled in the last days before the Second Coming, contains a number of them. Among other things, they are once again designed to serve as a wake-up call to the inhabitants of the earth so they can repent and prepare to meet the Lord as He comes to usher in the Millennium.

10. THE DEATH OF THE FIRSTBORN
Exodus 11:1–12:36

The final plague was the death of the firstborn among the Egyptians as well as their animals. You can see symbolism here; namely, just as the death of the firstborn among the Egyptians set the Lord's covenant people free from bondage, so also the death of the Firstborn of the Father (the firstborn spirit child of Heavenly Father in premortality—Jesus Christ) can set us free from the bondage of sin.

EXODUS 7

In this chapter, we will see Moses and Aaron go before Pharaoh as instructed. We will be shown that Satan has power to counterfeit God's miracles in order to deceive people. We will also see that God's power is greater than that of the devil. We will see the first of the ten plagues as the river turns to blood.

The JST helps significantly with the first four verses of chapter 7.

1 AND the LORD said unto Moses, See, **I have made thee a god to Pharaoh: and Aaron thy brother shall be thy prophet.**

2 **Thou shalt speak all that I command thee: and Aaron thy brother shall speak unto Pharaoh**, that he send the children of Israel out of his land.

JST Exodus 7:1–2

1 And the Lord said unto Moses, See, I have made thee a **prophet** to

Pharaoh; and Aaron thy brother shall be thy **spokesman**.

2 Thou shalt speak **unto thy brother** all that I command thee; and Aaron thy brother shall speak unto Pharaoh, that he send the children of Israel out of his land.

3 And **I will harden Pharaoh's heart**, and multiply my signs and my wonders in the land of Egypt.

JST Exodus 7:3

3 And **Pharaoh will harden his heart**, as I said unto thee; and thou shalt multiply my signs, and my wonders, in the land of Egypt.

Remember, every time you read anything to the effect that the Lord hardened Pharaoh's heart, in this chapter or elsewhere, it is an incorrect translation. The Lord does not harden our hearts. We do.

4 **But Pharaoh shall not hearken unto you,** that I may lay my hand upon Egypt [*punish Egypt*], and bring forth mine armies, and my people the children of Israel, out of the land of Egypt by great judgments [*plagues and punishments*].

JST Exodus 7:4

4 But Pharaoh will not hearken unto you, **therefore I will lay my hand upon Egypt,** and bring forth mine armies, my people, the children of Israel, out of the land of Egypt by great judgments.

5 And the **Egyptians shall know that I am the LORD,** when I stretch forth mine hand [*exercise My power*] upon Egypt, and bring out the children of Israel from among them.

6 And **Moses and Aaron did as the LORD commanded them**, so did they.

7 And **Moses was fourscore years old** [*80 years old*], and **Aaron fourscore and three years old,** when they spake unto Pharaoh.

Next, the Lord gives Moses and Aaron very specific instructions regarding their upcoming meeting with Pharaoh.

8 ¶ And **the LORD spake unto Moses and unto Aaron, saying,**

9 **When Pharaoh shall speak unto you, saying, Shew** [*pronounced "show"*] **a miracle** for you: then thou shalt say unto Aaron, Take thy rod, and cast it before Pharaoh, and it shall become a serpent.

JST Exodus 7:9

9 When Pharaoh shall speak unto you, saying, **Show** a miracle **that I may know you;** then thou shalt say unto Aaron, Take thy rod, and cast it before Pharaoh, and it shall become a serpent.

10 ¶ And **Moses and Aaron went in unto Pharaoh**, and they did so as the LORD had commanded: and **Aaron cast down his rod** before Pharaoh, and before his servants, **and it became a serpen**t.

11 **Then Pharaoh also called the wise men and the sorcerers:** now the magicians of Egypt, they also

did in like manner with their enchantments.

12 For they cast down every man his rod, and they became serpents: but **Aaron's rod swallowed up their rods.**

As you can see, in verses 11–12, above, and also in verse 22, one of the major messages of this chapter is the fact that Satan and his evil spirits who are upon the earth, have power to perform miracles. We are reminded of this in Revelation 16:14.

Revelation 16:14

14 For they are **the spirits of devils, working miracles**, which go forth unto the kings of the earth and of the whole world, to gather them to the battle of that great day of God Almighty.

This is a strong reminder that Satan in the "great counterfeiter."

He wanted to be the Redeemer (see Moses 4:1–3) and claimed to be the Only Begotten (see Moses 1:19). He succeeded in leading Cain to the frightful point of making a covenant in the name of "the living God" (Moses 5:29)—in other words, in the name of Jesus Christ—a counterfeit of covenants we make using the Savior's name.

We still see Satan attempting to deceive today, including the use of signs, covenants, and so forth involved in Satan worship, secret combinations, and the like.

Joseph Fielding Smith commented on the subject of miracles being performed by Satan and his evil hosts. He said:

"All down through the ages and in almost all countries, men have exercised great occult and mystical powers, even to the healing of the sick and the performing of miracles. Soothsayers, magicians, and astrologers were found in the courts of ancient kings. They had certain powers by which they divined and solved the monarch's problems, dreams, etc. One of the most striking examples of this is recorded in Exodus, where Pharaoh called 'the wise men and the sorcerers' who duplicated some of the miracles the Lord had commanded Moses and Aaron to perform. When Aaron threw down his rod, it became a serpent. The Egyptian magicians threw down their rods, and they also became serpents.

"The Savior declared that Satan had the power to bind bodies of men and women and sorely afflict them [*see Matthew 7:22–23; Luke 13:16*]. If Satan has power to bind the bodies, he surely must have power to loose them. It should be remembered that Satan has great knowledge and thereby can exercise authority and to some extent control the elements, when some greater power does not intervene." (Smith, *Answers to Gospel Questions,* 1:176, 178.)

By the way, did you notice that Aaron's rod swallowed up Pharaoh's magicians' rods, in verse 12? This is symbolic of the fact that God and His authorized servants have power over Satan and his followers.

13 And **he hardened Pharaoh's heart,** that he hearkened not unto them; as the LORD had said.

JST Exodus 7:13

13 And **Pharaoh hardened his heart,** that he hearkened not unto them; as the Lord had said.

Next, we will see the water turn to blood. It will be a disaster for the Egyptians.

14 ¶ And **the LORD said unto Moses, Pharaoh's heart is hardened,** he refuseth to let the people go.

15 **Get thee unto Pharaoh in the morning;** lo, he goeth out unto the water; and thou shalt stand by the river's brink against he come [*be there to meet him*]; and **the rod which was turned to a serpent shalt thou take in thine hand.**

16 And thou **shalt say unto him, The LORD God of the Hebrews hath sent me** unto thee, saying, **Let my people go,** that they may serve me in the wilderness: and, behold, hitherto thou wouldest not hear.

> Remember that the Egyptians believed in many gods (all false). And so, it makes sense for Moses to identify Jehovah as the one who sent him.

17 **Thus saith the LORD, In this thou shalt know that I am the LORD:** behold, I will smite with the rod that is in mine hand upon **the waters** which are in the river, and they **shall be turned to blood.**

18 And **the fish** that is in the river **shall die**, and **the river shall stink;** and **the Egyptians shall lothe to drink of the water of the river.**

> Next, we will see all of the Egyptians' water sources and supplies turn to blood.

19 ¶ **And the LORD spake unto Moses, Say unto Aaron, Take thy rod, and stretch out thine hand upon the waters of Egypt**, upon their **streams**, upon their **rivers**, and upon their **ponds**, and upon all their **pools** of water, **that they may become blood**; and that there may be blood throughout all the land of Egypt, both **in vessels of wood**, and **in vessels of stone**.

20 **And Moses and Aaron did so**, as the LORD commanded; and he lifted up the rod, and smote the waters that were in the river, **in the sight of Pharaoh, and in the sight of his servants;** and **all the waters** that were **in the river were turned to blood**.

21 And **the fish** that was in the river **died**; and **the river stank**, and **the Egyptians could not drink of the water of the river;** and there was blood throughout all the land of Egypt.

22 And **the magicians of Egypt did so with their enchantments:** and **Pharaoh's heart was hardened,** neither did he hearken unto them; as the LORD had said.

23 And **Pharaoh turned and went into his house**, neither did he set his heart to this also ["*paying no regard even to this*"—*see footnote 23a in your Bible*].

24 And **all the Egyptians digged round about the river for water to drink;** for they could not drink of the water of the river.

25 And **seven days were fulfilled, after** that **the LORD had smitten the river.**

EXODUS 8

In this chapter we will see the plagues of frogs, lice, and flies. Pharaoh will still not let the children of Israel go.

Notice that in verse 7, Pharaoh's magicians use their evil powers to duplicate the plague of frogs, but in verse 18, they are not able to replicate the plague of lice. Perhaps one lesson we see here is that God places limits upon Satan and his evil followers. This doctrine is taught, among other places, in the last two phrases of Moses 4:21:

Moses 4:21

21 And **I will put enmity** [*a natural dislike, intense distrust*] **between thee** [*Satan*] **and the woman, between thy seed** [*Satan's followers, including the one-third who followed him in premortality, as well as those who follow him here on earth*] **and her seed** [*Jesus Christ*]; **and he** [*Christ*] **shall bruise thy head** [*will crush Satan and his kingdom; in other words, He will triumph over Satan and ultimately cast him and his evil followers out completely (see Doctrine and Covenants 88:111–14)*], **and thou** [*Satan*] **shalt bruise his heel** [*will cause suffering, including causing evil men to crucify the Savior and causing pain and sorrow by leading people away from Christ and His gospel*].

And so, we can see that Satan can cause trouble, and indeed he does, but he cannot ultimately triumph over Christ and His work, including us, unless we let him. Another important message we see here is that the Lord gives the wicked many chances to repent and stop fighting against His work.

1 **AND the LORD spake unto Moses, Go unto Pharaoh, and say unto him, Thus saith the LORD, Let my people go, that they may serve me.**

2 And **if thou refuse to let them go, behold,** I will smite all thy borders with **frogs:**

3 And **the river shall bring forth frogs abundantly,** which shall go up and come **into thine house**, and into **thy bedchamber**, and upon **thy bed**, and into **the house of thy servants**, and **upon thy people**, and into **thine ovens**, and into thy **kneadingtroughs:**

4 And **the frogs shall come up both on thee, and upon thy people, and upon all thy servants.**

While it may or may not be pushing symbolism a bit too much in this context, it is nevertheless interesting to note that in Revelation 16:13, frogs are symbolic of evil spirits from the devil which will permeate society in the last days.

5 ¶ And **the LORD spake unto Moses, Say unto Aaron, Stretch forth thine hand with thy rod** over the streams, over the rivers, and over the ponds, **and cause frogs to come up upon the land of Egypt.**

6 And Aaron stretched out his hand over the waters of Egypt; **and the frogs came up, and covered the land of Egypt.**

7 **And the magicians did so with their enchantments**, and brought up frogs upon the land of Egypt.

8 ¶ **Then Pharaoh called for Moses and Aaron**, and said, Intreat the LORD, that he may take away the frogs from me, and from my people; and **I will let the people go**, that they may do sacrifice unto the LORD.

9 And Moses said unto Pharaoh, Glory over me [*to you I leave the honor of choosing the time*]: **when shall I intreat for thee**, and for thy servants, and for thy people, **to destroy the frogs from thee and thy houses, that they may remain in the river only?**

10 And **he said, To morrow. And he said, Be it according to thy word:** that thou mayest know that there is none like unto the LORD our God.

11 And **the frogs shall depart from thee**, and from thy houses, and from thy servants, and from thy people; **they shall remain in the river only**.

12 And Moses and Aaron went out from Pharaoh: and **Moses cried unto the LORD because of the frogs** which he had brought against Pharaoh.

13 And **the LORD did according to the word of Moses**; and the frogs died out of the houses, out of the villages, and out of the fields.

14 And they gathered them together upon heaps: **and the land stank**.

> Pharaoh is much like many wicked people who repent under pressure but never go through a deep change of heart. They revert quickly to their former ways after the immediate troubles are removed by the Lord.

15 **But** when **Pharaoh** saw that there was respite, he **hardened his heart**, and hearkened not unto them; as the LORD had said.

16 ¶ And **the LORD said unto Moses, Say unto Aaron, Stretch out thy rod, and smite the dust of the land, that it may become lice throughout all the land of Egypt.**

17 And **they did so**; for Aaron stretched out his hand with his rod, and smote the dust of the earth, and it became lice in man, and in beast; **all the dust of the land became lice throughout all the land of Egypt**.

18 And **the magicians did so** with their enchantments to bring forth

lice, **but they could not**: so there were lice upon man, and upon beast.

> Even Pharaoh's magicians now plead with him to yield to God, but his pride stands in the way.

19 **Then the magicians said unto Pharaoh, This is the finger of God:** and Pharaoh's heart was hardened, and **he hearkened not unto them**; as the LORD had said.

20 ¶ **And the LORD said unto Moses, Rise up early in the morning, and stand before Pharaoh**; lo, he cometh forth to the water; and **say unto him, Thus saith the LORD, Let my people go, that they may serve me.**

21 **Else, if thou wilt not let my people go, behold, I will send swarms of flies** upon thee, and upon thy servants, and upon thy people, and into thy houses: and the houses of the Egyptians shall be full of swarms of flies, and also the ground whereon they are.

> Next, the Lord says that, in effect, He will give Pharaoh obvious evidence that He is with the Israelites.

22 And **I will sever** [*separate*] in that day **the land of Goshen** [*the part of northern Egypt, on the Nile River Delta, where the children of Israel dwell*], **in which my people dwell, that no swarms of flies shall be there; to the end thou mayest know that I am the LORD** in the midst of the earth.

23 And **I will put a division between my people and thy people**: to morrow shall this sign be.

24 And **the LORD did so**; and there came a grievous swarm of flies into the house of Pharaoh, and into his servants' houses, and into all **the land of Egypt: the land was corrupted by reason of the swarm of flies**.

25 ¶ And **Pharaoh called for Moses and for Aaron, and said, Go ye, sacrifice to your God in the land** [*in other words, just do your sacrifices right here in Egypt*].

26 And **Moses said, It is not meet** [*it wouldn't be wise*] **so to do; for we shall sacrifice the abomination of the Egyptians** [*in sacrificing, we would be doing an abominable thing in the eyes of the Egyptians*] **to the LORD our God**: lo, shall we sacrifice the abomination of **the Egyptians** before their eyes, and **will** they not **stone us**?

27 **We will go three days' journey into the wilderness** [*so that we are far enough away from them so they won't see what we are doing*], **and sacrifice to the LORD our God, as he shall command us**.

> The concern of Moses and Aaron, in verses 26–27, above, lies in the fact that cows and bulls were sacred to the Egyptians, and it was an abomination in their eyes to kill them. Bulls were commonly used by the Israelites in their animal sacrifices. Thus, sacrificing within view of the Egyptians could lead to mob violence and stoning of many Israelites.

28 **And Pharaoh said, I will let you go**, that ye may sacrifice to the LORD your God in the wilderness; **only ye shall not go very far away**: intreat for me.

29 And **Moses said**, Behold, **I go out from thee, and I will intreat the LORD that the swarms of flies may depart** from Pharaoh, from his servants, and from his people, **to morrow**: but **let not Pharaoh deal deceitfully any more in not letting the people go to sacrifice to the LORD**.

30 And **Moses** went out from Pharaoh, and **intreated the LORD**.

31 And **the LORD** did according to the word of Moses; and he **removed the swarms of flies** from Pharaoh, from his servants, and from his people; **there remained not one**.

> Did you notice how completely the Lord removed the affliction of flies in verse 31, above. This can remind us of how merciful He is in forgiving us of sin and giving us completely new opportunities to be clean and free from past sins.
>
> Sadly, Pharaoh changes his mind yet again.

32 And **Pharaoh hardened his heart** at this time also, neither would he let the people go.

EXODUS 9

Next, we will see three more plagues, the death of the Egyptian's cattle (domesticated animals), the plague of boils and blains, and the plague of hail and fire. Still, Pharaoh will refuse to let the Lord's people go.

1 THEN **the LORD said unto Moses, Go in unto Pharaoh**, and **tell him, Thus saith the LORD God of the Hebrews, Let my people go**, that they may serve me.

2 For **if thou refuse** to let them go, and wilt hold them still,

3 Behold, **the hand of the LORD is upon thy cattle** [*domesticated animals*] which is in the field, upon the horses, upon the asses, upon the camels, upon the oxen, and upon the sheep: **there shall be a very grievous murrain** [*severe plague*].

4 And **the LORD shall sever** [*distinguish*] **between the cattle of Israel and the cattle of Egypt**: and **there shall nothing die of all that is the children's of Israel.**

5 And **the LORD appointed a set time,** saying, **To morrow the LORD shall do this thing** in the land.

6 And the LORD did that thing **on the morrow,** and **all the cattle of Egypt died: but of the cattle of the children of Israel died not one**.

7 And **Pharaoh sent**, and, behold, there was not one of the cattle of the Israelites dead. And **the heart of Pharaoh was hardened,** and **he did not let the people go.**

8 ¶ And **the LORD said unto Moses and unto Aaron, Take to you handfuls of ashes** of the furnace, and let Moses **sprinkle it toward the heaven in the sight of Pharaoh.**

9 And **it shall become small dust in all the land of Egypt,** and shall be **a boil breaking forth with blains** [*Blains were blisters, small inflammations of the skin that were filled with pus*] **upon man, and upon beast, throughout all the land of Egypt.**

10 And **they took ashes** of the furnace, and stood before Pharaoh; **and Moses sprinkled it up toward heaven**; and **it became a boil** breaking forth **with blains upon man, and upon beast.**

11 And **the magicians could not stand before Moses because of the boils;** for the boil was upon the magicians, and upon all the Egyptians.

12 And **the LORD hardened the heart of Pharaoh,** and he hearkened not unto them; as the LORD had spoken unto Moses.

JST Exodus 9:12

12 And **Pharaoh hardened his heart**, and he hearkened not unto them; as the Lord had spoken unto Moses.

13 ¶ And **the LORD said unto Moses**, Rise up early in the morning, and **stand before Pharaoh, and say unto him, Thus saith the LORD God of the Hebrews, Let my people go**, that they may serve me.

14 **For I will** [*NIV, "or I will"*] at this time **send all my plagues** upon thine heart, and upon thy servants, and upon thy people; **that thou mayest know that there is none like me in all the earth.**

15 **For now I will stretch out my hand, that I may smite thee and thy people with pestilence; and thou shalt be cut off from the earth.** [*NIV, "For by now I could have stretched out my hand and struck you and your people with a plague that would have wiped you off the earth."*]

16 And in very deed **for this cause have I raised thee up** [*NIV, "spared you"*], **for to shew in thee my power;** and **that my name may be declared throughout all the earth.**

17 **As yet exaltest thou thyself against my people, that thou wilt not let them go?**

JST Exodus 9:17

17 **Therefore speak unto Pharaoh the thing which I command thee, who as yet exalteth himself that he** will not let them go.

18 Behold, **to morrow about this time I will cause it to rain a very grievous hail,** such as hath not been in Egypt since the foundation thereof even until now.

19 **Send therefore now, and gather thy** [*Pharoah's*] **cattle, and all that thou hast in the field;** for upon every man and beast which shall be found in the field, and shall not be

brought home, **the hail shall come down upon them, and they shall die**.

> Next, in verses 20 and 21, we see that some of Pharoah's servants believed Moses and some did not.

20 **He that feared the word of the LORD among the servants of Pharaoh made his servants and his cattle flee into the houses:**

21 **And he that regarded not the word of the LORD left his servants and his cattle in the field**.

> Did you notice in verses 19–21, above, that the Lord is now reaching beyond Pharaoh to his people, allowing them to exercise their own agency to protect themselves and their livestock against the next plague, regardless of what Pharoah chooses to do?

22 ¶ **And the LORD said unto Moses, Stretch forth thine hand toward heaven, that there may be hail in all the land of Egypt**, upon man, and upon beast, and upon every herb of the field, throughout the land of Egypt.

23 And **Moses stretched forth his rod toward heaven**: and the LORD sent **thunder** and **hail**, and the **fire** ran along upon the ground; and **the LORD rained hail upon the land of Egypt**.

24 So **there was hail, and fire mingled with the hail**, very grievous, such as there was none like it in all the land of Egypt since it became a nation.

25 And **the hail smote** throughout all the land of Egypt all that was in the field, both **man and beast**; and the hail smote **every herb** of the field, and brake **every tree** of the field.

26 **Only in the land of Goshen, where the children of Israel were, was there no hail**.

> Next, Pharaoh makes quite an admission, but still, he will end up going back on his word (verses 34–35). Remember that the Lord loves him and his people, which is very evident in the number of chances He is giving them. This is quite an important message found in these verses. It probably applies to all of us as we time and again determine to change inappropriate behaviors but revert back to them when perceived consequences are no longer imminent.

27 ¶ And **Pharaoh sent, and called for Moses and Aaron, and said** unto them, **I have sinned this time: the LORD is righteous** [*NIV, "the Lord is in the right"*], and **I and my people are wicked**.

28 Intreat [*pray to*] the LORD (for it is enough) **that there be no more mighty thunderings and hail;** and **I will let you go**, and ye shall stay no longer.

29 And **Moses said** unto him, As soon as I am gone out of the city, **I will spread abroad my hands unto**

the LORD; and **the thunder shall cease**, **neither** shall there be **any more hail;** that **thou mayest know how that the earth is the LORD's.**

30 **But as for thee and thy servants, I know that ye will not yet fear the LORD God.**

31 And the **flax and the barley was smitten:** for the barley was in the ear, and the flax was bolled [*in the bud stage*].

32 **But the wheat and the rie** [*a type of wheat—see footnote 32b in your Bible*] **were not smitten: for they were not grown up**.

33 And **Moses** went out of the city from Pharaoh, and **spread abroad his hands unto the LORD:** and **the thunders and hail ceased**, and the rain was not poured upon the earth.

34 And when **Pharaoh** saw that the rain and the hail and the thunders were ceased, he **sinned yet more, and hardened his heart, he and his servants.**

35 And the **heart of Pharaoh was hardened, neither would he let the children of Israel** go; as the LORD had spoken by Moses.

EXODUS 10

In this chapter, we will see the plague of locusts and that of thick darkness. Again, we will see the translation in the Bible incorrectly indicate that the Lord hardened Pharaoh's heart.

Perhaps you've noticed that many people and cultures give God credit for everything. While such thinking can no doubt usually be credited to good intentions, it can be devastatingly wrong in situations such as this. The Lord does not inspire us to do wrong. The false doctrine of predestination can attain damaging credibility from such incorrectly translated segments of the Bible. The JST corrects verses 1, 20, and 27.

1 AND the LORD said unto Moses, Go in unto Pharaoh: for **I have hardened his heart, and the heart of his servants, that I might shew these my signs before him**:

JST Exodus 10:1

1 And the Lord said unto Moses, Go in unto Pharaoh; for **he hath hardened his heart, and the hearts of his servants, therefore I will show these my signs before him**;

Did you catch the significance of the JST change from "that," in verse 1, to "therefore?" As it stands in the Bible, one could develop a false belief that God sometimes inspires evil behavior in order to intervene and demonstrate His power. Some misguided individuals could take such thinking to extremes and teach that God is responsible for every thought and act, good or evil, thus confirming the false doctrine of predestination and effectively eliminating individual agency.

Next, we see that the Lord wants parents down through the ages to teach their children about these miracles in Egypt to build and strengthen testimonies.

2 And **that thou mayest tell in the ears of thy son, and of thy son's son, what things I have wrought in Egypt**, and my signs which I have done among them; **that ye may know how that I am the LORD.**

3 And **Moses and Aaron came in unto Pharaoh**, and said unto him, **Thus saith the LORD God of the Hebrews, How long wilt thou refuse to humble thyself before me?** let my people go, that they may serve me.

4 **Else**, if thou refuse to let my people go, behold, **to morrow will I bring the locusts** into thy coast:

> The plague of locusts will finish the devastation and destruction of crops started by the hail and fire in chapter 9.

5 And **they shall cover the face of the earth**, that one cannot be able to see the earth: and **they shall eat** the residue of **that** which is escaped, **which remaineth** unto you **from the hail, and** shall eat **every tree** which groweth for you out of the field:

6 And **they shall fill thy houses**, and **the houses of all thy servants,** and **the houses of all the Egyptians**; which neither thy fathers, nor thy fathers' fathers have seen, since the day that they were upon the earth unto this day [*it will be the worst infestation of locusts ever in the history of Egypt*]. And **he turned himself, and went out from Pharaoh.**

Pharaoh's servants now plead with him to give in to Moses before the plague of locusts is set loose. They beg him to face the reality of what has already happened to their land.

7 And **Pharaoh's servants said unto him, How long shall this man be a snare unto us? let the men go,** that they may serve the LORD their God: **knowest thou not yet that Egypt is destroyed?**

8 And **Moses and Aaron were brought again unto Pharaoh**: and **he said** unto them, **Go, serve the LORD your God: but who are they that shall go** [*which of your people do you plan to take with you*]?

9 And **Moses said, We will go with our young** and with our **old**, with our **sons** and with our **daughters**, with our **flocks** and with our **herds** will we go; for we must hold a feast unto the LORD.

10 And **he said unto them, Let the LORD be so with you, as** [*if—see footnote 10a in your Bible*] **I will let you go**, and your little ones: look to it; for **evil is before you** [*it is obvious that you are up to some mischief—see footnote 10b in your Bible*].

> In verse 10, above, it appears that Pharaoh is saying, in effect, that it would take an act of Moses's God indeed to get him to let Moses and Aaron go with all their people, including women and children. He suspects a plot to escape Egypt. Consequently, in verse 11, next, Pharaoh says, in effect, "Not a chance. Just take your men and go out and worship the

Lord." He then shows his contempt for them by having his servants drive them out from his court.

11 **Not so: go now ye that are men**, and serve the LORD; for that ye did desire. And **they were driven out from Pharaoh's presence**.

12 ¶ And **the LORD said unto Moses, Stretch out thine hand over the land of Egypt for the locusts**, that they may come up upon the land of Egypt, and eat every herb of the land, even all that the hail hath left.

13 And **Moses stretched forth his rod over the land of Egypt**, and the LORD brought an east wind upon the land all that day, and all that night; and **when it was morning, the east wind brought the locusts**.

14 And **the locusts went up over all the land of Egypt**, and rested in all the coasts [*borders*] of Egypt: very grievous were they; before them there were no such locusts as they, neither after them shall be such.

15 For **they covered the face of the whole earth**, so that the land was darkened; and they did eat every herb of the land, and all the fruit of the trees which the hail had left: and there remained not any green thing in the trees, or in the herbs of the field, through all the land of Egypt.

16 ¶ Then **Pharaoh called for Moses and Aaron in haste; and he said, I have sinned against the LORD your God, and against you**.

17 Now therefore forgive, I pray thee, my sin only this once, and intreat the LORD your God, that he may take away from me this death [*NIV, "this deadly plague"*] only.

18 And **he went out from Pharaoh, and intreated the LORD** [*prayed to the Lord*].

19 And **the LORD turned a mighty strong west wind, which took away the locusts**, and cast them into the Red sea; **there remained not one locust in all the coasts of Egypt**.

> There may well be some important Atonement symbolism in verse 10, above. When we truly turn to the Lord and repent, our sins are completely washed away.

20 But **the LORD hardened Pharaoh's heart**, so that he would not let the children of Israel go.

JST Exodus 10:20

> 20 But **Pharaoh hardened his heart**, so that he would not let the children of Israel go.

21 ¶ And **the LORD said unto Moses, Stretch out thine hand toward heaven, that there may be darkness over the land** of Egypt, even darkness **which may be felt**.

22 And Moses stretched forth his hand toward heaven; and there was a **thick darkness in all the land of Egypt three days** [*compare with 3 Nephi 8:20–23*]:

23 **They saw not one another, neither rose any from his place** for

three days: but all the children of Israel had light in their dwellings.

24 ¶ And **Pharaoh called unto Moses, and said, Go ye, serve the LORD; only let your flocks and your herds be stayed** [*remain here*]: let your little ones also go with you.

25 And **Moses said, Thou must give us also sacrifices and burnt offerings**, that we may sacrifice unto the LORD our God.

26 **Our cattle also shall go with us**; there shall not an hoof be left behind; for thereof must we take to serve the LORD our God; and we know not with what we must serve the LORD, until we come thither.

27 ¶ But **the LORD hardened Pharaoh's heart**, and he would not let them go.

JST Exodus 10:27

27 But **Pharaoh hardened his heart**, and he would not let them go.

One of the major messages we are seeing time and time again here, with Pharaoh's repeated going back on his word, is the fact that wickedness does not promote rational thought. Next, Pharoah is livid with rage and threatens Moses with death if he returns again to see him.

28 And **Pharaoh said unto him, Get thee from me**, take heed to thyself, **see my face no more; for in that day thou seest my face thou shalt die.**

29 And **Moses said, Thou hast spoken well** [*you are right*], **I will see thy face again no more**.

EXODUS 11

In this chapter, the final plague (the death of the firstborn) is introduced (it will take place in chapter 12). There is a reminder that the Lord keeps His word and has the power to deliver us from evil. Another lesson is that the promised blessings often come after the trial of our faith (Doctrine and Covenants 58:4).

1 And **the LORD said unto Moses, Yet will I bring one plague** *more* upon Pharaoh, and upon Egypt; **afterwards he will let you go hence** [*into the wilderness*]: when he shall let you go, **he shall surely thrust you out** hence altogether [*he will be very anxious to get you out of Egypt*].

In Exodus 3:20–22, the Lord told the Israelites that when they left Egypt, they would leave wealthy. The time for this prophecy to be fulfilled is now here. However, the use of the word "borrow," in verse 2, next, is unfortunate. It is a mistranslation of a Hebrew word in the original text. As it stands in the King James Version of the Bible, it makes the Israelites look like they took the things under false pretenses. In reality, the Egyptians, not the Israelites, had suffered so much because of the plagues that came upon them that they were glad to get rid of the Israelites and were eager to give them whatever necessary to get them to leave.

2 Speak now in the ears of the people, and **let every man borrow of his neighbour,** and **every woman of her neighbour, jewels of silver, and jewels of gold**.

> A much better word for "borrow," in verse 2, above, would be "ask," or "demand." Thus, there was no deception or dishonesty on the part of the Israelites; rather, they made a straightforward request for items to take with them. We will include a quote here from noted Bible scholar Adam Clarke in reference to the word "borrow" in verse 2. He said:
>
> "This is certainly not a very correct translation: the original word . . . shaal signifies simply to ask, request, demand, require, inquire, &c.; but it does not signify to borrow in the proper sense of that word, though in a very few places of Scripture it is thus used. In this and the parallel place, chap. xii. 35, the word signifies to ask or demand, and not to borrow, which is a gross mistake. . . . God commanded the Israelites to ask or demand a certain recompense for their past services, and he inclined the hearts of the Egyptians to give liberally; and this, far from a matter of oppression, wrong, or even charity, was no more than a very partial recompense for the long and painful services which we may say six hundred thousand Israelites had rendered to Egypt, during a considerable number of years. And there can be no doubt that while their heaviest oppression lasted, they were permitted to accumulate no kind of property, as all their gains went to their oppressors" (Bible Commentary, 1:307).

The first part of verse 3, next, points out that the Egyptians were very willing to give the children of Israel the things they requested. The verse also reminds us that Moses had attained great power among the people by this time.

3 And **the LORD gave the people favour in the sight of the Egyptians**. Moreover the man **Moses *was* very great in the land of Egypt, in the sight of Pharaoh's servants, and in the sight of the people.**

4 And **Moses said, Thus saith the LORD, About midnight will I go out into the midst of Egypt**:

5 And **all the firstborn in the land of Egypt shall die**, from the firstborn of Pharaoh that sitteth upon his throne, even unto the firstborn of the maidservant that *is* behind the mill; and all the firstborn of beasts.

6 And **there shall be a great cry throughout all the land of Egypt**, such as there was none like it, nor shall be like it any more.

7 **But against any of the children of Israel shall not a dog move his tongue, against man or beast**: that ye may know how that **the LORD doth put a difference between the Egyptians and Israel** [*so you know that there is a difference between the covenant people of the Lord and the Egyptians*].

> When we look at symbolism, there is a major message in verse 7, above. The children of Israel were the Lord's covenant people. All can become

covenant people of the Lord by conforming their lives to the gospel and making covenants with God. Egypt sometimes is used symbolically to represent the kingdom of the devil and worldly wickedness. Therefore, the last half of verse 7 can be understood to say that there is a tremendous difference between the ways of the world and the ways of the Lord.

The JST makes significant changes in the last three verses of this chapter.

8 And **all these thy servants** shall come down unto me [*Moses*], and bow down themselves unto me, saying, Get thee out, and all the people that follow thee: and after that I will go out. And **he went out from Pharaoh in a great anger**.

9 And the LORD said unto Moses, Pharaoh shall not hearken unto you; **that** my wonders may be multiplied in the land of Egypt.

10 And Moses and Aaron did all these wonders before Pharaoh: and **the LORD hardened Pharaoh's heart**, so that he would not let the children of Israel go out of his land.

JST Exodus 11:8–10

8 And **all these the servants of Pharaoh** shall come down unto me, and bow themselves down unto me, saying, Get thee out, and all the people that follow thee; and after that I will go out.

9 And the Lord said unto Moses, Pharaoh will not hearken unto you; **therefore** my wonders shall be multiplied in the land of Egypt.

10 And Moses and Aaron did all these wonders before Pharaoh, and **they went out from Pharaoh, and he was in great anger**. And **Pharaoh hardened his heart**, so that he would not let the children of Israel go out of his land.

EXODUS 12

This is a very significant chapter in Exodus. There is much Atonement symbolism here. Among other things, the death of the firstborn (Exodus 12:29–30) will lead to freedom from bondage. We will see the preparations required of the Israelites by the Lord in order to avoid the death of their own firstborn. We will be introduced to what will become known as the "Passover."

THE PASSOVER

One of the most important events in the Old Testament is the "Passover," the night when the Lord "smote all the firstborn in the land of Egypt" (Exodus 12:29) but "passed over" the homes of the Israelites, sparing their firstborn.

The Passover was such an important event that the Israelite calendar system was altered to make the month in which it took place become the first month in their calendar year (see Exodus 12:1–2). This month, Abib (later called Nisan), is the equivalent of late March or early April in our calendar system. Many Jews today continue to celebrate Passover.

As mentioned above, the preparation of the children of Israel for the "passing over" of the destructions and punishments of the Lord is filled with symbolism. In the first 28 verses, we will use **bold** to point out elements of the Passover and associated teachings.

You will see many "types" and "symbols." Remember that "types" is another word for "symbols." In other words, "types" are things that represent or symbolize something else—in this case especially, the mission and Atonement of Christ and what is required of us to have the Atonement work in our lives. First, the change in the Israelite calendar system, verses 1–2.

1 And the LORD spake unto Moses and Aaron in the land of Egypt, saying,

2 **This month** *shall be* **unto you the beginning of months: it** *shall be* **the first month of the year to you** [*change your calendar system to reflect this month as the first month of the year*].

3 ¶ Speak ye unto all the congregation of Israel, saying, In the tenth *day* of this month they shall take to them every man **a lamb** [*symbolic of the Savior*], according to the house of *their* fathers, a lamb for an house:

4 And if the household be too little for the lamb, let him and his neighbour next unto his house take *it* according to the number of the souls; every man according to his eating shall make your count for the lamb [*if a family is not big enough to eat a lamb themselves, join together with other families*].

5 Your **lamb shall be without blemish** [*the Savior was without blemish*], **a male of the first year** [*in the prime of life, symbolizing that the Savior was in the prime of His life when He was sacrificed*]: ye shall take *it* out from the sheep, or from the goats:

6 And ye shall keep it up until the fourteenth day of the same month: and the whole assembly of the congregation of Israel shall kill it in the evening.

7 And they shall **take of the blood** [*symbolic of the Savior's innocent blood*], and **strike** *it* **on the two side posts and on the upper door post** [*symbolic of having the mission and Atonement of Jesus Christ before us in all our comings and goings; also symbolic of the cleansing blood of Christ in our lives*] **of the houses, wherein they shall eat it**.

8 And they shall eat the flesh in that night, roast with fire, and **unleavened bread** [*symbolic of the urgency of following Christ now, not having time for the bread to rise before baking*]; *and* with **bitter *herbs*** [*symbolic of trials and tribulations that can come into the lives of followers of the* Savior] they shall eat it.

9 Eat not of it raw [*undercooked*], nor sodden [*boiled*] at all with water, but roast *with* fire; his head with his legs, and with the purtenance [*edible inner parts—see footnote 9b in your Bible*] thereof.

10 And ye shall **let nothing of it remain** [*take Christ completely into your lives, don't leave any of His gospel out*] until the morning; and that which remaineth of it until the morning ye shall burn with fire.

> Each element of the symbolism in verse 11, next, represents being prepared to leave in a hurry in order to effectively follow the Lord without delay. In other words, hurry to live the gospel!

11 ¶ And thus shall ye eat it; ***with your loins girded*** [*fully dressed, ready for action*], **your shoes on your feet**, and your **staff in your hand**; and ye shall **eat it in haste** [*hurry to live the gospel*]: it *is* the LORD's passover.

> If you look in the Bible Dictionary, under "Feasts," you will see that the Israelites were to eat the feast "standing, ready for a journey."

12 For I will pass through the land of Egypt this night, and will smite all the firstborn in the land of Egypt, both man and beast; and against all the gods of Egypt I will execute judgment: I *am* the LORD.

13 **And the blood shall be to you for a token** [*a sign or symbol that you have covenanted with Christ to live His gospel and follow His prophet*] **upon the houses where ye** *are:* **and when I see the blood, I will pass over you, and the plague** [*symbolic of the destructions and punishments that come upon the wicked*] **shall not be upon you to destroy** *you,* **when I smite the land of Egypt** [*symbolic of Satan and his kingdom*].

> Next, the Israelites are told to celebrate the Passover annually, every year thereafter. They are given details and instructions for how to go about this.

14 And **this day** [*Passover*] **shall be unto you for a memorial; and ye shall keep it a feast to the LORD throughout your generations**; ye shall keep it a feast by an ordinance for ever.

15 **Seven days** [*in biblical symbolism, the number seven represents completeness, perfection, the work of the Lord—compare with Matthew 5:48, footnote b in your Bible*] **shall ye eat unleavened bread** [*symbolizing readiness to follow God, not procrastinating*]; even the first day ye shall put away leaven out of your houses: for whosoever eateth leavened bread from the first day until the seventh day, that soul shall be cut off [*excommunicated*] from Israel.

16 And **in the first day *there shall be* an holy convocation** [*a meeting*], **and in the seventh day there shall be an holy convocation** to you; **no manner of work shall be done** in them, save [*except*] *that* which every man must eat, that only may be done of you [*in other words, no work except that required to prepare meals*].

17 And **ye shall observe *the feast of* unleavened bread**; for in this selfsame day have I brought your armies [*people, organized as groups according to the twelve tribes they*

belonged to] **out of the land of Egypt: therefore shall ye observe this day in your generations by an ordinance for ever.**

18 ¶ **In the first** *month,* **on the fourteenth day of the month at even** [*beginning in the evening*]**, ye shall eat unleavened bread, until the one and twenty-first day of the month at even** [*in the evening*]**.**

> In verse 18, above, it mentions, in effect, that the fourteenth day of the month begins in the evening. In our system, the next day begins at midnight, but in the Israelite system of days of the week, the day began in the evening and was over the next evening. The equivalent in our calendar system would be that if Tuesday began about 6 p.m. Monday, then Wednesday began about 6 p.m. Tuesday, and so on.

19 **Seven days shall there be no leaven** [*yeast was symbolic of sin and corruption, since it spoiled so easily*] **found in your houses: for whosoever eateth that which is leavened, even that soul shall be cut off from the congregation of Israel** [*symbolic of how personal sin and corruption can distance us from the Church and the Spirit*]**, whether he be a stranger, or born in the land.**

20 **Ye shall eat nothing leavened; in all your habitations shall ye eat unleavened bread.**

> We will include a quote from the *Old Testament Student Manual* that helps us understand the symbolism associated with "leaven" as used in Old Testament times:
>
> "Leaven, or yeast, was seen anciently as a symbol of corruption because it so easily spoiled and turned moldy. Jesus used this imagery when he warned the disciples of the 'leaven of the Pharisees' (Matthew 16:6), meaning their corrupt doctrine (see Matthew 16:6–12). In the law of Moses no leaven could be offered with the trespass offering (see Leviticus 6:17), suggesting that the offering must be without any corruption. For the Israelites, eating the unleavened bread symbolized that they were partaking of the bread which had no corruption or impurity, namely, the Bread of Life, who is Jesus Christ (see John 6:35). The careful purging of the household of all leaven (see Exodus 12:19) was a beautiful symbol of putting away all uncleanliness from the family. Paul drew on this imagery of the unleavened bread when he called upon the Corinthian Saints to put away sin from their lives (see 1 Corinthians 5:7–8)" (*Old Testament Student Manual: Genesis–2 Samuel,* page 119).
>
> Beginning with verse 21, next, Moses instructs the Israelites to begin actual preparations for what will become known as the Passover.

21 ¶ **Then Moses called for all the elders of Israel, and said unto them, Draw out** [*select from the flocks*] **and take you a lamb according to your families** [*for one or more families, depending on family size*]**, and kill the passover** [*the lamb*]**.**

22 And ye shall take a bunch of **hyssop** [*a plant associated with the Atonement of Christ—see John 19:29*], and **dip** *it* **in the blood** that *is* in the bason [*the bowl*], and **strike the lintel** [*the board or beam over the top of the doorway*] **and the two side posts with the blood** that *is* in the bason; and none of you shall go out at the door of his house until the morning.

> The symbolism of the spiritual protection provided by the "blood of the Lamb," for righteous followers of Christ, is seen clearly in verse 23, next.

23 For the LORD will pass through to smite the Egyptians; and **when he seeth the blood** [*symbolic of the blood of Christ*] upon the lintel, and on the two side posts, the LORD will pass over the door, and **will not suffer** [*allow*] **the destroyer to come in unto your houses to smite** *you*.

24 And **ye shall observe this thing** for an ordinance to thee and to thy sons **for ever**.

> Reading verse 24, above, might lead us to believe that the Passover should still be observed in the Church today. This is not the case. There is sometimes confusion about the use of the word "forever" as it appears in verse 24, as well as elsewhere in the Old Testament. Joseph Fielding Smith explains. He said:
>
> "The Feast of the Passover was fulfilled in that form in the crucifixion of Jesus Christ. The Passover was a law given to Israel that was to continue until Christ, and was to remind the children of Israel of the coming of Christ who would become the sacrificial Lamb. After he was crucified the law was changed by the Savior himself, and from that time forth the law of the sacrament was instituted. We now observe the law of the sacrament instead of the Passover because the Passover was consummated in full by the death of Jesus Christ. It was a custom looking forward to the coming of Christ and his crucifixion and the lamb symbolized his death. . . .
>
> "The word forever used in the Old Testament does not necessarily mean to the end of time but to the end of a period" (Smith, *Answers to Gospel Questions,* 5:153–54).
>
> In verse 25, next, the children of Israel are instructed to continue to celebrate Passover after they enter into the Promised Land (basically the Holy Land today) in about 40 years.

25 And it shall come to pass, **when ye be come to the land which the LORD will give you**, according as he hath promised, that **ye shall keep this service** [*the Passover*].

> Next, in verses 26–27, Moses reminds the people of the teaching opportunities they will have as parents as they keep the Passover in the future. It will become a great opportunity to teach the gospel to their children.

26 And it shall come to pass, **when your children shall say** unto you, **What mean ye by this service** [*what is the meaning of the Passover*]?

27 That **ye shall say, It *is* the sacrifice of the LORD's passover**, who passed over the houses of the children of Israel in Egypt, when he smote the Egyptians, and delivered our houses. And the people bowed the head and worshipped.

> Obedience is often referred to as "the first law of heaven" as implied in Doctrine and Covenants 130:20–21. In verse 28, next, we see an example of pure and simple obedience.

28 And **the children of Israel went away, and did as the LORD had commanded** Moses and Aaron, so did they.

> By way of summary, we will quote Elder Bruce R. McConkie as he teaches and reviews Atonement symbolism in the Passover. He said:
>
> "At the time appointed for their deliverance from Egyptian bondage, the Lord commanded each family in Israel to sacrifice a lamb, to sprinkle its blood on their doorposts, and then to eat unleavened bread for seven more days—all to symbolize the fact that the destroying angel would pass over the Israelites as he went forth slaying the firstborn in the families of all the Egyptians; and also to show that, in haste, Israel should go forth from slavery to freedom. As a pattern for all the Mosaic instructions yet to come, the details of the performances here involved were so arranged as to bear testimony both of Israel's deliverance and of her Deliverer. Among other procedures, the Lord commanded, as found in Exodus 12:
>
> "1. 'Your lamb shall be without blemish, a male of the first year,' signifying that the Lamb of God, pure and perfect, without spot or blemish, in the prime of his life, as the Paschal Lamb, would be slain for the sins of the world.
>
> "2. They were to take of the blood of the lamb and sprinkle it upon the doorposts of their houses, having this promise as a result: 'And the blood shall be to you for a token upon the houses where ye are: and when I see the blood, I will pass over you, and the plague shall not be upon you to destroy you,' signifying that the blood of Christ, which should fall as drops in Gethsemane and flow in a stream from a pierced side as he hung on the cross, would cleanse and save the faithful; and that, as those in Israel were saved temporally because the blood of a sacrificial lamb was sprinkled on the doorposts of their houses, so the faithful of all ages would wash their garments in the blood of the Eternal Lamb and from him receive an eternal salvation. And may we say that as the angel of death passed by the families of Israel because of their faith—as Paul said of Moses, 'through faith he kept the passover, and the sprinkling of blood, lest he that destroyed the firstborn should touch them' (Hebrew 11:28)—even so shall the Angel of Life give eternal life to all those who rely on the blood of the Lamb.
>
> "3. As to the sacrifice of the lamb, the decree was, 'Neither shall ye break a bone thereof,' signifying that when the Lamb of God was sacrificed on the cross, though they broke the legs of the two thieves to

induce death, yet they brake not the bones of the Crucified One 'that the scripture should be fulfilled, A bone of him shall not be broken.' (John 19:31–36.)

"4. As to the eating the flesh of the sacrificial lamb, the divine word was, 'No uncircumcised person shall eat thereof,' signifying that the blessings of the gospel are reserved for those who come into the fold of Israel, who join the Church, who carry their part of the burden in bearing off the kingdom; signifying also that those who eat his flesh and drink his blood, as he said, shall have eternal life and he will raise them up at the last day. (John 6:54.)

"5. As 'the Lord smote all the firstborn in the land of Egypt' because they believed not the word of the Lord delivered to them by Moses and Aaron, even so should the Firstborn of the Father, who brings life to all who believe in his holy name, destroy worldly people at the last day, destroy all those who are in the Egypt of darkness, whose hearts are hardened as were those of Pharaoh and his minions.

"6. On the first and seventh days of the Feast of Unleavened Bread, the Israelites were commanded to hold holy convocations in which no work might be done except the preparation of their food. These were occasions for preaching and explaining and exhorting and testifying. We go sacrament meetings to be built up in faith and in testimony. Ancient Israel attended holy convocations for the same purposes. Knowing that all things operate by faith, would it be amiss to draw the conclusion that it is as easy for us to look to Christ and his spilt blood for eternal salvation as it was for them of old to look to the blood of the sacrificed lamb, sprinkled on doorposts, to give temporal salvation, when the angel of death swept through the land of Egypt?

"It was, of course, while Jesus and the Twelve were keeping the Feast of the Passover that our Lord instituted the ordinance of the sacrament, to serve essentially the same purposes served by the sacrifices of the preceding four millenniums. After that final Passover day and its attendant lifting up upon the cross of the true Paschal Lamb, the day for the proper celebration of the ancient feast ceased. After that Paul was able to say: 'Christ our passover is sacrificed for us,' and to give the natural exhortation that flowed therefrom: 'Therefore let us keep the feast, not with old leaven, neither with the leaven of malice and wickedness; but with the unleavened bread of sincerity and truth.' (1 Corinthians 5:7–8.)" (*The Promised Messiah,* pages 429–31).

We will now continue with Exodus, chapter 12.

29 ¶ And it came to pass, that **at midnight the LORD smote all the firstborn in the land of Egypt**, from the firstborn of Pharaoh that sat on his throne unto the firstborn of the captive that was in the dungeon; and all the firstborn of cattle.

30 And Pharaoh rose up in the night, he, and all his servants, and all the Egyptians; and **there was a great cry**

in Egypt; for there was not a house where there was not one dead.

> Now, Pharaoh and his people are not only willing but anxious to have the children of Israel leave.

31 ¶ And **he called for Moses and Aaron by night, and said, Rise up, and get you forth from among my people**, both ye and the children of Israel; and go, serve the LORD, as ye have said.

32 Also **take your flocks and your herds, as ye have said, and be gone; and bless me also.**

33 And **the Egyptians were urgent** upon the people, that they might send them out of the land in haste; for they said, **We be all dead men.**

JST Exodus 12:33

> 33 And the Egyptians were urgent upon the people, that they might send them out of the land in haste; for they said, **We have found our firstborn all dead; therefore get ye out of the land lest we die also.**

34 And **the people took their dough before it was leavened** [*they ate unleavened bread, (which became a feature of the Passover feast later)*], **their kneadingtroughs being bound up in their clothes upon their shoulders.**

35 And **the children of Israel did according to the word of Moses; and they borrowed** [*asked for; see note regarding "borrow" after Exodus 11:2 in this study guide*] of **the Egyptians jewels of silver, and jewels of gold, and raiment:**

36 And **the LORD gave the people favour in the sight of the Egyptians, so that they lent** [*"let them have," see footnote 36b in your Bible*] unto them **such things as they required** [*asked for*]. And they spoiled [*received much from*] **the Egyptians** [*as prophesied and instructed in Exodus 3:22*].

37 ¶ And **the children of Israel journeyed from Rameses** [*an Egyptian treasure city located in far northern Egypt on the Nile River Delta*] **to Succoth** [*about 40–50 miles*], **about six hundred thousand** on foot that were **men, beside children.**

JST Exodus 12:37

> 37 And the children of Israel journeyed from Rameses to Succoth, about six hundred thousand men on foot, **besides women and children.**

38 **And a mixed multitude** [*a mixed blend of many other people—see footnote 38a in your Bible; apparently a number of people of other nationalities attached themselves voluntarily to the Israelites*] **went up also with them**; and flocks, and herds, *even* very much cattle.

> The question arises as to how many Israelites there were in this large group that left Egypt. Bible scholars vary in their answers. In the *Old Testament Student Manual,* we read a quote from a noted Bible scholar:
>
> "The most interesting, most difficult and (from the historian's point of

view) the most important question is the size of the Israelite population at the different stages of its history. The present texts indicate that the 70 souls of Joseph's day had risen to **two or three million** at the time of the Exodus (Numbers 1) and to at least five million in the time of David (2 Samuel 24:9; 1 Chronicles 21:5). With regard to the latter, R. de Vaux rightly says: '(2 Samuel) lists 800,000 men liable for military service in Israel, and 500,000 in Judah. . . . The lower total, in 2 Samuel, is still far too high: 1,300,000 men of military age would imply at least five million inhabitants, which, for Palestine, would mean nearly twice as many people to the square mile as in the most thickly populated countries of modern Europe.'

"The solution of the problem of the Exodus numbers is a long story. Suffice it to say that there is good reason to believe that the original censuses in Numbers 1 and 26 set out the numbers of each tribe, somewhat in this form:

Simeon: 57 armed men; 23 'hundreds' (military units).

This came to be written: 57 'lp; 2 'lp 3 'hundreds.'

"Not realizing that 'lp in one case meant 'armed man' [*one person*] and in the other 'thousand,' this was tidied up to read 59,300. When these figures are carefully decoded, a remarkably clear picture of the whole military organization emerges. The total fighting force is some 18,000, which would probably mean a figure of about **72,000** for the whole migration" (*Old Testament Student Manual: Genesis–2 Samuel,* page 194).

We will have to wait for a final answer regarding how many people left Egypt in the Exodus. Either way, it was a large expedition, with great numbers of animals along with huge amounts of equipment and supplies.

39 **And they baked unleavened cakes of the dough which they brought** forth out of Egypt, **for it was not leavened; because they were thrust out of Egypt, and could not tarry** [*wait for the dough to rise*], neither had they prepared for themselves any victual.

Next, we are told how long the children of Israel had lived in Egypt.

40 ¶ Now the sojourning of the children of Israel, who dwelt in Egypt, was **four hundred and thirty years**.

However, there is some question among Bible scholars as to whether the 430 years mentioned might include from the time that Abraham received the covenant to the time of the Exodus, as implied in Galatians 3:16–17. Whatever the case, the Israelites probably spent two hundred to three hundred years of their time in Egypt as slaves. If you keep this in mind, it will help you sympathize with Moses as he takes on the calling and challenge of leading this large group of people into the wilderness, whose cultural background and mind set is that of freed slaves who have a well-developed tendency to complain about their situation.

41 And it came to pass **at the end of the four hundred and thirty years**, even the selfsame day it came to pass, that **all the hosts of the LORD went out from the land of Egypt**.

42 It is a night to be much observed unto the LORD for bringing them out from the land of Egypt: **this is that night of the LORD to be observed of all the children of Israel in their generations**.

Verses 43–48, next, state, in effect, that no non-Israelites were allowed to partake of the Passover. Any who desired to do so were first required to make covenants—in other words, to join the church. This is similar to our day, in which the covenant of baptism is to be entered into before participating in the sacrament, temple worship, and so forth.

43 ¶ And the LORD said unto Moses and Aaron, **This *is* the ordinance of the passover: There shall no stranger** [*foreigner, non-Israelite, nonmember*] **eat thereof**:

44 **But every man's servant that is bought for money, when thou hast circumcised him** [*in other words, when he has entered into the Abrahamic covenant—see Genesis 17:10–11—and thus has become an Israelite*], **then shall he eat thereof** [*partake of the Passover meal and service*].

45 A **foreigner** [*non-Israelite*] **and an hired servant shall not eat thereof**.

In verse 46, next, we see that one of the requirements for proper preparation and handling of the lamb that was eaten at Passover was that none of its bones were to be broken.

46 **In one house shall it be eaten**; thou shalt not carry forth ought [*any*] of the flesh abroad out of the house; **neither shall ye break a bone thereof**.

This was symbolic and prophetic. It was symbolic of and a prophecy of the fact that none of the Savior's bones would be broken at the time of His crucifixion. It was a common practice among the Romans to break leg bones of crucifixion victims in order to speed up their death. We will quote John as he bears witness of this particular prophecy:

<u>John 19:32–36</u>

32 Then came **the soldiers**, and **brake the legs of the first** [*thief on the cross*], **and of the other** which was crucified with him.

33 **But when they came to Jesus**, and saw that he was dead already, **they brake not his legs**:

34 But one of the soldiers with a spear pierced his side, and forthwith came there out blood and water.

35 And he that saw *it* bare record, and his record is true: and he knoweth that he saith true, that ye might *believe*.

36 *For these thing*s **were done, that the scripture should be fulfilled** [*Exodus 12:46*], **A bone of him shall not be broken**.

Verse 47, next, is another reminder to the Israelites that all of them were to keep the Passover annually thereafter.

47 **All the congregation of Israel shall keep it** [*all members of covenant Israel are required to keep the Passover. This requirement will be done away with during the Savior's mortal ministry, when His great sacrifice fulfills the law of Moses*].

> In verses 48–50, next, we see a powerful principle that applies to our day too. When someone who is not a bloodline Israelite joins the Church by making the necessary covenant—in our case, baptism—and lives true to it, he or she becomes an Israelite, an heir to the blessings of Abraham, Isaac, and Jacob (contingent upon personal righteousness). There is no difference in the eyes of God between members of the Church who are bloodline Israel or who are not. This principle is illustrated in verses 48–50 and emphasized by the use of **bold**.

48 And when a stranger [*a non-Israelite*] shall sojourn [*remain*] with thee, and will [*desires to*] keep the passover to the LORD, let all his males be circumcised, and then let him come near and keep it [*participate in the Passover observance*]; and **he shall be as one that is born in the land** [*as one who is born an Israelite; in other words, there will be no difference between one who is a bloodline Israelite and one who joins the Lord's covenant people through circumcision*]: for no uncircumcised person shall eat thereof [*no nonmember is to participate in the Passover*].

49 **One law shall be** [*the same law of circumcision applies*] **to him that is homeborn** [*is born a bloodline Israelite*], **and unto the stranger** [*non-Israelite*] **that sojourneth** [*lives*] **among you.**

50 **Thus did all the children of Israel**; as the LORD commanded Moses and Aaron, so did they.

> Verse 51 shows that the Exodus was a well-organized operation.

51 And it came to pass the selfsame day, *that* **the LORD did bring the children of Israel out of the land of Egypt by their armies** [*in groups, organized according to which one of the twelve tribes they belonged*].

EXODUS 13

In this chapter, we see that the Israelites will be required to dedicate their firstborn sons to the Lord (see verses 1 and 12, for example). They are also reminded that they are to keep the Passover when they arrive in the promised land (verse 5). In verse 19, we see Moses keep the promise that his ancestors made to Joseph (who was sold into Egypt) that Joseph's remains would be taken to the land of promise.

One of the important applications for us, given symbolically in this chapter, is that the people are first required to follow the prophet (Moses). As they do so, they are brought into the presence of the Lord ("a pillar of a cloud" by day, and "a pillar of fire" by night—Exodus

13:21–22). This is a reminder that as we follow our Prophet today, we are preparing for the day when we will be brought into the direct presence God and dwell with Him in celestial glory forever.

1 AND the LORD spake unto Moses, saying,

2 **Sanctify unto me all the firstborn**, whatsoever openeth the womb among the children of Israel, both of man and of beast: it is mine.

3 ¶ And Moses said unto the people, **Remember this day** [*Passover*], **in which ye came out from Egypt**, out of the house of bondage; for by strength of hand the LORD brought you out from this place: **there shall no leavened bread** [*bread with yeast in it*] **be eaten**.

4 **This day came ye out in the month Abib** [*the first month of Spring—see footnote 4b in your Bible*].

5 ¶ **And it shall be when the LORD shall bring thee into the land of the Canaanites, and the Hittites, and the Amorites, and the Hivites, and the Jebusites** [*in other words, the promised land; the Holy Land; Canaan*], which he sware unto thy fathers to give thee, a land flowing with milk and honey, that **thou shalt keep this service** [*the feast of unleavened bread*] **in this month**.

6 **Seven days thou shalt eat unleavened bread,** and **in the seventh day shall be a feast to the LORD**.

7 **Unleavened bread shall be eaten seven days;** and **there shall no leavened bread be seen with thee, neither** shall there be leaven seen with thee **in all thy quarters** [*anywhere at all in your living quarters*].

8 ¶ And **thou shalt shew thy son** [*in other words, teach your children*] in that day, **saying, This is done because of that which the LORD did unto me when I came forth out of Egypt.**

9 And **it shall be for a sign unto thee upon thine hand** [*symbolic of action, acting in service of God*], **and for a memorial between thine eyes** [*forehead, symbolic of loyalty, total dedication, in this case to God; positive example: Revelation 14:1; negative example: Revelation 13:16*], **that the LORD's law may be in thy mouth** [*NIV: "on your lips"*]: **for with a strong hand hath the LORD brought thee out of Egypt.**

> The instructions in verse 9, above, eventually led to the practice of wearing phylacteries, little boxes with tiny scrolls inscribed with verses of scripture (top to bottom, Deuteronomy 11:13–21; Exodus 13:2–10, Exodus 13:11–16; Deuteronomy 6:4–9) inside, strapped to the forehead or to the left biceps. (See *Old Testament Student Manual, Genesis-2nd Samuel*, p 218.)

10 **Thou shalt therefore keep this ordinance in his season from year to year.**

11 ¶ **And it shall be when the LORD shall bring thee into the land of the Canaanites,** as he sware unto thee and to thy fathers, and shall give it thee,

> Next, the Lord instructs that the firstborn males of all of their domesticated animals are to belong to the Lord. Again, there is Atonement symbolism here, in that the "firstborn" males remind the people of the "Firstborn Son of God."

12 **That thou shalt set apart unto the LORD all that openeth the matrix** [womb]**, and every firstling that cometh of a beast** which thou hast; **the males shall be the LORD's.**

13 And **every firstling of an ass thou shalt redeem with a lamb**; and if thou wilt not redeem it, then thou shalt break his neck: and all the firstborn of man among thy children shalt thou redeem.

> We get some help understanding verse 13, above, through the following quote:
>
> "Every firstling of an ass thou shalt redeem with a lamb—Or a kid, as in the margin. In Numbers 18:15, it is said: "The first-born of man shalt thou surely redeem; and the firstling of an unclean beast shalt thou redeem." Hence we may infer that ass is put here for any unclean beast, or for unclean beasts in general. The lamb was to be given to the Lord, that is, to his priest (Numbers 18:8, Numbers 18:15). And then the owner of the ass might use it for his own service, which without this redemption he could not do; see Deuteronomy 15:19."
>
> (*Clarke's Commentary on the Bible*, Exodus 13:13.)
>
> The importance of teaching children about the Lord's blessings to their forebears is emphasized in the next verses.

14 ¶ **And it shall be when thy son asketh thee in time to come, saying, What is this?** that **thou shalt say** unto him, **By strength of hand the LORD brought us out from Egypt, from the house of bondage**:

15 **And** it came to pass, **when Pharaoh would hardly** [*NIV: "stubbornly refused to"*] **let us go, that the LORD slew all the firstborn in the land of Egypt,** both the firstborn of man, and the firstborn of beast: **therefore** [*this is why*] **I sacrifice to the LORD all that openeth the matrix** [*womb*]**, being males; but all the firstborn of my children I redeem** [*sacrifice a lamb in their place*].

16 And **it shall be for a token** upon thine hand, and **for frontlets** between thine eyes [*see note following verse 9*]: **for by strength of hand the LORD brought us forth out of Egypt**.

17 ¶ And it came to pass, **when Pharaoh had let the people go, that God led them not through the way of the land of the Philistines,** although that was near [*was a more direct route to the promised land*]; for God said, **Lest peradventure the people repent** [*for fear that they will change their minds*] **when they see war** [*are confronted with war*]**, and they return to Egypt**:

18 **But God led the people about, through the way of the wilderness of the Red sea**: and the children of Israel went up harnessed [*equipped for battle—see footnote 18c in your Bible*] out of the land of Egypt.

19 And **Moses took the bones of Joseph with him**: for he [*Joseph*] had straitly [*strictly*] sworn the children of Israel [*made them promise*], saying, God will surely visit you [*someday, God will set you free from Egypt*]; and ye shall carry up my bones away hence [*to the promised land*] with you.

20 ¶ And they took their journey from Succoth, and encamped in Etham, in the edge of the wilderness.

21 And **the LORD went before them by day in a pillar of a cloud**, to lead them the way; and **by night in a pillar of fire, to give them light; to go by day and night**:

22 **He took not away the pillar of the cloud by day, nor the pillar of fire by night**, *from* before the people.

> Perhaps you have noticed that the presence of the Lord is often denoted in the scriptures by a cloud (see Topical Guide, under "Cloud"). Much of the use of this symbolism stems from the Lord's presence being demonstrated through a cloud by day and fire by night as explained in verses 21–22, above. This imagery for the presence of the Lord is found throughout the scriptures. For example, the Second Coming of the Savior is sometimes depicted in prophecy as His coming in a cloud. We will give examples here:

Mark 13:26

> 26 And then shall they see the Son of man **coming in the clouds** with great power and glory.

Revelation 1:7

> 7 Behold, **he cometh with clouds**; and every eye shall see him, and they also which pierced him: and all kindreds of the earth shall wail because of him. Even so, Amen.

Doctrine and Covenants 34:7

> 7 For behold, verily, verily, I say unto you, the time is soon at hand that **I shall come in a cloud** with power and great glory.

This symbolism is one of the reasons you often see clouds in paintings of the Second Coming. They are Bible symbolism representing and emphasizing the presence of the Lord.

EXODUS 14

As you study chapter 14, you will see that Pharaoh, who can symbolically represent Satan, does not keep his promise to the Israelites and leads his armies into the wilderness in pursuit of Moses and his people. With this symbolism in mind, there are many applications we can see in this, including:

1. Satan and his followers don't keep their word.

2. Satan is relentless in trying to overcome us and place us in his bondage.

3. There is indeed "opposition in all things" (2 Nephi 2:11).

4. Quite often, just when we overcome one trial, another one comes up.

5. Satan and his forces appear domineering and frightfully powerful.

The counterbalancing side to all of the above is found in Pharaoh's defeat by the power of God, as he and his armies are drowned in the sea (see verse 28). One of the major themes of the scriptures is the absolute truth that the Lord has more power than Lucifer and that Satan will ultimately be defeated and banished to perdition (see Revelation 17:8; D&C 76:32) which is sometimes referred to as outer darkness or his "own place" (see Doctrine and Covenants 88:114). We also find symbolism in the fact that Pharaoh (symbolic of Satan) and his armies (symbolic of the armies of the wicked) were defeated by the waters of the Red Sea (symbolic of the waters of baptism, through which, if we truly repent, we can become completely clean and free from the bondage of past sins).

1 AND **the LORD spake unto Moses, saying**,

2 Speak unto the children of Israel, that they turn and encamp before Pi-hahiroth, between Migdol and the sea, over against Baal-zephon: before it shall ye **encamp by the sea**.

3 **For Pharaoh will say of the children of Israel**, They are entangled in the land, **the wilderness hath shut them in** [*they are trapped*].

4 And **I will harden Pharaoh's heart**, that **he shall follow after them; and I will be honoured upon Pharaoh** [*I will gain respect because of Pharaoh's behavior*], and upon all his host; that the Egyptians may know that I am the LORD. And they did so.

JST Exodus 14:4

4 And **Pharaoh will harden his heart**, and he shall follow after them; and I will be honored upon Pharaoh, and upon all his host; that the Egyptians may know that I am the Lord. And they did so.

5 ¶ And **it was told the king of Egypt that the people fled:** and the heart of Pharaoh and of his servants was turned against the people, **and they said, Why have we done this,** that we have let Israel go from serving us [*why have we been so foolish to let our slaves go*]?

6 **And he made ready his chariot, and took his people with him:**

> Pharaoh takes an intimidating army to recapture the Israelites.

7 And he took six hundred chosen chariots [*NIV "of the best chariots"*], and **all the chariots of Egypt, and captains over every one of them**.

8 And **the LORD hardened the heart of Pharaoh** king of Egypt, and he pursued after the children of Israel: and the children of Israel went out with an high hand [*boldly*].

JST Exodus 14:8

8 And **Pharaoh hardened his heart**, and he pursued after the children of

Israel; and the children of Israel went out with a high hand.

9 **But the Egyptians** pursued after them, all the horses and chariots of Pharaoh, and his horsemen, and his army, and **overtook them encamping by the sea,** beside Pi-hahiroth, before Baal-zephon.

10 ¶ And **when Pharaoh drew nigh, the children of Israel lifted up their eyes** [*saw the coming armies of Pharoah*], and, behold, the Egyptians marched after them; **and they were sore afraid:** and the children of Israel **cried out unto the LORD.**

> The depth of conversion and faith in Jehovah as well as loyalty to His prophet, Moses, are still very shallow in the hearts and minds of these liberated Israelite slaves. We see it here in their bitter, sarcastic complaining.

11 And **they said unto Moses, Because there were no graves in Egypt, hast thou taken us away to die in the wilderness** [*were there no graves in Egypt, so you brought us out here to die*]? **wherefore** [*why*] **hast thou dealt thus with us, to carry us forth out of Egypt?**

12 **Is not this the word that we did tell thee in Egypt**, saying, Let us alone, that we may serve the Egyptians? **For it had been better for us to serve the Egyptians, than that we should die in the wilderness.**

> Have you noticed that the Lord is willing to give us many, many witnesses of His power and love for us in order to enable us to become completely committed to the gospel path to salvation?

> One of the most difficult of situations in which to exercise self-control and kind feelings is one in which we have pure and honorable motives but are accused of having dishonorable intent and self-serving motives. This was the case for Moses here. Watch now as he responds to these angry false accusations. There is an important message in this for us.

13 ¶ And Moses said unto the people, **Fear ye not, stand still, and see the salvation of the LORD**, which he will shew to you to day: for the Egyptians whom ye have seen to day, ye shall see them again no more for ever.

14 **The LORD shall fight for you**, and ye shall hold your peace [*don't worry; you can relax*].

> We do not have an explanation or background for the question "Wherefore criest thou unto me?" in verse 15, next, but the command to "go forward" toward the sea is clear. It can remind us that we must often go forward in faith, before the desired blessings are even in sight.

15 ¶ And **the LORD said unto Moses,** Wherefore criest thou unto me? **speak unto the children of Israel, that they go forward**:

16 But **lift thou up thy rod, and stretch out thine hand over the sea, and divide it:** and **the children**

of Israel shall go on dry ground through the midst of the sea.

> Did you notice that part of the forthcoming miracle in verse 16, above, was that the children of Israel would be going on dry ground, rather than mired in mud on the sea bottom?

17 And I, behold, **I will harden the hearts of the Egyptians**, and **they shall follow them:** and **I will get me honour** [*My name will be magnified*] upon Pharaoh, and upon all his host, upon his chariots, and upon his horsemen.

JST Exodus 14:17

17 And I say unto thee **the hearts of the Egyptians shall be hardened**, and they shall follow them; and I will get me honor upon Pharaoh, and upon all his host, upon his chariots, and upon his horsemen.

18 **And the Egyptians shall know that I am the LORD** [*Jehovah*], when I have gotten me honour upon Pharaoh, upon his chariots, and upon his horsemen.

19 ¶ **And the angel of God,** which went before the camp of Israel, removed and **went behind them**; and **the pillar of the cloud** went from before their face, and **stood behind them** [*a dramatic demonstration that the power of the Lord stood between them and Pharoah's armies*]:

20 And it came **between the camp of the Egyptians and the camp of Israel;** and **it was a cloud and darkness to them**, but **it gave light by night to these: so that the one came not near the other all the night.**

JST Exodus 14:20

20 And it came between the camp of the Egyptians and the camp of Israel; and it was a cloud and darkness **to the Egyptians**, but it gave light by night **to the Israelites**, so that the one came not near the other all the night.

21 And **Moses stretched out his hand over the sea;** and **the LORD caused the sea to go back by a strong east wind all that night, and made the sea dry land, and the waters were divided.**

> Imagine the looks on the faces and the feelings in the hearts of the Israelites as they followed their prophet into the divided sea on dry ground with threatening walls of water on both sides. While it is likely that some were frightened, we hope that many were in awe of the obvious miracle being performed in their behalf.

22 And **the children of Israel went into the midst of the sea upon the dry ground**: and the waters were a wall unto them on their right hand, and on their left.

23 ¶ **And the Egyptians pursued, and went in after them** to the midst of the sea [*to the middle of the distance to be crossed*], even **all Pharaoh's**

horses, his chariots, and his horsemen.

24 And it came to pass, that **in the morning watch** [*2 a.m. until sunrise—see Bible Dictionary, under "Watches"*] **the LORD** looked unto the host of the Egyptians through the pillar of fire and of the cloud, and **troubled the host of the Egyptians,**

> The Lord's intervention became very obvious to the pursuing Egyptian armies.

25 And **took off their chariot wheels**, that they drave them heavily [*had difficulty driving*]: **so that the Egyptians said, Let us flee from the face of Israel**; for the LORD fighteth for them against the Egyptians.

> Next, under the direction of the Lord, the waters collapse in upon the Egyptian armies and they are completely destroyed (verse 28).

26 ¶ **And the LORD said unto Moses, Stretch out thine hand over the sea, that the waters may come again upon the Egyptians**, upon their chariots, and upon their horsemen.

27 And Moses stretched forth his hand over the sea, and **the sea returned to his strength** [*to normal*] when the morning appeared; and the Egyptians fled against it; and **the LORD overthrew the Egyptians in the midst of the sea.**

28 And **the waters returned, and covered the chariots, and the horsemen, and all the host of Pharaoh that came into the sea after them**; there remained not so much as one of them.

> Verses 29–31 are a review and summary.

29 But **the children of Israel walked upon dry land in the midst of the sea**; and the waters were a wall unto them on their right hand, and on their left.

30 Thus **the LORD saved Israel that day out of the hand of the Egyptians**; and Israel saw the Egyptians dead upon the sea shore.

31 And Israel saw that great work which the LORD did upon the Egyptians: **and the people feared the LORD, and believed the LORD, and his servant Moses**.

> We see additional symbolism in here the fact that the Israelites passed through the Red Sea on dry ground (verse 29). It can be symbolic of the truth that when we follow the Prophet, we are on "solid ground."

EXODUS 15

As you read the first twenty-one verses of chapter 15, you will see that the people praise the Lord for saving them from Pharaoh's armies. It is a time of great gratitude and rejoicing because of their deliverance from Egypt. But by the time you get to verse 24, the people are murmuring again! The Lord patiently and kindly solves their problem (see verse 25) and teaches a lesson about obedience and blessings (see verse 26).

EXODUS 15

1 **THEN sang Moses and the children of Israel this song** [*to "sing a song" is another way of saying "praised the Lord"*] unto the LORD, and spake, saying, I will sing unto the LORD, for he hath triumphed gloriously: the horse and his rider [*Pharaoh's armies*] hath he thrown into the sea.

2 **The LORD is my strength and song, and he is become my salvation:** he is my God, and I will prepare him an habitation; my father's God, and I will exalt him.

> The first two lines of verse 2, above, might remind you of one of our hymns in our Latter-day Saint hymn book, namely "The Lord Is My Light," hymn #89.

3 **The LORD is a man of war: the LORD is his name.**

4 **Pharaoh's chariots and his host hath he cast into the sea:** his chosen captains also are drowned in the Red sea.

5 **The depths have covered them:** they sank into the bottom as a stone.

6 Thy **right hand, O LORD, is become glorious in power:** thy right hand, O LORD, hath dashed in pieces the enemy.

> In biblical symbolism, "right hand" symbolizes power. It is also the "covenant hand." Thus, in verse 6, above, one implication is that the Israelites are saying that they are the Lord's covenant people and He is keeping His covenant to bless and save them.

7 And in **the greatness of thine excellency** thou hast overthrown them that rose up against thee: **thou sentest forth thy wrath, which consumed them as stubble** [*they didn't have a chance against Thy power*].

8 And with the blast of thy nostrils **the waters were gathered together,** the floods [*walls of water*] stood upright as an heap, and the depths were congealed [*the waters held firm*] in the heart of the sea.

9 **The enemy said, I will pursue, I will overtake, I will divide the spoil** [*I will profit by conquering these Israelites*]; my lust shall be satisfied upon them; I will draw my sword, my hand shall destroy them.

10 **Thou didst blow** with thy wind, **the sea** covered them: **they sank as lead** in the mighty waters.

11 **Who is like unto thee, O LORD,** among the gods? who is like thee, glorious in holiness, fearful in praises, doing wonders?

12 **Thou stretchedst out thy right hand** [*exercised thy power*], the earth swallowed them.

13 **Thou in thy mercy hast led forth the people which thou hast redeemed:** thou hast guided them in thy strength unto thy holy habitation.

> In the next several verses, Moses and the children of Israel show confidence that the Lord will likewise protect and bless them as they travel to the promised land.

14 The people shall hear, and be afraid: **sorrow shall take hold on the inhabitants of Palestina** [*the land of the Philistines—see footnote 14b in your Bible*].

15 Then **the dukes of Edom** [*country south of the Dead Sea*] **shall be amazed;** the **mighty men of Moab** [*country southeast of the Dead Sea*], **trembling shall take hold upon them; all the inhabitants of Canaan** [*inhabitants of the Holy Land; promised land*] **shall melt away.**

16 **Fear and dread shall fall upon them; by the greatness of thine arm** [*"arm" is symbolic of power and strength*] they shall be as still as a stone; till thy people pass over, O LORD, till the people pass over, which thou hast purchased [*ransomed, redeemed*].

17 **Thou shalt bring them in, and plant them** in the mountain of thine inheritance, in the place, O LORD, which thou hast made for thee to dwell in, in the Sanctuary, O Lord, which thy hands have established.

18 **The LORD shall reign for ever and ever.**

19 **For the horse of Pharaoh went in with his chariots and with his horsemen into the sea, and the LORD brought again the waters of the sea upon them; but the children of Israel went on dry land in the midst of the sea.**

20 ¶ And **Miriam** [*Moses's older sister*] **the prophetess** [*see Alma 32:23*], **the sister of Aaron**, took a timbrel [*tambourine—see Smith's Bible Dictionary, 1972, p 698*] in her hand; and **all the women went out after her with timbrels and with dances**.

21 And Miriam answered them, **Sing ye to the LORD**, for he hath triumphed gloriously; the horse and his rider hath he thrown into the sea.

22 **So Moses brought Israel from the Red sea**, and they went out **into the wilderness of Shur**; and they went three days in the wilderness, and found no water.

23 ¶ And when they came to Marah, **they could not drink of the waters of Marah, for they were bitter:** therefore the name of it was called Marah [*meaning "bitterness"—see footnote 23a in your Bible*] .

24 And **the people murmured against Moses**, saying, What shall we drink?

25 And **he cried unto the LORD; and the LORD shewed him a tree, which when he had cast into the waters, the waters were made sweet:** there he made for them a statute and an ordinance, and there he proved them,

> Next, we see an "if . . . then" phrase, in which the complaining Israelites are told that if they do their part, the Lord will do His part. It shows the important role of agency in obtaining desired blessings.

26 And said, **If** thou wilt diligently hearken to the voice of the LORD

thy God, and wilt do that which is right in his sight, and wilt give ear to his commandments, and keep all his statutes, **I will put none of these diseases upon thee, which I have brought upon the Egyptians**: for I am the LORD that healeth thee.

27 ¶ **And they came to Elim**, where were twelve wells of water, and threescore and ten [70] palm trees: and they encamped there by the waters.

EXODUS 16

The first twelve verses of chapter 16 are filled again with murmuring! It reminds us of Laman and Lemuel in the Book of Mormon. We will use bold to emphasize the Israelite murmuring. You will see the word "murmur" or a form of it at least eight times in these twelve verses!

Also, in this chapter, we see the miracles of water, manna, and quail, all reminders of the tender mercies of the Lord as He patiently strives to help these former slaves change from entitlement mentality to faithful members of covenant Israel.

1 **And they took their journey from Elim, and all the congregation of the children of Israel came unto the wilderness of Sin** [*in the south- central Sinai Peninsula*], which is between Elim and Sinai, on the fifteenth day of the second month after their departing out of the land of Egypt.

2 And **the whole congregation of the children of Israel murmured against Moses and Aaron** in the wilderness:

3 And the children of Israel said unto them, **Would to God we had died by the hand of the LORD in the land of Egypt, when we sat by the flesh pots** [*pots of meat, according to this verse in the NIV [(New International Version of the Bible)*], and when we did eat bread to the full [*in other words, when we were slaves in Egypt, at least we had plenty to eat*]; **for ye have brought us forth into this wilderness, to kill this whole assembly with hunger**.

4 ¶ **Then said the LORD unto Moses, Behold, I will rain bread from heaven** [*manna—see verse 15*] for you; and the people shall go out and gather a certain rate every day, that I may prove [*test*] them, whether they will walk in my law, or no.

5 And it shall come to pass, **that on the sixth day** [*on Fridays*] they shall prepare *that* which they bring in [*preparation for the Sabbath the next day*]; and **it shall be twice as much as they gather daily** [*on other days of the week*].

6 And **Moses and Aaron said unto all the children of Israel, At even** [*evening time*], then **ye shall know that the LORD hath brought you out from the land of Egypt**:

7 And **in the morning, then ye shall see the glory of the LORD** [*you will*

see evidence of the power of God]; for that he heareth your **murmurings** against the LORD: and **what *are* we, that ye murmur against u**s [*why are you treating us as if we were the ones who brought you out of Egypt, rather than the Lord*]?

8 And **Moses said**, *This shall be,* [*you will know that the Lord is in charge*] when **the LORD shall give you in the evening flesh** [*quail*] **to eat, and in the morning bread** [*manna*] **to the full;** for that the LORD heareth your **murmurings** which ye **murmur** against him: and what *are* we [*Moses and Aaron*]? **Your murmurings *are* not against us, but against the LORD**.

9 ¶ And Moses spake unto Aaron, Say unto all the congregation of the children of Israel, Come near before **the LORD**: for he **hath heard your murmurings.**

> In case you are wondering why Moses has Aaron do most of the talking to the people, remember that one of Moses's concerns when the Lord called him at the burning bush was that he was slow of speech. Consequently, the Lord called Aaron, his older brother, to be spokesman to the people for Moses (see Exodus 4:10–16).

10 **And it came to pass, as Aaron spake unto the whole congregation of the children of Israel, that they looked toward the wilderness, and, behold, the glory of the LORD appeared in the cloud** [*another obvious proof to all of them that the Lord was with them*].

11 ¶ And **the LORD spake unto Moses, saying,**

12 **I have heard the murmurings of the children of Israel:** speak unto them, saying, At even [*in the evening*] ye shall eat flesh [*quail*], and in the morning ye shall be filled with bread [*manna*]; and ye shall know that I *am* the LORD your God.

> At this point in their opportunity for spiritual progress, the Lord is very patient with the children of Israel. He has taken them at the level where they were spiritually when they left Egypt and is giving them much obvious evidence that He exists and that Moses is His prophet. Rather than punishment for murmuring here, additional direct evidence is given to them that God is indeed leading them through the wilderness toward the promised land.
>
> As you probably know, the time will come, yet future for these people, when they will have been taught sufficiently and given enough evidence of God's existence that they will become more accountable, and severe punishment will follow rebellion. All this is an important reminder that God is fair and reasonable.
>
> We will now see the miracle of the quail, followed by the miracle of manna. Notice that there are strict rules in conjunction with the gathering of manna. The Lord is blessing the Israelites and helping them while providing an opportunity for them to learn the value of strict obedience.
>
> First, large numbers of quail are miraculously provided as meat for

13 And it came to pass, that **at even the quails came up, and covered the camp**: and in the morning the dew lay round about the host.

> the Israelites. They come right into camp and wait to be caught.

> Next, manna is provided. Perhaps you have heard the phrase "manna from heaven," meaning sweet blessings from the Lord. The word "manna" comes from Hebrew "man-hu," meaning, "What is it." (See footnote 15a in your Bible).

14 And **when the dew that lay was gone up** [*had evaporated*], behold, **upon the face of the wilderness** *there lay* **a small round thing,** *as* **small as the hoar frost** [*crystals of frost*] **on the ground** [*in other words, the manna looked like small, round, flake-like things—see also footnote 14a in your Bible*].

15 And when the children of Israel saw *it,* they said one to another, **It** *is* **manna**: for they wist not [*knew not*] what it *was*. And **Moses said unto them, This** *is* **the bread which the LORD hath given you to eat**.

> We **find a description of manna in verse 31 and a description of it and how it was prepared to eat in Numbers.**

Exodus 16:31

31 And the house of Israel called the name thereof **Manna: and it** *was* **like coriander seed, white**; **and the taste of** it *was* **like wafers** *made* **with honey**.

Numbers 11:7–8

7 And **the manna** *was* **as coriander seed**, and the colour thereof as **the colour of bdellium** [*the color of amber*].

8 *And* the people went about, and gathered *it,* and **ground** *it* **in mills**, or **beat** *it* **in a mortar**, and **baked** *it* **in pans**, and **made cakes** of it: and the taste of **it was as the taste of fresh oil**.

> Next, we see instructions for gathering manna. Another opportunity to learn obedience.

16 ¶ This *is* the thing which the LORD hath commanded, **Gather** of it every man according to his eating, **an omer** [*about two quarts, according to the NIV Bible*] **for every man,** *according to* **the number of your persons**; take ye every man **for** *them* **which** *are* **in his tents**.

17 And the children of Israel did so, and gathered, some more, some less [*depending on how many were living in their tents*].

18 And when they did mete *it* [*measure it out*] with an omer, **he that gathered much had nothing over, and he that gathered little had no lack; they gathered every man according to his eating**.

> We see a lesson in faith being taught here as well as the avoiding of greed. There was to be no hoarding of extra manna. They were to have faith that the Lord would provide each day.

19 And **Moses said, Let no man leave of it till the morning** [*no one was to keep any until morning*].

> The Israelites have now arrived at the point in their opportunities for spiritual progress where disobedience is met with immediate punishment, as demonstrated by the wormy manna and the stench that came with it (see verse 20, next). These Israelites are being schooled in the early stages of knowledge, agency, and accountability.

20 **Notwithstanding** [*however*] **they hearkened not** [*were not obedient*] **unto Moses; but some of them left of it** [*kept some of it*] **until the morning**, and **it bred worms** [*grew maggots*], **and stank**: and **Moses was wroth** [*angry*] with them.

21 And they gathered it every morning, every man according to his eating [*according to their needs for meals*]: and **when the sun waxed** [*grew*] **hot, it melted** [*after they had gathered enough for their needs each day, the left over manna melted away*].

> Remember that, at this time, their Sabbath was on what we know as Saturday. It was their holy day. Sunday did not become the Sabbath Day until after the resurrection of the Savior (see Acts 20:7).

> The Israelites were being schooled by the Lord to make preparations on the day before the Sabbath, in order to more fully keep the Sabbath Day holy.

22 ¶ And it came to pass, *that* **on the sixth day** [*Friday*] **they gathered twice as much bread** [*manna*], two omers [*about four quarts*] for one *man:* and all the rulers of the congregation came and told Moses [*the leaders of the various congregations reported to Moses that their people were complying with the instructions*].

23 And he said unto them [*explained the reason for gathering twice as much manna on Friday*], This *is that* which the LORD hath said, **To morrow** *is* the rest of **the holy sabbath** unto the LORD [*tomorrow is a day of rest, the Sabbath on which we worship the Lord*]: bake *that* **which ye will bake** [*bake what you want*] *to day*, and **seethe** [*cook, boil*] **that ye will seethe**; and that which remaineth over lay up for you to be kept until the morning [*save the leftovers for tomorrow, the exact opposite of the normal rule—see verse 19, above*].

24 And **they laid** [*stored*] **it up till the morning, as Moses bade** [*they obeyed what the Prophet said to do*]: and **it did not stink, neither was there any worm therein** [*another obvious miracle, repeated weekly*].

25 And [*the next day*] Moses said, Eat that to day; for **to day** *is* **a sabbath unto the LORD: to day ye shall not find it in the field** [*there will be no manna in the field on the Sabbath, hence, no Sabbath day working*].

26 **Six days ye shall gather it; but on the seventh day,** *which is* **the sabbath, in it there shall be none**.

> Still learning their lessons. Some disobey again.

27 ¶ And it came to pass, *that* **there went out *some* of the people on the seventh day** [*the Sabbath*] **for to gather** [*to gather manna, even though they had been told by the prophet that there would be none*], **and they found none.**

> Earlier, we pointed out that the Lord was being very patient with these people who had come from a culture in Egypt that was far different than the culture of a Zion society. He gave them obvious evidence, time after time, that He was their God and Moses was His prophet. Yet some of them continued to disobey despite clear proof that disobedience is unwise (wormy manna, for example).
>
> There seems to be something missing in verses 28–29, next. From what we have read so far, Moses has been faithfully giving the word of the Lord to his people. Yet, as it stands, verse 28 indicates that Moses is being chastised. We wonder if perhaps something has been left out that would indicate that the Lord is instructing Moses to ask the question to the Israelites. In fact, the NIV indicates that "ye" in verse 28, in Hebrew, is the plural form. It thus implies that the Lord's concern is with the Israelites, not Moses.

28 And **the LORD said** unto Moses, **How long refuse ye to keep my commandments and my laws?**

29 See, for that **the LORD hath given you the sabbath, therefore he giveth you on the sixth day the bread of two days**; abide ye every man in his place [*everyone stay home on the Sabbath; don't go out looking for more manna*], **let no man go out of his place on the seventh day** [*a strict "schoolmaster"-type commandment—see Galatians 3:24*].

30 **So the people rested on the seventh day**.

31 And the house of Israel called the name thereof **Manna**: and it **was like coriander seed, white; and the taste of it was like wafers made with honey**.

> Next, Moses instructs to save about 2 quarts of manna in a pot for future generations to see, as a testimony of what the Lord did for their ancestors. It will be kept in the Ark of the Covenant (Exodus 25:21, including footnote 21b). It will not spoil.

32 ¶ And Moses said, This is the thing which the LORD commandeth, **Fill an omer of it to be kept for your generations;** that they may see the bread wherewith I have fed you in the wilderness, when I brought you forth from the land of Egypt.

33 And **Moses said unto Aaron, Take a pot, and put an omer full of manna therein,** and lay it up before the LORD, **to be kept for your generation**s.

34 As the LORD commanded Moses, so **Aaron laid it up before the Testimony** [*the Ark of the Covenant*], **to be kept**.

35 And **the children of Israel did eat manna forty years**, until they came to a land inhabited; they did

eat manna, until they came unto the borders of the land of Canaan [*the promised land*].

36 Now an omer is the tenth part of an ephah.

EXODUS 17

As you have already seen, there is much in the Old Testament that is symbolic of Christ. It is purposely designed to point the people's minds toward the Savior and His Atonement. Here in Exodus 17, you will again see examples of this as well as other important lessons taught with Biblical symbolism. We will point out some "types and shadows" (another name for symbolism) and then look at them in this chapter:

1. Christ is often referred to as the Rock, the sure foundation upon which we are invited to build our lives.
2. Christ is the "living water" (John 4:10) that cleanses our lives, refreshes our souls, and purifies us such that we can live satisfying and productive gospel lives during mortality and ultimately return to live with Him and the Father.
3. Christ, the Rock, was "smitten" for us (Isaiah 53:5) in order that we might live (be resurrected) and not die spiritually.
4. In order to lead His people, the Lord's prophet must be sustained by them.
5. When we sustain the prophet, we prevail against the enemies of our spirituality.

We will now point out the above five "types and symbols" in Exodus 17. The first three are seen in verse 6, after the Israelites have complained because they are they are out of water (verses 1–3).

1 AND all the congregation of the children of Israel journeyed from the wilderness of Sin [*an area in south central Sinai Peninsula*], after their journeys, according to the commandment of the LORD, and pitched [*pitched their tents*] in Rephidim: and **there was no water for the people to drin**k.

2 **Wherefore the people did chide with** [*complained to*] **Moses, and said, Give us water that we may drink.** And Moses said unto them, Why chide ye with me? wherefore do ye tempt the LORD? [*Perhaps meaning "Why are you challenging the Lord to prove He is with you?"—see end of verse 7*]

The people's complaining becomes quite caustic.

3 And the people thirsted there for water; and **the people murmured against Moses**, and said, Wherefore is this that thou hast [*why have you*] brought us up out of Egypt, to kill us and our children and our cattle with thirst?

We can sense that Moses is getting exasperated here.

4 **And Moses cried unto the LORD, saying, What shall I do unto this people? they be almost ready to stone me.**

5 And **the LORD said** unto Moses, **Go on before the people** [*go on*

ahead], and **take with thee of the elders** [*leaders*] **of** Israel; **and thy rod**, wherewith thou smotest the river, take in thine hand, and go.

6 Behold, **I will stand before thee there upon the rock in Horeb** [*symbolic of Christ as the "Rock," the sure foundation*]; and **thou shalt smite the rock** [*symbolic of the fact that Christ was to be smitten for our sins*], and **there shall come water out of it** [*symbolic of living water coming from Christ*], **that the people may drink**. And **Moses did so** in the sight of the elders of Israel.

> In this case, the people were literally threatened with physical death, because of lack of water in the wilderness. Symbolically, they were in jeopardy of spiritual death because of their failure to apply the gospel in their lives.
>
> "Desert" or "wilderness" is often used in scripture to symbolize apostasy, or the lack of the gospel in people's lives. Thus, the complaining, murmuring children of Israel were in double jeopardy. First, they were in danger of literally dying of thirst. Second, their lack of faith and their verbal attacks against the Lord's living prophet (see verses 2–3) put them in danger of losing their spirituality, a condition far more serious than physical death.

7 And **he called the name of the place Massah** [*the place of testing*], and **Meribah** [*the place of complaining*], because of the chiding of the children of Israel, and because they tempted the LORD, saying, Is the LORD among us, or not?

> No doubt you've noticed that there is plenty of opposition along the way as we strive to stay on the "strait and narrow path" (1 Nephi 8:20, meaning "narrow and narrowing as we get more righteous, path") to our "promised land" (celestial exaltation). We see this next, literally, as the Amalekites (a desert tribe that lived in the Wilderness of Paran in central Sinai Peninsula), under their leader, Amalek, attack the children of Israel as they strive to reach their promised land of Canaan.

8 ¶ **Then came Amalek, and fought with Israel** in Rephidim [*in the southwest part of the Sinai Peninsula*].

9 And **Moses said unto Joshua, Choose us out men, and go out, fight with Amalek: to morrow I will stand on the top of the hill with the rod of God in mine hand.**

10 So **Joshua did as Moses had said** to him, **and fought with Amalek:** and **Moses, Aaron, and Hur went up to the top of the hill.**

11 And it came to pass, **when Moses held up his hand**, that **Israel prevailed** [*began winning*]: **and when he let down his hand, Amalek prevailed** [*symbolic of the fact that without the leadership and keys of authority held by our living prophet, we cannot win against our spiritual enemies*].

12 **But Moses' hands** *were* **heavy** [*he got tired*]; and **they took a stone, and put** *it* **under him, and he sat**

thereon; and **Aaron and Hur stayed** [*supported*] **up his hands**, the one on the one side, and the other on the other side; and his hands were steady until the going down of the sun.

13 And **Joshua discomfited** [*disabled Amalek, won the battle against*] **Amalek and his people** with the edge of the sword.

> Examples 4 and 5, (in the background to this chapter) are found in the account of Amalek and his people engaging in war against the Israelites. As you can see in verses 8–13, above, Moses asked Joshua to take some men and fight against Amalek and his forces. Moses climbed a hill (symbolic of the Prophet's being on higher ground, thus closer to God than the people) with the rod of God in his hand (symbolic of power and authority from God to lead the people). As long as the living prophet held up his hand, Joshua's army was winning the battle, but when Moses got tired and let his hand drop, Amalek's army began winning. Through the support of the prophet by Aaron and Hur, the people of God won against their enemy.
>
> We see more symbolism in the last three verses. Victory comes through the power of the Savior and His Atonement.

14 And the LORD said unto Moses, Write this *for* a memorial in a book, and rehearse *it* in the ears of Joshua: for **I will utterly put out the remembrance of Amalek from under heaven** [*through Christ, we can completely triumph over all our enemies*].

15 And **Moses built an altar, and called the name of it Jehovah-nissi** [*Jehovah is my source of victory*]:

16 For he said, Because **the LORD hath sworn** [*covenanted*] *that* **the LORD *will have* war with Amalek from generation to generation** [*in effect, the Lord has covenanted that He will help us triumph over our enemies from generation to generation*].

EXODUS 18

It appears that sometime after Moses returned to Egypt with his wife, Zipporah, and their two sons (Exodus 4:20), he had sent them back to Midian to live with her father, Jethro (verse 2). Perhaps it was for their safety. Whatever the case, Jethro has now come to join Moses in the wilderness, bringing Zipporah and the children, Gershom and Eliezer (verses 5–6).

1 When **Jethro, the priest** of **Midian, Moses' father in law, heard of all that God had done for Moses, and for Israel** his people, **and that the LORD** had **brought Israel out of Egypt**;

JST Exodus 18:1

1 When Jethro, the **high priest** of Midian, Moses' father-in-law, heard of all that God had done for Moses, and for Israel his people, and that the Lord had brought Israel out of Egypt;

As you can see, in the JST, above, Jethro is referred to as "the **high** priest of Midian," whereas in the Bible it says "the priest of Midian." We thus know that Jethro was a high priest in the Melchizedek Priesthood. This is significant because we know from Doctrine and Covenants 84:6 that Moses received the Melchizedek Priesthood from Jethro.

2 Then Jethro, Moses' father in law, **took Zipporah**, Moses' wife, after he had sent her back,

3 **And her two sons**; of which the name of the one was **Gershom**; for he said, I have been an alien in a strange land:

4 **And** the name of the other was **Eliezer**; for the God of my father, said he, was mine help, and delivered me from the sword of Pharaoh:

5 And **Jethro, Moses' father in law, came with his sons and his wife unto Moses into the wilderness**, where he encamped at the mount of God:

6 **And he said unto Moses, I thy father in law Jethro am come unto thee, and thy wife, and her two sons with her.**

> Verse 7, next, shows us that this was indeed a tender reunion!

7 ¶ **And Moses went out to meet his father in law**, and did obeisance [*bowed down as a sign of respect*], **and kissed him; and they asked each other of their welfare**; and they came into the tent.

8 And **Moses told his father in law all that the LORD had done unto Pharaoh and to the Egyptians for Israel's sake**, and **all the travail** [*trouble and hardship*] that had come upon them by the way, a**nd how the LORD delivered them.**

9 And **Jethro rejoiced for all the goodness which the LORD had done to Israel, whom he had delivered out of the hand of the Egyptians**.

10 And **Jethro said**, Blessed be the LORD, who hath delivered you out of the hand of the Egyptians, and out of the hand of Pharaoh, who hath delivered the people from under the hand of the Egyptians.

11 **Now I know that the LORD is greater than all gods**: for in the thing wherein they dealt proudly [*NIV, "arrogantly"*] he was above them.

12 And **Jethro**, Moses' father in law, **took a burnt offering and sacrifices for God:** and Aaron came, and all the elders of Israel, to eat bread with Moses' father in law before God.

> After his arrival, Jethro watches as Moses carries out his daily work as prophet and leader of Israel and sees him wearing himself out trying to keep up with things that could reasonably be delegated to others. He offers some timely advice. This advice certainly can apply to all of us. In verses 13–26, we learn principles of delegation.

13 ¶ And it came to pass on the morrow, that **Moses sat to judge the people** [*went to his "office" to help*

solve problems, settle disputes, and so forth]: **and the people stood by Moses from the morning unto the evening** [in effect, people were lined up outside Moses's headquarters all day long, waiting for a turn to talk to him and receive help solving their problems].

14 And **when Moses' father in law saw all that he did to the people, he said**, What *is* this thing that thou doest to the people? **why sittest thou thyself alone** [why are you trying to do everything by yourself], and all the people stand by thee from morning unto even?

15 And Moses said unto his father in law, **Because the people come unto me to enquire of God** [because they all want me to get revelation from God to help them with their personal situations]:

16 **When they have a matter, they come unto me; and I judge between one and another** [I also help them solve disputes between one another], and **I do make** *them* **know the statutes of God, and his laws** [I also teach them the rules and laws of God].

17 And **Moses' father in law said** unto him, **The thing that thou doest** *is* **not good.**

18 **Thou wilt surely wear away**, both thou, and this people that *is* with thee: for **this thing** *is* **too heavy for thee** [you can't possible keep up with all this and do justice to it]; **thou art not able to perform it thyself alone**.

19 Hearken now unto my voice, **I will give thee counsel**, and God shall be with thee: **Be thou for the people to God-ward** [you represent the people to God—see footnote 19a in your Bible], that thou mayest **bring the causes unto God** [you plead with God for them]:

20 And thou shalt **teach them ordinances and laws**, and shalt **shew them the way wherein they must walk, and the work that they must do**.

> Verse 20, above, can remind us of the statement of Joseph Smith when, in answer to a question as to how he could lead so many people and keep such good order in the Church, he said, "I teach them correct principles and they govern themselves." (Millennial Star, Nov. 15, 1851, p 339.)
>
> Next, Jethro counsels Moses to delegate.

21 Moreover thou shalt **provide** out of all the people **able men** [select capable men], such as fear [respect and honor] God, men of truth, hating covetousness; and **place** *such* **over them** [organize and delegate much of this work to others, and make sure that they are good men with high standards themselves], **to be rulers of thousands**, *and* rulers of **hundreds**, rulers of **fifties**, and rulers of **tens** [organize the people into groups of tens,

fifties, hundreds, and thousands, and call leaders to preside over each]:

22 And **let them judge** [*preside and handle the problems of*] **the people at all seasons**: and it shall be, *that* **every great matter they shall bring unto thee** [*have them bring only the most difficult matters and issues to you*], but **every small matter they shall judge** [*let them handle the less-difficult matters*]: **so shall it be easier for thyself, and they shall bear *the burden* with thee** [*a key principle of delegation*].

23 **If thou shalt do this thing**, and God command thee *so* [*if God agrees with my counsel to you*], then **thou shalt be able to endure** [*you won't get so worn out*], and all **this people shall also go to their place in peace** [*the people will be much better served*].

24 So **Moses hearkened to the voice of his father in law**, and did all that he had said.

25 And **Moses chose able men out of all Israel, and made them heads over the people**, rulers of thousands, rulers of hundreds, rulers of fifties, and rulers of tens.

26 And they judged the people at all seasons: **the hard causes they brought unto Moses, but every small matter they judged themselves**.

As you read the above verses, you no doubt recognized many of the principles and practices that are used by the Lord in the Church today.

27 ¶ And **Moses let his father in law depart; and he went his way into his own land**.

EXODUS 19

It has now been fifty days since the Passover—see Smith's Bible Dictionary, p 499, under "Pentecost." The Passover took place as recorded in chapter 12, when the destroying angel "passed over" the children of Israel in the final plague before they left Egypt. This time of year will become known among the Israelites as "Pentecost," meaning fifty days after Passover. We will quote from the Bible Dictionary concerning Pentecost. You will find it under "Feasts."

Bible Dictionary: Pentecost

"Fifty days (Lev. 23:16) after the Feast of the Passover, the Feast of Pentecost was kept. During those 50 days the harvest of corn was being gathered in. It is called (Ex. 23:16) "the feast of harvest, the firstfruits of thy labours" and (Deut. 16:10) "the feast of weeks." The feast lasted a single day, which was a day of holy convocation (Lev. 23:21); and the characteristic rite was the new meal offering, that is, two loaves of leavened bread made of fine flour of new wheat. Special animal sacrifices were also made (Lev. 23:18) and freewill offerings (Deut. 16:10). The festival was prolonged in later times, and huge numbers of Jews attended it. Of this the narrative in Acts 2 is sufficient proof. It had the same evil reputation as the Feast of the Passover for tumults and massacres. We have no record of the celebration of this feast in the Old Testament."

One of the best-known events related to Pentecost is recorded in Acts 2, in the New Testament, which tells that the Holy Ghost descended upon the disciples and they spoke to the multitudes in various tongues.

Here in chapter 19, the children of Israel will be invited to prepare themselves to come into the presence of God. It could be, in effect, a temple experience for them. You will see some parallels between what they did and what we do in preparation to enter the temple. Sadly, they failed to prepare sufficiently and were stopped at the last minute from coming into His presence and seeing His glory. Still, they did hear His voice as He spoke the Ten Commandments from Sinai.

1 **IN the third month**, when the children of Israel were gone forth out of the land of Egypt, the same day **came they into the wilderness of Sinai**.

2 For they were departed from Rephidim, and were come to the desert of Sinai, and had pitched in the wilderness; and **there Israel camped before the mount** [*Mount Sinai*].

3 And **Moses went up unto God, and the LORD called unto him out of the mountain, saying, Thus shalt thou say to the house of Jacob**, and tell the children of Israel;

> Next, the Lord reminds the Israelites that He keeps His promises. He promised them that, if they followed His prophet, Moses, He would free them from bondage in Egypt. He did.

4 **Ye have seen what I did unto the Egyptians** [*I destroyed your enemies*], **and how I bare you on eagles' wings** [*I took you to great heights and carried you out of impossible difficulties*], **and brought you unto myself** [*and brought you to where you can safely worship Me without hindrance*].

> Atonement symbolism also appears in the phrase "and brought you unto myself" in verse 4, above. Through His atoning sacrifice, the Savior "purchased" us. We thus belong to Him. He has brought us unto Himself, and if we are willing to qualify to stay with Him, He will take us home to the Father.

> Perhaps you've noticed that a common format for making covenants with God is the "if . . . then" format. The Lords spells out what we must do (the "if") and tells us what blessings and privileges will attend our keeping of the covenant (the "then"). We see an example of this next.

5 Now therefore, **if ye will obey** my voice indeed, and keep my covenant, **then ye shall be a peculiar treasure unto me** above all people: for all the earth *is* mine:

> It is important that we understand the definition of the word "peculiar" as used in verse 5, above, and elsewhere in the scriptures. It applies to us. We will quote from the *Old Testament Student Manual Genesis-2 Samuel* for help with this (**bold** added for emphasis):

> "Today **the word *peculiar*** is used to mean something different and

unusual. Since Israel was to be a peculiar people in this sense also, Exodus 19:5 and similar scriptures (see Deuteronomy 14:2; 1 Peter 2:9) are often read in that way. The original word in both Hebrew and Greek, however, means 'property, wealth, private property, which is laid up or reserved; the leading idea is that of **select, precious, endeared; something exceedingly prized** and sedulously preserved'" (Wilson, *Old Testament Word Studies,* s.v. "peculiar," page 305; quoted in the *Old Testament Student Manual,* page 124).

We will also quote the Bible Dictionary for additional help in properly defining the word "peculiar," adding **bold** for emphasis:

Bible Dictionary: Peculiar

"One's **very own, exclusive, or special**; not used in the Bible as odd or eccentric. The Hebrew word *segullah,* which is translated *peculiar* in Deut. 14:2 and 26:18, is translated *special* in Deut. 7:6. Compare the various translations of the same word in Ex. 19:5; Ps. 135:4; Eccl. 2:8; Mal. 3:17. Titus 2:14 and 1 Pet. 2:9 should carry the meaning of the saints' **being the Lord's own special people or treasure**."

Through covenant keeping, we become a holy people, the Lord's people.

6 And [*through covenant making and keeping*] **ye shall be unto me a kingdom of priests, and an holy nation**. These are the words that thou shalt speak unto the children of Israel.

The next three verses of this chapter indicate that the people expressed a desire and willingness to make covenants and be the Lord's peculiar and holy people. Because of that, they were to be given a special witness of the Lord and of Moses, His prophet. They are invited to actually hear the voice of the Savior as He speaks (verse 9).

7 ¶ And **Moses** came and **called for the elders of the people, and laid before their faces all these words which the LORD commanded him**.

8 And **all the people answered together**, and said, **All that the LORD hath spoken we will do**. And Moses returned the words of the people unto the LORD.

9 And the LORD said unto Moses, Lo, **I come unto thee in a thick cloud**, that **the people may hear when I speak with thee, and believe thee for ever**. And Moses told the words of the people unto the LORD.

Because of the people's expressed desire and willingness to make covenants with the Lord, they are now instructed as to how to prepare to draw near to Him and hear His actual voice. Two of the personal qualifications for such precious privileges are given in verse 10. They are to:

1. Sanctify themselves. In other words, dedicate themselves spiritually to the Lord, doing their best to be pure and clean spiritually.

2. Be physically clean. Wash their clothes and do their best to be neat and tidy.

10 ¶ And the LORD said unto Moses, Go unto the people, and **sanctify them** to day and to morrow, and let them **wash their clothes**,

> Next, we see that the people were to be ready on the third day. Perhaps there is symbolism in the use of three days, possibly representing the time from the Crucifixion to the Resurrection of the Savior. In Biblical symbolism, the number 3 represents the Godhead and God's intervention to bless and help mankind.
>
> Also, as you continue to read, you will see that there were strict rules associated with this potential privilege. This can be symbolic of the fact that obedience is required for personal growth, as we progress toward eventually coming into God's presence. Unworthy individuals cannot survive the glory of the Lord.

11 And be ready against the third day: **for the third day the LORD will come down in the sight of all the people upon mount Sinai**.

12 And thou shalt **set bounds** unto the people round about, saying, Take heed to yourselves, that ye **go not up into the mount, or touch the border of it:** whosoever toucheth the mount shall be surely put to death:

13 **There shall not an hand touch it**, but he shall surely be stoned, or shot through; whether it be beast or man, it shall not live: **when the trumpet soundeth long, they shall come up to the mount.**

14 ¶ And **Moses went down from the mount unto the people, and sanctified the people; and they washed their clothes.**

15 And he said unto the people, **Be ready against the third day**: come not at your wives [*do not go near any woman with lust—see footnote 15a in your Bible*].

> Three days passed, and in the morning of the third day, the people were allowed to see obvious evidence of the presence of the Savior on Mount Sinai. We see this in verses 16–18.

16 ¶ And it came to pass on the **third day in the morning**, that there were **thunders** and **lightnings**, and **a thick cloud** upon the mount, and the voice of the **trumpet** exceeding loud; so that **all the people** that *was* in the camp **trembled**.

17 And **Moses brought forth the people out of the camp to meet with God**; and they stood at the nether part of [*foot of*] the mount.

18 And mount Sinai was altogether on a **smoke**, because the LORD descended upon it in **fire**: and the smoke thereof ascended as the smoke of a furnace, and **the whole mount quaked greatly**.

> It is interesting to note that ever since this marvelous event, smoke, fire, and shaking of the ground became symbolic of the presence of the Lord, in the minds of the Israelites.

Consequently, this symbolism of God's presence appears in the scriptures. One example is found in Isaiah's vision of the Savior. Isaiah is seeing the Lord, sitting on His throne in heaven and uses symbolism to tell his readers that the power and glory of the Lord filled heaven.

Isaiah 6:4

4 And the **posts of the door moved** [*the door frame shook*] at the voice of him that cried, and **the house** [*heaven*] **was filled with smoke** [*the glory of the Lord was present everywhere, as on Sinai—see Exodus 19:18*].

Without this understanding of symbolism, it might appear from Isaiah's vision that heaven is poorly constructed and that the air quality is substandard.

The Israelites also heard a trumpet, long and loud, heralding the coming of the Lord to Sinai. The same sound will be used to announce many other significant events, including the Second Coming (see Doctrine and Covenants 88:92).

19 And when the voice of **the trumpet sounded long, and waxed** [*grew*] **louder and louder, Moses spake, and God answered him by a voice.**

20 And **the LORD came down upon mount Sinai**, on the top of the mount: and the LORD **called Moses *up* to the top of the mount**; and Moses went up.

It appears to be the case, based on the next verse, that, at this point, many of the people are still unworthy. In fact, some are even considering attempting to force their way beyond the boundaries set for them (verse 12) in an attempt to get close enough to actually see the Lord. Therefore, Moses is told to hurry back down the mountain and warn the people not to do so. This must have been a big disappointment to this humble prophet.

21 And **the LORD said unto Moses, Go down, charge** [*warn*] **the people, lest they break through unto the LORD to gaze** [*to look at Him*], **and many of them perish** [*they would die if they did this*].

22 And **let the priests also**, which come near to the LORD, **sanctify themselves**, lest the LORD break forth upon them.

23 And **Moses said unto the LORD, The people cannot come up to mount Sinai:** for thou chargedst [*commanded*] us, saying, Set bounds about the mount [*verse 12*], and sanctify it.

24 And the LORD said unto him, **Away, get thee down** [*hurry down*], and **thou shalt come up**, thou, **and Aaron with thee** [*this will take place in Exodus 24:9–10*]: **but let not the priests and the people break through to come up unto the LORD, lest he break forth upon them.**

25 **So Moses went down unto the people, and spake unto them.**

Although some privileges were lost for the time being, these people still were blessed to hear the voice of the Lord as he spoke the Ten Commandments to them from Sinai. A summary of the lost privileges and marvelous blessings still received is given by Brother Ellis Rasmussen, who taught for many years in the Religion Department at Brigham Young University. He said (**bold** added for emphasis):

"If they had accepted all of the privileges offered them and followed the instructions which would have qualified them to receive the fulfillment of all God's promises, they could have been accorded the grandest of all revelations:

"He **offered to come down in the sight of all the people and let them hear when He spoke to Moses that they might know for themselves about His will and His law, and believe in Moses's future revelations from God, and revere the Lord evermore** (cf. Deuteronomy 4:10). Note the need of cleanliness and spiritual dedication in their preparation for this great spiritual experience.

"At the prearranged signal, the sounding of the trumpet 'exceeding long,' the people trembled in anticipation and awe, but **apparently they were not fully ready** to come up 'in the sight' of the Lord on the mount where Moses was, for the Lord told him to go down and warn them not to come up. Hints as to why this was so are found in the next chapter, 20:18–19, and in Doctrine and Covenants 84:21–25. **But even though their hearts were not fully prepared to endure His presence, they did hear the voice and the words of God as the Ten Commandments were given**, as will be seen later when we study Moses's review of these great events in his valedictory, in Deuteronomy 4:10, 12, 33, 36; 5:22–26. (Rasmussen, *Introduction to the Old Testament,* 1:83.)"

SOURCES

Book of Mormon Student Manual. Salt Lake City: The Church of Jesus Christ of Latter-day Saints, 1982.

Bryant, T. Alton. *The New Compact Bible Dictionary.* Grand Rapids, Mich.: Zondervan, 1981.

Clark, James R., comp. *Messages of the First Presidency of The Church of Jesus Christ of Latter-day Saints.* 6 vols. Salt Lake City: Bookcraft, 1965–75.

Conference Reports of The Church of Jesus Christ of Latter-day Saints. Salt Lake City: The Church of Jesus Christ of Latter-day Saints, 1898 to present.

Doctrines of the Gospel Student Manual. Salt Lake City: The Church of Jesus Christ of Latter-day Saints (Institutes of Religion), 2000.

Dummelow, J. R. *A Commentary on the Holy Bible.* New York: Macmillan, 1937.

Encyclopedia of Mormonism. Edited by Daniel H. Ludlow. 5 vols. New York: Macmillan, 1992.

German Bible, The Martin Luther Edition of. Wien (Vienna), Austria, 1960.

Hymns of The Church of Jesus Christ of Latter-day Saints. Salt Lake City: The Church of Jesus Christ of Latter-day Saints, 1985.

International Bible Society. *The Holy Bible: New International Version (NIV).* Grand Rapids, Mich.: Zondervan, 1984.

Josephus. *Antiquities of the Jews.* Philadelphia: John C. Winston Co., n.d.

Journal of Discourses. 26 vols. London: Latter-day Saints' Book Depot, 1854–86.

Kiel, C. F., and F. Delitzsch. *Commentary on the Old Testament.* 10 vols. Grand Rapids, Mich.: William B. Eerdmans Publishing, 1991.

Kimball, Spencer W. *Faith Precedes the Miracle.* Salt Lake City: Deseret Book, 1972.

Ludlow, Victor L. Isaiah: Prophet, Seer, and Poet. Salt Lake City: Deseret Book, 1982.

Maxwell, Neal A. *Deposition of a Disciple.* Salt Lake City: Deseret Book, 1976.

McConkie, Bruce R. *A New Witness for the Articles of Faith.* Salt Lake City: Deseret Book, 1985.

———. Doctrinal New Testament Commentary. 3 vols. Salt Lake City: Deseret Book, 1972.

———. *Mormon Doctrine.* 2d ed. Salt Lake City: Bookcraft, 1966.

———. *The Millennial Messiah.* Salt Lake City: Deseret Book, 1982.

———. *The Promised Messiah—The First Coming of Christ.* Salt Lake City: Deseret Book, 1978.

Nyman, Monte S. *Great Are the Words of Isaiah.* Salt Lake City: Bookcraft, 1980.

Ogden, Kelly D., and Andrew C. Skinner. *Verse by Verse—The Old Testament*, Volume 2, 1 Kings through Malachi. Salt Lake City, Deseret Book, 2013.

Old Testament Gospel Doctrine Teacher's Manual. Salt Lake City: The Church of Jesus Christ of Latter-day Saints (Institutes of Religion), 2001.

Old Testament Student Manual: Genesis–2 Samuel. Salt Lake City: The Church of Jesus Christ of Latter-day Saints (Institutes of Religion), 1981.

Old Testament Student Manual, I Kings–Malachi (Religion 302). Salt Lake City: The Church of Jesus Christ of Latter-day Saints, 1981.

Petersen, Mark E. *Moses, Man of Miracles.* Salt Lake City: Deseret Book, 1977.

Rasmussen, Ellis T. *An Introduction to the Old Testament and its Teachings.* 2d ed. 2 vols. Provo, Utah: BYU Press, 1972–74.

———. *A Latter-day Saint Commentary on the Old Testament.* Salt Lake City: Deseret Book, 1993.

Richards, LeGrand. *Israel! Do You Know?* Salt Lake City: Deseret Book, 1954.

Smith, Joseph. *History of The Church of Jesus Christ of Latter-day Saints.* Edited by B. H. Roberts. 2d ed. rev., 7 vols. Salt Lake City: The Church of Jesus Christ of Latter-day Saints, 1932–1951.

———. Joseph Smith's "New Translation" of the Bible. Independence, Missouri: Herald Publishing House, 1970.

———. *Teachings of the Prophet Joseph Smith.* Selected by Joseph Fielding Smith. Salt Lake City: Deseret Book, 1977.

About the Author

David J. Ridges taught for the Church Educational System for thirty-five years and taught for several years at BYU Campus Education Week. He taught adult religion classes and Know Your Religion classes for BYU Continuing Education for many years. He has also served as a curriculum writer for Sunday School, seminary, and institute of religion manuals.

He has served in many callings in the Church, including Gospel Doctrine teacher, bishop, stake president, and patriarch. He and Sister Ridges have served two full-time CES missions together. They are the parents of six children and grandparents of sixteen grandchildren so far. They make their home in Springville, Utah.

Scan to visit

www.davidjridges.com